Maintaining Financial Stability in Times of Risk and Uncertainty

Abhishek Behl
Indian Institute of Technology Bombay, India

Sushma Nayak
Symbiosis International University (Deemed), India

A volume in the Advances in Finance, Accounting, and Economics (AFAE) Book Series

IGI Global
DISSEMINATOR OF KNOWLEDGE

Published in the United States of America by
IGI Global
Business Science Reference (an imprint of IGI Global)
701 E. Chocolate Avenue
Hershey PA, USA 17033
Tel: 717-533-8845
Fax: 717-533-8661
E-mail: cust@igi-global.com
Web site: http://www.igi-global.com

Library of Congress Cataloging-in-Publication Data

Names: Behl, Abhishek, 1987- editor. | Nayak, Sushma, 1982- editor.
Title: Maintaining financial stability in times of risk and uncertainty / Abhishek Behl and Sushma Nayak, editors.
Description: Hershey : Business Science Reference, [2019]
Identifiers: LCCN 2018020717| ISBN 9781522572084 (hardcover) | ISBN 9781522572091 (ebook)
Subjects: LCSH: Finance, Public. | Risk management. | Uncertainty.
Classification: LCC HJ141 .M35 2019 | DDC 658.15--dc23 LC record available at https://lccn.loc.gov/2018020717

This book is published in the IGI Global book series Advances in Finance, Accounting, and Economics (AFAE) (ISSN: 2327-5677; eISSN: 2327-5685)

British Cataloguing in Publication Data
A Cataloguing in Publication record for this book is available from the British Library.

Advances in Finance, Accounting, and Economics (AFAE) Book Series

Ahmed Driouchi
Al Akhawayn University, Morocco

ISSN:2327-5677
EISSN:2327-5685

Mission

In our changing economic and business environment, it is important to consider the financial changes occurring internationally as well as within individual organizations and business environments. Understanding these changes as well as the factors that influence them is crucial in preparing for our financial future and ensuring economic sustainability and growth.

The **Advances in Finance, Accounting, and Economics (AFAE)** book series aims to publish comprehensive and informative titles in all areas of economics and economic theory, finance, and accounting to assist in advancing the available knowledge and providing for further research development in these dynamic fields.

Coverage

- Finance
- Development Economics
- Environmental and Social Accounting
- Economics Geography
- Economic Policy
- Taxes
- Microeconomics
- Accounting Standards
- E-finance
- Auditing

IGI Global is currently accepting manuscripts for publication within this series. To submit a proposal for a volume in this series, please contact our Acquisition Editors at Acquisitions@igi-global.com or visit: http://www.igi-global.com/publish/.

The Advances in Finance, Accounting, and Economics (AFAE) Book Series (ISSN 2327-5677) is published by IGI Global, 701 E. Chocolate Avenue, Hershey, PA 17033-1240, USA, www.igi-global.com. This series is composed of titles available for purchase individually; each title is edited to be contextually exclusive from any other title within the series. For pricing and ordering information please visit http://www.igi-global.com/book-series/advances-finance-accounting-economics/73685. Postmaster: Send all address changes to above address.

Titles in this Series

For a list of additional titles in this series, please visit: www.igi-global.com/book-series

Corporate Insolvency Law and Bankruptcy Reforms in the Global Economy
Amit Kashyap (Nirma University, India)
Business Science Reference • copyright 2019 • 261pp • H/C (ISBN: 9781522555414) • US $185.00 (our price)

Time Bank as a Complementary Economic System Emerging Research and Opportunities
Lukas Valek (University of Hradec Kralove, Czech Republic) and Vladimir Bures (University of Hradec Kralove, Czech Republic)
Business Science Reference • copyright 2019 • 208pp • H/C (ISBN: 9781522569749) • US $175.00 (our price)

Economic Dynamics of Global Energy Geopolitics
Ahmet Salih Ikiz (Muğla Sıtkı Koçman University, Turkey)
Engineering Science Reference • copyright 2019 • 305pp • H/C (ISBN: 9781522542032) • US $195.00 (our price)

Co-Manufacturing and New Economic Paradigms
Giulio Focardi (Osun WES, Italy) and Lorenza Salati (Osun WES, Italy)
Business Science Reference • copyright 2019 • 217pp • H/C (ISBN: 9781522570899) • US $185.00 (our price)

Handbook of Research on Microfinancial Impacts on Women Empowerment, Poverty, and Inequality
Ramesh Chandra Das (Katwa College, India)
Business Science Reference • copyright 2019 • 452pp • H/C (ISBN: 9781522552406) • US $275.00 (our price)

Emerging Economic Models for Global Sustainability and Social Development
Bryan Christiansen (Global Research Society, LLC, USA) Irina Sysoeva (Independent Researcher, Russia) Alexandra Udovikina (Independent Researcher, Russia) and Anna Ketova (Khabarovsk State Academy of Economics and Law, Russia)
Business Science Reference • copyright 2019 • 430pp • H/C (ISBN: 9781522557876) • US $225.00 (our price)

Techno-Social Systems for Modern Economical and Governmental Infrastructures
Alexander Troussov (The Russian Presidential Academy of National Economy and Public Administration, Russia) and Sergey Maruev (The Russian Presidential Academy of National Economy and Public Administration, Russia)
Business Science Reference • copyright 2019 • 351pp • H/C (ISBN: 9781522555865) • US $205.00 (our price)

IGI Global
DISSEMINATOR OF KNOWLEDGE

701 East Chocolate Avenue, Hershey, PA 17033, USA
Tel: 717-533-8845 x100 • Fax: 717-533-8661
E-Mail: cust@igi-global.com • www.igi-global.com

Editorial Advisory Board

Table of Contents

Detailed Table of Contents

A flood of corporate fraud has hit the market in the most recent decade, resuscitating attention to the impact of these incidences on corporate administration and stock market responses. Of particular relevance are Ponzi schemes that are considered practically the same as frauds. As more and more investors fall into the deep trap of Ponzi schemes, the situation is getting even more irrepressible. The reasons for a rise in the number of such swindles are mainly attributed to the breakdown in governance in different countries across the globe. This chapter dwells over the root causes of Ponzi schemes with specific focus on Asia and its developing regions. Through an in-depth study of the causes, the chapter looks to recommend possible solutions in mitigating the crisis, steps to ensure financial stability, and prevention of fraud risks.

This chapter briefly discusses the impact and policy implications of demonetization across the world. The main focus of the chapter is on the demonetization that occurred in India on 8th November 2016. The event is important due to the surprise effect and also due to the huge scale of impact that it had on the economy. The authors make a case for the demonetization from the policymaker's point of view. This chapter will introduce how demonetization has impacted the business sector as well as the financial sector of the economy. The aim of the chapter is not to estimate the impact of demonetization on the economy as whole but rather to discuss the impact of the policy on the different sectors of the economy and different stakeholders of the economy. This chapter would also explore demonetization as a policy tool for tax evasion and corruption. Finally, this chapter will introduce the concept of cashless economies around the world and whether it will be possible for the Indian economy to become a cashless economy anytime in the near future.

Importance of risk exposure and risk management practices have attracted the attention of companies, investors, and all other parties who benefit from performances of companies. Competitive environment and global effects force the companies to pay attention to manage their risks. Therefore, governmental bodies and international associations embarked on researches in risk management and as a result of these efforts regulations have been put in place. Germany, USA, and UK are the leading countries that made significant progress in risk management field by enacting laws, regulations, and issuing guidelines. But the subject is still new for some countries and difficult for companies, especially small and medium sized, to apply. The chapter starts with the benefits and importance of risk management. Then steps of risk management are explained with the examples.

The automatic use of heuristics, the effects of framing, and the tendency to procrastinate when combined with the risk and uncertainty inherent in the financial environment can lead to financial instability for ordinary investors. This chapter explores established behavioral tendencies with respect to financial decision making within the framework of behavioral economics: how and why heuristics are used to make decisions, how different choice frames influence decisions, the crucial impact of biases like loss aversion on decision outcomes. The chapter also explores critical factors that induce the tendency to procrastinate saving and investing. The chapter suggests strategies that investors can use to achieve long-term financial stability by achieving predetermined financial goals as well as protect their investments from depreciating in value in the context of financial market instability.

The world is full of financial risks and uncertainties even for those who have financial literacy. There are many factors to consider when planning financially: the stock market, hyperinflation, and climate change all play roles and are unpredictable. This chapter will focus on the actions that are being taken to establish financial literacy across the world and the impact these actions have on individual financial stability. Although financial literacy certainly cannot eliminate the risks and uncertainties that accompany unforeseen events, it is one way to prepare for these events. Even in times of normalcy, lack of financial literacy can put individuals at an increased risk of financial instability. This chapter presents a variety of recommendations and resources for financial literacy education as well as the risks and uncertainties that accompany their use.

Risk and uncertainty are disliked but inevitable. The nature of these has changed and new sources of risk have risen. To mitigate risk and maintain financial stability, the firms need to adapt. The world wide web and, within it, social media have had tremendous growth and wide coverage lately, making them determining forces in any economic activity. This has led to generation of large amount of data on myriad concerns. Recent developments in computing technology has thrown open the possibility of mining useful information from the enormous and dynamic data. The chapter outlines the growth of social media and social media analytics and its financial implications to businesses, consumers, and governments. It details how risk management and social media, two domains earlier considered more diverged than chalk and cheese are now inextricably linked and explains using various cases how social media analytics is used to manage risk and uncertainty. The authors also look at the emerging challenges with these developments.

Farm debt waivers have been introduced in India, from time to time, to provide relief to the indebted farmers. The chapter focuses on the viability of farm debt waiver in India—whether it serves as an ephemeral palliative (a temporary reassuring measure) or an enduring risk management tool (a permanent remedy to build resilience against a longstanding debt crisis)—for farmers by employing situation, actor, process, learning, action, performance (SAP-LAP) framework. Loan waivers occasionally appear as a quick fix to alleviate farmers' misery. They trigger moral hazard as the farmers make no attempts to repay the loans themselves with the expectation that an imminent waiver from the government would clear their debts, thus ruining the credit culture of the country. From a policy viewpoint, it is imperative to make agriculture sustainable by lessening inefficiencies, augmenting income, moderating costs, and affording protection through premeditated and well-defined insurance schemes.

To build an agrarian economy that guarantees sustenance and food security to a vast populace, raw material for its growing industrial base, surpluses for exports, and a just, even-handed, and reasonable rewarding system for the farming community, "commitment-driven" contract farming is undoubtedly a feasible unconventional farming model that offers a reliable and consistent input service to farmers and delivers preferred farm produce to the contracting firms. Contract farming is used as a risk management tool. Facilitation of contract farming requires support in terms of flexibility in legislation, offering effective mechanism to resolve conflicts between contracting parties, having an arbitration body for resolving conflicts and providing quality checking facilities. Proper design of the contract is critical in making contract farming more successful. Education and training in connection with contract farming should be provided extensively to companies and other government agencies. Governments should endeavor to encourage contract farming by means of appropriate legislation and facilitation, through a demand-driven approach. The chapter aims to examine contract farming as a risk mitigation tool for farmers in general and small farmers in particular by considering diverse cases of successes/failures in developed and developing countries. While doing so, the authors have also delved into the historical evolution of contract farming, types of contracts, benefits, and apprehensions of the contracting parties, and they offer solutions to make contract farming successful.

Globalization seems to have achieved ultimate penetration—the plethora of choice a consumer faces in any given product or service is only a testament to the fact. Worldwide, consumers are presented the options to choose between store brands (or generic/local brands, as they are sometimes known) and national brands. The choices consumers make are reflective of their perceptions about either brand and thus provide an insight into the perceived risks that consumers associate with store or national brands. This risk creates an uncertainty of consumer base and threatens the stability of market shares for brands. The chapter aims to study the various perceived risks consumers associate with brands across two product categories: consumer goods and hedonic goods. Consequently, solutions to change consumer perceptions or brand strategies have been provided so that brands may be able to reduce perceived risk associated with themselves and create a stable consumer base.

Buried pipelines are the most lucrative deal in today's transportation for transmission of vital fluids and liquids. However, with the advent of disasters, the continuous flow through these indispensable systems gets hampered. The purpose of this chapter is twofold: one is to develop a simulation approach to capturing the effect of risk/disaster due to unforeseen events on buried pipeline, and the second is to gauge financial losses due to such uncertain events. A simulation model considering hoop, longitudinal, and radial stresses on continuous flow carrying buried pipeline subjected to uncertain and risky events is developed in CAESAR II engineering software. The authors performed statistical analysis to carry node-based analysis to describe the repair cost associated with the individual node or throughout the whole pipeline system under study. Although with a limitation in terms of model accuracy and reliability as the actual scenario could differ from the simulated model, the study outlines financial gain over total repair cost using simulation modeling approach in face of disruptions.

Foreword

The global financial risk experiences have demonstrated that macroeconomic policymaking is expected to ensure monetary, fiscal and financial stability. Financial stability and risk management have assumed considerable importance, entailing for national authorities a constant need to monitor, identify and minimize the incidence of systemic risks. However, risks and uncertainties arise from unforeseen events and cause financial instability and losses.

This book explores a number of perspectives on how risks and uncertainties affect the financial stability of individuals and institutions, and also offers probable solutions to mitigate risk and achieve financial resilience under uncertainty. The fifteen topics in the book have been chosen carefully, providing a fine balance between global trends as well as policies and practices in India. All the chapters are topical. The chapters are well-balanced covering the experiences of emerging markets and measures taken by Central Banks, recent Indian policy measures such as demonetization, agriculture debt waiver and their effects, consumer financial behavior and sectoral analysis of crude oil buried pipeline system and emerging retail sector.

The chapters on recent banking crisis - Maintaining Financial Stability in Banking Sector: The Case of Turkey; Fragility of the Spanish Banking System; and Financial Exclusion, provide valuable insights on the causes of the risks, how challenges are getting addressed, and lessons for others. The chapter on the Effects of Macroprudential Policies on Financial Stability in Developing Countries analyses the policy instruments used by Central Banks in eleven select countries to manage current account deficit and concludes that excessive credit growth affects financial stability. The volume very aptly covers risks and regulatory approaches to risk mitigation. These are contemporary and relevant in the global context of increased frequency and severity of risk events.

Enabling the preparedness of individual consumers to face risks and uncertainities through financial literacy is gaining ground worldwide with Central Banks actively playing a role in finanical literacy of customers. The chapters on Addressing Financial Risks and Uncertainties through Financial Literacy Education and Behavioural Strategies to Achieve Financial Stability in Uncertain Times have useful information on how to achieve long term personal financial stability.

The agriculture debt waivers in India have been well analyzed and the recommendations to make agriculture sustainable by reducing inefficiencies, costs of operations and risk management through premeditated and well-structured insurance schemes are relevant. Agriculture risk management through contract farming draws lessons from global experiences.

The book *Maintaining Financial Stability in Times of Risk and Uncertainty* provides valuable insights for policy makers, researchers and practitioners alike. For students, this book offers essential reference material. Dr. Abhishek Behl, Researcher, Indian Institute of Technology Bombay and Ms. Sushma Nayak, Researcher, Symbiosis International (Deemed University) have done a commendable job as book editors in making the new research available for a wide audience.

Girija Srinivasan
Independent Researcher, India

Girija Srinivasan *is an expert in development finance and rural livelihoods with more than 30 years of extensive experience in development banking, consulting, technical assistance and studies. After an initial career as a development banker for 14 years, she then turned to build a successful international consulting practice in the areas of livelihoods and rural finance. She has been involved in design, supervision and evaluation of strategy and implementation of several unique development projects and ushered rural institutions in their growth process in India and abroad. Her areas of interest include rural livelihoods, rural banking, microfinance, financial inclusion and community-based organizations of women and farmers. Her experience spreads over almost all the states in India, South and South East Asia and the Middle-East. She has authored the India Social Performance Report in Microfinance for three years from 2012 to 2014, besides editing the report in 2011. These reports are regarded as 'must read' for MFI practitioners not just in India, but the world over. She has jointly authored, with N. Srinivasan (Central Banker and Development Banker for 30 years with Reserve Bank of India and National Bank for Agriculture and Rural Development (NABARD)), the State of India's Livelihoods Report for the years 2015, 2016 and 2017. She has also authored individually and collaboratively several books, undertaken pioneering studies in SHG bank linkage programme, and drafted the early manuals on adoption of SHG methodology in Government of India programmes. She has been on the Board of Friends of Women's World Banking. She is also involved in the industry bodies dealing with microfinance and rural livelihoods. As an international expert, she serves as a consultant and advisor to International Fund for Agricultural Development, GIZ, NABARD, Microsave, Frankfurt School and other institutions.*

Preface

OVERVIEW

Uncertainty, in the presence of vivid hopes and fears, is painful, but must be endured if we wish to live without the support of comforting fairy tales. — Bertrand Russell

Risks and uncertainties——market, financial, operational, social, humanitarian, environmental, and institutional——are the inherent realities of the modern world. Life is suffused with randomness and volatility; nearly everything momentous that occurs in the illustrious sweep of history, or in our individual lives, is an outcome of uncertainty. An important implication of such uncertainty is the financial instability engendered to the victims of different sorts of perils. For instance, the global financial crisis of 2007-2008 led to worldwide crashing of stock markets and adversely affected financial institutions across the globe, thus destroying investor confidence. During 2008-2009, Zimbabwe experienced the first hyperinflation of the 21st century that ruined the nation financially, drove many of its residents to poverty, and forced millions of nationals to emigrate. In November 2016, when India witnessed demonetization of its higher denomination currency, nearly 86% of the nation's legal tender was rendered worthless within few hours, thus sparking off a liquidity crisis. Furthermore, major events in 2016, including the Brexit vote in the United Kingdom and the Presidential Elections in the United States, rekindled the much-feared uncertainty for investors and financial authorities. Studies relating to Virtual Currencies (VCs) suggest that VCs produce sizeable risks as possible tools for money laundering, terrorist financing, tax evasion and swindle; also, additional risks to financial stability may eventually emerge as the new technologies become more extensively used.

Recent years have also witnessed a macabre series of natural disasters causing enormous losses to life and property, thus imperiling financial stability. Climate change affects financial stability in three major ways: physical risks relating to insurance obligations and valuation of financial assets emerging from climate- and weather-related shocks, for instance floods and hurricanes that damage/destroy property; liability risks that may possibly arise in the future if individuals experiencing loss from the effects of climate change seek recompense from those they hold responsible; transition risks in the form of financial risks that might result from the process of adjustment en route to a lower-carbon economy. Environmental risks reported in numerous countries worldwide have triggered off a livelihood crisis. In developing nations, the seasonal nature of agriculture causes unemployment for farmers for a major part of the year and detrimentally affects their incomes. Such unpredictable events have far-reaching ramifications which now constitute the subject of discussion for experts of diverse disciplines. The famous Black Swan theory that extends to erratic events within financial world as well as those beyond finance also encapsulates certain levels of risk. An important question nevertheless is, how does the economy in general, and individual economic agents in particular, respond to risks and uncertainties. On most occasions, it is observed that people are ill-equipped and unwary to deal with the consequences of such events and have to gradually develop unique methodologies to cope with them. But, can financial stability be realized through individual private actions alone or government intervention is necessary? Does financial stability merely necessitate the reliability and soundness of institutions, the steadiness and consistency of markets, least volatility that enhances greater confidence in the system — or somewhat more than this?

The book features contributors from a variety of disciplines, who bring in diverse perspectives and viewpoints of risks and uncertainties, and actions taken to cope with them from the standpoint of attaining financial stability.

OBJECTIVES

Risks and uncertainties arise from unforeseen events and are associated with adversity, financial instability and losses. The present book explores a number of perspectives on how risks and uncertainties affect the financial stability of individuals and institutions. In doing so, it provides means to encourage serious study of the origins and effects of unpredictable events on individuals and on society, providing a platform to explore different ways to establish financial stability and security. The book offers probable solutions to mitigate risk and achieve financial resilience under uncertainty.

TARGET AUDIENCE

The primary target audience of this book includes researchers, academicians and policy makers from a variety of disciplines interested in analysing and researching financial stability of individuals under risks and uncertainties. A secondary target audience consists of students and scholars pursuing advanced study in the social sciences.

ORGANIZATION OF THE BOOK

Chapter 1, "Deposit Insurance: Pre-Emptive Expediency Against Bank Runs or Propulsion of Moral Hazard? Economic and Political Implications in India," authored by Sushma Nayak, Abhishek Behl, and Aastha Behl, primarily focuses on the state of deposit insurance system in India. Considering the vulnerability of banking system in recent times and the weight accorded to deposit insurance to deal with this quandary, it is important to examine whether such insurance serves as a risk mitigating tool in the interests of depositors or it endangers the health of banking system by propelling moral hazard. The central question which the authors address in this chapter concerns with the impact of deposit insurance initiatives on financial stability, consistency and systemic progress, with India as a case in point. India is a country whose banking sector is known to have remained stable despite global cataclysm, thereby sustaining public confidence over the years. In the case of India, while Deposit Insurance and Credit Guarantee Corporation (DICGC) has been contributing appreciably to the stability of banking system by safeguarding depositors against possible loss of their entitled deposits with insured banks, the system is based on "paybox" mandate and affords limited conditional protection to depositors. Guided by the need for a stronger resolution mechanism, the Indian government introduced the Financial Resolution and Deposit Insurance (FRDI) Bill in August 2017, which had its own share of controversies, conceivably the most confounded provisions being the bail-in clause and omission of explicit declaration of maximum coverage. The economic and political pressures, however, led to the dropping of the Bill in July 2018, thus creating further vacuum in an already underprovided deposit protection. Therefore, in Indian milieu, it is important to examine the consistency and reliability of the prevailing and proposed (then shelved owing to political trepidations) arrangement of deposit insurance. For this purpose, the authors of the chapter have employed Delphi method and arrived at an important finding as regards how India needs a robust and reliable deposit insurance framework that shall secure the financial system against systemic crisis and sustain public confidence through financial stability.

Chapter 2, "Maintaining Financial Stability in Banking Sector: The Case of Turkey," authored by Meltem Gurunlu, analyses the Turkish banking system and points out challenges from a "Risk Management" perspective. It evaluates the developments in the Turkish banking system in conformity with the major banking crises during the period 1994-2017, by considering harmonization process with globally practiced standards of risk management – Basel Accords. Risk management in Turkey constitutes one of the major priorities due to developments in the international banking sector. When the main causes of banking crises in emerging market countries are examined, it is observed that inadequacy of capital, macroeconomic imbalances existing in the country, injection of hot money or short-term foreign cash inflows, and bad risk management environment with lack of supervisory authorities, have been major concerns. Presently, in the context of the Basel criteria, Turkish banking system competes strongly on a global scale with respect to capital adequacy and auditing standards. This position confirms a positive step for financial system in Turkey.

Chapter 3, "Measurement of Economic and Banking Stability in Emerging Markets by Considering Income Inequality and Nonperforming Loans," authored by Hasan Dinçer, Serhat Yüksel, Fatih Pınarbaşı, and İpek Tamara Çetiner, aims to measure the relationship between income inequality and nonperforming loans ratio. For this purpose, 20 different emerging economies are evaluated by using Pedroni panel cointegration and Dumitrescu Hurlin panel causality analysis. In addition to this aspect, annual data between the years 2000 and 2015 is considered in the analysis process. It is concluded that there is a long-term relationship between these variables. Therefore, it is proposed that these countries should initiate actions to improve the banking system. In other words, nonperforming loans ratio in banking sector can be decreased when banks in these countries can prudently choose their customers. Therefore, income inequality problem can be lessened in emerging economies.

Chapter 4, "Fragility of the Spanish Banking System and Financial Exclusion: Lessons Learned From the Global Crisis and New Challenges for the 21st Century Banking Sector," authored by Begoña Alvarez García and José Pablo Abeal Vázquez, focuses on how Spanish banking system has changed significantly over the last 20 years, both in quantitative as well as qualitative terms. The crisis has been the main driving force behind all these changes because it brought to light the weaknesses of the Spanish productive system and shook the foundations that sustained the banking system. As a consequence, a new banking system has emerged. This new banking system is more fragile, smaller in size, less profitable, less inclusive and faced with important financial and social challenges, which the authors draw attention to.

Chapter 5, "The Effects of Macroprudential Policies on Financial Stability in Developing Countries," authored by Sümeyra Gazel, aims to determine how macroprudential policies related to credit growth and exchange rate fluctuations affect the financial stability of developing countries with a current account deficit. The concept of financial instability is scrutinised with respect to policy instruments used by central banks. Although the policy instruments used in each country differ according to the country conditions, the standard factor among developing countries with a current account deficit problem is exchange rate volatility resulting from excessive credit growth and short-term capital movements. In this context, Argentina, Brazil, Chile, Colombia, Hungary, Indonesia, India, Mexico, Poland, South Africa, and Turkey are examined with regard to the effects of macroprudential policies on financial stability for the period between Q2 of 2006 and Q2 of 2017 by using the time-varying panel causality test developed by Dumitrescu and Hurlin. The results of the analysis indicate that excessive credit growth is a primary reason for the current account deficit.

Chapter 6, "The Threat of Ponzi Schemes: An Asian Perspective," authored by Sourya Mookerjee and Varun Sardesai, dwells over the root causes of Ponzi schemes with specific focus on Asia and its developing zones. Being crowned the world's economic powerhouse, Asia is the fastest growing region in the world. Nevertheless, it lacks the necessary grip over Ponzi schemes. There are numerous factors that have led to a growth in Ponzi schemes in Asia. But the major factors among them include financial literacy, financial inclusion, and financial regulation. The authors analyse these factors at length, discuss the prevailing loopholes, and further suggest the way forward for the region towards attaining the desired goals.

Chapter 7, "India Towards a Cashless Economy," authored by Abhinav Pal, Chandan Kumar Tiwari, and Tarun Khandelwal, discusses the impact of demonetization from a global standpoint in general and Indian perspective in particular. The aim of the chapter is to discuss the impact of the policy on the different sectors and different stakeholders of the economy, as well as explore demonetization as a policy tool for tax evasion and corruption. The authors discuss the implications of demonetization and suggest the improbability of ascertaining its influence on Indian economy in the long run. Furthermore, the chapter insinuates that there are lessons to be learnt from the experiences of other countries for moving towards a cashless economy, such as Korea, which transformed itself to a coinless economy; a similar transition for India may create better pathway for a cashless economy.

Chapter 8, "Importance of Risk Management and Risk Management Process," authored by Çağla Demir Pali, explores how risk is one of the fundamental elements that influences economic behaviour of people and businesses, and can arise due to umpteen reasons. Companies are exposed to a variety of risks: strategic, operational, compliance, internal audit, financial, fraud, market, credit, customer, supply chain, product and security risks. They are caused by the exposure to emerging markets, the toughening competition, and the fluctuations in the national and international markets, and have significant ramifications on the companies' financial performance and achievement of the plans. Companies are aware of the influence of such risks and risk management practices are being practiced accordingly. Risk management plays a critical role in determining how negative risks can be managed and converted to opportunities and also how likelihood of positive risks can be increased concurrently.

Chapter 9, "Behavioral Strategies to Achieve Financial Stability in Uncertain Times," authored by Ashlesha Khedekar-Swaminathan, discusses how the automatic use of heuristics, the consequences of framing, and the tendency to procrastinate, when coalesced with the risk and uncertainty inherent in the financial environment, can lead to financial instability for ordinary investors. The chapter scrutinizes established behavioural tendencies with respect to financial decision making within the framework of behavioural economics: how and why heuristics are used to make decisions, how different choice frames influence decisions, as well as the crucial impact of biases like loss aversion on decision outcomes. The chapter further investigates decisive factors that induce the tendency to procrastinate saving and investing.

Finally, the author suggests strategies that investors can use to achieve long term financial stability by realizing predetermined financial goals, as well as protect their investments from depreciating in value, in the context of financial market instability.

Chapter 10, "Addressing Financial Risks and Uncertainties through Financial Literacy Education: Recommendations, Resources, and Results," authored by Danielle McKain, discusses how financial risks and uncertainties being ubiquitous in nature, have an obvious impact on even those individuals who are financially literate. There are myriad factors to consider in financial planning—stock markets, hyperinflation, and climate change—all playing their respective roles and being grossly erratic in nature. This chapter focuses on the actions that are being taken to establish financial literacy across the world and the impact these actions have on individual financial stability. Although financial literacy cannot mitigate the risks and uncertainties that escort unforeseen events, it is one way to prepare for these events. Even in stable conditions, lack of financial literacy can put individuals at an increased risk of financial instability. The chapter presents a variety of recommendations and resources for financial literacy education, as well as, the risks and uncertainties that accompany their use.

Chapter 11, "Social Media Analytics for Maintaining Financial Stability," authored by Sebin Nidhiri and Sakshi Saxena, discusses how the World Wide Web, and within it, social media have had humongous growth and extensive coverage lately, making them decisive forces in any economic activity. This has led to generation of massive data on myriad concerns. Recent developments in computing technology have thrown open the possibility of mining useful information from the enormous and dynamic data. The chapter outlines the growth of social media and social media analytics and its financial implications to businesses, consumers and governments. It details how risk management and social media, two domains earlier considered more diverged than chalk and cheese, are now inextricably linked, and explicates using various cases how social media analytics can be employed to manage risk and uncertainty.

Chapter 12, "Farm Debt Waiver in India: An Ephemeral Palliative or an Enduring Risk Management Tool? A SAP-LAP Analysis," authored by Sushma Nayak and Shrabana Mukherjee, discusses the impact and implications of farm debt waivers in India. Farm debt waivers have been introduced in India, from time to time, to provide relief to the indebted farmers. The chapter focuses on the viability of farm debt waiver in India—whether it serves as an ephemeral palliative (a temporary reassuring measure) or an enduring risk management tool (a permanent remedy to build resilience against a longstanding debt crisis)—for farmers, by employing Situation, Actor, Process, Learning, Action, Performance (SAP-LAP) framework. Loan waivers occasionally appear as a quick fix to alleviate farmers' misery. They trigger moral hazard as the farmers make no attempts to repay the loans themselves with the expectation that an imminent waiver from the government would clear their debts, thus ruining the credit culture of the country. The authors suggest that from a policy viewpoint, it is imperative to make agriculture sustainable by lessening inefficiencies, augmenting income, moderating costs and affording protection through premeditated and well-defined insurance schemes.

Chapter 13, "Agricultural Risk Management Through Contract Farming Ventures: An Exploration of Cross-Country Evidences," authored by Isha Gole and Neha Sharma, considers how contract farming is a viable avantgarde farming model, which offers a reliable and consistent input service to farmers and delivers preferred farm produce to the contracting firms. The chapter examines contract farming as a risk mitigation tool, for farmers in general, and small farmers in particular, by considering diverse cases of successes/failures in developed and developing countries. While doing so, the authors also delve into the historical evolution of contract farming, types of contracts, benefits and apprehensions of the contracting parties, and offer solutions to make contract farming a success.

Chapter 14, "Evaluating Emerging Indian Retail Scenario: Consumer Preferences, Perceived Risks, and Uncertainties – Store Brands vs. National Brands," authored by Shivali Pande and Aishwarya Narayan, explores how globalization seems to have achieved ultimate penetration – the plethora of choice a consumer faces in any given product or service. Globally, consumers are offered the options to choose between store brands (or generic/local brands) and national brands. The choice consumers make are reflective of their perceptions about either brand and thus provide an insight into the perceived risks that consumers associate with store or national brands. This risk creates an uncertainty of consumer base and threatens the stability of market shares for brands. The chapter examines the various perceived risks consumers associate with brands across two product categories: consumer goods and hedonic goods. Consequently, solutions to change consumer perceptions or brand strategies have been provided so that brands may be able to reduce perceived risk associated with themselves and create a stable consumer base.

Chapter 15, "Financial Risk Analysis for Crude Oil Buried Pipeline System," authored by Narendra Gade, Ravi Suryavanshi, Pravin Suryawanshi, Arati Barik, and Rahul Bhalerao, discusses how buried pipelines are lucrative in transportation for transmission of vital fluids and liquids. However, with the advent of disasters, the continuous flow through these indispensable systems gets hampered. The purpose of the chapter is twofold: one, to develop a simulation approach for capturing the effect of risk/disaster due to unforeseen events on buried pipeline; second, to gauge financial losses due to such uncertain events. A simulation model considering hoop, longitudinal, and radial stresses on continuous flow carrying buried pipeline, subjected to uncertain and risky events, is developed in CAESAR II engineering software. The authors conduct statistical inquiry to carry Node-based analysis for describing the repair cost associated with the individual node or throughout the whole pipeline system under study.

Abhishek Behl
Indian Institute of Technology Bombay, India

Sushma Nayak
Symbiosis International University (Deemed), India

Acknowledgment

The editors of the book would like to express their gratitude to each and everyone who directly or indirectly supported us in finalizing our idea, nurturing it and helping us finish our project. We would like to thank all our academic associations and researchers who have contributed in the intellectual capital of the book. It was always their support because of which we were able to take decisions and improve the quality of the book. An extended thanks to all the authors who worked hard in offering their time and intellect to write chapters which would serve the readers. We would also like to appreciate their hard work and diligence with which they shaped the content of the chapters.

It would not have been easy without constant support and mentoring by Dr. Rameshwar Dubey who symbolizes excellence in research and writing. We are really thankful to him for mentoring us on this project.

We would like to thank the Almighty for guiding us with mature thoughts and an ability to take right decisions for the success of the book. The support of family remains unparalleled in any success and the same goes here as well. We would like to thank our parents, family members and friends who helped us stay motivated during the entire course of the book.

Lastly, we would like to express our gratitude to the editorial advisory board members who helped us with their timely reviews and the team of IGI who supported us constantly at every phase of the book.

Abhishek Behl
Indian Institute of Technology Bombay, India

Sushma Nayak
Symbiosis International University (Deemed), India

Chapter 1
Deposit Insurance:
Pre-Emptive Expediency Against Bank Runs or Propulsion of Moral Hazard? Economic and Political Implications in India

Sushma Nayak
Symbiosis International University (Deemed), India

Abhishek Behl
Indian Institute of Technology Bombay, India

Aastha Behl
Pranveer Singh Institute of Technology, India

ABSTRACT

Deposit insurance is intended for providing security to depositors from the standpoint of averting bank runs. It is crucial for nations to examine their institutional environment, banking structure, and regulatory framework before insuring deposits in the interest of maintaining market discipline. In the case of India, while Deposit Insurance and Credit Guarantee Corporation (DICGC) has been contributing appreciably to the stability of Indian banking system by safeguarding depositors against possible loss of their entitled deposits with insured banks, the system is based on "paybox" mandate and affords limited conditional protection to depositors. Guided by the need for a stronger resolution mechanism, the Indian government introduced the Financial Resolution and Deposit Insurance (FRDI) Bill in August 2017, which had its own share of controversies, conceivably the most confounded provisions being the bail-in clause and omission of explicit declaration of maximum coverage. The economic and political pressures, however, led to the dropping of the Bill in July 2018, thus creating further vacuum in an already underprovided deposit protection.

DOI: 10.4018/978-1-5225-7208-4.ch001

INTRODUCTION

Banks play a significant role in the process of financial intermediation in an economy. One of the primary functions of banks is to accept deposits 'payable on demand or at short notice' thereby constituting 'liquid liabilities,' while the other is granting loans 'non-recallable on demand' thus constituting 'illiquid assets.' In this fashion, banks act as key players with respect to maturity transformation (Allen & Carletti, 2008; Havrylchyk & Verdier, 2018). The divergence in maturity — of deposits and loans — exposes banks to liquidity crisis or the odds of self-fulfilling bank runs, with a probability of all/several depositors attempting to withdraw funds at once (Bryant, 1980; Diamond & Dybvig, 1983; Demirgüç-Kunt & Detragiache, 1997; Ennis & Keister, 2009; Calvo, 2012; Iyer & Puri, 2012; Gertler & Kiyotaki, 2015; Andolfatto, Nosal, & Sultanum, 2017; Dijk, 2017; Mattana & Panetti, 2017; Havrylchyk & Verdier, 2018). Such bank runs are generally a product of 'herd behavior' or 'mob mentality' or 'mass hysteria,' when depositors press on panic button to pull out their deposits due to: an outbreak of news — real or rumor — concerning the banks' financial health (fiscal irregularities) or a downturn following recessionary economic tendencies (downward spiral) when there are qualms that banks may be unable to meet their obligations to depositors owing to cash crunch.

A question that arises is: Why do banks accept short-term deposits payable on demand that make them susceptible to apparent runs? The answer to this lies in the fact that more often than not, only some depositors aim to withdraw funds during a given period, so it is generally practicable to meet such demands without really having liquid assets backing every deposit. The drawback, however, as mentioned earlier, is the susceptibility of such a system to self-fulfilling panics (Diamond & Dybvig, 1983). If people suppose that a bank will fail, every depositor would, in effect, be desperate to withdraw funds in one fell swoop — and since the bank's assets are illiquid, attempting to cater for those demands may, in fact, cause the bank to fail. This connotes that even healthy banks are prone to panics and flusters, popularly known as bank runs. In a nutshell, the link among depositors appears as a coordination game with two Nash equilibria: one in which nobody tries to withdraw their deposits because they believe no one else will try to withdraw their deposits, and one in which everybody would try to withdraw their deposits because they believe everyone else will try to withdraw their deposits (Diamond & Dybvig, 1983). Banks faced with bank runs frequently seal the shutters and refuse to permit more than a few withdrawals during a given period, which is known as 'suspension of convertibility' (Diamond & Dybvig, 1983; Gorton, 1985; Engineer, 1989; Villamil, 1991; Samartin, 2002; Chen & Hasan, 2008; Bordo & Haubrich, 2010; Diamond, Kashyap, & Rajan, 2017). Suspension of convertibility as a provisional measure to reinstate stability may work in the interests of the concerned bank, but is detrimental to the interests of depositors, who are deprived access to their own funds held with the bank. It further indicates the inefficiency of the banking system to create confidence among depositors concerning a reliable investment climate that can stand the tests of safety and liquidity. In such a scenario, the only possible recourse to avoid bank runs is an assurance that the depositors would get their funds back, even if the bank fails (Martinez Peria & Schmukler, 2001). Can there be one such arrangement?

Diamond & Dybvig (1983) contend that suspension of convertibility may not be the most favorable apparatus for averting bank runs. A finer way of forestalling bank runs is deposit insurance backed by the government or central bank. Such insurance compensates depositors for all or part of their losses in the case of a run. Albeit, if depositors know that they will recover their money even in the event of a bank failure, they are not motivated to take part in the run. Hence, adequate deposit insurance can eliminate the likelihood of bank runs. Deposit insurance, in a way, serves as a risk management tool in the interests of depositors. It prevents bank runs and ensures faith in the banking system. This view was further maintained by Nobel Laureate Paul Krugman when he stated that banking, left to its own mechanisms, innately poses risks of destabilizing runs. In his words, he described: "banks as we know them — institutions that issue promises to pay money on, or almost on, demand, while holding liquid assets that cover only a fraction of that potential demand — are inherently subject to runs, self-fulfilling losses of confidence" (Krugman, 2014). On a fundamental level, keeping up a deposit insurance program is probably not going to be exceptionally expensive for the administration: to the extent that bank runs are forestalled, deposit insurance shall never be required to be disbursed.

Countries across the world, such as those in Asia and Europe, which have pursued liberalization to enhance the competence and effectiveness of their financial systems, have taken up deposit insurance (Gallego, Herrero, & Salas, 2002). The number has particularly risen after the global financial crisis of 2008 (Schich, 2008; Demirgüç-Kunt, Kane, & Laeven, 2015). Arguments persist that although deposit insurance can impede bank runs, when undone cautiously, explicit deposit insurance can fuel bank crises by offering banks perverse incentives to take unwarranted risks in the form of indiscriminate lending without due diligence, also known as 'moral hazard' (Anginer, Demirgüç-Kunt, & Zhu, 2014; Kim, Kim, & Han, 2014; Allen, Carletti, Goldstein, & Leonello, 2015; Ngalawa, Tchana &, Viegi, 2016). Globally, the debate still continues regarding what constitutes the appropriate coverage threshold for insuring deposits. Limited coverage can enfeeble financial stability. During financial crises, a majority of depositors, if not sufficiently protected, participate in bank runs, whether such banks are sound or weak. On the contrary, if most depositors were to be fully covered, it would create a moral hazard. Deposit insurance, categorically, is a double-edged sword (Cull, Senbet, & Sorge, 2002). While it can help restrain the propensity of depositors to flee at the earliest signs of breakdown at any bank, it also jeopardizes the discipline of the insured bank and drives amplified risk taking (Berger & Turk-Ariss, 2014).

Therefore, following the global financial crisis, countries such as Austria, Australia, Belarus, Denmark, Singapore, India, as well as few others, have been working out ways of redesigning the prevalent Deposit Insurance System (DIS) from the standpoint of modifying government guarantees. As an elaboration, in India, the current practice of deposit insurance, channeled through Deposit Insurance and Credit Guarantee Corporation (DICGC) — a subsidiary of Reserve Bank of India (RBI) — works to compensate depositors up to Rs. 1 lakh in the event of bank failure. This implies depositors holding deposits more than a lakh with a failing bank would lose the residual amount. However, depositors can niftily diversify their deposit holdings with the same bank in different right, different capacity, or across diverse banks to enjoy the optimum deposit insurance cover. Depositors, who are well educated, are more inclined to diversify deposits across accounts corresponding to the insurance cap, thus signifying that financial sophistication is allied to stronger responses (Iyer, Jensen & Johannesen, 2016). This, though, is further contingent upon information accessibility and financial literacy of the depositors.

To replace the existing system with the intent of making it more depositor-friendly, the Indian government tabled the Financial Resolution and Deposit Insurance (FRDI) Bill in the lower house of the Parliament in August 2017. The main statement of the bill spelled out: "An Act to establish a framework to carry out the resolution of certain categories of financial service providers in distress, to provide deposit insurance to consumers of certain categories of financial services and for designation of Systemically Important Financial Institutions by the Central Government for resolution; and whereas it is necessary to establish a corporation with the objective of protecting consumers of covered service providers and public funds to the extent possible thereby contributing to the stability and resilience of the financial system; and for matters connected therewith or incidental thereto" (Department of Economic Affairs,

Government of India, 2016). In addition to a series of cautionary procedures to consolidate the banking system, it involved a provision of 'bail-in' — a way to rescue an ailing bank by making its creditors and depositors take a loss on their holdings. The proposed bill could empower the government to use depositors' money to save a bank on the brink of liquidation, subject to close scrutiny and parliamentary oversight. The bill, however, after being open to a host of discussions and debates of its possible ramifications, was finally dropped in July 2018, out of government's fear of far-reaching nihilism among the public, need to appease edgy investors, and eschew any widespread backlash prior to the 2019 general elections. One argument cited for its abandonment is the 'fallacy and misapprehension' that battered public trust and resulted in panic withdrawal of cash by depositors. The question still remains: is deposit insurance, in any form, a definitive and reasonable solution for risk management in the event of a bank failure?

Considering the vulnerability of banking system in recent times and the weight accorded to deposit insurance to deal with this quandary, it is important to examine whether such insurance serves as a risk mitigating tool in the interests of depositors or it endangers the health of banking system by propelling moral hazard. The central question which the authors address in this chapter concerns with the impact of deposit insurance initiatives on financial stability, consistency and systemic progress, with India as a case in point. India is a country whose banking sector is known to have remained stable despite global cataclysm, thereby sustaining public confidence over the years. Therefore, in Indian milieu, it is important to examine the consistency and reliability of the prevailing and proposed (then shelved owing to political trepidations) arrangement of deposit insurance. For this purpose, the authors of the present chapter shall employ Delphi method — mutual assessment and forecasting method that relies upon independent investigation with major use of opinion, feedback, judgment and comments for developing consensus among experts who act together anonymously. The Delphi technique is a consensus-building practice encompassing structured communiqué among members of an expert panel by means of autonomous responses to iterative rounds of opinion poll (Sahakian, 1997). Such a method is deemed appropriate for a study which involves questions of policy making or social relevance, with a view to establish (or accomplish) consensus on contentious topics (Linstone & Turoff, 1975).

The rest of the chapter is organized as follows. Section 2 gives an extensive background of the subject under consideration by examining literature relating to the underpinnings of deposit insurance, brings out the contentions and controversies surrounding it, focuses on the mandates and core principles for its effective implementation, and discusses the ways in which it is enacted in various countries of the world, particularly after the financial crisis of 2008. Section 3 describes at length the current DIS in India and explicates the modification proposed in it by means of FRDI. It further expounds the outcomes of expert inquiry, draws inferences from the findings of the survey, and delves into the reasons responsible for the annulling of FRDI. Section 4 proposes solutions to manage systemic risks from the standpoint of ensuring market discipline in the banking sector. Section 5 outlines directions for future research and Section 6 sketches out concluding remarks.

BACKGROUND

Deposit Insurance: Theoretical Backdrop, Contentions and Controversies

Deposit insurance is extensively offered by numerous countries as an element of fiscal safety net to enhance stability (Anginer, Demirgüç-Kunt & Zhu, 2014). It has evolved as an inexorably utilized apparatus by governments to safeguard the stability of banking systems and shield bank investors from incurring massive losses owing to bank failures (Demirgüç-Kunt, Kane & Laeven, 2015; Calomiris & Jaremski, 2016). The presence of insurance influences the investment decisions of individuals, banks, and firms (Pennacchi, 2006). Likewise, an increase in the amount of deposit insurance coverage and upsurge in funding provisions helps buoy up financial stability (Iyer, Jensen & Johannesen, 2016). The global financial crisis of 2007–08 brought to fore noteworthy policy lessons for DIS. The emergence of the crisis accentuated the significance of sustaining depositor confidence and the decisive role that DIS plays in preserving it. In some nations, blanket guarantees — off the cuff extension of deposit insurance in addition to the limited coverage already committed earlier — were issued by the authorities. Regardless of the nature of insurance protection, policymakers acclaim its merit in guaranteeing depositors' faith in the financial system.

Critics claim that deposit insurance is a guarantee against loss; in the event that losses bring about a failure, a bank is assured that the burden will be borne by the government or insuring agency and the depositors will be recompensed. This incentivizes banks to take riskier decisions by offering high interest rates to attract deposits and attempt to earn the money to pay those high interest rates by making high-risk advances, eventually resulting in stressed assets for banks (Lambert, Noth & Schüwer, 2017). Several arguments persist which underscore the fact that big banks primarily contribute to systemic risk, briefly discussed as follows:

- **Unstable Banking Argument:** Big banks are predisposed to undertake risky activities by financing them through short-term debt, thus exposing them to liquidity crisis and fire sales (Kashyap, Rajan & Stein, 2002; Shleifer & Vishny, 2010; Shleifer & Vishny, 2011; Gennaioli, Shleifer & Vishny, 2013; Laeven, Ratnovski & Tong, 2014).
- **Too-Big-to-Fail Argument:** Regulators are averse to shutting down big banks, thus fueling moral hazard that leads these banks to assume undue risks in the anticipation of government bailouts (Farhi & Tirole, 2012; Laeven, Ratnovski & Tong, 2014).
- **Agency Cost Argument:** Big banks no longer perform only lending and depository functions. They have a large-scale diversification in their work portfolios, which leads to agency problems, feeble corporate governance and enhanced risks of systemic failures (Bolton, Freixas & Shapiro, 2007; Laeven & Levine, 2007; Laeven, Ratnovski & Tong, 2014).

It is therefore imperative for nations to examine their institutional environment, banking structure and regulatory framework before insuring deposits in the interest of maintaining market discipline (Demirgüç-Kunt & Kane, 2002). Effective supervision, regulation and control can lessen the unintentional ramifications of deposit insurance (Keeley, 1990; Anginer, Demirgüç-Kunt & Zhu, 2014), an argument which has been challenged by Calomiris & Jaremski (2016). Risk-adjusted premiums may serve the purpose of limiting moral hazard (Allen, Davidson, Hein & Whitledge, 2017), a practice followed by countries such as Italy, Peru and United States (Demirgüç-Kunt & Kane, 2002). Additionally, depositors can exert influence on the performance of banks and discipline them by punishing the latter through withdrawal of deposits and demanding higher interest rates, something that is widely evident in countries such as Argentina, Chile and Mexico (Martinez Peria & Schmukler, 2001). A possible contention here is: are these tendencies for risky behavior limited by the banks' vigilance toward their goodwill and brand-name, their pursuit for sustaining the trust, loyalty and security of depositors, and the structural difficulties they would have to face in the case of losses due to risky behavior. Can these be sufficiently limiting factors in banks pursuing overly risky activities? While their risk appetites may increase marginally due to deposit insurance, the aversion to large risks may still persist. Literature insinuates that deposit insurance may not essentially diminish market discipline (Martinez Peria & Schmukler, 2001) as depositors would, still be, more vigilant while depositing their money and banks would be required to be more careful while deploying those funds in search of higher yields. Depositors effectively differentiate banks on the basis of their riskiness and have a propensity to move their deposits to safer havens (Calomiris and Wilson, 2004).

While the tax system prevalent in a country plays a critical role in determining whether deposit insurance is likely to be provided ex-ante or ex-post (Cooper & Kempf, 2015), deposit insurance protection can assume either of the two forms — implicit deposit insurance or explicit deposit insurance (Demirgüç-Kunt & Kane, 2002; Schich, 2008; Demirgüç-Kunt, Kane & Laeven, 2015). Implicit deposit insurance is flexible and non-obligatory. In such an arrangement, the government's protection of depositors is optional as there are no prescribed laws or official regulations concerning the reimbursement to depositors in the aftermath of bankruptcy. The defrayal amount and the nature of protection are contingent upon ad hoc judgments exclusively made by the government in the event of a bank failure. The government has the discretion to make direct payments to depositors or organize and initiate the merger of a weak bank with a strong bank or bail out the ailing bank through capital infusion. This arrangement has its obvious downside as it engenders uncertainty about how, when, and whether or not depositors will be repaid. Funding, to a great extent, is subject to government's capacity to access funds after bank crash. Thus, implicit coverage is purely conjectural and is largely subject to political motivations that evoke a government's response to sizeable or extensive banking mess. This makes taxpayer bailouts of insolvent banks seem imminent.

Explicit deposit insurance, on the contrary, has precise directives to offer coverage and scrupulous guidelines to institute fundamental features of the DIS. In such an arrangement, premiums to be collected from member banks, coverage limits — whether 100 percent coverage or lesser than that, ways of financing the system, methodology of reimbursing depositors in the event of a bank failure or systemic crisis, institutions and bodies liable to offer protection, deposits entitled for protection, membership — whether voluntary or enforced, are decided beforehand through an Act of Parliament. The settlement can assume the form of a pay-out or the transfer of insured deposit.

Research indicates that implicit deposit insurance or instating an extemporized DIS is not an ideal method of dealing with a banking crisis (Kane, 2000). Depositors from countries with implicit guarantee exhibit greater withdrawal risk; implicit policy, therefore, may be partially successful as compared to explicit policy (Boyle, Stover, Tiwana & Zhylyevskyy, 2015). Studies also suggest that corrupt nations are inclined to take up implicit policy while explicit insurance system exposes them to default risk, liquidation, and adverse macroeconomic shocks, a manifestation of frail and feeble institutions, as well as unhealthy competitive tendencies (Egbuna, Oduh, Ujunwa & Okoyeuzu, 2018). In any case, a reasonably high deposit insurance cap is crucial to boost depositor confidence during a financial crisis (Iyer, Jensen & Johannesen, 2016), while a good deal of systemic stability depends upon how effective the mandates are (suite of legitimate directives describing the roles and responsibilities of deposit insurers) and core principles governing such an insurance system.

Mandates and Core Principles for Efficient Deposit Insurance

Recent developments around the globe, such as the financial crisis of 2008, have necessitated the evolution of distinct mandates for insurers, as illustrated in Table 1.

While these mandates serve as an essential guideline to insurers, it is further important to discuss the core principles for effective DIS introduced in the year 2009 through the collaborative efforts of International Association of Deposit Insurers (IADI) and the Basel Committee on Banking Supervision (BCBS). As the Basel Committee is committed towards improving the resilience of global banking system, these fundamental principles are used by countries across the world as a yardstick or a point of reference to appraise the quality of deposit insurance offered by them, identifying lacuna in their DIS, and adopt simultaneous measures to address them. A detailed description of these principles is given in Table 2.

In view of the importance of these core principles, several changes have been introduced in the DIS of numerous countries across the world, particularly after the global financial crisis of 2008, discussed in the next segment.

Deposit Insurance: A Global Overview

The role of deposit insurance and its nature as well as scope have undergone considerable changes since the global financial crisis of 2008. Convictions about the intent of deposit protection in maintaining financial stability have intensified and its merit in the safety net has been expounded and validated a great deal (Micajkova, 2013). The improvement in deposit insurance was influenced in one or more of the six ways exhibited in Figure 1.

There has been a massive increase in countries adopting deposit insurance after the crisis. The number of explicit insurance providers increased to112 in the year 2013 as against a meager 84 in the year 2003 (Demirgüç-Kunt, Kane & Laeven, 2015). Table 3 discusses the major changes brought about in the DIS of a few countries post-2008 crisis.

Deposit insurance became a subject of contentions and controversies during the global financial crisis, 2008. Uncertainty sparked off panic responses and breakdown of banks. Under these conditions, deposit insurance appeared as a critical element of financial safety net in arresting the panic response. Nations with enough resources afforded to expand their insurance coverage and extended the financial safety net to reinstate buoyancy in their financial system. Exceptionally, a few countries failed to keep

Table 1. Distinct mandates for deposit insurance providers

Mandate	Description
Pay Box	The insurance provider is accountable for the repayment of insured deposits only.
Pay Box Plus	The insurance provider is additionally accountable for providing definite resolutions (e.g. financial assistance).
Loss Minimizer	The insurance provider is actively involved in choosing from a variety of minimal-cost resolution policies.
Risk Minimizer	The insurance provider has extensive risk minimization obligations which involve risk estimation / management, a wide range of timely intervention practices, resolution authority, and on some occasions, prudential supervision tasks as well.

Source: World Bank, n.d.

Table 2. Core principles for effective deposit insurance systems

Number	Core Principle	Description
1.	Public policy objectives	In the larger interests of financial stability and depositor protection, it is essential to draw well-defined objectives, detail them, and integrate them into a comprehensible DIS.
2.	Mandate and authority	The mandate as well as authority held by the deposit insurer should be in conformity and consistency with the public policy objectives, and manifestly described in the legislation.
3.	Governance	The deposit insurer should be functionally autonomous, objective, evenhanded, transparent, responsible, and completely insulated from external intervention – political, industrial, or any other.
4.	Associations and interactions with other safety-net participants	A formal and all-inclusive framework should be instituted to ensure cohesion, close co-ordination and continuous information flow among the deposit insurer and other financial safety-net participants.
5.	Cross-border concerns	The presence of foreign banks in a jurisdiction should be sustained through effective co-ordination and continuous information flow among the deposit insurers in pertinent jurisdictions. In situations involving more than one deposit insurer for coverage, it is imperative to ascertain which deposit insurer or insurers will be liable for the repayment and settlement process.
6.	Deposit insurer's role in contingency planning and crisis management	The deposit insurer should be alert and responsive by setting up a system that involves policies and measures to counter the risks of bank failures through: i. being a member of a framework that secures constant communication and synchronization among financial safety-net participants for systemic crisis vigilance and management; ii. ensuring active involvement and participation of all safety-net participants.
7.	Membership	All banks should, by compulsion, be members of DIS.
8.	Coverage	The amount of deposit covered by insurance should be clear and well-defined. Coverage should be adequate; neither too less to endanger financial stability, nor too more to threaten market discipline. It should be consistent and in harmony with the public policy objectives. At the point when a nation chooses to transition from a blanket guarantee to a restrictive DIS, the transition ought to be as fast as a nation's conditions allow. Blanket guarantees can have various unfavorable impacts if held very long, strikingly moral hazard. Policymakers should give careful consideration to public outlook and expectations during the period of transition.
9.	Funding	The deposit insurer should have enough funds to promptly reimburse depositors in case a situation of payout arises. The onus for bearing the cost of deposit insurance should rest with the banks.
10.	Information dissemination to the general public	The public should be, on a regular basis, informed about the rudiments, benefits and constraints of DIS.
11.	Legal safeguards	The deposit insurer and people, working presently or previously for the deposit insurer, must be shielded from liability emerging from activities, cases, claims, legal actions, moves or exclusions, enacted in good faith in accordance with the fulfillment of their responsibilities. Legal protection to these parties should be outlined in legislation.
12.	Dealing with parties responsible for bank failure	The deposit insurer should be empowered to initiate necessary action against parties held responsible for bank failure.
13.	Early detection and well-timed intervention	The deposit insurer should be a part of the framework that allows for early detection and recognition of when a bank is likely to fail or get itself into some sort of serious trouble and take necessary steps before the actual failure.
14.	Failure resolution	There should be an active and exclusive failure resolution plan that can be put into action to protect depositors and reinstate financial stability.
15.	Compensating depositors	There should be prompt settlement and repayment to depositors in the event of bank failure. Any delays in this regard may shatter the confidence of the public.
16.	Recoveries	The deposit insurer should enjoy rights to claim the proceeds from the assets of the failing bank, guided by economic and commercial considerations.

Source: International Association of Deposit Insurers (IADI) (2014)

Figure 1. Upgrades in deposit protection following 2008 global financial crisis
Source: Demirgüç-Kunt, Kane & Laeven (2015)

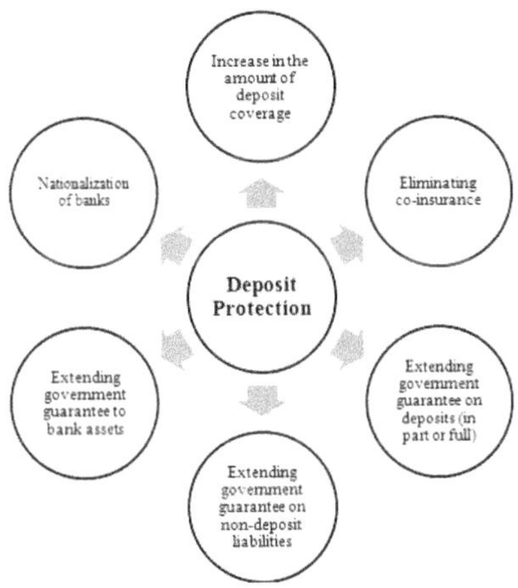

Table 3. Major changes in DIS following 2008 global financial crisis

Country/Continent	Major Changes in DIS Following 2008 Global Financial Crisis	Source
Australia	• Explicit deposit insurance was introduced.	Micajkova, 2013; Demirgüç-Kunt, Kane & Laeven, 2015
	• In October 2008, the government extended guarantee to deposits held with all the banks for the following three years in addition to providing funds to local banks for a definite period.	Schich, 2008
Austria, Denmark, Germany, Hong Kong, Iceland, Singapore, Slovak Republic	• There was an unlimited raise in the amount of deposit coverage.	Schich, 2008
Belgium, Greece, Luxembourg, Netherlands, Portugal, Spain, Switzerland, United Kingdom, Czech Republic, Finland, Hungary, Poland, Sweden, Russia	• There was a well-defined raise in the amount of deposit coverage as compared to what prevailed before the crisis.	Schich, 2008
Belgium, Iceland, Ireland, Netherlands, United Kingdom	• There was a sizeable nationalization of banks.	Demirgüç-Kunt, Kane & Laeven, 2015
Chile, Czech Republic, Dominican Republic, Lithuania, Paraguay, United Kingdom	• Blanket guarantee was extended on a bank-selected basis	Laeven & Valencia (2008) as cited in Ognjenovic (2017)
Ireland	• In September 2008, the government of Ireland extended interim guarantee to deposits, bonds, senior subordinated debt and dated subordinated debt held with six largest banks, with the commitment to cease the guarantee in September 2010.	Schich, 2008
New Zealand	• In October 2008, the government instituted an opt-in retail deposit scheme which was discontinued in December 2010.	Schich, 2008; Demirgüç Kunt, Kane & Laeven, 2015
Republic of Macedonia	• Deposit insurance coverage was increased from EUR 20,000 to EUR 30,000.	Micajkova, 2013
United States	• A guarantee program was introduced to cover money market funds for a definite period of two years effective from September 2008. • In October 2008, the cap on insurance provided by Federal Deposit Insurance Corporation (FDIC) was temporarily raised from USD 100,000 to USD 250,000 per depositor, per insured bank. • FDIC extended interim conditional guarantee to senior unsecured debt of all FDIC-insured institutions.	Schich, 2008
	• The payout speed was enhanced and reimbursement was initiated within a couple of business days after the closure of the failed institution.	Micajkova, 2013

Source: Various sources

their assurances: Iceland did that on insured deposits while Cyprus inflicted sizeable losses on their uninsured depositors (Demirgüç-Kunt, Kane & Laeven, 2015). However, as against international financial markets which got debilitated owing to crisis of confidence, countries such as India remained immune to the far-reaching stresses and shocks of the global catastrophe, thanks to the coherent fiscal and monetary measures initiated by the government and the monetary authority. As a consequence, no special measures were needed to expand the deposit insurance coverage or raise the premium. A detailed discussion of India's DIS forms the mainstay of forthcoming segments.

MAIN FOCUS OF THE CHAPTER

The chapter focuses on the present state of deposit insurance in India with specific emphasis on the existing protection afforded by DICGC and the limpidity and loopholes involved in it, as well as the nuances of the FRDI Bill, 2017, which led to the latter's abolition before seeing the light of the day. As is popularly known: "The institutions that enhance people's economic lives such as central banks, deposit insurance and stock exchanges are not the products of careful designs in calm times, but are cobbled together at the bottom of financial cliffs. Response to the crisis follows a familiar pattern - it starts with a blame. New parts of the financial system are vilified: a new type of bank, investor or asset is identified as a culprit and is then banned or regulated out of existence" (Singh, 2015). These words hold particularly true in a country like India which has a vast and diverse network of banks such as commercial banks — public sector banks, private sector banks, foreign banks, regional rural banks — and co-operative banks, spread across the length and breadth of the country. Although each one of these performs independent activities, they are mutually interconnected and influence each other through their diverse transactions. Consequently, the performance of one bank is likely to influence the performance of another bank on account of interbank transfers and related functions. In such a scenario, even if one single bank fails to deliver efficiently, it will have an adverse impact not only on its own customers, but also on its banking partners, thus enhancing the risk of systemic failure. An effective DIS that strikes a balance of objectives — depositor confidence vs. moral hazard — thus becomes imperative, which constitutes the crux of the present chapter.

DEPOSIT INSURANCE SYSTEM IN INDIA

Present Status of DIS in India

In India, the responsibility of insuring bank deposits is vested in Deposit Insurance and Credit Guarantee Corporation (DICGC), a wholly-owned subsidiary of Reserve Bank of India, which was instituted in 1962 through an Act of the Parliament — DICGC Act, 1961. The details of the functions performed by this body are covered in Table 4.

Table 5 indicates the holdings of DICGC during the period 2007-2008 to 2016-2017. The fund surplus has been increasing over the years, whereas the outstanding liability for claims is exhibiting an erratic trend: a rising picture in the aftermath of the financial crisis, followed by a decline (with minor exceptions) in subsequent years.

Table 4. Current status of deposit insurance protection in India as provided by DICGC

Particulars	Details
Mission	"To contribute to financial stability by securing public confidence in the banking system through provision of deposit insurance, particularly for the benefit of the small depositors"
Vision	"To be recognized as one of the most efficient and effective deposit insurance providers, responsive to the needs of its stakeholders"
Historical prominence	Second oldest deposit insurer of the world
Type	Ex-ante
Mandate	Pay box
Governance	Operationally self-governing
Insured banks	All commercial banks, local area banks, regional rural banks, co-operative banks functioning in India
Insured deposits	Current deposits, savings deposits, recurring deposits, fixed deposits, etc.
Non-insured deposits	Government deposits, inter-bank deposits, overseas deposits of Indian banks, any others as may be specifically exempted by DICGC with prior approval of RBI
Maximum insurance	Rupees one lakh inclusive of principal and interest held in the same right and same capacity with a given bank
Premium payment	Every six months by the insured bank
Nature of premium	Flat rate
Delay in paying premium	Imposition of penalty at 8 per cent over the bank rate from the commencement of financial half year till the date of payment
Non-payment of premium	Cancellation of registration of insured bank on a lapse for three periods in succession
Reimbursement to depositors	Upon liquidation of a bank or reconstruction/amalgamation/merger of a bank
Duration of reimbursement	Within two months from the receipt of claim from the liquidator

Source: DICGC (2017)

Table 5. Deposit insurance fund of DICGC (2007-08 to 2016-17) (In Rs. Crore)

	2007–08	2008–09	2009–10	2010–11	2011–12	2012–13	2013–14	2014–15	2015–16	2016–17
Deposit insurance fund	13,362	16,156	20,152	24,704	30,093	36,120	40,617	50,453	60,254	70,155
Of which										
Fund balance (actuarial)	1,553	1,817	3,275	3,774	4,768	5,265	5,068	5,207	5,412	5,598
Fund surplus	11,809	14,339	16,877	20,930	25,325	30,855	35,549	45,246	54,842	64,557
Outstanding liability for claims	488	1075	764	603	689	905	392	314	252	222

Source: DICGC Annual Reports [as cited in (Bose, 2017)]

While DICGC has been contributing appreciably to the stability of Indian banking system by safeguarding depositors against possible loss of their entitled deposits in insured banks under unforeseen circumstances, the Indian government decided to broaden the scope of DIS in India through introduction of FRDI Bill in August 2017, guided by the need for a stronger resolution mechanism that emerged after the 2008 global financial crisis. However, the controversial bill was later scrapped in July 2018 for reinstating public confidence and securing vote bank in the milieu of the 2019 general elections. Indian economy continues to be dominated by political contemplations, proved time and again. This constitutes the subject of discussion in the next segment.

The Financial Resolution and Deposit Insurance (FRDI) Bill: Arrived and Left, but Never Stayed

The FRDI Bill was introduced in the lower house of the Indian Parliament on August 10, 2017. The primary objective was to broaden the coverage of regulatory command and control for the entire financial system, rather than merely keeping it confined to the banking sector. Its major emphasis was on resolution mechanism to identify and discipline the weaker institutions, way before they land themselves in a situation of virtual collapse. Towards this end, a Resolution Corporation (RC) would be set up with the responsibility of classifying banks and other financial service providers — insurance companies, non-banking financial companies, stock exchanges, and payment systems — on the basis of risk exposure ranging from low, moderate, material, imminent, and critical risk to viability (Halan, 2017). Once a financial institution would come into the material risk or imminent risk category, it would be required to propose a restoration strategy to the regulating body and a resolution tactic to the RC within a span of 90 days of identification (Bose, 2017). Such an institution would then be supervised by RC and its performance would be periodically assessed to scrutinize if it violates the critical risk to viability criteria. If a financial institution would land itself in the 'critical risk' category, it could be an alarming sign for the RC to immediately take over. It would assume control over the administration of that firm and might deploy any one or more of the five options to deal with the quandary:

1. transfer the assets and liabilities of the vulnerable firm to a stronger firm;
2. facilitate merger or acquisition of the firm;
3. create a bridge entity to take possession of the firm's assets, liabilities and management;
4. bring into action the bail-in provision of converting creditors' (including depositors') debt into equity; or lastly,
5. liquidate the firm altogether.

Although the proposed arrangement was deemed to be a farsighted step to safeguard the stability of the entire financial system, it had its own share of controversies and debates following mass hysteria over the proposed bail-in clause. Conceivably, the most confounded provision in the FRDI Bill was the bail-in clause, which resulted in apprehensions among people that deposits being liabilities would be written down in case of a default. However, bail-in could be realized only if depositors gave away consent to the bank by agreeing to do so through signing deposit forms, an aspect which either failed to reach out clearly to the masses or missed the mark in its accurate interpretation by the latter. The RC was also supposed to be empowered to insure bank deposits by setting a ceiling in consultation with the

RBI. Nevertheless, a major snag of the FRDI Bill was the omission of explicit declaration of maximum deposit insurance amount.

The loopholes in the bill were widely censured because they defeated the very purpose for which it was introduced — restoring public confidence and *maintaining financial stability in times of risk and uncertainty*. The bill in reality led to bank runs. "As per Reserve Bank of India (RBI) data, aggregate deposits of all scheduled commercial banks fell from Rs. 116.84 lakh crore in April 2018 to Rs. 116.52 lakh crore by end of May 2018. The demand and time deposits also fell from Rs. 1,53,000 crore to Rs. 1,52,100 crore. While all this cannot be attributed entirely to fears over the FRDI Bill, it could still point to a trend" (Sridhar, 2018). This led to the termination of the bill which was heralded by experts as an aperture in the legal make-up for resolution, alongside liquidation, of financial firms in the country — a matter that the Centre would have to take up at a later date.

RESEARCH METHODOLOGY

The authors began their study by reviewing scholarly articles relevant to 'deposit insurance' published during the period 1983-mid 2018. The year 1983 was chosen as the initial year because the seminal paper on this subject by Diamond and Dybvig was published in the same year. All, or most of the articles reviewed by authors, predominantly discussed 2 aspects:

1. The role of deposit insurance in forestalling bank runs and arresting systemic crisis;
2. The odds of moral hazard triggered by deposit insurance in the absence of enough supervision and oversight by the regulatory authorities.

These two aspects came under rigorous consideration during the global financial crisis, a picture which held nearly true for the entire world. However, Indian banking system remained largely immune to these developments owing to a strong regulatory framework. As a result, there were no major revisions in the DIS afforded by banks in India; arrangements continued to remain pretty much the same as they were before the crisis. It was only when the Indian government tabled the FRDI Bill in the lower house of the Parliament in August 2017 that the issue of DIS became a subject of significant arguments and controversies. This bill, as discussed earlier, had its own set of strengths and weaknesses which led to apprehensions among depositors about the safety of their funds parked with banks. In several parts of the country, particularly in Telangana and Andhra Pradesh, people participated in bank runs by claiming to have lost faith in the banking system following the proposed FRDI Bill that vehemently provided for a bail-in clause (The Economic Times, 2018). Initially, to control this situation, bank officials and authorities had to come forward to notify customers against excessive withdrawals with a word of assurance that the FRDI Bill is still a bill and the depositors will be protected. However, the assurances were not enough and the bill had to be dropped later in July 2018.

Motivated by these factors, the authors of this chapter aimed at:

- Establishing the credibility and credence of having a DIS in place;
- Assessing the way DIS currently functions in India in the form of protection extended by Deposit Insurance and Credit Guarantee Corporation; and

- Identifying the limitations/strengths of the abandoned FRDI Bill from the standpoint of renewing the DIS in India and bolstering the financial system.

For this purpose, Delphi method/expert survey, involving two rounds, was undertaken with a view to gather and integrate opinions for attaining a degree of convergence. Delphi method essentially involves inviting opinions and systematizing judgments, especially in complex issues which necessitate intuitive construal of evidence or informed deductions. It requires at least two rounds. A majority of the studies employ two or three rounds. According to Walker and Selfe (1996) as cited in Thangaratinam & Redman (2005), "repeated rounds may lead to fatigue by respondents and increased attrition." The number of experts recruited in the process and the fact that conflicting opinions are to some extent hidden behind the main converging one, make it an established and plausible approach for policy makers.

Selection of the Expert Panel and Panel Size

An expert may be considered as one who has pertinent knowledge and experience in a particular discipline. There are no predetermined rules regarding a definite panel size. Linstone (1978) as cited in Thangaratinam & Redman (2005) proposes that "a suitable minimum panel size is seven" although panel sizes may essentially range from four to three thousand. As a result, it appears that the decision concerning panel size is experiential and pragmatic, with due consideration to aspects such as time and budget.

For the present study, Academicians, Independent Researchers working within the domain of financial sector, Bankers, and Members of Parliament (policy makers) were recruited to constitute the panel. The experts were chosen based on their expertise and willingness to participate in the study. Most of the panelists (85%) had over ten years of teaching/work/research experience in the banking sphere; while the rest had relatively less, although not lower than 5 years. Figure 2 exhibits the composition of the expert panel and panel size.

Questionnaire Preparation

First Round Questionnaire

The first-round questionnaire was an open-ended one and developed from content analysis of major findings and relevant claims exposed in extant literature. It elicited responses for the following concerns:

1. **Role and Scope of Deposit Insurance:** The experts were asked whether they thought deposit insurance can serve as a mechanism to avoid bank runs or it is an insufficient measure to avoid runs if customers can claim only a certain percentage (capped amount) of their deposit back in the event of bank failure. They had to further comment on the scope of deposit insurance with respect to its necessity or otherwise and its role in strengthening/degrading the financial system.
2. **Moral Hazard:** Experts had to answer whether deposit insurance triggers moral hazard or there is no possibility of information asymmetry in this regard.
3. **Monitoring and Supervision of Banks in the Absence of Deposit Insurance:** Experts were asked if they thought whether in a system without deposit insurance, depositors and bank creditors would have an incentive to monitor their bank's behavior to ensure it does not act in a manner that endangers its solvency.

Figure 2. Composition of the expert panel and panel size
Source: Authors

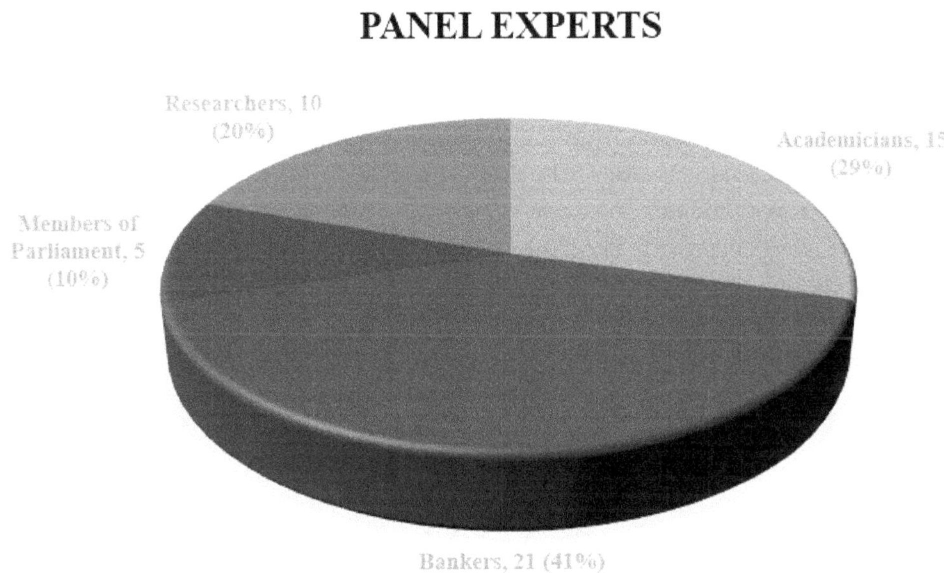

4. **Present Status of DIS in India:** Under the current system of DIS in India provided through Deposit Insurance and Credit Guarantee Corporation Act, 1961, any amount more than Rs. 1 lakh in a deposit account can be forfeited in the event of a bank failure. This limit was placed in 1993, nearly 25 years ago. The experts were asked whether this is an adequate amount or needs reconsideration in the present-day context from the standpoint of inflation and cost of living.
5. **Proposed Legislation for Revised DIS in India**: The experts were finally asked if the formerly proposed legislation through FRDI Bill could have served as a better arrangement over the current one provided by DICGC. This inquiry was important to explore how DIS in India could be improved in the context of obliteration of FRDI and with due consideration to the inadequacies of DICGC with respect to deposit protection.
6. **Additional Comments:** The experts were given discretion to share any additional comments, over and above their responses to structured questions covered in the questionnaire.

The questionnaire was e-mailed to the experts with a request to respond within four days. However, the same was accomplished with an extended deadline of seven days and constant follow-up by authors. The responses to the open-ended questions were analyzed and interpreted qualitatively by sorting, classifying and grouping of common items.

Second Round Questionnaire

Based on responses and arguments presented by the experts in the first round, the second-round questionnaire was drawn with new items that were not covered in the first-round questionnaire. It was based on five-point Likert Scale and included 44 indicator statements which invited responses by choosing any one of the five options: totally agree, agree, partially agree, disagree, and totally disagree. This questionnaire was shared with the experts through email, and all technical terms, acronyms and jargon were clarified in the mail.

Analysis

Quantitative analysis was undertaken from the responses derived in the second Delphi round, which was the final round of seeking responses. The authors established the interpretation of 'consensus' in conformity with the aims of the study. An iterative two-stage process was deemed sufficient to elucidate and build up the quality of consensus. The method of analysis was adopted from Bourgeois, Kanoute & Faye (2014) by classifying the degree of consensus into seven categories, illustrated in Figure 3.

Results

The experts appraised and responded to the second-round questionnaire by selecting one of the five options for each indicator statement. The authors have sorted the 44 indicator statements into three groups:

1. The credibility and credence of instituting a deposit insurance system (presented in Table 6).
2. Existing status of DIS in India in the form of protection extended by Deposit Insurance and Credit Guarantee Corporation (presented in Table 7).
3. Exploring the weaknesses/strengths of FRDI Bill from the standpoint of future renewal of DIS in India and strengthening the financial system (presented in Table 8).

As illustrated in Table 6, three levels of agreement were observed with respect to 19 questions: strong agreement (16 indicator statements), weak agreement (2 indicator statements), scattered toward agreement (1 indicator statement). Strong disagreement was identified with respect to 1 question.

Figure 3. Categorization of level of consensus among experts
Source: Bourgeois, Kanoute & Faye (2014)

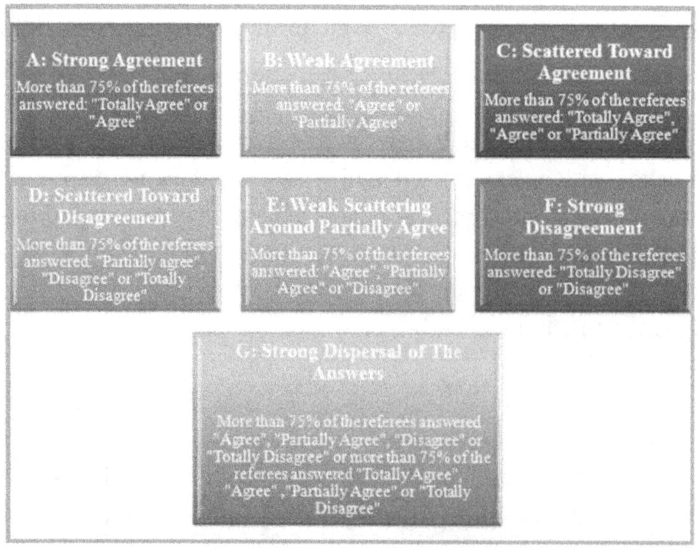

Deposit Insurance

Table 6. Credibility and credence of instituting a deposit insurance system

#	Indicator Statement	Level Consensus						
		A	B	C	D	E	F	G
1.	Explicit deposit insurance serves as a mechanism to avoid bank runs.	*						
2.	DIS is not a sufficient remedy to avoid bank runs.	*						
3.	Bank run is an economic as well as behavioral phenomenon – an outcome of herd mentality.	*						
4.	Decisions concerning deposit insurance need to be taken before a banking crisis because instating an extemporized DIS to deal with an existing banking crisis can be perilous.	*						
5.	During a crisis, countries with DIS experience lesser bank risk and better systemic stability.		*					
6.	DIS is more likely to protect small depositors than big depositors in the case of partial coverage of bank deposits.	*						
7.	Unless capital adequacy, risk bearing and risk tolerance of insured institutions are scrutinized gingerly, DIS may result in excess risk taking and diminish bank stability in the long run.	*						
8.	Although deposit insurance is in place, banks may be dissuaded from engaging in excessively risky activities owing to their attentiveness to goodwill, brand name, trust, and customer loyalty.	*						
9.	The prevalence of DIS reduces the incentive of depositors to monitor banks and thus fuels moral hazard wherein the bank will be prompted to take higher risks (reckless lending and investment decisions), knowing it well that the government shall be obliged to rescue the former if it should fail.	*						
10.	In the absence of DIS, depositors have a larger incentive to monitor their banks' activities (by demanding higher deposit interest rates or by withdrawing their deposits). However, this is subject to depositors' financial knowledge and the obscure nature of banking transactions.	*						
11.	If DIS is not credible or if there are costs involved in recovery of deposits following a bank failure, insured depositors will be compelled to monitor banks further.		*					
12.	Although absence of DIS will make depositors more vigilant while depositing their money and banks more careful while deploying those funds in search of higher yields, it may correspondingly reduce the liquidity in the financial system.			*				
13.	In the absence of DIS, although individuals have the incentive, they may not necessarily be able to monitor bank behavior, or correctly evaluate risky behavior in the event it occurs.	*						
14.	DIS, despite its tendency toward moral hazards, does strengthen the financial system and must continue to exist as it provides stability to the entire financial system by increasing its capability to withstand shocks. Quoting the age-old adage, "half a loaf is better than none," even though insufficient, the existence of such a mechanism is important, which can later be improved based on the responses and the scenario.	*						
15.	The "moral hazard effect" of DIS is prominent when the economy is doing well and experiencing optimistic trends, while the "stabilization effect" of DIS is evident when the economy is experiencing downward spiral.	*						
16.	Arbitrarily extending government guarantees and similar forms of bailout encourage shoddy bankers and discipline good ones.	*						
17.	The unfavorable consequences of DIS may be contingent upon the institutional environment prevalent in a country and could possibly be alleviated by means of effective bank regulation. Such checks and controls can counteract the perverse incentives created by DIS so that moral hazard need not be a concern.	*						
18.	Account-holders should "coinsure" a fraction of their deposits implying an obligation, by convention, to endure a portion of their banks' accrued losses upon failure.						*	
19.	A bank's deposit insurance premium should be finely tuned, sensitive and responsive to the risk exposure of the bank.	*						
20.	While an explicit and unequivocal DIS must incorporate a "paybox" function that gives payout to depositors in case of bank failure, nations may likewise choose to consolidate the DIS with resolution functions or that of a watchdog or banking regulator or controller, known to as "paybox plus."	*						

*Indicates level of consensus among experts

Source: Authors

Table 7. Existing status of DIS in India as extended by Deposit Insurance and Credit Guarantee Corporation

#	Indicator Statement	Level Consensus						
		A	B	C	D	E	F	G
1.	In a nation like India, where there is considerable degree of financial exclusion, and small depositors, in particular, are concerned about the safety of their deposits, DIS is crucial for financial inclusion and thus acts as a catalyst.	*						
2.	In India, there is not enough awareness of DIS.	*						
3.	DICGC should have a significant role to play in regulation and control for timely detection of bank failures and initiating definitive measures from the standpoint of safeguarding public deposits as well as maintaining financial stability.	*						
4.	It is vital to widen the mandate of DICGC from "pay-box" to "pay-box plus."	*						
5.	RBI should have authority and influence to resolve a bank before liquidation.	*						
6.	DICGC should identify ways and means to speed up the repayment process to depositors of failed banks in order to retain the latter's confidence in banking system.	*						
7.	It is essential to raise the deposit insurance cap beyond INR 1 lakh as it has remained unaltered since last 25 years i.e. from 1993.	*						
8.	From the viewpoint of enhancing the financial strength of DICGC, an organization which primarily exists to serve the interests of small depositors, it is necessary to exempt the corporation from tax payments, as has been the practice followed by other countries across the globe.		*					
9.	DICGC should move away from flat rate premium system to risk-sensitive differential premium system.	*						
10.	DICGC, in collaboration with the RBI, should build up a superior and sophisticated sensory framework for quick recognition of crisis and first-rate exigency planning, with sufficient funds at all times, to arrest the crisis early on and preserve depositors' interests.	*						
11.	DICGC should strive towards attainment of one of the core principles viz., cross border coordination.	*						

*Indicates level of consensus among experts
Source: Authors

As illustrated in Table 7, two levels of agreement were observed with respect to 11 questions: strong agreement (10 indicator statements) and weak agreement (1 indicator statement).

As illustrated in Table 8, three levels of agreement were observed with respect to 12 questions: strong agreement (6 indicator statements), weak agreement (4 indicator statements) and scattered toward agreement (2 indicator statements). For one statement, there was weak scattering around partially agree.

DISCUSSION

The use of Delphi as a method of data collection has assumed popularity over the last 30 years; studies particularly suggest that internet and its applications have lessened Delphi limitations and brought forth its best outcomes (Donohoe, Stellefson & Tennant, 2012). In the present study too, it enabled the authors to derive consensus on various aspects of DIS in general and DIS in India in particular.

Experts believe that a premeditated explicit DIS is necessary to avoid bank runs and maintain financial stability, earlier confirmed by Demirgüç-Kunt, Kane & Laeven (2015); Calomiris & Jaremski (2016); Iyer, Jensen & Johannesen (2016). If depositors are aware that they will get back their funds to the extent

Table 8. Limitations/strengths of the abandoned FRDI Bill

#	Indicator Statement	Level Consensus						
		A	B	C	D	E	F	G
1.	There were several ambiguities surrounding the FRDI Bill and government's clarifications regarding these were vague, which resulted in its eventual collapse.		*					
2.	The establishment of Resolution Corporation to identify definite factors for categorization of banks and other financial institutions into five categories of risk (stretching from low, moderate, material, imminent and critical risk to viability) would have ensured that there is a systematic and methodical apparatus for measurement, supervising, and managing impending failures even before they occur.	*						
3.	The bill upheld the interests of depositors by safeguarding the value of the weak bank (most likely to fail) through prompt detection and a premeditated action plan.		*					
4.	The bill afforded a greater probability for depositors to claim their funds, if the bank exhibited higher propensity to fail.		*					
5.	FRDI allowed effective supervision and categorization of banks thus tagging their status and guaranteeing adoption of pre-emptive measures to forestall a failure. This made the bill a sizeable improvement and upgrade from the existing system of DICGC.			*				
6.	The FRDI bill provided a more dynamic mechanism of addressing the incidence of any bank failure. The bill sought to take corrective actions and decisions on individual case basis. This is much different from the many outdated precedents stated in the DICGC.	*						
7.	FRDI bill could have attained its objective if the government had amplified the deposit insurance ceiling to protect 80–90% of deposits.	*						
8.	FRDI Bill was more a restatement of the status quo with minor upgrades.			*				
9.	A Resolution Corporation with retained DICGC benefits would be a win-win situation for depositors, banks and the regulators.	*						
10.	The proposed feature of "bail in" does not make the depositors worse off because they would still get the insured amount.					*		
11.	The FRDI Bill seemed to work on theory and paper, the success of which would have ultimately been in the hands of the executive.	*						
12.	While the measure had a good intention, it might not have been a sound method to ensure customer's safety as well as save the bank from failure.		*					
13.	The government must introduce more pragmatic and crystal-clear policies to infuse faith among the public and initiate banking sector reforms without leaving room for contentions and disputations.	*						

*Indicates level of consensus among experts
Source: Authors

of the insured amount, DIS can actually hold back financial contagion. The level of awareness among depositors is critical as bank runs are not merely economic upshots, but behavioral too, and a lot depends on how the public as a whole think and respond collectively as a herd (Ricciardi, 2017). However, DIS may not be sufficient by its own to serve the purpose (Demirgüç-Kunt & Kane, 2002) because it further depends on strong financial structures (Kleftouri, 2013) and the capped amount or the maximum amount insured. In case of partial coverage of deposits, there is higher probability of a bank run as depositors have large incentive to withdraw the amount over and above the insured amount, which may not hold true in the case of full coverage. In any case, DIS works largely in favour of small depositors (Demirgüç-Kunt & Kane, 2002) who are likely to enjoy insurance protection for the entire amount.

DIS has the capacity to ensure greater systemic stability in times of crisis subject to the nature of insurance protection (explicit/implicit/blanket guarantee) afforded by a country (Anginer, Demirgüç-Kunt & Zhu, 2014). However, a major drawback of DIS is the probability of moral hazard (Kusairi, Sanusi & Ismail, 2018). Those banks, which least care about their brand name and goodwill, may be motivated to take undue risks and be reckless in their lending and investment decisions considering the possibility of a bailout in the event of a failure. Depositors too may be less vigilant in monitoring their banks in the presence of DIS. This can be effectively checked through organized supervision and control on the part of the regulating body (by initiating timely action) as well as the depositors (by imposing a cost while dealing with risk prone banks) (Martinez Peria & Schmukler, 2001). Another important measure could be introducing a practice of risk based differential premium in place of flat rate premium; the higher the risks taken by a bank, more should be the insurance premium payable and vice versa (Allen, Davidson, Hein & Whitledge, 2017). A nation must opt for "paybox plus" mandate of deposit insurance protection which comes into action to establish control even before a bank fails (Ognjenovic, 2017). All these steps taken together may yield desired outcomes to ensure market discipline.

As pointed by experts, co-insurance is not an ideal arrangement as depositors should not be made to bear the incidence of bank's losses (Boyle, Stover, Tiwana & Zhylyevskyy, 2015), although it is meant to caution depositors make more prudent bank choices while placing their deposits (Demirgüç-Kunt, Kane, Karacaovali & Laeven, 2008). Co-insurance is a threat to financial stability.

In the case of India, DICGC has a significant role to play in safeguarding the interests of small depositors, but the level of awareness and financial literacy amid depositors is still a matter of concern. DICGC needs to improve in five major spheres: increase awareness among depositors, raise the deposit insurance limit to more than a lakh with due consideration to inflation and cost of living (the cost of living has increased manifold since 1993), introduce risk-based differential premium, move from "paybox" to "paybox plus" mandate, and ensure quick disbursement of funds to depositors of failed banks. An important amendment to strengthen DICGC could be exemption from tax payments, although a better way could be introduction of risk-based differential premium, which is likely to expand resources for the insuring body as well as impart discipline to shoddy banks.

According to experts, FRDI Bill had several aces over the existing arrangement. It could have been an ideal arrangement likely to be tested by time had it become an Act. Although there were several ambiguities surrounding this bill, particularly with respect to maximum amount insured, it was based on "paybox plus" mandate, a much-needed arrangement for India in the present-day context. One of its most crucial aspects was active monitoring and classification of banks thus tagging their status, and ensuring pre-emptive measures to avoid a failure. And even though there could be a failure, there were proper measures proposed to attempt revival and a definite timeframe for resolution, which is lacking in the existing system. The Resolution Corporation with incredible powers could have definitely acted in extended capacity compared to DICGC. Nonetheless, the bail-in clause didn't fit well on account of a possible threat to market discipline. It is difficult to ascertain whether depositors would be willing to have their deposit cancelled from the bank's liability if the failure of the bank is due to its own risky financial decisions. The trust of the customers in the bank would be eroded. Therefore, while the measure had a good intention, it failed to ensure customers' safety as well as saving the bank from imminent failure.

SOLUTIONS AND RECOMMENDATIONS

Based on the findings of the study, it may be clearly stated that government's provision of financial safety net to banks and other financial institutions is imperative. In case a crisis arises, it may be deemed essential to overlook the moral hazard aspect, since the pressing need then is to restore confidence. Guarantees/assurances can be effective in this respect. DIS, therefore, must be "optimally funded" — "able to fulfill its main task and enable fast and efficient access to deposits when they become unavailable, based on DIS's risk awareness, a proactive financial management policy and adjustments of established benchmarks and funding in accordance with the DIS's needs" (Ognjenovic, 2017). DIS in India should continue to be explicit in nature but with an escalation in maximum amount covered for all banks, founded on "paybox plus" mandate, adherence to all the core principles, institution of risk based differential premium by having banks pay for adopting a higher risk profile, allowing quick disbursement of funds to depositors of failed banks, and providing cross border coordination arrangements.

It must be further noted that institutional failures are most often triggered by a single or few big deals undertaken without sufficient due diligence, which has large scale ramifications, frequently unfavorable. Thus, in-depth qualitative monitoring of massive deals and credit related due diligence norms should have wider emphasis than merely focusing on a single figure for insurance cover.

As the integration of Indian economy with the rest of the world has enhanced further, it is necessary to secure the system as a whole in order to protect sudden vulnerable impacts to the economy. Banks, in order to be globally sustainable, need to maintain a reasonably minimum buffer capital stock for raising their loss absorption capacity.

There should be an arrangement, which pronounces risk exposures of banks in public domain for depositors to assess the risk-return matrix of the concerned bank before deciding to place deposits. The publicly available knowledge and easily comprehensible risk measures can facilitate depositors to choose a more suitable bank in sync with their risk appetites and expectations for returns.

The existing framework to deal with banks and other financial firms in India is insufficient, given the size and growing nature of the industry. In Indian scenario, it is important to enhance the overall security of the banking and financial system. However, it must be ensured that any policy, if rolled out, is done smoothly, and sufficient clarification regarding all the provisions is provided in advance. It must come out as a mechanism which builds trust and stability in the banking sector and not otherwise.

FUTURE RESEARCH DIRECTIONS

A good deal of research has been undertaken with respect to diverse aspects of deposit insurance at a global level; however, there is paucity of enough research concerning the same with respect to India. Although DICGC is one of the oldest deposit insuring bodies across the globe, the level of insurance protection extended is not at par with global standards. Future research may focus on a comparison of India's deposit insurance practices with the rest of the world. It is necessary to examine the nature of institutional environment prevalent in India, the extent of financial exclusion, the level of public awareness and the expectations of depositors from an effective DIS. Similarly, future research should identify the performance of DICGC till date, its efforts at disciplining banks for non-compliance with prescribed conventions, and its efficiency with respect to reimbursement to depositors of failed banks. These findings shall assist judgments on the espousal of best deposit insurance practices from the standpoint of *maintaining financial stability in times of risk and uncertainty.*

CONCLUSION

The concept of deposit insurance is based on providing security to depositors with the objective of averting bank runs. Historically, it has been observed that uninsured depositors are most likely to participate in runs. Therefore, it is indispensable to have DIS in place in a country, although, the amount of insurance coverage provided is critical. If it is too high, there is a risk of moral hazard, while if it is too low, it fails in preventing runs. The amount must be such that an individual feels their earnings are secured, and amount lost, if any, is an acceptable risk. The core challenge of DIS arises from the need to strike a fine balance between the incentives of averting crises and the costs involved in regulating risky behavior by banks and customers. It is therefore crucial for nations to examine their institutional environment, banking structure and regulatory framework before insuring deposits in the interest of maintaining market discipline. Effective supervision, regulation and control can lessen the unintentional ramifications of deposit insurance. Risk-adjusted premiums too may serve the purpose of upholding market discipline. In the case of India, while DICGC has been contributing appreciably to the stability of Indian banking system by safeguarding depositors against possible loss of their entitled deposits in insured banks, the system is based on "paybox" mandate and affords conditional protection only up to Rs. 1 lakh, which has remained unchanged since 1993. The Indian government, therefore, decided to broaden the scope of DIS through introduction of FRDI Bill, guided by the need for a stronger resolution mechanism. The primary objective was to expand the coverage of regulatory command and control for the entire financial system, rather than merely keeping it confined to the banking sector. It had its own share of controversies and debates, conceivably, the most confounded provision being the bail-in clause, which resulted in apprehensions among people that deposits being liabilities would be written down in case of a default. A major downside of the bill also occurred in the omission of explicit declaration of maximum deposit insurance amount. These loopholes and lacuna led to the dropping of the bill altogether, resulting in an aperture in the legal make-up for resolution and/or liquidation of financial firms in the country — a matter that the Centre would have to take up at a later date. India needs a robust and reliable DIS that shall secure the financial system against systemic crisis and sustain public confidence through financial stability.

ACKNOWLEDGMENT

The authors express gratitude to Prof. Urvashi Dhingra, Ms. Mahica Vinod and Ms. S. Nandhini of Symbiosis International (Deemed University) for their unflinching help and support throughout the completion of this chapter. The authors further thank all the experts who extended their cooperation and assistance by being part of the Delphi study.

REFERENCES

Allen, F., & Carletti, E. (2008). *The Role of Liquidity in Financial Crises*. SSRN Electronic Journal. doi:10.2139srn.1268367

Allen, F., Carletti, E., Goldstein, I., & Leonello, A. (2015). Moral Hazard and Government Guarantees in the Banking Industry. *Journal of Financial Regulation*, *1*(1), 30–50. doi:10.1093/jfr/fju003

Allen, K., Davidson, T., Hein, S., & Whitledge, M. (2017). Dodd–Frank's federal deposit insurance reform. *Journal of Banking Regulation*, 1-16. doi:10.105741261-017-0050-3

Andolfatto, D., Nosal, E., & Sultanum, B. (2017). Preventing bank runs. *Theoretical Economics*, *12*(3), 1003–1028. doi:10.3982/TE1970

Anginer, D., Demirguc-Kunt, A., & Zhu, M. (2014). How does deposit insurance affect bank risk? Evidence from the recent crisis. *Journal of Banking & Finance*, *48*, 312–321. doi:10.1016/j.jbankfin.2013.09.013

Berger, A., & Turk-Ariss, R. (2014). Do Depositors Discipline Banks and Did Government Actions During the Recent Crisis Reduce this Discipline? An International Perspective. *Journal of Financial Services Research*, *48*(2), 103–126. doi:10.100710693-014-0205-7

Bolton, P., Freixas, X., & Shapiro, J. (2007). Conflicts of interest, information provision, and competition in the financial services industry. *Journal of Financial Economics*, *85*(2), 297–330. doi:10.1016/j.jfineco.2005.06.004

Bordo, M., & Haubrich, J. (2010). Credit crises, money and contractions: An historical view. *Journal of Monetary Economics*, *57*(1), 1–18. doi:10.1016/j.jmoneco.2009.10.015

Bose, P. (2017, December 27). *FRDI Bill, 2017: Inducing Financial Instability*. Retrieved from http://www.epw.in/engage/article/frdi-bill-2017-issues-and-concerns

Bourgeois, D., Kanoute, A., & Faye, D. (2014). Strategies to promote better research on oral health in Africa: A Delphi consensus study. *Contemporary Clinical Dentistry*, *5*(1), 13. doi:10.4103/0976-237X.128654 PMID:24808689

Boyle, G., Stover, R., Tiwana, A., & Zhylyevskyy, O. (2015). The impact of deposit insurance on depositor behavior during a crisis: A conjoint analysis approach. *Journal of Financial Intermediation*, *24*(4), 590–601. doi:10.1016/j.jfi.2015.02.001

Bryant, J. (1980). A model of reserves, bank runs, and deposit insurance. *Journal of Banking & Finance*, *4*(4), 335–344. doi:10.1016/0378-4266(80)90012-6

Calomiris, C., & Jaremski, M. (2016). Deposit Insurance: Theories and Facts. *Annual Review of Financial Economics*, *8*(1), 97–120. doi:10.1146/annurev-financial-111914-041923

Calomiris, C., & Wilson, B. (2004). Bank Capital and Portfolio Management: The 1930s "Capital Crunch" and the Scramble to Shed Risk. *The Journal of Business*, *77*(3), 421–455. doi:10.1086/386525

Calvo, G. (2012). Financial crises and liquidity shocks a bank-run perspective. *European Economic Review*, *56*(3), 317–326. doi:10.1016/j.euroecorev.2011.12.005

Chen, Y., & Hasan, I. (2008). Why Do Bank Runs Look Like Panic? A New Explanation. *Journal of Money, Credit and Banking*, *40*(2-3), 535–546. doi:10.1111/j.1538-4616.2008.00126.x

Cooper, R., & Kempf, H. (2015). Deposit insurance and bank liquidation without commitment: Can we sleep well? *Economic Theory*, *61*(2), 365–392. doi:10.100700199-015-0897-4

Cull, R., Senbet, L., & Sorge, M. (2002). The effect of deposit insurance on financial depth: A cross-country analysis. *The Quarterly Review of Economics and Finance*, *42*(4), 673–694. doi:10.1016/S1062-9769(02)00120-5

Demirgüç-Kunt, A., & Detragiache, E. (1997). The Determinants of Banking Crises: Evidence From Developing and Developed Countries. *IMF Working Papers*, *97*(106), 1. doi:10.5089/9781451947175.001

Demirgüç-Kunt, A., & Kane, E. (2002). Deposit Insurance Around the Globe: Where Does It Work? *The Journal of Economic Perspectives*, *16*(2), 175–195. doi:10.1257/0895330027319

Demirgüç-Kunt, A., Kane, E., Karacaovali, B., & Laeven, L. (2008). Deposit Insurance around the World: A Comprehensive Database. *Deposit insurance around the world: Issues of design and implementation*, 363. doi:10.7551/mitpress/9780262042543.003.0011

Demirgüç-Kunt, A., Kane, E., & Laeven, L. (2015). Deposit insurance around the world: A comprehensive analysis and database. *Journal of Financial Stability*, *20*, 155–183. doi:10.1016/j.jfs.2015.08.005

Department of Economic Affairs, Government of India. (2016). *The Financial Resolution and Deposit Insurance Bill, 2016*. Delhi: Ministry of Finance, Government of India. Retrieved from https://dea.gov.in/sites/default/files/FRDI%20Bill-27092016_1.pdf

Diamond, D., & Dybvig, P. (1983). Bank Runs, Deposit Insurance, and Liquidity. *Journal of Political Economy*, *91*(3), 401–419. doi:10.1086/261155

Diamond, D., Kashyap, A., & Rajan, R. (2017). Banking and the Evolving Objectives of Bank Regulation. *Journal of Political Economy*, *125*(6), 1812–1825. doi:10.1086/694622

DICGC. (2017). *A Guide to Deposit Insurance*. Retrieved from https://www.dicgc.org.in/FD_A-GuideToDepositInsurance.html

Dijk, O. (2017). Bank run psychology. *Journal of Economic Behavior & Organization*, *144*, 87–96. doi:10.1016/j.jebo.2017.08.005

Donohoe, H., Stellefson, M., & Tennant, B. (2012). Advantages and Limitations of the e-Delphi Technique. *American Journal of Health Education*, *43*(1), 38–46. doi:10.1080/19325037.2012.10599216

Egbuna, E., Oduh, M., Ujunwa, A., & Okoyeuzu, C. (2018). Does deposit insurance promote moral hazards and adverse selection? Evidence from Sub-Saharan Africa. *International Journal of Managerial Finance*, *14*(2), 150–169. doi:10.1108/IJMF-10-2016-0196

Engineer, M. (1989). Bank runs and the suspension of deposit convertibility. *Journal of Monetary Economics, 24*(3), 443–454. doi:10.1016/0304-3932(89)90031-7

Ennis, H., & Keister, T. (2009). Bank Runs and Institutions: The Perils of Intervention. *The American Economic Review, 99*(4), 1588–1607. doi:10.1257/aer.99.4.1588

Farhi, E., & Tirole, J. (2012). Collective Moral Hazard, Maturity Mismatch, and Systemic Bailouts. *The American Economic Review, 102*(1), 60–93. doi:10.1257/aer.102.1.60

Gallego, S., Herrero, A. G., & Salas, J. S. (2002). *The Asian and European Banking Systems: The case of Spain in the quest for development and stability* (No. 217). Banco de España, Servicio de Estudios. Retrieved from http://econwpa.repec.org/eps/fin/papers/0304/0304007.pdf

Gennaioli, N., Shleifer, A., & Vishny, R. (2013). A Model of Shadow Banking. *The Journal of Finance, 68*(4), 1331–1363. doi:10.1111/jofi.12031

Gertler, M., & Kiyotaki, N. (2015). Banking, Liquidity, and Bank Runs in an Infinite Horizon Economy. *The American Economic Review, 105*(7), 2011–2043. doi:10.1257/aer.20130665

Gorton, G. (1985). Bank suspension of convertibility. *Journal of Monetary Economics, 15*(2), 177–193. doi:10.1016/0304-3932(85)90063-7

Halan, M. (2017, December 13). *FRDI Bill is not going to hike the risk to your deposits*. Retrieved from https://www.livemint.com/Opinion/WHC48EQMgIucC8ve5d38FM/FRDI-Bill-is-not-going-to-hike-the-risk-to-your-deposits.html

Havrylchyk, O., & Verdier, M. (2018). The Financial Intermediation Role of the P2P Lending Platforms. *Comparative Economic Studies, 60*(1), 115–130. doi:10.105741294-017-0045-1

International Association of Deposit Insurers. (2014). *IADI Core Principles for Effective Deposit Insurance Systems*. IADI. Retrieved from https://www.iadi.org/en/assets/File/Core%20Principles/cprevised-2014nov.pdf

Iyer, R., Jensen, T., & Johannesen, N. (2016). *The Run for Safety: Financial Fragility and Deposit Insurance*. SSRN Electronic Journal. doi:10.2139srn.2780073

Iyer, R., & Puri, M. (2012). Understanding Bank Runs: The Importance of Depositor-Bank Relationships and Networks. *The American Economic Review, 102*(4), 1414–1445. doi:10.1257/aer.102.4.1414

Kane, E. (2000). *Designing Financial Safety Nets to Fit Country Circumstances*. World Bank. Retrieved from http://documents.worldbank.org/curated/en/423381468764432839/pdf/multi-page.pdf

Kashyap, A., Rajan, R., & Stein, J. (2002). Banks as Liquidity Providers: An Explanation for the Coexistence of Lending and Deposit-taking. *The Journal of Finance, 57*(1), 33–73. doi:10.1111/1540-6261.00415

Keeley, M. C. (1990). Deposit insurance, risk, and market power in banking. *The American Economic Review*, 1183–1200. Retrieved from https://www.jstor.org/stable/2006769?seq=1#page_scan_tab_contents

Kim, I., Kim, I., & Han, Y. (2014). Deposit Insurance, Banks' Moral Hazard, and Regulation: Evidence from the ASEAN Countries and Korea. *Emerging Markets Finance & Trade*, *50*(6), 56–71. doi:10.1080/1540496X.2014.1013875

Kleftouri, N. (2013). Deposit protection system's design and effectiveness. *Journal of Banking Regulation*, *16*(1), 51–63. doi:10.1057/jbr.2013.21

Krugman, P. (2014, April 26). Is a banking ban the answer? [Blog]. Retrieved from https://krugman.blogs.nytimes.com/2014/04/26/is-a-banking-ban-the-answer/

Kusairi, S., Sanusi, N., & Ismail, A. (2018). Dilemma of deposit insurance policy in ASEAN countries: Does it promote banking industry stability or moral hazard? *Borsa Istanbul Review*, *18*(1), 33–40. doi:10.1016/j.bir.2017.08.006

Laeven, L., & Levine, R. (2007). Is there a diversification discount in financial conglomerates? *Journal of Financial Economics*, *85*(2), 331–367. doi:10.1016/j.jfineco.2005.06.001

Laeven, L., Ratnovski, L., & Tong, H. (2014). *Bank Size, Capital, and Systemic Risk: Some International Evidence*. SSRN Electronic Journal. doi:10.2139srn.2508910

Laeven, M. L., & Valencia, F. (2008). The use of blanket guarantees in banking crises (No. 8-250). International Monetary Fund.

Lambert, C., Noth, F., & Schüwer, U. (2017). How do insured deposits affect bank risk? Evidence from the 2008 Emergency Economic Stabilization Act. *Journal of Financial Intermediation*, *29*, 81–102. doi:10.1016/j.jfi.2015.07.001

Linstone, H. (1978). *The Delphi technique. In Handbook of Futures Research* (pp. 271–300). Westport, CT: Greenwood.

Linstone, H., & Turoff, M. (1975). *The Delphi method*. Reading, MA: Addison-Wesley Pub. Co., Advanced Book Program.

Martinez Peria, M., & Schmukler, S. (2001). Do Depositors Punish Banks for Bad Behavior? Market Discipline, Deposit Insurance, and Banking Crises. *The Journal of Finance*, *56*(3), 1029–1051. doi:10.1111/0022-1082.00354

Mattana, E., & Panetti, E. (2017). *The Welfare Costs of Self-Fulfilling Bank Runs* (No. 2017/17). ISEG-Lisbon School of Economics and Management, REM, Universidade de Lisboa. Retrieved from https://rem.rc.iseg.ulisboa.pt/wps/pdf/REM_WP_017_2017.pdf

Micajkova, V. (2013). Deposit insurance in times of financial crisis. *South Eastern European Journal of Economics, 2*, 165–176. Retrieved from https://ojs.lib.uom.gr/index.php/seeje/article/viewFile/5502/5530

Ngalawa, H., Tchana, F., & Viegi, N. (2016). Banking instability and deposit insurance: The role of moral hazard. *Journal of Applied Econometrics*, *19*(2), 323–350. doi:10.10161514-0326(16)30013-7

Ognjenovic, D. (2017). *Deposit Insurance Schemes: Funding, Policy and Operational Challenges* (1st ed.). Palgrave Macmillan. doi:10.1007/978-3-319-51143-6

Pennacchi, G. (2006). Deposit insurance, bank regulation, and financial system risks. *Journal of Monetary Economics*, *53*(1), 1–30. doi:10.1016/j.jmoneco.2005.10.007

Ricciardi, V. (2017). The Role of Group Psychology in Behavioural Finance: A Research Starting Point for Banking, Economic, and Financial Historians. In K. Schönhärl (Ed.), *Decision Taking, Confidence and Risk Management in Banks from Early Modernity to the 20th Century*. Cham: Palgrave Macmillan. doi:10.1007/978-3-319-42076-9_12

Sahakian, C. (1997). *The Delphi method*. The Corporate Partnering Institute.

Samartin, M. (2002). Suspension of Convertibility versus Deposit Insurance: A Welfare Comparison. *Review of Finance*, *6*(2), 223–244. doi:10.1023/A:1020147632508

Schich, S. (2008). Financial crisis: Deposit insurance and related financial safety net aspects. *OECD Journal: Financial Market Trends, 2008*(2), 1-39. doi:10.1787/fmt-v2008-art12-en

Shleifer, A., & Vishny, R. (2010). Unstable banking. *Journal of Financial Economics*, *97*(3), 306–318. doi:10.1016/j.jfineco.2009.10.007

Shleifer, A., & Vishny, R. (2011). Fire Sales in Finance and Macroeconomics. *The Journal of Economic Perspectives*, *25*(1), 29–48. doi:10.1257/jep.25.1.29

Singh, J. (2015). *Changing Mandate of Deposit Insurance Systems*. Retrieved from https://www.dicgc.org.in/pdf/Speeches/ChangingMandatesOfDepositInsurance.pdf

Sridhar, G. (2018, July 19). FRDI Bill fiasco: More caution needed in policy-making. *The Hindu Businessline*. Retrieved from https://www.thehindubusinessline.com/economy/policy/frdi-bill-fiasco-more-caution-needed-in-policy-making/article24464067.ece

Thangaratinam, S., & Redman, C. (2005). *The Delphi technique*. Retrieved from https://obgyn.onlinelibrary.wiley.com/doi/pdf/10.1576/toag.7.2.120.27071

The Economic Times. (2018, March 29). *What is a bank run? It's in full swing in Telangana and Andhra Pradesh*. Retrieved from https://economictimes.indiatimes.com/news/politics-and-nation/what-is-a-bank-run-its-in-full-swing-in-telangana-and-andhra-pradesh/articleshow/63531528.cms?utm_source=WAPusers&from=mdr

Villamil, A. (1991). Demand deposit contracts, suspension of convertibility, and optimal financial intermediation. *Economic Theory*, *1*(3), 277–288. doi:10.1007/BF01210565

Walker, A., & Selfe, J. (1996). The Delphi method: A useful tool for the allied health researcher. *British Journal of Therapy and Rehabilitation*, *3*(12), 677–681. doi:10.12968/bjtr.1996.3.12.14731

World Bank. (n.d.). *Current Developments in Deposit Insurance*. Retrieved from http://pubdocs.worldbank.org/en/586861477065128589/16-Current-Development-in-Deposit-Insurance.pdf

ADDITIONAL READING

Aldunate, F. (2015). *Deposit Insurance, Bank Risk Taking and Failures: Evidence from Early 20th Century State Deposit Insurance Systems*. SSRN Electronic Journal; doi:10.2139srn.2692131

Bao, W., & Ni, J. (2017). Could Good Intentions Backfire? An Empirical Analysis of the Bank Deposit Insurance. *Marketing Science*, *36*(2), 301–319. doi:10.1287/mksc.2016.1009

Boyle, G., Stover, R., Tiwana, A., & Zhylyevskyy, O. (2015). The impact of deposit insurance on depositor behavior during a crisis: A conjoint analysis approach. *Journal of Financial Intermediation*, *24*(4), 590–601. doi:10.1016/j.jfi.2015.02.001

Calomiris, C., & Jaremski, M. (2016). *Stealing Deposits: Deposit Insurance, Risk-Taking and the Removal of Market Discipline in Early 20th Century Banks*. SSRN Electronic Journal; doi:10.3386/w22692

Cooper, R., & Kempf, H. (2015). Deposit insurance and bank liquidation without commitment: Can we sleep well? *Economic Theory*, *61*(2), 365–392. doi:10.100700199-015-0897-4

Dewenter, K., Hess, A., & Brogaard, J. (2017). Institutions and Deposit Insurance: Empirical Evidence. *Journal of Financial Services Research*. doi:10.100710693-017-0271-8

Enkhbold, E., & Otgonshar, B. (2013). The Effect of Deposit Insurance on Risk Taking in Asian Banks. *Asian Journal of Finance & Accounting*, *5*(1). doi:10.5296/ajfa.v5i1.3023

Fungáčová, Z., Weill, L., & Zhou, M. (2016). Bank Capital, Liquidity Creation and Deposit Insurance. *Journal of Financial Services Research*, *51*(1), 97–123. doi:10.100710693-016-0240-7

Martin, C., Puri, M., & Ufier, A. (2018). *Deposit Inflows and Outflows in Failing Banks: The Role of Deposit Insurance*. SSRN Electronic Journal; doi:10.3386/w24589

Qian, N., Zhang, K., & Zheng, C. (2017). *How Do Regulatory Ability and Banking Market Structure Affect Explicit Deposit Insurance Scheme Adoption and Banks Risk Taking?* SSRN Electronic Journal; doi:10.2139srn.3060943

KEY TERMS AND DEFINITIONS

Blanket Guarantee: An announcement of additional protection to certain deposits and financial instruments by concerned authorities, over and above the security extended by premeditated limited coverage.

Bridge Bank or Bridge Entity: A financial institution set up to provisionally to take over and keep up definite assets, liabilities and procedures of a failed bank as a part of the resolution mechanism.

Ex Ante Funding: Deposit insurance system that allows funding arrangements to secure deposits before a crisis occurs.

Ex Post Funding: Deposit insurance system that allows funding arrangements to secure deposits after a bank failure or systemic crisis.

Herd Behavior: Behavior exhibited by a vast majority of the population, not guided by their own instinct or intuition, but purely as a reaction/response to other people's actions and behavioral tendencies. Also, alternatively known as 'mob mentality' that results in mass hysteria.

Mandate: Power and influence available with a deposit insurer through a set of official guidelines concerning its roles and obligations.

Moral Hazard: A phenomenon that guides one party in a transaction to take risks, motivated by the fact that the costs of such actions shall be borne by another party.

Risk-Based Premium: Premium linked with risk taking ability of banks.

Self-Fulfilling Prophecy: A customary phrase which implies that people expecting something positive or negative to happen, behave in a way that makes the expectation come true even though it was not supposed to.

Chapter 2
Maintaining Financial Stability in the Banking Sector:
The Case of Turkey

Meltem Gurunlu
Istanbul Arel University, Turkey

ABSTRACT

Maintaining financial stability in the banking sector through a well-functioning risk management system is a strategic approach in today's global world where the risks have become much more diversified than ever. This chapter was undertaken in order to investigate the risk management topic by focusing on the experiences learned from the banking crises up-to-date and implications of the Basel Accords which outlined capital adequacy standards to prevent such crises. With paying special attention to the case of Turkish banking system, main challenges and possible solutions are also discussed.

INTRODUCTION

A healthy risk management system is crucial for banking system as it enables banks to effectively measure their specific market, credit and operational risks and adjust their capital accordingly. In an environment with ever increasing volatility as well as more complex financial risks, establishment of internal risk control systems and regulations by both public and international institutions are rising concerns for most emerging market economies.

The present chapter aims to analyse the "Turkish banking system" and points out challenges from a "Risk Management" perspective. In other words, it aims to evaluate the developments in the Turkish banking system in line with the major banking crises during the period commencing from 1994 until 2017, by taking into account harmonization process with the globally practiced standards of risk management – Basel Accords.

The chapter proceeds as follows. To begin with, the chapter briefly explores the main characteristics of the Turkish banking system emphasizing the need for a strong risk management system. Then, risk management process with all its relevance to banking system shall be considered. The next section

DOI: 10.4018/978-1-5225-7208-4.ch002

concentrates on banking crises and constructs the links with risk management, underscoring the most significant crises which have affected the Turkish banking system till date and caused structural changes in the system. Finally, international capital adequacy standards set by Basel Accords and their implications for the Turkish banking system are briefly discussed. Subsequently, solutions and recommendations for the issue under consideration and possible future research directions will be given. The concluding remarks are presented in the final section of this chapter.

BACKGROUND

Risks are usually defined by the adverse impact on the profitability arising out of several distinct sources of uncertainty (Bessis, 2010, pp: 3-12). Banks are subject to a wide array of risks in the course of their operations. Effective risk management comprises four phases: identification of risks, evaluation of risks, management of risks and controlling of risks. Risk Management provides protection against the possibility of damages on the investments of banks that can result from future uncertainties, by means of hedging or neutralizing the financial risks that result from one or a series of transactions.

The events in the Turkish economy during the crises of 1994, end-2000 and 2008 have shown the importance of proper and integrated risk management systems in the Turkish banking system. This was a period which ca be characterized by increasing vulnerability to the shocks and financial crises. For example, the weakness of banking system has caused the collapse of the previous International Monetary Fund (IMF)-sponsored plans. Especially, after the crises in 1994 and end-2000, there was better realization that a banking system may bear huge amount of losses, face insurmountable capital erosion and be a burden on the entire economy. Hence, the establishment of a more stable banking platform with proper risk management framework to withstand macro shocks is imperative. This contributes to stability of the overall economy because banking system is the backbone of the economic system of a country. An integrated risk management system constitutes effective market, credit and operational risk management. How Turkish banks can develop and enhance their market, credit and operating risk measurement and management capabilities is a critical strategic tool for creating and sustaining competitive advantage. Banking in today's environment is the business of managing risk - not just the business of borrowing and lending funds as it used to be traditionally done in the past. Better risk management systems allow banks to deploy their capital more efficiently and provide a source of competitive advantage.

Market risk management measures potential profit or loss by means of Value at Risk (VaR) models and stress testing and is especially important after the illiquidity crisis of 2001. Credit risk management is critical in the milieu of the fact that the volume of commercial credit will expand due to the target that inflation will decrease and the rising importance of harmonization with European standards. Credit risk management systems which are based on risk grading and portfolio management ought to be developed in order for banks to be profitable after the decrease in net interest rate margin. Operational risk management is also important, because banking instruments and operations are becoming more complex and sophisticated and the risks encountered due to operational failure of people, process or technology should be measured and managed. Most typically, Turkish banks face market risk which is caused by interest rate and foreign exchange rate volatilities because their portfolios are mostly composed of government securities funded by their short positions in foreign currency. They sell foreign currency against domestic currency in order to benefit from high returns of governmental debt instruments. But, this triggers the demand for foreign currency when their foreign currency denominated liabilities come due because their borrowings are in terms of foreign currency. The volatility of foreign exchange rate, hence becomes the core risk for the Turkish banks. But in more developed markets where inflation rate and public sector borrowing requirement (PSBR) are low, the most common type of risk for commercial banks is credit risk which means the risk of customers' default.

For all the aforementioned reasons, the establishment of risk management system and functions in Turkey assumes greater credence as well as the steps to be taken for the establishment of a culture that accepts risk management as a strategic approach. The underlying importance of this study is to make contribution to the establishment of risk management culture by analysing different approaches to the subject; how it may add to the competitive advantage of banks as well as contribute to a sounder financial system and well-being of the economy as a whole.

MAIN FOCUS OF THE CHAPTER

International financial markets have witnessed a drastic transition for the last thirty years. While volatility in markets has increased with the emergence of more complex financial instruments like derivatives, market participants of this highly dynamic and competitive sector, are exposed to bigger and far more diversified risks. There are many reasons behind these developments that have made the financial sector further risk sensitive than ever.

First and the most important reason to be mentioned is the *globalization of international markets*. A major development that deeply affected banking sector by the 1990s is the rising importance of emerging markets and flow of financial funds in the developed countries with lower risks and lower returns through emerging market instruments with higher returns, but higher risks. This was undeniably vital for the development of emerging markets but, on the other hand, this brought together the severe fluctuations in the global market place. With the effect of deregulation on international financial flows across countries, local markets became more prone to systemic crises which spread epidemically from one market to another with a domino effect. This has been experienced heavily during Russian and Asian crises. The turbulence in emerging markets – starting in Mexico in 1995, continuing in Asia in 1997 and spreading to Russia and Latin America in 1998 – has further extended the interest in risk management to companies outside the traditional sphere of banking and insurance. The world of commercial banking underwent a deep transformation as a result of marketable instruments, competing with loans and demand deposits. Increasing competition has forced banks to search for more income by embracing more risks. The increasing competition in credit markets, involvement of non-financial institutions and availability of low cost credits from the capital markets have forced banks to expand their liabilities in order to compete with the narrowing profit margins.

The second reason is that the *international financial markets are increasingly volatile*. Volatility, which is defined as the standard deviation of unexpected outcomes, is one of the primary sources of financial risks (Jorion, 2006, pp: 63-67). Losses can occur through combination of two factors: the volatility in the underlying financial variables and exposure to the underlying source of financial risk. Whereas banks have no direct control on volatility of financial variables, they may adjust their exposure to these risks. VaR methodology, which is brought by the rapid progress of information technology in recent years, captures the combined effect of underlying financial volatility and exposure to risks. VaR is the maximum potential loss that can occur in the value of a portfolio having a certain investment horizon under a certain probability. It permits comparison of the market risk of different investment instruments so that portfolio performance can be evaluated in terms of the risks undertaken. This model has become a necessity in many countries and financial institutions in determining capital adequacy and the use of it is encouraged by the Bank for International Settlements (BIS).

Another major reason behind those developments that necessitates risk management is the *new investment alternatives*. This entails the use of derivative instruments in order to hedge complex structured investment positions. Derivative instruments provide controlled exposure to risks by disaggregating risks; those that users are willing to bear and those that they are willing to transfer. Thus, derivatives are aimed at hedging or minimizing losses. But because of the leverage effect of derivative instruments, when they are used for speculative purposes overwhelmingly and where the risks are not hedged rightfully, they may lead to realization of huge losses in case of an unpredictable environment and even lead to a collapse of the bank. The leverage of any position is the gain or loss in its value relative to the change in the underlying risk factor. The risk factor may be a price, an interest or exchange rate or an index such as stock index. The bigger the leverage, the higher the profit is if the underlying price moves the right way and the bigger the loss if it moves against the hedger (Jorion, 2006, pp: 23-38).

All these surrounding factors have led to publication of investigative reports on good risk management practice by both academic and professional circles like Group of Thirty (G-30), Derivatives Policy Group, International Swaps and Derivatives Organization (ISDA), Risk Grading Institutions like Moody's, Standard and Poor's and regulatory bodies like Bank for International Settlements (BIS) and International Organization of Securities Commission (IOSCO) and other interested parties. These reports have made a number of sensible recommendations that have rapidly become benchmarks (industry standards) for modern financial risk management. They tend to focus particularly on derivative risks but their recommendations apply not just to derivatives providers and investment banks but to other financial institutions and corporates as well. The main recommendations of these reports are much the same: the need for an independent risk management function that reports directly to the senior management and the use of internal or VaR models for measuring and managing financial risks across the institution.

As a result, the changes in economic environment are opening up new opportunities for institutions operating in the financial markets. But it also confronts them with new risks. The future of numerous different financial markets will be decided by whether market participants succeed in transforming the new risks into new opportunities or otherwise. Only those financial institutions that succeed in retaining their strengths and eliminating their weaknesses will maintain their positions.

Risk Management Process

Like every profit-oriented organization, banks face macroeconomic shocks (such as recessionary tendencies) and microeconomic shocks (such as new competitive threats). In addition to these general risks, banks, also, have some peculiar or characteristic risks; they have to manage risks which are originating from their on-balance sheet and off-balance sheet activities. They have additional types of risks, because of their most distinctive feature, their intermediary role between economic units and payments function.

Two areas of management have, now, been critical to the success of banking in line with the structural changes in the banking industry:

- **Effective Performance or Profitability Management:** The management of expectations on profitable markets
- **Risk Management:** Defining, measuring, eliminating and transferring risks

The ultimate goal of bank's performance – the maximization of shareholder's wealth – is a common goal for both areas of management. Theoretically, these critical areas of management are taken independently. But a new strategy which integrates both the performance and the risk management is vitally important for banks. The *Risk-based strategic planning* aims at enhancing performance as well as focusing on potential risks (Van Greuning & Bratanovic, 2009). All uncertainties eventually lead to fluctuations in a financial institution's profitability. For this reason, it is important to identify different types of risks as precisely as possible, quantify these risks and understand how they affect the profitability of a bank's capital investments. The amount of capital that a bank holds should be directly proportional to the risks it faces. Theoretically, a bank that takes no risk and has certain streams of revenue and expense would have no need or limited need for capital. Conversely, a bank that experiences significant fluctuations in its revenues, expenses or losses would need sizeable levels of capital.

In recent years, *Risk Adjusted Profitability Measurement* (RAPM) methodologies are being used by banks to compute the *economic capital* which is defined as the aggregate amount of equity capital that is required as a cushion for a bank's unexpected losses due to all of its risks, and this is different from *regulatory capital* – capital required by the regulators and calculated by limiting the maximum level of a bank's risky assets and off-balance sheet commitments to a fixed multiple of its capital and the *book capital* – the capital computed by subtracting the total liabilities from total assets; it is an accounting measure of how much capital a bank has rather than how much it should have. The calculation of economic capital by defining and measuring all risks on a component and aggregated basis and on a desired level of confidence provides the following advantages:

- Profitability can represent true measurement of the risks incurred
- Improved decision making for capital allocation and strategic planning
- A clear link between business performance and shareholder value creation
- Consistent information on pricing.

RAPM transforms the risk management process from risk measurement to risk optimization, with risk being managed to increase the shareholders' value and gain a competitive advantage by allowing management to evaluate the performance of activities with widely differing risk/return profiles on a consistent and comparative basis. Risk is the standard deviation or degree of volatility of net cash flows. Bank profitability depends on the management of risks related to products and services which are supplied in the course of bank's intermediation and payment functions. Within the context of financial theory, risk is the difference between expected return and present value of the cash flows of the related position. If present value of cash flow is bigger than its expected return, then risk arises. The key problems are defining and measuring risks and their relations. The operational objective of risk management is to identify, quantify and properly balance the elements of financial risks which are subject to complex interdependencies that may significantly increase a bank's risk profile. In developing economies, the unstable market environments significantly increase the range and the magnitude of bank exposure to financial risk. Such conditions render risk management even more complex and make the need for effective risk management process further acute.

The main types of financial risks include credit risk, interest rate risk, currency risk and liquidity risk. Market risk occurs as a result of interactions among these fundamental risk types. These four types of risks have direct effects on the profitability of a bank and they also have indirect effects on capital adequacy and the market share. If a bank manages its risks in an optimum way, then it is able to strengthen its financial structure by adding to its shareholders' equity and by the same token it is able to increase its market share. Accordingly, the major aims of good risk management in banking can be mentioned as follows:

- Enhancing net income
- Obtaining capital adequacy
- Expanding market share

Banking Crises and Risk Management

The last three decades are mainly characterized by currency and banking crises. A currency crisis may be said to occur when a speculative attack on exchange value of national currency results in devaluation of the currency or forces the authorities to defend the currency by using large volumes of international reserves or by sharply increasing interest rates. A bank failure, on the other hand, refers to a situation in which the excessively rising liquidity, credit, interest rate or exchange rate risk pushes the bank to suspend the internal convertibility of its liabilities. If the bank failure problem undermines the entire banking system, the crisis turns out to be systemic (Kibritcioglu, 2002). Systemic risk refers to the risk or probability of breakdowns (losses) in an entire system as opposed to breakdowns in individual parts or components and is evidenced by co-movements (correlation) among most or all the parts. Thus, systemic risk in banking is evidenced by a high correlation and clustering of bank failures in a country, a number of countries, or globally; and in currencies by a clustering of depreciations in exchange rates in a number of countries (Kaufman & Scott, 2003).

The Bank for International Settlements (BIS) defines systemic risk as "the risk that the failure of a participant to meet its contractual obligations may in turn cause other participants to default with a chain reaction leading to broader financial difficulties" (Basel Committee on Banking Supervision,1993). According to another definition, systemic risk is "the likelihood of a sudden, usually unexpected, event that disrupts information in financial markets, making them unable to effectively channel funds to those parties with the most productive investment opportunities." To exemplify, bank A defaults on a loan, deposit, or other payment to bank B that produces a loss greater than B's capital and forces it to default on a payment to bank C with losses that are larger than C's capital, and this goes on down the chain. The smaller a bank's capital-asset ratio, the more leveraged it is and the more it is likely to be driven into insolvency by insolvencies of banks located earlier on the transmission chain and to transmit losses to banks located later on the chain (Kaufman, 2000).

Banks are intermediaries which aim to earn profits in financial markets by acquiring funds, and by using these funds to make investment or lending them to borrowers. Their liabilities are the funds that they acquire from savers in the form of deposits or as borrowings, while their assets mainly include reserves, marketable securities and loans. The difference between the assets and liabilities of a bank equals its net worth which in fact shows the bank's residual value or equity capital after meeting all of its liabilities. That is, bank's net worth includes the capital contributed by the bank's shareholders and accumulated profits from doing business as intermediary in financial markets. When the net worth of the bank turns negative, the bank becomes insolvent. It is explicit that a bank is exposed to risk that the values of its assets and/or liabilities change in financial markets. That is, all banks are exposed to different types of economic risks (Kibritcioglu, 2002), such as:

- Liquidity risk (massive bank runs)
- Credit risk (rising non-performing loans)
- Exchange rate risk (banks' increasing unhedged foreign currency liabilities)
- Market risk

Therefore, bank's net worth, and hence, a bank failure, basically can be linked to excessive risk taking of bank managers. In fact, several empirical studies in literature show that massive bank runs and withdrawals, enormous lending booms, and high increases in foreign liabilities of banking sector are among the major leading indicators of banking crises (Caprio et al., 1999). In the absence of regulations limiting banks' open foreign currency positions, banks are likely to be motivated to take excessive risk by acquiring funds from international markets. If domestic banks have large amounts of unhedged foreign currency debt, then a sudden devaluation may cause a sharp fall in the net worth of banks thereby increasing the vulnerability of domestic banking sector (IMF, 1998)

The Financial Crises in Turkey and Risk Management

The causes of Turkish crises do not differ from those experienced elsewhere, at least in theory. Poor banking practices, inadequate capital, poor assessment of credit risks, lending to connected enterprise or insiders, excessive maturity and/or currency mismatches and excessive risk taking are common causes for any country experiencing problems in the financial sector (Caprio & Klingebiel, 2003.

This section will have a closer look at the development of Turkish banking sector in the period 1994-2009 – a period which can be characterized by tremendously increasing vulnerability to the shocks and financial crises that can be attributed to the absence of full-fledged risk management systems in banking sector. Especially, after the crises in 1994 and end-2000, there was better realization that a banking system may bear huge amount of losses, face insurmountable capital erosion and be a burden on the entire economy if it failed to measure its risks in the event of unpredictability and thereby attempted to control them; the need for proper risk management practices and measures thus needed emphasis. In this period, it has been observed how excessive risk takings in the name of making high profits in the banking sector have turned out to be a failure.

The Financial Crisis in 1994

The period 1990-1994 witnessed the rise both in interest rate and foreign exchange risks in parallel with these developments occurred especially, in the second half of the 1980's. The Turkish banking system went through a transformation process during the 1980's after the stabilization programme which was based on principles of free market economy. The banking system has progressed by the introduction of new markets – the foreign exchange and gold markets; improvements in the capital markets and in the financial instruments –, and the liberalization of the foreign exchange regime and interest rates. All these structural changes were targeted at reconstructing of the economy by giving more emphasis to the market forces, promoting foreign investment and inflow of foreign capital and improving the competition among the banks. Because, foreign currency funding became an increasingly critical issue for Turkish banks and they began to back their fixed rate, high yielding government security investments by running short positions in foreign currency that they borrowed from abroad. 1994 was a year when all excessive risk takings in the sector resulted in losses. Despite the accumulated public-sector deficit, the expansionist policies to decrease interest rates led both domestic and international investors to leave the Turkish Lira (TL) instruments. The illiquid market forced interest rates to rise to maximum levels and unavoidably a TL devaluation was made by the government. In this phase, the total assets in the whole banking system decreased to $52.6 billion from $72.4 and the amount of capital erosion was $2.4 billion: from $ 6.7 billion to $4.3 billion (TBAT, 2000). The confidence depression in the financial markets were overcome at the expense of introducing full deposit insurance scheme which caused moral hazard and initiated the aggressive risk taking by small and mid–sized banks to enjoy high profitability in the form of high interest margins and caused unfair competition of unsound banks in the system.

Consequentially, the credit ratings of the banks which are essential for foreign currency borrowing were downgraded and made Turkey a net payer of foreign debt. After the fast recovery of economy in 1995, banking sector began to grow. High real interest rates captured the attraction of investors to TL denominated instruments and the substitution effect of national currency with foreign currencies slowed down; however, it did not turn positive. Funding with foreign currency and running open positions in foreign assets started once again, but this time at higher costs while the maturity for the foreign liabilities was getting shorter.

With the introduction of new taxes imposed upon foreign currency and TL borrowings, repos and forward transactions gained importance and open positions based on non-cash credit increased. Because of the increasing regulatory requirements, banking sector became involved in off-shore banking where there were no liquidity and cash ratios, no legal reserves for deposits and banks could enjoy the advantage of exemption from national taxes. So, banks expanded their off-balance sheet activities. The exposure of Turkish banks to risks in the financial environment further increased. The ratio of off-balance sheet transactions to total assets increased from 41.4% in 1992 to 100.8% in 2000 (TBAT, 2000). In the second half of 1998, the staff monitoring agreement with IMF brought limitation to open positions and forward transactions and gave the signals of enhancement of supervisory regulations on the banks' activities. This caused increased tension among investors about the contraction of the liquidity and banks began to close their huge and risky open positions in foreign currency. The taxation of securities income and stoppage tax on interbank transactions shocked the investors in an environment where the Russian banking sector's declaring moratorium caused negative impacts on funds flow to emerging economies. In this panic environment, the riskiness of Turkish banks and their heavy exposure to market risks – mainly to interest rate and foreign exchange rate risks – were felt deeply.

At the end of 1999, the total assets of the banking sector increased by 14 percent in USD terms and reached USD 133.5 billion when compared to the previous year. Despite the diminishing effect of the re-increase of repo transactions and increased transparency in the balance sheets of banks in the Saving Deposits Insurance Fund (SDIF), the ratio of total assets to GNP increased from 69 percent in 1998 to 92 percent in 1999 (TBAT, 2000).

The Financial Crisis in the End-2000

The seeds of the banking crisis that broke in Turkey in November 2000 were sown over many years. Apart from poor banking practices and deficiencies in supervision, typical symptoms of a banking crisis include lending booms, deterioration of banks' lending portfolios, decreasing levels of capitalization, insufficient loan loss provisions, increasing short-term foreign liabilities, which are common themes in all crises (De Luna Martinez, 2000). The following three factors significantly contributed to the end-2000 crisis:

- *Unfair competition* from state banks and reluctance of authorities to let non-viable banks fail hampered the development of a commercially-oriented banking system. Unfair competition from unsound banks destroyed bank profitability. Government and Central Bank involvement in the rescuing of troubled banks led to financial and fiscal problems, since with such operations, banks could undertake riskier lending and offer higher returns to attract funds than otherwise (Neyaptı & Dincer, 2004).
- *The capital deficiency* of many banks implied little risk of further loss and significant upside gains to bank's stockholders. With little or no capital at stake, many banks undertook risky investments.
- *Liquidity risk from short-term foreign debt* further increased fragility and made banks vulnerable to any shocks to their capital flow.

At the end of 1999, Turkey embarked upon an ambitious stabilization programme to cure the chronic inflation problem. Firm monetary and exchange rate policies were set out so as to reduce the inflationary expectations. Despite the significant progress which have been made throughout 2000, a severe banking crisis blew up in the November 2000 which was accompanied by a massive capital outflow. This crisis revealed the vulnerability of the banking sector and sensitivity of foreign confidence to a widening current account deficit. The crisis resulted in high real interest rates which put a burden on the banking system. Obviously, it witnessed that strengthening of the banking system was a key element for the success of the stabilization programme.

The end-2000 crisis developed as a result of the emergence of some mid-sized banks which had positioned themselves aggressively for continuing declines in interest rates via longer term investments which were highly leveraged by short-term funds. These banks were forced to sell their government bond holdings at loss to maintain liquidity in the face of increasing cost of the TL funds. Consistent with its monetary goals, the Central Bank was at first constrained from stepping in to ease the liquidity problems. The illiquid banks spread and first-tier banks cut their lines of credit to the interbank market and international participants exited the overnight market, unwilling to except Turkish banks' risks. This exacerbated market pressures and portfolio losses of the exposed banks (OECD, 2001).

Following the announcement of the disinflationary programme and serious decline in treasury bill rates, banks gave different responses according to their risk-taking strategies. Some banks deemed the declining returns on repo positions not attractive enough to compensate for a risk of sudden rise in funding costs and they lowered their maturity mismatch. When interest rates decrease, returns on repo positions decline and if maturity mismatch is not lowered, then the bank becomes very vulnerable to sudden interest rate hikes. As an alternative strategy, some other banks believed that a realized increase in short-term interest rates could cause distress on bank margins and cause even greater exposure to risk if compensation is attempted through risky lending and increased leverage and extended maturity mismatch. The deterioration of the programme in the medium term led to the withdrawal of funds by foreign investors from treasury bill market and the illiquidity problem caused a sudden rise in the short-term interest rates. Banking Regulation and Supervision Agency of Turkey (BRSA) took over the sixth largest private bank (Demirbank) which had been the main source of the liquidity problem, under the deposit insurance fund.

The business mix of Turkish banks at the interest income can be broadly divided into three categories: spread on Turkish Lira deposits; spread on foreign currency liabilities, and income generated on currency mismatch or running open position. The Turkish banking industry was generally heavily dependent on foreign currency funding and average maturity of deposits in the system was short-term.

The cost of collecting foreign currency and Turkish Lira deposits was one of the main drivers of bank margins. The margins and earnings would drop sharply as banks lost their inflation profits arising from float income (the profit on high-yielding uncovered bond arbitrage) and high-risk premium on government debt as the country stabilised. In fact, net interest margins of Turkish banks were twice as high as those in comparable OECD countries. This can be attributed to inflation profits. The main argument was that Turkish banks would lose if inflation was stabilised, based on the notion that with lower inflation, the risk on the treasury bill would fall and the banks would lose their gains from float revenues. High profitability in banking industry in the form of high net interest margins was indeed a common feature of all high inflation economies. Demirgüç-Kunt and Huizinga (1999) reported in their study covering 80 countries over 1988-1995 period that interest margins in high inflation countries were twice as high as those in low inflation countries. In Turkey, interest income constitutes the bulk of bank income. But the problem is that high margins reflect high nominal margins rather than real margins if there is no inflation accounting. Turkish banks were vulnerable before the implementation of the stabilization programme as earnings with the effect of inflation stripped out were not sufficient to provide a positive return on equity.

Turkish banks had significantly small levels of interest-earning assets. This was a structural problem within the Turkish banking industry and directly related to banks' decision to deploy their capital to investments in affiliated companies rather than their core banking business. Second, although Turkish banks enjoyed higher margins, they showed low levels of fee income, particularly when a sizeable portion of their non-interest income could be attributable to trading gains, which should normally be considered part of the net interest margin. Since the introduction of the IMF-sponsored stabilization programme at the end of 1999, banks have shifted their asset mix to longer maturity and fixed rate assets while their liabilities remained short-term. This was reflected on the balance sheets of banks in the form of large maturity mismatches. 67% of banks' funding was short-term with a maturity of less than three months, a disproportionately large percentage of these funds was invested in assets in longer maturities (TBAT, 2000). In brief, we can examine the significant factors that mostly contributed to the end-2000 crisis in Turkish banking sector under three main headings:

- Weak capital base
- Heavy reliance on foreign borrowing
- Unfair competition and government intervention

The Global Financial Crisis in 2008

The global crisis which began in September 2008 in the United States includes the deterioration of the structure of mortgage lending, mismatch of interest rates, swelling in housing prices, tightness in funding securities, growth of credit derivative markets, and credit rating issues. The 2008 global financial crisis has caused serious losses to both the developed and developing countries' stock markets; most currencies lost value, risk premiums increased, foreign capital flows and the debts of the banks fell seriously. After the global financial crisis that began at the end of 2008, the rise in exchange rates affected Turkish economy negatively. In this period, foreign exchange borrowers with more debt than receivables in the same currency faced exchange rate volatility risk.

A package of measures was designed to address the global crisis and soften the impact of the negative consequences of the crisis in Turkey. This package overlaps with measures taken around the world and involves the measures to mobilize the economy, reduce the problem of liquidity caused by diminished foreign demand, increased domestic demand, ensure economic growth and address the problem of unemployment. The crisis package included various supporting schemes (for example; liquidity, tax, credit and guarantee support for production and exportation) and a new investment incentive legislation. The main objectives of these measures taken by the government were to increase consumption expenditures, employment, capital inflows from abroad, domestic investments and encouraging the production and exportation of Small & Medium Sized Enterprises (SMEs).

The banking system was described both domestically and abroad in 2009 as the "Turkey's best story" (TBAT, 2009). The main reasons were the sound balance sheet structure, strong equity and high reliance on Turkish Lira. A significant portion of the Bank's resources were deposits of residents in Turkey and TL deposits constituted two-thirds of the deposits. In addition, after the 2001 crisis, the BRSA introduced strict regulations for open positions so the banking system was less influenced by the 2008 global financial crisis than the 1994 and 2001 crises and faced no major damage. Through the domestic debt swap undertaken to achieve a healthier structure in the private banking system, the foreign currency open positions had been substantially closed, necessary measures were taken for the banks identified to have capital inadequacy through a capitalization program, the balance sheets of private banks have been made more transparent by applying inflation accounting, and their capital structures have been strengthened. Arrangements had been made for the instruction of mechanisms to accelerate the settlement of bad assets (BRSA, 2010). The Turkish banking system has not felt the effects of the global crisis in this environment due to some structural differences. In particular, structural changes such as the restructuring of public banks after the 2001 crisis, consolidation of regulatory and supervisory frameworks, strengthening of the capital base of the banking sector and elimination of weak banks from the system have made the system immune to possible crises. In the face of the global crisis in 2008, one of Turkey's advantage was the absence of regularly functioning and complex mortgage system such as the one in the United States. Since there was no such developed mortgage system, banks did not invest in the mortgage-based derivatives, so they never took any risks and were unaffected from the crisis for a long time.

Figure 1. Capital adequacy ratios in the Turkish banking system, 2005-2017 (%)
Source: Banking Regulation & Supervision Agency of Turkey (BRSA) Financial Sector Report, 2017

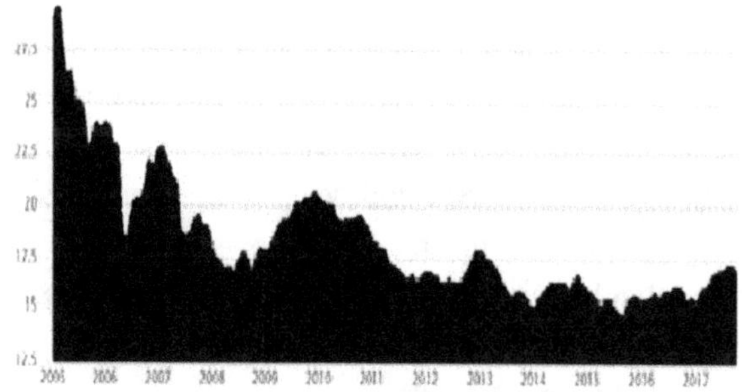

Basel Accords and Their Implications for the Turkish Banking System

Bank capital serves four primary functions. First, it inspires public confidence in the bank's viability by absorbing unanticipated losses. Second, it protects uninsured depositors in the event of bank insolvency. Third, it pays for the acquisition of physical plants and other resources necessary to operate the bank. Finally, it serves as a regulatory restraint on unjustified asset growth by excessive risk taking. Since adequate capital is a necessary condition for solvent banks, and solvent banks are fundamental to the world economy, adequate bank capital is thus essential for a sound economy. Because adequate bank capital is a vital component of economic stability, it has become a subject of concern for financial regulatory bodies around the world. Many regulators firmly believe that "capital standards help to ensure the financial strength of internationally active banks while promoting greater competition."

As a result, "*financial globalization and liberalization*" created a need for banks and banking supervisors to adopt international standards rather than following a series of purely domestic regulations. The Basel Committee on Banking Supervision, played an architectural role in outlining global capital adequacy standards that are currently enforced, and evaluating proposals to change the present regulatory regime.

Basel I

With the implementation of Basel I, adopted in 1988, issues such as establishment of Turkish banks' risk culture, and completion of the technological investments have gained importance. Turkey, due to the reason that the provisions were easy to practice, adapted Basel I easily. Basel I criteria with low risk sensitivity due to the use of only four different risk weights have been defined as "one size dress for all," because all banks with different fields of activity applied the risk weights in the same way. Another shortcoming of the Basel I criteria due to the rapid rate of change in markets was that the innovations in secondary markets and derivative markets had not been foreseen. Many banks were able to show their debts less than they were in in real terms by selling their securities through securitization or by taking positions in derivative markets. Many banks entered into very risky investments compared to their capital and showed a lower level of risk than they were through such transactions. This has been influential in the banking crises in the following years (Matten, 2000).

The 1988 agreement also defined a common measure of solvency - *The Cooke Ratio* – which only covers credit risks and requires that bank capital should be equal to at least to 8 percent of the total risk-weighted assets of the bank (Basel Committee on Banking Supervision, 1988) This "one size fits all" standard model, as well as, providing simplicity for risk management also bears some disadvantages like, not providing the accurate measure of a bank's risk. This may be said, because, it does not take into account diversification effects across risk types and it does not make reference to actually experienced volatilities. Over the time, the limitations of the 1988 accord become apparent because the regulatory measure of bank risk as stipulated by the risk weights can differ substantially from the actual risks that the bank faces. After more than a decade of inaccurate capital ratios leading to regulatory arbitrage and the international credit crunch, regulatory bodies and bankers from nearly all participating nations lost their confidence for the 1988 Accord and petitioned for change.

Basel II

The Basel Committee's proposals of 2001 – **"The New Capital Accord or Basel II"** – constitute a root and branch reform of the 1988 Capital Accord. The new framework intends to provide approaches which are more comprehensive and more sensitive to risks than the 1988 Accord, while maintaining the overall level of regulatory capital. Capital requirements that are more in line with underlying risks will allow banks to manage their businesses more efficiently. The new framework is less prescriptive than the original Accord. At its simplest, the framework is somewhat more complex than the old but it offers a range of approaches for banks capable of using more risk-sensitive analytical methodologies which require more detail in their application.

The three mutually reinforcing pillars - which together should contribute to safety and soundness in the financial system (Basel Committee on Banking Supervision, 2001):

1. The standardized approach to credit risk measurement is modified to make it more risk sensitive; the risk weights are refined by reference to an external credit assessment institution where under the 1988 Accord, the risk weights depend on the broad category of borrower (sovereigns, banks, or corporates). For example, for corporate lending, the 1988 Accord provides only one risk weight category of 100% but the new Accord will provide four categories (20%, 50%, 100%, and 150%)
2. Two new methods – foundation methodology and advanced methodology – for the internal ratings-based approach which banks are allowed to use their internal estimates of borrower creditworthiness to assess credit risk in their portfolios, are mentioned. So, under both the foundation and advanced internal ratings-based approaches, the range of risk weights will be more diverse than those of the standardized approach, resulting in greater risk sensitivity.
3. The 2001 proposal develops a suitable capital charge for operational risks (like the risk of loss from computer failures, poor documentation and fraud). Presently, many major banks allocate 20% or more of their internal capital to operational risks. The three different approaches – *Basic Indicator, Standardized and Internal Measurement Approaches* – are identified. The basic indicator approach utilizes one indicator of operational risk for a bank's total activity. The standardized approach specifies different indicators for different business lines. The internal measurement approach requires banks to utilize their internal loss data in the estimation of required capital.

Figure 2. The changes in the New Basel Accord or Basel II

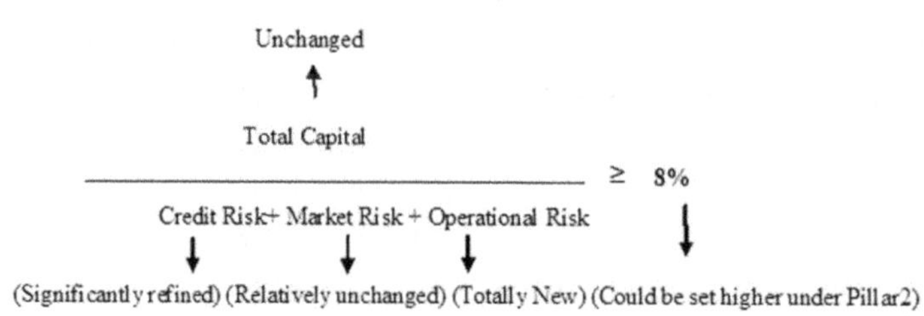

The areas for senior management attention can be considered under a number of headings:

- Strategic issues
- Credit risk management
- Operational risk management
- Implications for regulatory relation and supervisory review
- Market discipline

The Basel compliant risk-based capital adequacy legislation framework was brought into force in 2006; however, the minimum capital adequacy standard ratio of banks had been set as 8% since 1998 in Turkey. The BRSA is authorised to increase such ratio taking into consideration internal systems, assets and financial conditions of the banks and to impose different minimum statutory capital adequacy ratios to different banks. The BRSA announced a target capital adequacy ratio of 12% in 2006 and banks are expected to achieve and maintain a capital adequacy ratio that is higher than 12%. In addition, banks in Turkey are also required to implement an Internal Capital Adequacy Assessment Process (ICAAP) which shall be used to internally calculate the capital adequate to cover current and future risks by banks. Specifically, the ICAAP for each bank shall assess its internal capital adequacy level and produce an internal capital requirement ratio based on that bank's risk profile and appetite and the volume and complexity of its transactions. In the calculation of such internal capital requirement ratio, banks should include both internal capital requirements based on risks not captured by the statutory capital requirements and a capital planning buffer amount determined on the basis of stress tests and scenario analysis. As a result, the Turkish financial sector reached high capital adequacy levels as of March 2017, the capital adequacy ratio of the Turkish financial sector hit 16.1% consisting of high quality assets (85% qualifies as Tier I or Core Capital).

Basel III

The 2008 global financial crisis has been very costly and disconcerting . In order to ensure that banking system is more resistant to future crises, some reforms like increasing liquidity, capital quality and capital adequacy ratio have been essential. As a result of these efforts, the Basel banking audit committee published Basel III. The Basel III criteria do not completely change the Basel II criteria but they aim to overcome the shortcomings of the 2008 crisis.

The arrangements made for this purpose are:

- Increasing the minimum capital both in quantity and quality
- Regulations on minimum liquidity ratios
- Making changes in capital adequacy calculations related to trading accounts
- Change in calculation of counter party credit risk
- Development of cross-border banking rules
- Revision of effective banking supervision and development of standard supervision practices

These applications are not entirely different from Basel II but show a feature that further increases the obligations of banks. Basel III accord has reduced the risk of failure in individual banking but banking activities have become costlier. The effects of the Basel III criteria on the Turkish banking system can be summarized as follows:

- The difference between the capital adequacy ratio of the Turkish banking system and the core capital adequacy ratio is lower than in the U.S. and European banks. In 2008 global economic crisis, Turkey was the only country that did not need public's patronage of capital in the banking sector among OECD countries.
- When the Basel III criteria are examined, it has been seen that the regulations related to liquidity and capital buffer in particular are similar to proactive measures taken by BRSA before the crisis. Thanks to proactive measures such as the application of target capital adequacy ratios, the extremely robust Turkish banking system in the recent crisis has echoed the whole world.
- Cyclical capital buffering and capital protection buffering practices, which are among the criteria of Basel III would require additional capital requirements and they will adversely affect banks' equity reserves in the short-term but likely to have a positive impact on economic growth in the medium and long term.
- Perhaps the most significant impact of the Basel III criteria will manifest itself in the narrowing of the informal economy, which will make the banking surveillance system work more efficiently.
- Significant changes in the risk appetite and perception of banks will come into play. Banks' customer portfolio preferences will change in the direction of sound companies with good creditworthiness and good rating and it will be possible to use credits with lower than the average credit interest rate for the firms with good credit ratings.

When the capital structure of the Turkish banking system is evaluated, it is seen that the ratio of capital-like credits in equity is low, and the items such as paid-in capital, profit back-ups and undistributed profits are higher (90% of legal capital is composed of core or Tier 1 capital). Tier 3 or sub-supplementary capital stock which will be extracted from equity calculations in Basel III applications is not already existing in the Turkish banking system and will not affect the existing conditions. As a result, Turkish banking system has adequate capital support. So, due to the Turkish banking system's sound capital structure, high liquidity level, low leverage ratio and deposit-based funding structure provided by modern risk management, effective audit and internal control system, it is likely that there will not be a problem for the implementation of Basel III criteria. The assessment team relating to Basel Committee on Banking Supervision Regulatory Consistency Assessment Programme ("RCAP") also determined and announced in its March 2016 report that Turkey is in compliance with the Basel III risk-based capital standards with all underlying components (Basel Committee on Banking Supervision, 2016).

SOLUTIONS AND RECOMMENDATIONS

Whether it is a developed or an emerging country, the weakness of banking system poses a significant threat, both to the financial system of that country and the stability of international financial markets. The crises taking place in international markets have their own characteristics. Although pre-crisis indicators differ, results are always the same because the fall in national income leads to the impoverishment of the public and the fluctuations in financial markets cause the investors to lose money.

Banking system is a system in which competition is intense. Each financial enterprise determines its growth and development strategy in line with its vision and mission. In this sense, the definition of financial risk is made separately for each bank. An important question could be "how the vision and the mission of a bank can be formulated in an equation involving macroeconomic risks, sector and company-based risks?" In order to answer this, the reliability of the figures used primarily in determining economic activities should be questioned. One can wonder if economic data and corporate balance sheets reflect the truth or not. Whether the items that credit demanding companies show as collateral and their balance sheets reflect the reality or not should be questioned before risk management.

Another question could be "Are banks adhering to corporate governance principles completely when conducting risk analysis?" Transparency is critically important. If market participants have enough knowledge, this will contribute to the stabilization of the markets. Deficiencies in transparency increase uncertainty. At the same time, transparency also forces the decision makers to be accountable and thus helps to understand the underlying causes of the decision. Taking all this into consideration, even today the risk management of any bank alone cannot create ideal conditions for success. Therefore, banking system should be in accordance with transparency criteria and this should be adopted by other related parties such as real sector firms.

FUTURE RESEARCH DIRECTIONS

In line with the above findings, the framework for an integrated risk management which covers all possible risk components should be improved in order to achieve optimum capital levels for a given bank. Further research in this area is needed to ensure that the economic capital calculated by banks is equal to the regulatory capital required by banking authorities.

The models which take into account the conditions for an emerging market should also be improved in order to calculate the exposed risk by banks more accurately. The market price sensitivity to macroeconomic stability and political developments is much higher in emerging economies such as Turkey and large fluctuations are observed more frequently. Historical observations show that the return variances of the risk measurement models do not fit the normal distribution. There is a fat tail problem in the yield changes. The fact that this condition is not taken into account by the reason of the normal distribution leads to a small value of the calculated risk and capital adequacy measurements. In a market where volatility is so high, adjustments based on risk factors need to be made.

CONCLUSION

Risk management in Turkey due to the developments in international banking sector constitutes one of the major agenda items in the economic structure. When the main causes of banking crises in emerging market countries are examined, it can be obviously seen that the inadequacy of capital, macroeconomic imbalances existing in the country, injection of hot money or short term foreign cash inflows increasing the fragility of the overall economic system and bad risk management environment with lack of supervisory authorities have been the major causes. As of today, in the context of the Basel criteria, Turkish banking system competes on a global scale in terms of capital adequacy and auditing standards. This position confirms a positive step for financial system in Turkey.

On the other hand, Turkey's aforementioned ability to adapt to international rules will lead to even more positive results for sustainable growth, economic development and structural transformation of the country if resolution of structural problems and macroeconomic instability could be achieved. The Basel criteria are extremely important as guidelines that are considered to be mandatory by countries accepting these criteria but are more guiding because they do not coincide with national legislation simultaneously.

As a result, in a competitive banking sector, the capital base, asset quality, risk management capability, liquidity, and maturity mismatch should act as filters to eliminate those unsound banks from the system which create systemic risk and threaten the entire economic structure. As the economic stabilization is achieved, the economic profits on arbitrage opportunity of government securities will decline and the funds will be directed to real sector for the aim of increasing production and economic growth. In this environment of more intense competition, only the banks which implement strategic risk management techniques accurately and have adjustable cost structures will survive in the long-run.

REFERENCES

Banking Regulation & Supervision Agency of Turkey (BRSA). (2017). *Financial Sector Report.* Istanbul: BRSA. Retrieved from: https://www.bddk.org.tr/WebSitesi/turkce/Raporlar/TBSGG/16031tbs_temel_gostergeler_raporu_mart_2017.pdf

Basel Committee on Banking Supervision. (1993). *The supervisory treatment of market risks.* BIS. Retrieved from: https://www.bis.org/publ/bcbs11a.pdf

Basel Committee on Banking Supervision. (2001). *The New Basle Capital Accord: an explanatory note.* BIS. Retrieved from: https://www.bis.org/publ/bcbsca01.pdf

Basel Committee on Banking Supervision. (2016). *RCAP Report, Assessment of Basel III risk-based capital regulations in Turkey.* BIS. Retrieved from: https://www.bis.org/bcbs/publ/d359.pdf

Basle Committee on Banking Supervision. (1988). *Internal Convergence of Capital Measurement and Capital Standards.* BIS. Retrieved from: https://www.bis.org/publ/bcbs04a.pdf

Bessis, J. (2010). *Risk management in banking.* Wiley.

Caprio, G., Hunter, W., Kaufman, G., & Leipziger, D. (Eds.). (1999). Preventing banking crises: lessons from recent global bank failures. Economic Development Institute of WB.

Caprio, G., & Klingebiel, D. (2003). *Episodes of systemic and borderline financial crises.* World Bank.

De Luna Martinez, J. (2000). *Management and resolution of banking crises.* WB Discussion Paper, 413. doi:10.1596/0-8213-4723-3

Demirgüç-Kunt, A. & Huizinga, H. (1999). Determinants of commercial bank interest margins & profitability: An international evidence. *WB Economic Review, 13*, 379-408. doi:10.1093/wber/13.2.379

IMF. (1998). *World Economic Outlook.* International Monetary Fund. Retrieved from:http://www.imf.org/en/Publications/WEO/Issues/2016/12/31/Financial-Crises-Causes-and-Indicators

Jorion, P. (2006). *Value At Risk: The new benchmark for controlling market risk.* McGraw-Hill.

Kaufman, G. (2000). Banking and currency crises and systemic risk: Lessons from recent events. *Economic Perspectives, 24*(3), 9–20. Retrieved from https://www.chicagofed.org/publications/economic-perspectives/2000/3qepart2

Kaufman, G., & Scott, K. (2003). What is systemic risk and do bank regulators retard or contribute to it? *Independent Review, 7*(3), 371–391. Retrieved from http://www.independent.org/pdf/tir/tir_07_3_scott.pdf

Kibritcioglu, A. (2002). *Excessive risk-taking, banking sector fragility and banking crises.* University of Illinois, Commerce and Bus. Admin. Working Paper No. 02-0114. doi:10.2139srn.317491

Matten, C. (2000). *Managing bank capital: Capital allocation and performance measurement.* John Wiley & Sons, Ltd.

Neyapti, B., & Dincer, N. (2004). *Measuring the quality of bank regulation and supervision, with an application to transition economies. Discussion Paper, Turkish Economic Association, No. 2004/2*. Ankara: Turkish Economic Association. Retrieved from https://www.econstor.eu/bitstream/10419/83282/1/dp_2004-02.pdf

OECD. (2001). Policy reassessment in the light of the end-2000 financial crisis. In *OECD Economic Surveys: Turkey.* Paris: OECD. Retrieved from: http://www.oecd.org/turkey/1886247.pdf

The Banks Association of Turkey (TBAT). (2000). *The Banking Sector Report.* Istanbul: TBAT.

The Banks Association of Turkey (TBAT). (2009). *The Financial system and banking sector in Turkey.* Istanbul. TBAT. Retrieved from: https://www.tbb.org.tr/Dosyalar/Arastirma_ve_Raporlar/The_Financial_System_and_Banking_Sector_in_Turkey.pdf

Van Greuning, H., & Bratanovic, S. B. (2009). *Analyzing banking risks: A new framework for assessing risk management.* World Bank. doi:10.1596/978-0-8213-7728-4

ADDITIONAL READING

Altunbas, Y., Kara, A., & Olgu, O. (2009). *Turkish banking: Banking under political instability and chronic high inflation.* Palgrave Mcmillan. doi:10.1057/9780230582064

Banking Regulation & Supervision Agency of Turkey (BRSA). (2010). From Crisis to Financial Stability. Ankara: BRSA. Retrieved from: https://www.bddk.org.tr/WebSitesi/english/Reports/Working_Papers/8675from_crisis_to_financial_stability_turkey_experience_3rd_ed.pdf

Crouhy, M., Galai, D., & Mark, R. (2014). *The essentials of risk management.* USA: McGrawhill.

Gallati, R. (2003). *Risk management and capital adequacy.* USA: McGrawhill.

IMF. (February 2017). Turkey financial sector assessment program: Detailed assessment of observance - Basel core principles for effective banking supervision. IMF country report 17/46, Washington: International Monetary Fund. Retrieved from: https://www.imf.org/en/Publications/CR/Issues/2017/02/08/Turkey-Financial-Sector-Assessment-Program-Detailed-Assessment-of-Observance-of-the-Basel-44641

Jorion, P. (2009). *Financial risk manager handbook.* USA: Wiley.

Laurens, F. (2012). Basel III and prudent risk management in banking: Continuing the cycle of fixing past crises. *Journal of Risk Governance & Control, 2*(3), 17–22. doi:10.22495/rgcv2i3art1

Scannella, E., & Blandi, G. (2015). Operational risk in bank governance and control: How to save capital requirement through a risk transfer strategy, evidences from a simulated case study. *Journal of Risk Governance & Control, 5*(2), 142–159. doi:10.22495/rgcv5i2c1art8

KEY TERMS AND DEFINITIONS

Bank for International Settlements (BIS): An international organization based in Basel, Switzerland that acts as a bank for central banks of major industrial countries.

Basel Committee: Joint committee of banking supervisory agencies in the 12 major industrial countries organized in 1975. The Basel Committee promotes uniform policies for bank capital and supervision of financial institutions.

Capital Adequacy: Requirement that banks maintain equity capital sufficient to protect depositors from losses and support asset growth. Capital adequacy measures financial leverage; as leverage increases, less capital is available to cover unexpected losses. Thus, highly leveraged banks have more volatile earnings than banks with adequate capital, and are more closely monitored by banking regulators.

Deposit Insurance Scheme: Deposit insurance is a measure implemented in many countries to protect bank depositors, in full or in part. Deposit insurance in Turkey is handled by Savings Deposit Insurance Fund.

Domino Effect: Usually associated with financial crises, domino effect can be manifested as negative externalities diffused from one crashing market to another.

Economic Capital: Aggregate amount of equity capital that is required as a cushion for a company's unexpected losses due to all of its risks.

High Yielding Uncovered Bond Arbitrage: This happens when banks sell foreign currency against domestic currency in order to benefit from high returns of government debt instruments. But this triggers the demand for foreign currency when their foreign currency denominated liabilities come due because their borrowings are in terms of foreign currency. The volatility of foreign exchange rate, hence becomes the core risk for Turkish banks.

Regulatory Capital: Capital required by the regulators and calculated by limiting the maximum level of a bank's risk assets and off-balance sheet commitments to a fixed multiple of its capital.

Risk Adjusted Profitability: The financial services sector uses two common risk-adjusted profitability measurement models; risk-adjusted return on capital (RAROC) and return on risk-adjusted capital (RORAC).

Systemic Risk: Possibility that failure of one bank to settle net transactions with other banks will trigger a chain reaction, depriving other banks of funds and preventing them from closing their positions in turn.

Value at Risk (VaR): VaR is a measure of how much money the bank might lose over a period of time in the future. It provides standardized measure of market risks and estimate better the risk/return profile of individual assets or asset classes.

Chapter 3
Measurement of Economic and Banking Stability in Emerging Markets by Considering Income Inequality and Nonperforming Loans

Hasan Dinçer
Istanbul Medipol University, Turkey

Serhat Yüksel
İstanbul Medipol University, Turkey

Fatih Pınarbaşı
İstanbul Medipol University, Turkey

İpek Tamara Çetiner
İstanbul Medipol University, Turkey

ABSTRACT

Economic and banking instability are the factors that can affect each other significantly. This chapter aims to measure the relationship between income inequality and nonperforming loans ratio. For this purpose, 20 different emerging economies are evaluated by using Pedroni panel cointegration and Dumitrescu Hurlin panel causality analysis. In addition to this aspect, annual data between the years 2000 and 2015 is considered in the analysis process. It is concluded that there is a long-term relationship between these variables. Hence, it can be said that these countries should take some actions to improve banking system. In other words, nonperforming loans ratio in banking sector can be decreased when banks in these countries can choose customers more effectively. Therefore, income inequality problem can be minimized in emerging economies.

DOI: 10.4018/978-1-5225-7208-4.ch003

INTRODUCTION

Income inequality is a very significant problem facing countries. It has a negative influence in many different aspects (Jenkins, 2017). Firstly, income inequality may cause social problems. The main reason behind this situation is that some people have high living standards whereas some others have financial problems in case of income inequality. Therefore, this situation may increase the crime rate in these countries (Lee and Lee, 2018). Furthermore, income inequality may also cause economic problems in the country. When there is income inequality, some people become unemployed. Because this situation decreases consumption amount, it affects economic development negatively (Lindauer, 2017).

In addition to these aspects, it is also important to understand which factors lead to income inequality of the countries. For example, it is thought that income inequality increases when minimum wage level in the country is low. The main reason is that the income of employees is low whereas employers' revenue goes up in case of low minimum wage level. Moreover, it is also accepted that another factor that causes income inequality is differences in regional development. In this case, the income of the people in high developed regions is quite high while people can earn much less in other regions (Dabla-Norris et al., 2015).

Instability of the banking system is also accepted as a significant indicator of income inequality. When banks give loans to the people who have low credibility, this situation increases nonperforming loans ratio of the banks (Dinçer et al., 2018). Hence, banks may be unwilling to give loans if they have high nonperforming loans ratio. This situation has a negative impact on investment ratio and it declines the profitability of the companies. If the companies have lower profit, they will fire some employees and it increases unemployment ratio in the companies (Yüksel, 2016).

By looking at the points emphasized above, it can be understood that analyzing the relationship between economic and banking stability is very important. Parallel to this aspect, in this study, it is aimed to measure the relationship between income inequality and nonperforming loans ratio. Within this context, 20 different emerging economies are examined with the help of Pedroni panel cointegration and Dumitrescu Hurlin panel causality analysis. As a result, it can be possible to give recommendation for these companies to minimize economic and banking instability.

This study consists of 5 different parts. After this introduction part, similar studies in the literature are shared in the second part. In addition to them, the third section explains the general concepts about income inequality and nonperforming loans ratio. For this purpose, GINI coefficient is explained in a detailed manner. Moreover, the fourth part gives information about the application on emerging economies. Additionally, the final part underlines the analysis results and recommendations in order to minimize the problems of economic and banking instability.

LITERATURE REVIEW OF RESEARCH AND DEVELOPMENT

Income inequality is a very popular topic in the literature. In addition to this aspect, the subject of nonperforming loans also attracts the attention of the researchers. Some selected studies with respect to these aspects are detailed on Table 1.

Berisha et al. (2015) focused on trying to find a relationship between household debt and income inequality as it may influence one another. They refer to the results of Atkins, Piketty, and Saez as they continue the research. Using the Johansen and Engle–Granger methodology, United States of America

Table 1. Studies related to income inequality and non-performing loans

Author	Method	Scope	Results
Podpiera & Weill (2008)	Granger- Causality Model	Czech Republic	When there is bad management in the banking industry there is an increase in NPLs. Also, it has been seen that foreign investment positively affect the NPLs.
Caliskan (2010)	Descriptive Statistics	Turkey	Economic growth cannot be the only solution to income inequality in the country of Turkey.
Louzis et.al (2012)	Panel Data Methods	Greek Banking Sector	Macroeconomic factors have a direct effect on the NPL in the Greek banking sector.
Kauko (2012)	Regression	Emerging 34 EU Countries	When there is a shortfall in an account, it can be said that there is a risk of NPLs.
Mukhopadhaya (2013)	Gini decomposition methodology,	China	Disposable income directly affects the income inequality in China.
Abid et.al (2014)	Panel Data Methods	16 Tunisian Banks	Macroeconomic variables and bad decision making in management in Tunisia are two reasons of NPLs.
Clark & Ambrosio (2015)	Descriptive Studies	World	People get influenced by the level of income of others and when they earn less it is seen that this causes the status discrimination.
Rougoor & Marrewijk (2015)	Scenario Analysis	137 Countries - Six Continents	Income inequality will eventually decrease by 2027.
Berisha et.al (2015)	Johansen and Engle–Granger methodology	USA	Households have a strong influence on income inequality
Yağcılar and Demir (2015)	Panel Data Analysis	Turkey	Non-performing loans have some negative and positive relations with some variables such as; negative relations with the stock market, measurement, loan/deposit ratio, liquidity and active profitable. Positives: foreign banks and sufficient investments. On the other hand, there were some variables such as interest rates and inflation where no relations were found.
Cheung and Lucas (2015)	Regression	USA	People indirectly get affected by the income of their surroundings, which can potentially influence social skills
Ghosh (2015)	Sensitivity Analysis	US States	High funding, liquidity risks, low quality in credit, bad cost efficiency and the size of the banking industry can all result in high non-performing loans.
Cifter (2015)	Panel Data Analysis	Central and Eastern European Countries	In central and Eastern European countries bank concentration and NPL do not have any kind of relation ultimately. However, this does not necessarily mean the loan liability factor does not play a role in the matter.
Bumann & Lensink (2016)	Regression	Sub-Saharan Countries	For emerging markets where the deepness of finance is very low, most probably the income inequality will increase.
Florida and Mellander (2016)	Regression	USA	While it can be thought that wage inequality is directly related with income inequality, the study shows that there is a relation. There are other factors such as competency, educational background and skill sets that set the tone for the wage inequality. On the other hand, income inequality could be affected by ethnic backgrounds and low income.
Genç and Aşmaz (2016)	Hatemi-J Cointegration	Turkey	GDP, BIST 100 Index, commercial loan interests, and reel currency are some of the macroeconomic indicators of the non-performing commercial loans.
Rajha (2016)	Regression	Jordan	Non-performing loans in Jordan are directly affected by the increasing prices in services and goods along with the economical size.
Zhang et.al (2016)	Panel Regression Model	60 city Commercial Banks 16 State Owned Banks 11 Rural Commercial Banks	When there is a high amount of risk in the NPLs, this also influences the character of the loans itself.
Konstantakis et.al (2016)	VAR & VEC Model	Greek Banking Sector	The financial industry in Greece is significantly affected by the NPLs.

continued on following page

Table 1. Continued

Author	Method	Scope	Results
Yang & Greaney (2016)	Engle - Granger	China, Japan, South Korea, United States	Income inequality has a positive effect on Japan, China, and the United States. Also, trade openness has some effects in each country in a different way.
Stuckyet.al. (2016)	Spatial analysis	USA	According to the study, some aggressive acts such as violence and crime is directly affected by income inequality.
Vilhjalmsdottir et.al. (2016)	Similarity Analysis	Iceland	Income inequality has negative effect on social relations.
Tao et.al. (2016)	Regression	Europe to Latin America, North America and Asia	There has been a model showing the income inequality for different countries.
Seven & Coskun (2016)	Regression	Emerging Countries	The growth of banks and stock markets do not affect poverty positively.
Vithessonthi (2016)	Panel Regression GMM Regression	Japan	During the financial crisis in 2007 the growth of loans and non-performing loans are positively related.
Dimitrios et.al (2016)	Augmented Dickey Fuller	Euro- Area	Both management skills and risk preferences have a direct effect on the outcome of NPLs.
Destek et.al (2017)	ARDL Limitation Test & Granger Causality Test	Turkey	According to the study, when the value of money decreases over time the inequality in income increases. Also, the increase in governmental expenditure can be shown as if it has direct effect on the matter.
Meyer and Sullivan (2017)	Descriptive Statistics	USA	The differences between income inequality and consumption inequality can be seen in single homes and/or single individuals.
Ngamaba et.al (2017)	Descriptive Statistics	OECD	Income inequality depends on the economic strength of a country.
Anderson et.al. (2017)	Regression	90 Countries	The emotional belongingness of a citizen depends on the income inequality in a country. As the income inequality increases wealthy people are less likely to serve their country. On the other hand, when income inequality is at minor levels the wealth is no longer a variable of the emotional belongingness in a country.
Ayyıldız (2017)	Regression	15 Countries	Income taxes, population, and foreign investments have a direct association with income inequality.
Bağce et. al. (2017)	Descriptive Statistics	161 Different Countries	According to the study, countries with a democratic approach in management are less likely to have income inequality.
Karluk and Unal (2017)	Descriptive Statistics	Turkey	Income inequality has a direct effect on fraud.
Us (2017)	Panel Data Analysis	Turkey	After economical turning points, the motive of the non-performing loans has changed. The quality of a loan is a sign of strong economic status.
D'Onofrio et.al (2017)	Regression	Italy	As the banks develop themselves locally the income inequality decreases
Gründler & Köllner (2017)	Regression	OECD Countries	When there is a use of the inequality measures both market inequality and redistribution increase.
Kennedy et.al (2017)	Panel Regression	Australia	Financial growth is affected by income inequality both in Europe and USA.
Haan & Sturm (2017)	Dynamic Panel Model	121 Countries	Both financial development and political institutions are a reason of income inequality when it comes to the impact of liberalization.
Neaime & Gaysset (2017)	Generalized Methods of Moments (GMM) & Generalized Least Squares (GLS)	Eight MENA Countries	When individuals do not become a part of financial systems in MENA countries the income inequality decreases.
Tarchouna et.al (2017)	Principal Component Analysis GMM Panel Regression	184 US Commercial Banks	As the volume of the bank decreases, the risks of NPLs also decrease.
Alandejani & Asutay (2017)	GMM	Commercial Banking in GCC Countries	Islamic banks focusing sector-specific financing has a direct negative impact on the NPLs.
Ghosh (2017)	Logit	100 Largest Commercial Banks in the US	US housing pricing, real GDP growth, and housing starts are the variables that get affected by the NPLs.

was their sampling during their research. As a result, it was found that households have a strong relation to income inequality. According to Caliskan (2010), the level of poverty and income inequality has dramatically taken a toll in developing countries. Especially in Turkey, based on the economic growth (although it has become better compared to the last years), the country is at disadvantage. He claims that this issue has not been given priority to. As a result, he claims that the dependency on the economic growth of a country cannot be the only way income inequality deserves a solution. With the panel data analysis, Cifter (2015) tried to show the relation between the concentrations of the banks and the non-performing loans. He focused on the Central and Eastern European countries. It was found that in central and Eastern European countries bank concentration and NPL do not have any kind of relation ultimately. However, this does not necessarily mean the loan liability factor does not play a role in the matter.

Destek et.al (2017) aimed to find the effects of the modules of the Gini by using various variables such as the GDP, financial development, government expenditures, and inflation, the main purpose of the study is to focus on the effects of these variables on the Gini directly ARDL Limitation Test & Granger Causality Test was used to analyze the data. According to the study, when the value of money decreases over time the inequality in income increases. Also, the increase in governmental expenditure can be shown as if it has direct effect on the matter. Florida and Mellander (2016) focused on the income inequality depending on the regions in the United States. As there are differences in the wages in state systems, the paper aims to focus both on wage inequality and income inequality across the nation. During the study the regression method was applied to analyze the data. As a result, while it can be thought that wage inequality is directly related with income inequality, the study shows that there is a relation. There are other factors such as competency, educational background and skill sets that set the tone for the wage inequality. On the other hand, income inequality could be affected by ethnic backgrounds and low income.

Meyer and Sullivan (2017) believe that there has not been an accurate measurement in the income inequality between certain years. According to them, there are various areas that needs to be taken under consideration before income inequality can be measured clearly. Using the descriptive studies in the USA, it was found that the difference between income inequality and consumption inequality can be seen in single homes and/or single individuals. According to Ngamaba et.al. (2017), to increase the well-being of people it is important to decrease the level of income inequality.

Anderson et.al. (2017) tries to show the issue of income inequality from a different perspective by focusing on a more patriotic approach. They think that the sacrifice and commitment people will give to their countries depends on their income level. As a result of this study, focusing on 90 countries, the emotional belongingness of a citizen depends on the income inequality in a country. As the income inequality increases wealthy people are less likely to serve their country. On the other hand, when income inequality is at minor levels the wealth is no longer a variable of the emotional belongingness in a country for the poor.

The aim of Ayyildiz (2017) in this research is to find the causes of income inequality in the given countries (White Russia, Brazil, Bulgaria, China, Colombia, Costa Rica, Dominique Republic, Georgia, Paraguay, Peru, Romania, Russia, Thailand, Turkey). By using the regression methods to analyze the data, it was found that income taxes, populations, and foreign investments have a direct association with income inequality. Also, Bagce et.al. (2017) focuses on income inequality based on the countries managed by the parliament, presidential, and semi-presidential countries. 161 different countries were involved in the study, using descriptive statistics. According to the study, countries with democratic approaches in management are less likely to have income inequality.

Cheung and Lucas (2015) claims the direct positive relationship between high level of living and life satisfaction, although it does mention the subjectivity in the matter. The aim of the study is to find the link between income and life satisfaction in a mechanical matter. In the USA it was found that the income of their surroundings indirectly affects people. This can eventually and/or potentially influence social skills. Furthermore, Genc and Asmaz (2016) identified that banks take big risk when they provide loans to customers. However, they also believe that there must be some deeper reasons. Therefore, they seek to see the bigger Picture by using various methods. The concentration of the sampling is in Turkey.

Karluk and Unal (2017), for the first time in literature combine the Gini Index and the corruption perception index in order to measure the relationship between poverty, income, and corruption. They found that income inequality has a direct effect on fraud. The study used descriptive statistics sampling Turkey only. According to Mukhopadhaya (2013), the income inequality in China depends on both national and international investments. However, he also claims that these kinds of investments eventually lead to the decrease of unemployment. Therefore, the decrease of unemployment may result in low levels of income inequality. The aim of the paper is to focus on the differences between in rural and urban areas when it comes to income inequality. The methodology used in this study is the Gini decomposition. As a result, it was found that disposable income directly affects the income inequality in China.

Rajha (2016) defines that non-performing loans in general could be the main reason of the banking crisis in the world. In order to prevent this, the aim of the study focuses on the reasons of the non-performing loans in Jordan. The methodology of the study is Regression. At the end, the non-performing loans in Jordan are directly affected by the increasing prices in services and goods along with the economical size. Furthermore, according to Stucky et.al. (2016), there is general perception of income inequality being one of the major reason of crimes. Although it is claimed in this study that the ratio of the crimes will increase in underprivileged neighborhoods, it is challenging to say that income inequalities is an affect. Looking at the neighborhoods considered to be in the poverty category in the United States, the authors used the spatial analysis to get accurate results in the matter. As a result, some aggressive acts such as violence and crime are directly affected by the income inequality.

Tao et.al. (2016) focuses on the empirical observation of the expanding laws. The aim of the research is to show the relation between income inequality and relevant policies in the matter. Using the regression method, the study focuses on countries from Europe to Latin America and from North America to Asia. There has been a model showing the income inequality for different countries. Us (2017) aims to find the changes in non-performing loans after a crisis. With the panel data analysis, it can be seen a change in the non-performing loans with the economical turning points. The quality of the loan rather than the quantity has been taken into consideration. Also, it was found that the quality of a loan is a sign of strong economic status. Vilhjalmsdottir et.al. (2016) found the relationship between income inequality and the stress level it causes on adults. In this study, it is identified that although it is not clear how income inequality may affect the mental health, income inequality has negative effect on social relations in Iceland.

Also, Yagcılar and Demir (2015) states that risk management in the banking industry is a delicate issue that should be handled with care. When there is an increase in non-performing loans in a country, the risk management department in banks needs to be questioned. With the regression model, D'Onofrio et. al. (2017) tried to show the relation between local banks and income inequality. the other hand, the relationship between finance and inequality is seen as the region becomes enlarged. Additionally, Bumann & Lensink (2016) defined that when the financial deepness rises above 25 a decrease in income inequality can be seen. According to Clark & Ambrosio (2015) regardless of the situation of income inequality, it can be said that the behaviors and thoughts towards the topic can be explained with only one perspective.

Moreover, Rougoor & Marrewijk (2015) tried to determine the fluctuations of income equality at the given years. They concluded that income inequality will eventually decrease by 2027. On the other side, Gründler & Köllner (2017) focused on the analysis of income inequality and redistribution by reviewing development levels and subjective perspectives. They reached the conclusion that the affiliation between market inequality and redistribution increases when there is a use of the inequality measures. Seven and Coskun (2016) aimed to determine the correlation between income inequality with the bank and stock market incline. It is found that banks and stock markets do not work on benefit of solving poverty in any way

Kennedy et.al. (2017) focused on to find the answer to see if somehow income inequality has a negative impact on the growth of the economy. It is determined that the financial growth both for Europe and the United States if affected by income inequality. Yang and Greaney (2016) tried to find the relationship between the income inequality and the growth of the economy in the big four markets by using the Engle-Granger Method. It is defined that there is a direct impact of income inequality and financial growth in China, Japan, and the United States. Haan & Strum (2017) aimed to find the correlation between financial liberalization, financial development, and banking crisis with income inequality. They claim that income inequality is affected by the financial development and liberalization, and also by crisis.

Podpiera and Weill (2008) suggests that there is an incline in non-performing loans when there is bad management. Moreover, when there is an affiliation with foreign investment in the banking industry, a positive repercussion was seen and therefore, it is suggested by the study to focus on foreign ownerships. Ghosh (2015) aimed to analyze the factors effecting NPLs through both state-level and regional banking. It is identified that high funding, liquidity risks, low quality in credit, bad cost efficiency and the size of the banking industry can all result in high non-performing loans. Vithessonthi (2016) aimed to evaluate the relationship between the growth of bank credits and NPLs when there is an economic pressure. It is defined that that during the financial crisis in 2007 the growth of loans and non-performing loans are positively related. However, he adds that the positive relation changes direction after the crisis. Dimitrios et.al. (2016) tried to find the factors of NPLs in Europe for the given years of 1990-2015. With the model of GMM, it is determined that both management skills and risk preferences have a direct effect on the outcome of NPLs.

Kauko (2012) analyzed the decline in the credit quality during crisis. Using the regression method, it is concluded that when there is a shortfall in an account it can be said that there is a risk of non-performing loans. In other words, between the years of 2000-2005 there was no direct negative effect of NPLs until a shortage was seen. Tarchouna et.al. (2017) evaluated the direct effect of corporate management on NPLs using both the component analysis and panel data methods. It can be understood that as the volume of the bank decreases, the risks of NPLs also decreases due to their low-risk management styles. On the other hand, banks with high size in the United States, do face some challenges when it comes to NPLs due to their high risk-taking strategies. Using the panel data method, Abid et.al (2014) claims that NPLs in Tunisian banks are affected by two factors; macroeconomic variables and bad decision making in management.

Furthermore, Louzis et.al. (2012) aimed to find the reasons of the NPLs in Greece between independent loan categories. It is seen that macroeconomic factors have a direct effect on the NPLs in Greece. On the other hand, the character of management also plays a role in the NPLs as well. Also, Zhang et al. (2016) looked at the actions taken regarding the NPLs in China. It is defined that when there is a high amount of risk in the NPLs, it also influences the character of the loans itself. Alandejani and Asutay (2017) have found that as Islamic banks focus on industry specific financing, the risk they take is higher than conventional banks, which has a direct negative impact on the NPLs. In other words, when the risk is distributed at a gain-loss contract the probability of having lower NPLs can be seen. Ghosh (2017) stated that US housing prices, real GDP growth, and housing starts were the variable that get affected by the NPLs the most.

While analyzing the studies in the literature, it can be seen that income inequality is analyzed in many different studies. In addition, it is also identified that nonperforming loans ratio is considered by many different authors as well. On the other side, it is understood that many different methodologies are considered in these studies, such as regression, ARDL, GMM, logit. Nevertheless, it can be defined that there is a need for a new study in which the relationship between economic and banking stability is evaluated.

GENERAL INFORMATION ABOUT INCOME INEQUALITY AND NONPERFORMING LOAN RATIO IN EMERGING ECONOMIES

In this part, income inequality and non-returning loans will be addressed in the context of emerging economies. Income inequality refers to unbalanced/disproportional distribution of total national income between households (Todaro & Smith, 2014). According to Human Development Report 2016, income amount is rising around the world, but rising of income comes with expanding of inequality along. On the other hand, developing regions are converging and this brings about narrowing of income inequality as a whole in worldwide (UNDP, 2016). Nonperforming loans represent loans that have passed the default or similar status after a certain period of time. According to Rajan and Dhal (2003), financial stability is key factor of rapid and sustained economic progress. There are various indicators of financial stability, but non-performing loans have an important role among them; because they point out to credit risk, asset quality and other factors.

Once these concepts have been fundamentally addressed, the question of what is meant by “emerging” economies and which economies are those economies should be answered. Emerging economies refers low-income economies which have rapid growth. These economies use economic liberalization method as the main source for their growth (Hoskisson et al., 2000). There are many different classification categories of “emerging” economies. This study will be based on the classification of the International Monetary Fund (IMF). According to the report of the International Monetary Fund (IMF) in 2010, there are 23 emerging economy blueprints. These countries and their geographical locations on the world are listed in Table 2.

According to the classification of the International Monetary Fund, a list of 23 different countries arises when countries are listed. An assessment of these countries, with their geographical location on the globe, allows the subject to be addressed in a geographical context. This list includes 9 countries from Asia, 6 from South America, 6 from Europe, 1 from North America and 1 from Africa. When the results of these ranks are examined, the results are consistent with the economic development in the world. In terms of the strength of the European and North American continent in economic development, and the fact that the countries of Africa are behind in this respect, it is a matter of course.

Table 2. List of emerging economies by Continents (IMF ranking)

Country	Continent	Country	Continent
Argentina	South America	Pakistan	Asia
Bangladesh	Asia	Peru	South America
Brazil	South America	Philippines	Asia
Bulgaria	Europe	Poland	Europe
Chile	South America	Romania	Europe
China	Asia	Russia	Asia
Colombia	South America	South Africa	Africa
Hungary	Europe	Thailand	Asia
India	Asia	Turkey	Europe
Indonesia	Asia	Ukraine	Europe
Malaysia	Asia	Venezuela	South America
Mexico	North America		

Source: http://www.imf.org/external/pubs/ft/weo/2015/02/pdf/text.pdf

Definition of GINI Coefficient

The measurement of inequality is one of the basic stages for other relevant work. Inequality measure refers to a numerical and scalar representation which shows the differences in income for a specific population (Cowell, 2011). Gini coefficient is one of the measures used to measure the inequality. Gini coefficient is an aggregate numerical aggregate measure about income equality whose values are ranging from 0 to 1. The value 0 refers to perfect equality and on the other side 1 value refers to perfect inequality. Thus, when coefficient reaches high values it means income is not being distributed equally. The opposite is true, namely income is distributed more evenly when the coefficient is low (Todaro & Smith, 2014).

GINI Values of Emerging Economies

GDP coefficients are among the most important indicators for emerging economies. In this study, the coefficients of GINI will be examined firstly in terms of emerging economies, then G7 countries will be evaluated. Gini coefficient values of the 23 countries included in the list of emerging economies can be found in Table 3. Gini coefficient is distributed in a quite wide range of 25.5 to 63.4, in emerging economies. The table also indicates that the country with the highest GINI coefficient is South Africa with a 63.4 GINI coefficient, while the country with the lowest GINI coefficient is Ukraine with a coefficient of 25.5. The highest GINI coefficients are listed in Brazil (51.3), Colombia (51.1) and Mexico (48.2), respectively. The lowest GINI coefficients are Romania (27.5), Pakistan (30.7) and Hungary (30.9).

The Place of Emerging Economies With Respect to Income Inequality

emerging economies can be divided into 3 groups in themselves regarding GINI coefficient. The first group countries are countries with a GINI coefficient below 35. The second group countries are those with a GINI coefficient between 35 and 45. Lastly, the third group countries can be expressed as countries

Table 3. GINI coefficients of emerging economies

Country	GINI Coefficient	Date of Source	Country	GINI Coefficient	Date of Source
Argentina	42,7	2014	Pakistan	30,7	2013
Bangladesh	32,1	2010	Peru	44,3	2015
Brazil	51,3	2015	Philippines	40,1	2015
Bulgaria	37,4	2014	Poland	32,1	2014
Chile	47,7	2015	Romania	27,5	2013
China	42,2	2012	Russia	37,7	2015
Colombia	51,1	2015	South Africa	63,4	2011
Hungary	30,9	2014	Thailand	37,8	2013
India	35,2	2011	Turkey	41,2	2014
Indonesia	39,5	2013	Ukraine	25,5	2015
Malaysia	46,3	2009	Venezuela	46,9	2006
Mexico	48,2	2014			

Source: World Bank. (2018). GINI index (World Bank estimate). World Bank Open Data: https://data.worldbank.org/indicator/SI.POV.GINI

with a GINI coefficient above 45. The countries in the third group can be expressed as a red group, since the GINI coefficient is close to 1 indicating that the inequality is too high. Malaysia, Venezuela, Chile, Mexico, Colombia, Brazil and South Africa are countries with a GINI coefficient of over 45 and are in a negative position relative to other emerging economies in the sense of economic inequality. Among them, South Africa is far behind in the nearest Emerging economy, Brazil.

The countries in the second group do not have as negative conditions as the countries in the third group but are not as positive as those in the first group, so the countries in the second group can be expressed as the blue group. Peru, Argentina, China, Turkey, Philippines, Indonesia, Thailand, Russia and Bulgaria are countries with GINI coefficients between 35 and 45. The countries in the first group can be expressed as a green group because the GINI coefficient of 0 means perfect equality and the first group countries have lower coefficients than the other two group countries. India, Poland, Bangladesh, Hungary, Pakistan, Romania and Ukraine are the first group countries with a GINI coefficient below 35. Once the GINI coefficients have been examined in terms of emerging economies, it will be useful to examine them within the G7 countries. The Gini coefficients of the G7 countries are distributed in a narrow range of 31.4 to 41. Within this range, the highest GIN coefficient among the G7 countries is in the United States, and the lowest GINI coefficient is in Germany.

Definition of Nonperforming Loans

Non-performing loan status occurs when borrower does not pay agreed debt more than 90 days (European Central Bank, 2018). According to Nkusu (2011), deterioration in loan portfolio of banks is one of major factors for economic crises and banking system distress. This deterioration has validity for both advanced and developing economies. Dornbusch (2001) provides example of combination of nonperforming loans and emerging economies in his study. Thailand and Malaysia are these examples and he indicates that two countries had substantial nonperforming loans in 1997. Thailand has nonperforming loans in real estate and consumer finance. On the other hand, Malaysia had stock market credits that have caused the market boom. Unwillingness to raise of mandated lending rates give rise to an offshore market, the pressure on the currency came to fruition. The economic crisis took place as result. In this section, as in the GINI coefficient section, information on emerging economies will also be examined on non-performing loans (Yüksel, 2017).

Information About Nonperforming Loan Ratio in Emerging Economies

Interpreting nonperforming loans contains referring to nonperforming loan ratio. Table 4 shows the data on bank performance loans to total gross loan ratios for emerging economies.

The highest NPL / TGL rate is found in Ukraine, while the lowest rate is in Malaysia. Countries with the highest NPL / TGL ratio are Brazil, Romania, Hungary and Pakistan; on the other hand, the lowest NPL / TGL countries are China, Argentina, Chile and Philippines.

The Comparison of Emerging Countries With Others Regarding Nonperforming Loans

Emerging economies are divided into two groups, green and blue, with the ratio being below 6 percent and above. The green group countries are Malaysia, China, Argentina, Chile, Philippines, Indonesia, Mexico, Thailand, Colombia, Turkey, South Africa, Bulgaria, Peru, Poland and India. The blue group countries are Russia, Bangladesh, Pakistan, Hungary, Romania and Brazil. In this classification, Ukraine, which is quite different from other countries, and Venezuela, whose data cannot be reached, are separated. Ukraine is the country with the highest ratio with 28.03%.

Table 4. Bank nonperforming loans to total gross Loans (%) in emerging countries (2015)

Country	NPL / TGL	Country	NPL / TGL
Argentina	1,736841818	Pakistan	11,35888408
Bangladesh	8,397907814	Peru	3,925485924
Brazil	14,61205086	Philippines	1,885478208
Bulgaria	3,31178796	Poland	4,341512013
Chile	1,874663267	Romania	13,50621927
China	1,673880164	Russia	8,347232397
Colombia	2,847672788	South Africa	3,121685643
Hungary	11,66312603	Thailand	2,682830867
India	5,883522274	Turkey	2,987723292
Indonesia	2,431042481	Ukraine	28,03477147
Malaysia	1,601390954	Venezuela	N/A
Mexico	2,523211904		

Source: World Bank. (2018). Bank nonperforming loans to total gross loans (%). World Bank Open Data: https://data.worldbank.org/indicator/FB.AST.NPER.ZS

Evaluation of the NPL / TGL ratios of the G7 countries after the NPL / TGL ratios of emerging economies is also important for comparison. The NPL / TGL ratios of the G7 countries are generally less than 10%, while only Italy has 17.11% ratio, higher than other countries. Given the combination of emerging economies and G7 countries, G7 countries have similar NPL / TGL ratios to the first group of countries in Emerging economies. The only exception is Italy from the G7 countries. Italy has a NPL / TGL ratio of 17.11%, even higher than the second group of countries in the developing world.

AN APPLICATION ON E7 COUNTRIES

Data Set and Scope

In this study, the causality relationship between income equality and nonperforming loans are evaluated. For this purpose, all emerging economies are intended to analyze. However, only 20 of these countries can be included in the analysis process due to the data availability problem. The details of these countries are given on Table 5.

On the other side, annual data of these countries for the periods between 2000 and 2015 is considered. This data is provided from the data source of World Bank.

Pedroni Panel Cointegration Analysis

The aim of cointegration analysis is to understand whether there is a long-term relationship between the variables. In order to reach this objective, 7 different tests are performed which are Panel v-Statistic, Panel rho-Statistic, Panel PP-Statistic, Panel ADF-Statistic, Group rho-Statistic, Group PP-Statistic and Group ADF-Statistic. In these 7 tests, if the probability values of more than 3 are lower than 0.05, it is concluded that these variables have long run relationship (Pedroni, 2001).

Dumitrescu Hurlin Panel Causality Tests

Dumitrescu Hurlin panel causality test is used to understand the causal relationship between some different variables. It is the form of Granger causality analysis which can be used for panel data. There is a requirement of this test that all variables should be stationary. The equation of this approach is given below (Dumitrescu and Hurlin, 2012).

Table 5. List of emerging countries analyzed in the study

Argentina	Armenia	Bolivia	Brazil	Colombia
Costa Rica	Dominican Republic	Georgia	Honduras	Kazakhstan
Kyrgyz Republic	Moldova	Panama	Peru	Paraguay
Russian Federation	Thailand	Turkey	Ukraine	Uruguay

$$Y_{i,t} = a_i + \sum_{k=1}^{K} Y_i^k Y_{i,t-k} + \sum_{k=1}^{K} B_i^k X_{i,t-k} + \varepsilon_{i,t} \tag{1}$$

In the equation (1), it is aimed to understand whether there is a causality analysis between x and Y. Furthermore, K refers to the the optimum lag interval. Also, α gives information about the constant term and B explains to the coefficient of the variables.

Analysis Results

In the analysis process, firstly, Im, Pesaran and Shin panel unit root test is conducted to see whether the variables have unit root or not. The details of this test are given on Table 6.

Table 6 shows that all variables have unit root because their probability values are greater than 0.05. Additionally, it can also be seen that by taking the first differences of them, they become stationary. Therefore, it is identified that these two variables are appropriate for panel cointegration analysis. Table 7 gives information about the results of Pedroni panel cointegration analysis.

Table 7 shows that out of 7 different tests, probability values are lower in 6 tests. This situation explains that there is a long-term relationship between income inequality and nonperforming loans in emerging countries. On the other side, Dumitrescu Hurlin panel causality analysis is also performed to see whether there is a causality relationship between these variables. The details are demonstrated on Table 8.

Table 8 gives information about the Dumitrescu Hurlin panel causality test results for 3 different lags. In this process, 2 different ways of causality relationship are aimed to identify. First of all, it is tried to understand whether income inequality has a causal impact on nonperforming loans. As it can be seen from this table that probability values are greater than 0.05 for all different lags. This means that income inequality does not cause nonperforming loans in emerging economies. Secondly, a different causality

Table 6. Im, pesaran and shin panel unit root test results

Variables	Level Value (Prob)	First Difference Value (Prob)
Income Inequality	0.9636	0.0000
Nonperforming Loans	0.4746	0.0000

Table 7. Pedroni panel cointegration test results

Relationship Type	Test Name	Probability Values
The relationship between income inequality and nonperforming loans	Panel v-Statistic	0.9999
	Panel rho-Statistic	0.0000
	Panel PP-Statistic	0.0000
	Panel ADF-Statistic	0.0000
	Group rho-Statistic	0.0035
	Group PP-Statistic	0.0000
	Group ADF-Statistic	0.0000

Table 8. Dumitrescu hurlin panel causality analysis results

The Way of the Relationship	Lag	Probability Values	Results
Income Inequality → Nonperforming Loans	1	0.8304	Income inequality does not cause nonperforming loans.
	2	0.5499	
	3	0.5940	
Nonperforming Loans Ratio → Income Inequality	1	0.0141	Nonperforming loans ratio does not cause income inequality.
	2	0.8024	
	3	0.9737	

analysis is also performed to see if nonperforming loans ratio has a causal influence on income inequality. For the first lag, it is defined that the probability value is lower than 0.05. However, for the second and third lag, these values are greater than 0.05. Therefore, it can be understood that nonperforming loans ratio does not cause income inequality for these countries. In conclusion, it can be said that there is a long-term relationship between nonperforming loans ratio and income inequality for emerging economies. This situation was also emphasized in some studies in the literature (Yağcılar and Demir, 2015; Ghosh, 2017). Nevertheless, it is identified that it is not a causal relationship.

While considering these aspects, it can be understood that there is a significant relationship between nonperforming loans and income inequality for emerging economies. In other words, when income is distributed negatively in these countries, people cannot pay back their credit debts to the banks effectively. This situation has a negative effect on the financial performance of the banks. When banks' profitability decreases, they may be more reluctant to give new loans to the consumers and investors. Hence, it can have a negative influence on the consumption and investment amount of the countries. Moreover, it may cause lower economic growth for these emerging economies. Therefore, the governments in these countries should take an immediate action in order to solve unfair income distribution problem.

SOLUTIONS AND RECOMMENDATIONS

This study aims to identify the relationship between nonperforming loans ratio and income inequality in emerging economies. As a result of Pedroni panel cointegration and Dumitrescu Hurlin panel causality analyses, it is determined that there is a long term relationship between these two variables. Therefore, it can be said that these countries should take some actions to improve banking system. With the help of these implementations, banks in these countries can choose customer more effectively so that nonperforming loans ratio in banking sector can be decreased. This situation has a positive effect on decreasing income inequality in these emerging economies.

FUTURE RESEARCH DIRECTIONS

This study evaluates the relationship between income inequality and nonperforming loans ratio in emerging economies. By underlining a significant topic for these countries, it is aimed to make contribution to the literature. On the other side, a new study may also be conducted to see this relationship for developed economies. In addition to this issue, this relationship can also be evaluated by using a different methodology, such as regression and Toda Yamamoto causality analysis.

CONCLUSION

Economic instability is accepted as an important indicator of banking instability. On the other side, the instability in the banking sector may also cause economic problems for the countries. In this study, it is aimed to evaluate the relationship between income inequality and nonperforming loans ratio. Within this framework, 20 different emerging economies, which have necessary data, are analyzed. In addition to these issues, Pedroni panel cointegration and Dumitrescu Hurlin panel causality analysis are taken into the consideration to reach this objective.

In the first phase of the analysis process, Im, Pesaran and Shin panel unit root test is conducted so as to understand whether the variables have unit roots. As a result, it is understood that the variables are not stationary on their level values because their probability values are greater than 0.05. Thus, the first differences of these variables are used in the analysis. After the stationary analysis, Pedroni panel cointegration analysis is performed. It is concluded that there is a long-term relationship between income inequality and nonperforming loans in emerging countries.

In addition to them, Dumitrescu Hurlin panel causality analysis is also performed to see whether there is a causality relationship between these variables. According to the results, it is determined that income inequality does not cause nonperforming loans in emerging economies. On the other hand, it can also be understood that nonperforming loans ratio does not cause income inequality for these countries since the probability values are higher than 0.05. Consequently, it can be said that although there is long term relationship between these variables, they cannot be accepted as the main cause of the another one.

By looking at the results of the analysis, it can be seen that income inequality has an important effect on nonperforming loans for emerging economies. This shows that in case of unfair income distribution in these countries, people may not be successful to pay back their credit debts to the banks effectively. Therefore, this aspect leads to decrease in the financial performance of the banks. The credit amount given by the banks to the consumers and investors decreases when they have lower financial performance. This situation causes to lower economic improvement for emerging economies.

It can be understood that unfair income distribution in emerging economies can cause crucial financial problems. Thus, the governments in these countries should take an immediate action in order to solve unfair income distribution problem. Within this framework, they may decrease the taxes to attract the investors so that there can be higher investment in the countries. This situation provides new employment opportunities for the people, so it may have a decreasing effect on unemployment. Therefore, this issue has a powerful effect to minimize income inequality problem for the emerging economies.

REFERENCES

Abid, L., Ouertani, M. N., & Zouari-Ghorbel, S. (2014). Macroeconomic and bank-specific determinants of household's non-performing loans in Tunisia: A dynamic panel data. *Procedia Economics and Finance, 13*, 58–68. doi:10.1016/S2212-5671(14)00430-4

Alandejani, M., & Asutay, M. (2017). Nonperforming loans in the GCC banking sectors: Does the Islamic finance matter? *Research in International Business and Finance, 42*, 832–854. doi:10.1016/j.ribaf.2017.07.020

Anderson, C., Getmansky, A., & Hirsch-Hoefler, S. (2017). Burden Sharing: Income, Inequality, and Willingness to Fight. *British Journal of Political Science*.

Ayyildiz, F. V. (2017). *Gelir Adaletsizliginin Sebeplerinin Arastirilmasi*. Ampirik Analiz.

Bağce, H. E. (2017). Parlamenter ve Başkanlık Sistemiyle Yönetilen Ülkelerde Gelir Dağılımı Eşitsizliği ve Yoksulluk. *İnsan&İnsan*, 5.

Berisha, E., Meszaros, J., & Olson, E. (2015). Income inequality and household debt: A cointegration test. *Applied Economics Letters, 22*(18), 1469–1473. doi:10.1080/13504851.2015.1039698

Bumann, S., & Lensink, R. (2016). Capital account liberalization and income inequality. *Journal of International Money and Finance, 61*, 143–162. doi:10.1016/j.jimonfin.2015.10.004

Cheung, F., & Lucas, R. E. (2016). Income inequality is associated with stronger social comparison effects: The effect of relative income on life satisfaction. *Journal of Personality and Social Psychology, 110*(2), 332–341. doi:10.1037/pspp0000059 PMID:26191957

Çifter, A. (2015). Bank concentration and non-performing loans in Central and Eastern European countries. *Journal of Business Economics and Management, 16*(1), 117–137. doi:10.3846/16111699.2012.720590

Clark, A., & D'Ambrosio, C. (2013). *Attitudes to income inequality: experimental and survey evidence*. Academic Press.

Cowell, F. (2011). *Measuring inequality*. Oxford University Press. doi:10.1093/acprof:osobl/9780199594030.001.0001

D'Onofrio, A., Minetti, R., & Murro, P. (2017). Banking development, socioeconomic structure and income inequality. *Journal of Economic Behavior & Organization*. doi:10.1016/j.jebo.2017.08.006

Dabla-Norris, M. E., Kochhar, M. K., Suphaphiphat, M. N., Ricka, M. F., & Tsounta, E. (2015). *Causes and consequences of income inequality: A global perspective*. International Monetary Fund.

de Haan, J., & Sturm, J. E. (2017). Finance and income inequality: A review and new evidence. *European Journal of Political Economy, 50*, 171–195. doi:10.1016/j.ejpoleco.2017.04.007

Destek, M. A., Okumus, İ., & Manga, M. (2017). Türkiye'de Finansal Gelişim ve Gelir Dağılımı İlişkisi: Finansal Kuznets Eğrisi. *Dogus University Journal, 18*(2).

Dimitrios, A., Helen, L., & Mike, T. (2016). Determinants of non-performing loans: Evidence from Euro-area countries. *Finance Research Letters, 18*, 116–119. doi:10.1016/j.frl.2016.04.008

Dinçer, H., Yuksel, S., & Adalı, Z. (2018). Relationship Between Non-Performing Loans, Industry, and Economic Growth of the African Economies and Policy Recommendations for Global Growth. In *Globalization and Trade Integration in Developing Countries* (pp. 203–228). IGI Global. doi:10.4018/978-1-5225-4032-8.ch009

Dornbusch, R. (2001). *A primer on emerging market crises (No. w8326)*. National Bureau of Economic Research. doi:10.3386/w8326

Dumitrescu, E. I., & Hurlin, C. (2012). Testing for Granger non-causality in heterogeneous panels. *Economic Modelling*, *29*(4), 1450–1460. doi:10.1016/j.econmod.2012.02.014

European Central Bank. (2018). *What are non-performing loans (NPLs)?* European Central Bank. Retrieved from https://www.ecb.europa.eu/explainers/tell-me/html/npl.en.html

Florida, R., & Mellander, C. (2016). The geography of inequality: Difference and determinants of wage and income inequality across US metros. *Regional Studies*, *50*(1), 79–92. doi:10.1080/00343404.2014.884275

Gastwirth, J. L. (2017). Is the Gini index of inequality overly sensitive to changes in the middle of the income distribution? *Statistics and Public Policy (Philadelphia, Pa.)*, *4*(1), 1–11. doi:10.1080/2330443X.2017.1360813

Genç, E., & Sasmaz, M. Ü. (2016). Takipteki Banka Kredilerinin Makroekonomik Belirleyicileri: Ticari Krediler Örnegi/Macroeconomic Determiners Of Non-Performing Loans: Commercial Loans Sample. *Selcuk Üniversitesi Sosyal Bilimler Enstitüsü Dergisi*, (36), 119.

Ghosh, A. (2015). Banking-industry specific and regional economic determinants of non-performing loans: Evidence from US states. *Journal of Financial Stability*, *20*, 93–104. doi:10.1016/j.jfs.2015.08.004

Ghosh, A. (2017). Sector-specific analysis of non-performing loans in the US banking system and their macroeconomic impact. *Journal of Economics and Business*, *93*, 29–45. doi:10.1016/j.jeconbus.2017.06.002

Hoskisson, R. E., Eden, L., Lau, C. M., & Wright, M. (2000). Strategy in emerging economies. *Academy of Management Journal*, *43*(3), 249–267.

International Monetary Fund. (2015). *World Economic Output*. International Monetary Fund.

Jenkins, S. (2017). The measurement of income inequality. In *Economic inequality and poverty: International perspectives* (pp. 17–52). Routledge.

Karluk, S. R., & Unal, U. (2017). *Türkiye Ekonomisinde Yoksulluk*. Yolsuzluk ve Gelir Dağılımı İlişkisi.

Kauko, K. (2012). External deficits and non-performing loans in the recent financial crisis. *Economics Letters*, *115*(2), 196–199. doi:10.1016/j.econlet.2011.12.018

Kennedy, T., Smyth, R., Valadkhani, A., & Chen, G. (2017). Does income inequality hinder economic growth? New evidence using Australian taxation statistics. *Economic Modelling*, *65*, 119–128. doi:10.1016/j.econmod.2017.05.012

Köllner, S., & Gründler, K. (2016). *Determinants of Governmental Redistribution: Income Distribution*. Development Levels, and the Role of Perceptions.

Konstantakis, K. N., Michaelides, P. G., & Vouldis, A. T. (2016). Non-performing loans (NPLs) in a crisis economy: Long-run equilibrium analysis with a real time VEC model for Greece (2001–2015). *Physica A*, *451*, 149–161. doi:10.1016/j.physa.2015.12.163

Lee, C. C., & Lee, C. C. (2018). The Impact of Country Risk on Income Inequality: A Multilevel Analysis. *Social Indicators Research*, *136*(1), 139–162. doi:10.100711205-016-1534-8

Lindauer, D. L. (2017). Maintaining Perspective on the Economic Issues of Today. *Society*, *54*(1), 2–3. doi:10.100712115-016-0090-9

Louzis, D. P., Vouldis, A. T., & Metaxas, V. L. (2012). Macroeconomic and bank-specific determinants of non-performing loans in Greece: A comparative study of mortgage, business and consumer loan portfolios. *Journal of Banking & Finance*, *36*(4), 1012–1027. doi:10.1016/j.jbankfin.2011.10.012

Meyer, B. D., & Sullivan, J. X. (2017). *Consumption and Income Inequality in the US Since the 1960s (No. w23655)*. National Bureau of Economic Research. doi:10.3386/w23655

Mukhopadhaya, P. (2013). Trends in income inequality in China: The effects of various sources of income. *Journal of the Asia Pacific Economy*, *18*(2), 304–317. doi:10.1080/13547860.2013.778158

Neaime, S., & Gaysset, I. (2017). Financial inclusion and stability in MENA: Evidence from poverty and inequality. *Finance Research Letters*.

Ngamaba, K. H., Panagioti, M., & Armitage, C. J. (2017). Income inequality and subjective well-being: A systematic review and meta-analysis. *Quality of Life Research: An International Journal of Quality of Life Aspects of Treatment, Care and Rehabilitation*, 1–20. PMID:29067589

Nkusu, M. M. (2011). Nonperforming loans and macrofinancial vulnerabilities in advanced economies (No. 11-161). International Monetary Fund.

Pedroni, P. (2001). Fully modified OLS for heterogeneous cointegrated panels. In *Nonstationary panels, panel cointegration, and dynamic panels* (pp. 93–130). Emerald Group Publishing Limited.

Podpiera, J., & Weill, L. (2008). Bad luck or bad management? Emerging banking market experience. *Journal of Financial Stability*, *4*(2), 135–148. doi:10.1016/j.jfs.2008.01.005

Rajan, R., & Dhal, S. C. (2003). Non-performing loans and terms of credit of public sector banks in India: An empirical assessment. *Occasional Papers, 24*(3), 81-121.

Rajha, K. S. (2016). Determinants of Non-Performing Loans: Evidence from the Jordanian Banking Sector. *The Journal of Finance*, *4*(1), 125–136.

Rougoor, W., & Van Marrewijk, C. (2015). Demography, growth, and global income inequality. *World Development*, *74*, 220–232. doi:10.1016/j.worlddev.2015.05.013

Seven, U., & Coskun, Y. (2016). Does financial development reduce income inequality and poverty? Evidence from emerging countries. *Emerging Markets Review*, *26*, 34–63. doi:10.1016/j.ememar.2016.02.002

Stucky, T. D., Payton, S. B., & Ottensmann, J. R. (2016). Intra-and inter-neighborhood income inequality and crime. *Journal of Criminal Justice*, *39*(3), 345–362.

Tao, Y., Wu, X., Zhou, T., Yan, W., Huang, Y., Yu, H., . . . Yakovenko, V. M. (2016). *Universal Exponential Structure of Income Inequality: Evidence from 60 Countries.* arXiv preprint arXiv:1612.01624

Tarchouna, A., Jarraya, B., & Bouri, A. (2017). How to explain non-performing loans by many corporate governance variables simultaneously? A corporate governance index is built to US commercial banks. *Research in International Business and Finance, 42*, 645–657. doi:10.1016/j.ribaf.2017.07.008

Todaro, M., & Smith, S. (2014). *Economic Development (12 b.).* Pearson.

UNDP. (2016). *Human Development Report 2016.* Author.

Us, V. (2017). The Determinants of Non-Performing Loans Before and After the Crisis: Challenges and Policy Implications for Turkish Banks. *Emerging Markets Finance and Trade.*

Vilhjalmsdottir, A., Gardarsdottir, R. B., Bernburg, J. G., & Sigfusdottir, I. D. (2016). Neighborhood income inequality, social capital and emotional distress among adolescents: A population-based study. *Journal of Adolescence, 51*, 92–102. doi:10.1016/j.adolescence.2016.06.004 PMID:27337213

Vithessonthi, C. (2016). Deflation, bank credit growth, and non-performing loans: Evidence from Japan. *International Review of Financial Analysis, 45*, 295–305. doi:10.1016/j.irfa.2016.04.003

World Bank. (2018a). *Bank nonperforming loans to total gross loans (%).* World Bank Open Data. Retrieved from https://data.worldbank.org/indicator/FB.AST.NPER.ZS

World Bank. (2018b). *GINI index (World Bank estimate).* World Bank Open Data. Retrieved from https://data.worldbank.org/indicator/SI.POV.GINI

Yagcilar, G. G., & Demir, S. (2015). Türk Bankacılık Sektöründe Takipteki Kredi Oranları Üzerinde Etkili Olan Faktörlerin Belirlenmesi. *Uluslararası Alanya İşletme Fakültesi Dergisi, 7*(1).

Yang, Y., & Greaney, T. M. (2017). Economic growth and income inequality in the Asia-Pacific region: A comparative study of China, Japan, South Korea, and the United States. *Journal of Asian Economics, 48*, 6–22. doi:10.1016/j.asieco.2016.10.008

Yüksel, S. (2016). *Bankacılık Krizlerinin Erken Uyarı Sinyalleri: Türkiye Üzerine Bir Uygulama.* Ankara: Akademisyen Yayınevi.

Yüksel, S. (2017). Determinants of the Credit Risk in Developing Countries After Economic Crisis: A Case of Turkish Banking Sector. In *Global Financial Crisis and Its Ramifications on Capital Markets* (pp. 401–415). Cham: Springer. doi:10.1007/978-3-319-47021-4_28

Zhang, D., Cai, J., Dickinson, D. G., & Kutan, A. M. (2016). Non-performing loans, moral hazard and regulation of the Chinese commercial banking system. *Journal of Banking & Finance, 63*, 48–60. doi:10.1016/j.jbankfin.2015.11.010

KEY TERMS AND DEFINITIONS

Developed Country: It refers to the country which has high economic performance in comparison with the developing and least developed countries.

Dumitrescu Hurlin Panel Causality Analysis: It is an advanced form of Granger causality analysis in which panel data is analyzed.

Emerging Economies: They refer to the countries whose economies are not developed yet. However, they have a potential to be a developed country.

GINI Coefficient: It is an aggregate numerical aggregate measure about income equality whose values are ranging from 0 to 1.

Nonperforming Loans: They refer to the loans which are not paid by the customers more than 90 days.

Nonperforming Loans Ratio: It is the ratio of nonperforming loans to the total amount of the loans.

Chapter 4
Fragility of the Spanish Banking System and Financial Exclusion:
Lessons Learned From the Global Crisis and New Challenges for the 21st Century Banking Sector

Begoña Alvarez García
University of A Coruña, Spain

José Pablo Abeal Vázquez
University of A Coruña, Spain

ABSTRACT

Since the outbreak of the financial crisis in 2007, Spain entered a period of wide-ranging economic and social changes. Spanish financial institutions have been implicated in the real-estate bubble, and they were highly exposed to uncertainty and the steady decline of real estate businesses. As a result, the Spanish banking system has undergone a major transformation process. It has been necessary to restructure many institutions, so today the sector is smaller, and it has been forced to rethink its business strategy to survive. The social cost of all these changes has been particularly high, and financial exclusion has increased in Spain from the beginning of the crisis. This chapter shows the changes that have taken place in the Spanish banking system from the beginning of the crisis, the social implications ensued, and the challenges currently faced by the new banking industry that has emerged since the crisis.

INTRODUCTION

There is wide consensus in literature about the general idea that if citizens access basic financial services like opening a bank account, borrowing money or making and receiving transfers, then they are better able to save money, start and expand businesses, invest in education, deal with unforeseen needs or irregular incomes, avoid exploitative financing, etc. (Beck, Demirgüç-Kunt, & Levine, 2005; Tuesta,

DOI: 10.4018/978-1-5225-7208-4.ch004

Sorensen, Haring, & Cámara, 2015). For these reasons, the fight against Financial Exclusion (FE) is one of the priority challenges within the agendas of governments, financial authorities, and international institutions and forums such as the World Bank, the International Monetary Fund (IMF), the OECD, the G-20 group (Cámara & Tuesta, 2014; Sarma & Pais, 2011; Demirgüç-Kunt & Klapper, 2013; Cull, Ehrbeck, & Holle, 2014). In the academic world there is also desire to study FE and Financial Inclusion (FI). As a result, over the last decade, efforts have increasingly concentrated on assessing what sort of situations the different countries are in and how to improve their FI (Beck & Levine, 2004; Levine, 2005; Beck, Demirgüç-Kunt, & Martínez Peria, 2007; Donou-Adonsou & Sylwester, 2016; Haan & Sturm, 2017). In this sense, one recent achievement is that the World Bank has been building a database of global financial inclusion (Global Findex) since the year 2011, which includes indicators comparable throughout the world, those indicators being related to the way in which people save, apply for loans or make payments. To date, according to the data collected in the Global Findex (Demirgüc-Kunt, Klapper, Singer, & Van Oudheusden, 2015), some 2 billion working-age adults globally do not use formal financial services, and these people are mostly concentrated in countries with lower-middle and lower per capita incomes. This data could lead us to think that the most developed countries, those with the highest per capita incomes and highest percentages of banked people, do not suffer from FE; nevertheless, in these countries, there are also sectors of the population excluded for a wide variety of reasons, e. g. people with low or not stable incomes experiencing difficulty in raising finance, ethnic minority communities that live at the margins of formal financial services, unemployed people, persons with a history of bad debt, people that do not feel confident about bank services, etc.

This chapter aims to analyze how inclusive the Spanish financial system is and how it has developed in recent years. The case of the Spanish financial system has special interest because it has undergone a major transformation since the beginning of the financial crisis in the year 2008 (one of the biggest in Europe and in the world) and, as a result, the Spanish society had to pay a very high price in economic and social terms. In this research, emphasis is placed on the social consequences, with special reference to FI and the reasons that have caused significant retrogression in inclusiveness. For this purpose the chapter is structured as follows:

- Background section defines FI and reference is made to several indicators used for assessing it, such as the number of banked people or the number of bank branches per 1000 population. Reference is also made to the relationship between finance, growth, and inequality.
- The main focus of the chapter section shows the organizational structure of the Spanish banking system and describes how it has changed over the last 20 years, explaining the causes and consequences of the transformation experienced. Additionally, some indicators used in literature to assess FI are presented, although they are not enough depiction of the real social and economic situation. This is why the solutions and recommendations focus on other indicators for the purpose of showing a comprehensive picture of FI in Spain.
- Finally, some future research directions are presented alongside the challenges that the Spanish banking system have to overcome to deal with the economic and social requirements of the 21st century financial sector.

BACKGROUND

Although in general terms FE can be understood as one of the dimensions of social exclusion that refers to the lack of capacity of some citizens to gain access to basic formal financial services, a variety of definitions have been proposed in literature. Some of these definitions are useful in understanding the implications of FI and FE, and how they develop. For example, Mohan (2006) points out, emphasizing the qualities that financial services should offer, that FE "signifies the lack of access that certain segments of society have to appropriate, low-cost, fair and safe financial products and services from mainstream providers." Additionally, Amidzic, Massara, and Mialou (2014) indicate, focusing more on the reasons for FI, that it "can be broadly defined as an economic state where individuals and firms are not denied access to basic financial services based on motivations other than efficiency."

Two important insights can be drawn from the definitions above. The first one is that even though some authors talk about FE and others about FI, it is necessary to clarify that they are referring to the same social phenomenon. From the viewpoint of exclusion, the focus is more on the negative consequences arising from it, while from the angle of inclusion the focus is more on the advantages of being able to have access to financial services. The second one is that there are several reasons which led to FE. According to Kempson, Atkinson, and Pilley (2004) there are six main explanations: (1) legal obstacles such as identity requirements, (2) the terms and conditions of bank accounts, (3) levels of bank charges, (4) physical access problems, (5) refusal by banks, and (6) psychological and cultural barriers. These reasons are related to both the provision/conditions-of-provision of bank services and the demand for these bank services. Therefore, FI is a complex phenomenon, which has several dimensions (Sarma & Pais, 2011; Amidzic et al., 2014).

This complexity becomes evident while trying to evaluate FI. Traditionally FI was measured with variables such as the number of banked persons, often proxied by the average number of bank accounts per 1000 population, and other indicators as the number of automated teller machines (ATMs) or the number of bank branches per 1000 population.

Nevertheless, as indicated by Sarma and Pais (2011), multidimensional measures are necessary to assess the different dimensions of FI. For this reason, Sarma (2008) has designed a multidimensional index of FI which incorporates three different dimensions – accessibility, availability, and usage of banking services – and Cámara and Tuesta (2014) have developed a methodology to measure the extent of FI for a country or region by considering both demand-and supply-side information from the perspective of banked as well as unbanked people.

The complex nature of the FI phenomenon becomes also evident when analyzing why it is important to foster FI or, in other words, when analyzing what impact FI is having on growth and poverty, and what is the relationship between the development of banking systems and FI.

In principle, financial development may affect the poor through two channels: aggregate growth and changes in the distribution of income.

Concerning the finance growth nexus, most authors show evidence that financial development promotes growth by enabling the efficient allocation of capital and reducing the borrowing and financing constraints. Some of these researchers have analyzed the aggregate effect of the development of credit markets and stock markets on economic growth (e.g., Arestis, Demetriades, & Luintel, 2001; Beck & Levine, 2004; Cheng, 2012), other researchers have focused on the credit markets effect (e.g., Berthelemy & Varoudakis, 1996), and finally others have focused on the stock markets effect (e.g., Andersen &Tarp, 2003). A complete overview about this subject is made by Levine (2005) and a detailed survey is made by Durusu-Ciftci, Ispir, and Yetkiner (2017). Against this background, other authors observe a different relationship between financial development and growth, in particular an inverted U-shape effect that signifies that the level of financial development is good up to a point, after which the relationship reverses (e. g. Cecchetti & Kharroubi, 2012; Arcand, Berkes, & Panizza, 2012; Beck, Georgiadis, & Straub, 2014). Specifically, Arcand et al. (2012) show that finance starts having a negative effect on output growth when the credit to the private sector reaches 100% of GDP.

Concerning the finance reducing-inequality nexus, different conclusions have also been reached in empirical works. Many authors show that better developed financial markets lead to a reduction in income inequality (e.g., Banerjee & Newman, 1993; Galor & Zeira, 1993; Beck et al., 2007). In addition to finding evidences that financial development reduces income inequality, Beck et al. (2007) show that financial development boosts the growth rate of the income share of the poorest quintile. In contrast to the latter, Greenwood and Jovanovic (1990) develop a model that predicts a nonlinear relationship between financial development, income inequality, and economic development. They show that at all stages of economic development, financial development improves capital allocation, boosts aggregate growth, and helps the poor through this channel. However, the distributional effect of financial development, and hence the net impact on the poor, depends on the level of economic development. At early stages of development, only the rich can afford to access and directly profit from better financial markets. However, at higher levels of economic development, many people can access financial markets so that financial development helps a larger proportion of citizens. More recently Jauch and Watzka (2016) find a positive relationship between financial development and income inequality within countries. They consider that all income groups within a country benefit from more financial development but the wealthier groups are benefitting more and this is why the income inequality increases. More specifically they point that an increase in the provision of credit by 10% leads to an average increase in the Gini coefficient by 0.22 for the sample of 138 countries that they study during the period 2000-2004.

In the most recent works about the finance reducing-equality nexus, the authors include several dimensions of the financial system. Naceur and Zhang (2016) use a sample of 143 countries (covering both developing and developed countries) from 1961 to 2011 to study the effect of five different dimensions of financial development (financial access, financial deepening, financial efficiency, financial stability and financial liberalization) on income inequality and poverty. These authors find evidences that the first four dimensions can help reduce inequality and poverty, while the last one has the opposite effect on the global average. They also show that banking sector development has a stronger positive effect on income distribution than stock market development. Haan and Sturm (2017) use a sample of 121 countries from 1975 to 2005 to analyze the impact of financial development, financial liberalization, and banking crisis on poverty. They find evidences that these three dimensions of financial activity increase income inequality. Therefore, Haan and Sturm (2017) contradict the conclusions of Naceur and Zhan (2016) about the impact of banking system development. The effect of banks has also been analyzed by Donou-Adonsou and Sylwester (2016) that observe a positive relationship between banks and poverty, but a non-significant impact of microfinance interventions (MFI) on poverty.

In addition, it should be considered (as pointed out by Tuesta et al., 2015) that the dynamics followed by economic growth, financial development, and FI depend also on several non-financial factors – such as TIC development, cultural aspects or the specific politics of financial consumer protection developed by authorities – that directly affect the quality and usability of financial services. FI is, therefore, a complex phenomenon that needs to be analyzed by considering several factors. In this light, to study the Spanish case is necessary to explain in next section what the specificities of the Spanish banking system are and how it has changed since the onset of the financial crisis.

MAIN FOCUS OF THE CHAPTER

The main objective of this chapter is to evaluate the economic and social consequences stemming from the transformation seen in recent times in the Spanish banking system. To this end, it is previously necessary to show how the organizational structure of the Spanish banking system is and what the reasons leading such a significant transformation are.

Organizational Structure of the Spanish Banking System

The Spanish banking system is composed primarily of banks, savings banks, and credit unions. There are important differences among them in their legal status and their business model, therefore the main characteristics of them are presented below.

Banks

They are limited liability companies, so the share capital belongs to shareholders who participate in shareholders' meetings with a voting power proportional to the number of shares held. The business model of Spanish banks is oriented towards commercial and retail banking and it has maintained close links with the industry.

Savings Banks

They are limited companies that were set up as private foundations. This foundational nature has been having major implications in savings banks activity:

- They had legal restrictions to raise Tier 1 capital by ways different from retained earnings.
- Once they had covered the reserve required to guarantee their credit activities, they had to invest the surplus funds toward social cause.

This investment in social development together with the saving banks business model are the two most significant reasons why savings banks have played historically a leading role in the social sphere and in the fight against social and financial exclusion. Concerning the saving banks' business model, it should be noted that:

- It was much more focused on retail banking and geographical proximity to customers. In fact, savings banks offered financial services in geographical areas (like the rural ones) that were not covered by banks for profitability reasons. For many years, the financial activity of savings banks was limited to their region of origin. Subsequent to the entry of Spain in the European Economic Community[1], which is currently the European Union (EU), they were allowed to compete out of their region of origin and this change led them to expand the number of branches and compete more among them (Somoza López, 2015)

- Savings banks' activities were very focused on encouraging saving among the general population and give financial support to self-employed entrepreneurs and small and medium size businesses (SMEs).

Due to the legal status and business model of savings banks, they were able to integrate social commitment with financial objectives by giving back a part of their profits to society. This means that savings banks fulfilled an important social obligation that complemented the State's social programmes. Nevertheless, the management teams of savings banks were less professionalized than the management teams of banks. This is because the General Assembly of savings banks comprised representatives of (1) depositors, (2) local public administrations, (3) founding entities and (4) employees. Having local public administrations in the General Assembly means that the representatives of political parties were involved in decision making, even if they lacked in many cases, the adequate expertise and academic education.

Credit Unions

They are private mercantile societies that perform a double condition: (i) they are cooperative societies and (ii) they are deposit entities (comparable to other banking institutions). They aim to serve the financial needs of their members and third parties through activities undertaken by the credit institutions. Each member of the cooperative has one vote, regardless of the capital held. Credit unions usually develop their activities in a local setting and, in most cases, the business model is focused on their region of origin, with a straightforward social objective often associated with rural development.

General Situation Before the Financial Crisis

At the beginning of 1990s, the Spanish banking system moved towards a process of concentration that mainly affected savings banks and credit unions. These financial institutions wanted to gain size in terms of market share to be in a better position to tackle both the challenges defined by being a part of the EU and the changes related to EU's own development.

Little by little, the barriers to the free expansion of national entities throughout the country and the barriers to entry for foreign financial institutions were removed, the euro was introduced as the single currency for 11 countries, the single banking market of the EU was being set up and some savings banks and credit unions decide to merge to gain size and become more competitive (Corral Delgado, Domínguez Martínez, & López del Paso, 2011).

According to the Census of Spanish banking institutions (Figure 1), in the year 1998, the total number of institutions in Spain was 301 (153 banks, 51 savings banks, and 97 credit unions). This number was slightly reduced since then until the year 2007 when the total number of institutions was 279 (151 banks, 46 savings banks, and 82 credit unions), representing a decrease of 9% in the total number of savings banks and a decrease of 15% in the total number of credit unions.

This process of concentration did not in the least mean a reduction in the overall installed capacity. In the year 1998, there were 38,768 banking offices across the country and they were increasing gradually to 45,747 offices in the year 2007. The largest increase took place in the period 2004-2006, at a time when the country experienced phenomenal growth (the annual GDP growth rate in these years was over

Figure 1. Number of Spanish banking institutions before the financial crisis
Source: Bank of Spain

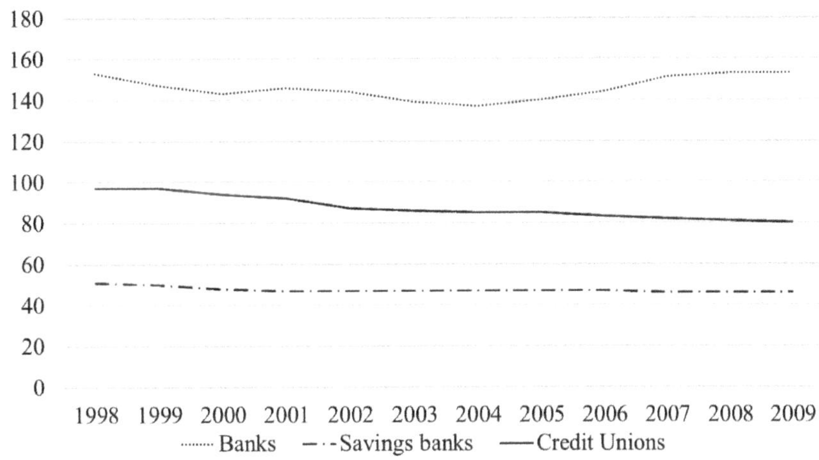

3%). Quantitative differences are observed among banks, savings banks and credit unions when they are analyzed separately (Figure 2).

The decrease in the number of offices in banks was 11% during the period 1998-2007, while the number of savings banks and credit unions increased respectively up to 40% and 37%. Therefore, the growth in the sector was driven mainly by the territorial expansion of savings banks and credit unions. This different behavior shows that banks applied a cost containment strategy, while savings banks gave priority to expand their activity beyond their region of origin and managed to increase their presence by more than 7 percentage points in these years (Corral Delgado et al., 2011). It was such a growth in savings banks in the years 2004, 2005 and 2006 that 914, 1014, and 1,180 offices were opened respectively, which means opening almost 3 offices a day during the years 2004 and 2005 and more than 3 offices a day during the year 2006.

Figure 2. Number of Spanish banking branches before the financial crisis
Source: Bank of Spain

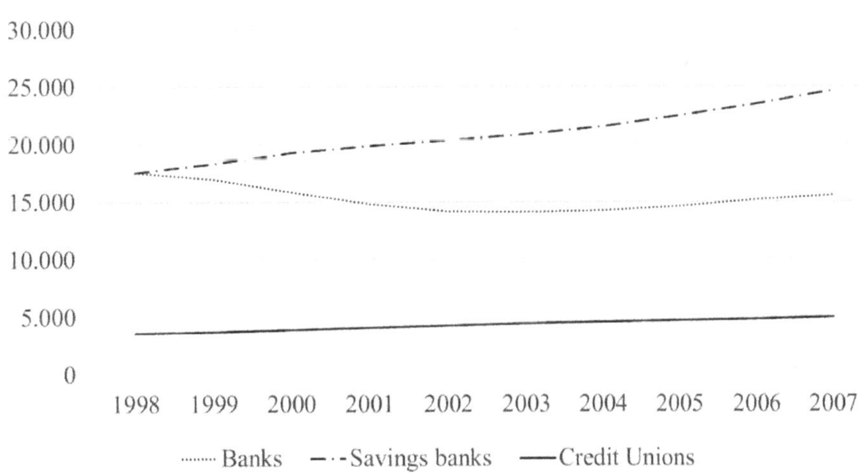

The development in the number of offices is also reflected in the number of employees (Figure 3). On the whole, during the period 1998-2007, the recruitment for jobs increased in the sector by 11%, although such increase was mainly driven by the expansion policy of savings banks and credit unions. Whilst banks reduced the number of employees by 13%, savings banks increase staff by 40. 6% and credit unions by 53. 7%. This different behavior is explained by the disappearance of the barriers to the free expansion across the country that historically have been applied to savings banks and credit unions. Banks did not have these barriers to operate at national level, so their geographical coverage has always been biggest. However, savings banks seize the moment to expand their activities outside their region of origin.

In those years, the banking sector's profits increased noticeably (Figure 4). It was a period that can be described, as indicated by Tajadura Garrido (2015), as a moment of "authentic financial exuberance." In fact, the overall earnings before taxes in the whole sector are multiplied by 3.6 times over the period 1998-2007, from a total of 8,159 million euros to a total of 29,573 million euros. During those years, banks made an accumulated net gain of 9,462 million euros, more than the savings banks which made an accumulated net gain of 8,980 million euros. These results are logical because savings banks were bearing important expansion costs in these years, while banks were benefiting more from the already installed capacity. However, very soon it became clear that growth has been excessive and the excesses of this period were going to have severe consequences for the future of the banking sector. The banking sector growth was hiding important weaknesses that came abruptly to light with the onset of the crisis.

Crisis and Transformation

Since the outbreak of the international financial crisis, which started in the USA in the year 2008, everything has changed. The crisis has affected almost all the developed countries of the world, although

Figure 3. Number of employees of the Spanish banking institutions before the financial crisis
Source: Bank of Spain

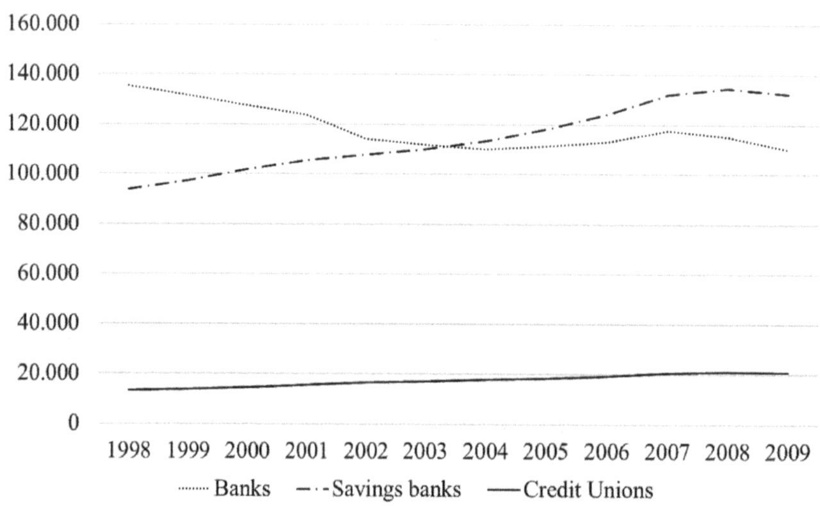

Figure 4. Earnings before tax (million) of the Spanish banking institutions
Source: Bank of Spain

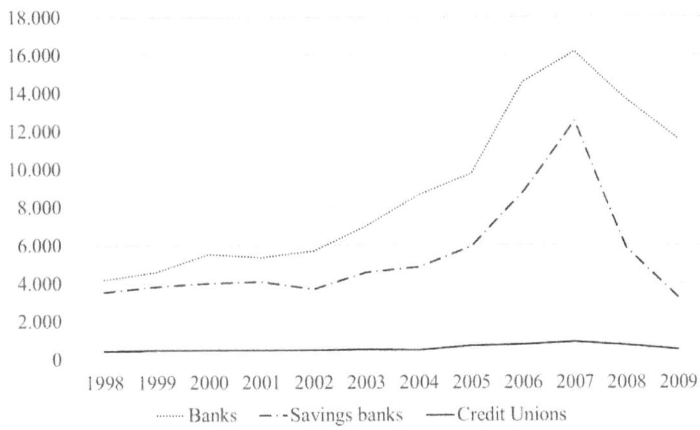

the severity of the implications has not been similar for the countries concerned (Maudos, 2012; Maroto, Mulas Granados, & Fernández Álvarez, 2012; Calvo Bernardino & Martín de Vidales Carrasco, 2014). In the Spanish case, the crisis has been very deep and it is till recently that clear signs of improvement are being noticed. Despite the image of creditworthiness shown by the Spanish financial institutions in the first months of the crisis (Álvarez, 2008; García Montalvo, 2014; Bank of Spain, 2017), some weaknesses became apparent soon such as the sharp deterioration of the credit portfolios related to the real estate sector, the lack of liquidity caused by the difficulties in obtaining finance in international markets, and a poor management of some problems like the preferred shares that definitely broke the customers' confidence in the sector.

In many countries, the crisis was sparked and subsequently aggravated by the accumulation of toxic assets in the financial institution portfolios; nevertheless, in the Spanish case, the roots of the problem were more related to the imbalances built up in previous years. According to Maudos (2012), to find these roots it is necessary to look into the combination of the following factors:

- An intensive growth of public and private indebtedness that could be funded by the abundance of liquidity available in the international markets in a scenario of low interest rates. The level of private debt grew in Spain from 97.2% of GDP in 1999 (at that moment the Euro area average was 112%) to 225% of GDP in 2009 (at that moment the Euro area average was 165%).
- A high growth in bank credit. The Spanish banking system emerged second in the whole Euro area that extended highest credit to private sector between 2000 and 2007, falling just below Ireland.
- An excessive concentration of real estate assets in bank's balance sheets. An important part of the banking credit was allocated to the financing of the real estate development and construction industry. House prices rose sharply, boosting speculative behaviors that favored the development of a real estate bubble. When the bubble burst, the prices began to fall provoking rapid deterioration of credit portfolios and a ripple effect on the rest of the economy.
- Huge growth in the installed capacity mainly due to the savings banks and credit unions increase in the number of offices and employees.

To these factors, there should be an addition of inadequate evaluation and management of risks and even some episodes of malpractice in the activities of certain banking institutions. Some examples of malpractice include: the application of "floor clauses" that prevent the mortgage interest rate from going below a baseline minimum or the marketing of risky financial products without properly informing the customers. The last one is the case of preference shares. Preference shares are hybrid products between bonds and equities (the agreed compensation is received as an interest payment but this payment depends on the issuing company's performance). During the years of high performances, the preference shares were offering high returns, but due to the outburst of the crisis the performance diminished significantly and investors got locked into an investment that had an undefined maturity. The customers of banks and savings banks that had invested in preference shares felt totally cheated causing discontent in society and a great deal of distrust towards the financial system.

The country risk increased sharply in these years (risk premium grew exponentially reaching 631 basis points in July 2012) and the macroeconomic conditions steadily worsened. The gravity of the situation reached such a magnitude that in the year 2012, the Spanish Government was compelled to apply for financial assistance, so the Spanish and European authorities signed a Memorandum of Understanding (MoU) on the conditions of Sectorial Financial Policy as well as Financial Assistance Framework Agreement (Carbó Valverde & Rodríguez Fernández, 2014; Urbaneja Cillán, 2014). The MoU marked the start of a drastic process of change in the financial system, characterized by:

- The recapitalization, restructuring and resolution of banks and savings banks that performed worse in stress tests
- The transfer of the damaged assets of the credit institutions that required public support to a new assets management company (called the Company for the Management of Assets proceeding from Restructuring of the Banking System) founded in November, 2012.

The process of restructuring and resolution of financial institutions has been so intense (Table 1) that it is an unprecedented process in Spain and also one of those of greatest impact in EU (Berges & Ontiveros, 2013; Fernández de Lis & Rubio, 2013; Tajadura Garrido, 2015; Gutiérrez Fernández, Fernández Torres, & Palomo Zurdo, 2016).

According to data shown in Table 1, more than 18,000 banking offices were closed in Spain between the years 2008 and 2017, which means a decrease of 40.3% in the global installed capacity. This reduction was much sharp in the period 2010 and 2012, which coincides with the worst years of the crisis.

Germany and Italy made also substantial adjustments, but the levels were not so high in such a short period of time. 9,459 offices were closed in Germany in these years (which means a decrease of 23% between 2008 and 2017) and 6,795 offices were closed in Italy (which means a decrease of 19.9% in the same period).

The closure of banking offices has been accompanied by staff adjustment measures that have further aggravated the crisis and the feeling of helplessness of many citizens. In the period 2008-2017, more than 93,000 jobs were lost in the Spanish banking system (i.e., a reduction of 33.8%). Nothing similar has been seen in the other Eurozone countries, highlighting the seriousness of the situation and the fragility of the Spanish banking system.

The new banking system that has emerged after the restructuring process is: (1) smaller in size, (2) less profitable, and (3) more concentrated. The total assets of the sector in year 2017 represent 46% of the total in year 2008, less than the half. This trend in the sector contrasts with the developments in other

Table 1. Evolution of financial institutions in Europe

SPAIN	2008	2009	2010	2011	2012	2013	2014	2015	2016	2017
Number of branches	46,065	44,431	43,164	40,103	38,142	33,713	31,999	31,087	28,807	27,480
Number of employees	276,497	267,383	261,389	245,956	234,292	215,953	201,656	196,556	186,982	183,016
Total assets of branches	230,146	221,158	203,003	204,290	191,213	131,381	104,075	94,479	105,947	108,124
Shares of the 5 largest in total assets	42.4%	43.3%	44.3%	48.1%	51.4%	54.4%	58.3%	60.2%	61.8%	63.7%
ITALY	**2008**	**2009**	**2010**	**2011**	**2012**	**2013**	**2014**	**2015**	**2016**	**2017**
Number of branches	34,169	34,030	33,631	33,561	32,872	31,759	30,723	30,475	29,335	27,374
Number of employees	338,035	323,407	321,081	316,360	309,478	306,607	299,684	298,473	295,305	281,928
Total assets of branches	265.454	229.375	249.626	283.180	283.239	242.030	249.231	255.942	232,669	207,947
Shares of the 5 largest in total assets	31.2%	31.0%	39.8%	39.5%	39.7%	39.6%	41.0%	41.0%	43.0%	43.43%
GERMANY	**2008**	**2009**	**2010**	**2011**	**2012**	**2013**	**2014**	**2015**	**2016**	**2017**
Number of branches	39,531	38,851	38,149	37,675	36,239	36,155	35,284	34,001	32,026	30,072
Number of employees	685,550	673,500	668,500	663,800	659,100	655,600	649,900	637,238	619,621	597,319
Total assets of branches	156,185	151,784	164,883	189,429	257,255	185,858	196,033	252,254	309,763	325,278
Shares of the 5 largest in total assets	22.7%	25.0%	32.6%	33.5%	33.0%	30.6%	32.1%	30.6%	31.4%	29.7%
FRANCE	**2008**	**2009**	**2010**	**2011**	**2012**	**2013**	**2014**	**2015**	**2016**	**2017**
Number of branches	39,467	38,311	38,784	38,433	38,359	37,862	37,623	37,567	37,261	37,209
Number of employees	424,536	416,772	412,933	426,336	421,037	416,262	408,726	406,701	410,925	398,516
Total assets of branches	138,772	129,961	119,290	124,320	124,804	104,367	119,368	128,903	130,338	144,827
Shares of the 5 largest in total assets	51.2%	47.2%	47.4%	48.3%	44.6%	46.7%	47.6%	47.2%	46.0%	45.4%
BELGIUM	**2008**	**2009**	**2010**	**2011**	**2012**	**2013**	**2014**	**2015**	**2016**	**2017**
Number of branches	4,316	4,201	3,973	3,881	3,819	3,738	3,607	3,508	3,347	3,195
Number of employees	65,985	63,723	61,861	61,197	60,068	58,237	56,666	55,774	54,657	53,002
Total assets of branches	45,378	41,219	43,814	79,153	89,724	108,478	147,518	131,659	140,248	62,877
Shares of the 5 largest in total assets	80.84%	77.12%	74.86%	70.77%	66.35%	63.99%	65.79%	65.45%	66.19%	68.8%
PORTUGAL	**2008**	**2009**	**2010**	**2011**	**2012**	**2013**	**2014**	**2015**	**2016**	**2017**
Number of branches	6,417	6,532	6,587	6,501	6,259	5,987	5,938	5,453	4,928	4,692
Number of employees	62,377	61,593	61,504	59,911	57,348	55,820	53,888	50,687	46,584	46,238
Total assets of branches	28,122	33,261	38,241	42,996	45,182	33,253	30,808	23,998	19,339	19,202
Shares of the 5 largest in total assets	69.1%	70.1%	70.9%	70.8%	69.9%	70.3%	69.2%	72.3%	71.2%	73.1%

Source: (European Central Bank (2018). European Central Bank Database)

countries such as Germany or Belgium. The number of offices and staff were reduced in Germany although the banking business increased, and in the case of Belgium the weight of total assets multiplied by 1.3.

The Spanish banking shrinkage becomes evident through of the figures (Table 1): the weight of the shares of the 5 largest credit institutions in total assets increases in more than 20 percentage points (much more than in the other European countries) and the number of entities has fallen from 280 to 207 in the period 2008-2017 (European Central Bank, 2018).

It is worth noting that restructuring has not affected the different kind of financial institutions in the same way (Somoza López, 2015). Savings banks have experienced the greatest transformation during this process, with the ensuing repercussion on the social work that they were carrying out. Savings banks, that were able to balance financial objectives and a social commitment for more than 100 years and were an indispensable pillar of the Spanish financial system, have disappeared: the only 2 that remain have very small dimensions and very limited geographical scope. The another 44 have been forced, by law, to become banking or ordinary foundations (resulting in the "bancarization" of savings banks) and they have been exposed to several waves of mergers and take-overs. The final outcome is the convergence towards just 11 entities of larger size.

Consequences of the Restructuring Process

The analysis of the process of transformation described above cannot be reduced only to the number of assets, global installed capacity or earnings. A more in-depth analysis is necessary to understand the social implications of the restructuring process and how FI has evolved through time. In order to give a complete and more detailed portrait of FI in Spain, some economic and social indicators not directly related to the banking system (henceforth non-banking indicators) are considered along with some indicators directly related to the banking system (henceforth banking indicators).

Non-Banking Indicators

The unemployment rate, the Gini coefficient, the GDP per capita or even the mortgage foreclosures are generally used indicators to study the living conditions of citizens and the incidence of social exclusion.

Looking at the Spanish case, it should be noted that Spain reached the highest unemployment rate in OECD countries during the crisis and, hence, many families found themselves unable to cover their current liabilities and came close to the risk of social exclusion. Additionally, default rate increased notably, as well as the number of mortgage foreclosures (Table 2). In this context, social inequalities grew significantly (as indicated by the sharp increase of Gini coefficient) and the living/financial conditions of many citizens worsened because they were left jobless and homeless.

These social and economic indicators show a very complicated situation since the beginning of the crisis and they are in line with the evolution described above.

Banking Indicators

Prior to the crisis, Spain was one of the most inclusive countries in the world in the financial area. Sarma and Pais (2011) assessed the Index of Financial Inclusion (IFI) and the Human Development Index (HDI) in 49 countries for the year 2004 and Spain was at the 4th position in IFI (only surpassed by Austria, Belgium, and Denmark) and the 7th position in HDI (only surpassed by Norway, Belgium, Austria,

Table 2. Non-banking indicators for Spain since the outbreak of the financial crisis

	2008	2009	2010	2011	2012	2013	2014	2015	2016
Unemployment rate (%)	13.79	18.66	20.11	22.56	25.77	25.73	23.70	20.90	18.63
GINI coefficient	32.4	32.9	33.5	34	34.2	33.7	34.7	34.6	34.5
GDP per capita (€)	24,300	23,300	23,200	22,900	22,562	22,518	22,780	23,300	24,100
Mortgage foreclosures	58,686	92,319	93,636	77,854	91,622	82,68	80,749	68,165	48410

Source: (World Development Indicators, Spanish General Council of Judiciary, Spanish National Institute of Statistics)

Denmark, France and Italy). Additionally, the Data from the Global Findex developed by the World Bank (Table 3) give us an idea of what has happened from the year 2011. These data show that despite the severity of the crisis and the dramatic changes experienced, Spain remains one of the countries in the world with a major percentage of banked people and with a major percentage of people that have a debit or a credit card. These two banking indicators, the number of banked people and the number of people owning financial products, are the two one most commonly used to assess FI.

Based on the figures of Table 3, it could be concluded that hardly anything has happened in the Spanish financial system in recent years (the number of people aged over 15 having an account increased from 93% in the year 2011 to 94% in the year 2017) or even that financial conditions have improved based on indicators such as "borrowed to start, operate, or expand a farm or business", "borrowed from a financial institution", and "borrowed from family or friends". Therefore, there seems to be a contradiction

Table 3. Global Findex indicators for Spain

	2011	2014	2017
Account (% age 15+)	93%	98%	94%
Account, in labor force (% age 15+)	96%	NA	98%
Account, out of labor force (% age 15+)	89%	NA	84%
Account, income, poorest 40% (% ages 15+)	92%	97%	93%
Account, income, richest 60% (% ages 15+)	94%	98%	94%
Account, rural (% age 15+)	93%	98%	94%
Saved to start, operate, or expand a farm or business (% age 15+)	NA	14%	18%
Saved at a financial institution (% age 15+)	35%	48%	51%
Saved any money in the past year (% age 15+)	NA	67%	68%
Outstanding housing loan (% age 15+)	NA	36%	36%
Debit card ownership (% age 15+)	62%	83%	85%
Credit card ownership (% age 15+)	42%	54%	54%
Borrowed to start, operate, or expand a farm or business (% age 15+)	NA	6%	36%
Borrowed from a financial institution (% age 15+)	11%	18%	18%
Borrowed from family or friends (% age 15+)	12%	22%	17%

Source: (The World Bank)

between the picture shown by the chosen non-banking indicators and the picture shown by the chosen banking indicators. This is the issue raised in this chapter. FI is a complex phenomenon that cannot just be measured as the number of banked people or the number of people owning banking products. In addition to these widely disseminated indicators, it is important to see how the real living conditions of citizens have changed and use some banking indicators in line with the non-banking ones to capture the true financial situation of citizens.

SOLUTIONS AND RECOMMENDATIONS

The financial crisis that started in 2008 has caused a significant deterioration in the living conditions of citizens from almost all developed countries. In the case of Spain, the crisis has also led to a great fragility of the financial system, which in turn has contributed to an increase in social and financial exclusion. In order to alleviate these issues and prevent a similar crisis in the future, various solutions have been proposed from different fronts:

- On the one hand, the political and financial authorities have implemented legal measures aimed at strengthening the financial system and controlling/reducing global risks. Some examples are financial directives such as MiFID II (Markets in Financial Instruments Directive) or MiFIR (Markets in Financial Instruments Regulation), which impose additional requirements on financial institutions to increase their levels of transparency and security.
- On the other hand, citizens have mobilized both individually to demand changes and collectively to create NGOs for promoting the social and financial inclusion of the most disadvantaged groups.

Recommendations for the future go through two different routes:

- The first one, promoting measures to improve the FI of citizens, which, in turn, means reducing poverty levels and inequalities, and increasing the protection of the most vulnerable groups.
- The second one, knowing the true about the FI level by counting on appropriate indicators that show a complete picture of the evolution of the financial system and its social and financial consequences. The indicators traditionally used to assess FI are the number of banked people or the number of people with financial products. However, these indicators are not enough to show the reality of FI. Therefore, using more indicators that reflect demand and supply of banking services is recommended.

This is why some additional indicators that help the reader to understand the current situation of FI are presented below.

Banking Indicators From the Demand Side

From the demand side it is important to consider to what extent the clients use financial services in their everyday activities. An indicator that may give an idea of the acceptance of the financial services is the number of credit and debit cards requested, on average, per customer (Table 4).

Table 4. Number of credit and debit cards

	2008	2009	2010	2011	2012	2013	2014	2015	2016
Cards per customer > 16 years	2.6	2.5	2.4	2.4	2.3	2.3	1.6	1.6	1.7

Source: (Bank of Spain)

There is a notable decrease in the number of credit and debit cards per customer, which means that customers are more austere when using banking services. This indicator is clearly showing a decline since the year 2008, reflecting the fact that customers are changing their habits and reducing the consumption of banking products. Behind this data, there are also the economic difficulties of some clients and the lack of confidence in the financial sector.

Banking Indicators From the Supply Side

From the supply side, it is also advisable to use one or several indicators that enable the researcher to get a wide overview of both the global financial sector and the relationship with customers. Three key indicators are proposed to this purpose. These indicators are related to:

1. Geographical proximity to clients.
2. Credit availability for businesses and households.
3. Spending in both social work and social action.

Concerning the geographical proximity to the client (Table 5), it is clear that banking concentration has resulted in the worsening of indicators such as the number of banking offices /10,000 people > 16 years and the number of ATMs /10,000 people > 16 years. The first banking offices closed were the less profitable ones (mainly the offices located in rural areas or in small communities with scarce economic activity). This is why behind this data lies the fact that many clients of rural or depressed areas no longer have a banking office in their neighborhood or an ATM to make financial transactions out of working hours.

Concerning credit availability, it is worth noting that, despite the important role of financial markets, in Spain the banking system is the main catalyst of credit towards the real economy. The lack of liquidity in international markets and the internal difficulties of banking institutions pushed them to turn off the

Table 5. Geographical proximity to the client

	2008	2009	2010	2011	2012	2013	2014	2015	2016
Banking offices/10,000 people > 16 years	12.0	11.6	11.2	10.4	10.0	8.9	8.3	8.0	7.4
ATMs/10,000 people > 16 years	16.0	15.6	15.4	14.6	14.1	13.4	12.1	12.0	11.6

Source: (Bank of Spain)

credit tap very sharply (Figure 5) and the credit to private sector fell by 58 percentage points between the years 2008 and 2016.

The decline in private credit affected either businesses or households. The very serious situation of the Spanish economy becomes clearer when comparing the magnitude of the reduction of credit to the SMEs with other EU countries (Table 6). In the case of Spain during the period 2008-2014 there was a drop of 62% in loans to SMEs, which in Spain make up 99.88% of all businesses. The trend was similar for households (Figure 5): the household debt decreases from 87.83% of GDP to 69.13% of GDP in the period 2009 -2016. These figures show the large impact that a weak banking system may have on both real economy and the financing capacity of citizens.

Concerning the spending on social work, it should be pointed out that this spending was mainly made by savings banks. Since savings banks are the institutions more affected by the restructuration, the important social work that they were carrying on diminished significantly (Table 7).

Figure 5. Domestic credit to private sector (% of GDP)
Source: World Bank

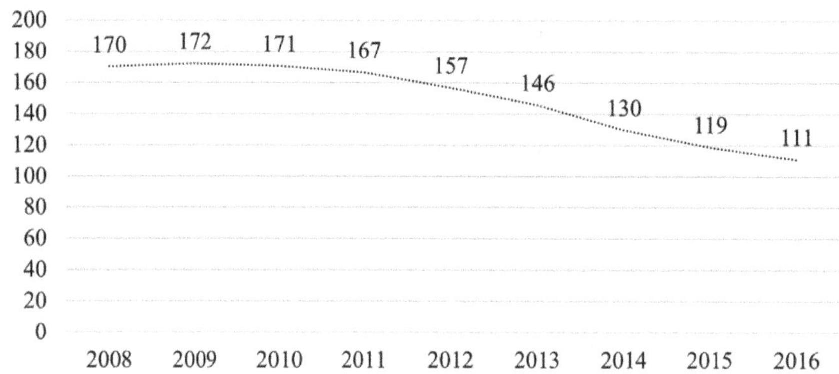

Table 6. Total loans to SMEs (millions)

	Spain	Change	France	Change	Italy	Change	Portugal	Change
2007	394,000		158,386		173,938			
2008	357,000	**-9.4%**	166,076	4.9%	176,772	1.6%		
2009	263,000	**-26.3%**	165,396	**-0.4%**	176,408	**-0.2%**	87,707	
2010	210,000	**-20.2%**	172,573	4.3%	186,268	5.6%	85,923	**-2.0%**
2011	174,000	**-17.1%**	183,063	6.1%	180,399	**-3.2%**	79,915	**-7.0%**
2012	146,000	**-16.1%**	187,694	2.5%	174,704	**-3.2%**	69,974	**-12.4%**
2013	135,000	**-7.5%**	189,283	0.8%	164,021	**-6.1%**	61,980	**-11.4%**
2014	146,000	8.1%	192,025	1.4%	153,816	**-6.2%**	58,630	**-5.4%**
2015	166,000	13.7%	195,433	1.8%	146,546	**-4.7%**	55,955	**-4.6%**

Source: (OECD Statistics)

Table 7. Expense of savings banks in social work (2004-2016)

Year	Expenses (Thousand €)	Change	Number of Activities	Change	Number of Beneficiaries	Change
2004	1,163,498		120,275		79,960,788	
2005	1,338,253	15.0%	139,938	16.3%	87,403,568	9.3%
2006	1,524,629	13.9%	140,319	0.3%	106,019,968	21.3%
2007	1,824,295	19.7%	176,563	25.8%	128,679,516	21.4%
2008	2,058,971	12.9%	201,607	14.2%	141,859,675	10.2%
2009	1,775,926	**-13.7%**	199,724	**-0.9%**	162,575,931	14.6%
2010	1,462,366	**-17.7%**	155,031	**-22.4%**	99,025,636	**-39.1%**
2011	1,124,918	**-23.1%**	124,498	**-19.7%**	79,105,529	**-20.1%**
2012	818,589	**-27.2%**	105,424	**-15.3%**	49,688,353	**-37.2%**
2013	647,729	**-20.9%**	88,439	**-16.1%**	32,013,290	**-35.6%**
2014	709,905	9.6%	119,965	35.6%	36,015,435	12.5%
2015	717,385	1.1%	91,927	**-23.4%**	30,378,921	**-15.7%**
2016	734,546	2.4%	102,132	11.1%	30,795,190	1.4%

Source: (Social Work Memories of CECA from 2004 to 2016)

The expenses of savings banks in social work are allocated in 5 categories of activities: 1) social care and health (also known as social action), 2) culture and heritage, 3) education and research, 4) environment, 5) local development and employment creation, and 6) sports and leisure. Before the crisis the expense in social work increased very much, with an annual growth rate of over 10% and an accumulated growth rate of 77% from 2004 to 2008. These figures highlight the important role played by savings banks have in the social sphere and in the fight against social and financial exclusion. However this positive trend is reversed since the outbreak of the crisis. In spite of the adverse economic situation, savings banks continued doing a great deal to maintain the expense in social work, although this expense diminished sharply, decreasing steadily until the year 2013 and increasing gently from that moment. From the year 2008 to 2013 the expense in social work has fallen by approximately 69%, from 2,058 million euros to 647 million euros. Looking at the share of these expenses allocated to social action (table 8), the following should be highlighted:

- Social action is also on a downward trend since the year 2008, with large reductions being recorded in the years of greatest changes in savings banks.
- Despite expense in social action diminishing, it represents a growing proportion of the total expense in social work during the crisis, ranging between 40% and 50%. The fall in the number of beneficiaries between the years 2008 and 2013 was also smaller in social action (71%) than in total social work (77%). Therefore, these figures show that the savings banks' efforts were mainly focused on social action rather than on the other activities.

The three banking indicators described did not equally affect every individual:

- Geographical proximity to clients. People in rural areas or small towns in recession were the most affected by the office closures arising from the fragility of the banking system, so that the crisis contributed to increasing their geographical and social marginalization. One example is the case of Liberbank bank that closed its offices in the localities of fewer than 500 inhabitants, leaving 33 towns without any bank branch at all.
- Decrease in credit. Credit squeeze affected thousands of self-employed people and SMEs, particularly those that were running into difficulty and could not apply for financial support to overcome the economic problems. In the same vein, people with smaller borrowing capacity (such as those who suddenly lost their jobs) were the most affected by the credit squeeze. It is worth noting that the percentage of households in which all members were unemployed increased from 4.15% in the first quarter of 2008 to 15% in the first quarter of 2013.
- Reduction in social spending. People who used to benefit from the savings banks' spending on social work belonged to disadvantaged groups or groups at risk of exclusion (such as unemployed people, immigrants, ethnic minorities, ex-prisoners, etc.). This is why the cut in social work spending was particularly detrimental to the most disadvantaged people.

Therefore, it can be concluded that the crisis and the fragility of the Spanish banking system have led to a worsening in the FI of the Spanish society, although those who have suffered the most are the most vulnerable.

FUTURE RESEARCH DIRECTIONS

FI is a complex phenomenon. Such complexity is the reason why it is not always easy to show a true picture of both the FI developments and the driving factors that move it in one direction or in another. That is why in addition to the most known and used indicators of FI, other indicators have been proposed in this chapter to complement them and to provide information related to both the demand and supply of financial services. These indicators also give an idea of the robustness and the organizational structure of the banking system, as well as the medium-term business strategy pursued by financial institutions. Nevertheless, FI depends on many factors such as the technological innovation or cultural aspects. On this issue, the future lines of research should contribute to take into account these additional elements, in particular the ones related to the impact that ICT has on the financial area.

CONCLUSION

The Spanish banking system has changed significantly over the last 20 years both in quantitative as well as qualitative terms. The crisis has been the main driving force behind all these changes because it brought to light the weaknesses of the Spanish productive system and shook the foundations that sustained the banking system. As a consequence, a new banking system has emerged. This new banking system is more fragile, smaller in size, less profitable and less inclusive. In addition, this new banking system has to deal with important challenges. From a financial point of view, some of the challenges to be met are:

- Being competitive in an environment of very low interest rates, which reduces the business margins. This is why the banking sector is diversifying its operations into more profitable activities, such as consumer credits in which the interest rates are higher though at the cost of very high competitiveness.
- Focusing more on controlling global risk. The over-confidence of pre-crisis years together with an inadequate evaluation of the risks have led to a completely distorted perception of the real risks assumed. Hence, an efficient evaluation and management of the risks to which financial institutions are exposed (especially the systemic ones) are now considered of vital importance.
- Adapting itself to a new and rapidly changing regulatory regime. Multiple regulative reforms have been implemented to prevent future repetition of the failures that led to the crisis which is why the banking system is constantly changing to adapt itself to the new requirements.
- Playing a leading role in the technological innovation arising from the significant ICT penetration in the financial activity.

From a social point of view, some of the challenges to be met are:

- Improving the FI of citizens and continuing to maintain the important social work that savings banks have been building for more than 100 years.
- Winning back the confidence of citizens. The large responsibility of the banking system for the crisis has broken the confidence of citizens in the sector. For this reason the banking system should come closer to its clients and focus more on social activities that restore the confidence again.
- Focusing more on the client's needs and improving the financial consumer protection.

Concerning the social challenges it is difficult to improve without appropriate and comprehensive indicators that capture the current status before designing the way forward in relation to these issues.

ACKNOWLEDGMENT

This research was supported by the University of A Coruña.

REFERENCES

Álvarez, J. A. (2008). La banca española ante la actual crisis financiera. *Estabilidad Financiera*, *15*, 21–38.

Amidzic, G., Massara, A., & Mialou, A. (2014). *Assessing Countries' Financial Inclusion Standing—A New Composite Index* (IMF Working Paper No. 14/36). Retrieved from International Monetary Fund website: https://www.imf.org/en/Publications/WP/Issues/2016/12/31/Assessing-Countries-Financial-Inclusion-Standing-A-New-Composite-Index-41385

Andersen, T. B., & Tarp, F. (2003). Financial liberalization, financial and economic growth in LDCs. *Journal of International Development*, *15*(2), 189–209. doi:10.1002/jid.971

Arcand, J.-L., Berkes, E., & Panizza, U. (2012). *Too much finance?* (IMF Working Paper WP/12/161). Retrieved from International Monetary Fund website: https://www.imf.org/external/pubs/ft/wp/2012/wp12161.pdf

Arestis, P., Demetriades, P. O., & Luintel, K. B. (2001). Financial development and economic growth: The role of stockmarkets. *Journal of Money, Credit and Banking*, *33*(1), 16–41. doi:10.2307/2673870

Banerjee, A. V., & Newman, A. F. (1993). Occupational choice and the process of development. *Journal of Political Economy*, *101*(2), 274–298. doi:10.1086/261876

Bank of Spain. (2017). *Informe sobre la Crisis Financiera y Bancaria en España. 2008-2014*. Retrieved from https://www.bde.es/f/webbde/Secciones/Publicaciones/OtrasPublicaciones/Fich/InformeCrisis_Completo_web.pdf

Beck, R., Georgiadis, G., & Straub, R. (2014). The finance and growth nexus revisited. *Economics Letters*, *124*(3), 382–385. doi:10.1016/j.econlet.2014.06.024

Beck, T., Demirgüç-Kunt, A., & Levine, R. (2007). Finance, inequality and the poor. *Journal of Economic Growth*, *12*(1), 27–49. doi:10.100710887-007-9010-6

Beck, T., Demirgüç-Kunt, A., & Martínez Peria, M. S. (2007). Reaching Out: Access to and Use of Banking Services across Countries. *Journal of Financial Economics*, *85*(2), 234–266. doi:10.1016/j.jfineco.2006.07.002

Beck, T., & Levine, R. (2004). Stock markets, banks, and growth: Panel evidence. *Journal of Banking & Finance*, *28*(3), 423–442. doi:10.1016/S0378-4266(02)00408-9

Berges, A., & Ontiveros, E. (2013). Sistema bancario español: Una transformación sin precedentes. *Harvard Deusto Business Review*, *229*, 16–28.

Berthelemy, J., & Varoudakis, A. (1996). Economic growth convergence clubs and the role of financial development. *Oxford Economic Papers*, *48*(2), 300–328. doi:10.1093/oxfordjournals.oep.a028570

Calvo Bernardino, A., & Martín de Vidales Carrasco, I. (2014). Crisis y cambios estructurales en el sector bancario español: Una comparación con otros sistemas financieros. *Estudios de Economía Aplicada*, *32*(2), 535–566.

Cámara, N., & Tuesta, D. (2014). *Measuring Financial Inclusion: A Muldimensional Index* (BBVA Working Paper No. 14 (26)). Retrieved from BBVA website: https://www.bbvaresearch.com/wp-content/uploads/2014/09/WP14-26_Financial-Inclusion2.pdf

Carbó Valverde, S., & Rodríguez Fernández, F. (2014). Has bank restructuring in Spain and Europe paid off? *Spanish Economic and Financial Outlook*, *3*(3), 5–13.

Cecchetti, S., & Kharroubi, E. (2012). *Reassessing the impact of finance on growth* (BIS Working Papers No 381). Retrieved from Bank for International Settlements website: https://www.bis.org/publ/work381.pdf

Cheng, S. (2012). Substitution or complementary effects between banking and stock markets: Evidence from financial openness in Taiwan. *Journal of International Financial Markets, Institutions and Money*, *22*(3), 508–520. doi:10.1016/j.intfin.2012.01.007

Corral Delgado, S., Domínguez Martínez, J. M., & López del Paso, R. (2011). El nuevo mapa del sistema financiero español. *Extoikos*, *3*, 65–77.

Cull, R., Ehrbeck, T., & Holle, N. (2014). *Financial inclusion and development: Recent impact evidence.* Retrieved from http://www.cgap.org/publications/financial-inclusion-and-development-recent-impact-evidence

Demirgüç-Kunt, A., & Klapper, L. (2013). Measuring Financial Inclusion: Explaining Variation Across and Within Countries. *Brookings Papers on Economic Activity*, *44*(1), 279–321. doi:10.1353/eca.2013.0002

Demirguc-Kunt, A., Klapper, L., Singer, D., & Van Oudheusden, P. (2015). *The Global Findex Database 2014* (World Bank Policy Research Working Paper No 7255). Retrieved from World Bank website: http://documents.worldbank.org/curated/en/187761468179367706/pdf/WPS7255.pdf

Donou-Adonsou, F., & Sylwester, K. (2016). Financial development and poverty reduction in developing countries: New evidence from banks and microfinance institutions. *Review of Development Finance*, *6*(1), 82–90. doi:10.1016/j.rdf.2016.06.002

Durusu-Ciftci, D., Ispir, M. S., & Yetkiner, H. (2017). Financial development and economic growth: Some theory and more evidence. *Journal of Policy Modeling*, *39*(2), 290–306. doi:10.1016/j.jpolmod.2016.08.001

European Central Bank. (2018). *European Central Bank Database.* Retrieved June 1, 2018 from https://www.bis.org/publ/work381.pdf

Fernández de Lis, S., & Rubio, A. (2013). *Tendencias a medio plazo en la banca española* (BBVA Working Paper No. 13/33). Retrieved from BBVA website: https://www.bbvaresearch.com/publicaciones/tendencias-a-medio-plazo-en-la-banca-espanola/

Galor, O., & Zeira, J. (1993). Income distribution and macroeconomics. *The Review of Economic Studies*, *60*(1), 35–52. doi:10.2307/2297811

García Montalvo, J. (2014). Crisis financiera, reacción regulatoria y el futuro de la banca en España. *Estudios de Economía Aplicada*, *32*(2), 497–528.

Greenwood, J., & Jovanovic, B. (1990). Financial development, growth, and the distribution of income. *Journal of Political Economy*, *98*(5), 1076–1107. doi:10.1086/261720

Gutiérrez Fernández, M., Fernández Torres, Y., & Palomo Zurdo, R. (2016). De la Transformación a la Bancarización de las Cajas de Ahorros españolas: Un análisis de los resultados perseguidos. *REVESCO*, *122*, 86–109.

Haan, J., & Sturm, J.-E. (2017). Finance and income inequality: A review and new evidence. *European Journal of Political Economy*, *50*, 171–195. doi:10.1016/j.ejpoleco.2017.04.007

Jauch, S., & Watzka, S. (2016). Financial development and income inequality: A panel data approach. *Empirical Economics*, *51*(1), 291–314. doi:10.100700181-015-1008-x

Kempson, E., Atkinson, A., & Pilley, O. (2004). *Policy level response to financial exclusion in developed economies: Lessons for developing countries.* Retrieved from http://www.bristol.ac.uk/media-library/sites/geography/migrated/documents/pfrc0409.pdf

Levine, R. (2005). Finance and growth: theory and evidence: 12. In P. Aghion & S. Durlauf (Eds.), *Handbook of economic growth* (pp. 865–934). Amsterdam: Elsevier; doi:10.3386/w10766

Maroto, R., Mulas Granados, C., & Fernández Álvarez, J. (2012). *Crisis financiera y rescates bancarios en Europa. Ideas sobre el caso español.* Madrid: Fundación Ideas.

Maudos, J. (2012). El impacto de la crisis en el sector bancario español. *Cuadernos de Información Económica, 226*, 155–163.

Mohan, R. (2006, November). *Economic growth, financial deepening and financial inclusion.* Paper presented at the Annual Bankers' Conference 2006. Retrieved from http://rbidocs.rbi.org.in/rdocs/Speeches/PDFs/73697.pdf)

Naceur, S. B., & Zhang, R. (2016). *Financial Development, Inequality and Poverty: Some International Evidence* (IMF Working Papers No. 16/32). Retrieved from International Monetary Fund website: https://www.imf.org/en/Publications/WP/Issues/2016/12/31/Financial-Development-Inequality-and-Poverty-Some-International-Evidence-43718

Sarma, M. (2008). *Index of financial inclusion* (ICRIER Working Paper No. 215). Retrieved from Indian Council for Research on International Economic Relations website: http://www.icrier.org/pdf/Working_Paper_215.pdf

Sarma, M., & Pais, J. (2011). Financial inclusion and development. *Journal of International Development, 23*(5), 613–628. doi:10.1002/jid.1698

Somoza López, A. (2015). Algunas consideraciones sobre el proceso de reestructuración en las cajas de ahorro españolas: Una referencia al caso alemán. *Análisis Financiero, 129*, 20–33.

Tajadura Garrido, C. (2015). El sistema financiero español tras la crisis: Menor en tamaño. más seguro y menos rentable. *Análisis Financiero, 127*, 1–19.

Tuesta, D., Sorensen, G., Haring, A., & Cámara, N. (2015). *Financial inclusion and its determinants: The case of Argentina* (BBVA Research Working Paper No. 15/03). Retrieved from the BBVA website: https://www.bbvaresearch.com/wp-content/uploads/2015/01/WP_15-03_Financial-Inclusion-in-Argentina.pdf

Urbaneja Cillán, J. (2014). La Reestructuración del Sistema Financiero Español. El proceso de reforma tras la asistencia financiera a la Banca Española. *Revista Jurídica de Castilla y León, 32*, 1–46.

ADDITIONAL READING

Bordo, M. D., & Meissner, C. M. (2012). Does inequality lead to a financial crisis? *Journal of International Money and Finance, 31*(8), 2147–2161. doi:10.1016/j.jimonfin.2012.05.006

Demirgüç-Kunt, A., Beck, T., & Honohan, P. (2008). Finance for all? Policies and pitfalls in expanding access. Retrieved from https://siteresources.worldbank.org/INTFINFORALL/Resources/4099583-1194373512632/FFA_book.pdf. doi:10.1596/978-0-8213-7291-3

Kappel, V. (2010). The effects of financial development on income inequality and poverty (CER-ETH Working Paper, No. 10/127). Retrieved from the website: https://www.econstor.eu/bitstream/10419/39977/1/293_kappel.pdf

Pagano, M. (1993). Financial markets and growth: An overview. *European Economic Review*, *37*(2-3), 613–622. doi:10.1016/0014-2921(93)90051-B

Rioja, F., & Valev, N. (2004). Does one size fit all? A reexamination of the finance and growth relationship. *Journal of Development Economics*, *74*(2), 429–447. doi:10.1016/j.jdeveco.2003.06.006

Wu, J., Hou, H., & Cheng, S. (2010). The dynamic impacts of financial institutions on economic growth: Evidence from the European Union. *Journal of Macroeconomics*, *32*(3), 879–891. doi:10.1016/j.jmacro.2009.09.003

KEY TERMS AND DEFINITIONS

Bancarization of Spanish Savings Banks: The process, forced by law, of conversion of Spanish savings banks into banks.

Banking System: The structural network of institutions that offer financial services within a county. The members of the banking system and the functions they typically perform include (1) commercial banks that take deposits and make loans, (2) investment banks which specialize in capital market issues and trading, and (3) national central banks that issue currency and set monetary policy.

Finance Growth Nexus: Relationship between the development of financial activities and the economic growth in a country.

Finance Reducing-Inequality Nexus: Relationship between the development of financial activities and institutions, and the reduction of the poverty.

Financial Exuberance: The quality of the financial system of growing profusely.

Indicator: Measurable variable used as a representation of an associated (but non-measured or non-measurable) factor or quantity. For example, consumer price index (CPI) serves as an indicator of general cost of living which consists of many factors some of which are not included in computing CPI. Indicators are common statistical devices employed in economics. See also economic indicators and measure.

Retrogression in Inclusiveness: The process of returning to a worse situation in terms of inclusiveness.

Unbanked: Not having access to the services of a bank or similar financial organization.

ENDNOTE

1 Spain joined the European Economic Community in the year 1986, after signing in June 1985 the Act of Accession.

Chapter 5
The Effects of Macroprudential Policies on Financial Stability in Developing Countries

Sümeyra Gazel
Bozok University, Turkey

ABSTRACT

In this chapter, the concept of financial instability is examined in terms of the policy instruments used by central banks. Although the policy instruments used in each country differ according to the country conditions, it is thought that the common factor among developing countries with a current account deficit problem is exchange rate volatility resulting from excessive credit growth and short-term capital movements. In this context, Argentina, Brazil, Chile, Colombia, Hungary, Indonesia, India, Mexico, Poland, South Africa, and Turkey are examined with regard to the effects of macroprudential policies on financial stability for the period between Q2 of 2006 and Q2 of 2017 by using the time-varying panel causality test developed by Dumitrescu and Hurlin. The results of the analysis indicate that excessive credit growth is a cause of the current account deficit. The same findings are also valid for interest rate. There is no obvious link between the exchange rate and the current account deficit.

INTRODUCTION

The idea that macroeconomic risks are affected by global financial markets in open economies has become increasingly widespread with the advent of globalization. Changes in risk perception owing to expansionary monetary policies by developed countries after the 2008 global financial crisis and capital flows becoming excessively volatile as a result of this approach are deemed as major macroeconomic risks. Capital flows are mostly directed towards developing countries, implying that domestic currencies of developing countries become overvalued and banks reach excessive credit levels. In other words, emerging economies encounter additional challenges owing to their vulnerability to inconsistent international capital flows. This situation has led to increased imports and an imbalance in demand, followed by the rapid deterioration of current account balances for developing countries. Disruption of

DOI: 10.4018/978-1-5225-7208-4.ch005

short-term capital inflows, credit expansion and current account balances have caused financial fragility post-2008 financial crisis, thus leading many countries to re-examine their existing economic policies (CBRT, 2015; Hannoun, 2010) At this point, the most important change is the abandonment of the idea that financial stability will occur spontaneously when price stability is attained. At the same time, this idea has led to central banks using diverse and highly complex policy tools. Individual countries have developed different policy tools according to their circumstances to mitigate the effects of the global crisis. In this context, many countries have attached particular importance to variables such as credit growth and exchange rate, and have thus developed new policy instruments that can control these variables in order to provide financial stability. These instruments, which have been used to provide financial stability, together with price stability policies, used to monitor and mitigate the risks that may arise in the financial system, are included in macroprudential policies. These policies are mainly designed to reduce the adverse effects on the financial system and the real economy of the risks that may arise owing to financial problems. Financial sector stability plays a vital role in achieving sustainable economic growth. Overcoming market friction and encouraging economic growth is realized through effective financial institutions and markets.

In this chapter, the aim was to determine how macroprudential policies related to credit growth and exchange rate fluctuations affect the financial stability of developing countries with a current account deficit. The rest of the chapter is organized as follows. In the next section, the concept of financial stability is defined and the importance of financial stability is addressed. In the third section, the roles of central banks in ensuring financial stability are discussed and policy tools are examined. In the fourth part, a time-varying panel causality test is applied to 11 countries with a current account deficit. In the final section, the findings are summarized and recommendations for future research are provided. This chapter will make an important contribution as it assesses financial stability in terms of central bank policies.

BACKGROUND

Financial Stability and Macroprudential Policy

The 2008 global financial crisis created an environment in which most of the known facts about the dynamics of the economy were questioned in many countries and it was realized that focus on individual institutions alone could not efficiently counter the systemic risk to the financial market. Since the financial crisis, some of the most commonly asked questions are how to detect systemic risk and what steps would be taken to avoid such a formidable crisis again. The Financial Stability Board, the International Monetary Fund and the Bank for International Settlements (2009) describe systemic risk as "a risk of disruption to financial service that is caused by a deterioration of all parts of the financial system and has the potential to have important negative results for the real economy." The most general definition of systemic risk is the failure of the whole system, which seriously impairs financial markets and damages the economy widely because of the links and interdependencies between entities. In spite of doubts about how to manage systematic risk, there are opinions in the literature about how best to do so. For example, the Group of Thirty analysts (G-30, 2010) suggest using some macroprudential tools, such as avoiding systematically high leverage levels, providing the necessary liquidity for sound operation of the market, regulating market actions, and overcoming excessive credit growth. Clement (2010) stated that macroprudential policy is defined as "the use of prudential tools with the obvious objective of supporting the stability of the financial system as a whole, not necessarily of the individual institutions within it." In other words, the goal of macroprudential policy should be to help to ensure financial stability within the whole system.

Financial Stability

Financial systems, which include institutions, products, and markets, are so complex that there is no consensus for defining financial stability. Although financial stability has been among the primary targets of many countries in recent years, it still remains an elusive concept. The Central Bank of the Republic of Turkey (CBRT, 2015) defines financial stability as the resilience of the economy against unexpected situations that may disrupt the balance of the financial system. According to The European Central Bank (ECB, 2012), "financial stability refers to resistance to shocks, thus decreasing the likelihood of disruption in the financial intermediation process, in which savings are not usually directed at profitable investment opportunities". Another definition, provided by Foot (2003), is that financial stability is the ability of a significant part of the financial markets and institutions in the economy to safely perform their operations (as cited in Schinasi, 2004, p.14). In other words, financial stability implies the absence of relative price movements in real or financial assets.

Policy makers and investors are interested in the actual relationship between financial stability and volatility or uncertainty. Essentially, volatility is a necessary element of a well-functioning financial system. Volatility in financial markets frequently depends on a higher degree of uncertainty in the financial markets. As the underlying factors affecting asset prices change, asset prices will either increase or decrease, and volatility will thus emerge. In this respect, asset prices generally reflect their "true" profitability. Therefore, a market without risk and volatility would lead to ossified financial markets with no opportunity to provide investment capital for the real economy. Neither macroprudential policy nor any other measures seek to exterminate risk and volatility entirely. Nevertheless, in extraordinary situations, such as a bubble in asset prices, price movements may not always reflect fundamental factors. While identifying that it is impossible to quantify exactly how much risk and volatility are economically optimal, policymakers try to increase the flexibility of the financial system and attempt to forestall risk and volatility from reaching a point that could result in a highly costly financial crisis (Knütter, Mohr, & Wagner, 2011; G-30, 2010).

Over the last 30 years, regulations aimed at preventing the risks and fragilities that may occur in the financial system have been predominantly based on microprudential policies, taking into account the soundness of the financial structure. The 2008 global financial crisis showed that traditional economic policies, financial regulations, micro-risk-reduction policies, and financial security nets consisting of the deposit insurance system are inadequate for detecting systemic risks that could lead to the disruption of some part of the financial system or the whole system. In this context, the importance of financial stability has increased. It has become clear that both macroprudential and traditional policy tools are necessary in order to ensure and protect financial stability. Hannoun (2010) compared the two models—traditional and new—for financial stability, as summarized in Table 1.

According to Table 1, financial decision makers should be able to use both monetary policy and fiscal policy in combination with microprudential policy to ensure to global financial stability. Financial stability is an indication that there is sustainable confidence in the financial dimension. With the new paradigm, it is easier to provide the three conditions defined by the ECB (2012): (i) resources can be transferred effectively and smoothly from savers to investors in the financial system; (ii) financial risks

Table 1. Financial stability paradigms

Traditional Model	New Model
Monetary policy based on price inflation	Monetary policy targeting price inflation, but also taking into account financial imbalances
Microprudential policy based on individual banks	Microprudential policy focused on systemic risk and considered together with macroprudential policy
Trust in domestic risk management and market discipline	Higher bank capital, better management, more regulation
Fiscal policy lacks financial stability concerns	Countercyclical fiscal policy
More domestic policy	More universal coordination

Source: Hannoun, 2010.

should be considered and well managed; and (iii) real and financial economic surprises or shocks can be easily absorbed by the financial system. In short, the new paradigm takes into account the financial instability of each unit of the economy and broadens the functions of monetary policies.

The Importance of Financial Stability

With changes to the architecture of the financial system, the concept of financial stability has become more important, especially since the global crisis. It is now understood that the disruptions that may occur in the financial system can seriously affect the real economy. Financial stability has notably contributed to global financial markets, the economies of individual countries and parliamentary policy.

Losses by some market participants owing to economic fluctuations within any country may have a contagion effect on other market participants. In a financial system where inter-country integration is high; the given negative effects can spread quickly to foreign countries and cause a systemic risk. The cost of a systemic financial crisis can be much higher than the cost of maintaining stability before the crisis. Hence, financial stability is essential for global financial markets. In addition to this, financial stability ensures a healthy continuation of the transfer of funds required to enable savings owners and investors to carry out their activities effectively and reduces the vulnerability of the economy by providing a balanced distribution of risks. Financial stability is also crucial for the effectiveness of monetary policy because it expands the central bank's area of action in the implementation of monetary policy. For example, if financial stability is not achieved in a country's economy, monetary policy tools cannot be used as desired and the anticipated effects of the applied policies may not be achieved. Fluctuations in credit availability and exchange rates threaten financial stability and can disrupt resource allocation in the economy. In this way, reaching excessive levels of liquidity surplus or openness also weakens the monetary transmission mechanism. The predictability of the monetary transmission mechanism in all dimensions is important in order to provide a better estimate of the effects of central banks' monetary policies. Central banks may not be able to provide the desired outcome in order to maintain price stability if there is high uncertainty within the transfer mechanism (CBRT, 2015).

Sources of Financial Instability

It is thought that describing financial instability is much easier than defining financial stability. Financial instability can be defined as sudden and extreme fluctuations in asset prices, the failure of financial institutions to fulfill their functions in the system, and the deterioration of the operation of the national or international credit system. At the same time, previous examples show that excessive volatility of asset prices is frequently associated with financial instability. Volatility is an inherent phenomenon of the markets. It is well-known that interest rates and/or asset prices can change by the hour and even by the minute, but not all volatility is a sign of market instability. In other words, the changes can describe the normal workings of financial markets and may not indicate financial instability, even though they are sometimes very significant.

What, in that case, separates changes in financial conditions that signal instability from these other changes that take place continuously? Such instability has a damaging effect on the economy in various ways in a manner that the flow of finance to them becomes limited. At the same time, it can harm the operations of specific financial enterprises and markets so that they have difficulties in funding the rest of the economy. Are there events that menace financial stability different from those that do not? Any shock influencing the financial sector to a degree that significantly disrupts the continuing productive ability of the economy can be defined as financial instability (Chant, Lai, Illing, & Daniel, 2003). The channeling of funds to profitable investment opportunities, which is the most fundamental task of the financial system, does not take place and financial instability can then arise when the shocks to the financial system prevent the flow of information. Actually, when financial instability is strong, the functioning of financial markets can be completely distorted and a financial crisis can occur. According to Mishkin (2000), there are four important factors that cause increases in asymmetric information problems and financial instability: increases in interest rates, deterioration of balance sheets with the change of asset prices, corruption of financial sector balance sheets, and increased uncertainty. These four factors can be considered as leading to a financial crisis in which the effects of uncontrollable financial instability are seen across a wide area and the markets are unable to fulfill their functions.

Macroprudential Policies

Macroprudential policies have increased in importance since the 2008 global crisis. Even though there are different definitions and emphases, a consensus has been formed whereby macroprudential policy aims to restrict the risks and costs of systemic crises. According to Kawai & Morgan (2012), macroprudential supervisions and regulations are used to decrease systemic risks and maintain systemic financial stability. Macroprudential policies help to detect the vulnerabilities of the financial system and forestall a crisis by addressing those vulnerabilities with policy actions in a timely manner. The Group of Thirty analysts (G-30, 2010) defined the aim of macroprudential policy as "reducing systemic risks by strengthening the financial system's flexibility in the face of economic downturns and resisting procyclical behaviors." As an alternative view, according to Borio & Drehman (2009), the risk of system-wide distress is restricted by macroprudential policy. It is clear that macroprudential policy cannot entirely eliminate systemic risk. The application of a strong macroprudential policy regime may not prevent a financial crisis, but a crisis can be contained at less cost when macroprudential policies are used. For this reason, an expectation of eliminating all systemic risks by the use of macroprudential policies is not realistic (G-30, 2010).

Caruana (2010) discussed the time and cross-sectional dimensions of macroprudential policy. The first dimension is associated with increasing aggregate risk. The other dimension deals with the distribution of the aggregate risk within the financial system at a point in time. Although macroprudential policies have attracted a great deal of attention in recent times in the monetary policy literature, macroprudential policy research is not so much an analytical foundation for policy frameworks. This might be attributed to three fundamental reasons. Primarily, the macroprudential approach has recently begun to draw attention in policy debates and there is no consensus about the definition of financial stability or the determination of macroprudential policy aims. Secondly, the interactions between the financial system and macroeconomy are not clear. Finally, the definition of and the relationship between microprudential and macroprudential policy are still not clear (Galati & Moessner, 2011).

The relationship between macroeconomic policy and macroprudential policy is a topic of particular interest. Actually, both macroeconomic policy and macroprudential policy take the whole economic system into account, rather than individual establishments. However, macroeconomic policy considers the interactions between interest rate and inflation, and macroprudential policy pays attention to systemic risk; macroeconomic policy is not concerned with systemic risk (G-30, 2010). In brief, it is assumed that macroprudential policies, which focus on reducing systemic financial risks, are among the most useful tools of advanced and especially emerging countries. Nonetheless, but there is not enough evidence of their effectiveness or efficiency (Claessens, Ghosh, & Mihet, 2013).

Macroprudential Policies in Emerging Countries

The policies applied by developed countries to overcome the 2008 global crisis have increased liquidity and this liquidity has created capital inflows to developing countries. Capital flows provide many benefits to emerging market economies, especially economic growth and development: financing necessary investment, smoothing consumption, and diversifying risks are among the benefits. However, Kawai & Takagi (2008) pointed out that large capital flows can bring three types of risks for capital-recipient countries, especially if not managed correctly. The first is macroeconomic risk. The increase in capital flows might cause growth in the volume of domestic credit, leading to economic overheating, including inflation. Moreover, capital flows can adversely affect the real exchange rate. In this way, economic growth and price stability targets may not be realized. The second risk, and one of the most important causes of financial instability, is that capital inflows have maturity dates and the possibility of not being paid. When payments are not made on time, equity and other asset prices increase with currency inconsistency in the balance sheets of private sector debt, potentially decreasing the quality of assets. This situation causes greater financial fragility. The third risk is sudden terminations. When capital inflows stop suddenly, this situation can lead to rapid reserve decumulation or strong currency depreciation. For this reason, developing economies mostly use foreign exchange-related macroprudential policies while developed economies use borrower-based policies because developing economies are more exposed to external shocks and are less perfect. Developing countries with their usually less liberalized financial systems are more exposed to market failures. Therefore, the effects of external shocks are felt less in financially advanced and open markets. In this case, both developed economies and developing markets can learn about the effectiveness of macro-prudential policies from each other. The most commonly used tools by advanced countries are CONC (concentration limits), INTER (limits on interbank exposures), and LEV (leverage ratios). Developing economies usually use the following tools: LTV (loan-to-value ratio), RR(reserve requirement ratios, FC (limits on foreign currency loans), DP (time-varying loan-loss provisioning), and CG (limits on domestic currency loans) (Cerutti, Claessens & Laeven, 2017). Some emerging Latin American countries have been using the macroprudential measures detailed in Table 2.

According to Table 2, Latin America countries prefer to use policies that target larger and more volatile capital inflows to enable them to cope with systematic liquidity risk.

Table 2. Macroprudential measures used recently by some Latin American countries

Country and Measure	Policy Tool	Motivation-Objective
Brazil (long-term consumer loan market, 2010)	Capital requirements	Decelerate credit growth
Bolivia (2008), Colombia (2007), Peru (2008)	Dynamic provisioning	Countercyclical tools
Colombia (2008), Peru (1997)	Liquidity requirements	Tools to govern liquidity risk
Peru (2011), Brazil (2010), Uruguay (2009-2011)	Reserve requirements on bank deposits	Restrict credit growth, manage liquidity, and complete monetary policy to reach macroprudential goals
Peru (2010, 2011)	Reserve requirements on foreign liabilities of banking institutions	Increase the cost of bank financing with the goal of shifting the funding structure towards the longer term
Peru (2010), Uruguay (2010)	Tools to manage foreign exchange credit risk	Assist financial institutions to internalize foreign exchange credit risk related to lending to un-hedged borrowers
Brazil (Reserve requirements on short spot dollar positions, 2011), Peru (on net FX derivate contract)	Limits on foreign exchange positions	Manage foreign exchange risk
Peru (restrict to foreign investments by domestic pension funds, 2010)	Other	Facilitate capital outflows and simplify pressure on the currency, domestic demand, and consumer prices

Source: Tovar, Escribano, & Martin, 2012

THE ROLE OF CENTRAL BANKS IN FINANCIAL STABILITY AND POLICY OPTIONS

Central banks use various tools to provide financial stability, such as monetary policy tools and macroprudential policy tools. The intended aim of these tools is to avoid and mitigate the effects of crises. Open-market operations and reserve ratio requirements as monetary policy tools are used to regulate the demand and supply of money. In a crisis, the role of central banks as the lender of last resort can simply be considered as an excessive type of open-market operation. According to Kawai & Morgan (2012) "the primary aim of macroprudential policies is to reduce systemic financial risk, usually by limiting growth of bank credit". The process of achieving and sustaining financial stability involves the interaction of macroeconomic policies with other policies. Although the fact that price stability and financial stability targets may conflict in the short-term can sometimes create a dilemma in terms of monetary policy, macroprudential policies can give monetary policy room to maneuver in some periods. Similarly, structural measures to be implemented in the field of fiscal policy can be used in conjunction with macroeconomic policies to help achieve the targeted results (CBRT, 2015).

Financial Stability or Price Stability

The 2008 crisis demonstrates that price stability does not ensure macroeconomic stability. In several countries, dangerous financial imbalances (for instance, large foreign-exchange exposures or fast credit growth) advanced under low inflation. To provide macroeconomic stability, policies have to contain financial stability (IMF, 2013). The central banks should provide a balance between continuing price stability, as their primary objective, and supporting financial stability, which is a more general objective. Monetary policy is generally applied for a period of 2 to 3 years, depending on the economic cycle, but the risks and imbalances in the financial system occur over a longer period, causing the so-called financial cycle, which can include several economic cycles. A solution to this inconsistency could be expanding the timescale for the price stability objective (Criste & Lupu, 2014). To do so, central banks must know the sources of instability very well and must continuously monitor the current state of the financial system to implement monetary policy in conformity with the macroeconomic objectives (Chant, Lai, IIling & Daniel, 2003).

Macroprudential policies have an important place in achieving financial stability. Macroprudential policies can serve the purpose of financial stability if they are coordinated with other policies A policy has to contain financial stability as an extra objective to ensure macroeconomic stability. Although financial stability is one of the most important goals, the use of both monetary and macroprudential policies is nevertheless limited. Experiences from countries such as Brazil, Korea, Israel, Sweden, Poland, Turkey, and the United States illustrate the difficulties with using both policies in conjunction. However, it also demonstrates that well-targeted macroprudential policies can assist monetary policy in achieving both price and financial stability. For example, in Brazil, capital and reserve requirements were used together in the post-crisis period (2010–2011) to forestall an overheating of the economy and to limit risks from rapid credit growth (IMF, 2013).

Monetary and Fiscal Policy Tools

During ordinary times, central banks sell short-term government papers for cash under open-market operations. However, in situations such as a liquidity trap, central banks can implement the so-called 'unconventional' measures. For instance, if the types and maturities of assets to be purchased are expanded by open-market operations, then they can become unconventional measures. Credit easing (or qualitative easing) is used to ease credit conditions in the markets. Sometimes central banks make statements about the expected trends of future monetary policies to influence market expectations (Kawai & Morgan, 2012). Fiscal policy is also an important tool in terms of securing and protecting financial stability. First, the public spending and tax policies can act as an automatic balancer, contributing to the avoidance of financial imbalances. Second, tight fiscal policy that is monitored during periods of strong economic growth may slow down the rate of credit expansion and reduce the bubbles that can occur in asset prices. Finally, fiscal policy can be used for sectors where financial imbalances are likely to occur and bubbles are starting to form. The application of tax policies in addition to macroprudential measures, such as limiting credit expansion to specific sectors, contributes to the prevention of financial imbalances (CBRT, 2015). If monetary and financial stabilization policies are better understood, financial sector uncertainty may decrease and, in this situation, financial market participants can make investment decisions more easily. Furthermore, during periods of irrational exuberance in financial markets, central banks can help change the enhanced perception of risk with a convenient communication (Knütter & Wagner, 2010).

Currency and Capital Flow Management

The period of financial liberalization, which began in the 1980s and gained momentum with the inclusion of most countries in the 1990s, states that many developing countries transition to a flexible exchange rate system. Through this period, integration in financial markets increased thanks to improvements in computer and communication technologies, and capital flows within countries began to affect each other considerably. According to CBRT (2015), market players, in order to increase their income, borrow in a currency with low borrowing costs and tend to trade the funds by converting to another currency with higher returns. These activities, so-called carry trades, have led to accelerated capital flows to the markets of higher-yielding countries. However, uncertainty arising as a result of such factors as the lack of adequate information in the market, fluctuations in the market and macroeconomic instability cause sudden capital outflows in some countries. In this context, short-term capital flows have transformed a risk factor that threatens financial stability by reducing the resistance of countries to shocks. It is not easy to manage capital inflows, so regulatory authorities must watch for unwanted flows to manage capital inflows. Recent capital control measures for some Asian countries are as follows: one month holding period on Bank Indonesia Certificates(SBIs), limits on foreign exchange derivative contracts (Korea), and limits on commercial banks related to net foreign currency exposure (Thailand) (Kawai & Morgan, 2012). In brief, exchange rate movements accelerated by global liquidity abundance—as a result of short-term capital inflows—have the potential to increase macroeconomic and financial imbalances by distorting the efficient distribution of resources in the economy. Policies relating to currency and capital flow management aim to deter market players from short-term speculative capital inflows and to limit macroeconomic risks that could lead to a sudden stop in the global risk appetite (Başçı & Kara, 2011).

Macroprudential Policy Tools

Macroprudential policy tools are used to limit systemic risk and to prevent systemic financial crises in this framework. Macroprudential policies generally have three objectives (IMF, 2011): (i) Reducing the impact of shocks by creating a buffer against systemic shocks, thus protecting the financial system from systemic shocks and ensuring the continuity of the economy credit flow; (ii) preventing systemic fragility that may occur over time by reducing the cycle between credit and asset prices, limiting the use of intensive leverage and reducing funding from unsustainable sources; and (iii) checking fragilities that may arise from interdependence in the financial system and identifying key institutions that should not be allowed to go bankrupt. Central banks use a variety of toolkits, such as limits on loan growth, debt-service-to-income ratios, loan-to-value ratios, and credit exposure limits on certain sectors to achieve these goals (Kawai & Morgan 2012). Some of these tools aim to manage aggregate risk by considering procyclicality, but others propose controlling aggregate risk with systemic oversight. When the countries that use the tools are examined, it is clear that the majority are in the developing country category. For instance, while China, Hong Kong, Malaysia, Thailand, and Indonesia use loan-to-value ratios, Hong Kong and Korea prefer to use debt-service-to-income ratios. Because a country's exposure level to shocks and risks and financial market characteristics can change, the preferred use of macroprudential policies will be different.

It should not be overlooked that the use of policies may create side effects on other policy targets. If financial distortions change exogenously, each policy can sustain its goals without being affected by side effects (IMF, 2013). Therefore, macroprudential supervisors must cautiously set the use of these tools to the specific economy in which they are used because the differing economic environment of other financial systems may make that tool impractical or inefficient. Moreover, macroprudential regulators must be aware of the adverse effects on the economy, which can occur when macroeconomic policies are applied together (G-30, 2010).

In brief, financial stability is a common goal of central banks, but the policy tools to be used vary according to the conditions of the country. As seen in the literature section of the study, earlier studies often emphasize the importance of use of different tools according to the level of development of the countries.

Literature Review

Although the concept of financial stability has been an important target for many central banks for a very long time, after the 2008 global financial crisis it became almost an obligatory target. Numerous studies on the concept of financial stability have been published before the crisis, but much of the work has been carried out in the post-crisis period. The effectiveness of macroprudential measures in different countries, mostly applied after the 2008 crisis, has been compared in these studies. For this reason, the present section mainly focuses on the key studies carried out in the post-crisis period.

One of the important studies carried out after the 2008 global financial crisis was conducted by Lim et al. (2011). They investigated whether macroprudential policies affected credit and leverage levels. According to their results, a reduction in the procyclicality of credit and leverage was linked to ceilings on credit growth and reserve requirements, as well as limits on debt-to-income and loan-to-value ratio. Peersman (2011) applied a structural vector autoregressive model for the Euro area economy. The sample period covers January 1999 to December 2009. The results of the analysis demonstrate that multiple instruments can be used together as monetary policy tools in order to influence macroeconomic variables. Gertler & Karadi (2011), developed a quantitative monetary model to evaluate the effects of the central bank using unconventional monetary policy to struggle a simulated financial crisis. According to their evaluations, central banks use unconventional monetary policy tools to offset a disruption of private financial intermediation. A study by IMF (2013) examined several countries (Korea, New Zealand, Spain, Switzerland, Ireland, and the United Kingdom) in terms of the relationship between policy changes, financial vulnerabilities, and the real economy. According to their findings, credit growth and loan-to-value limits are significantly and negatively related to capital requirements and reserve requirements. Dedola, Karadi & Lombardo (2013) researched the international dimension of unconventional policies in open economies. Consumption, investment, national income, leverage ratios, bank assets, bond yields were analyzed by VAR method in the study. According to results, that national policies that do not internalize the national influences of non-traditional policies may be insufficient against shocks. Shin (2013) surveyed 57 countries using panel regressions and more than three decades of data. He examined the impact of nine non-interest rate policy tools on house prices and housing credit. The results reveal that housing credit growth is affected by housing-related taxes, the maximum loan-to-value ratio and the maximum debt-service-to-income ratio. Tovar, Escribano, & Martin (2012) examined the effects of reserve requirements and other macroprudential policies on credit growth, with panel data Vector Auto Regression (VAR), using information from five Latin American countries over the period from January 2003 to April 2011. The results suggest that the reserve requirement has a short-term effect on credit growth. Dell'Ariccia et al. (2012) carried out one of the most comprehensive studies examining the impact of macroprudential policy tools on credit growth by using a dataset covering 170 countries over the period 1970–2010. The authors determined that credit growth is associated with economic growth and financial reform. Claessens, Ghosh & Mihet (2013) examined 2,800 individual banks from 48 countries for the period 2000–2010. They found that measures aimed at borrowers are effective in decreasing the growth in banks' leverage and asset liabilities. Gambacorta, Hoffman & Peersman

(2014) examined the macroeconomic effects of non-traditional monetary policies for USA, UK, Japan, Euro Area, Canada, Norway, Switzerland and Sweden. In the study, Panel VAR analysis was used and January 2008-June 2011 period examined. According to the findings, when an increase in the assets of central banks is realized, the level of economic activity and prices increase temporarily. Also, the macroeconomic effects of non-traditional monetary policies applied in different countries were found to be similar. Cerutti, Claessens & Laeven (2017) contributed to the existing literature by examining a broad set of macroprudential policies in 119 countries and by separating the effects on different segments of the credit markets and house prices. Their results showed that the relationship between macroprudential policy and credit growth varies from country to country. They found weaker associations in financially more open economies.

According to the related literature, macroprudential policies, especially after the 2008 crisis, have an important place in ensuring financial stability. This study attempts to determine the role of macroprudential policies in ensuring financial stability in countries that face the problem of a continuous current account deficit. A time-varying panel causality test is used to determine whether the relationship between macroprudential policies and financial stability has changed over time. No studies on countries with current account deficits could be found in the related literature. It is also believed that it is the first time that this method has been applied on the subject under consideration. Thus, it is expected that this study willmake a useful contribution to the literature.

AN EMPIRICAL ANALYSIS OF EFFECTS OF MACROPRUDENTIAL POLICIES ON FINANCIAL STABILITY IN EMERGING COUNTRIES

In this section, firstly the datasets used in the analysis are introduced, and secondly, the empirical model used in this work is presented. In the last part, the findings of the analysis are discussed.

Empirical Analysis

Data Used for Analysis

In this study, the effects of macroprudential policies applied by central banks to ensure financial stability have been examined for emerging economies, which usually have current account deficits. Financing of current account deficits has great importance for countries that generally have current account deficits. Because short-term credits and capital inflows are mostly used in financing the current account, it is thought that in the case of any shock, financial markets may be adversely affected, leading to financial instability. In this context, an econometric analysis has been carried out on developing countries. Argentina, Brazil, Chile, Colombia, Hungary, Indonesia, India, Mexico, Poland, Turkey, and South Africa will be examined with credit growth, the real effective exchange rate, the policy rate, and current account balance data. Total credit to the private non-financial sector from banks is used to measure the credit growth. Although central banks have not used common instruments to provide financial stability after the 2008 global crisis, variables such as loan growth and exchange rate volatility have been included in the analysis because they serve a common purpose. In other words, central banks aim to limit credit growth and reduce exchange rate volatility, although the instruments that they use to achieve financial stability are different. The period from Q2 2006 to Q2 2017 has been examined by using time-varying panel causality test to determine the effect of the pre-crisis period in 2008. . Analysis based solely on causality does not make it possible to make strong conclusions about the central bank policies prescription but the time-varying causality analysis helps us to gain a general viewpoint related to the impact of central bank policies in terms of the changing relationship over the research period.

Empirical Model

The time-varying panel causality analysis was based on the panel causality analysis developed by Dumitrescu and Hurlin (2012). The test is strong against cross-section dependency and the β_i s for each country to be different; that is, the coefficients must be heterogeneous. For this reason, homogeneity tests need to be carried out before the models can be established. Dumitrescu and Hurlin (2012) state that their test was based on the causality test developed by Granger (1969), further converted to apply to panel data. The model for causality analysis is shown in Equation 1 (Dumitrescu & Hurlin, 2012).

$$y_{i,t} = \alpha_{i,t} + \sum_{k=1}^{K} \gamma_i^{(k)} y_{i,t-k} + \sum_{k=1}^{K} \beta_i^{(k)} x_{i,t-k} + \varepsilon_{i,t} \tag{1}$$

Here, x and y represent two variables that are being investigated for a causality relationship, while k represents the lag. γ and β indicate the lag coefficients of the dependent and independent variables, respectively. The analysis requires that the data be stable. If not, non-stationary variables must be included by taking first differences. The test hypotheses are as follows:

$H_0 : \beta_i = 0, \forall_i = 1, ..., N$ (There is no causality for all units)

$H_1 : \beta_i = 0, \forall_i = 1, ..., N_1$ (There is causality for some units)

$\beta_i \neq 0, \forall_i = N_1 + 1, \mathrm{N}_1 + 2, ..., N$

Wald $(W_{N,T}^{Hnc})$ and $(\mathrm{Z}_{N,T}^{Hnc})$ statistics were developed by Dumitrescu and Hurlin (2012) to test these hypotheses, as shown in Equations 2 and 3.

$$(\mathrm{W}_{N,T}^{Hnc}) = \frac{1}{N} \sum_{i=1}^{N} W_{i,T} \tag{2}$$

$$(Z_N^{Hnc}) = \frac{\sqrt{N}[W_{N,T}^{Hnc} - N^{-1} \sum_{i=1}^{N} E(W_{i,T})]}{\sqrt{N^{-1} \sum_{i=1}^{N} Var(W_{i,T})}} \xrightarrow[N,T\to\infty]{d} N(0,1) \quad (3)$$

The null hypothesis is rejected if the statistics calculated in the Dumitrescu and Hurlin (2012) test are greater than the critical values or if the probability values for the test statistics are below the associated significance levels, for example, 10% or 5%. In other words, it means that there is causality for some units. The time-varying causality test is based on the fact that the causality relation between two variables may not be stable over the study period. There may be some causality for some sub-periods but not others when considering the entire study period. For this reason, the authors also tested whether the causality is stable using this test. The number of windows (sub-period) in this study has been set at 15 to catch any causality that could occur and the Dumitrescu and Hurlin causality test has been applied to the sub-periods using the rolling window method. In this way, 31 cycles of causation have been established. Then, the probability values of the causality test statistical values calculated for each sub-period have been taken and figures have been drawn with a level of significance of 10%. Periods below the 10% level of significance show the causality relationship between variables for the period and the 15 quarters before that period. For this study, the data set includes observations from Q2 2006 to Q2017 and start date has been identified according to availability of data for the countries. Q2 2006–Q4 2009, Q2 2006–Q1 2010, and Q4 2006–Q2 2010 can be given as examples of the sub-periods used for analysis. As seen in the example, the analyzed periods progress by rolling in turn and each sub-period progresses quarter-by-quarter. Due to the applied period, this analysis is called a time-varying panel causality test. The causality relationships between the macroprudential policies and financial stability in developing countries with a current account deficit have been investigated for the defined sub-periods using this method. Thus, rather than taking into account the whole period studied, differences that have taken place in the sub-periods have been assessed to determine any changes of causality that occurred over time.

Results and Discussion

As previously mentioned in data section, it is necessary to carry out a few tests before the time-varying panel causality test. One of the tests is related to the determination of the cross-section dependence. Whether there is a cross-section dependence of the variables has been determined by the Breusch–Pagan Lagrange Multiplier (LM), bias-corrected LM, Pesaran scaled LM and Pesaran Cross-Sectional Dependence (CD) tests. Then, the stability levels of the variables for each model have been identified with the aid of unit root tests. The cross-section dependency test results are presented in Table3.

According to the results of cross-section dependency tests, the null hypotheses of the tests are rejected because the calculated test statistics are statistically significant. In other words, it is seen in all variables. In this case, cross-section dependency must be taken into consideration in the analysis. Because of the cross-section dependency in the variables, Cross-Sectionally Augmented Dickey-Fuller (CADF) test, which is one of the second-generation tests developed by Pesaran (2007), is used. Table 4 shows the unit root test results of the variables.

Table 3. Cross-section dependency test results

Test	Credit Growth		Current Account Deficit		Interest Rate		Real Effective Exchange Rate	
	Test Statistic	Prob.	Test Statistic	Prob.	Test Statistic	Prob.	Test Statistic	Prob.
Breusch–Pagan LM	132.30*	0.00	88.49*	0.00	262.05*	0.00	117.34*	0.00
Pesaran Scaled LM	7.370*	0.00	3.193*	0.00	19.742*	0.00	5.944*	0.00
Bias-Corrected Scaled LM	4.683*	0.00	9.220*	0.00	10.47*	0.00	11.544*	0.00
Pesaran CD	-1.247	0.10	-2.984*	0.00	1.619*	0.05	-4.162*	0.00

Note: * Shows cross-section dependency at 5% significance.

Table 4. Results of bootstrap panel unit root test

CADF				
	Level		1st Difference	
	Constant (CIPS-Stat)	Constant and Trend	Constant	Constant and Trend
Credit Growth	-1.872	-2.44	-4.362*	-4.312*
Current Account Deficit	-2.023	-2.375	-4.971*	-4.985*
Interest Rate	-1.752	-2.396	-3.126*	-3.163
Real Effective Exchange Rate	-2.389*	-2.852*	-4.683*	-4.714*

Note: * Shows stability at a significance level of 5%. Critical Cross-Sectionally Augmented IPS (CIPS) values are -2.33 for the intercept-only model and -3.78 for the intercept and trend model. The number of bootstrap cycles is 5000.

The unit root analysis revealed that the variables are stationary in their differences, except for the real effective exchange rate. However, these findings show the results for the all data period in order to make a general evaluation about variables. In the present analysis, the authors performed unit root tests for each window and the causality test was performed according to each test result. Additionally, the time-varying analysis of causality is based on the Bootstrap Toda-Yamamoto causality test which Hacker & Hatemi-J (2006) developed from the Toda-Yamamoto (1995) causality test. As known, there is no importance whether there is a cointegration relationship or not in Toda-Yamamoto (1995) causality test (Ertekin & Kırca, 2017, p.57). For this reason, the analysis of the time-varying panel causality has been performed by taking the differences of the variables for period containing unit root. The number of windows has been determined as 15 quarters and a total of 31 periods have been examined. Furthermore, a lag of 1 has been applied to analyze the Dumitrescu and Hurlin causality. The country's parameter coefficients must be different for each country for this analysis. The homogeneity test results are shown in Table 5.

The homogeneity test results demonstrate that the slope coefficients of each country are not homogeneous. In this case, it has been found that the coefficients of the countries, which are a necessary condition for the analysis of causality, are different. In this instance, a causality analysis has been applied for

Table 5. Results of homogeneity test

Model	$\tilde{\Delta}$		$\tilde{\Delta}_{adj}$	
	Test Stat.	Prob.	Test Stat.	Prob.
Credit Growth – Current Account Deficit	18.052*	0.00	18.671*	0.00
Current Account Deficit – Credit Growth	17.591*	0.00	18.194*	0.00
Credit Growth – Real Effective Exchange Rate	21.420*	0.00	22.155*	0.00
Real Effective Exchange Rate – Credit Growth	20.411*	0.00	21.111*	0.00
Real Effective Exchange Rate – Current Account Deficit	12.375*	0.00	12.800*	0.00
Current Account Deficit – Real Effective Exchange Rate	12.035*	0.00	12.447*	0.00
Interest Rate – Current Account Deficit	23.805*	0.00	24.622*	0.00
Current Account Deficit – Interest Rate	21.179*	0.00	21.906*	0.00
Interest Rate – Real Effective Exchange Rate	14.643*	0.00	15.145*	0.00
Real Effective Exchange Rate – Interest Rate	16.950*	0.00	17.532*	0.00

Note: * Indicates heterogeneity at 5% significance.

each period and the figures for the periods have been formed according to the statistics obtained from the causality test. Probability values that are below the 10% level of significance indicate that there is a causality relation between variables for that period and the previous 14 quarters.

Figure 1 presents the results of the bilateral time-varying panel causality analysis for credit growth and current account deficit. According to Figure 1, statistically significant causality has been found in the periods of Q2 2006–Q4 2009, Q3 2006–Q1 2010, and Q4 2006–Q2 2010 from credit growth to current account deficit. Then, it seems that the causality disappeared until Q1 2012–Q3 2015. It can be seen that the causality from credit growth to current account deficit continues until the end of the study period, whereas a causality from current account deficit to credit growth is not the case in any period. The results show that the central banks' credit growth interventions as a macroprudential policy have affected the current account deficit.

Figure 2 displays the results from the time-varying panel causality analysis for both credit growth to real effective exchange rate and real effective exchange rate to credit growth. The figure shows that there is causality from real effective exchange rate to credit growth in a significant portion of the study period. Causality from the real effective exchange rate to the credit growth seems to have occurred in some periods, such as Q2 2006–Q4 2009, Q1 2008–Q3 2011, Q2 2011–Q4 2014.

The time-varying causality relationship between real effective exchange rate and current account deficit is presented in Figure 3. According to the figure, a causality from the real effective exchange rate to the current account deficit was detected during the period of Q2 2006–Q2 2012, but no findings of causality were obtained afterward, whereas a causality in the opposite direction was not detected in the analyzed period.

Figure 4 shows the time-varying causality relationship between interest rate—one of the most important instruments of central banks from the past to the present—and current account deficit. Figure 4 shows that the causality from the interest rate to current account becomes evident after the crisis in the analyzing period. Countries seem to have achieved their targets of influencing the current account deficit with interest rate policies.

Figure 1. Credit growth and current account deficit
Source: Author's calculations.
Note: Dashed line indicates Dumitrescu–Hurlin test statistical probability value for causality from credit growth to current account deficit while dotted line shows vice versa.

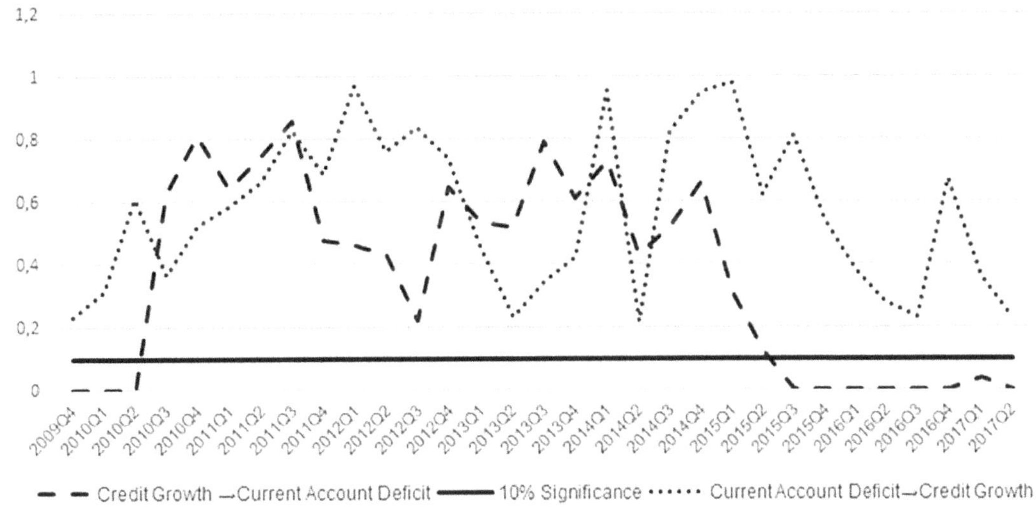

Figure 2. Credit growth and real effective exchange rate
Source: Author's calculation.
Note: Dashed line indicates Dumitrescu–Hurlin test statistical probability value for causality from credit growth to real effective exchange rate while dotted line shows vice versa.

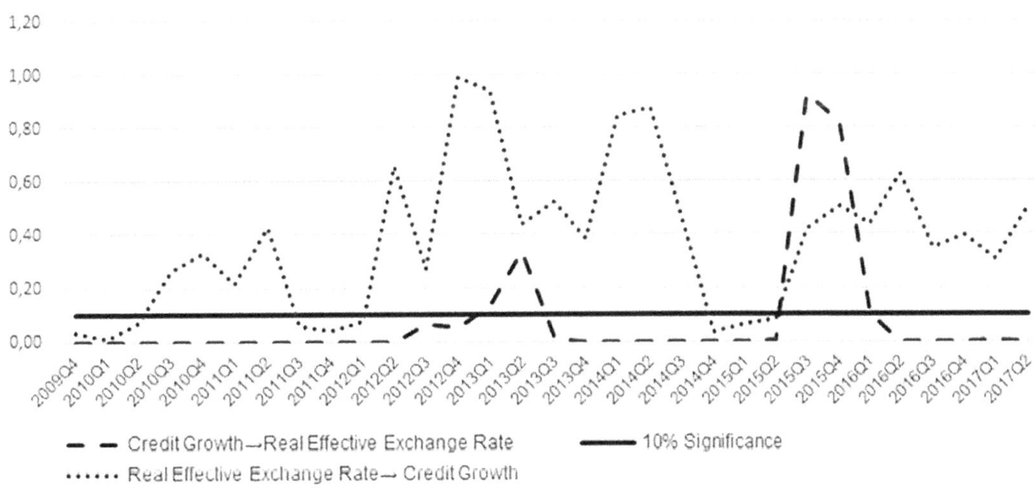

Figure 5 shows the results of the bilateral time-varying panel causality analysis between interest rate and real effective exchange rate. According to Figure 5, there is causality from interest rate to real effective exchange rate throughout most of the study period, and especially the post-crisis period. This result shows that interest rate policies are effective at controlling real effective exchange rates. The figure also shows that causality from real effective exchange rate to interest rate occurs before Q1 2014.

Figure 3. Real effective exchange rate and current account deficit
Source: Author's calculation.
Note: Dashed line indicates Dumitrescu–Hurlin test statistical probability value for causality from the real effective exchange rate to the current account deficit while dotted line shows vice versa.

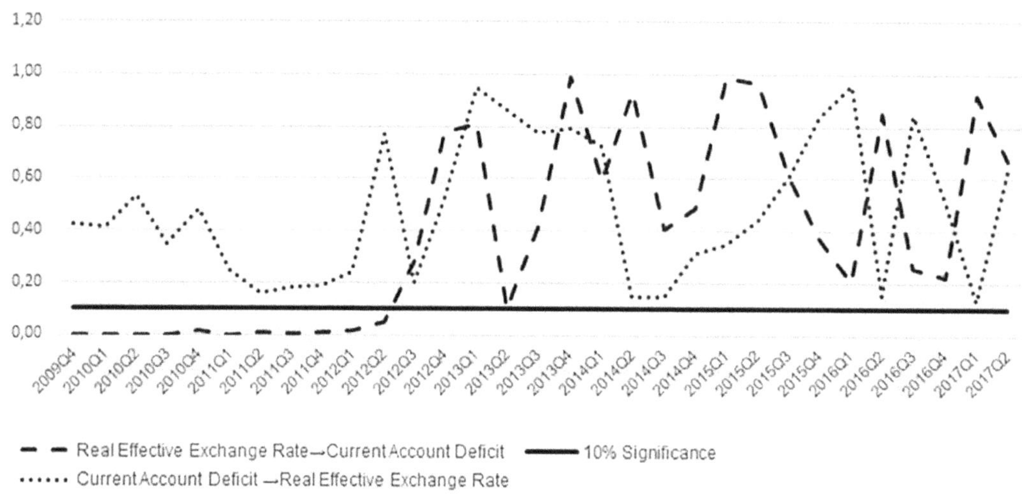

Figure 4. Interest rate and current account deficit
Source: Author's calculation
Note: Dashed line indicates Dumitrescu–Hurlin test statistical probability value for causality from the interest rate to the current account deficit while dotted line shows vice versa.

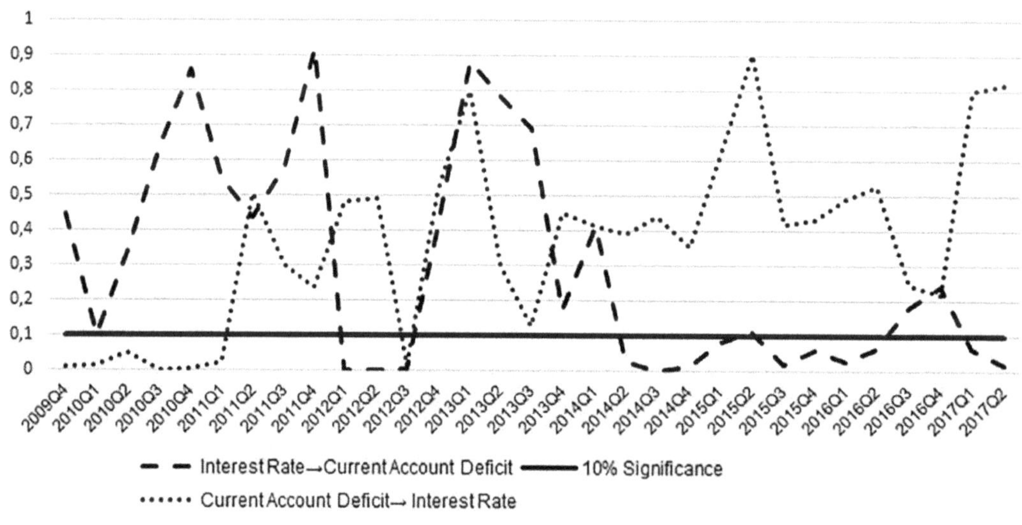

The results of this analysis show that the central bank policies of the studied countries ensure the intended aim of financial stability because a causality relationship between credit growth and current account deficit has been detected in the post-crisis period. It is possible to see a similar causality between interest rate and current account deficit. Thus, interest policies have been shown to affect the current account deficit, especially in the post-crisis period.

Figure 5. Interest rate and real effective exchange rate
Source: Author's calculation
Note: Dashed line indicates Dumitrescu–Hurlin test statistical probability value for causality from the interest rate to the real effective exchange rate while dotted line shows vice versa

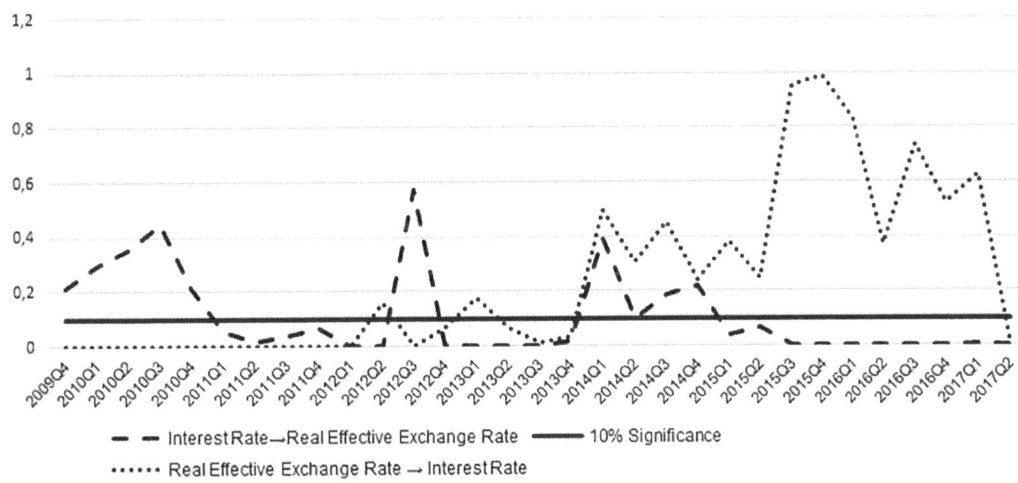

SOLUTIONS AND RECOMMENDATIONS

The concept of financial stability is often discussed with the concepts of avoiding financial crisis and managing systemic risk. Obviously, managing systematic risk means that the possibility of encountering a financial crisis decreases. Although the concept of financial stability has become more well-known in developed countries as a result of the recent crisis, emerging countries have come forward with wider macroeconomic policies to ensure their financial stability, because developing countries are more vulnerable to commodity price shocks and other risks, especially volatility in international capital flows. Exchange rate movements caused by short-term capital inflows and accelerated by an abundance of global liquidity have the potential to increase macroeconomic and financial imbalances, especially by disrupting the efficient distribution of resources in emerging economies. In fact, emerging economies are more complicated than developed economies when considering the process of overcoming a financial crisis. Although the role of central banks in financial stability was discussed frequently before the 2008 financial crisis, it has now become common for central banks to play an important role in ensuring financial stability after the crisis. Central banks are now using exchange rate management and monetary policy instruments, especially macroprudential policies, to reduce systematic risk. In this context, it can be said that effective monetary and macroprudential policies support each other. The policy composition can be seen as an appropriate strategy to mitigate the impact of short-term capital movements on macroeconomic imbalances, especially in countries with high current account deficits. It is necessary to take into account the main features of the structure of the financial system such as depth, the nature of capital movements, and the state of economic conjuncture while policies design against short-term capital movements. Besides, the institutional setup and to international coordination are necessary for efficient policies.

FUTURE RESEARCH DIRECTIONS

Many researches have been carried out about macroprudential policies until now but there is still room for future research. Subsequent studies should group countries with similar policy instruments together. In addition, an asymmetric impact response function, which has recently attracted attention in economic literature, can be used to assess the asymmetric effect.

CONCLUSION

In this study, the concept of financial stability has been examined in terms of central bank policy tools. Developing countries that have a current account deficit and use various policy instruments to ensure financial stability have been selected because the financial vulnerabilities of these economies are thought to be higher than in other developing countries. Argentina, Brazil, Chile, Colombia, Hungary, Indonesia, India, Mexico, Poland, South Africa, and Turkey have been examined in terms of credit growth, real effective exchange rate, interest rate, and current account deficit data. The time-varying panel causality method has been applied to determine whether post-crisis policies have had an effect on current account deficits compared to the pre-crisis period, and also to capture the possible changes in the post-crisis period with a lag of 1. The time-varying panel causality test results include similar findings to those reported in the literature. In other words, the control of credit growth of developing countries with macroprudential policies seems to have been successful during the analysis period. It is also possible to say that the central banks have affected the current account deficit after the crisis period by using interest rate as a policy tool. However, a causality from the real effective exchange rate to the current account deficit has not been established for the studied countries. This may be owing to the fact that exchange rate policies differ from country to country for the analysis period and therefore there is no universal effect across the studied countries. In sum, a meaningful causality relationship between the credit growth and the current account deficit especially after the crisis emphasizes the importance of "credit growth" as one of the main indicators for financial stability. In this case, credit growth may be in the forefront of the indicators that central banks should pay attention. Moreover, the second analysis shows that there is a causality relation over the almost whole period from credit growth to real effective exchange rate. These results can be considered as a preliminary evidence that credit growth may also be related to other macroeconomic variables. The results of the causality relation between interest rate and current account deficit show that the relationship becomes more clear especially after the crisis.

REFERENCES

Başçı, E., & Kara, H. (2011). Finansal İstikrar ve Para Politikası. *İktisat, İşletme ve Finans, 26*, 9-25.

Borio, C., & Drehmann, M. (2009). *Towards an Operational Framework for Financial Stability: 'Fuzzy' Measurement and Its Consequences* (Working Paper No. 284). BIS. Retrieved Dec 12, 2017, from https://www.bis.org/publ/work284.htm

Caruana, J. (2010). Grappling with systemic risk. *The Finsia Journal of Applied Finance*, *2*, 6-10. Retrieved Dec 5, 2017, from https://www.finsia.com/docs/default-source/jassa-new/jassa-2010/6_10.pdf?sfvrsn=bec1de93_6

Cerutti, E., Claessens, S., & Laeven, L. (2017). The Use and Effectiveness of Macroprudential Policies: New Evidence. *Journal of Financial Stability*, *28*, 203–224. doi:10.1016/j.jfs.2015.10.004

Chant, J., Lai, A., IIling, M., & Daniel, F. (2003). *Essays on Financial Stability* (Technical Report No. 95). Bank of Canada, Retrieved from https://www.bankofcanada.ca/wp-content/uploads/2010/01/tr95.pdf

Claessens, S., Ghosh, S. R., & Mihet, R. (2013). Macro-Prudential Policies to Mitigate Financial System Vulnerabilities. *Journal of International Money and Finance*, *39*, 153–185. doi:10.1016/j.jimonfin.2013.06.023

Clement, P. (2010). The term "macroprudential": Origins and Evolution. *BIS Quarterly Review*. Retrieved Feb 18, 2018, from https://www.bis.org/publ/qtrpdf/r_qt1003h.pdf

Criste, A., & Lupu, I. (2014). The Central Bank Policy Between the Price Stability Objective and Promoting Financial Stability. *Procedia Economics and Finance*, *8*, 219–225. doi:10.1016/S2212-5671(14)00084-7

Dedola, L., Karadi, P., & Lombardo, G. (2013). Global Implication of National Unconventional Policies. *Journal of Monetary Economics*, *60*(1), 66–85. doi:10.1016/j.jmoneco.2012.12.001

Dell'Ariccia, G., Igan, D., Laeven, L., Tong, H., Bakker, B., & Vandenbusseche, J. (2012). *Policies for Macrofinancial Stability: How to Deal with Credit Booms?* IMF Staff Discussion Note. Retrieved from https://www.imf.org/external/pubs/ft/sdn/2012/sdn1206.pdf

Dumitrescu, E. I., & Hurlin, C. (2012). Testing for Granger non-Causality in Heterogeneous Panels. *Economic Modelling*, *29*(4), 1450–1460. doi:10.1016/j.econmod.2012.02.014

Ertekin, M., & Kırca, M. (2017). Türkiye'de Kentleşme ve İktisadi Büyüme İlişkisinin Zamanla Değişen Nedensellik Analizi Yöntemiyle İncelenmesi. *Journal of Emerging Economies and Policy*, *2*(2), 44–63. Retrieved from http://dergipark.gov.tr/download/article-file/430140

European Central Bank (ECB). (2012). *Financial Stability Review, What is Financial Stability*? Financial Stability Report. Retrieved Feb 15, 2018, from https://www.ecb.europa.eu/pub/pdf/other/ecb.financialstabilityreview201711.en.pdf?7a775eed7ede9aee35acd83d2052a198

Financial Stability Board, International Monetary Fund and Bank for International Settlements. (2009). *Guidance to Assess the Systemic Importance of Financial Institutions, Markets and Instruments: Initial Considerations*. Washington, DC: IMF. Retrieved from https://www.imf.org/external/np/g20/pdf/100109.pdf

Foot, M. (2003). *What is 'Financial Stability and How Do We Get it?* The Roy Bridge Memorial Lecture. Financial Services Authority.

Galati, F., & Moessner, R. (2011). *Macroprudential Policy-A Literature Review* (Working Paper No. 337). BIS. Retrieved from https://www.bis.org/publ/work337.pdf

Gambacorta, L., Hoffman, B., & Peersman, G. (2014). The Effectiveness of Unconventional Monetary Policy at the Zero Lower Bound: A Cross- Country Analysis. *Journal of Money, Credit and Banking*, *46*(4), 615–642. doi:10.1111/jmcb.12119

Gertler, M., & Karadi, P. (2011). A Model of Unconventional Monetary Policy. *Journal of Monetary Economics*, *58*(1), 17–34. doi:10.1016/j.jmoneco.2010.10.004

Granger, C. (1969). Investigating Causal Relations by Econometric Models and Cross-Spectral Methods. *Econometrica*, *37*(3), 424–438. doi:10.2307/1912791

Group of Thirty (G-30). (2010). *Engancing Financial Stability and Resilience - Macroprudential Policy, Tools and Systems for the Future*. Retrieved from http://group30.org/images/uploads/publications/G30_EnhancingFinancialStabilityResilience.pdf

Hacker, R. S., & Hatemi-J, A. (2006). Tests for Causality between Integrated Variables Using Asymptotic and Bootstrap Distributions: Theory and Application. *Applied Economics*, *38*(13), 1489–1500. doi:10.1080/00036840500405763

Hannoun, H. (2010). *Towards A Global Financial Stability Framework*. (Working Paper No. 284). BIS. Retrieved from https://www.bis.org/speeches/sp100303.pdf

International Monetary Fund (IMF). (2011). *Macroprudential Policy: An Organizing Framework*. Washington, DC: IMF. Retrieved from https://www.imf.org/external/np/pp/eng/2011/031411.pdf

International Monetary Fund (IMF). (2013). *Key Aspects of Macroprudential Policy-Background Paper*. Washington, DC: IMF. Retrieved from https://www.imf.org/external/np/pp/eng/2013/061013C.pdf

Kawai, M., & Morgan, P. J. (2012). *Central Banking for Financial Stability in Asia* (Working Paper No. 377). ADBI. Retrieved from https://www.adb.org/sites/default/files/publication/156232/adbi-wp377.pdf

Kawai, M., & Takagi, S. (2008). *A Survey of The Literature on Managing Capital Inflows* (Discussion Paper No. 100). ADB. Retrieved from https://www.adb.org/sites/default/files/publication/156738/adbi-dp100.pdf

Knütter, R., Mohr, B., & Wagner, H. (2011). *The Effects of Central Bank Communication on Financial Stability: A Systematization of the Empirical Evidence* (Discussion Paper No.463). FernUniversitat in Hagen. Retrieved from http://www.fernuni-hagen.de/wirtschaftswissenschaft/download/beitraege/db463.pdf

Lim, C., Columba, F., Costa, A., Kongsamut, P., Otani, A., Saiyid, M., ... Wu, X. (2011). *Macroprudential Policy: What Instruments and How to Use Them? Lessons from Country Experiences. (Working Paper No. 238)*. Washington, DC: IMF. Retrieved from https://www.imf.org/external/pubs/ft/wp/2011/wp11238.pdf

Mishkin, F. S. (2000). *Financial Stability and the Macroeconomy (Working Paper No. 9)*. Central Bank of Iceland. Retrieved from http://hpi.uw.hu/pdf/wp9.pdf

Peersman, G. (2011). *Macroeconomic Effects of Unconventional Monetary Policy in The Euro Area. (Working Paper No. 1397)*. ECB. Retrieved from https://www.ecb.europa.eu/pub/pdf/scpwps/ecbwp1397.pdf?99ef78cb1aa613f60d8716d0db59b585

Pesaran, M. H. (2007). A Simple Panel Unit Root Test in the Presence of Cross-Section Dependence. *Journal of Applied Econometrics*, *22*(2), 265–312. doi:10.1002/jae.951

Schinasi, G. J. (2004). *Defining Financial Stability*. (Working Paper No. 04/187). Washington, DC: IMF. Retrieved from https://www.imf.org/en/Publications/WP/Issues/2016/12/31/Defining-Financial-Stability-17740

Shin, H. S. (2013). Adapting Macroprudential Approaches to Emerging and Developing Economies. In O. Canuto & S. R. Ghosh (Eds.), *Dealing with the Challenges of Macro Financial Linkages in Emerging Markets* (pp. 17–55). Washington, DC: World Bank.

The Central Bank of the Republic of Turkey (CBRT). (2015). *Finansal İstikrar - Türkiye'de Finansal İstikrar Gelişmeleri*. Ankara: CBRT.

Toda, H. Y., & Yamamoto, T. (1995). Statistical Inference in Vector Autoregressions with Possibly Integrated Processes. *Journal of Econometrics*, *66*(1-2), 225–250. doi:10.1016/0304-4076(94)01616-8

Tovar, C. E., Escribano, G. M., & Martin, V. M. (2012). *Credit Growth and the Effectiveness of Reserve Requirements and Other Macroprudential Instruments in Latin America* (Working Paper No. 12/142). Washington, DC: IMF. Retrieved from https://www.imf.org/external/pubs/ft/wp/2012/wp12142.pdf

ADDITIONAL READING

Akinci, O., & Olmstead-Rumsey, J. (2018). How Effective are Macroprudential Policies? An Empirical Investigation. *Journal of Financial Intermediation*, *33*, 33–57. doi:10.1016/j.jfi.2017.04.001

Amorello, L. (2018). *Macroprudential Banking Supervision & Monetary Policy: Legal Interaction in the European Union*. United Kingdom: Palgrave Macmillan; doi:10.1007/978-3-319-94156-1

Barwell, R. (2013). *Macroprudential Policy: Taming the Wild Gyrations of Credit Flows, Debt Stocks and Asset Prices*. United Kingdom: Palgrave Macmillan; doi:10.1057/9781137274465

Barwell, R. (2017). *Macroeconomic Policy after the Crash: Issues in Microprudential and Macroprudential Policy*. United Kingdom: Palgrave Macmillan; doi:10.1007/978-3-319-40463-9

Bruno, V., Shim, I., & Shin, H. S. (2017). Comparative Assessment of Macroprudential Policies. *Journal of Financial Stability*, *28*, 183–202. doi:10.1016/j.jfs.2016.04.001

Choi, S. M., Kodres, L., & Lu, J. (2018). *Friend or Foe? Cross-Border Linkages, Contagious Banking Crisis, and "Coordinated" Macroprudential Policies*. Washington, DC: IMF.

Krishnamurti, D., & Lee, Y. C. (2014). *Macroprudential Policy Framework: A Practice Guide*. Washington, DC: World Bank.

Lee, M., Gaspar, R., & Villaruel, M. L. (2017). *Macroprudential Policy Frameworks in Developing Asian Economies*. (Working Paper No. 510). Philippines: Asian Development Bank.

Mizen, P., Rubio, M., & Turner, P. (2018). *Macroprudential Policy and Practice*. United Kingdom: Cambridge University Press; doi:10.1017/9781108304429

KEY TERMS AND DEFINITIONS

Credit Boom: The quick expansion of lending by financial institutions.

Credit Easing: A monetary policy that a central bank aims to increase liquidity by purchasing financial assets or commodity.

Financial Stability: A condition in which financial system as a whole is flexible that the financial institutional system is resistant to economic shocks and fulfill their main functions properly.

Macroprudential Policies: Measures and regulations for the whole financial system to reduce systemic risk.

Price Stability: A situation in economy that the prices of goods and services change very slowly or don't change at all.

Short-Term Capital Flows: Private and official capital flows that carry maturities of less than 1 year in order to benefit from interest and foreign currency arbitrage.

Sudden Stop: An abrupt stop in the flow of foreign capital into an economy.

Systemic Risk: The possibility that an event at the industry or company level could trigger strong instability or collapse an entire economy.

Chapter 6
The Threat of Ponzi Schemes: An Asian Perspective

Sourya Mookerjee
Trinity College Dublin, Ireland

Varun Sardesai
Symbiosis International University (Deemed), India

ABSTRACT

A flood of corporate fraud has hit the market in the most recent decade, resuscitating attention to the impact of these incidences on corporate administration and stock market responses. Of particular relevance are Ponzi schemes that are considered practically the same as frauds. As more and more investors fall into the deep trap of Ponzi schemes, the situation is getting even more irrepressible. The reasons for a rise in the number of such swindles are mainly attributed to the breakdown in governance in different countries across the globe. This chapter dwells over the root causes of Ponzi schemes with specific focus on Asia and its developing regions. Through an in-depth study of the causes, the chapter looks to recommend possible solutions in mitigating the crisis, steps to ensure financial stability, and prevention of fraud risks.

INTRODUCTION

Ever since the 2008 global meltdown, there has been an inevitable focus on curbing financial misuse. Maintaining financial stability becomes an arduous task during times of uncertainty. Following the major events in 2016, including the Brexit vote in the United Kingdom and the Presidential Elections in the United States, the much-feared uncertainty for investors and financial authorities is back again. Such outcomes were earlier perceived to be a consequence of globalization, involving issues like immigration and trade, both of which play a pivotal role in determining the financial flows around the global economy. Thus, this makes the issue of maintaining financial stability in today's uncertain world even more pertinent. Studies conducted in recent years amplify how self-seeking aspirations and cupidity can make pioneers lose sight and validate unethical and deceitful practices (Bishop, 2013). A flood of corporate frauds has hit the market in the most recent decade, resuscitating attention to the impact of

DOI: 10.4018/978-1-5225-7208-4.ch006

these incidences on stockowner value, corporate administration and stock market responses (Bonini & Boraschi-Diaz, 2013). The reasons for a rise in the number of such swindles are mainly attributed to the breakdown in governance in different countries across the globe (Rajagopalan & Zhang, 2009).

Of particular relevance are Ponzi schemes that are considered practically the same as frauds (Gabel, 2011). It is named after Charles Ponzi, the con man who masterminded it for the first time (Zuckoff, 2006; Frankel, 2012; Lewis, 2015). Lewis (2015) explains that in a Ponzi scheme, the promoter of the plan guarantees financiers/investors an appealing quantifiable yield and announces it to be safe, yet in all actuality, no genuine venture happens. Individuals are urged to place resources into the plan, and the capital accumulated by the initial patrons is utilized for disbursing preliminary returns until investors feel confident and choose to contribute more. Numerous investors then persuade their kith and kin to join, boosting the inflow of assets. In the long run, in any case, the plan goes bust in light of the fact that the promoter begins to spend the cash too rapidly; old investors pull back their funds, and the consortium of new investors flees. If the plan lives longer, more investors reinvest their proceeds and it is less likely that anybody explores its niceties, thus permitting the felon to wheedle out and squander more funds (Levmore, 2012). Nonetheless, sooner or later, when such "pyramid" schemes get too huge, the promoter can't jack up enough capital from new investors to reimburse former investors, and many individuals lose their wealth (Sec.gov, 2013). Thus, a Ponzi plan can't work for eternity as the fund is a restricted asset and will dry in the long run; the malefactor must realize that the plan will in the end crumple due to failure to pull in new investors (Tanner, 2011).

"A Ponzi scheme is an investment fraud that pays existing investors with funds collected from new investors. Ponzi scheme organizers often promise to invest their money and generate high returns with little or no risk. But, the money is not invested at all. Instead, it is used to pay those who invested earlier and keeping the rest for themselves" (U.S. Securities and Exchange Commission, 2018). Ponzi plan is oft known as "pyramid scheme" because it is made viable by a pyramidal configuration in which funds from numerous investors at the base are utilized to pay exceptional yields to few investors at the pinnacle (Cortés, Santamaría & Vargas, 2016).

A growing phenomenon that was a corollary of the 2008 recession was fraud risk arising from Ponzi schemes. These schemes, by nature, are unrealistic entities for which investors devote their money in expectation of nearly doubling their initial investments within very short periods of time and with lowest possible risks associated (Investopedia, 2017). There is a correlation between the level of Ponzi schemes unraveled and the performance of our economy. When there is an economic slowdown, there are less people likely to invest and more people wanting to withdraw their invested capital, thereby leading to a collapse of such deceptive investments (Wilber, 2009). Although these schemes first came to be known by the notorious actions of Charles Ponzi, the Bernie Madoff Investment Scandal post the 2008 crisis, could not have made it anymore infamous. The $18 billion fraud by Madoff shook the world and proved to be an inflection point. It was after this event that the issue of Ponzi schemes became one of the prime focus for financial regulators, just as terror had become one of the main challenges for all governments post 9/11 (Rhee, 2009).

Ponzi schemes are among the most notorious investments prevailing in today's times. These schemes lure investors by offering attractive returns with little or no risk. Essentially, the success of a Ponzi scheme, such as the Bernie Madoff Scandal, majorly lies on the principal of 'more money coming in than going out'.

Let us look at an example to understand this concept more clearly. Company X Pvt. Ltd. starts a new scheme promising to double the investor's returns every year, with A being their first investor, putting in about $10,000. Table 1 will help deciphering the phenomenon step by step.

In Year 2, the company sends a statement showing the doubling of A's money to $20,000, whereas it is still at the $10,000 mark and the company has not invested it at all. On seeing this, A goes to meet his friends at their town club and briefs them about how efficiently he was successful in doubling his investments in such a short period of time. This incentivizes B to put in $15,000. The investors perceive the total investment with the company at $35,000, but it is much lesser at $25,000. In Year 3, the statement from the company reflects a doubling of the investments of both A and B, and both incentivize their mutual friend C to join the party. For personal reasons, A decides to withdraw his accumulated balance of $40,000 in this year. The company faces no problem in paying off A as the investment from B and C is sufficient enough to cover the costs. On successful receipt of the maturity by A, more and more investors like D and E put in their money perceiving this scheme as a legitimate business. As can be noticed, the scheme is not generating any revenue at all. It is just paying off old investors by the money coming in from the new one. Hence, as a result, in a Ponzi scheme, the actual value is much lesser than the perceived value, and this is what the Ponzi operators strive to conceal. This inference also solidifies the fact as to why most of the dubious Ponzi schemes collapse during recessionary periods, owing to unusually large withdrawals. This point shall be explained further in the chapter.

One of the major factors leading to a rise in such schemes is undoubtedly the dearth of financial knowhow and the structures governing them (Ulrich, 2008). To all veterans in the field of investing, characteristics of a Ponzi scheme would naturally appear suspicious and hence would have the possibility in successfully decoding its true nature. And this, as we can see, is only possible through a financially well-literate and financially well-informed population. According to a recent report by the Nigeria Watch International, 'herd mentality' is a prominent reason for investors falling into the trap, as they rather prefer investing by following their herd without evaluating the schemes pragmatically (International, Nigeria Watch, 2017). Similarly, a strong regulatory environment with well crystallized accountability and transparency can heavily crack down fraud schemes operating within the market.

Jacobs & Schain (2011) delve into the reasons for the inevitable attraction of the Ponzi schemes which entices not only lesser financial expertise, but also people from well informed backgrounds.

Table 1. Example of Ponzi scheme operation

	Year 1	Year 2	Year 3	Year 4
Investors				
A	10,000	20,000	40,000	-
B		15,000	30,000	60,000
C			35,000	70,000
D				100,000
E				150,000
Total Perceived Value	10,000	35,000	105,000	380,000
Total Actual Value	10,000	25,000	60,000	270,000

Source: Author

Even though the duped investors in the Charles Ponzi and the Bernie Madoff scandals consisted mainly uninformed investors, yet there was some proportion of the investors from well-educated background as well. Gullibility and influence are the major reasons for people falling prey to Ponzi schemes (Jacobs & Schain, 2011). The irrational approach of investors is underscored by emotions and family pressures while investing. The close bonding between families in China leads to similar investment patterns as too (The Economist, 2018). As a result, the investors fail to analyse the schemes nominally and end up being a victim of the herd mentality. This is the precise loophole which the Ponzi operators have been successful in employing.

The former Governor of the Reserve Bank of India, Raghuram Rajan, has emphasized the need to increase financial inclusion for curbing Ponzi schemes (ET Bureau, 2014). This statement comes in the wake of the Saradha Chit Fund scheme in West Bengal that shook the entire nation. According to reports by Fernandes (2013) and Kaul (2014), Saradha Group, centred in West Bengal, administered chit funds or collective investment schemes and enticed numerous investors to place their savings in its plans with massive promotions through lustrous pamphlets and the guarantee of exceptionally significant yields. The plans were straightforward and appealing. An investor could contribute a very small sum, even as less as Rs. 100, and there was no ceiling on the amount of deposit. Saradha assured incomprehensible returns – ranging from 15-50%. It likewise assured land and other gratifying privileges at all times, with the affirmation that in the event it fell short of keeping its promises, it would refund the money. There were contract agents who were hired for getting in more clients. Celebrities were roped in to endorse the schemes. The money collected from the investors was never utilized by the fund for productive investment in real estate (as asserted earlier) that could have generated sizeable returns, but was circulated amongst the investors; precisely, deposits mobilized from one were utilized to compensate the other. Thus, there was every probability that the funds would dry some day and they did. However, the foremost reason attributed for the fund to have survived longer than anticipated is the political affiliations of Saradha Group with the regional party that was then ruling in the state. As pointed by Kaul (2014), Saradha, tried its best to prove its authenticity by furnishing capacious documents other than those sought by capital market regulator Securities and Exchange Board of India (SEBI). Nevertheless, the party ended when SEBI asked Saradha to submit digital evidences and found a number of dubious transactions in its several dealings into alternative forms of business. Eventually, Saradha met the fate of a typical Ponzi scheme – a collapse. Saradha deviated from ethical obligations on more occasions than one by not keeping its promises to the investors. A scam involving nearly 25 billion rupees caused a loss to nearly 17 lakh investors that ran into several crores (Roy, 2015). Few investor suicides were reported as well according to revelations from a member within SEBI, who had been closely following the case (Shrivastava and Chakraborty, 2014). In a conference held by the state secretaries and financial regulators of India, it was decided to enable the free flow of information throughout the economy and the banking system to mitigate this fraud risk arising from Ponzi schemes. The conference also decided to develop a website dedicated solely for the benefit of investors and publish regular updates about dubious schemes operating in the market. The chairman of the Securities and Exchange Board of India urged the states to enact the Depositors' Investor Protection Act and further solidify the enforcement mechanism.

Deason, Rajgopal, & Waymire (2015) conducted an empirical analysis to ascertain the characteristics of people falling prey to Ponzi frauds. One of the major conclusions of the paper recognizes the ignorant and complacent behaviour of investors. Owing to less financial knowhow among many investors, they often rely on word of mouth rather than facts. This was the prominent phenomenon during the Bernie Madoff investment scandal. The paper analyses the case of the United States of America where there is considerably greater level of financial inclusion. But despite being in the formal arena financial markets, people continued being attracted to dubious investment schemes in America, which kept flourishing and growing unchecked. This is where the role of the financial regulators came into question. Thus, the conclusion by (Deason, Rajgopal, & Waymire, 2015) reasserts the importance for financial literacy, financial inclusion, and financial regulation as among the prime components for ponzi schemes.

Monroe, Carvajal, & Pattillo (2010) outline the impact Ponzi schemes have had on developing countries. The paper argues that monitoring Ponzi schemes require strong and effective regulatory framework, which the developing countries lack.

The paper has presented Table 2 above showing the extent of impact Ponzi schemes have had on developing economies. The Ponzi collapse in Jamaica had costed the economy 12.5 percent of its GDP whereas Albania suffered a whopping 79 percent of its GDP to Ponzi schemes. This is the reason why the paper emphasizes pertinently over the issue of Ponzi schemes. It can also be noticed from the table that most of the schemes had collapsed during recession years of 2007-08, thereby justifying the earlier explanation of the author in the explanation of Ponzi scheme concept. However, it can be noticed that there has been no mention of any Asian country in the data, which hosts the largest cohort of developing nations in the area. The two biggest developing economies of the world, China and India, are in this region and it is notoriously famous for the magnitude of Ponzi schemes prevalent in their regions. But unfortunately, there is complete absence of a centralized data on the incidences of Ponzi schemes in the Asian region, and the only reliable source prevailing are the newspaper reports.

In Asia, Ponzi schemes have become a growing menace. Owing to lesser financial knowhow especially within developing economies, the problem makes the proliferation of Ponzi schemes even more endemic. The Saradha Chit Fund Scandal in the Eastern Indian State of West Bengal to the Yucheng Group Scandal in China simply depicts the enormity of the problem. Being predominantly cash based economies, Ponzi operators in countries like India and China easily get away with such frauds without providing their investors with any verifiable tracking pedagogue of their money (ET Bureau, 2012). Facts and figures from Standard & Poor, World Bank database, and Bank of International Settlements portray the relation between the level of financial integrity and the incidence of Ponzi schemes between developed and developing regions in Asia. It is reported by prominent media sources that the Yucheng Group Scandal of China was estimated at a whopping $7.6 billion, yet there has hardly been much coverage on the incident (Ning, 2017). However, there are now comparatively more measures being taken by

Table 2. Snapshot of Ponzi breakouts in developing countries

Country	Name(s)	Year of Collapse	(U.S. Dollars)	(Percent of GDP)
Antigua and Barbuda	Stanford Financial Group	2009	8 billion	N.A.
Grenada	SGL Holdings	2008	30 million	5
Jamaica	OLINT, Cash Plus, World Wise	2008	1 billion	12.5
Colombia	DRFE, DMG,	2008	1 billion	0.4
Lesotho	MKM Burial Society	2007	42 million	3
Albania	VEFA, Gjallica, Kamberi	1997	1.7 billion	79

Source: Monroe, Carvajal & Pattillo (2010)

authorities to prevent the rise of any further swindling of investors' money in countries like India. With the Digital India initiative, Pradhan Mantri Jan Dhan Yojana, mandatory KYC norms, all aimed for even greater financial inclusion by the Indian government, things are looking relatively optimistic. But there still lies a loophole even from a hierarchical aspect as evident from the recent tussle between the SEBI and the State Governments. The SEBI intends to abrogate from being the sole regulator of financial operators including Ponzi schemes, and is passing the buck over to the State Governments (Rajagopal, 2016). This evidently presents the obstacles towards managing any deep-rooted problem as the Ponzi schemes flourishing unchecked in developing Asian economies like India and China.

Keeping this objective in mind, the chapter shall now embark to study the specific factors of financial literacy, financial inclusion, and financial regulation from an Asian perspective. After a thorough analysis, the paper intends to analyse and discuss the prevailing loopholes, and further suggest the way forward for the region towards attaining the desired goals.

BACKGROUND

The incidences of Ponzi schemes have gone up in recent years and so has been their revelation in published works. Johnson (2012) reports of a Ponzi scheme in the U.S. wherein regardless of many cautioning signs, none of the impending guardians and the watchdog intervened to safeguard the interests of investors. Fletcher and Herrmann (2012) bring out instances of corrupt practices across the world by focusing on their extent and influence as well as actions to counter them. According to Deason et al. (2015), Ponzi schemes are more prone to happen in states where the populace is innately gullible and naïve, and where there are limited options for native investment. The masterminds of Ponzi schemes are shrewd onlookers of the financial system, who are well acquainted with the potential unexploited markets and people's intense urge to move up the social ladder, are adept to take benefit of prevalent circumstances to make themselves wealthier – explicitly manipulating the financially excluded segment of the population (Krige, 2012). Considering the amount of loss to investors, Christensen (2012) suggests "rescission and restitution" approach to be adopted by the legal system for imparting justice to the victims of Ponzi schemes; victims should be compensated by the breaching party according to the losses incurred by them.

Ever since the origination of Ponzi schemes by its first architect, Charles Ponzi, this fraudulent activity has been growing at an increasing pace. In the article reported by Altman (2008), it states the series of the biggest Ponzi schemes in the financial world that have taken place post the Charles Ponzi scandal. The Madoff Scandal amounted to a whopping $50 billion which was pulled off very tactically by the former NASDAQ chairman Bernard Madoff. The intention was to conceal the insolvency of his company by paying off the new coming investors with the proceeds received from the earlier entrants. However, this cycle did not last long as once the markets began to tumble, investors increasingly withdrew from the schemes, and the whole business collapsed like a house of cards. The article also goes on to dethrone Charles Ponzi as the 'founder' of this 'malicious phenomenon. In the year 1899, a New York based grifter named William Miller, had allegedly duped $1 million from investors, amounting to approximately $25 million in today's dollars. Miller used to promise an astonishing return of '520 percent' to his investors. After his racket was exposed by newspapers, he was sentenced to ten years in prison. So, as it can be noticed, the malevolent Ponzi schemes originated earlier than history herself. Even though the Charles Ponzi scandal is infamously credited to be its founder in 1930s, the phenomenon existed much earlier from 1899. However, the menace of Ponzi schemes began much later than the deportation of Charles Ponzi in 1934 to his native in Italy. During the financial boom of the 1980s and 1990s, by developing increasingly complex investment models, traders were able to con thousands of investors during this period. In 1985, a San Diego based currency trader had fleeced more than 1,000 investors with investments worth $85 million. In 1990, there was another major Ponzi scandal in Florida, which duped more than 20,000 people with investments to the tune of $500 million. However, this phenomenon slowly began to spread away from United States to elsewhere in the world. With the fall of the Soviet Union and the independence attained by the newly formed Eastern European nations, there was an urge to get rich quickly by citizens of these new sovereignties to enjoy the freedom from communist rule. Owing to this, people of these regions started investing heavily into schemes that promised attractive rates of return, and Eastern Europe ended up losing a breathtaking $1.2 billion into Ponzi schemes by 1996. Hence, this article pertinently shows the spread of the Ponzi venom across the world, which was initially a phenomenon predominant in the United States. Thus, this gave commencement to Ponzi schemes as a worldwide threat.

Coming over to Africa, the article by Mahama (2016) explores the correlation between financial literacy and Ponzi schemes in the nation of Ghana. The nation's financial system has been hit by a slew of financial frauds arising out of collapse of Ponzi schemes. As like in any other nation, the society in Ghana started pointing fingers to all possible culprits in the system. Some blamed the careless attitude of the financial regulators in Ghana, while others blamed the greed of the investors devoting their money into such schemes blindly without thorough introspection of the nature. The article further goes on to highlight several points to be remembered before investing into such schemes. The investors should be cautious about the phrase 'high returns and no risk'. An investment, by nature, is bound to entail some risk or the other, else it is not an investment at all. The article also points fingers towards the nature of 'herd mentality' in Ghana. In many developing nations like Ghana, where there is a lack of financial knowledge, people often tend to go by word of mouth and follow the herd. As a result, when the con is pulled, it becomes a domino effect. Further, the author highlights that investors much watch out for consistent returns. In a world today with continuously fluctuating market, it is nearly impossible for any investment model in achieving the same level of return for a varied period. Hence, if the investment is continuously reaping good returns, it must be investigated, and the source of such proceeds must be ascertained. The author concludes the article by underlining the need of financial literacy in Ghana and across the developed world. Financial literacy is the tool that can empower people in making rational decisions towards investments, savings, and insurance. The void of financial literacy can lead to bad financial decisions which in turn affect the financial health the individual and the economy. No matter how strong the regulation may be, if the society is not financially equipped to make the correct decisions, even the most stringent laws may stand to be helpless during need of the hour.

An urge by Solli (2017) in the journal underscores the insufficiency present today in the market to protect investors from arising frauds. The write up gives an example of the series of Ponzi schemes in Albania that shook the economy in the 1990s. The Ponzi schemes in Albania were estimated to be a whopping 79 percent of the nations' GDP. This further led to a collapse of the state government and civil unrest following it. Similarly, the Ponzi schemes in the Caribbean too were nothing insignificant, with Jamaica being hit by Ponzi schemes worth 25 percent of its GDP in 2008-09, and Grenada losing 5 percent of its GDP to Ponzi schemes in the same period. The article further goes on to blame the technology and digital world which have catalyzed the spread of Ponzi schemes across all regions of the world. It emphasizes the need for regulators to step up the digital market monitoring efforts.

In an interview to Press Trust of India (2014) by Ashish Kumar Chauhan, Managing Director and CEO of Bombay Stock Exchange, he suggests that financial regulation will be the key to curbing the menace of Ponzi schemes in rural areas. Even 70 years after the nations' independence, formal finance like the banks, insurance, mutual funds, stocks, are yet to reach the rural pockets of the country. This leaves the rural people of no other option but to get lured away by fraudulent Ponzi operators offering attractive returns and taking advantage of the monopoly. A presence of a bank can help to mitigate this phenomenon by immediately reporting the operations of such fraudulent activities to the top authorities in their region. Chauhan also goes on to blame the city-centric attitude of the financial institutions which has also exacerbated this problem, leaving less options for the rural people. C.S.Mohapatra, Adviser to the Department of Economic Affairs in the Ministry of Finance, also commented in the article by defining Ponzi schemes as an occurrence due to the loopholes in the laws and regulations of the system. Hence, the regulators must get better at adopting innovative standards.

Coming now to Asia, the Ponzi schemes have been a truly uncontrollable menace, In the article by Chow (2018), it explores the reasons for China falling repeatedly to malicious Ponzi schemes despite increase in crackdowns. The article states that not everyone in China is attached to the magnificent growth story of the country. The wealthiest one percent of the country own a third of the nations' wealth, whereas the poorest 25 percent own just 1 percent of the nation's wealth. This creates a desperation among the poor and desolated regions in China to earn more wealth by joining companies operating a Ponzi racket. The employees are reportedly 'brainwashed' towards believing the benevolence of the opportunity and incentivized into devoting long working hours. An anonymous labourer from Xinhua province of China reveals his experience while working for a Ponzi firm. During his work, he noticed increasing number of workers for the company but hardly any profits or revenue being generated. Later it was revealed that the company kept running so long on devotions and capital only without accruing any actual income, thereby leaving thousands of employees out of jobs and millions of investors duped. This is just one story from thousands of such instances in China, or rather in Asia itself.

Being crowned the world's economic powerhouse, Asia is the fastest growing region in the world. It is home to 60 percent of the global population, with China and India together accounting for 37 percent of the total global population alone (The World Bank, 2018). But unfortunately, there is an infamous rise in some activities that the region cannot be proud of, and among them is the Ponzi schemes. As can be inferred from the preceding paragraphs, there are a variety of factors that lead to a growth in the Ponzi schemes. But the major factors among them include the financial literacy, financial inclusion, and financial regulation. It is often argued that demographics in Asia is much different from the ones around the world. The mechanism which was a success in say Europe may not give the same result in the case of Asia. In Asia, there is a vast economic, cultural, and social disparity. The average population in Asia is much larger than rest of the world. It is almost certain that tackling the menace of Ponzi schemes will entail a multilateral approach rather than a unilateral one. This implies that multilateral approaches must be adopted in each of the forty-eight nations of Asia to tackle the problem of Ponzi schemes (The World Bank, 2018).

MAIN FOCUS OF THE CHAPTER

On analyzing the background of the topic, the main factors which determine the level of Ponzi and fraudulent schemes are financial literacy, fiscal inclusion, financial regulation, of Ponzi cases. There seems to be an evident correlation between the three mentioned factors with the incidence. Unfortunately, there have not been sufficient literature and discussion over the level of these factors in the context of Asia and relating it with the incidence of Ponzi schemes. This chapter shall now discuss the factors with specific emphasis over the Asian context.

Financial Literacy

Financial Literacy is a combination of awareness, knowledge, skill, attitude, and behaviour necessary to make sound financial decisions and ultimately achieve individual financial wellbeing. (OECD, 2011)

Financial literacy has been eminently proven as one of the major causes for people falling into Ponzi traps. The financial literacy of a person corresponds more to the environment he or she resides in. This comprises of a variety of factors, namely financial inclusion in the society, the general literacy level, and socio-economic development in the society. An interesting study by Yoshina, Morgan, & Wignaraja (2015) of the Asian Development Bank, explicitly states that many a times, the financial literacy also depends on the economic experiences of their nations and states. For example, an average Japanese citizen would be able to elaborate on inflation than a Swedish citizen whose country has always held a track record of negative inflation. Similarly, an average Indian citizen will be able to able to answer better on the aspect of demonetization than citizens of any other country. This one-time phenomenon is possibly the most popular concept of Economics in India today than many other concepts taking place their daily lives. This is natural to occur, as not everyone is a student of economics, and learn about other disciplines only when they have faced an experience pertaining to it. According to the report, the general level of financial literacy in the Asia-Pacific is lower than their counterparts in the West. Many of the Western nations, especially the Nordic countries, conduct a mandatory financial literacy session every week from the school level itself. Whereas, in Asia, more impetus is given towards their own respective specialization only.

Financial literacy has become an increasingly important discipline for individuals to be aware of. Everyone, irrespective of their profession, work hard towards just one motivation, that is earning money and building their financial resources. People also resort to investing into various schemes, and sometimes become victims of Ponzi schemes too. Without any fault of theirs they still face the brunt. There are numerous reasons as to why a person may not be able to attain the expected level of financial literacy, and they are certainly not to be blamed for that. Hence, this chapter strongly emphasizes the need for financial literacy among investors and individuals to prevent them from getting lured by the malicious Ponzi schemes. It should also be noted that Ponzi operators find the lack of financial literacy as the main weakness to be taken advantage of.

In the Asian pacific, countries of Singapore and New Zealand fare highly in the financial literacy index whereas the parameters are still lacking in India and Indonesia. It is noticed that the South Asian region predominantly occupies the lower half of the ranking index for financial education in Asia. As reported by Maierbrugger (2015), financial education in the South Asian region is among the lowest in the world. This region includes countries like India which hosts one-fifth of the world's population.

The study conducted by Wingfield (2016) analyses several factors which affect the financial literacy discrepancies, using quantitative techniques and empirical models. The target sample included university students from diverse fields and backgrounds. Factors considered are gender, race, religion and family income. On running the regression model, the output turned to show a statistical significant effect on

Figure 1. MasterCard literacy financial scorecard, 2013
Source: (Yoshina, Morgan, & Wignaraja, 2015)

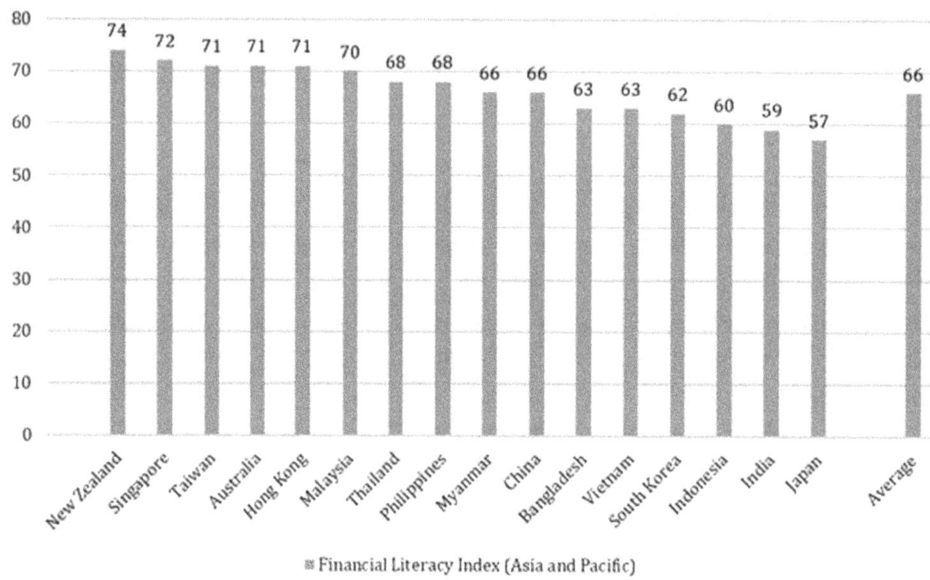

financial literacy of the student with any difference in the variables considered. The paper in its conclusion duly acknowledges qualitative and diverse factors to be a key cause in the differences towards financial literacy levels.

Similarly, using the pedagogue of study employed by Wingfield (2016), the causes for financial literacy discrepancies in the Asian continent can be deciphered to quite an extent. First, the level of demography in Asian nations is much higher when compared with the European countries and the United States. It is a much arduous task for the Asian governments in implementing and ensuring a level of financial literacy per capita with the Western nations as their benchmark. For example, New Zealand and Singapore both top the list of financial literacy in Asia-Pacific, whereas densely populated nations of India and Bangladesh occupy the bottom rankings. Even though in absolute terms, India may carry a greater number of financially educated individuals than Singapore, but in percentage terms it always loses out owing to its humungous population that is factored in. Second, Asian countries lack the implementation of a dedicated national strategy towards financial education specifically. The policies of education and literacy adopted in many nations do miss out hugely in incorporating the financial aspect of learning. Furthermore, in a federal system of government, there arises varied statistics within the country itself. For example, in the federal structure of India, with States having considerable autonomy towards framing education policies for their respective jurisdictions, there occurs a significant gap in literacy rates. The level of literacy in the southern Indian state of Kerala with over ninety percent beats many of the Western nations itself. Whereas, northern Indian states of Bihar and Uttar Pradesh constitute the lowest literate regions in the world. Such a disproportionate statistic occurs within the country itself. Hence, implementing a financial literacy scheme in a federal structure like India entails a daunting challenge which many a times is tough to undertake.

The socio-economic structure of the society is another factor which leads to a lower financial literacy rate in some areas of Asia. Anyone familiar with India and its societal strata can certainly expect such a result. Females in India by custom were not allowed to venture outside and she was meant to stay within closed doors and serve the husband. It was even considered a taboo to educate a girl child. However, things are changing now and the attitudes towards women is increasingly moving towards a positive direction. But this positive change is only limited as they are more noticed in the urban cities and towns of India. There are millions of Indian women in rural areas of the country who still suffer under this stereotypical hostility.

In neighbouring China too, there is a huge disproportion of literacy levels between the Western Tibet and Eastern regions of the country. The financial hubs of Shanghai, Shenzen, Beijing, etc. continue to prosper and reap the fruits of China's economic growth whereas the mountainous and arid regions of Tibet have been perpetually neglected by the Chinese regime. And as one can expect, the level of literacy in Tibet is much less than Mainland China. Yoshina, Morgan, & Wignaraja (2015) correctly points out that education policies in Asia are less broad based and more marginalized and restricted to some communities only. Hence, unless the Asian economies seriously consider the urgent need to strengthen their financial literacy policy and develop a more inclusive policy on the same, Ponzi schemes shall continue to flourish, and more victims shall fall into this trap.

Fiscal Inclusion

Financial inclusion is the process of ensuring access to appropriate financial products and services needed by vulnerable groups such as weaker sections and low income groups at an affordable cost in a fair and transparent manner by mainstream institutional players. (OECD, 2011)

As was discussed comprehensively on the financial literacy levels in Asia, there is another significant factor causing the low performance for the continent, and that is the level of fiscal inclusion. It is a common saying that the human nature as such learns lesser from the from the four walls in the classroom and more from the real world outside. The same applies for the financial system too. The more humans interact and engage with the financial system, the more efficient and knowledgeable they can grow about it. Unfortunately, in some areas, even this factor is lacking along with education infrastructure which makes matters even more worse. Financial inclusion indicates the level of financial penetration in a country, whether be it in the form of banks or lending institutions, so on and so forth.

Several parts of the world, especially the less developed and developing nations lack in financial penetration. For example, even today in many areas of India, the nearest bank is sometimes situated at about fifteen to twenty kilometres, and in some cases even longer. This often prevents people from depositing their savings into the bank through which they could have earned some interest. Instead, owing to less knowhow, they are attracted by dubious schemes offering to doubt their investments in a very brief period, and that is how the victims are lured towards such schemes. The report by Ayyagiri & Beck (2015) puts Singapore, South Korea, Hong Kong on the top of the table. The report puts the developing Asian region at 26.7% adults holding a bank account with a formalized institution. This level is much lower than the global median of 40%. In the developing Asian region, there are only 17.7 ATMs per 100,000 adults and 10.6 commercial branches per 100,000 adults. This statistic too is significantly lower than the European average of 51.6 ATMs per 100,000 adults and 23.3 commercial banks per 100,000 adults. The enterprises in developing Asian region holding current and savings account stood at 84.24%, close to the African subcontinent which had 83.94% of its enterprises holding a current or savings account. The figure for European enterprises however stood at 92.13%. Within developing Asia, the East Asian and Pacific region had a financial use by its firms at a rate of 91.80% and 94.56% respectively. Whereas in South Asia, it was 79.72%. It must be remembered that the regions with higher ranking figures also correspond to the countries holding the upper rankings in the financial inclusion index.

The paper also dwells upon the reasons as to why the numbers are lower for the Asian region. An overwhelming 76.22% of the respondents chose 'lack of money' as their main reason for not depositing their money with a bank. Every savings account entailed a minimum balance to be maintained, which is often higher than the money the rural earners can save after meeting their basic requirements. Both 'Transportation' and 'Too Far Away' are the next following reasons for not depositing their money. This reasoning is completely justified given the meagre amount of money that the rural earners are able to save, and a significant chunk of that share as well would be spent in travelling to the nearest bank, which

Figure 2. ATMs per 100,000 adults
Source: (Ayyagiri & Beck, 2015)

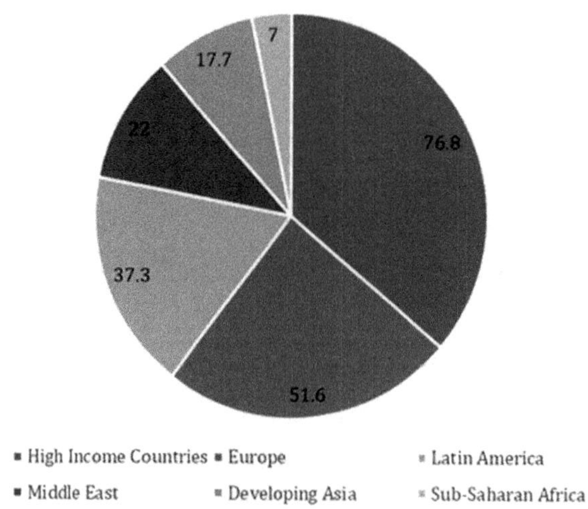

**For a more accurate representation see the electronic version.*

Figure 3. Bank branches per 100,000 adults
Source: (Ayyagiri & Beck, 2015)

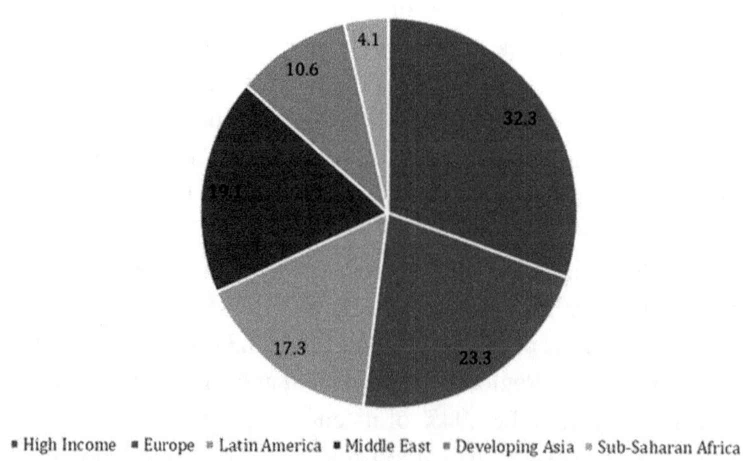

**For a more accurate representation see the electronic version.*

is often miles away. It should be noted that 'Religious Reasons' at 6.16% occupies the lowest cause of not depositing money with the bank. It clearly indicates that people are today more willing to break their superstitions and devote their money to formalized financial institutions but owing to the structural barriers in undertaking the same, they are unable to do so.

Not only individuals, but also firms operating within the rural and lesser developed areas of developing Asia find it difficult to use formal financial institutions. Being a predominantly cash based economic system, 55% of the firms felt 'no need' of maintain a formalized bank account. Following this was the reason of 'unfavourable interest rates'. In such areas, there is a high prevalence of private money lenders and microfinance institutions which charge a reasonable rate of interest. Hence, all these factors keep the firms from accessing the formal financial institutions.

India is a country with a major chunk of the population residing in rural areas having restricted access to banking facilities (The Economic Times, 2015). As an outcome, the habits of thrift, economy, prudence and saving are less developed among the people. The financially excluded are also not learned enough to make the right financial choices (UNDP India, 2012). Due to limited financial knowledge and lack of alternative investment options, it becomes easy for swindlers to lure the people for investing in Ponzi schemes by promising them amazingly high returns; no wonder India ranks among top three countries with respect to shadow banking (Shrivastava and Chakraborty, 2014; Sinha, 2016).

However, there has been a gradual improvement in India towards financial inclusion. Post the last census in 2011, The Reserve Bank of India (2013) presented its assessment report on the financial inclusion in India. According to the report, as early as 1951, 69.7% of the rural households had access to informal sources and a mere 3.9% had access to formal sources. Over the decades, that figure changed dramatically. As of 2011, 58.4% of the rural households held access to formal institutions and only 31.2% had to informal institutions.

Figure 4. Barriers to account penetration in developing Asia, 2011
Source: (Ayyagiri & Beck, 2015)

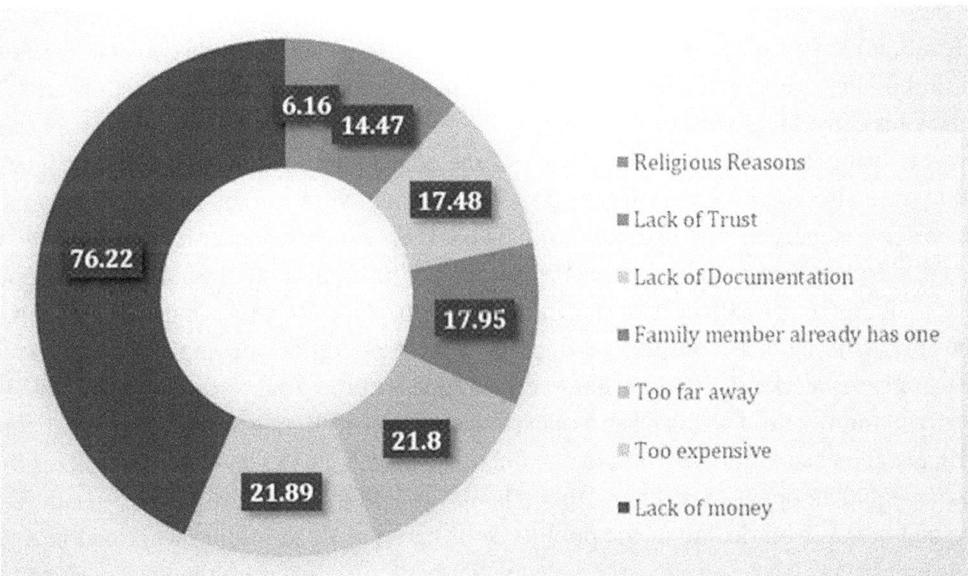

**For a more accurate representation see the electronic version.*

Figure 5. Access to formal and informal sources of credit by rural households in India
Source: (The Reserve Bank of India, 2013)

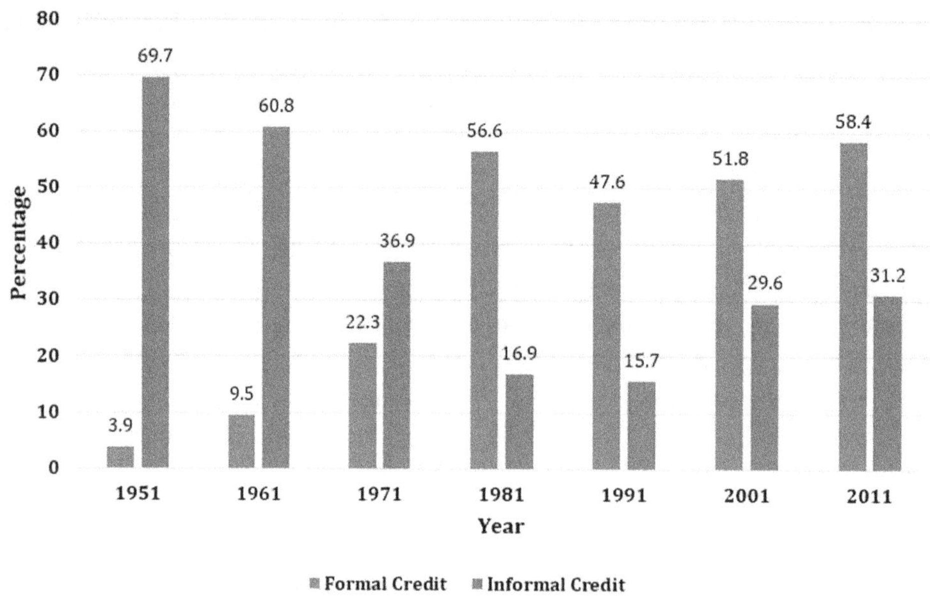

This is certainly a tectonic shift towards a positive and inclusive direction. But, there still is a long way to go. One can notice that there still lies around 10% of the rural households in India that do not have access to any financial institutions at all. The Government of India and the Reserve Bank of India have launched a mandatory provision in their policies and budget for strengthening the financial inclusion and financial literacy in the country. As stated in the article titled 'Role of banks in financial inclusion in India', the banks prove to be a key player in achieving the required objectives. Many parts of the country, especially in Gujarat and Maharashtra, evolved the cooperative banking system. This system of banks involved much lesser hassle for the rural inhabitants towards opening their bank account, and as a result, it led to a widespread access to banking facilities across these two states. But not every region of the country was benefitted with such a system. The current Prime Minister of India, Narendra Modi, during his early days in office had launched the Pradhan Mantri Jan Dhan Yojana. The aim of this scheme was to bring the entire rural population of the country into formalized banking. The poor and rural people were also given the option to open a bank account with zero balance. This scheme went on to set a record of opening 3 crore (30 million) new bank accounts within a span of ten days. Guinness Book of World Records designated this performance as 'The highest number of bank accounts opened in one week' (India Today, 2015). Along with these new bank accounts, a total of 65,000 crore rupees were deposited with the banks despite the poor having the option of opening a zero-balance account. This is yet another evidence which describes the willingness of the rural communities in Asia to join the formalized banking system. The Jan Dhan Yojana has truly been a huge success and the most popular case study of financial inclusion for the world today. But as Newton's second law of motion states that 'Every action has an equal an opposite reaction', this schemes too was not spared from criticism. Opposition parties argued the over-burdening of the public-sector banks with additional workload in a short span of time. Another significant point to note is that while bank officials were themselves deployed on the ground to facilitate the opening of these bank accounts, the later follow-up by the new customers posed to be a problem (Unnikrishnan, 2016). There is still an infrastructure deficit in the rural areas with the nearest bank branch being miles away, and hence it is still preventing people from accessing their bank accounts. For the time being, they just have an account registered under the scheme for the government to boast about without any actual utility owing to continuing barriers.

Financial Regulation

Financial Regulation is the supervision of financial markets and institutions. Financial regulations necessitate financial institutions to certain requirements, restriction and guidelines. The primary purpose of a financial regulation is to maintain the integrity of the financial system. Financial regulation protects investors, maintain orderly markets and promote financial stability. (US Legal, 2018)

The Asian Financial Crisis during the years 1997-98 highlighted the urgent need for stricter financial regulation in the region. It was a crisis that crippled the Southeast Asian economies, with many of them declaring emergency and bankruptcy with the international institutions. The 2008 Global Financial Crisis in the United States of America portrayed that this is a shared problem faced by nations all over the world. Financial regulations are made based on the nature of the economy and the problem that are needed to be addressed. For example, the Federal Reserve in the United States may not find it very difficult to reduce interest rates whereas India, having control of inflation as its main objective, the Reserve Bank of India maintains a very tight control of the interest rates over the fiscal years. In this context, Kawai & Morgan (2014) presents a study analyzing the regulatory framework between the countries in the European Union and Asia.

Figure 6. Regulatory quality in European Union (Percentile Ranking)
Source: (Kawai & Morgan, 2014)

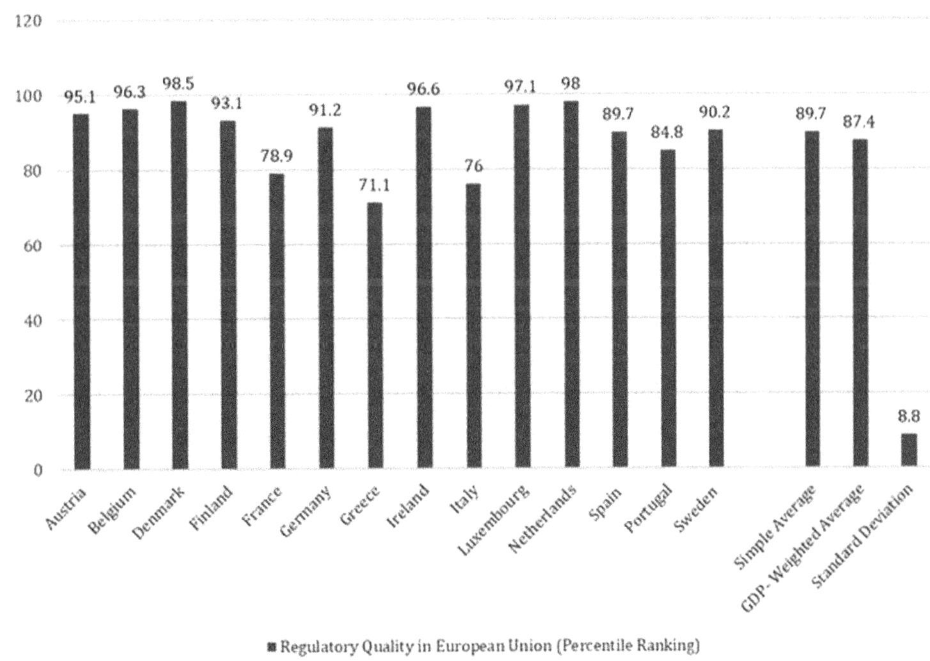

The paper notes a considerable lower quality of fiscal regulation in Asia than it is in the European Union. The percentile average ranking for Europe stands at 89.7 whereas for Asia, it is merely 58.1. Ironically, the highest percentile rank obtained is by an Asian country, which is 100 obtained by Singapore followed by Australia at 97.1. India stands at 34 and China 43.5. However, there also lies a greater level of diversity among the rankings attained by the Asian nations when compared with the European nations. The standard deviation of rankings for Europe is 8.8 whereas for Asia it is as high as 29.9. The paper cites greater economic diversity among Asian economies as the sole reason for this discrepancy. Europe is united by a common monetary framework, thereby leading to much lesser differences. Whereas, in Asia, there is no such centralization, and a great degree of diversity in terms of income and financial development prevails in the region. The paper highlights that the Eurozone has by far the most highly developed financial regulations in the world. Though there are still a few shortcomings and loopholes in this framework as became evident during the Eurozone debt crisis. The certain cultural difference between member nations has been preventing the region from attaining a complete uniform financial regulation. However, the continent still is at a much better position in the world, certainly better than Asia. The paper then goes on to recommend steps to correct the factors that is causing Asian nations to lack behind in the domain of financial regulation. By giving impetus to ASEAN, the paper highlights that there is a greater level of transparency required in the region. The members of ASEAN must increasingly adhere to the international standards and there should also be greater cooperation between the financial regulators. The paper strongly recommends ASEAN members to harmonise trading platforms, foreign exchange regulations, and other indirect infrastructures including financial services. The paper urges to promote the Asian Financial Stability Dialogue. This would not only ensure a mechanism to keep the financial stability in check but also promote dialogue and debate among nations to harmonise relations between the countries.

The World Bank has studied the financial sector regulation in India. The presentation identifies the growing conglomerate feature within the financial sector of India. It cites the example of ICICI, SBI and HDFC. Though these are considered as different entities, in real practice a significant edge is given to these companies by the financial regulators as they operate a much larger business. This nature ignores the small operators who are not given the same advantage by the system. This is dangerous as a similar phenomenon had taken place in South Korea in the 1980s. The financial system gave rise to a select group of companies termed as 'Chaebol'. When the group were losing out on their business, it crippled the entire economy of not only South Korea, but the entire region of South-East Asia. The Ponzi schemes have become a growing menace in India, and it is simply the absence of any stern regulator at the ground level that has caused the menace to grow. Initially, the Securities and Exchange Board of India was handed over the task to monitor and prevent the operation of Ponzi schemes in the country. However, SEBI, being a centralized authority and having only one office in Mumbai, is finding it increasingly difficult to reach the grassroot level across the country and prevent this problem. Finally, the board has put the onus on the State Government of protecting their region's investors. Another argument presented by SEBI is that it is essentially an agency formed by an Act of Parliament, which puts the board at the boots of the central government. Even though the ban of Ponzi schemes is an act of the central government, it is the responsibility of the state governments to enforce this law. If each state dedicates a separate wing in their jurisdictions tasked with the responsibility to protect their investors and crackdown on such fraudulent schemes, it will lead to a considerable drop in the incidence of Ponzi schemes. It will lead to a lesser area of monitoring with each state level agency looking after their own jurisdiction, thereby enabling a greater crackdown on the culprits. This project might sound to be a highly expensive affair,

Figure 7. Regulatory quality in Developing Asia
Source: (Kawai & Morgan, 2014)

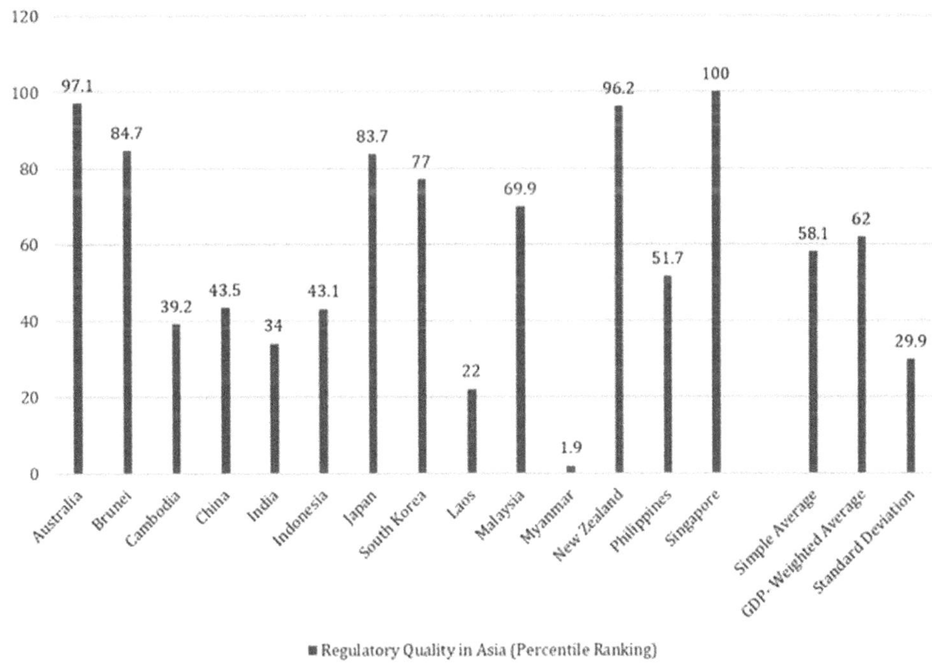

but if the nation is to save crores of money being swindled away by Ponzi operators, a big investment such as this is necessary. Recently the Bitcoin was banned by the Indian Government. The Ministry of Finance and the Reserve Bank have warned investors from trading in such instruments. However, there have been reports of illegal bitcoin trading taking place in some pockets of the country. This could have been mitigated only if there is a financial regulation agency at the state levels too.

India lacks an integrated regulatory system to impede Ponzi schemes. Ponzi schemes are barred under the Prize Chit and Money Circulation (Banning) Act, 1978 and the respective government in the State is the watchdog for the same (Rajagopal, 2016). This may lead to lack in uniformity in the way such schemes may be tackled in different states. Consequently, there are further evidences of such frauds from time to time. In this regard, it is noteworthy to mention the Ponzi scheme wangled by Pearls Agrotech Corporation Ltd (PACL) that is known to have deceived more than 5 crore investors (Javaid, 2016).

On 20th February 2018, the union cabinet of India headed by the Prime Minister Modi passed the Unregulated Deposit Schemes and Chit Funds (Amendment) Bill. This has been perceived as a step towards the prevalence of illegal schemes which deeply exploit the loopholes in the system and dupe the hard-earned money of thousands of investors (Press Information Bureau, 2018). One of the most prominent features of the bill includes a complete ban on any activity which may lead to a flourishing of unregulated schemes. As a part of this clause, the bill bans promoting, operating, issuing advertisements or accepting deposits in any unregulated deposit activity. Some of the other features of this bill includes the attachment of property as a collateral which registering and accepting deposits, to ensure realization of investors' money in case of default. In the event of failure to abide by this law, heavy fines and penalty shall be imposed to offenders, including imprisonment in some cases. Lastly, this implementation of this bill has been entrusted to the State Governments, to further enhance the spirit of cooperative federalism in dealing with this situation (Press Information Bureau, 2018).

SOLUTIONS AND RECOMMENDATIONS

In the summary paper by Wood (2006), analyses the role of cooperative federalism in today's markets. Wood (2006) cites the Enron Corporation scandal and the World Com crash which has shaken the corporate world. It gave birth to the Sarbanes-Oxley Act in 2002 in the United States that sought to strengthen corporate accounting principles in all organization and promote transparency of information to all stakeholders. However, regardless of this act, financial frauds continued to persist in the economy as there was not enough impetus provided towards implementation of the law, which needed more interaction between the States and Congress. The symposium thereby concluded cooperative federalism as the only solution in today's diverse world. The paper encourages active information sharing between authorities, and more delegation of power to the lower levels to increase efficiency and ensure successful implementation of financial laws.

From the main focus, it can be inferred that Asia in lacking in the necessary grip about Ponzi schemes. There is no doubt that Ponzi schemes is a worldwide phenomenon and not only limited to Asia. It is in fact a menace which originated in the United States, and gradually spread throughout various parts of the world using many pedagogues available in today's generation. In parameters of financial literacy, financial inclusion, financial regulation, and Ponzi reporting, Asia is lacking majorly when compared with the Western and other OECD economies. It must also be noted that there lies a wide gap amongst Asian nations themselves. There is a much greater deviation from the average in the case of Asia than say Europe. For example, even though the average rate of fiscal inclusion for Asia is lesser than Europe, there are few Asian nations performing significantly better than European nation. Singapore attains a percentile ranking of 100 towards financial inclusion, whereas the highest attained by any European nation is 97 percentiles. Similar is the story for nations ranking at the bottom of the table. Thus, this reveals the diverse nature of Asian economies, whether be it economically, or socially or religious beliefs. It is interesting to note that major predominant religions in the world today have originated from Asia. Hence, for tackling any problem within this region, there requires a significant amount of cooperation and unity between neighbouring nations. And the same enthusiasm is required for tackling the menace of Ponzi schemes as well. Today there exists three different major associations within the same Asian continent, namely – Association of South East Asian Nations (ASEAN), South Asian Association for Regional Cooperation (SAARC), and Organisation of the Petroleum Exporting Countries (OPEC). These associations are merely regional bodies. But Asia, as a continent, stands lack of any common associations thereby signaling no unity. Of course, it is a mammoth task to bring all forty-eight Asian nations to the table and work upon a common association. But this is the only solution in today's time which Asia needs. A continent which stands to be the powerhouse of the world today cannot afford to remain in dis-unity while individually attempting to solve their own problems without interaction. For tackling the menace in Ponzi schemes and any other prevailing issues as well, the entire Asian region needs to stand united. This chapter urges the need for a common forum for Asian nations to meet, interact, and uniformly find solutions to the problems plaguing the continent. It need not be a complete monetary union like in Europe, but a strong and dedicated forum for members to rely upon always and promote brotherhood among its people.

This chapter proscribes a step by step approach towards tackling the menace of Ponzi schemes. The method encourages a cooperative and federal approach.

- Empower the states/districts/provinces in every Asian nation with the necessary regulatory infrastructure. For example, all states in India should form their own financial regulatory bodies with considerable autonomy, but reporting to the authorities like the SEBI, the RBI, and the Ministry of Finance. Similarly, China also should adopt a similar mechanism in each of their provinces.
- There must be free flow of information and reporting carried out between the states/districts/provinces within the nation. In case of any reported Ponzi schemes, swift action can be implemented with directions from the central authorities, and the culprits can be brought to task saving the investments of millions of investors.
- Between nations, there should be a smooth flow of information between financial institutions. There could be conferences, summits, workshops, etc. of financial regulators where they could meet and discuss upon the various problems facing their economies, and the corrective action to be taken without disrupting the financial stability in their countries and in the Asian region as well.
- A joint effort of all forty-eight Asian nations must be initiated to create a forum for the continent. This forum would provide an ideal platform for all the nations, be it underdeveloped, developing, and developed, to come together and put forward their concerns surrounding the day-to-day affairs.
- New common institutions must be formed in Asia and the existing ones should be strengthened to monitor the entire region. For example, as was discussed under the Main Focus of the Asian Development Bank reports, countries of South Asia, East and South-East Asia and Pacific alone were covered in the surveys. There were hardly any facts and figures from the West Asian and the Middle-Eastern nations
- The common Asian forum must stand as a united force in the world. So long, the hegemony of important global decisions was executed by the Western powers owing to their stronger unity. The proposed Asian forum will partly act to balance and stabilize both the sides.

DIRECTIONS FOR THE FUTURE

As this chapter has kept its focus towards the Asian context, there is undoubtedly ample scope towards a study from other domains also. As it could be observed through the course of this study, there is a unique correspondence between the level of per-capita income and the financial literacy as well. The developing regions with lower per capita income also tend to be the most vulnerable targets for Ponzi schemes owing to their lower financial knowhow. The possible future context of research must give prior emphasis towards analyzing the problems the lower and middle-income economies face while tackling Ponzi schemes. This shall not only broaden the scope of the study, but also encourage awareness among the target groups about the possible risks posed by financial frauds.

CONCLUSION

To conclude, there lies an ample opportunity for tapping into while dealing with the multiple problems in the world today. Owing to the fast changing and dynamic nature of this world that we reside in, nations and institutions must become increasingly adaptable and flexible to tackle the given situation. Especially today, there has been a rising threat posed by protectionism and regionalism. This is an expected reaction which has spilled over from certain perils of globalization. It is difficult to maintain the co-existence of cooperation and regionalism at the same time. Because of globalization, the problems facing the world today are global problems too. Be it terrorism, climate change, cybercrime, and now Ponzi schemes too. To overcome the global problems, there must be an adoption of global solutions too. The growth of technology has had some bane as well. For example, the phenomenon of Ponzi schemes exacerbated since the advent of digital space in 1980s and 1990s, and it spread across all parts of the world. But the boon from technology is the more connected that people have become across borders. The society must uphold this unity and go forward in fighting the problems facing the world today. As the saying goes, 'United we stand, divided we fall'. This chapter urges its readers to continue the spirit of cooperation and unity. As it is seen from this chapter, the possible solution remaining for fixing the Asian Ponzi crisis is a spirit of cooperation and federalism. There exists a barrier between cultures, communities, and even interaction. This is the advantage taken up by the fraudsters operating such programs. There are many other problems in the financial world. But the common cause for all of them is the various barriers prevailing between the victims affected. Thus, interaction, cooperation, stronger and larger unity, is the key to tackle the challenges posed for maintaining financial stability in today's times of risk and uncertainty.

REFERENCES

Altman, A. (2008). A Brief History of Ponzi Schemes. *Time*.

Asian Development Bank Institute. (2014). *Financial Inclusion in Asia*. Asian Development Bank.

Ayyagiri, M., & Beck, T. (2015). *Financial Inclusion in Asia: An Overview*. Asian Development Bank.

Bishop, W. (2013). The Role of Ethics in 21st Century. *Journal of Business Ethics*, *118*(3), 635–637. doi:10.100710551-013-1618-1

Bonini, S., & Boraschi-Diaz, D. (2013). The Causes and Financial Consequences of Corporate Frauds. In R. Cressy (Ed.), *C. D & M. C, Entrepreneurship, Finance, Governance and Ethics* (pp. 295–314). Springer. doi:10.1007/978-94-007-3867-6_13

Bureau, E. T. (2012, November 26). *What is a Ponzi Scheme and how investors are trapped*. Retrieved from The Economic Times: https://economictimes.indiatimes.com/analysis/what-is-a-ponzi-scheme-and-how-investors-are-trapped/articleshow/17348270.cms

Bureau, E. T. (2014). Financial inclusion can curb ponzi schemes: RBI Governor Raghuram Rajan. *The Economic Times*.

Chow, E. (2018, March 9). *Why China keeps falling for pyramid schemes*. Retrieved from The Diplomat: https://www.realclearworld.com/2018/03/09/why_china_keeps_falling_for_pyramid_schemes_190718.html

Christensen, G. (2012). Allocating loss in Securities Fraud. *William & Mary Business Law Review, 3*(2), 310-339.

Cortes, D., Santamaria, J., & Vargas, J. (2016). *Economic Shocks and Crime: Evidence from the crash of Ponzi Schemes*. Bogota: Universidad del Rosario. Retrieved from http://repository.urosario.edu.co/bitstream/handle/10336/11880/dt185.pdf?sequence=3

Deason, S., Rajgopal, S., & Waymire, G. (2015). *Who Gets Swindled in Ponzi Schemes?* Atlanta: Emory University. Retrieved from https://www0.gsb.columbia.edu/mygsb/faculty/research/pubfiles/12962/ponzi%20draft%20may%2013%202015.pdf

Fernandes, J. (2013). *Chit fund scam: How Saradha duped its investors?* Retrieved from http://www.ndtv.com/india-news/chit-fund-scam-how-saradha-duped-its-investors-520076

Fletcher, C., & Herrmann, D. (2012). *The Internationalisation of Corruption*. Surrey: Gower.

Frankel, T. (2012). *The Ponzi Scheme Puzzle*. New York: Oxford University Press. doi:10.1093/acprof:osobl/9780199926619.001.0001

Gabel, J. (2011). Midnight in the Garden of Good Faith: Using Clawback Actions to HArvest the Equitable Roots of Bankrupt Ponzi Schemes. *Case Western Reserve Law Review, 62*(1), 19-79.

India Today. (2015, January 21). *Pradhan Mantri Jan Dhan Yojana Made it to the Guiness Book of World Records*. Retrieved from India Today: https://www.indiatoday.in/education-today/gk-current-affairs/story/pradhan-mantri-jan-dhan-yojana-made-it-to-guinness-world-records-a-record-11.5-cr-accounts-opened-236741-2015-01-21

Investopedia. (2017). *Ponzi Scheme*. Retrieved from Investopedia: https://www.investopedia.com/terms/p/ponzischeme.asp

Jacobs, P., & Schain, L. (2011). *The Never Ending Attraction of the Ponzi Scheme*. Fairfield: Sacred Heart University.

Kaul, V. (2014). *Another Sahara: How Sahara built a 'brand' and duped people*. Retrieved from http://www.firstpost.com/investing/another-sahara-how-saradha-built-a-brand-and-duped-investors-724287.html

Kawai, M., & Morgan, P. (2014). *Regional Financial Regulation in Asia*. Asian Development Bank Institute. doi:10.4337/9781783472208.00012

Krige, D. (2012). Fields of dreams, fields of schemes: ponzi finance and multi-level marketing in South Africa. *International African Institute, 82*(1), 69-92.

Levmore, S. (2012). Rethinking Ponzi-Scheme Remedies in and out of Bankruptcy. *BUL Review, 92*, 969.

Lewis, M. (2015). *Understanding Ponzi Schemes: Can Better Financial Regulation Prevent Investors from Being Defrauded?* Edward Elgar Publishing. doi:10.4337/9781782549109

Mahama, W. (2016, February 4). *Ponzi Schemes and Financial Literacy in Ghana*. Retrieved from Ghana Web: https://www.ghanaweb.com/GhanaHomePage/features/Ponzi-schemes-and-financial-literacy-in-Ghana-412808

Maierbrugger, A. (2015). *South Asia has world's lowest financial literacy*. The Gulf Times.

Monroe, H., Carvajal, A., & Pattillo, C. (2010). *Perils of Ponzis*. IMF.

Nigeria Watch International. (2017, January 23). MMM Nigeria Ponzi Scheme And the Curse of 'Herd Mentality'. *Vigilance-Security Magazine*. Retrieved from http://www.vigilance-securitymagazine.com/news/general/nigeria-watch-international/8722-mmm-nigeria-ponzi-scheme-and-the-curse-of-herd-mentality

Ning, D. (2017, September 12). *Owner of China's Biggest Ponzi Scheme Sentenced to Life in Jail*. Retrieved from Bloomberg News: https://www.bloomberg.com/news/articles/2017-09-12/owner-of-china-s-biggest-ponzi-scheme-sentenced-to-life-in-jail

OECD. (2011). *Financial Inclusion as Defined by RBI*. OECD.

OECD. (2011). *Mesauring Financial Literacy*. OECD.

Press Information Bureau. (2018, February 20). *Cabinet approves New Bill to ban Unregulated Deposit Schemes and Chit Funds (Amendment) Bill, 2018*. Retrieved from Press Information Bureau: http://pib.nic.in/newsite/PrintRelease.aspx?relid=176677

Press Trust of India. (2014). *Formal Finance to curb ponzi schemes*. Business Standard.

Rajagopal, K. (2016). *Ponzi schemes not under our purview: SEBI*. Retrieved from http://www.thehindu.com/news/national/Ponzi-schemes-not-under-our-purview-SEBI/article14559017

Rhee, R. (2009). *The Madoff Scandal, Market Regulatory Failure, and the Business Education of Lawyers*. Gainesville, FL: University of Florida.

Roy, I. (2015). *The Saradha chit fund scam*. Retrieved from http://www.rediff.com/news/special/explained-the-saradha-chit-fund-scam/20150107

SEC.gov. (2013). *Pyramid Schemes*. Retrieved from https://www.sec.gov/answers/pyramid

U.S. Securities and Exchange Commission. (2018). *Ponzi Scheme*. Washington, DC: U.S. Securities and Exchange Commission.

Shrivastava, B., & Chakraborty, S. (2014). *Sahara to Saradha spur SEBI's Rs.64,000 crore Ponzi Schemes Crackdown*. Retrieved from http://www.livemint.com/Money/74gd93JfsVVrUZKCj0ABXL/Sahara-to-Saradha-spur-Sebis-Rs64000-crore-Ponzi-schemes-c

Solli, J. (2017, March 15). *'Buyer Beware' is insufficient financial protection*. Retrieved from Center for Financial Inclusion: https://economictimes.indiatimes.com/news/economy/finance/financial-inclusion-can-curb-ponzi-schemes-rbi-governor-raghuram-rajan/articleshow/40906102.cms

Tanner, M. (2011). *Social Security, Ponzi Schemes, and the Need for Reform*. Washington, DC: Cato Institute. Retrieved from https://object.cato.org/sites/cato.org/files/pubs/pdf/PA689.pdf

The Economist. (2018). Pyramid schemes cause huge social harm in China. *The Economist.*

The Reserve Bank of India. (2013). *Financial Inclusion in India - An Assessment.* Mumbai: RBI.

The World Bank. (2018, April). *Asia Pacific Economic Update.* Retrieved from The World Bank: http://www.worldbank.org/en/region/eap/publication/east-asia-pacific-economic-update

Ulrich, C. W. (2008, December 15). *Ponzi Schemes: Know How To Protect Yourself.* Retrieved from CNBC: https://www.cnbc.com/id/28239456

Unnikrishnan, D. (2016, April 8). *Jan Dhan Reality Check.* Retrieved from First Post: https://www.firstpost.com/business/jan-dhan-reality-check-manmohan-singhs-criticism-is-indeed-right-but-only-partially-2718642.html

US Legal. (2018). *Financial Regulation Law and Legal Definition.* Retrieved from US Legal: https://definitions.uslegal.com/f/financial-regulation/

Wadhwa, V. (2017). Why Bitcoin is the largest ponzi scheme in human history. *The Hindustan Times.*

Wilber, D. Q. (2009, June 12). *Economic Downturn Speeds Collapse of Ponzi Schemes.* Retrieved from Washington Post: http://www.washingtonpost.com/wp-dyn/content/article/2009/06/11/AR2009061103993.html

Wingfield, B. (2016). *The relationship between demographic factors and financial literacy among students at a South African University.* Pretoria: University of Pretoria.

Wood, C. (2006). *Federalism in Securities Regulation: A Brief Introduction and Reflection.* San Francisco: University of San Francisco.

Yoshina, N., Morgan, P., & Wignaraja, G. (2015). *Financial Education in Asia: Assessment and Recommendations.* Asian Development Bank Institute.

Zuckoff, M. (2006). *Ponzi Schemes: The True Story of a Financial Legend.* Random House.

Chapter 7
India Towards a Cashless Economy

Abhinav Pal
Symbiosis International University (Deemed), India

Chandan Kumar Tiwari
Symbiosis International University (Deemed), India

Tarun Khandelwal
Symbiosis International University (Deemed), India

ABSTRACT

This chapter briefly discusses the impact and policy implications of demonetization across the world. The main focus of the chapter is on the demonetization that occurred in India on 8th November 2016. The event is important due to the surprise effect and also due to the huge scale of impact that it had on the economy. The authors make a case for the demonetization from the policymaker's point of view. This chapter will introduce how demonetization has impacted the business sector as well as the financial sector of the economy. The aim of the chapter is not to estimate the impact of demonetization on the economy as whole but rather to discuss the impact of the policy on the different sectors of the economy and different stakeholders of the economy. This chapter would also explore demonetization as a policy tool for tax evasion and corruption. Finally, this chapter will introduce the concept of cashless economies around the world and whether it will be possible for the Indian economy to become a cashless economy anytime in the near future.

INTRODUCTION

Demonetization basically refers to discontinuation of old currency units of an economy which would render the old currency value less and replace the old currency units with new currency units having value. The Prime minister of India on behalf of the government of India, cited three primary reasons for implementing demonetization as a policy move. Firstly, one of the most vital reasons for implementing such a drastic move was to keep a check on the proliferating stash of black money, which would be

DOI: 10.4018/978-1-5225-7208-4.ch007

mainly be kept in the higher denominations of currency like ₹500 and ₹1000. Secondly, as expressed by the Prime minister demonetization would help in dealing with rising menace of fake currency notes that would be circulating in the economy, according to the RBI's annual report of 2015-16, 63% of the counterfeit notes are in the form of ₹500 and ₹1000. The third reason cited by the government for this drastic policy move was to curb the terror funding which is mostly carried out by a stash of black money and counterfeit notes.

The decision to implement such a huge and impactful policy step was kept completely confidential, and only two key government officials were aware of this policy move, the finance minister, and the RBI governor. The confidentiality of this decision was very necessary to ensure this decision is effective, as lack of confidentiality would have resulted in people making pre-emotive measures of making prior arrangements for handling their black money. Therefore, it was an imperative that this decision was carried out in full confidentiality and secrecy (Paliwal, 2017).

Such a sudden policy decision which could have a huge impact on the day to day functioning of the general public is generally met with both criticisms and praises. In the subsequent aftermath that followed the policy decision of demonetization due to the sudden nature of its implementation many public surveys and media reports garnered praises for the move, while many noted economists severely criticized the policy, including Nobel laureate, Dr. Amartya Sen as he felt that impact, such a policy would have on the nation's economic life will be detrimental, more so against the backdrop that the Indian economy is cash-intensive in nature (Masiero, 2017). Post the announcement, the central government experienced major and visible backlash from the general public, small traders and shop owners for the economic disruptions that stemmed due to demonetization and completely changed the industry dynamics within the markets. Lahiri, (2016) pointed out that there was the severe persistence of shortage of cash post the policy decision was implemented and this led to the various detrimental impact on the various sectors of the economy. The section of the society that was most badly hit by demonetization was that of the poor and vulnerable which carried out majority of its transactions in cash and without a proper safety net in the form of proper provisions made for the lack of cash, they were bound to suffer majorly due to this policy decision which led to this situation of cashlessness. Implementation of the policy was immediately put into effect, the moment the Prime Minister made his announcement on the broadcast, on November 8, 2017, while addressing the Indian nation in lieu of the old currency notes, RBI introduced new currency notes of 2000 and fresh denominations of ₹500 were introduced on 22nd December, 2016 and ₹1000 ceased to exist altogether. The policy stated that old currency notes could be exchanged for new currency notes by visiting the banks. Even people who did not have bank accounts could exchange the old currency notes by providing a valid identity proof that they possessed. The process of exchanging old currency notes in return of the new ones was available till the 30th December 2016, post that no person would be able to obtain the new currency in return of the old currency. However, old currency notes could have been used before the 30th December for making certain payments such as hospital bills, fees, petrol pump payments and various penalties liable to be paid to the state and central government (Nam & Bhat, 2016). The initial withdrawal limit was set at ₹2000 from ATMs, which were later increased to ₹4000. While banks had a withdrawal limit of ₹10,000 per day with an overall weekly limit of ₹20,000 (Choudhury & Dwarakanath, 2017). From the point of view of the people of the Indian economy, these rules of exchanging old currency with new currency and the limits that were attached to these exchanges were most critical and crucial changes in terms of policy of demonetization that was implemented and it would change the way the majority of the public carried out their day to day activities and transactions. The RBI had issued a number of notifications and orders governing the exchange and deposit process of old currency notes in return of the new currency notes, and also many notifications were declared regarding the cash withdrawal process which added much to the confusion and anger of the people of the Indian Economy. The abruptness of demonetization led to sharp rise in demand for the new currency notes, given the Indian economy is a cash intensive economy where 90% of the transactions are carried out in cash and the inadequate supply of these new currency notes and older smaller denominations notes led to long queues and large lines of people waiting outside banks and ATMs which led to a lot of frenzy and chaos among the people who were desperately trying to obtain the new currency notes (R. K. Singh, 2016). Since RBI had not made proper arrangements of supply of new currency notes, therefore ATMs and banks ran out of the new currency notes pretty quickly which further compounded the problems that were faced by the people in the economy. The chaos and frenzy that followed the policy move also claimed many lives, just ten days post demonetization almost 55 deaths were reported due to overexertion due to extended standing in long lines and queues near banks and ATMs (Shekhar, 2016). People that resided in the rural area suffered the most due to low penetration of banks in such areas and lack of bank accounts maintained by the people residing in rural area coupled with limited access to financial services led to major troubles for the rural population as it meant the majority of people would have to travel to far off places to exchange the older notes in return of the new ones. Also, due to the absence of digitization of finances in the rural areas, constrained financial access and lack of financial literacy, a large proportion of transactions in rural areas were majorly carried out in cash, which meant that ill effects of demonetization would prominently impact the rural areas of the country the most. Further, making the situation worse and compounding the confusion faced by the rural population was the fact that RBI made different rules for cash deposit and withdrawal process for District central cooperative banks, primary agricultural societies and primary financial institutions which were majorly used by the rural population of India (Kumar, 2017a).

History of Demonetization in India

It was not the first time that the Indian economy has experienced demonetization as a policy tool. India has witnessed two more currency ban in the past which were as follows:

1. **First Currency ban in 1946:** Currency notes of ₹500 and ₹1000 and four years later ₹10000 notes were introduced as well. However, in the year 1946, both ₹1000 and ₹10,000 ceased to exist as currency notes, but they were later introduced back in circulation along with ₹5000 (Hari, 2017).
2. **The Second Currency ban in 1970's:** Then the prime minister Mr. Morarji Desai followed the recommendations of the Wanchoo committee set up by the Planning commission of India and banned the currency notes of ₹1000, ₹5000 and ₹10,000 by taking them out of circulations. The policy decision was taken to tackle the growth and spread of black money proliferating in the economy and to halt the generation of black money in the economy (Hari, 2017).

Many economists have pointed out various similarities between demonetization of 1978 and 2016, which were as follows:

1. Both the prime ministers, Mr. Morarji Desai and Mr. Narendra Modi had implemented the note ban to tackle the problem of growth of black money and halt the generation of black money.

2. Mr. Morarji Desai had declared the decision of demonetizing over a public broadcast on the radio. Similarly, Mr. Narendra Modi announced the ban over a broadcast that was aired on all news channels.
3. Both times the policy decision was implemented in secrecy and the decision was kept absolutely confidential before its implementation.

The policy move of demonetization is not new to economies, various countries have experienced or undergone the consequences of demonetization as a policy tool. Few countries have even witnessed economic success with demonetization. History of demonetization dates way back to 1880-1885 when the French had implemented demonetization for the first time. Countries like Myanmar, Nigeria, Soviet Union and South Korea have implemented demonetization in the past to keep a check on the growth of black money and banish the black market from their economies. The economy of Zimbabwe had taken the decision to apply the note ban to tackle the issue of hyperinflation and stabilization of the economy. While Ghana had made use of the policy tool to curb tax evasion in their economy. While demonetizing their currency helped the Australian economy to deal with counterfeit currencies (Kumar, 2017b).

Russia had also experienced demonetization. The impact of Russian demonetization is very profound. The Soviet Union inherently was used to barter exchanges. The situation was amplified between 1994 to 1998. The surge in the barter trade rose from 10 percent to 50 percent of the industrial transaction between the said period. In Russia, due to the demonetization there was a surge in the different forms of money surrogates. As a result of the demonetization and use of money surrogates, the cost of the transaction had increased, markets were fragmented and this also caused problems in implementation of the tax laws and other regulation. Some of the important forms were direct barter, offsets and other paper securities. The direct barter in case of Russia, ranged from the simple barter trade to complex chains of delivery. Offsets basically involved cancellation of mutual debts. They also ranged from simple to complex arrangement (Litwack & Sutherland, 2000). Major causes of Russian demonetization were the changes in macroeconomic policies, problems and delays in the structural reforms and other factors inherited from Soviet Union (Commander & Mumssen, 1998; Gaddy, Gaddy, & Ickes, 2016).

However, in case of India, the brief period of demonetization in which India had banned the use of ₹500 and ₹1000 notes, other modes of payment gained popularity. These other modes include the payment via e-wallets such as Paytm, Freecharge and others (which are also explained later in the chapter). There was no as such creation of barter trade or use of other payment mechanism which did not involve the valuation of the goods and services in non-rupee terms. Hence, Indian experience was very different than the Russian experience if compared in terms of implications.

Many economies have witnessed economic success with this policy move, while for others demonetization's costs have outweighed the benefits that are accrued to the economy. In the Indian Scenario, many economist and policymakers have severely criticized the policy of demonetization over the weak and poor implementation arrangements made by the government for successfully carrying out the policy of demonetization which led to massive inconvenience to the general public of India. The former prime minister even went ahead and declared the policy move as "Monumental Mismanagement" which has caused great inconvenience and pain to the people of India and also led to disastrous economic consequences for the Indian Economy in terms of disruption of business environment and fall in the GDP of India.

The next two broad sections of this chapter discuss the impact of demonetization on the various sectors of the Indian Economy and various aspects of a cashless economy in the Indian context.

IMPACT OF DEMONETIZATION ON INDIAN ECONOMY

Demonetization is considered to be a major step in the growth of our economy. It was mainly aimed to eradicate counterfeit currency, curb tax evasion and inflation and keep control over black money and terror funding. Moreover, this move was also aimed at the promotion of organized business sector and making India cashless economy. In India, the size of cash relative to GDP is the highest whereas the size of electronic transactions in total transactions is lowest in the world. The impact of demonetization was highly significant as the demonetized currency represented over 85% of the currency in circulation. Despite affecting the life of a common man, however, it was observed that significant mass of common people supported the government move to demonetize higher denomination currency notes of ₹500 and ₹1000 (Beyes & Bhattacharya, 2016). Some people have opposed the decision where some were skeptical about the move. This decision of Government has received mixed responses. There have been problems of liquidity shortage, loss of growth due to a temporary halt to major economic activities.

The short-term consequences of currency-scrapping were quite severe, which has disrupted the life of the common man for several weeks after the announcement. More than 90 percent of the rural population have not used digital transactions. (R. Singh, 2017). A major portion of the citizens of the country use cash. Only very tiny portion use other mediums of exchange for their requirements. Therefore, along with urban population, rural society was negatively affected by a such move. The authors will study the impact of demonetization on macroeconomic variables and impact on various sectors of the economy.

Impact on Macroeconomic Variables

The Impact of Demonetization on various macroeconomic variables can be studied as below.

Liquidity

As of Nov. 4, 2016, over 86 percent of notes in circulation were the higher denomination of ₹500 and ₹1000 constituting 11 percent of GDP (Hari, 2017). Currency scrapping of higher denomination notes along with the imposition of withdrawal limits resulted in an acute shortage of money supply causing a liquidity crunch for the country in the short term.

Inflation

Declaring of ₹500 and ₹1000 currency notes as illegal tender eradicated illegal cash piled in our system from several numbers of years. This has lowered inflation especially in semi-urban and rural areas where the share of cash transactions is very high (Joshi, 2018). However, over a period of time sluggish production have caused a decline in supply leading to inflation.

Gross Domestic Product

Demonetization severely affected the Indian economy as it is cash-based economy. Shortage of liquidity in cash-intensive industries have undermined consumption and business activity posing a challenge to the growth momentum of the Indian economy (Joshi, 2018). The growth in industries namely cement, steel, and refinery products, constituting 38% of the Index of Industrial Production (IIP), declined (Mounika

& Kadhirvel, 2017). This has adversely affected the banking industry as the current account holders demand large sums of cash. Moreover, lack of payment mechanism due to cash shortage disrupted the consumption and business activity leading to lag in growth.

Credit Creation

Due to demonetization, money outside the system was brought back to the financial system which is used by the banks for several productive purposes in the economy. This has significantly improved bank deposits. More and more coming into the formal banking system has increased the bankability to lend. This has improved the profitability of banks along with the reduction of interest rates. This has also solved the problem of NPA with banking to a certain extent.

Taxation

Finance Minister Arun Jaitley announced that both direct taxes as well as indirect taxes including excise duty, service tax, and customs duties levied by the union government had registered a significant growth from the pre-demonetization era, indicating the limited impact of demonetization on commercial activity (Joshi, 2018).

Impact of Demonetization of Various Sectors

The impact of demonetization was severe on all those sectors where transactions are mostly backed by cash. All informal sectors have been duly affected by such move of the government.

Farming and Fishing Industry

The sector typically deals with high cash transactions. Due to cash crunch, farmers found difficult to buy seeds and fertilizer and selling crops and perishable products. Consequently, reduction in demand led to a decline in the prices of crops. Further, demonetization led to a scarcity of cash to pay for food products. Farmers started facing difficulty in recovering even their cost of transportation and dumped their products in desperation (Mounika & Kadhirvel, 2017). Agricultural products including food grains, vegetables, sugarcane, milk, eggs were dumped on the ground. The poultry and fishing industry which mostly runs on cash transactions suffered a bad deal. Overall, agricultural and allied business activities faced tough times in the short run.

Manufacturing Sector

Scrapping higher currency notes of ₹500 and ₹1000 in November 2016 hit the manufacturing sector output. The Nikkei India Manufacturing Purchasing Managers' Index (PMI) fell below 50- mark for the first time in 2016 to 49.6 in December. It was above 50 in prior months. A reading below 50 indicates contraction while one above 50 specifies expansion (Joshi, 2018). Being cash driven sector, almost all companies observed new production and output dip for the first time in 2016. This, in turn, resulted in lower employment.

Jewelry and Real Estate

The impact of demonetization on jewelry and real estate is apparent. As these, sectors transact with lot more cash, the liquidity squeeze caused by demonetization has a negative impact on these sectors. Real estate is considered to be a sector with high black money involvement. Hence, a cash crunch has brought short-term instability. The companies in these sectors due to low demand faced a high level of debt and therefore loan defaults. It also had a negative wage implication due to the involvement of the casual workforce.

Automobiles

Shortage of cash led to a decline in domestic sales of two-wheelers sharply. Customers started delaying the purchases, affecting the automobile sector negatively (Joshi, 2018). The companies in this sector due to low demand found liquidity and profitability crunch where debt management became a problem.

Consumer Durables

Wholesalers, as well as retailers, deal with a large amount of cash transaction in this segment. Cash crunch created a problem for the customers as well as dealers leading to slag in the short run. This created a problem for working capital management with these companies.

Microfinance Institutions

The Government decision to demonetize the large denomination notes of ₹500 and ₹1000 led to a decline in disbursement rate of Micro Finance Institutions providing financial assistance to micro- business (Mali, 2016). Micro-Finance Institutes being the major source of the capital provider to micro business have negatively affected both these institutions. There has been difficulty in especially cash disbursement and delay in collection of loan installments from the small business ventures.

Micro, Small and Medium Enterprise (MSME)

Indian Micro Small and Medium Enterprise (MSME) sector have a significant share in the Gross Domestic Product of our economy. The businesses like restaurants, salons, textiles including seasonal business are low capital ventures working on the basis of liquidity preference. The workforce in this sector is not highly educated and tech-savvy. Due to a preference for cash, the demand for such informal sectors has gone down. Small firms, as well as the Informal sector, suffered badly due to demonetization.

Daily Wage Workers

There exists a significant proportion of informal sector. This sector employs a huge amount of workforce. This sector is highly dependent on cash to meet working capital requirements. Demonetization has resulted in the closure of many of this business due to a shortage of cash resulting in a loss of employment in this sector.

Services Sector

Affected severely by demonetization, there has been worst slump in the services sector post demonetization due to squeeze of new orders and spending cut by customers resulting from cash shortages.

Business declined in hotels, logistics, and restaurants due to a cash shortage. Along with agriculture and manufacturing, service sectors also have a large number of cash transactions (Joshi, 2018).

E-Commerce

Due to demonetization, companies in the e-commerce sector faced up to 30% decline in Cash on Delivery order. Successful online retailers in India including Amazon, Flipkart, and others halted offering cash on delivery services temporarily (Mali, 2016). It was observed that out of the total orders 70% of the e-commerce orders are still paid in cash. Therefore, such an announcement on 8th November has negatively affected the volume of these businesses as cash on delivery is the most sort mode of payment for buyers in India. Some of these companies also put a cap on the maximum value of Cash on Delivery causing inconvenience to shoppers. This sector has highly encouraged buyers to use debit cards and credit cards enabled by the point of sales devices carried by delivery personnel. This led to an increase in demand for Card Swipe Machines. Furthermore, use of e-payment and e-wallet gained popularity after such a move.

Digital Wallet

A digital wallet or e-wallet allows an individual to make online transactions like shopping, bill payments or online booking etc. There has been a significant increase in the electronic payments made via these e-wallets. Paytm, MobiKwik, Freecharge, and others e-wallet companies have been the biggest beneficiaries of government move of demonetization (Mali, 2016). There has been a significant boom in the business of these companies. Digital transactions are recorded which promotes white money leading to increasing the government's tax revenue.

Financial Sector

The financial sector had a mixed effect. Our central bank, Reserve Bank of India, domestic earning declined as it had to pay interest of crores of rupees after it mopped up excess liquidity in the banking system after demonetization. The currency printing cost also increased because of the move. For commercial banks, the increase in current account and savings accounts deposits resulted in a sizable increase in liquidity with the banks resulted in increased profitability. A study found that there was no significant impact of demonetization on the stock market. However, the scrapping exercise affected the stock market for a shorter duration, but it recovered soon (Chauhan & Kaushik, 2016).

Information Technology Sector

Demonetization had an adverse effect on the grey channel market in order to prevent illegal money lending and money laundering. This move has helped to reduce the use of cash to purchase fake products and buy Chinese products. Use of new age payments like Paytm, PayUMoney, Mobikwik along with the use of online banking has increased since then, and there has been a significant boost to several IT startup and

Fintech companies providing a platform for online payments for buyers (Mounika & Kadhirvel, 2017). This has also helped the government bodies and interested parties to trace financial information and electronic KYC (Know Your Customer) from income tax departments. Usage of Aadhar and promotion of several government schemes and benefits have enabled banking and financial institutions to be tech savvy and thereby provide growth momentum to the IT industry. To promote digital India is one of the prime goals of the present government.

Other Impact

There has been a significant reduction in other social and economic evils including black money, counterfeit currency, and hawala trade. Demonetization had put a halt on these activities leading India to more sustainable growth.

Black Money

It is observed that only a small portion of the black money is held in the form of cash and the majority is in the form of physical assets namely gold, land and building. Demonetization had withdrawn black money and brought back to the Indian financial system where the notes of ₹500 and ₹1000 were deposited to the banks (Mounika & Kadhirvel, 2017). It had taken out mostly all black money kept in the form of cash and imposed heavy penalties on the black money hoarders thereby punishing the offenders.

Counterfeit Currency

Before demonetization, it was estimated that 250 out of every million Indian banknotes were fake. The new currency notes of ₹500 and ₹2000 have been issued with advanced security features which are less vulnerable to counterfeiting. This had badly affected domestic terrorism including Maoist and Naxalites increasing the surrender rate for these groups. At the same time, smuggling of arms and money laundering to promote internal, as well as external terrorism, is being highly scrutinized (Mounika & Kadhirvel, 2017).

Hawala Traders

Hawala is a method of transmitting money from different countries to India in Indian currency denominations. Through this process, people of different countries convert their black money into white money. The scrapping of high denominations currency notes made existing notes available with hawala traders null and void. This has ultimately led to end of hawala racket and decline in real estate prices in the country (Mounika & Kadhirvel, 2017).

Undoubtedly, demonetization negatively impacted almost all business sectors including the financial sector at least in short- run. There was a major setback in the form of liquidity and profitability to all the sector of the economy. Due to demonetization, short to medium term scenario does not look good as almost all the economic indicators exhibited unhealthy performance.

However medium to long-term approach has a different story to tell. Significantly, it is expected that the tax and interest rates on loans will come down. This will result in higher tax collections due to better compliance resulting in reduced rates in the long term. It will also drive up the disposable income.

This can give a positive impact on consumption demand in the long term, enhancing employment and standard of living. Also, curbing counterfeit currency, black money, and improved bank deposits will lead to sustainable development in the long run which is yet to be measured. The government can use this money for developing infrastructure including educational institutions, hospitals, roads and other amenities for the needy and poor section of the society (Nerkar, 2016).

Further, there is significant growth to digital transactions which is a government effort to promote cashless society. Digital push is successful mostly in metros and urban India. However, still, it has not catered to the rural areas which resemble the largest population. The government is required to go away with the absence of banking facilities, financial illiteracy and inadequate infrastructure for financial transactions to penetrate digitally and make India cashless society.

CASHLESS ECONOMY

Introduction: About Money

Yap Island in the Pacific had large discs of limestone as currency. The size of these discs were at times as large as six feet in radius. These large discs of limestone were used for purposes such as marriage, inheritance and other transactions. Given, the size of these discs it would require a lot of effort to physically transfer disc from one person to another. Because of this most of the times, villagers just used to acknowledge the new owner of the disc. According to Yap lore, one of the limestone discs was lost at sea, while it was being transported from the quarry. Everyone in the village believed that one of the disc was there in the sea, so someone was granted the claim over the value of the disc. The disc at the bottom of the sea was also considered for the transactions (Furness, 1910).

This story conveys a very important idea. The money on this island was a disc of limestone, which had to be transferred from person to another person for the transactions. But the transfer of disc was done by just transferring the ownership rather than a physical transfer of limestone disc. Money is a medium of exchange. The most tangible form of money is cash. The replacement of cash with the substitutes such as debit cards, credit cards, and other forms have existed for a more than a decade. In the current times, especially when we purchase an expensive product or service, the change of the money does not happen physically but rather the claim on the money changes from one to another. Like for example when a purchase is made via debit card, the claim on the money in the bank changes. This is an example of a cashless transaction. The value of cash comes from the information it contains, more specifically the information about the purchasing power, and therefore, we can say that it is an information good. Since cash is an information good, we can be replaced via digital substitute (Becker, 1999). According to Chakravorti (2016), the cashless economy is where financial transactions are not conducted with money in the form of cash (currency notes and coins) but is conducted via the digital form. One of the reasons for demonization was to move towards the cashless economy. According to the Rogoff (2015), cashless society has to phase out cash starting from the large denomination bills and eventually coins. One of the main reasons for going cashless to reduce the size of the shadow economy.

One of the flagship programs of the Government of India is digital India launched in 2015, with a vision to transform India (Ministry of Electronics & Information Technology, 2015). According to the Ministry of Electronics and Information Technology (Cashless India. (2018)., "The Digital India programme is a flagship programme of the Government of India with a vision to transform India into a digitally empowered society and knowledge economy. "Faceless, Paperless, Cashless" is one of the professed role of Digital India." For this government is promoting cashless transactions via various ways such as bank cards, e-wallets, UPI, and others.

There are some costs as well as benefits from the cashless economy, but before discussing it lets first focus on various ways of achieving the cashless economy.

Path Towards a Cashless Economy

There are two main ways to approach the cashless economy. The first one is a top-down approach. In this central bank stops issuing the currency bills and coins and thereby, paving the way for the cashless economy. The central bank further provides the substitutes to cash. This should take cash from society and hence, making it a cashless society. This top-down approach may not be practical due to political pressure. In a democracy, it will be very tough for any political party to get the bill passed in the assembly. However, some advanced economies may be able to accomplish this. One of the major reasons why this kind of policy may be practiced is to pursue the negative interest rate policy (we talk about this in the next section). However, this kind of approach will lead to inconvenience to the public.

The second way to make the economy cashless is a bottom-up approach. In this central bank can allow private agents to economize the use of cash. For example, some telecom operators offer discounts on recharges and other promotional schemes to attract the consumers to use mobile payment instead of cash. As the consumers become more and more familiar with them, the acceptability of these payment portals are increased like to purchase of groceries, movie tickets and so on.

Either way, if the government is trying to make the economy cashless, it has to have the proper infrastructure for it. The infrastructure would require good internet connectivity for mobile wallet use. This transition would require that system should be easy to enough to be deciphered by all the individuals in the country. The transactions are very important, and therefore, if the system of cashless economy is excluding even a small proportion of the population, it may not be a good idea to move towards the cashless economy.

Need for Cashless Economy

In the twenty-first century, where we have all sorts of payments alternatives to cash available for making the payments, but we still use cash. There are various reasons to move towards the cashless economy. The important reasons are as follows

Check on the Shadow Economy

One of the features of the cash is anonymity. This makes the currency one of the preferred way of dealing with the shadow economy and also for illegal activity. Kiyotaki & Wright (1989), pointed a very important property of physical cash that makes it the most accepted form of payments for tax evasion and illegal transactions. The buyer and seller do not know about the history, giving it full anonymity.

The size of the black economy in India is estimated around 62 percent of the gross domestic product of India (Kumar, 2017b). Given this backdrop, it is quite important for India to reduce the size of the black economy. One of the most important features of the black economy is that there is no tax revenue generated from it. Further, if the government can effectively tax the black economy, the budget of the government will also improve. In India, before demonetization, the 500 and 1000 denomination currency notes worth ₹15.4 trillion were in circulation, which represented the 86.9 percent of the total money in circulation (B. Singh & Roy, 2017).

Negative Interest Rates

Paper currency makes it difficult for central banks to push the interest rate below zero. This has become more relevant in contemporary times. According to Blanchard, Dell'Ariccia, & Mauro (2010), in the developed economies, low and stable inflation rates have pushed the interest rates towards the lower bound, i.e. zero. For central banks, this means that in case of a deflationary shock it cannot reduce the interest rate to level it likes to reduce due to the lower cap.

Keeping cash at an individual level has some cost associated with it. These costs include the risk of theft, therefore keeping cash with the bank and thereby using the digital money payments is easier. However, when the central bank tries to push the rate of interest to sub-zero levels, there may be a tendency of the people to hoard cash. This kind of behavior will make it tough for the central bank to pursue a negative interest rate policy. As Blanchard et al., (2010) discussed because of the lower bound, the central banks may have to rethink the targeted inflation rates from 2% to 4%. This would leave some room for the central banks to use monetary policy.

The Natural Shift Towards the Cashless Society

The society will automatically gradually tend towards the use of non-cash modes of the transaction as they become more economical to use. There are broadly three ways to measure it. Firstly, from the perspective of the individual payer. When a transaction takes place, the payer wants to maximize his utility from the transaction. There are factors that affect the mode of payment such as the wealth of the household, consumer preferences and transaction-specific factors (Mantel, 2001). Here, his decision will be constrained by the instruments that payee is willing to accept. For example, a payer has to pay some amount say, ₹427, here he can pay via cash, credit card, mobile wallets and other non-cash payment methods. But he can only pay using non-cash methods only when the payee is accepting the other methods of payment. On the payer side, he may be interested in paying in non-cash modes because of the convenience not carrying cash as well as not requiring to deal with change. This may also lead to saving in terms of time as well.

Secondly, when we include all the parties to the transactions (Evans, 2002). This gives a social benefit of the transaction, where both buyer and seller are trying to maximize the benefit. Here, for example in the case of payment via cheque, there is a float period of a few days, which gives the buyer credit of few days and seller has to bear the cost of float. Hence, there is no net change in social benefit. However, if we assume that buyers are waiting in a queue, and a specific payment method is requiring more time than the other payment methods (for example due to poor connectivity, there is a delay in approval from banks in case of debit cards, in this case, that causes an externality, which increases the wait time for everyone).

Lastly, all the components for cast and benefit should be included. For example, when we are talking about the cash, transactions there is the cost of printing and circulating the cash within the economy. The central bank has to mint the cash and transport it banks (Bauer, 1998). And then banks will further store it and distribute to ATMs, where people can withdraw cash and use it further. There are costs associated with the procuring and maintaining of the ATMs as well. All this are the part of a cash transaction. There is also cost associated card payment as well. In case of card payment, there are some saving in terms of cost as the merchant is required handle cash, nor he is required to deposit the same. However, there is a cost associated with card payments which are bank charges and some fixed cost for the card sweeping machine (Garcia-Swartz, Hahn, & Layne-Farrar, 2004).

Cashless Economy: Problems

The Decrease in the Transactions

As we have already discussed that for black economy, cash is the ideal mode of the transaction as there is inherent anonymity, however as the people shift from cash to non-cash modes of transaction, there will be a reduction in the economic activity. This reduction in economic activity can be controlled, if the government can provide a digital mode of payment which keeps this essential property of anonymity cash intact, then the loss of economic activity can be taken care off. However, as Rogoff (1998), pointed out that this can also set-off even if the small fraction of black economy pays the taxes.

Technological Challenge

The process of shifting to a completely cashless society requires an infrastructure that would allow the cashless society to function. Here there has to significant infrastructure in terms of information technology as well as the FinTech is required (Worthington, 2006).

Changing the Existing System

Changing the current state of things from cash to completely non-cash can disturb the whole economic system. This can affect the economy in unexpected ways (Rogoff, 2014). This can lead to a decline in demand for debt.

Cyber Threat

If we transit completely from cash to non-cash, it would mean a lot of dependence on information technology as well as power. If there is a grid failure or cyber-attack the whole economy will be in affected and hence, it will make the system more vulnerable to such attacks. Further, paper cash reduces the impact of these cyber-attacks.

India's Shift Towards the Cashless Economy

On 8th November 2016, India demonetized ₹500 and ₹1000 currency bills which represented the 86.9% of the total currency in circulation (Mali, 2016). As discussed above this kind of step is more closely related to the top-down approach to promote cashless society. Given this demonetization in the economy, digital payment portals that existed before demonetization such as Paytm, Freecharge and others experienced the surge in the volume. Further due to this, there have been new competitors entering the market of digital payments such as BHIM, Google Tez (now known as Google Pay), Phone Pe and others.

Table 1. Payment system indicators – annual turnover

Item	Volume (million)			Value (₹ billion)		
	2014-15	2015-16	2016-17	2014-15	2015-16	2016-17
Systemically Important Financial Market infrastructures (SIFMIs)						
1. RTGS	92.8	98.3	107.8	7,54,032	8,24,578	9,81,904
Total Financial Markets Clearing (2+3+4)	3	3.1	3.7	7,52,000	8,07,370	10,56,173
2. CBLO	0.2	0.2	0.2	1,67,646	1,78,335	2,29,528
3. Government Securities Clearing	1.1	1	1.5	2,58,917	2,69,778	4,04,389
4. Forex Clearing	1.7	1.9	1.9	3,25,438	3,59,257	4,22,256
Total SIFMIs (1 to 4)	95.8	101.4	111.5	15,06,033	16,31,948	20,38,077
Retail Payments						
Total Paper Clearing (5+6+7)	1,196.50	1,096.40	1,206.70	85,434	81,861	80,958
5. CTS	964.9	958.4	1,111.90	66,770	69,889	74,035
6. MICR Clearing	22.4	0	0	1,850	0	0
7. Non-MICR Clearing	209.2	138	94.8	16,814	11,972	6,923
Total Retail Electronic Clearing (8+9+10+11+12)	1,687.40	3,141.50	4,205.00	65,366	91,408	1,32,255
8. ECS DR	226	224.8	8.8	1,740	1,652	39
9. ECS CR	115.3	39	10.1	2,019	1,059	144
10. NEFT	927.5	1,252.90	1,622.10	59,804	83,273	1,20,040
11. Immediate Payment Service (IMPS)	78.4	220.8	506.7	582	1,622	4,116
12. National Automated Clearing House (NACH)	340.2	1,404.10	2,057.30	1,221	3,802	7,916
Total Card Payments (13+14+15)	1,737.70	2,707.30	5,450.10	3,326	4,483	7,421
13. Credit Cards	615.1	785.7	1,087.10	1,899	2,407	3,284
14. Debit Cards	808.1	1,173.60	2,399.30	1,213	1,589	3,299
15. Prepaid Payment Instruments (PPIs)	314.5	748	1,963.70	213	488	838
Total Retail Payments (5 to 15)	4,621.60	6,945.20	10,861.70	1,54,126	1,77,752	2,20,634
Grand Total (1 to 15)	4,717.40	7,046.60	10,973.20	16,60,158	18,09,701	22,58,711

Note:
1. Real Time Gross Settlement (RTGS) system includes customer and inter-bank transactions only.
2. Settlement of Collateralised Borrowing and Lending Obligation (CBLO), Government securities clearing and forex transactions are through the Clearing Corporation of India Ltd. (CCIL). Government Securities includes Outright trades and both legs of Repo transactions.
3. Consequent to total cheque volume migrating to the cheque truncation system (CTS), there is no Magnetic Ink Character Recognition (MICR) Cheque Processing Centre (CPC) location in the country as of now.
4. The figures for cards are for transactions at point of sale (POS) terminals only.
5. The National Automated Clearing House (NACH) system was started by the National Payments Corporation of India (NPCI) on December 29, 2012, to facilitate inter-bank, high volume, electronic transactions which are repetitive and periodic in nature.
6. Figures in the columns might not add up to the total due to rounding off of numbers.
Source: Annual Report of the RBI, 2018

As India had chosen the top-down approach, it had to face certain problems in promoting the digital payments. However, instead of choosing the top-down approach, India could have chosen the bottom-up approach, as chosen by South Korea, as they are experimenting with the coinless society. There are certain advantages with the bottom-up approach over the top-down approach, i.e., similar to South Korea. Firstly, there would have been savings in terms of coin minting. Secondly, it would have allowed the general public to get acquainted with the electronic payment systems. Thirdly, it would have allowed the FinTech to develop and would have also tested the preparedness of the society to shift a non-cash mode of transactions (Moon, 2017). India's demonetization although did increase the non-cash mode of payment in the country. As shown in the table below, there has been a surge in the electronic clearing growth, in terms of the value of transaction of 39.84 percent from 2014-15 to 2015-16 and 44.69 percent from 2015-16 to 2016-17. Further, there has also an increase in the usage of cards for the payments. The of the value of transaction using the card for payment grew at 38.79 percent from 2014-15 to 2015-16 and 65.54 percent from 2015-16 to 2016-17(Reserve Bank of India. (2018)).

CONCLUSION

Demonetization just like any other economic reform would have certain costs and drawbacks which are very apparent and immediate, along with benefits which are diffused and would only be gauged over a period of time and not immediately. Whether this bold policy decision would be beneficial for the Indian economy in the long run is completely hinging on the plan of action of the government for the future to tackle the menace of black money. In economics, one of the aspects of cost and benefit evaluation of any policy is to ask those who have been harmed whether they have been properly compensated for the same, in this regard it is pretty evident that the current government has fallen short of the mark, and there was a lack of an action plan to help the section of the society which was most inconvenienced. Also, there are lessons to be learned from the experiences of other countries for moving towards the cashless economy. There are lessons to be learned from Korea, which transformed itself to a coinless economy. The similar transition for India may create better pathway for a cashless economy. It would be interesting to see how India transforms itself in a cashless economy.

REFERENCES

Bauer, P. W. (1998). *Currency: time for change?* Federal Reserve Bank of Cleveland, Economic Commentary.

Becker, W. E. (1999). Carl Shapiro and Hal R. Varian. Information Rules: A Strategic Guide to the Network Economy. *The Journal of Economic Education*, *30*(2), 189–190. doi:10.1080/00220489909595956

Beyes, P., & Bhattacharya, R. (2016). *India's 2016 demonetisation drive: A case study on innovation in anti-corruption policies, government communications and political integrity*. OECD Global Anti-Corruption Integrity Forum. Retrieved from https://www.oecd.org/cleangovbiz/Integrity-Forum-2017-Beyes-Bhattacharya-India-demonetisation-drive.pdf

Blanchard, O., Dell'Ariccia, G., & Mauro, P. (2010). *Rethinking Macroeconomic Policy: Getting Granular. IMF Staff Position Note* (Vol. 10). IMF eLibrary. doi:10.1111/j.1538-4616.2010.00334.x

Chakravorti, B. (2016). *The Cost of Cash in the United States*. The Fletcher School Tufts University. Retrieved from http://fletcher.tufts.edu/CostofCash/~/media/Fletcher/Microsites/Cost of Cash/CostofCashStudyFinal.pdf

Chauhan, S., & Kaushik, N. (2016). Impact of Demonetization on Stock Market: Event Study Methodology. *Indian Journal of Accounting*, 127.

Choudhury, S. D. C., & Dwarakanath, B. (2017, January 16). India central bank relaxes cash withdrawal limit with immediate effect. *Reuters*. Retrieved from https://in.reuters.com/article/us-india-modi-corruption-withdrawal/india-central-bank-relaxes-cash-withdrawal-limit-with-immediate-effect-idINKBN1501GQ

Commander, S. J., & Mumssen, C. (1998). *Understanding barter in Russia*. Academic Press.

Evans, D. S. (2002). The Antitrust Economics of Two-Sided Markets. *Ssrn*, *20*, 325. doi:10.2139srn.332022

Furness, W. H. (1910). *The island of stone money, Uap of the Carolines, by William Henry Furness, 3d ... with illustrations from photographs by the author*. London: J.B. Lippincott Company.

Garcia-Swartz, D. D., Hahn, R. W., & Layne-Farrar, A. (2004). *The economics of a cashless society: An analysis of the costs and benefits of payment instruments*. AEI- Brooking Joint Center For Regulatory Studies.

Hari, G. R. (2017). *Demonetisation*. Retrieved from http://www.mca.co.in/images/Demonetisation_MCA.PDF

Joshi, V. (2018). Impact of Demonetization on Indian Economy with Respect to Real Estate Sector. *Ssrn*, *7*(3), 20–28. doi:10.2139srn.3120188

Kumar, A. (2017a). Economic Consequences of Demonetisation Money Supply and Economic Structure. *Economic and Political Weekly*, *150*(1).

Kumar, A. (2017b). *Understanding the Black Economy and Black Money in India*. RUA Publications. Retrieved from https://books.google.co.in/books?id=DB6UnQAACAAJ

Lahiri, A. K. (2016). *Demonetization, the Cash Shortage and the Black Money*. Academic Press.

Litwack, J. M., & Sutherland, D. (2000). The Demonetisation of the Russian Economy: Causes and Policy Options. *OECD Economic Survey of Russia: 1999-2000*. Retrieved from https://www.imf.org/external/pubs/ft/seminar/2000/invest/pdf/litwack.pdf

Luo, G. Y. (1998). The evolution of money as a medium of exchange. *Journal of Economic Dynamics & Control*, *23*(3), 415–458. doi:10.1016/S0165-1889(98)00029-3

Mali, V. (2016). Demonetization: A step towards modified India. *International Journal of Commerce and Management Research International Journal of Commerce and Management Research Issue, 2*(12), 2455–1627.

Mantel, B. (2001). *Why Don't Consumers Use Electronic Banking Products? Towards a Theory of Obstacles, Incentives, and Opportunities*. doi:10.2139srn.256736

Masiero, S. (2017). New routes to cashlessness ? ICTs, demonetisation, and the Indian informal economy. *Dsa2017*.

Ministry of Electronics & Information Technology. (2015). *Digital India*. Retrieved April 16, 2018, from http://digitalindia.gov.in/content/introduction

Ministry of Electronics and Information Technology (MeitY). (n.d.). *Cashless India*. Retrieved April 16, 2018, from http://cashlessindia.gov.in

Moon, W. (2017). A Coinless Society as a Bridge to a Cashless Society: A Korean Experiment. In *Cash in East Asia* (pp. 101–115). Springer; doi:10.1007/978-3-319-59846-8_7

Mounika, D., & Kadhirvel, R. (2017). Impact Of Demonetization In E-Banking. *International Journal of Trend in Research and Development*, 1–3.

Nam, R., & Bhat, S. (2016, December 21). FACTBOX - RBI rolls back curbs on cash deposits. *Reuters*. Retrieved from https://in.reuters.com/article/india-demonetisation-latest/factbox-rbi-rolls-back-curbs-on-cash-deposits-idINKBN14A12A

Nerkar, A. D. (2016). Demonetisation: Impact on Indian Economy. *International Journal of Advanced Engineering Research and Science, 3*(12), 281–283. doi:10.22161/ijaers.3.12.50

Paliwal, B. (2017, April). 30 Days of Demonetization in India. *Cornell Policy Review*. Retrieved from www.cornellpolicyreview.com/30-days-of-demonetization-in-india/?pdf=3449

Rogoff, K. (1998). Blessing or curse? Foreign and underground demand for euro notes. *Economic Policy, 13*(26), 261–303. doi:10.1111/1468-0327.00033

Rogoff, K. (2014). *Costs and Benefits to Phasing Out Paper Currency*. doi:10.3386/w20126

Rogoff, K. (2015). Costs and Benefits to Phasing out Paper Currency. *NBER Macroeconomics Annual, 29*(1), 445–456. doi:10.1086/680657

Shekhar, P. (2016, November 18). Demonetisation: Could private hospitals have saved 55 lives with old notes? *India Today*. Retrieved from https://www.indiatoday.in/india/story/demonetisation-private-hospitals-old-currency-notes-352711-2016-11-18

Singh, B., & Roy, I. (2017). *Mint Street Memo No. 01 Demonetisation and Bank Deposit Growth*. Academic Press.

Singh, R. (2017, November 27). Demonetisation: Why the challenge to take digital payment to rural India is as huge as the opportunity. *Economic Times*, pp. 1–10. Retrieved from http://economictimes.indiatimes.com/news/economy/policy/sunday-et-making-rural-india-pay-digitally-and-challenges-post-demonetisation/articleshow/55640316.cms

Singh, R. K. (2016, November 30). Indian economy racing before Modi removed oxygen of cash. *Reuters*. Retrieved from https://in.reuters.com/article/us-india-economy-gdp/indian-economy-racing-before-modi-removed-oxygen-of-cash-idINKBN13P1X8

Worthington, S. (2006). *The cashless society The European plastic payment card*. The Cashless Society; doi:10.1108/09590559510095260

ADDITIONAL READING

Balaji, K. C., & Balaji, K. (2017). A Study on Demonetization and its Impact on Cashless Transactions. *International Journal of Advanced Scientific Research & Development*, 58-64.

Bayero, M. A. (2015). Effects of Cashless Economy Policy on financial inclusion in Nigeria: An exploratory study. *Procedia: Social and Behavioral Sciences*, *172*, 49–56. doi:10.1016/j.sbspro.2015.01.334

Betz, F., Anderson, T. R., & Puthanpura, A. K. (2017). Modeling Currency Flow in an Economy: The Case of India's Demonetization in 2016. *Theoretical Economics Letters*, *7*(04), 1001–1014. doi:10.4236/tel.2017.74068

Dash, A. (2017). A Study on Socio Economic Effect of Demonetization in India. *International Journal of Management and Applied Science (IJMAS)*, 13-15.

Ganesan, G., & Gajendranayagam, B. (2017). Impact of demonetization on Indian Economy. *IJAR*, *3*(9), 433–436.

Ramdurg, A. I., & Basavaraj, D. (2016). Demonetization: Redefining Indian economy. *International journal of commerce and management research*, *2*(12), 07-12.

Rani, G. (2016). Effects of demonetization on retail outlets. *International journal of applied research*, *2*(12), 400-401.

Shukla, M., & Bose, M. S. (2017). Impact of Digitalization in Economy and The effects of Demonetization: An Overview. *ELK Asia Pacific Journals-978-93-85537-02-8 NMC*.

Sinha, A., & Rai, D. (2016). Aftermath of demonetization on rural population. *International Journal of Research in Economics and Social Sciences*, *6*(11), 223–228.

Woodruff, D. (1999). Barter of the bankrupt: The politics of demonetization in Russia's federal state. *Uncertain transition: Ethnographies of change in the postsocialist world*, 83-124.

KEY TERMS AND DEFINITIONS

Cashless Economy: Cashless economy refers to the economy where transactions are done using digital payment methods instead of using cash.

Demonetization: Demonetization basically refers to discontinuation of old currency units of an economy which would render the old currency value less and replace the old currency units with new currency units having value.

Digital Wallet: A digital wallet or e-wallet allows an individual to make online transactions like shopping, bill payments, or online booking.

Hawala: Hawala is a method of transmitting money from different countries to India in Indian currency denominations.

Inflation: Inflation refers to sustained increase in the price level of goods and services in the economy over a period of time.

Microfinance Institution: Microfinance institutions are finance institutions that provide financial services to lower income segments of the population.

Chapter 8
Importance of Risk Management and Risk Management Process

Çağla Demir Pali
TYH Textile, Turkey

ABSTRACT

Importance of risk exposure and risk management practices have attracted the attention of companies, investors, and all other parties who benefit from performances of companies. Competitive environment and global effects force the companies to pay attention to manage their risks. Therefore, governmental bodies and international associations embarked on researches in risk management and as a result of these efforts regulations have been put in place. Germany, USA, and UK are the leading countries that made significant progress in risk management field by enacting laws, regulations, and issuing guidelines. But the subject is still new for some countries and difficult for companies, especially small and medium sized, to apply. The chapter starts with the benefits and importance of risk management. Then steps of risk management are explained with the examples.

INTRODUCTION

Risk is one of the fundamental elements that influences economic behavior of people and businesses and has been studied in different areas such as accounting, finance, economics, safety, and health. Since researchers have approached risk from different dimensions, several definitions of risk are used in literature. Usta (2012) defined risk as a positive or negative difference between a realized value and an expected value depending on the future alternatives. In financial markets, "risk" and "uncertainty" are used interchangeably but they are basically different concepts. In a simple way, the measurable part of uncertainty is called risk and it shows the probability of occurrence of an event and whether the result will be good or otherwise (Usta, 2012).

Graham (2008) stated that risks can arise due to various reasons. They can be related to internal factors such as management (accounting system, management style, and the like), technology (production methods), people (staff, customers and suppliers), or adequacy of controls as well as external reasons such as business environment, political issues, regulations and policies, country and industry they operate

DOI: 10.4018/978-1-5225-7208-4.ch008

in. In addition to the risks these factors can cause individually, interactions among them can also raise some other risks. For example, risks related to employees can have an impact on the risks associated with management or adequacy of controls; meanwhile managerial risks are also affected by technological risks. Likewise, economical risks (government regulations, exchange risks, political stability) also have an impact on the financial risks (foreign currency risks, interest risks, liquidity risks, credit risks) of the entities. Global factors have effect on businesses or business environment directly and this link continues with operations, reputation and infrastructure of the company, respectively.

With the emergence of new risks, changes in their effects can be more brutal now because of the exposure, volume and volatility in the markets. On the other hand, companies are more aware of the negative effects of risks. Therefore, they are trying to manage risks they are exposed to. But not all kinds of risks can be managed effectively; accordingly, risks are classified as controllable risks and non-controllable risks. The business structure and the business-specific risks arising from the industry in which they operate are the risks under the control of the entities and can be avoided or their effects can be reduced or increased with actions taken. The risks that are not under the control of the companies are generally country related or worldwide affected risks.

In this chapter, the importance and benefits of risk management practices is emphasized and the steps of risk management processes are explained. This chapter starts with literature review and the bases of the related regulations have been explained and supported by relevant reports. Benefits and objectives of risk management are discussed to reason the importance of the risk management practices. Then a general overview of risk management is given and steps of the process is detailed with the examples. Finally, future research opportunities are discussed.

BACKGROUND

Risks caused by the exposure to emerging markets, the toughening competition in markets, and the fluctuations in the national and international markets have significant effects on the companies' financial performances and future expectations. On the other hand, companies cannot avoid all the risks they are exposed to. Therefore, adaptations to changes and fluctuations, elimination of potential negative effects and evaluation of opportunities for possible future benefits have significant impact on the future success of companies.

Additionally, changes in the financial sector and developments in the banking system in recent years have also changed the market dynamics. Instability in the markets have affected companies' financial results and has made them less predictable. Since they cannot be easily predictable and controllable, more precarious financial results are experienced and they have become a threat to countries and economies. Because of these, the financial crises are experienced, and they are one of the factors that draw attention to the importance of risk management and risk disclosures. Linsley (2011, p. 5) has reached the following results in a study on risk disclosures of banks relating to pre-financial crisis he has made:

In all cases prior to the crisis the narratives portray the banks as having a sound awareness of the risk environment and a propensity to adapt their risk management approaches as the risk environment changes. They display a confidence in their ability to manage the risks they are confronted with and there is no forewarning that a crisis may be imminent within these narratives.

The analysis of the tone of the risk narratives indicates that there is an increasing optimism as the pre-crisis period progresses. This potentially influences readers to adopt a relatively more accepting and unquestioning stance towards the risk view of the banks as they (unconsciously) absorb this optimism. However, given the complex nature of risk, it would be more appropriate for readers to adopt a proactive and questioning attitude towards the risk view of the banks. The mood of optimism noted in respect of the pre-crisis risk disclosures dissipates post-crisis. The certainty aspect of their tone, which is associated with ideas of resolve and perseverance, tends to decrease over the pre-crisis period and then increases post-crisis. A similar pattern, albeit to a lesser extent, is noted in respect of the activity aspect of their tone. The decrease in certainty and activity tones pre-crisis are likely to be connected with the increased mood of optimism, for if there is a belief that 'all is well' then managers feel less pressure to convey determination to undertake decisive actions. Conversely, the banks' managers adopting an attitude of certainty and activity post-crisis can serve to reassure readers that they are acting determinedly to manage the risks associated with the crisis.

As can be seen, the confidence of the banks in their risk management abilities and the optimistic environment have brought about the destructive effects of the financial crises. This, yet again, reveals the importance of risk management and the negative results of inadequate practices.

After the financial crisis in 2008, companies became more aware of the implications of risks and the methods that can be adopted to manage them. Identifying and assessing risks, selecting and implementing risk management strategies and evaluation and control of the process is known as risk management. These steps are established and understood especially in developed countries. But risk management practices are still rare in some developing and under-developed countries because of the challenges in implementation and insufficient guidance offered by the regulatory bodies.

Due to a lack and inadequacy of risk management practices, businesses, business owners and stakeholders have suffered various damages. For this reason, many national or international institutions have conducted various studies and prepared reports.

In the report "Observations on Risk Management Practices during the Recent Market Turbulence" (Senior Supervisors Group, 2008) it is studied whether insufficiencies in risk management practices of banks investigated had an impact on the losses they incurred. It is observed in the report that, due to economic instabilities, the banks opted to improve their risk management practices, and for some companies that helped in delivering better outcomes.

Another important point to note here is that the risks exist for all businesses, regardless of their size. All small, medium or large businesses are exposed to risks, although, the impact or consequences of those risks may vary. For example, both a large retail chain and a pop and mom store are exposed to similar risks. These risks include: the risk of inventory being stolen, the risk of damage to inventory, the risk of damage to building used for business operations, theft, and increase in the cost of goods sold, etc. Similarly, enterprises operating in agriculture business are exposed to risks regardless of their size. Unusual seasonal conditions or unexpected changes in weather create a risk for all businesses operating in the sector and need to be carefully examined and managed. Risk management is necessary for businesses of various sizes, but it is important to consider the company specifics and size of the companies when setting the risk management practices, since large and small companies cannot implement the same practices totally. Since businesses have different risk appetites and risk levels, the company size will cause changes in practices. Also, cost and benefit analysis should be done, company sizes should be taken into consideration and the most effective and most appropriate methods for the company should be identified when there is a risk.

OBJECTIVES AND BENEFITS OF RISK MANAGEMENT

Recently numerous companies have suffered damages or have been fined because of the inadequacy or ineffectiveness of risk management practices in various countries. For example, Wells Fargo paid $185 million penalty for inappropriate sales practices (such as setting up accounts without customer consent, generating overdraft charges, etc.), and stock price of Volkswagen decreased by 40% and lawsuits were filed for not meeting the compliance standards. Both mistakes could be prevented by the existence of effective and appropriate risk management practices.

There are risks for all companies, but the types of these risks can vary depending on the countries, sectors or company-specific factors. Risks exposed can have positive or negative effects on the entities in accordance with their nature. The direction of the risks can be changed by the measures taken through risk management practices. Risk management is used to assess opportunities that can prevent or mitigate the risks through preliminary determination of the uncertainties that might have an adverse effect on the future performance of the businesses, and to take necessary precautions. Risk management has been an increasingly important issue recently and various countries are working on it; they intend to encourage risk management practices through the work of regulatory agencies.

Risk management is important for companies to achieve their objectives and to improve the future operational and financial performance. It is also important for investors to have confidence on their investment decisions and protect their invested money.

By risk management:

- The negative risks can be managed and converted to opportunities;
- The negative risks or their effects can be eliminated or reduced;
- The likelihood of positive risks can be increased.

Risk management aims to identify, analyze and examine possible future effects of risk factors and to allocate these effects to appropriate accounts and transactions. In an entity with an effective risk management system, it is assumed that the managers have knowledge of the risk factors, corporate risk management and the possible effects of these risks on future performance (Dobler, 2008).

Usta (2012) summarizes some factors that make risk management necessary:

- Globalization of financial resources and increasing international competition and the internationalization of goods and capital movements;
- Increase in financial market transactions;
- The emergence of new financial products;
- Increase in technological needs and continuity of technological changes;
- Political changes;
- The effects of central banks;
- The emergence of banks that are trading risks;
- Development and dissemination of risk management practices.

In the research conducted by Deloitte and Touche LLP (2015) some benefits of risk management models are identified and those are given below:

- To increase the chance to get more benefit from opportunities;
- To support the identification and management of risks at the institutional level;
- Reduces operational losses and surprises to a minimum level;
- More improved risk-taking decisions;
- Combining the risk factor with performance and growth.

The Committee of Sponsoring Organizations of the Treadway Commission ("COSO") (2009) emphasized the benefits of a good understanding of risks for management. By understanding risk categories and concentrations, they could evaluate their risk capabilities and vulnerability against crises. Also, it would help them to see whether a company could work effectively in managing certain types of risks, and if so, they could accept more risks on a specific area while tolerating others from the standpoint of allocating their resources effectively.

RISK MANAGEMENT PROCESS

Risk management is a process consisting of three steps of determining, evaluating and managing risks by a systematic approach. Since risk management is a dynamic process rather than a static one, the risk management process continues with the control and improvement, after the implementation of the prepared plan has started. It is necessary to constantly review the process and to follow the updated risks and effectiveness of the measures taken against the identified risks (Merna, Al-Thani, 2008).

Success of companies is affected not only by internal factors but also external factors, and those factors play an important role in the achievement of targets identified. These factors mostly include the possible events that will affect the way the companies operate and needs to be controlled by risk management practices.

Risk management is a complex and indirect process and starts with the understanding of what risk is. At this point the following issues stated by Graham (2008, p. 14) should be kept in mind:

- Risk is about the future;
- Risk is based on the notion of probability of an event happening;
- Risk is then assessed in the intensity or impact of that event;
- Once you decide on probability and impact you can then compare various risks you are facing and set priorities;
- After that it is all about mitigating, managing and controlling your risks.

Graham (2008) summarized risk management in two stages and six steps in which risk management starts with risk analysis. Risk analysis consists of three steps: identifying the risks, analyzing risks and prioritizing them based on their importance. First, the risks that companies are exposed to must be found and identified. After identifying the risks that have effect on business, it is necessary to analyze them qualitatively and quantitatively and rank the possible effects. The ranking step is known as prioritization. In this way, it will be possible to allocate resources starting from the elements with high risk and to use them in the most efficient manner by avoiding the waste of resources. In this process, monitoring of each step is crucial to establish a better risk analysis process.

The process defined by Graham (2008) continues with the development of risk management plan that is the second stage with three steps. In this stage, the data obtained in risk analysis process is used. All risks should be considered in the preparation of the risk management plans by considering the priority order set in the risk analysis section. And risk interactions between identified risks should be considered to see their effects in aggregate. For example, if a risk is increased when another risk is decreased, the two risks must be assessed together, and unnecessary resource spending should be avoided by setting up independent strategies. During the implementation of the plan, risk management practices should be monitored and the risks that the entity is exposed to should be reviewed continuously. This way, usefulness of the plan will be tested. These reviews should not only be limited to the implementation of the risk plan but should also include reviewing the identified risks and determining whether they continue to be valid and whether there are any potential new risks. By these reviews, additional actions can be taken or some precautions can be eliminated to avoid unnecessary resource spending. Also, if new risks are identified new strategies should be established.

As it is explained above, risk management process can be divided into different steps and further details can be added. But in general, the explained process is summarized in four steps as:

1. Risk identification
2. Risk Assessment
3. Selection and Implementation of Risk Management Strategies
4. Evaluation of the Process and Reporting

The steps of risk management are explained below in detail. Examples will also be given using Company G, a zipper manufacturer. Company G is a family owned business that purchases raw materials in US dollars ($) from abroad and sells its products in Euro (€) after making the necessary customizations. Additionally, since it applies 'make to order' production method, it does not have a high amount of raw material and purchases raw materials according to the orders received. Finally, 62% of its sales are made to a specific customer. It has an outstanding bank loan of $1,000,000 which will be paid in next 5 years.

Step 1: Risk Identification

Risk identification is the first step of risk management process and is crucial since it is necessary to identify all risks that could affect the future activities of the entity either positively or negatively.

Identification of risks is a process that requires extensive review. For this reason, it is not sufficient to examine only the significant items in the balance sheet and income statement. All factors that affect those accounts should be considered carefully and in detail. For example, an entity which has the risk of foreign exchange exposure should not only look at foreign currency accounts, but also should consider all accounts that will be affected by possible changes in exchange rates. In cases where raw material prices increase due to the changes in the exchange rates, suppliers that could become more attractive should be identified and new supplier agreements should be made beforehand. (Brodeur, Buehler, Patsalos-Fox & Pergler, 2010) Exchange rate changes can also affect sales units by the change in sales prices (to foreign customers) in the long term. So, the effect on sales revenue will be both in dollars and in units.

It is important that all departments should work cohesively in risk identification process. While many entities generate risk maps, they follow the path of bringing the risks from different departments together. The different naming of the same or similar risks in different departments may lead to the problem of not assessing these risks together and may prevent the identification of greater risks faced by enterprises. (Brodeur, Buehler, Patsalos-Fox & Pergler, 2010. If a risk is related to more than one department, its effect will be extensive and must be treated carefully. Therefore, same or similar risks must be considered in the same way. They can be overlooked if they are viewed separately (because their combined affect can be missed). This way importance of the interdepartmental risks will be noticed and risks will be prioritized properly. And by considering two risks together, actions taken to counter them will be set more effectively by avoiding to waste resources to manage these risks separately.

A group of UK based risk management organizations came together and conducted a study about risk management in 2002. The study was published as "A Risk Management Standard" by Institute of Risk Management (IRM). (IRM, 2002) The study incorporated the opinions of a wide range of organizations related to risk management and identified the steps of risk management. The standard is the basis for further work and was used in recent studies as a starting point. Despite the publication of ISO 31000 Risk Management in 2018 it is still supported by IRM. A list of risk identification techniques is determined in the report and a revised version of the list is given below:

- Questionnaires/Interviews
- Expert judgements
- Brainstorming
- Risk assessment workshops
- Scenario analysis
- Process oriented business studies which describe the internal processes and external factors that have influence on those processes,
- Auditing and inspection
- Incident investigation
- SWOT (Strength, Weakness, Opportunities and Threats) analysis

Identified risks must be reevaluated because it is important to be mindful to avoid following mistakes: predicted results, working on the same risks for years, taking into account unnecessary/outdated risks (past related losses), focusing on the risks that are easy to manage, overestimating the risk projecting an isolated case to whole entity, using unreliable sources (identifying risks based on unacceptable evidence), to assume things are all right (thinking that there is no significant risk for the company) (Graham, 2008). Concentrating on insignificant risks can cause to overlook significant risks. By doing so companies can both waste their resources (effort, time and money) and miss the chance to manage important risks that can affect companies' future performances.

Example: The Company first, held extensive reviews. Meetings were held with employees from various departments to identify the risks that they were exposed to and obtain their opinions using surveys and scenario analysis. Risk maps were prepared.

The risks identified were as follows:

- Foreign currency risk (Company G buys inventory in US $ but sells finished goods in Euro);
- Raw material shortage risk (Company uses 'make to order' production method thus there is no safety stock);
- Customer concentration risk (Company G relies on one big client);
- Political risk (Company G has business relations with more than one country so political changes can affect custom agreements);
- Risks related to management techniques (Company G is a family owned business, thus most of the management practices are old fashioned and decisions are made by the owner without consultation);
- The risk of shift in customer preferences (Company G is in fashion business thus changing trends can affect the demand);
- Liquidity risk (Company G has a bank loan);
- New competitors in the market.

Step 2: Risk Assessment

Risk assessment is a systematic process for analyzing identified risks that can affect companies' objectives in a positive or negative direction. These events can be results of external (economic trends, rules, regulations, competitive environment) or internal (operations, staff, procedures) factors. Establishing a strong risk assessment process enables the management to identify and evaluate risks in a better way, as well as identify the risks that can be used for the benefit of business and ensure that the necessary controls are effectively and efficiently placed in operation. In risk assessment process, objectives of the entity, the distribution of responsibilities, timing, and the necessary inputs and outputs are considered. Then, planning is done by using this information. A well-implemented risk assessment process provides the basis for how an entity can provide risk appetite data and respond to risks that they are exposed to. (Price Waterhouse Coopers, 2008)

Entities that are exposed to structural risks should clearly identify how much risk they can accept (risk appetite), what risks they can afford to take, and how much they can benefit from these risks (opportunities arise from the risks). A company's risk appetite is determined by assessing the risk capacity. Risk capacity is the ability to avoid undesirable effects when they are faced to. (Brodeur, Buehler, Patsalos-Fox & Pergler, 2010) COSO (2009) mentioned that risk capacity is related to liquid assets, capital or borrowing capacity of the companies. It is also noted that risk appetite should be sufficiently below the risk capacity for better results.

Some examples of these risks are cancellation of projects, postponement of repair and maintenance work, loss of reputation, decrease in product quality, failure to fulfill obligations and failure to pay debts. Once these limits are set, management should determine whether more risk can be taken. In this process, it is very important to consider the nature of the company and the risk profile. (Brodeur, Buehler, Patsalos-Fox & Pergler, 2010)

COSO (2009) emphasizes that risk appetite must be set at the optimum level to meet stakeholder expectations and also those of the management and board of directors. The accepted risk level will change with the companies' risk-taking policy as low risk appetite is better for risk averse companies while high risk takers should set a higher risk appetite. Boards' understanding of risk appetite is critical in this process since lack of that understanding will prevent the board from constraining management's willingness to take excessive risks that goes beyond the stakeholders' appetite for risk. In the aforementioned study, COSO companies' policy of entering international markets is given as an example for risk appetite. Some companies refuse to enter certain countries or international markets because of exposure to more risks while others think it is necessary to enter the markets or work in international markets to achieve long-term success. As in this example, risk appetite changes depending on the companies' policy.

It is also advised that in risk appetite determination process, the impacts of past events and the reactions of key stakeholders must be considered. Understanding the stance of employees, creditors, customers, shareholders and regulators who are the stakeholders of the companies is important to see their perspective on risk acceptability. Estimating hypothetical future events and their potential effect should also be helpful in this determination.

Price Waterhouse Coopers (2008, pp. 21-32) summarized risk assessment process in six steps as follows:

1. Identify relevant business objectives;
2. Identify events that could affect the achievement of objectives;
3. Determine risk tolerance;
4. Assess inherent likelihood and impact of risks;
5. Evaluate the portfolio of risks and determine risk responses;
6. Assess residual likelihood and impact of risks.

Various studies call these steps with different names but even if the naming is different the descriptions are essentially similar. The steps of risk assessment process are briefly described below. (Price Waterhouse Coopers, 2008; Deloitte & Touche LLP, 2012; Brodeur, Buehler, Patsalos-Fox & Pergler, 2010).

1. **Identification of Relevant Business Objectives:** Risk assessment process starts with identifying relevant business objectives. By that, entities can focus on the right risks and ensure that the risk assessment plan is targeted to the correct/relevant/prioritized objectives of the companies. It is easy to identify business objectives since they are already included in annual reports, presentations prepared by the analysts, unit strategy reports, and other management reports related to operations.

In this step, business objectives and related risks should be categorized as operational, financial, strategic or managerial risks. Also, subcategories can be helpful to assess much in detail such as market, liquidity, and exchange risks or financial risks category related to financial objectives. Assessment of different types of risks will be explained later in detail.

If the business objectives and related risks are categorized, it would be possible to work on and treat them separately. Also, related employees must be involved in the process. By their contribution, companies can benefit from the experience and specialization of the employees and focus on the right risks with an extensive background.

In the process of determination of the objectives of the company, the effects of the risks identified (about financial position of the entity, its reputation or the staff) and the realization of the probabilities should be considered. In this way, the resources of the companies are used efficiently to meet business objectives.

2. **Identification of Events that Could Affect the Achievement of Objectives:** The second step in risk assessment process is to identify events that can affect the achievement of the objectives identified. These "events" are incidents that have occurred in the past, are happening now, or are

likely to have a chance to affect the realization of the objectives in the future in a positive or negative direction. These events can depend on the internal or external factors.

3. **Determination of Risk Tolerance:** Risk tolerance refers to the level of risk that can be tolerated by the entity. To determine the tolerance levels, companies should consider the likelihood of occurrence of risks and their effects and their relations with company specifics and the industry companies operate in. This is one of the most important steps that can restrain the companies' growth potential by setting limits on their risk-taking potential. As it is mentioned before, avoiding risks is not always a good option for the companies. Therefore, determination of risk tolerance is crucial to take optimum risks. In the optimum level, companies take maximum risk they can afford to and not miss opportunities while they do not take unnecessary risks. This step must be held carefully to determine the risk management plan. Also, the calculations and considerations must be evaluated periodically and if necessary changes should be made.
4. **Assessment of Inherent Likelihood and Impact of Risks:** Potential events affecting the achievement of the business objectives of the entities are considered as negative risks. And the probability of occurrence and the effects of these risks on the business must be determined. First, the probabilities and effects of each risk are determined separately then they are brought together later. By that total effect will be calculated.

In the first step it was mentioned that companies should get the employees involved in the identification of the business objectives; they should be involved in this step too. But assessment is a tricky job to do since the standards can be subjective. Therefore, a common set of criteria must be set beforehand to evaluate and assess all possibilities fairly. It will give guidance for assessors who are responsible for working on the likelihood and impact of risks and provide a set of rules for the controllers who control the assessors' work. Also, it can be useful to divide this step into two stages. In the first stage initial risk monitoring can be performed by using qualitative techniques. Then, in the second stage more quantitative methods can be used to evaluate the most important risks.

5. **Evaluation of the Risk Portfolio and Determination of Risk Responses:** Risk management strategies are presented on how to respond to risks by considering the probabilities and effects of identified risks (which were calculated in the previous step). These strategies are determined by considering risk tolerance. Risk response strategies might be "accept," "share," "decrease," or "avoid" and all these actions are taken for each risk separately.

In evaluation of risk portfolio, risk interactions must be considered carefully. An insignificant risk can create significant opportunity or cause great damage when it interacts with another. To see the interactions between risks, risk interaction matrices can be used.

Determination of risk responses stage in this step is also related to next step of risk management: selection of risk management strategies. But here companies just decide what action they should take for which risk. Therefore, they must evaluate all the risks separately and together to see their importance by considering their potential effect. The potential effect mentioned is not just financial but also includes non-financial issues such as reputational effect, safety problems, and vulnerability.

6. **Assessment of Residual Likelihood and Impact of Risks:** Ideal responses may not be detected for all risks all the time. In some cases, only the odds of some risks or only the effects can be reduced. For this reason, risks that have not been responded must be reevaluated. By that, effectiveness of risk strategies and risk coverage ratio can be calculated and evaluated.
7. **Monitoring the Risk Assessment Process:** Monitoring and accountability are important for the assignment of responsibilities and allocation of resources effectively. For this reason, after establishing the risk assessment process, it should be supervised and controlled regularly. These steps must include effective risk identification, continuous monitoring and taking steps for necessary measurements.

Risks can be detected in different departments or levels of the company; therefore, risk assessment process covers more than one department and held by different people and groups. Risk assessment is divided into risk groups and these risk groups are explained below (Brodeur, Buehler, Patsalos-Fox & Pergler, 2010):

- **Assessment of Strategic Risks:** This refers to examining the risks related to mission and strategic objectives of the company. They are usually carried out by senior management at strategic planning meetings.
- **Assessment of Operational Risks:** This refers to examining the risk of loss that may result from insufficient or unsuccessful internal control processes, staff errors, systematic internal problems or external factors. These risks can be assessed in daily work routine or an independent assessment can be held specifically for this purpose.
- **Assessment of Compliance Risks:** This refers to examination of the risks to compliance with regulations, laws, rules, policies, procedures, ethics, contractual conditions that must be followed by the entity. These assessments are made as part of the entity's compliance efforts held in general compliance procedures.
- **Assessment of Internal Audit Risks:** These assessments reveal the effects of the risks related to shareholder value which form the basis of the internal audit plan.
- **Assessment of Financial Risks:** Information related to these assessments is basically gathered from independent auditing firm the companies work with. The auditors assess the risks of material misstatement in the financial statements in accordance with the information obtained from the internal audit department and operations. In this process, characteristics of the financial statement elements (such as materiality, suspicious accounts and transactions) and the effectiveness of the basic controls held are reviewed.
- **Assessment of Fraud Risks:** This refers to examination of the risks associated with fraudulent transactions that may affect ethics and compliance standards applied and integrity on financial reporting process. It is an assessment spread across the entity and can be made by support from specialists outside the company.
- **Assessment of Market Risks:** This refers to evaluation of market movements (risks related to options, commodities, interest rates and foreign currency) that may affect the performance of entities. Risks that companies are exposed to are assessed in this process. It is usually done by specialists outside the company who has market expertise.

- **Assessment of Credit Risks:** This refers to evaluation of the risks that lenders are exposed to. If the borrower cannot meet the contractual obligations, it will cause a liquidity problem for the lender. In this assessment, the loan accounts and transactions are examined one by one, as well as the portfolio is analyzed in a general perspective. This examination is held by the experts in the area.
- **Assessment of Customer Risks:** This refers to investigating the risks related to customers. Customer risks may have a significant impact on companies' reputation and financial performance. Customers' intentions, credibility, connections and other relevant factors are considered in these assessments and they are held by parties responsible for customer relations within the companies.
- **Assessment of Supply Chain Risks:** Assessments related to the selection and management of suppliers are included in this step. Identification of product and service inputs and the provision of necessary support are assessed by the staff who work in relation to supply chain.
- **Assessment of Product Risks:** This refers to examination of risks related to the products. This process starts from product design and development and covers the entire production, distribution, usage and disposal processes. In these evaluations, not only the product revenue and costs are considered but also the impact on the brand value of the relevant products, the interaction with other products, dependence on third parties and other related factors. These evaluations are usually made at product management level.
- **Assessment of Security Risks:** This refers to examination of the risks related to security breaches of the physical assets and information systems. These breaches can result from practices, activities, staff and business structure. This assessment is usually carried out by security departments and technology departments which have expertise in the subject.

Example: In risk assessment step, Company G started by identifying its business objectives and possible risks identified in the previous step that could affect the achievement of these objectives. Then they analyzed their risk appetite and risk capacity, and risk matrices were prepared for all identified risks and the responses below were decided:

- Foreign currency risk - Avoid
- Raw material shortage risk - Accept
- Customer concentration risk - Avoid
- Political risk - Accept
- Risks related to management techniques - Share
- The risk of shift in customer preferences - Accept
- Liquidity risk - Decrease
- New competitors in the market – Accept

Step 3: Selection and Implementation of Risk Management Strategies

Identification of "key risk indicators" is the first step in preparation of risk management strategies. Potential risks that various sections of the business may be exposed to can be detected early by using these indicators. In addition to providing early preparation for possible opportunities, these key risk indicators also offer the opportunity to take early precautions for possible problems. Establishing an effective set of key risk indicators will have a significant impact on the ability of the entity to achieve its objectives, and therefore the objectives of the entity must be clearly defined. Then, the risks that prevent the achievement of these objectives from being realized are identified (Beasley, Branson, Hancock, 2011).

One of the most effective ways to determine the key risk indicators is to analyze events one by one. One of the best ways to do that is to start analysis of an event that has affected the business in the past (or affecting right now) and causes increase of occurrence of a risk. Then, the detected event should be examined and the reasons of the event causing the business to suffer a loss or profit missed should be investigated. Finally, steps can be taken to minimize the risk of undesirable effects. For example, a business that wants to take precautions about the risk of failing to meet the terms of the loan agreement should primarily identify the factors that may create a risk for the company. For this reason, the first step is to determine whether the company will breach a contract. Once these events, known as key risk indicators, have been identified, company will have an opportunity for early detection of the risk and may go a long way towards reducing the negative effects or eliminate the risk. If there are conditions such as limits for net profit or interest coverage ratio specified in the terms of the contract, lower amount of sales revenue can be called as key risk indicator. The next step is to determine the precautions to be taken to avoid exposure and these measures may be requested to negotiate with the lender and to modify the terms (Beasley, Branson, Hancock, 2011). As it is seen, key risk indicators offer the opportunity to act before the risk event takes place. If these indicators are determined, when the main risk indicators in the form of a drop in sales or an unexpected large payment arise, companies can act quickly since they are ready.

It must be noted here that key risk indicators are not just negative cues. They can be used for as potential opportunities. If a potential gain is noticed, companies should determine which actions should be taken to realize the gain and then assess. Probability of occurrence of an event (that can cause positive results) can be considered and by taking early actions its occurrence can be guaranteed.

Further steps can be taken to examine the key risk indicators and identify "key factors" which will offer a chance to companies to detect the risks much earlier. Continuing with the same example, external sources like industrial reports or economic conditions can be used for the identification of the key factors that would produce the above-mentioned intermediate indicators (decrease in sales revenue). By identifying key factors (which are components of the key risk indicators), early measures can be taken using internal resource data such as facility capacity, staff status, input prices, and turnover rate of key personnel. Thus, negative risk elements can be eliminated totally or used to convert them to opportunities. (Beasley, Branson, Hancock, 2011). After the identification of key factors and key risk indicators, risk management strategy can be established. But addition to those factors and indicators, risk tolerance of companies must be considered.

In the selection of risk management strategies there are many options can be chosen. Some of them are listed and explained below (Her Majesty's Treasury, 2004):

1. **Tolerate the Risk:** If the risk exposed can be tolerated by the company, the first option will be tolerating the risk and taking no further action. In some cases, even if the risk is not tolerable, company's options might be limited or taking actions against the risks can cost more than the potential benefit. In such cases, companies are prone to tolerate the risk and focus on more 'treatable' risks.
2. **Treat the Risk:** After the identification and assessment of the risk-taking actions, to constrain the risk to a desired or acceptable level is known as risk treatment. In risk treatment, risks can be divided in subgroups to address different actions for each separately. For this option, there are four different kind of controls: preventive controls, corrective controls, directive controls, and detective controls.

a. **Preventive Controls:** Most of the controls implemented in companies to treat risks fall in this category. Preventive controls are designed to set limits to the possibility of an unwanted outcome being realized. Proper authorization and separation of duties are the examples of these controls.

b. **Corrective Controls:** These controls are put in place against the outcomes which have been already realized. The purpose of their use is to recover the damage and loss. Insurance is a good example of corrective controls.

c. **Directive Controls:** They are designed to achieve determined results. To avoid accidents, wearing protective clothing by employees who work in dangerous jobs is an example of directive controls.

d. **Detective Controls:** These controls are applied "after the event" to detect the undesirable consequences. Taking a physical count of inventory and reconciliation of accounts are the examples in this group.

3. **Transfer the Risk:** Risk treatment is a costly and complex way to manage risks. This way, intolerable and hard to treat risks can be transferred to a third party. Paying a third party to undertake the risk or getting insurance are the tools that might be used to transfer risk. Transferring a risk does not always mean that the company cannot manage the risk; in some cases risks are transferred to a third party because it is more capable of managing the risk effectively. Even if some companies are better than others in risk management, not all risks can be totally transferrable such as reputational risk.
4. **Terminate the Risk:** If costs of treating or transferring the risk are higher than its benefits, companies should consider putting an end to the activity that causes the risk.
5. **Take the Opportunity:** This option is different than others. The first four options are used to avoid the effect of risks, but this one is about to increase the probability of occurrence or effects of risks.

Example: Company G determined the below risk strategies:

- **Foreign Currency Risk**: Company G decided to use derivative instruments to hedge risk.
- **Raw Material Shortage Risk:** After extensive considerations, it was decided that 'make to order' production method is the optimum way. Furthermore, Company G decided to accept this risk (but negotiations would be done with the clients to place the orders earlier).
- **Customer Concentration Risk:** It was decided to undertake negotiations with potential clients to gain new customers. If necessary, Company G would shift the production capacity to new customers from the biggest customer to prevent concentration.
- **Political Risk:** Company G could not avoid this risk, furthermore it decided to accept the risk.
- **Risks Related to Management Techniques:** Company G decided to hire professional managers and advisors to improve the company's managerial capabilities and reach better decisions; also, it was decided that directors' and officers' liability insurance would be purchased.
- **The Risk of Shift in Customer Preferences:** Company G could not avoid this risk; so, it decided to accept the risk.
- **Liquidity Risk:** The company decided not to take new loans after repaying the existing one, it also decided to assign someone for synchronization of cash flows.

- **New Competitors in the Market:** Company G could not avoid this risk; therefore, it decided to accept. However, it was further decided that the relations with the customers should be re-evaluated and the relations with the profitable customers should be strengthened.

Step 4: Evaluation of the Process and Reporting

Establishing an efficient and effective strategy is not enough on its own as its implementation must be evaluated and then the results of the evaluations should be reported. If any error or missing part is detected after the reviews, risk management system can be modified. Even in cases when risk management process works as intended, some improvements can be made after the evaluations to ensure a better performance and increase the efficiency.

To explain the reasons for demanding more and better risk reporting, analogies are made with products and services used in daily life. For example, it is expected to put a warning label on the packages of hot products or warnings about possible changes in the value of investments. While most of this information provides data to parties such as consumers and investors, the information disclosed is not sufficient to meet the needs of users completely. It is not preferred by companies to disclose more information than what is demanded by the regulators. The same reasons apply to risk disclosures, which are part of corporate reporting. Meanwhile, in recent years, companies make more risk disclosures than in the past. The reasons for this increase are the changes in the business environment and the risky nature of these changes. Especially, the increasing use of financial instruments in the last 30 years and the high amount of money invested in them attract attention to importance of risk disclosures. Because of the limitations of historical financial reporting information, information users demand more information for better decision-making opportunities. Financial and non-financial information disclosures in the future must compensate these limitations to meet the demand (Institute of Chartered Accountants in England and Wales, 2011, p. 4).

Beasley, Branson, Hancock (2011) advised that the following issues should be attended in the review of risk management process to make improvements in the system, if necessary; whether there are new risks that may arise, whether there is a change in the probabilities and/or effects of the existing risks, changes in the priority of risks managed, whether previously identified risks are still valid and whether the controls are effective. By internal reporting of risk management practices, top management will be kept informed and shall have knowledge about the risk management process. This will help to expand their view to see the companies' risk exposure level and its possible effects on the company. By that, new decisions can be made by considering their risk acceptance level.

For external reporting purposes, risks and risk management practices are generally stated in annual reports of the entities, and these reports are presented to outside users of the information such as investors, creditors, customers or governmental bodies. The main party who uses the risk management information in this group is the investors of the entities and those who make their decisions by considering the risks of the entities to measure the risks they are exposed to.

It is important to note that companies cannot always reach the targets they determined by risk management practices. Graham (2008) listed and explained the following reasons of the failure of risk management applications:

- **Too Narrow a Focus on Risk:** Looking for risks that are easy to acquire or manage should be avoided.

- **Failure to Manage Risk Complexity and Materiality:** Partial application opportunities should be recognized but a consistency that is spread across the enterprise should be emphasized. Considering the risk tolerance, the materiality level (used to determine the amounts to be examined) should be identified and parameters should be determined to focus on the most important ones. Focusing on all the risks will be a time and resource consuming activity that must be avoided.
- **Complex Reporting and Communications:** Easy-to-implement plans should be used such as simple, code-based tables and reports.
- **Unclear Accountability for Risk:** Accountability usually arises after the event occurs. For this reason, it is advantageous to go for early action. To establish accountability, there must be an assigned executive who has control over the activities, has explicitly expressed responsibilities and established compensation mechanisms.
- **Undefined Roles and Responsibilities:** The executive committee should set guidelines and strategies and accept the possible remaining risks. Senior management should accept risk of liability and provide risk policy and support through guidelines, tools and metrics. The identification, evaluation, reduction, monitoring and disclosure of risks are the responsibility of the management responsible for the operation and the system. Additionally, periodic controls, evaluation and assurance should be carried out by management.

Example: Company G identified and assessed its risks and set appropriate risk strategies. Then the effectiveness of the implemented strategies was evaluated and improvements in the company's risk profile was observed. For the next period, new objectives were set and plans were made, it was also decided to repeat the control procedures applied. Finally, the risk management strategies applied were disclosed through the Company's website and annual report.

SOLUTIONS AND RECOMMENDATIONS

As mentioned earlier, the importance of risk management practices has drawn attention of the companies and they are starting to work on this field or if they already have risk management practices they are trying to get better. Because of this, importance of theoretical work on the area is increasing. Companies can be guided by directories and manuals to be prepared, and they can be shed light on their work in the areas they are challenged.

Another important issue to note is that companies should be encouraged to make an effort about risk management practices. Especially for small-sized companies, the potential cost of risk management applications may seem to be more than the potential cost of not having any risk management system. For this reason, workshops and seminars to be held in order to show the importance of the issue to companies of any size will have a significant impact.

Finally, it would be useful to encourage, or even challenge, especially large companies to apply risk management practices. In this way, companies will be able to benefit from these applications and will avoid crises in the future that could result from not managing risks.

FUTURE RESEARCH DIRECTIONS

Especially in the last 15 years, the importance of risk management has increased and the subject has begun to attract the attention of regulators and academicians. Various countries have made regulations, guidelines for practitioners have been prepared and attention has been paid to the importance of risk management. However, despite the benefits of risk management practices, it is not implemented by all companies. Therefore, it is useful to examine why companies do not give due importance to risk management practices or why they prefer not to use it. This way, it will be possible to identify the reasons that deter companies from adopting such practices and to encourage businesses to apply risk management practices.

In addition to analyzing why companies do not have risk management practices, examining the benefits gained by the companies that implement risk management practices and identifying deficiencies in their implementations will be helpful in making progress in risk management practices.

Finally, although in countries like UK, US, Germany and Canada, there are guidelines prepared by regulatory bodies to help the companies in risk management, in other countries there is no such guidance provided for companies. To see the difference between level of country practices, comparative studies and research might be helpful.

Also, quality of risk management practices should be measured. By this way, the guidelines that will be prepared might be more streamlined and success oriented.

CONCLUSION

Risk is one of the fundamental elements that influences economic behavior of people and businesses and can arise due to various reasons. Companies are exposed to a variety of risks: strategic, operational, compliance, internal audit, financial, fraud, market, credit, customer, supply chain, product and security risks. They are caused by the exposure to emerging markets, the toughening competition, and the fluctuations in the national and international markets and have significant effects on the companies' financial performances and achievement of the plans.

Companies are more aware of the importance of risks and risk management practices are being carried out. As it was mentioned before by risk management the negative risks can be managed and converted to opportunities, the negative risks or their effects can be eliminated or reduced, and the likelihood of positive risks can be increased.

The steps of risk management are as follows:

1. **Risk Identification:** Risk identification is the first step of risk management process and requires extensive review. All factors that affect balance sheet and income statement items should be considered carefully. All departments should work in coordination and help each other to identify all risks separately and their effects in total.
2. **Risk Assessment:** Risk assessment is a systematic process for analyzing identified risks and establishing a strong risk assessment process enables the management to identify and evaluate risks in a better way. In this step, objectives of the entity, the distribution of responsibilities, timing, and the necessary inputs and outputs are considered and planning is done by using this information. Price Waterhouse Coopers) 2008 summarized the process in six stages as i*dentify relevant business*

objectives, identify events that could affect the achievement of objectives, determine risk tolerance, assess inherent likelihood and impact of risks, evaluate the portfolio of risks and determine risk responses and *assess residual likelihood and impact of risks.*

3. **Selection and Implementation of Risk Management Strategies**: Setting a risk management strategy starts with identification of "key risk indicators" and "key factors" that can help to detect early signs of potential losses or gains. After they are identified possible actions against those events should be decided to act better to manage the related risks. Options for companies are as follows: tolerate the risk, treat the risk, transfer the risk, terminate the risk and take the opportunity.
4. **Evaluation of the Process and Reporting:** Establishing an effective and efficient risk management strategy is just a starting point. Therefore, the strategy established must be reevaluated periodically and if there are any missing or wrong items in the process it must be modified.

The guides to be prepared can guide the companies in risk management applications. In addition, companies can be protected by making risk management practices mandatory, so that countermeasures against possible crises could be taken.

REFERENCES

Beasley, M. S., Branson, B. C., & Hancock, B. V. (2011). *Developing Key Risk Indicators to Strengthen Enterprise Risk Management*. Retrieved December 21, 2017 from https://mgt.ncsu.edu/vol2/erm/ee/i/weblogs/research-documents/coso-kri-paper-jan2011.pdf

Brodeur, A., Buehler, K., Patsalos-Fox, M., & Pergler, M. (2010). *A Board Perspective on Enterprise Risk Management*. McKinsey Working Papers on Risk, Number 18. Retrieved December 15, 2017 from https://www.mckinsey.com/~/media/mckinsey/dotcom/client_service/risk/working%20papers/18_a_board_perspective_on_enterprise_risk_management.ashx

Deloitte & Touche LLP. (2012). *Risk Assessment in Practice*. Retrieved December 6, 2017 from https://www2.deloitte.com/content/dam/Deloitte/global/Documents/Governance-Risk-Compliance/dttl-grc-riskassessmentinpractice.pdf

Deloitte & Touche LLP. (2015). *Türkiye*. İstanbul: Türkiye'de Borsaya Kote Olmayan Şirketlerde Kurumsal Yönetim Uygulamaları.

Dobler, M. (2008). Incentives for Risk Reporting – A Discretionary Disclosure and Cheap Talk Approach. *The International Journal of Accounting*, *43*(2), 184–206. doi:10.1016/j.intacc.2008.04.005

Graham, A. (2008). *Integrated Risk Management - Implementation Guide*. Retrieved December 1, 2017 from http://post.queensu.ca/~grahama/publications/TEXTPDF.pdf

Her Majesty's Treasury. (2004). *The Orange Book: Management of Risk-Principles and Concepts*. Retrieved December 21, 2017 from https://assets.publishing.service.gov.uk/government/uploads/ system/uploads/attachment_data/file/220647/orange_book.pdf

Institute of Chartered Accountants in England and Wales. (2011). *Reporting Business Risks: Meeting Expectations*. Retrieved December 2, 2017 from http://www.icaew.com/~/media/corporate/files/technical/financial%20reporting/information%20for%20better%20markets/ifbm/rbr%20final.ashx.

Institute of Risk Management (IRM). (2002). *A Risk Management Standard*. Retrieved January 1, 2018 from https://www.theirm.org/media/886059/ARMS_2002_IRM.pdf

International Organization for Standardization. (2018). *ISO 31000 Risk management — Guidelines*. Retrieved August 28, 2018 from https://www.iso.org/obp/ui#iso:std:iso:31000:ed-2:v1:en

Linsley, P. M. (2011). *UK Bank Risk Disclosures in the Period Through to The Onset of the Global Financial Crisis – Briefing*. Retrieved December 10, 2017, from https://www.icaew.com/-/media/corporate/files/ products/financial-services/cbp-uk-bank-risk-disclosures-in-the-period-through-to-the-onset-of-the-global-financial-crisis.ashx

Merna, T., & Al-Thani, F. (2008). *Corporate Risk Management*. West Sussex, UK: John Wiley & Sons Ltd.

PriceWaterhouseCoopers. (2008). *A Practical Guide to Risk Assessment*. Retrieved December 15, 2017 from https://web.actuaries.ie/sites/default/files/erm-resources/a_practical_guide_to_risk_assessment.pdf

Senior Supervisors Group. (2008). *Observations on Risk Management Practices during the Recent Market Turbulence*. Retrieved January 12, 2018 from https://www.sec.gov/news/press/2008/report 030608.pdf

The Committee of Sponsoring Organizations of the Treadway Commission. (2009). *Strengthening Enterprise Risk Management for Strategic Advantage*. Retrieved December 5, 2017 from https://www.coso.org/documents/COSO_09_board_position_final102309PRINTandWEB FINAL_000.pdf

Usta, Ö. (2012). *İşletme Finansı ve Finansal Yönetim*. Ankara: Detay Yayıncılık.

ADDITIONAL READING

Fier, S. G., & Liebenberg, A. P. (2014). The Market for Directors' and Officers' Insurance. *Risk Management & Insurance Review*, *17*(2), 215–239. doi:10.1111/rmir.12023

Financial Reporting Council. (2009). *Going Concern and Liquidity Risk: Guidance for Directors ok UK Companies 2009*. Retrieved August 28, 2018 from https://www.frc.org.uk/getattachment/079e9ca2-7153-4831-8248-5de419041f6c/Going-concern-and-liquidity-risk-guidance-for-directors-of-uk-companies-093.pdf

Financial Reporting Council. (2014). *Guidance on Risk Management, Internal Control and Related Financial and Business Reporting*. Retrieved August 28, 2018 from https://www.frc.org.uk/getattachment/d672c107-b1fb-4051-84b0-f5b83a1b93f6/Guidance-on-Risk-Management-Internal-Control-and-Related-Reporting.pdf

Hull, J. C. (2015). *Risk Management and Financial Institutions*. New Jersey: Wiley.

Institute of Risk Management. (2017). *Risk Appetite Statements*. Retrieved August 28, 2018 from https://www.theirm.org/media/3296897/0926-IRM-Risk-Appetite-12-10-17-v2.pdf

Institute of Risk Management. (2018). *A Risk Practitioners Guide to ISO 31000: 2018*. Retrieved August 28, 2018 from https://www.theirm.org/media/3513119/IRM-Report-ISO-31000-2018-v3.pdf

Institute of Risk Management. (2018). *Internal Model Industry Forum: Aligning Operational Risk and Insurance*. Retrieved August 28, 2018 from https://www.theirm.org/media/3524205/IMIF_Aligning-Operational-Risk-and-Insurance_v5.pdf

Institute of Risk Management. (2018). *Internal Model Industry Forum: The Journey from Model Validation to Model Risk Management*. Retrieved August 27, 2018 from https://www.theirm.org/media/3497273/IRM_Model-Risk-Management_FINAL.pdf

International Corporate Governance Network. (2015). *Guidance on Corporate Risk Oversight*. Retrieved August 27, 2018 from https://www.icgn.org/sites/default/files/ICGN%20Corp%20 Risk %20 Oversight-web_0.pdf

Razek, M. A. (2014). The Association Between Corporate Risk Disclosure and Firm Performance in Emerging Country – The Case of Eqypt. *Journal of Empirical Studies*, *1*(3), 105–115. https://ideas.repec.org/a/pkp/joestu/2014p105-115.html Retrieved August 27, 2018

KEY TERMS AND DEFINITIONS

Brainstorming: It is a type of meeting where members of the team exchange ideas and produce new ideas.

Probability: This is the likelihood whether a risk will occur.

Risk: The uncertainty involved in the possibility of an event occurring.

Risk Appetite: The extent of risk a company is willing to take.

Risk Capacity: The amount of risk companies can take while avoiding the negative effects.

Risk Interaction Matrix: A tool used to measure probability or possible effects of risks in interaction with each other.

Risk Management: Consists of risk identification, risk assessment, selection and application of risk management strategies, and evaluation and reporting of the process.

Risk Matrix: A tool used to measure probability or possible effects of risks.

Risk Tolerance: The amount of risk that can be tolerated by the company without taking any precautions against.

Scenario Analysis: It is a type of meeting that members of the team examine possible scenarios and discuss possible effects for the future.

Chapter 9
Behavioral Strategies to Achieve Financial Stability in Uncertain Times

Ashlesha Khedekar-Swaminathan
Symbiosis International University (Deemed), India

ABSTRACT

The automatic use of heuristics, the effects of framing, and the tendency to procrastinate when combined with the risk and uncertainty inherent in the financial environment can lead to financial instability for ordinary investors. This chapter explores established behavioral tendencies with respect to financial decision making within the framework of behavioral economics: how and why heuristics are used to make decisions, how different choice frames influence decisions, the crucial impact of biases like loss aversion on decision outcomes. The chapter also explores critical factors that induce the tendency to procrastinate saving and investing. The chapter suggests strategies that investors can use to achieve long-term financial stability by achieving predetermined financial goals as well as protect their investments from depreciating in value in the context of financial market instability.

INTRODUCTION

Instability in the economic and financial environment is unavoidable in current times. The main sources of market instability tend to be the unknown factors in the environment. These unknown factors or events can be referred to as market uncertainty (Slovik, 2011). Ellsberg (1961) defined an event as uncertain if it had unknown probability. Knight (1921) defined uncertainty as being characterized by randomness that cannot be measured precisely and therefore cannot be insured. Under these definitions, an uncertain event can be characterized as an event whose probability is unknown and immeasurable. With respect to uncertainty in financial markets, the efficient market hypothesis (Fama, 1970) provides another perspective. The theory states that market prices include all known information and instantly reflect any new information. This implies that in an efficient market, any unknown information cannot be reflected in market prices. This unknown information set represents market uncertainty.

DOI: 10.4018/978-1-5225-7208-4.ch009

In current times, uncertainty can stem from events such as measures taken by governments and central banks like demonetization; changes in tax policies or trade relations; unexpected changes in international frameworks like the British vote to exit the European Union; political upheavals; as well as effects on business caused by natural disasters like floods or hurricanes or war-like situations. Such events are exogenously determined and are therefore difficult to predict even for experts. Uncertainty can also stem from unique events created by firms or individuals like conceiving Ponzi schemes, cooking the books, large scale financial frauds, announcement of mergers, acquisitions or hostile takeovers.

Globalization of business and cross border investments have increased the domestic impact of international events. Therefore, domestic financial markets, and consequently investors in an open economy, can expect to experience market instability that can be a result of local or international erratic/ uncertain incidents. When uncertain factors or events become more certain, or rather, their probability becomes more measurable, the new information will be reflected or adjusted in asset prices, and this adjustment can be positive or negative. The period of adjustment typically involves some degree of instability in asset prices until prices settle at some new level. This adjustment can be sudden or may take place over a period of time (Rigotti & Shannon, 2005; Slovik, 2011). Such an unanticipated change in prices can be perceived as instability in the financial markets. Another significant aspect of market uncertainty, from the perspective of market stability is the degree of market uncertainty (Slovik, 2011). Changes in prices would implicitly reflect the changes in the degree of confidence investors have in an estimate of the probability of an event's occurrence (Ramsay, 1926; Ellsberg, 1961).

Media cascade was described by Kahneman (2011) as the extensive media coverage of uncertain or unpredictable events which tends to influence decision making. A media cascade focuses most investors' attention on stock price movements, market developments and related news, thus informing the investors' estimations of the probability of an event's occurrence and prediction of values (Tversky & Kahneman, 1974) i.e. indirectly determining the unknown and known information sets for decision making. By extension, it can be assumed that a media cascade can also influence the degree of uncertainty of an event. Thus, investors tend to be unaware of or pay less attention to the gradual development of events outside the known information set and are subsequently taken by surprise when an uncertain event occurs or its probability of occurrence apparently increases suddenly (Tversky & Kahneman, 1974; Wilson & Brekke, 1994).

Although all financial markets are sensitive to the instability with a varying degree, this chapter focuses on stock markets rather than commodities markets, bond markets or currency markets. Stock markets are more accessible; therefore, they are relatively more attractive to ordinary investors (as opposed to experienced traders) (Jiwarajka, 2017; Investment Company Institute, 2017). For example, 83% of retail investors in India prefer to invest directly in stocks (Businessworld, 2017). An ordinary investor may invest directly in stocks or via mutual funds with the objective of increasing their wealth (Buch, 2017; Times of India, 2017). Instability in this financial market can adversely affect the wealth creation of participating investors due to its vulnerability to associated market uncertainties. As a reaction to changes in prices, an ordinary investor may restructure their investment portfolio or withdraw funds from the market. Given the risk-reward matrix in financial markets, should the investor choose to shift funds into products perceived as less risky, they would be implicitly accepting a lower return on their investment.

Literature in economics and finance distinguishes between uncertainty and risk wherein risk, characterized by randomness, can be measured precisely (Ellsberg, 1961), but ordinary investors tend to treat them synonymously. This is because uncertainty is not just a necessary condition for risk; the dynamic nature of risk also introduces uncertainty (Gough, 1988). Gough (1988) argues that the distinction between uncertainty and risk hinges on the probability of occurrence. Likewise, an individual's perception of risk is based on subjective probabilities which introduce uncertainty. In the context of decision making, both uncertainty and risk affect an individual's behavior (Ellsberg, 1961). Tversky and Fox (1995) posited that people tend to be less sensitive to uncertainty than risk. Further, they found that people prefer to bet on known rather than unknown probabilities, where known probabilities lie in their domain knowledge and unknown probabilities lie in the set of "uncertain" events and thus they tend to exhibit ambiguity aversion. This implies that people prefer to bet in their area of competence (Tversky & Kahneman, 1992). As discussed by Tversky and Fox (1995), certainty and impossibility are the two end points on the scale of probability and people prefer chance over uncertainty because the probabilities associated with uncertainty are imprecise. These findings can be understood in the domain of financial markets wherein investors prefer to invest in stocks because they have some degree of knowledge in this area. In addition, risk in financial markets is usually measurable and quantifiable (Knight, 1921) and therefore can be managed with appropriate strategies, whereas uncertainty cannot. In the backdrop of people's preference for ambiguity aversion, this chapter discusses the approach to the risks involved in investing, as risk can be measured. Ordinary investors with limited financial knowledge and acumen can be advised on how to manage risk: by diversifying their investment portfolio or by investing in assets with varying degrees of risk.

Individuals are also aware that they must insulate themselves from erratic incomes, business cycles and economic uncertainty such as company bankruptcy or shutdown, takeovers, mergers, government policy changes that can result in downsizing. In addition to the uncertainty involved in maintaining earnings, individuals must also protect their investments from eroding due not only to financial market fluctuations but also inflationary pressures and regulatory changes. In order to be financially stable in the long term and successfully accumulate wealth, strategic financial planning and execution are critical.

In the context of popular understanding of investment, the goal of an investor is to navigate through financial markets in order to achieve financial stability and accumulate wealth in the long term. The continuous reporting of events by business news and media keeps investors updated on events. Tversky and Kahneman (1974, 1992) discussed how people tend to give more decision weight to outcomes which are uncertain, more than their probability justifies. They explained that the decision weight reflects how much an individual is worrying about it: the more they worry, the higher the probability of its occurrence. It can thus be assumed that the extended media coverage of a particular event can influence an investor to panic or assign more decision weight to the negative outcome of the event. Thus, an investor is likely to make changes to their portfolio in order to avoid losses and protect their wealth. These changes can possibly override any benefit provided by strategic planning and threaten financial stability.

Strategies on how to navigate market uncertainty in order to achieve financial stability tend to be based on financial theories, such as the rational expectations theory and the efficient market hypothesis, which assume that investors are rational decision makers and will not act irrationally. All investors are also human and are therefore susceptible to emotions. Behavioral economics incorporates this human aspect in its approach and assumes people to be "boundedly" rational. By extension, investors are boundedly rational and susceptible to seemingly irrational and emotional decisions. Further, the use of heuristics can reduce the cognitive effort involved in financial planning and decision making (Khedekar-Swaminathan & Kulkarni, 2018). Procrastination is another relevant behavioral tendency that can impact financial stability for an ordinary investor (Thaler, 1980; Gilovich & Medvec, 1995; Ackert, Church, & Deaves, 2003; Lynch & Zauberman, 2007). Through an examination of how the use of certain heuristics and the tendencies to procrastinate play a role in investor decision making, it is possible to adjust financial strategies which counter market uncertainty by including this perspective of rationality.

This chapter explores at length behavioral tendencies in decision making with regard to investment. Thus, it provides a theoretical foundation to achieve financial stability for ordinary investors by applying them to financial decision making. The chapter focuses on the group of ordinary investors as they tend to rely largely on salary income to create savings that will be invested; they may not be financially savvy or have significant trading experience; but as discussed above, their wealth creation is vulnerable to market instability. The final decision regarding execution of strategies to navigate the instability lies with them and as such they may require a behavioral strategy to avoid a suboptimal financial decision.

Why not simply advocate financial education instead of nudging? From the perspective of cognitive psychology, in order to learn from experience, we need frequent practice and immediate feedback because learning takes practice (Hayes, 2004). Assuming that learning a behavior is crucial in decision making, when the financial stakes are higher, the decision-making quality is likely to go down (Lotto, 2017). This kind of trial and error learning can be detrimental to the investor's wealth. Therefore, rather than recommending financial learning or education, which is likely to take time and is cognitively cumbersome to understand and implement, this chapter suggests using behavioral insights to provide easily usable, learnable and replicable strategies for ordinary investors.

The following section of this chapter discusses the relevant heuristics and biases which can impact the outcome of financial decision making. The subsequent section discusses procrastination of investing for long term goals and its impact on financial stability. The last section discusses strategies which can be used to achieve financial stability. These strategies are derived from the understanding of the use of the selected heuristics as well as the tendency to procrastinate.

BACKGROUND

Heuristics and Biases in Financial Decision Making

Heuristics

Heuristics are mental shortcuts or cues that people use to make decisions. They can be considered as problem solving techniques that an individual develops based on past experience. Heuristics assist in making decisions or choices quickly with minimal mental effort. The formation and use of heuristics are largely spontaneous or involuntary i.e. there is no conscious cognitive effort involved to create them or recall them (Kahneman, 2011). People tend to use heuristics because of two important tendencies of the human mind: 1) the human mind tends to categorize experiences in order to use the stored information in the future and 2) the tendency to prefer cognitive ease in decision making (Kahneman, 2011). The combination of these two tendencies results in the formation of heuristics for decision making. The theoretical explanation for the use of heuristics in financial decision making is explained by the concept of bounded rationality.

The concept of bounded rationality in economic decision making was introduced by Herbert Simon in as early as 1956 (Simon, 1956). Bounded rationality implies that an economic agent's decisions may not always be "rational". Simon stressed that individual decision makers have no choice but to make decisions under the constraints of limited cognitive resources. Cognitive limitations can include access to necessary information as well as the ability to accurately analyze the available information (Simon, 1956). Being subject to these limited cognitive resources, the individual resorts to heuristics to make judgments and decisions, particularly when faced with risk and uncertainty. In their seminal work on heuristics in economic decision making, Tversky and Kahneman (1974) explain how using heuristics can lead to predictable bias in choices, especially in the context of risk and uncertainty. Since risk and uncertainty are inherent in decision making with respect to investing in financial products, it is not surprising that use of heuristics has been observed to play a significant role in economic and financial decision making.

The use of heuristics involves a cognitive process. If this cognitive process is faulty or suboptimal, there is likely to be an impact on the decision outcome. The decision outcome can be suboptimal because of implicit cognitive biases in the faulty cognitive process which produces the heuristic. A cognitive bias can be described as a systematic pattern of deviation from rationality in judgment, reasoning and evaluation (Blanco, 2017).

Research in the areas of behavioral economics and finance has identified a number of different heuristics which investors commonly tend to use while making financial decisions. The heuristics which are predominantly used in investment decision making are explained in detail below. The biases associated with these heuristics and the manner in which they affect investors and their wealth accumulation goals are also discussed.

Affect Heuristic

Financial and economic theories assume investors to be critical and impassive in making decisions. Cognitive psychology assumes that people are not rational and one of the factors influencing human behavior is the emotional response to a stimulus (Slovic et al., 2002).Investors are human, so it can be assumed that it may be difficult for them to approach financial decisions involving risk and uncertainty with the normative rationality (Lerner, Small, & Loewenstein, 2004).The heuristic wherein emotions influence decision making is known as the *affect heuristic* (Slovic et al., 2002; Kahneman, 2011).The investor consults their feelings or assesses the emotional response to the outcome of the decision, while making a decision regarding an investment. This heuristic is used reflexively, usually with little or no cognitive deliberation (Kahneman, 2011). The emotions that are typically observed in investment decisions are fear of loss, fear of risk and regret of a negative outcome. The use of the affect heuristic results in biases in the outcome of the decision. For example, a person may choose to invest in a particular stock because they have encouraging sentiments about the company. Or an investor may put money into a particular mutual fund because it has been recommended by someone they have positive feelings for. Investors have been observed to avoid buying stocks when prices have recently fallen out of fear of further downward movement, when in reality the prudent strategy is to buy when prices are low (Lerner, Small, & Loewenstein, 2004; Belsky & Gilovich, 2010; Guiso, Sapienza, & Zingales, 2013). The use of the *affect heuristic* has increased relevance in the context of market instability as the instability can heighten the experience of emotional responses and exert a greater influence on an investor's decision. The behavioral responses resulting from the use of the *affect heuristic* in the decision-making process and their resulting biases are explained below.

Loss Aversion

Using the affect heuristic to plan implies that an investor is likely to consider his/her feelings about the outcome of that decision. When an investor compares the current amount of wealth to the amount of wealth likely to be attained after an investment decision; if the new amount of wealth is likely to be less than the current amount, then he/she is unlikely to invest. Kahneman and Tversky (1979) explained in their seminal paper on Prospect theory that people tend to feel the pain of a loss more than the pleasure of a gain of the same amount i.e. losses loom larger than gains. Prospect theory explains how the positive or negative change in the state of wealth is crucial for decision making. The emotional response to the expected change in one's state of wealth will determine the decision to invest and investors choose to avoid incurring a possible loss. This tendency is identified as the bias of *loss aversion* (Kahneman &Tversky, 1979). This bias therefore favors stability over change. The preference for stability can result in the investor deciding not to invest, decision paralysis or only investing when the probability of a gain is significantly higher than the probability of a loss (Kahneman & Tversky, 1984). As it is difficult to predict outcomes for ordinary investors, the loss aversion bias can deter them from earning returns on existing wealth or limiting possible profitable investment options. Loss aversion can also damage existing wealth as an investor may not wish to close a loss-making investment. This tendency is another bias related to loss aversion known as the *disposition effect* (Shefrin & Statman,1985; Odean & Barber, 2000). It occurs in two ways. First, if a particular investment is incurring a loss i.e. the current price is lower than the purchase price, the optimal or rational decision would be to book the loss so as not to incur any further loss on the investment. But investors are observed to be prone to hold on to loss making investments, in the hope that the position would reverse and they may be able to exit the investment at a small profit or zero loss. The disposition effect may even result in further reduction of existing wealth. Second, the disposition effect is also said to be at work when investors tend to sell profit making investments too early, in order to "book" the profit. This tendency implies that the investor may be missing out on potential further gains. Again, this bias prevents investors from accumulating more wealth.

Regret Aversion

Regret is another powerful emotion which influences investors; they would therefore try to avoid any decision that will result in regret about the outcome (Loewenstein, Weber, Hsee, & Welch, 2001). As people tend to have a stronger emotional reaction to an outcome that is produced by an action rather than if it was produced by inaction, they tend to feel more regret for a negative outcome if it is the result of having taken some action rather than doing nothing (Kahneman, 2011). Therefore, it can be understood that the regret associated with losing money after having acted on a decision to invest, can deter an individual from deciding. The bias to avoid feeling regret for an outcome resulting from a suboptimal decision is regret aversion. Regret aversion plays a significant role in financial decision making as regret can colour an investor's disposition and can lead to detrimental financial behavior such as postponing booking of losses or deciding to not restructure an existing portfolio (Thaler, 1980; Gilovich & Medvec, 1995; Ackert, Church, & Deaves, 2003). Investors who are influenced by the anticipated regret of the decision tend to invest in less risky assets as this behavior reduces the potential to regret poor outcomes, but it also reduces the potential for a significant return on investment.

Risk Aversion

Risk aversion is the tendency to avoid risk in the context of uncertainty (Kahneman & Tversky, 1984). The outcome of any form of investment involves uncertainty. In the context of instability of financial markets, there is a tendency to be more sensitive to risk or more risk averse. Behavior in risky situations results in part from direct emotional influences and in part from the result of a cognitive assessment (Loewenstein et al., 2001). The cognitive assessment of risk depends on the probabilities of possible outcomes and the assessment of the outcome's severity. The use of the *affect heuristic* in decision making elicits emotional responses to the probable out comes which in turn produce behavioral responses that may depart from what an individual may view as the best course of action. The results of the combination of emotional response and rational judgment may be in opposition to one another i.e. there may be a divergence between the cognitive assessment and the automatic emotional response to risk and this divergence can hinder decision making (Loewenstein et al., 2001). For example, even if an individual cognitively understands that assuming some risk in an investment decision can garner a better reward, the feeling of fear induced by the risk can stop him from making an investment or delay the decision. Risk averseness can also impact the decision regarding how much an individual is willing to pay or invest for a stock or other asset (Ackert, Church, & Deaves, 2003). Investors have been observed to consider the risk of a particular investment in isolation rather than with reference to the risk profile of their existing portfolio (Rabin & Thaler,2001). Thus, this bias can result in choosing less risky investments which can lead to a lower accumulation of wealth in the long term.

Representativeness Heuristic

In order to make decisions efficiently and swiftly, people tend to use associative reasoning when faced with uncertainty. They do this by mentally categorizing events and objects into groups by focusing on the similarities that the object or event shares with a larger group. The objective is to determine the probability of whether the object or event belongs to that larger group (Tversky & Kahneman, 1974; Kahneman, 2011). This automatic categorization is known as the *representativeness heuristic*. Such tendency leads to a number of judgment errors or biases in the decision-making process. These include substituting similarity for probability, ignoring statistical base rates of the larger population, insensitivity to the randomness of an event occurring, misconceptions of chance and illusions of validity (Tversky & Kahneman, 1974; Rizzi, 2008; Szyszka, 2011). In the context of investing, this heuristic can manifest as "trend chasing" by investors. Investors believe that studying the past performance of an asset can give an indication of the future performance. They intentionally search for a pattern in the past price performance which they assume is a valid basis on which to predict the future price movement. By doing so, they ignore the probability of a random event occurring that may change the continuation of the "pattern" of performance. This implies that they are substituting similarity of the pattern for the probability that the pattern will recur (Szyszka, 2011). Financial advisors have been observed to use the past performance of mutual funds to encourage new investments in a particular fund. The use of *representativeness heuristic* can also result in "herd mentality" which is often observed in financial markets (Rizzi, 2008; Szyszka, 2011). The simple explanation is that because the individual identifies himself/herself as an investor when other investors are buying or selling a particular stock, he/she should do the same. The decision is without reference to the size of the sample under consideration. Loss aversion impacts the investors' decision as they do not wish to miss out on a good investment opportunity and follow the behavior of the group. Another manifestation is the assumption that if a company has high quality management, strong reputation and consistent earnings, it must be a good company to invest in. In theory, these aspects of the company should already be accounted for in the market price of the company's stock. Thus, the decision to invest becomes biased because of the misconception of the chances of the stock rising as well as the illusion that the said information is valid. The investor should ideally be considering the net present value of discounted cashflows using an appropriate risk adjusted discount rate. But this is a cognitively effortful task, hence the heuristic is used, and the investment decision outcome becomes biased.

Substitution Heuristic

When faced with a question or problem which requires a complex or complicated calculation to be done or the consideration of a number of variables, people tend to substitute the question with a simpler one which is easier to answer (Kahneman, 2011). This tendency to substitute difficult questions with easier ones is known as the *substitution heuristic*. In the context of investing, this heuristic is commonly used to make decisions regarding the distribution or allocation of funds across asset classes. The calculation of the amount of savings required from one's monthly income also requires a complex calculation as the amount saved acts as the principal on which returns will be earned. Research indicates that people tend to substitute doing these calculations by using percentages in multiples of 5 to determine the portion of their salary to be saved each month (Benartzi & Thaler, 2007). Diversifying investments into various financial products to balance the risk and return of an investment portfolio is a common investment strategy employed by investors as well as financial advisors. Calculating the proportion in which the investable funds are to distributed requires a complex calculation as well as a study of the vast information on each available financial product. In addition, the investors' risk profile and return requirements should be considered in this calculation. The accuracy of this calculation becomes critical in order to accumulate the desired wealth through optimal investments, in the long term. Unfortunately, investors tend to use a "naïve diversification" strategy which is the result of the *substitution heuristic*. Benartzi & Thaler (2007) observed that when people were asked to distribute their savings between various assets, they tended to use strategy of simply dividing the available amount equally between a given number of options instead of conducting any detailed calculation. This bias for cognitive ease in decision making can result in suboptimal returns and wealth accumulation and possible financial instability.

Availability Heuristic

People tend to determine the likelihood or probability of an event occurring, based on how easy it is to recall a similar event (Tversky & Kahneman, 1974). This tendency results in prediction of events that are easier to recall as more likely to occur and conversely those events that are not easy to recall as less likely to occur. Further, recent events are predicted as more likely to occur than events that have occurred far in the past (Tversky & Kahneman, 1974). This mental shortcut to predict the probability of an event occurrence is known as the *availability heuristic*. The use of this heuristic by investors can influence their decision to invest in a particular financial product or stock (Shiller, 1998; Barber & Odean, 2007). This heuristic also affects the choice of industry or firm for investing (Jarell & Peltzman, 1985; Shelor et al., 1992; Bosch et al., 1998). Positive news regarding a particular financial product, company or industry can influence investors' purchase decisions. The role of the media and investor networks play an important part in the automatic use of this heuristic. Significant positive or negative developments in a particular company or industry tend to be reported by various media outlets and catch the eye of investors. Repeated reports make the information more salient in the investors' decision process as the information becomes easier to recall. On the other hand, smaller news about the same company or industry may not reach the media and hence is unintentionally kept out of the investors' search set for the decision process. Further, using this heuristic makes people include scenarios that are easier to imagine in the search set whereas scenarios that are difficult to imagine are not. Thus, this heuristic can influence younger investors particularly, as they may not have experienced a particular event like a financial crisis, fraud or asset bubble burst and will therefore tend to assign lower probability to such an occurrence which can be damaging for long term financial stability.

In the context of financial decision, availability bias is observed to be especially strong. The constant stream or cascade of information from business and financial media has a significant unconscious influence on investors. This bias manifests in a number of ways. Investors are observed to consider investing only in stocks that come to their attention not only through media but also friends and family, or other sources outside their own research (Shiller, 1984,1987). *Familiarity bias* is a result of increase in advertising by financial product issuers as it attracts new investors through easy recall of such products. The increased ability to recall information tends to get substituted by positive feelings regarding the product, leading to this bias. It has also been observed that investors prefer familiar or well-known investments despite the seemingly obvious gains from diversification. The investors will prefer investing in familiar rather than unfamiliar stocks and bonds when diversifying investments as these lie outside their familiarity and are therefore categorized as uncertain. This can lead to sub-optimally diversified portfolios with a greater a risk of losses.

Anchoring Heuristic

In any decision-making process, people use an anchor or a reference point against which they compare choice options. The use of an anchor as a short cut in the decision-making process is known as *anchoring* and it is widely used for decisions relating to purchases and estimation of risk and uncertainty (Tversky & Kahneman, 1974). An anchor can be identified by the individuals themselves or even be suggested by an external source. A person identifies an anchor value by internally accessing consistent information, making intuitive approximations, and may also use the substitution heuristic if a relevant anchor value is not easily available (Epley & Gilovich, 2001). If the anchor is suggested by an outside source, an individual will tend to conduct an internal validity check of the anchor value and also consider the credibility of the source suggesting the anchor. An externally suggested anchor reduces the cognitive effort involved in evaluation (Epley & Gilovich, 2010). People tend to be more vulnerable to the anchoring heuristic when they have limited knowledge about the commodity being considered (Furnham & Boo, 2002). The anchoring heuristic can be used in different aspects of a financial decision such as determining the amount to be invested, expected returns and for decisions to purchase or sell assets. In the purchase or sale decision process, once the anchor has been identified, the next step is to evaluate the current price of the product or asset by adjusting from the anchor value. The bias resulting from the identification of an anchor is known as the *anchoring effect*. Typically, individuals will tend not to adjust sufficiently away from the anchor while considering a proposition because of the influence of the anchor (Kahneman, 2011; Tversky & Kahneman, 1974).

If an investor is earning 10% return on a particular investment, this rate of return can become his anchor while comparing other investment returns and influence his decision to buy or sell. The investor should evaluate returns on different asset classes like debt, equity or property with reference to that particular class as the risk profile of each class is different. If this is anchored at a 10% return across investments, the investor may prefer to invest in assets which yield a return of 10% or more and may ignore other important decision factors like risk and liquidity. Simonsohn & Loewenstein (2006) found that with respect to property investments, people who moved to cities anchored on real estate prices from their previous market. People moving from expensive cities to cheaper ones tended to buy houses that were larger than what they needed and vice versa because they were anchored on the amount previously invested. The use of the anchoring heuristic can result in a bias known as *confirmation bias*. *Confirmation bias* predisposes an investor who has anchored himself/herself on a decision to buy or sell a particular asset to selectively filter information and pay more attention to information that supports their decision while ignoring opposing or contrary information; the investor, in this case, derives "utility" from the preferred outcome (Kahneman, 1994). This bias tends to skew the information in the investors search set and results in yielding incomplete information regarding the stock being considered, leading to a likely suboptimal decision. Another bias resulting from anchoring and loss aversion is the *endowment effect* (Kahneman, Knetsch & Thaler, 1991). When fixing the selling price of an owned asset, like property, investors tend to anchor on a price which is usually higher than the market rate and refuse offers at the market price because they are lower than the anchor value. This tendency can result in holding the asset for too long and missing the opportunity to sell it at a profitable price. Thus, an investor's financial stability can be threatened by the combination of using incorrect anchors and the resulting biases.

Framing Effects in Financial Decision Making

Framing of a decision choice implies the manner in which choices and their outcomes are represented to a decision maker. One of the determinants of a person's decision utility is how the decision outcomes are framed (Kahneman, 1994). Decision makers tend to frame the possible outcomes of the decision by determining the probability of each outcome and whether the outcome entails positive or negative utility (Tversky & Kahneman, 1981). Research has indicated that they are likely to choose that outcome which has the highest probability of giving them a positive utility (Read, Loewenstein & Rabin, 1999; Kahneman, 2011). Individuals' investment decisions also depend on how various investment options and their outcomes are framed. The framing of the choice may be done either by investors themselves or by an external source like an advisor or broker. Another aspect of framing is the type of choice frame used. The use of abroad or narrow frame can affect the outcome of a financial decision (Read et al., 1999). When using a broad choice frame, individuals consider all the possible consequences of available options, compare them and choose those options which maximize their utility. When using a narrow choice frame, each investment option along with its inherent risk is considered separately from other options. Therefore, decision outcomes will be biased by which choice frame was used. Evaluating multiple investments either individually or together can influence the risk assessment of an individual investment. A loss averse investor may unwittingly take on more than the desirable amount of risk if he evaluates many investment products together rather than considering one at a time. Broad framing encourages diversity in choice. An investor using a broad choice frame may adopt a combination of risky strategies to avoid losses (Tversky & Kahneman,1981; Read et al., 1999; Thaler, 1999). A notable observation in the use of narrow framing is that people generally evaluate risks in terms of a narrow frame because it simplifies evaluation and reduces cognitive strain (Kahneman & Lovallo, 1993). When using a narrow choice frame, decision makers are prone to neglecting both the statistics of the past as well as the multiple options of the future. This tendency to consider each choice in isolation makes these choices susceptible to the bias of isolation errors (Kahneman & Lovallo,1993). Treating each investment in isolation can result in naïve diversification strategies of the portfolio as a whole.

In the field of investing, framing effects can have real consequences to wealth accumulation. Employees tend to prefer investing in company stock rather than a mutual fund. This is a very narrow decision frame which fails to consider the risk of loss of wages or income in addition to the amount invested in stock, if the company shuts down (Benartzi & Thaler,2007). Investors may also create narrow frames of prior investments or "old" money and recent investments or "new" money. Investors are known to adjust allocations of new money rather than old money (Benartzi & Thaler, 2007). Broad framing can also result in ignoring or underweighting small amounts of money relative to a larger amount. The underlying preference for hedonism in framing results is the tendency to integrate smaller losses with larger ones (Thaler, 1999). So, commissions charged by a share broker may be neglected during evaluation of trading gains or losses (Read et al., 1999) but these charges reduce the net income of the investor.

The tendency to sell assets which are losing money is a bias known as *myopic loss aversion. Myopic loss aversion* is another example of investors' narrow framing. Myopic loss aversion can lead to an investor increasing the frequency of monitoring portfolio performance and restructuring the portfolio in order to minimize any loss. Benartzi & Thaler (1995) found that the more frequent the evaluation of the investment position, the more likely the investor is to act. If an individual has invested money to achieve a long-term financial goal, the appropriate strategy would be to review the portfolio after longer time intervals i.e. aligning the review frequency to the time horizon of the goal. Using a narrow frame of a shorter time horizon for portfolio evaluation can lead to myopic loss aversion which can prompt an investor to sell a loss-making investment too early in order to make the account position more favourable. In addition, the commission cost involved in frequent trading or buying and selling can negate or reduce the amount of returns on the portfolio in total. Benartzi & Thaler (1994) described how investors who reviewed their portfolios too often make changes to the portfolio more often, and pay more in commissions than those who do not.

Procrastination of Financial Decision Making

Most people face multiple demands on their time and effort, and are also confronted with numerous deadlines to meet. In a situation where one must make the cost-benefit tradeoff between completing a particular task today or postponing for a future date, a person may choose to delay completing some tasks. Despite the awareness of the possibility of being worse off due to delaying a particular task, many people voluntarily procrastinate doing it (Steel, 2007). Regular saving and investment, and portfolio review are important tasks for wealth accumulation. Conventional wisdom encourages individuals to start early and continue saving to be able to achieve long term financial stability. In the backdrop of market instability and uncertainty, it is an apparently prudent long-term strategy to follow. As instability in financial markets is not easily predictable and there is a tendency towards procrastinating behavior, it can be inferred that procrastination of financial planning and investment in the context of financial instability can be detrimental for an individual investor's long-term financial stability. It consequently becomes prudent in the study of investor behavior to examine the features of tasks that lead to procrastination in the context of saving and investment decision making

Research on procrastination has identified a combination of two task characteristics that induce procrastination: timing of rewards and task aversiveness (Silver & Sabini, 1982; Froese, Nisly & May, 1984; Dewitte & Schouwenberg, 2002; Ferrari, Mason & Hammer, 2006; Steel, 2007, 2010).

Task Aversion

People tend to procrastinate when a task is perceived as aversive. The aversive or unpleasant attributes of a task can include the requirement to put in a large amount of effort as well as a high difficulty level (Froese, Nisly & May,1984; Ferrari, Mason & Hammer, 2006). Financial planning involves tasks which require complicated calculations involving calculation of monthly savings, estimations of future requirements, predictions of future inflation and interest rates, allocation of funds between asset classes and risk reward decisions (Lussardi, 2003); these are all tasks that require a high level of effort and involve a high difficulty level particularly for investors who have limited knowledge of finance. An investor incurs a *psychic cost* in the present, in terms of time and effort of doing the unpleasant task while the benefit of doing the task will accrue in the future (Akerlof, 1991). *Psychic costs* refer to those costs that are imposed on an individual in the form of stress or unhappiness which arise from emotions like fear, frustration and regret (Elster, 1998; Ochsner & Gross, 2003). People tend to have emotional reactions to decision outcomes (Damasio, 1994; Slovic, 2002; Kahneman, 2011), therefore controlling one's actions or forcing oneself to execute a difficult or unpleasant task which is in opposition to such emotions. This involves a psychic cost of doing the task now.

The presence of too many choices also increases cognitive effort for a decision maker. Financial planning involves allocation of funds in various assets to achieve an acceptable risk-reward ratio. Allocations have to be done after considering the multiple options available within and between various asset classes and financial products. The need to choose between many options can add to the aversiveness of the task resulting in procrastination (O'Donoghue & Rabin, 1998).

Timing of Benefits

An individual will conduct a cost-benefit analysis where the present psychic and actual costs of performing a task are weighed against the future benefit(s) (Akerlof, 1991). When faced with multiple demands on time and effort in the present, a current cost-benefit analysis may result in postponing those tasks which have an immediate cost but do not have an immediate benefit (Steel, 2007), like saving for future financial goals or making investment decisions for wealth accumulation. As the benefit of doing this task is in the future, the decision tradeoff is between present costs of performing a task and the future costs of performing it. As the present cost is more salient in comparison to the future cost (Akerlof, 1991) the probability that an individual will procrastinate important decisions regarding investments, insurance, tax planning, saving etc,. is high.

Temporal Distance

The fact that future financial goals are typically a) to be achieved over the course of time and b) provide a benefit at some point far in the future, also induces procrastination. The farther away an event is temporally, the less impact it has on current decisions and people tend to postpone completion of that task (Dewitte & Schouwenberg, 2002; Ferrari, Mason & Hammer, 2006; Steel, 2007). For investors, the time that the funds will be needed is so far in the future that they may not feel the urgency to complete the financial planning task in the present.

Planning Fallacy and Overconfidence

Planning fallacy is the tendency to erroneously predict the completion of a task by a pre-determined date (Kahneman, 2011). It is the result of using the substitution heuristic and anchoring heuristic combined with narrow framing and tends to lead to overconfidence. People tend to use a narrow decision frame (Kahneman & Lovallo, 1993) that can result in their considering only the time and effort involved to complete this task, ignoring any other possible demands on time and effort. Further, they tend to substitute the complex assessment of the various factors required for the task's completion with their positive intention of completing the project. This positive intention becomes their anchor for predicting the time period for project completion (Kahneman, 2011). This context results in overly optimistic plans or scenarios to successfully complete the task. The individual tends to neglect considering a more realistic assessment based on their own past performance or situational factors which may not be as positive or possibly negative, in this assessment. This is due to the tendency to give more decision weight to the current intention as compared to situational or contextual factors in the decision context (Griffin, Dunning & Ross, 1990; Koehler, 1991; Kahneman & Lovallo, 1993; Koehler & Poon, 2006; Skinner, 2007). Not only do people tend to base their predictions of task completion on outcome scenarios that reflect their hopes of successfully completing the task, they also base them on one or very limited number of outcome scenarios that depict progression of the present to the future, even though the future is uncertain (Kahneman, 1993; Newby-Clark et al., 2000).

These tendencies contribute to a person's overconfidence and optimistic predictions about the future. This inaccurate self-prediction of future behavior can therefore lead to decision choices in the present that may be regretted in the future. In the context of financial planning, overconfidence about one's ability to successfully make and execute a financial plan to achieve future financial goals combined with the tendency to neglect considering the possibility of any adverse events in the interim can lead to procrastination in executing the plan. This not only heightens the possibility of not achieving the goals but also experiencing financial instability in the long term.

SOLUTIONS AND RECOMMENDATIONS

Behavioral Strategies to Achieve Financial Stability

Strategies to Overcome Affect Heuristic Biases

One useful strategy an ordinary investor can adopt is to pre-decide investment decision rules. In effect, replace emotionally created heuristics with unemotional thumb rules which can be used for quick and efficient decision making.

1. **Pre-Decided Profit and Loss Achievement Prices:** At the time of purchase of the stock or asset, an investor can decide what amount of loss he/she is comfortable with bearing and set a rule that if this level of loss is breached then the asset must be sold. For example, the investor can pre - decide

the price at which to sell the stock, such as 10% lower than the purchase price. When purchasing the stock, a standing order may be left with the broker to exit the position at the pre-decided rate. Similarly, to book profit on an investment, an order to sell the stock may be negotiated if the stock reaches a certain price level, for e.g. the price reaches 15% higher than the purchase price. This simple strategy can be used to overcome loss aversion and the disposition effect explained earlier.

2. **Pre-Decide Portfolio Fund Distribution Between Assets With Different Risk Profiles:** As discussed earlier, risk assessment tends to be influenced by emotions. Research has indicated that when a person is experiencing negative emotions like anger, fear or disgust, they tend to assess an investment at high risk (Loewenstein et al., 2001). Conversely, when a person is experiencing positive emotions, they tend to underestimate risk (Ackert, Church & Deaves, 2003). It can be understood from these observations that an investor's mood can influence the risk profile of their portfolio. To overcome this bias, one recommended strategy is to pre-decide the percentage distribution of the portfolio funds in different risk categories. An ordinary investor may choose to allocate portfolio in the following manner: 35% in high risk assets, 40% in medium risk assets and 25% in low risk assets. As the investor will not change this pre-decided distribution, when evaluating any new asset for investment, the investor will be required to determine whether the new asset will alter their pre-decided portfolio distribution. If it does, necessary restructuring will have to be done to maintain the risk distribution. By using this broader frame or context for decision making, the investor is avoiding considering the risk of the new investment in isolation. Further, by assessing the risk of new investments and comparing in this manner, the investor develops a better understanding of risk and may tend to become less risk averse with time.

Strategies to Overcome Availability Heuristic biases

It is important for ordinary investors to understand and recognize the influence media has on their decision making. Not only ordinary investors, but experienced traders also tend to use the availability heuristic (Shiller, 1987).

1. **"Cool Off":** When a large group of investors sells or buys a particular stock or asset, the change in the demand is reflected as large movement in the price. The consequent media coverage of the significant price change and speculation on the possible reasons can influence other investors to follow this "herd mentality" (Rizzi, 2008; Szyszka, 2011). The consequences of this behavior can include the possibility of ordinary investors buying at a high price or selling at a low price. It is suggested that as a rule, ordinary investor should not react to market news immediately. It is recommended that the investor should follow a brief 24 hour "cooling off" period for the market price to stabilize before taking any decision.
2. **Look for Opposing Information:** In order to overcome the familiarity bias, ordinary investors should as a rule, intentionally find and assess contrary information to that which is received from advertisements, marketing brochures or other sources. This behavior will assist the investors in creating a comprehensive, unbiased information set based on which they can decide.

Strategies to Overcome Framing Biases

As observed earlier, the decision or choice frame used by a decision maker can result in particular biases in the decision outcome. Additionally, current trading in financial markets tends to be dominated by computers, institutional investors and other large investors who have better information, more experience and deeper pockets than the ordinary investor.

1. **Review the Portfolio as a Whole:** In the above context, it would be difficult for an ordinary investor to try to increase their wealth by trading in such a market. A preferred strategy may be to buy and hold investments for the long term (Thaler, 2015). A long-term investor can fix a rule to review their portfolio performance once every year rather than more frequently i.e. they can use a broad time frame for portfolio review rather than a narrow time frame. This behavior strategy should also result in countering myopic loss aversion as the investor will make less frequent portfolio adjustments and may learn to focus on making regular investments to build wealth rather than curtailing losses.
2. **Framing as a Gain:** Losses on investments are at times inevitable. An investor may consider that the upside of incurring losses on investments is that these losses can be claimed at the time of filing income tax returns. Intentionally, hedonically framing these losses as gains can be a useful way for ordinary investors to overcome loss aversion.

Consulting an Expert

Consulting a financial advisor or planner is the most recommended strategy to avoid behavioral biases in financial decision making and achieving financial stability in the long term (Khedekar-Swaminathan & Kulkarni, 2018). Financial planners charge for their services which may deter ordinary investors from availing their services. In the long run, this cost could work out to be less than the cost of inefficient allocation of funds or erroneous calculations of savings required to maintain the investor's financial stability. Collaborating with an expert on investment decisions leaves an ordinary investor limited scope to use heuristics to make a decision. A brief explanation is given below:

1. If an investor consults a professional financial advisor, the former would be required to fix appointments to review their investment portfolio in advance. Fixing an appointment tends to reduce the potential for procrastinating the portfolio review resulting in a systematic review process and an optimal wealth accumulation plan.
2. Financial advisors and planners are trained to assess their clients' requirements objectively and allocate the available funds in an optimal manner. They are equipped with the necessary tools or software to make the required complex calculations. This professional approach implies that an ordinary investor does not need to reflexively use the substitution heuristic to predict amounts required in the future or optimum risk distribution. Absence of using heuristics means outcomes would not be subject to the associated biases.
3. Financial experts are trained professionals and least likely to allow emotions to enter the decision-making process. An ordinary investor can refer to an expert to overcome the disposition effect and also the endowment effect as it pertains to decisions regarding purchase and sale of assets which may garner emotional attachment like property or commodities like gold.

4. Further, as a financial planner or advisor is objective in their approach, any emotions attached to the investors' financial goals or to their perceptions of financial products and markets would be regulated. This reduces the influence of loss aversion, regret aversion and risk aversion in the decision process, thus, increasing the probability of a finically stable outcome for the long term.

FUTURE RESEARCH DIRECTIONS

Two broad areas of future research have emerged from the current body of knowledge in the area of behavioral finance. The first area of study is the behavioral tendency to procrastinate saving for future financial goals and the second area is investor psychology.

Potential studies on procrastination could focus on aspects of self-control which explore saving for the future vs. spending in the present within the context of intertemporal choice. The choice an investor makes regarding whether to save or spend in the present is likely to have an impact on their long-term financial wellbeing.

The robust body of research on the behavioral tendencies of investors within the existing behavioral finance literature recognizes investor biases in investment decision making and explains the potential detrimental effects of these biases on investors' wealth. Therefore, future studies could explore the ordinary investor's overconfidence and susceptibility to planning fallacy with regard to financial goal achievement.

The overarching objective of such studies could be to encourage investors to approach, work with and trust financial advisors in order to achieve their long-term financial goals as well as financial stability.

CONCLUSION

This chapter has defined financial instability for ordinary investors as a situation where in the investments made are insufficient to achieve the desired amount of financial buffer to tide over periods of uncertainty that may involve no or low income as well as long term financial wealth goals. In order to achieve financial stability, ordinary investors should protect their investments from erosion due to market fluctuations, inflationary pressures and regulatory changes. This chapter has discussed the inherent limitations faced by retail investors in taking optimal financial decisions with the objective of protecting their wealth in times of uncertainty. The discussed limitations result in biases in the decision outcomes which are caused by emotional, cognitive heuristics and behavioral tendencies like procrastination. The strategies suggested aim to encourage responsible financial behavior and avoid financial instability during times of uncertainty with reference to stock market investments. By setting the recommended rules and regularly following them, the investor is only replacing the heuristics they use for financial decision making. These behavioral techniques are cognitively easier, faster to adopt and implement than gaining the financial knowledge and experience required to become a savvy investor. The result is the ability to achieve long term financial stability despite financial market uncertainties and the ensuing market instability. The limitations of these strategies lie in the investor's ability to adhere to the "new" rules by overcoming their reflexive emotions and behaviors. Further, the strategies are generic and may require adjustment for the unique circumstance of an individual investor.

REFERENCES

Ackert, L., Church, B., & Deaves, R. (2003). *Economic Review Section Quarterly*. Federal Reserve Bank of Atlanta.

Akerlof, G. (1991). Procrastinantion and Obedience. *The American Economic Review*, *81*(2), 1–19.

Barber, B., & Odean, T. (2007). All that Glitters: The Effect of Attention and News on the Buying behavior of Individual and Institutional Investors. *Review of Financial Studies*, *21*(2), 785–818. doi:10.1093/rfs/hhm079

Belsky, G., & Gilovich, T. (2010). *Why Smart People make Big Money Mistakes*. New York: Simon and Schuster.

Benartzi, S., & Thaler, R. (1995). Myopic loss aversion and the equity premium puzzle. *The Quarterly Journal of Economics*, *110*(1), 73–92. doi:10.2307/2118511

Benartzi, S., & Thaler, R. (2007). Heuristics and biases in retirement savings behavior. *The Journal of Economic Perspectives*, *21*(3), 81–104. doi:10.1257/jep.21.3.81

Blanco, F. (2017). *Cognitive Bias. In Encyclopedia of Animal Cognition and Behavior*. Springer International.

Bosch, E., Eckard, W., & Singal, V. (1998). The Competitive Effect of Air Crashes: Stock Market Evidence. *The Journal of Law & Economics*, *41*(2), 503–519. doi:10.1086/467399

Buch, H. (2017). *As stock market heats up retail investors slake thirst with mutual fund sips*. Retrieved from https://www.moneycontrol.com/news/business/mutual-funds/as-stock-market-heats-up-retail-investors-slake-thirst-with-mutual-fund-sips-2385439.html

Businessworld. (2017). *Investors prefer equities survey*. Retrieved from http://www.businessworld.in/article/84-Retail-Investors-Prefer-Equities-Survey/19-07-2017-122408

Damasio, A. (1994). *Descartes' Error: Emotion, Reason and the Human Brain*. New York: Putnam Publishing.

Dewitte, S., & Schouwenberg, H. (2002). Procrastination, Temptation and Incentives: The struggle between the present and the future in procrastinators and the punctual. *European Journal of Personality*, *16*(6), 469–489. doi:10.1002/per.461

Ellsberg, D. (1961). Risk, Ambiguity and the Savage Axioms. *The Quarterly Journal of Economics*, *75*(4), 643–669. doi:10.2307/1884324

Elster, J. (1998). Emotions and economic theory. *Journal of Economic Literature*, *36*(1), 47–74.

Epley, N., & Gilovich, T. (2010). Anchoring unbound. *Journal of Consumer Psychology*, *20*(1), 20–24. doi:10.1016/j.jcps.2009.12.005

Epley, N., & Golivich, T. (2001). Putting adjustment back in the anchoring adjustment heuristic: Differential processing of self-generated & experimenter provided anchors. *Psychological Science*, *12*(5), 391–396. doi:10.1111/1467-9280.00372 PMID:11554672

Fama, E. (1970). Efficient capital markets: A review of theory and empirical work. *The Journal of Finance*, *25*(2), 383–417. doi:10.2307/2325486

Ferrari, J., Mason, C., & Hammer, C. (2006). Procrastination as a predictor of task perceptions: Examining delayed and non-delayed tasks across various deadlines. *Individual Differences Research*, *4*(1), 28–36.

Froese, A., Nisly, S., & May, R. (1984). The effects of task interest and difficulty on Procrastination. Kansas Academy of Science, 87(3-4), 119-128. doi:10.2307/3627847

Furnham, A., & Boo, H. C. (2002). A literature review of the anchoring effect. *Journal of Socio-Economics*, *40*(1), 35–42. doi:10.1016/j.socec.2010.10.008

Gilovich, T., & Medvec, V. (1995). The experience of Regret: What, when and why. *Japanese Psychological Review*, *102*(2), 519–595. doi:10.1037//0033-295x.102.2.379 PMID:7740094

Gough, J. (1988). *Risk and uncertainty. Information Paper no.10.* Center for Resource Management, University of Canterbury and Lincoln College.

Griffin, D., Dunning, D., & Ross, M. (1990). The role of construal processes in overconfident predictions about the self and others. *Journal of Personality and Social Psychology*, *59*(6), 1128–1139. doi:10.1037/0022-3514.59.6.1128 PMID:2283587

Guiso, L., Sapienza, P., & Zingales, L. (2013). *Time varying risk aversion.* CEPR Working Paper.

Hayes, S. C. (2004). Acceptance and commitment therapy, relational frame theory and the third wave of behavioral and cognitive therapies. *Behavior Therapy*, *35*(4), 639–665. doi:10.1016/S0005-7894(04)80013-3 PMID:27993338

Investment Company Institute. (2017). *US mutual funds, Chapter 3.* Investment Company Fact Book. Retrieved from http://www.icifactbook.org/ch3/18_fb_ch3

Jarell, G., & Peltzman, S. (1985). The Impact of Product Recalls on the Wealth of Sellers. *Journal of Political Economy*, *93*(3), 512–536. doi:10.1086/261313

Jiwarajka, G. (2017). *Increasing the base of retail investors.* Retrieved from http://www.primedatabase.com/article/2017/41.Article-Gopal%20Jiwarajka.pdf

Kahneman, D. (1994). New Challenges to the Rationality Assumption. *Journal of Institutional and Theoretical Economics*, *150*(1), 105–124.

Kahneman, D. (2011). *Thinking Fast and Slow.* New York: Farrar, Straus and Giroux.

Kahneman, D., Knetsch, J., & Thaler, R. (1991). Anomalies: The endowment effect, loss aversionand status quo bias. *The Journal of Economic Perspectives*, *5*(1), 193–206. doi:10.1257/jep.5.1.193

Kahneman, D., & Lovallo, D. (1993). Timid choices and bold forecastes: A cognitive perspective on risk taking. *Management Science*, *39*(1), 17–31. doi:10.1287/mnsc.39.1.17

Kahneman, D., & Tversky, A. (1979). Prospect Theory: An analysis of decision under risk. *Econometrica*, *47*(2), 263–291. doi:10.2307/1914185

Kahneman, D., & Tversky, A. (1984). Choices, Values and Frames. *The American Psychologist*, *39*(4), 341–350. doi:10.1037/0003-066X.39.4.341

Khedekar-Swaminathan, A., & Kulkarni, S. (2018). Behavioral challenges for retirement planning: A study of employees of the Information Technology industry in Pune, Maharashtra. *International Journal of Applied Behavioral Economics*, *7*(2), 15–29. doi:10.4018/IJABE.2018040102

Knight, F. (1921). *Risk, Uncertainty and Profit*. Boston: Houghton Mifflin.

Koehler, D. (1991). Explanation, Imagination & Confidence in Judgment. *Psychological Bulletin*, *110*(3), 499–519. doi:10.1037/0033-2909.110.3.499 PMID:1758920

Koehler, D., & Poon, C. (2006). Self-predictions overweight strength of current intentions. *Journal of Experimental Social Psychology*, *42*(4), 517–524. doi:10.1016/j.jesp.2005.08.003

Lerner, J., Small, D., & Loewnstein, G. (2004). Heart strings and purse strings. *Psychological Science*, *15*(5), 337–341. doi:10.1111/j.0956-7976.2004.00679.x PMID:15102144

Loewenstein, G., Weber, E., Hsee, C., & Welch, N. (2001). Risk as feeling. *Psychological Bulletin*, *127*(2), 267–286. doi:10.1037/0033-2909.127.2.267 PMID:11316014

Lotto, B. (2017). *Deviate: The science of seeing differently*. London: Weidenfeld & Nicolson.

Lussardi, A. (2003). *Planning and Saving for Retirement*. Dartmouth College Working Paper.

Lynch, J. Jr, & Zauberman, G. (2007). Construing consumer decision making. *Journal of Consumer Psychology*, *17*(2), 107–112. doi:10.1016/S1057-7408(07)70016-5

Newby Clark, I., Ross, M., Buehler, R., Koehler, D., & Griffin, D. (2000). People focus on optimistic scenarios and disregard pessimistic scenarios while predicting task completion times. *Journal of Experimental Psychology. Applied*, *6*(3), 171–182. doi:10.1037/1076-898X.6.3.171 PMID:11014050

O'Donoghue, T., & Rabin, M. (1998). *Procrastination in preparing for retirement*. UCLA Berkley Working paper.

Ochsner, K., & Gross, J. (2003). *Thinking makes it so: a social cognitive neuroscience approach to emotion regulation. In The Handbook of Self-Regulation*. The Guilford Press.

Odean, B., & Barber, T. (2000). Trading is hazardous to your wealth: The common stock investment performance of individual investors. *The Journal of Finance*, *55*(2), 773–806. doi:10.1111/0022-1082.00226

Rabin, M., & Thaler, R. (2001). Anomalies: Risk Aversion. *The Journal of Economic Perspectives*, *15*(1), 219–232. doi:10.1257/jep.15.1.219

Ramsay, F. P. (1926). Truth and Probability. In R.B. Braithwaite (Ed.), The Foundations of Mathematics and other logical essays. New York: Harcourt Brace.

Read, D., Loewenstein, G., & Rabin, M. (1999). Choice bracketing. *Journal of Risk and Uncertainty*, *19*(1), 171-197.

Rigotti, L., & Shannon, C. (2005). Uncertainty and risk in financial markets. *Econometrica*, *73*(1), 203-243. doi:.00569.x doi:10.1111/j.1468-0262.2005

Rizzi, J. (2008). Behavioral bias of the financial crisis. *Journal of Applied Finance (JAF), 18*(2), 84–96.

Shefrin, H., & Statman, M. (1985). The disposition to sell winners too early and ride losers too long: Theory and evidence. *The Journal of Finance, 40*(3), 777–790. doi:10.1111/j.1540-6261.1985.tb05002.x

Shelor, R., Anderson, D., & Cross, M. (1992). Gaining from Loss: Property Liability Insurer Stock Values in the aftermath of the 1989 California Earthquake. *The Journal of Risk and Insurance, 59*(3), 476–488. doi:10.2307/253059

Shiller, R. (1987). Fashions, fads and bubbles in financial markets. In J. Coffee (Ed.), Knights, Raiders and Targets: The impact of the hostile takeover. Oxford, UK: Oxford University Press.

Shiller, R. (1998). *Human Behavior and the Efficiency of the Financial System.* NBER Working Paper.

Shiller, R., Fischer, S., & Friedman, B. M. (1984). Stock prices and social dynamics. *Brookings Papers on Economic Activity, 2*(2), 457–498. doi:10.2307/2534436

Silver, M., & Sabini, J. (1982). When it's not really procrastination. *Psychology Today, 16*(1), 39–42.

Simon, H. (1956). Rational choice and the structure of the environment. *Psychological Review*, Vol.63, compiled in, and quoted from, de. *Simon, 1957*, 241–260.

Simonsohn, U., & Loewenstein, G. (2006). Mistake #37: The effect of previously encountered prices on current housing demand. *Economic Journal (London), 116*(508), 175–199. doi:10.1111/j.1468-0297.2006.01052.x

Skinner, J. (2007). *Are you sure you're saving enough.* NBER, Working Paper 12981.

Slovic, P., Finucane, M., Peters, E., & MacGregor, D. (2002). The Affect Heuristic. In Heuristics and Biases: The Psychology of Intuitive Judgment (pp. 397–420). New York: Cambridge University Press. doi:10.1017/CBO9780511808098.025

Slovik, P. (2011). Market uncertainty and market instability. IFC Bulletin No. 34, Bank for International Settlements.

Steel, P. (2007). The Nature of Procrastination: A meta analytical and theoretical review of quintessential self-regulatory failure. *Psychological Bulletin, 133*(1), 65–74. doi:10.1037/0033-2909.133.1.65 PMID:17201571

Steel, P. (2010). Arousal avoidant and decisional procrastinators: Do they exist? *Personality and Individual Differences, 48*(8), 926–934. doi:10.1016/j.paid.2010.02.025

Szyszka, A. (2011). Behavioral anatomy of the financial crisis. *Journal of Centrum Cathedra*, 121–135.

Thaler, R. (1980). Toward a positive theory of Consumer Choice. *Journal of Economic Behavior & Organization, 1*(1), 39–60. doi:10.1016/0167-2681(80)90051-7

Thaler, R. (1999). Mental accounting matters. *Journal of Behavioral Decision Making, 12*, 183–206. doi:10.1002/(sici)1099-0771(199909)12:3<183:aid-bdm318>3.0.co;2-f

Thaler, R. (2015). *Misbehaving: The making of behavioral economics.* New York: W.W. Norton & Company.

Times of India. (2017). *19 lakh new investors in mutual funds added in April-May*. Retrieved from https://timesofindia.indiatimes.com/business/india-business/19-lakh-new-investors-in-mutual-funds-added-in-april-may/articleshow/59161430.cms

Tversky, A., & Fox, C. (1995). Weighing risk and uncertainty. *Psychological Review*, *102*(2), 269–283. doi:10.1037/0033-295X.102.2.269

Tversky, A., & Kahneman, D. (1974). Judgment under Uncertainty: Heuristics and Biases. *Science New Series*, *185*(4157), 1124–1131. doi:10.1126cience.185.4157.1124 PMID:17835457

Tversky, A., & Kahneman, D. (1992). Advances in prospect theory: Cumulative representation of uncertainty. *Journal of Risk and Uncertainty*, *5*(4), 297–323. doi:10.1007/BF00122574

Tvesky, A., & Kanheman, D. (1981). Framing decisions & the psychology of choice. *Science New Series*, *211*(4481), 453–458. doi:10.1126cience.7455683 PMID:7455683

Wilson, T., & Brekke, N. (1994). Mental contamination and mental correction: Unwanted influences on judgment and evaluations. *Psychological Bulletin*, *116*(1), 117–142. doi:10.1037/0033-2909.116.1.117 PMID:8078969

ADDITIONAL READING

Ackert, L. F., & Deaves, R. (2009). *Behavioral finance: Psychology, decision making, and markets*. Boston, Massachusetts: South-Western Cengage Learning.

Akerlof, G. A., & Shiller, R. J. (2009). *Animal Spirits: How human psychology drives the economy, and why it matters for global capitalism*. Princeton, New Jersey: Princeton University Press.

Gul, F., & Pesendorfer, W. (2001). Temptation and self-control. *Econometrica*, *69*(6), 1403–1435. doi:10.1111/1468-0262.00252

Loewenstein, G., & Thaler, R. (1989). Anamolies: Intertemporal Choice. *The Journal of Economic Perspectives*, *3*(4), 181–193. doi:10.1257/jep.3.4.181

Lusardi, A., & Mitchell, O. S. (2005). Financial Literacy and planning: Implications for retirement well-being. De Nederlandsche Bnak Working Paper 78

Montier, J. (2007). *Behavioral Investing: A practitioner's guide to applying behavioral finance*. New Jersey: John Wiley & Sons Inc. doi:10.1002/9781118673430

O'Donoghue, T., & Rabin, M. (1999a). Doing it now or later. *The American Economic Review*, *89*(1), 103–124. doi:10.1257/aer.89.1.103

Pompian, M. (2006). *Behavioral finance and wealth management: How to build optimal portfolios that account for investor biases*. New Jersey: John Wiley & Sons Inc.

Read, D. (2004). *Intertemporal Choice. The Blackwell Handbook of Judgment and Decision Making, Derek J. Koehler and Nigel Harvey. (424–43)*. Oxford: Blackwell.

KEY TERMS AND DEFINITIONS

Aversion: A strong disinclination towards the possibility or probability of occurrence of a particular outcome.

Bounded Rationality: A concept that explains behavior that diverges from the standard assumption of a fully rational economic agent. It occurs due to limitations of cognitive ability and access to information for decision making.

Framing: The manner in which an individual constructs mental representation of the decision choices and outcomes.

Instability: Large variations in monetary value.

Media Cascade: The constant flow of information from various media sources which focuses on a particular event.

Ordinary Investor: An individual who is inexperienced in making investment decisions or who makes investment decisions infrequently.

Overconfidence: The feeling of being more capable that prior evidence suggests.

Strategy: A plan to execute pre-decided actions in order to achieve a long-term objective or goal.

Temporal Distance: The amount of time that separates an individual's present time and a target event in the future.

Chapter 10
Addressing Financial Risks and Uncertainties Through Financial Literacy Education:
Recommendations, Resources, and Results

Danielle McKain
Beaver Area School District, USA

ABSTRACT

The world is full of financial risks and uncertainties even for those who have financial literacy. There are many factors to consider when planning financially: the stock market, hyperinflation, and climate change all play roles and are unpredictable. This chapter will focus on the actions that are being taken to establish financial literacy across the world and the impact these actions have on individual financial stability. Although financial literacy certainly cannot eliminate the risks and uncertainties that accompany unforeseen events, it is one way to prepare for these events. Even in times of normalcy, lack of financial literacy can put individuals at an increased risk of financial instability. This chapter presents a variety of recommendations and resources for financial literacy education as well as the risks and uncertainties that accompany their use.

INTRODUCTION

Despite the increase in access to financial information, people all over the world struggle to make educated financial decisions. The purpose of the present chapter is to highlight the current need for financial literacy education, resources available for the same, and contemporary research on the impact of such education. There are national and international organizations that provide information on financial literacy education. This chapter concentrates on information provided by the Organisation for Economic Cooperation and Development (OECD), International Network on Financial Education (INFE), the Consumer Financial Protection Bureau (CFPB) of the United States, and the Ontario Securities Commission (OSC) of Canada. There are a variety of resources and curriculums available for financial literacy

DOI: 10.4018/978-1-5225-7208-4.ch010

education. Many of these resources are free and can be incorporated into courses or used independently. Using these resources could be the first step to financial risk mitigation.

People all over the world of all ages are underprepared for financial planning. Many people lack the financial literacy to make decisions for saving, investing, making major purchases, and retirement plans. Organizations and governments have acted to impart financial literacy, but research is lacking in effective practices. Studies show that people around the world lack financial literacy (Lusardi & Mitchell, 2011). The United States Department of Labor National Longitudinal Survey of Youth revealed that financial literacy was low among adolescents ages 12 to 16 from a nationally representative survey sample of 9,000 adolescents. Less than one-third of young adults in the United States had basic knowledge of interest rates, inflation, and risk diversification (Lusardi, Mitchell, & Curto, 2010).

Many programs and resources have been developed to increase financial literacy and there is a push to teach financial literacy in schools. In 2015, the Financial Industry Regulatory Authority (FINRA), a private corporation in the United States, found that teaching financial skills prior to college is critical for adulthood with respect to financial security and success (Engard, 2016). Schools focus on teaching reading, writing, and math, but often fail to teach financial literacy. They strive to prepare students for adulthood, yet many adults struggle with financial knowledge and planning. While math is a major component of high school curriculums, the required courses are typically based on Algebra and Geometry and lack foundational financial education. However, there are many resources available to incorporate financial education into courses.

Based on available literature, this chapter will focus on data and resources for financial education collected from the Organisation for Economic Cooperation and Development (OECD), International Network on Financial Education (INFE), the Consumer Financial Protection Bureau (CFPB), and the Ontario Securities Commission (OSC). These sources provide elaborate data and recommendations relating to financial literacy. Throughout the chapter, this data will be correlated to other resources, programs, research, results, and recommendations. Lastly, this information will be used to establish how future research can include financial capabilities to account for variations in the economy.

The objectives of this chapter include:

1. **Need for Financial Literacy Education:** Providing data supporting the need for financial literacy education from OECD, CFPB, and OSC;
2. **Recommendations for Financial Literacy Education:** Providing recommendations for financial literacy education from OECD and CFPB;
3. **Resources for Financial Literacy Education:** Providing resources for financial literacy education from CFPB, OSC, and other additional resources;
4. **Results of Financial Literacy Education:** Providing data related to the effects of financial literacy education from CFPB and other research studies;

BACKGROUND: NEED FOR FINANCIAL LITERACY EDUCATION

Financial literacy has the potential to create stability in times of financial risk and uncertainty. "Starting Early for Financial Success" was a special issue of *The Journal of Consumer Affairs* that focused on financial education, financial inclusion, and financial well-being. The journal identified three main concerns that contribute to current financial issues: everyday financial decision making is increasingly complex, serious financial decisions occur at a younger age, and many families struggle financially (Sherraden & Grinstein-Weiss, 2015). The articles in the journal suggest that early commencement of financial education can lead to financial success. Greenspan (2005) suggests that the complexity of the financial world today makes the need for financial education important. Computers, access to credit, and advances in technology make financial planning vary across the world.

Recessions, increasing prices, foreclosures, bankruptcies, decreasing savings, and poverty are global concerns (McCormick, 2009). Unfortunately, those living in developing countries do not usually have the option to plan financially. Without access to resources, financial literacy and planning is nearly impossible; thus, Johnson and Sherraden (2007) refer to the access to financial resources as financial capability. The best methods for financial preparation are complicated, but individuals living in developed countries are often in control of their own financial decisions. While some of these factors cannot be controlled, it may be possible to prepare for them. The unknown risks and uncertainties of the future place pressure and stress on individuals. To prepare for these unknown exigencies, individuals can take control of their finances and prepare themselves as much as possible through education.

The next section of this chapter will review the Organisation for Economic Cooperation and Development (OECD), International Network on Financial Education (INFE), the Consumer Financial Protection Bureau (CFPB), and the Ontario Securities Commission (OSC). The resources and information provided by these organizations provide opportunities for financial literacy and education planning.

OECD/INFE: International

The Organisation for Economic Co-operation and Development (OECD), established in 1961, provides a forum for governments to compare and exchange policy experiences, identify good practices, and promote decisions and recommendations. The mission of OECD is to support policies that improve the social and economic well-being of people around the world and produce better policies for better lives (About the OECD, 2018). The OECD analyzes aspects such as taxes, social security, leisure time, school systems, and pensions. They set international standards for subjects of social relevance such as agriculture, tax, and chemical safety, help governments establish public finances for future economic growth, support new sources of growth through innovation, and promote skills for work productivity in future jobs.

In 2008, the International Network on Financial Education (INFE) was created by the OECD as a network of public experts on financial education. INFE gathers 220 public institutions from almost 100 countries to meet twice a year to develop analytical work on priority policy issues, guidelines, and good practices (International Gateway for Financial Education, 2012). In 2012, G20 leaders endorsed the OECD/INFE High-level Principles on National Strategies for Financial Education. The principles serve as international guidelines for policymakers to develop evidence-based, coordinated approaches to financial education.

The National Strategies for Financial Education OECD/INFE Policy Handbook is a result of countries that have implemented national strategies from the guidelines. Over 110 economies of OECD/INFE with 65 direct contributors provided in-depth analysis of challenges faced when implementing national strategies for financial education (National Strategies for Financial Education: OECD/INFE Policy Handbook, n.d.). As of June 2015, a national strategy was being revised or a second national strategy was being implemented in 11 countries (Australia, Czech Republic, Japan, Malaysia, Netherlands, New Zealand, Singapore, Slovak Republic, Spain, United Kingdom, and the United States). A first national strategy was being implemented in 23 countries (Armenia, Belgium, Brazil, Canada, Croatia, Denmark,

Estonia, Ghana, Hong Kong (China), India, Indonesia, Ireland, Israel, Korea, Latvia, Morocco, Nigeria, Portugal, Russian Federation, Slovenia, South Africa, Sweden, and Turkey). Furthermore, a national strategy was being designed in 24 countries (Argentina, Chile, China, Colombia, Costa Rica, El Salvador, France, Guatemala, Kenya, Kyrgyzstan, Lebanon, Malawi, Mexico, Pakistan, Paraguay, Peru, Poland, Saudi Arabia, Serbia, Tanzania, Thailand, Uganda, Uruguay, and Zambia), and planned in 6 countries (Austria, FYR Macedonia, Philippines, Romania, Ukraine, and Zimbabwe).

The OECD/INFE Policy Handbook provides case studies for the following countries: Australia, Brazil, Canada, Denmark, Hong Kong (China), India, Indonesia, Japan, Malaysia, Mexico, Netherlands, New Zealand, Peru, Portugal, Singapore, South Africa, Spain, Thailand, Turkey, United Kingdom, and United States. The case studies provide modalities of instruction, teacher development, and pedagogical material developed and certified by public institutions.

The following information is from the OECD handbook providing more insight to the various strategies countries that are using the OECD/INFE High-level Principles on National Strategies for Financial Education to address financial literacy (National Strategies for Financial Education: OECD/INFE Policy Handbook, n.d.). More information concerning these examples is provided in the OECD handbook. Many of these programs are new, but as they are established and implemented, evaluation and monitoring will provide valuable information for future research.

- **Australia:** A key component of Australia's financial education strategy is how personal circumstances determine financial decisions. The Australian Securities and Investments Commission (ASIC) researched financial behavior to identify five indicators associated with personal finances. National Financial Literacy Strategy is the national website (www.financialliteracy.gov.au).
- **Brazil:** The Citizen Financial Education Project uses technology to promote financial education and reach those living in poverty. Ten low-income communities in Brazil will be part of the project that is expected to include 5000 families. The project uses tablet computers that are pre-loaded with financial education content. The project is coordinated through the Central Bank of Brazil (BCB) and the University of Bahia's Solidarity Economy and Territorial Developmental department (ITES/UFBA). Brazil has multiple national websites including Life and Money (www.vidaedinheiro.gov.br), ENEF week (www.semanaenef.gov.br), and Financial Education Programme in Schools (www.edufinanceiranaescola.gov.br).
- **Czech Republic:** Financial education is included in primary school.
- **Denmark:** The Money and Pension Panel coordinates financial education activities; personal finance and economics are part of the Common Objectives, which are required to be taught through the 2012 Folkeskole Act.
- **Estonia:** Estonia includes financial education in primary and secondary schools.
- **Hong Kong, China:** The Investor Education Centre (IEC) started in 2012. The national website is Investor Education Centre (www.hkiec.hk).
- **India:** The Government and Reserve Bank have recently made banking services a priority and are working on a national strategy for financial education.
- **Indonesia:** A national strategy for financial education was launched in 2013. As part of the national financial customer protection framework, the mandate from the Indonesia Financial Services Authority (OJK) provides financial information and education.
- **Ireland:** Financial literacy is covered in secondary math, home economics, and business classes.

- **Japan:** Financial literacy is part of the national curriculum and is covered in social studies, home economics, and moral classes. Teachers attend seminar trainings.
- **Lebanon:** Financial literacy is part of the national curriculum. Teachers are trained through the Ministry of Education.
- **Malaysia:** The Pengurusan Wang Ringgit Anda (POWER!) program is used to teach young individuals financial knowledge and skills. Pre and post surveys are used to measure financial knowledge, attitudes, and behavior.
- **New Zealand:** A Financial Behavior Index is a quick online survey that is used to track financial behavior.
- **Peru:** The Ministry of Education (MINEDU), Peruvian Superintendence of Banking, Insurance and Private Pension Funds (SBS), the National System of Evaluation, and the Accreditation and Certification of Educational Quality (SINEACE) created a financial education framework to update the national curricula that included financial education competence.
- **Portugal:** The National Council of Financial Supervisors coordinates the Portuguese National Plan for Financial Education. The council sponsors a national school competition that promotes financial education.
- **Singapore:** The national financial education program in Singapore is called Money SENSE through the Financial Education Steering Committee (FESC). The program includes workshops, talks, and e-learning modules.
- **South Africa:** The Human Science Research Council (HSRC) conducts both an annual and baseline survey to determine financial literacy levels of various groups. The National Treasury and National Consumer Financial Education Committee (NCFEC) have a national strategy for financial education. The national website www.mylifemymoney.co.za is designed to help consumers make the most out of their money.
- **Spain:** The Financial Education program, part of the national strategy of Financial Education Plan, has shown positive results in schools. The national website www.finanzasparatodos.es provides information for financial decisions.
- **Turkey:** The National Strategy for Financial Access was started in 2014. The strategy includes surveys to measure development in financial literacy and promote financial awareness.

In 2012, financial literacy became an optional component of the OECD Programme for International Student Assessment (PISA). This assessment tests 15-year-olds in mathematics, problem-solving, reading, and science in 65 countries every three years. The addition of a financial literacy assessment provides the opportunity to further research factors associated with financial literacy levels.

In 2015 BSJG China (refers to Beijing, Shanghai, Jiangsu and Guangdong), Belgium (Flemish), Canadian provinces (refers to the seven provinces in Canada that participated: British Columbia, Manitoba, New Brunswick, Newfoundland and Labrador, Nova Scotia, Ontario and Prince Edward Island), Russia, Netherlands, Australia, United States, Poland, Italy, Spain, Lithuania, Slovak Republic, Chile, Peru, and Brazil participated in the financial literacy portion of the PISA test. China, Belgium, Canadian provinces, Russia, and the Netherlands were the top 5 performing countries, followed by Australia, then the United States. The results found that among the countries and economies that participated, 22% of students did not have basic financial skills.

Approximately 48,000 15-year-olds in 15 participating countries participated in the test (OECD PISA financial literacy assessment of students, n.d.). Results of the 2015 PISA study found 12% of 15-year-old students were top performers in financial literacy. The results also found approximately 56% of 15-year-old participants had a bank account and those students who held a bank account tended to perform better in financial literacy than students of similar socioeconomic status who did not have a bank account. Advantaged students scored 89 points higher in financial literacy than disadvantaged students, showing financial skills are strongly related to the social-economic background of the family. More than 70% of students in Australia, Belgium (Flemish), the Canadian provinces and the Netherlands hold a bank account. In most countries/economies there was no difference in financial literacy by gender. Immigrant students scored lower in financial literacy than native-born students of similar socioeconomic status. Of those who participated, 19% have a prepaid debit card, 64% earn money working, 31% have the skills to manage a bank account, and 84% discuss money with their parents. Mathematics or reading skills could not explain almost 40% of the variation in financial literacy in the study. Two-thirds of the participating countries and economies are implementing a national strategy for financial education specifically addressing young people among their targeted audiences. In 2018, 21 countries will be participating in the PISA financial literacy: Australia, Brazil, Bulgaria, Canada, Chile, Estonia, Finland, Georgia, Indonesia, Italy, Latvia, Lithuania, Netherlands, Peru, Poland, Portugal, Russian Federation, Serbia, Slovak Republic, Spain, United States.

Consumer Financial Protection Bureau (CFPB): United States

The Consumer Financial Protection Bureau is a United States government agency that makes sure banks, lenders, and other financial companies treat people fairly (Consumer Financial Protection Bureau, n.d.). The mission of CFPB is to empower consumers to take control of their financial lives. To improve financial capability through education, CFPB has worked to define, measure, and study what contributes to financial well-being. This starts with defining financial capability as the ability to manage financial resources effectively based on skills, knowledge, and accessibility (Building Blocks to Help Youth Achieve Financial Capability, n.d.).

The National Financial Well-Being Survey for adults, developed and conducted through the CFPB, Abt Associates, the University of Wisconsin-Madison's Center for Financial Security, and GfK, was used to produce the Financial Well-Being in America report in 2017. The survey measured individuals' financial well-being and also included individual, household, and family characteristics, income, employment, savings, safety nets, financial experiences, financial behaviors, skills, and attitudes (Financial Well-Being survey, n.d.).

After asking people across the United States, the CFPB determined that financial well-being means having financial freedom of choice and financial security, in both the present and the future. Financial well-being is further defined by (1) having control over day-to-day and month-to-month finances (2) the ability to deal with a financial shock (3) being on track to meet financial goals and (4) having the financial freedom to choose things that bring enjoyment (Financial Well-Being survey, n.d.).

The average score for financial well-being for over 6,000 U.S. adults was 54 (out of 100). With approximately one-third of adults surveyed scoring 50 or below, one-third scoring between 51 and 60, and one-third scoring 61 or above. One-third scoring 50 or below indicates that they have difficulty making ends meet, and approximately 20% have a difficult time paying for food, housing, and medical care. Individuals with more financial knowledge and skills had higher average financial well-being scores.

In addition, employment, income, and education also had a strong correlation with financial well-being scores. The study found that older adults had higher financial well-being scores. Geography and gender did not have an impact on financial well-being scores, but racial/ethnic groups did reveal small differences (Financial Well-Being survey, n.d.).

The strongest relationships were determined to be related to savings and safety nets. Using non-bank short-term credit, being denied credit, and being contacted by a debt collector were strongly related to low financial well-being scores. Higher financial well-being scores were strongly correlated with habits of savings, routine money management, long-term planning, and confidence in financial goals. Those with higher financial well-being scores had the financial skills and knowledge found in many financial education curriculums. Due to the variation within almost all groups and subgroups, the study concluded that many factors determine one's financial well-being (Financial Well-Being survey, n.d.).

Individual opportunities for foundational financial attitude, skill, and knowledge, can influence financial well-being (Financial Well-Being survey, n.d.). Financial educators are encouraged to help build financial skills, confidence, and effective money management behaviors. The data from the National Financial Well-Being Survey provides correlations with characteristics based on individual situations that could be used to predict future financial well-being and may be used to help other countries formulate national strategies for financial education as outlined in the OECD section.

Ontario Securities Commission (OSC): Canada

The Ontario Securities Commission (OSC) is an independent Crown corporation that is responsible for regulating the capital markets in Ontario (OSC About, 2018). They protect investors and contribute to financial system stability by regulating firms, public companies, investment funds, and marketplaces. The operation is separate from the government and funding is through market participants. The goals of the OSC are to provide regulation, protection, compliance, enforcement, and supervision. In addition, they provide innovation, accountability, and organization. The OSC has performed a variety of investor research surveys and studies to improve knowledge and understanding. The following examples provide insight into the types of surveys that other countries may be using to formulate national strategies for financial education as outlined in the OECD section.

The Ontario Securities Commission (OSC) conducted a study, *Financial life stages of older Canadians* and found older Canadians found value in understanding future income needs (68%), so that they would not outlive their money (67%), preparation for health issues (66%), generation of income in retirement (63%), and the impact of inflation (62%) (Financial Life Stages of Older Canadians, n.d.). The survey also revealed that there was a lack of knowledge for how much income would be needed for retirement and Canadians were not saving enough for retirement.

Missing Out: Millennials and the Markets research study found that 80% of Ontario millennials were saving, but only 50% were investing (MISSING OUT: Millennials and the Markets, n.d.). Reasons for not investing included: other financial priorities, lack income, lack of investment knowledge, and fear of losing money. The OSC site provides resources for learning about investing. Topics include investing basics, investment products, planning your future, and savings plans.

An Ipsos Reid poll, *Canadians' obstacles to saving and investing,* found that Canadians' primary issues for managing and investing money are not enough income (48%), fear of losing money (23%), too much debt (22%), lack of financial knowledge (20%), lack of confidence (14%), and lack of time (12%) (Omnibus poll: Canadians' obstacles to saving and investing, n.d.). As for budgeting, 46% of those surveyed said they always budget their money, and 24% said they don't budget at all. Furthermore, 17% responded that they only budget for major purchases, and 13% said they budget for emergencies. Women (49%) were more likely to budget their money than men (43%), and middle-aged (44%) and seniors (45%) were less likely to budget than young adults (49%).

In 2012, the *Benchmarking Financial Knowledge Survey* found that a little over one-third of Ontarians passed basic financial concepts application (Benchmarking Financial Knowledge Survey, n.d.). While those surveyed demonstrated financial knowledge, there were problems applying that knowledge to real life scenarios. Financial planning, including inflation, long-term savings, and retirement planning, were found to be the weakest areas of financial knowledge.

RECOMMENDATIONS FOR FINANCIAL LITERACY EDUCATION

Financial literacy has the potential to help individuals overcome financial risks. The following are recommendations for financial literacy education from OECD and CFPB.

OECD Recommendations

In 2005, the OECD recommended that financial education is essential to be taught in schools and starts as early as possible. Since financial education is a long-term process, incorporating it into curriculums early provides the opportunity for children to build on knowledge and promote responsible financial behavior. The importance of financial education is recognized, and countries are adding financial education into school curriculums; however, the barriers include lack of political will, lack of resources, extensive curriculums, and insufficient expertise. Many of the countries that are implementing financial education follow the INFE guidelines that are supported by OECD (National Strategies for Financial Education: OECD/INFE Policy Handbook, n.d.):

1. A coordinated national strategy should place financial education in schools.
2. A learning framework at the national, regional, or local level should set goals, content, learning outcomes, resources, and evaluation plans. The content should cover attitudes, values, skills, and knowledge.
3. The strategy should begin with a sustainable source of funding.
4. Financial education should begin early and continue throughout students' schooling.
5. Financial education should be part of the school curriculum and may or may not be taught as a separate subject.
6. Teachers should be trained and supported throughout the process.
7. Schools and teachers should be provided with resources.
8. Students should be assessed and rewarded for achievements.

OECD recommends evaluating the impact of financial literacy initiatives in and outside of school. They also advise addressing the needs of low-performing students and tackling socioeconomic inequalities early. Equal opportunities should be provided for boys and girls, and students should be taking advantage of learning opportunities at school. OECD encourages advising parents and providing safe opportunities for learning outside of school (National Strategies for Financial Education: OECD/INFE Policy Handbook, n.d.).

CFPB Recommendations

The Consumer Financial Protection Bureau (CFPB) in the United States has been trying to approve a national requirement for financial literacy education in both elementary and secondary schools. There are five recommendations for financial literacy education established by CFPB (Engard, 2016):

1. Financial literacy should start early and be taught as an isolated subject for high school students.
2. Personal finance questions should be on standard exams.
3. Students should be provided with hands-on learning opportunities.
4. Teachers should be trained and offered incentives for teaching personal finance.
5. Parents should be supplied with tools to use at home.

RESOURCES FOR FINANCIAL LITERACY EDUCATION

Individual financial stability can be established through financial literacy. The following section provides resources from CFPB and OSC. In addition, a variety of additional resources will be presented. These resources were chosen by the author of this chapter based on quality and availability. Through education, individuals could become more aware of potential risks and how do deal with uncertain situations.

CFPB Resources

The Federal Deposit Insurance Corporation (FDIC) and Consumer Financial Protection Bureau (CFPB) of the United States strive to make it easier for schools to provide financial education by providing lesson plans, videos, and other resources on their site (Federal Deposit Insurance Corporation, n.d.). Money Smart is a four-level (PreK-2, 3-5, 6-8, 9-12) curriculum series that can be downloaded. Additionally, Money Smart News is the FDIC's quarterly newsletter that features teaching tips and success stories. There are also links to implementation ideas and suggestions to help educators use and promote Money Smart (Federal Deposit Insurance Corporation, n.d.).

CFPB offers a variety of Consumer Tools, Practitioner Resources, and Data and Research.

Individuals can find out their financial well-being by answering ten questions that will measure present financial well-being and provide steps that can be taken to make improvements (Find out your financial well-being, n.d.). CFPB describes financial well-being as how much your financial situation and money choices provide you with security and freedom of choice. The questions do not ask for specific data like income, mortgage, or credit score.

OSC Resources

The Ontario Securities Commission (OSC) website offers financial tools such as a savings calculator, compound interest calculator, and pay down debt tools (Get Smarter About Money, 2018). These tools are for people to use so that they can make better financial choices. The site also provides numerous research studies and reports concerning the habits and needs of Canadians concerning personal finance, money management, and investing.

ADDITIONAL RESOURCES

Canadian Foundation for Economic Education (CFEE)

The Canadian Foundation for Economic Education (CFEE) started in 1974 as a charitable, non-profit, non-partisan organization in Canada (Canadian Foundation for Economic Education Resources, n.d.). CFEE seeks to make economic and financial capabilities as it works with education systems, to provide free programs. In addition, CFEE works with the Association of Asia Pacific Countries and the Child and Youth Finance International in Amsterdam. CFEE supports improved financial literacy. They partnered with BMO Financial Group to offer "Talk with Our Kids About Money Day" to integrate financial education into 7th grade curriculums. They also offer free curriculum and activities for teachers all year.

Jump$tart

The JumpStart Coalition for Personal Financial Literacy publishes National Standards in K-12 Personal Finance Education. The National Standards establish guidelines for the personal finance knowledge young people should have in elementary and high school to become adult consumers that are independent and prepared to make good financial decisions. The goal is to help students achieve financial literacy and become financially capable consumers (Jumpstart Clearinghouse, n.d.). The Jump$tart Coalition defines financial literacy as the ability to use skills and knowledge to manage financial resources effectively for a lifetime of financial security (Jumpstart Clearinghouse, n.d.). The 2015 standards consist of six major categories Spending and Saving, Employment and Income, Credit and Debt, Investing, Financial Decision Making, and Risk Management and Insurance. Each standard is broken down with overall competency and knowledge statements.

The JumpStart Coalition believes that financial literacy is a continuum of abilities, subject to variables throughout life (JumpStart Who We Are, 2018). Furthermore, financial literacy is more than just knowledge, but more importantly, the ability to use knowledge to make financial choices. As individual and economic circumstances change, financial literacy can enable one to respond appropriately. Moreover, the primary goal of JumpStart is not that a student can recite definitions of financial terms, but rather evaluate situations based on financial knowledge to make educated decisions for them to become financially capable consumers.

EverFi

EverFi offers an online Financial Literacy resource that provides videos and interactive activities to bring concepts to life. Progress and knowledge are tracked individually, and students receive a certificate upon completion. The course consists of nine modules: banking, saving, credit cards & interest rates, credit score, financing higher education, renting vs. owning, taxes & insurance, consumer protection, and investing. It is free for students and teachers. The resources, designed for high school students, can be used in an Algebra, Economics, Business, Family and Consumer Science, or AVID course (Financial Literacy, n.d.).

The EverFi Financial Literacy course, *Building Financial Foundations* builds a foundation for students' future. Each of the nine modules contains instructional animations. Real-life financial scenarios and documents are used to break down information in an easy to follow format. Each module, aligned with Jumpstart Standards and U.S State Financial Literacy Standards, takes approximately 40-50 minutes to complete. Teachers receive student score reports, lesson plans, alignment guide with state standards, answer keys, and discussion guides. Students receive practice activities, performance-based games, and an interactive learning format. The course begins with a Pre-Survey, followed by a prediction Pre-assessment, learning activities, post-assessment, and finally, a post-survey. The pedagogy is based on Universal Design for Learning (UDL) and Teach for Understanding (TFU) frameworks. Example modules include filling out the Free Application for Federal Student Aid (FAFSA) form, understanding your paycheck, and buying a new car. Over 10 million students have used the EverFi resources.

Khan Academy

The non-profit organization, Khan Academy is free and offers education pertaining to Personal Finance, Finance and Capital Markets, College Admissions, Careers, Entrepreneurship, Microeconomics, and Macroeconomics (Khan Academy, n.d.). Personal Finance course topics include Interest and Debt, Saving and Budgeting, Income, Investment Vehicles and Retirement, Auto, Housing, Paying for College, Taxes, and Keeping your Information Safe. Finance and Capital Markets course topics include Housing, Interest and Debt, Taxes, Inflation, Stocks and Bonds, Accounting and Financial Statements, Investment Vehicles, Money, Insurance and Retirement, Options, Banking and Central Banks, Futures, Swaps, CDOs and other Derivatives, MBSs, and Current Economics. College Admissions course topics include Making High School Count, Getting Started, Applying to College, Exploring College Options, Wrapping Up, Paying for College, and Life After College. Careers course topics include Introduction, Support Health and Wellness, Serve Your Community, Design, Start a Business, Perform, Create, Educate, Conduct Research, Build and Fix Things, Travel and Explore, Manage People and Processes, and Analyze and Advise. The entrepreneurship section includes 50 interviews with entrepreneurs.

Khan Academy offers Learner, Teacher, and Parent accounts. Teachers can create accounts and invite students by email or a course code. Once students enroll in a course, teachers (coaches) can make assignments and track activity and progress. Class progress, as well as individual student progress, can be analyzed to identify strengths and weaknesses. There are instructional videos, lessons and interactive practice exercises. Students can see their progress, activity, and time. Coaches can receive weekly student highlight emails for each class and students can receive a weekly progress summary email. Khan Academy offers special content through partnerships with NASA, Bank of America, The Museum of Modern Art, The California Academy of Sciences, and MIT. Khan Academy offers French, Spanish, and Brazilian Portuguese versions of their site. Additionally, resources can be translated into over 36 languages.

Bank of America offers Better Money Habits through Khan Academy. Topics include Saving & Budgeting, Credit, Debt, Auto, Homeownership, College, Retirement, Taxes & Income, Privacy & Security, and Personal Banking. There are three initial questions (1) What is your stage in life? A.) Just starting out B.) Working and growing C.) Nearing Retirement D.) Living in Retirement (2) What is your work situation? A.) Working Full-Time B.) Self-employed C.) Currently a Student D.) Active military or a veteran E.) Working part-time F.) Not currently working (3) What is most important to you?

A.) Finances: Saving for retirement, paying off student loans, buying a car, reducing debt, improving credit, building up savings, received windfall B.) Family: Getting married/ living together, welcoming a child, saving for college, caring for adult children or aging parents, teaching kids about money, getting divorced C.) Work: starting a new job, prepping for taxes, working in retirement D.) Home: buying a home, refinancing a home, renting. Based on responses to these three questions, the site will provide articles, videos, and infographics.

Junior Achievement (JA)

Junior Achievement is a non-governmental organization. The mission of JA is to inspire and prepare young people to succeed in a global economy (Junior Worldwide, n.d.). JA Worldwide includes JA Africa, INJAZ Al-Arab, JA Americas, JA Asia Pacific, JA Europe, and JA USA and is dedicated to educating youth and preparing them for future academic and economic success. According to JA, 36% of Americans say that they have felt their financial situation was out of control at some point in their lives. JA USA offers many programs to prepare students for the real world. Junior Achievement is used in over 200,000 classrooms and after-school locations reaching more than 4.8 million students per year. Volunteers teach the nonprofit programs across the United States. JA Worldwide serves more than 10 million students in over 100 countries. JA reinforces the value of education. Teachers can reach out to a local JA Office and a Program Manager will reach out to coordinate a JA volunteer visit. The volunteer will visit the classroom for an entire day or about an hour a day for a week. JA programs align with national, state, and district standards and are designed for elementary, middle, or high school. Junior Achievement's purpose is to "inspire and prepare young people to succeed in a global economy" (Junior Worldwide, n.d.).

JA offers a variety of programs for elementary, middle, and high school (Junior Achievement Programs, n.d.). Elementary school programs offered include BizTown, More than Money, Our City, Our Community, Our Families, Our Nation, Our Region, and Ourselves. Middle school programs include Economics for Success, Finance Park, Global Marketplace Blended Model, Global Marketplace, It's My Business! Blended Model, It's My Business! and, It's My Future. High school programs include Be Entrepreneurial, Career Success, Company Program Blended Model, Economics, Exploring Economics, Finance Park, Job Shadow, Launch Lesson, Personal Finance Blended Model, Personal Finance, and Titan.

The JA site presents concepts and skills for each program, as well as an overview of each session. For example, Finance Park is designed to help students build a foundation in financial skills to make good financial decisions in their future. The program includes 13 lessons and hands-on budgeting simulation. There is a traditional format offered for middle school students and a Project-Based Learning (PBL) for high school students. Finance Park lessons include Income and taxes, Career exploration, Managing risk, Saving and investing, Debt, Credit, and Budgeting (Junior Achievement Finance Park, n.d.).

Council for Economic Education (CEE)

The Council for Economic Education (CEE) is a non-profit organization that focuses on the economic and financial education for students in elementary and high school. They strive to educate educators and provide curriculum resources and support (Council for Economic Education, 2018). In the United States, educational requirements are determined by each state and furthermore, by each school district. Financial education requirements vary from district to district and state to state. It is unlikely that the country would adopt national standards, but with so many resources there can be some consistency established.

The CEE conducts research on K-12 financial and economic education in the United States and releases the Survey of the States every two years to represent the progress of economic and personal finance education. CEE provides standards in economics and personal finance, as well as, assessments and online resources to support and promote requiring economics and personal finance education. As of 2018, 17 states require high school students to take a course in personal finance (Survey of the States, 2018). The CEE suggests requesting promoting standards and course requirements at the state level and teacher training.

CEE's Master Teacher Program is for teachers who wish to teach professional development workshops to other educators in their districts or at national conferences in an effort to increase the number of students who take personal finance and economic courses (Master Teacher Program, n.d.). Five years of full-time classroom instruction is required to become a master teacher. In addition, teachers must complete 6 hours of CEE Professional Development and demonstrate experience presenting at professional development workshops and conferences.

RESULTS OF FINANCIAL LITERACY EDUCATION

There are many resources available for teaching financial literacy that it makes educating young adults to seem simple. Financial literacy education should prepare young adults to make educated financial decisions in their future. This section of the chapter will present the results of current financial education research. There are many questions about financial literacy education; more research is necessary to determine the specific components, timing, impact, and accessibility of these programs.

CFPB

The 2016 CFPB report, *Building Blocks to Help Youth Achieve Financial Capability*, presented results of research on where and when children and adolescents acquire financial capability foundations (Building Blocks to Help Youth Achieve Financial Capability, n.d.). The report reveals critical attributes, abilities, and opportunities that are established from a young age through adulthood and begin the development of financial capability. The results helped create a skills-based model that can to be used to enhance financial education, as well as develop and test new financial educational strategies.

The research found that (1) executive function, (2) financial habits and norms, and (3) financial knowledge and decision-making skills are the three components of youth development that lead to adult financial capability. The study indicates the importance of starting financial education early and to continue throughout high school. The research indicates that focusing on personal financial knowledge is only one component of future financial well-being and that focusing on it alone will not result in adult financial capability. CFPB provides a youth personal finance pedagogy tool for educators to use.

Families, communities, and schools are all important to build these three components of financial capability. Not all students have the same opportunities to develop these components; thus, CFPB developed four recommendations for ways to apply these components to financial education programs. The first recommendation is to focus on developing executive function skills in early childhood. The second recommendation is to help parents and caregivers be active influences on financial socialization.

The third recommendation is to provide children and youth opportunities for experiential learning. The fourth recommendation is the teach financial research skills to youth.

The CFPB states that financial education in high schools can lead to improved credit scores. Thus, in 2015, they released a guide for policymakers for advancing K-12 financial education to connect policymakers with tools, information, and insights for K-12 financial education planning. The guide provides an easy-to-follow framework that includes three sections: Building initiative, Laying the groundwork, and Extending the impact. Each section is broken down further into modules that provide current efforts, examples, resources, and case studies.

Positive Results of Financial Literacy Education

Lack of financial literacy combined with unpredictable events could undoubtedly increase risk and uncertainty. The Financial Industry Regulatory Authority (FINRA), a private self-regulatory corporation in the United States, found that student credit scores increased as much as 5.2 percent two years after financial literacy education was mandated; furthermore, they found a decrease of as much as 8.4 percent in the number of students who were 90 days or more delinquent on credit card payments (Engard, 2016). Brown, Collins, Schmeiser, and Urban (2014) studied the credit behavior of young adults after state-mandated financial education and found that after implementing a financial education requirement, young people had higher relative credit scores and lower relative delinquency rates than those in states that do not have mandated financial education.

In 2015, the RMC (Research Making Change) Research Corporation, provides research on programs and performs evaluations for government agencies, foundations, and organizations seeking improvements in education, well-being, and health. RMC used a pre-post comparison-group design to evaluate the JA Finance Park Curriculum. Data collected included pre-and post-program student surveys, a teacher survey, a volunteer survey, and site visits to four JA areas. The research found students who participated in JA Finance Park acquired financial literacy knowledge and demonstrated more financial literacy knowledge than students who did not participate (Curriculum Evaluation, 2016). Students affirmed the value of JA Finance Park and teachers perceived a substantial impact on students (Curriculum Evaluation, 2016).

Smart X is a comprehensive program through CEE's Financial Fitness for Life series that focuses on engaging schools, school districts, and states to enhance and extend personal finance education and incorporate financial literacy lessons in all grade levels (SmartX, n.d.). Smart X offers professional development for teachers and focuses on both pedagogy and content. Lessons are activity based on developing good decision-making skills based on saving, education, money management, spending, and credit. There is also a parent component to promote financial education discussions at home. Lessons are aligned to Common Core Math and English Language Arts. Pre and post-test outcomes are provided and have been nationally normed. Four of the fifty states have implemented Smart X. Tennessee has used it the longest and has reached more than 85,000 students. Pre and post-test results show meaningful student achievement gains (SmartX, n.d.).

Never Too Young: Personal Finance for K-5 Learners, offered through CEE, is an elementary program that creates a real-world understanding of personal finance and economics. It was developed based on the demand to teach students about finances outside of the regular school day (Never Too Young, n.d.). The approach of this program considers a range of age and ability levels, non-classroom setting, inconsistent attendance, and non-traditional teachers. The program consists of 12 units and teaches the cost of having a family, basics of banking and credit, and the importance of cost-benefit analysis in making purchases. Nearly 6,000 students in 15 states have participated in the program. In New York City, 86% of participants came from schools with a significant number of students eligible for free and reduced lunches. A pre and post-test showed a 19% improvement for the 3rd to 5th graders who participated (Never Too Young, n.d.).

Negative Results of Financial Literacy Education

Some research has found that financial education does not result in better financial behavior. Willis (2008) wrote about the disadvantages of financial literacy education. He argues that the benefits are not worth the costs. A 2009 study of 79 high school students found that those who completed a financial management course were not more financially literate 1 to 4 years later. Additionally, there was not significant difference in the financial behavior of students who took the course did not seem and those who did not take the course (Mandell & Klein, 2009).

Fernandes, Lynch, & Netemeyer (2014) conducted research analyzing 168 papers and 201 studies on the relationship between financial literacy and financial education to financial behaviors. They found that interventions that intend to improve financial behavior only explain 0.1% of the variance in financial behaviors. Financial education was found to have severe limitations especially when 20 months or more passed since the time of education. This suggests that education at the time of the financial decision could be more beneficial, which is appropriate when making credit card or mortgage decisions, but challenging when considering investing or retirement planning.

The impact of implementing financial literacy education is debatable. Some research suggests implementing such programs results in better financial planning and security, while others would suggest financial literacy education does not equate to better financial planning and security. More research is necessary to determine the long-term impact of financial literacy education.

SOLUTIONS AND RECOMMENDATIONS

Many challenges accompany financial literacy education. In the quickly changing and uncertain times we live in, it is important to acknowledge possible steps that can be taken to better prepare individuals for future financial decisions. Many countries are focusing on promoting financial literacy. Although promising, financial literacy comes with many challenges, as well as risks and uncertainties.

OECD and CFPB make similar recommendations for financial literacy education. These recommendations are only applicable if there is a financial literacy program that can be put into practice. The solution to addressing financial risk and uncertainty through financial literacy education is to make financial literacy education appropriate and meaningful. Worldwide, the solution starts with access to financial services. The World Bank addresses this concept by reducing poverty and thus creating stability.

The World Bank has 189 countries in a global partnership seeking sustainability to reduce poverty and build prosperity. World Bank Group offers financial products to help countries end poverty and promote economic growth through education, water, energy, sanitation, and health care for people. In 2013 the Global Survey on Financial Consumer Protection and Financial Literacy (CPFL) provided insight from 114 countries. The report highlights that poverty can be reduced through access to financial services and recent financial crises show the need for consumer protection for financial stability (Mylenko, 2014). Policies should increase the ability to manage risks and consumers should be protected from policies that could create financial instability. The report also explains that it is essential for countries with emerging markets to protect consumers. In Peru and Bangladesh, the number of new depositors over doubled from 2005 to 2011 (Mylenko, 2014). As more low- and middle-income economies gain access to financial systems, the need for financial literacy increases.

The Financial Capability and Consumer Protection survey was part of the 2013 CPFL and was broken down into four categories, Behavior and Attitudes, Financial Knowledge, Financial Inclusion, and Consumer Protection (Surveys, n.d.). The results from the survey can be easily displayed with the graphing tool on the website that allows selection of a country and topic. It is recommended that this data along with the information from the OECD handbook can be used as a starting point for future research. The needs of each country are uniquely complex. As more emphasis is placed on financial literacy, it is essential to research what has already been done and the resources that are available. Comparing and sharing data and results is one way to organize and strategize for future programs to promote financial stability and minimize risk.

FUTURE RESEARCH DIRECTIONS

Financial risks and uncertainties are everywhere. Although financial literacy education seems like an obvious starting point, research is limited. There are many programs and resources available, but many are new and do not have data for research. Also, financial literacy education is challenging to study due to the many variables that are involved. Economy, parental influence, the timing of education, measuring financial knowledge and planning, and specific components can all be unique to each situation. Additionally, the implementation of financial literacy programs varies and long-term studies are rare. Studies involving children and adolescents are less common, making research even more challenging.

Financial stability varies significantly around the world. The magnitude of financial risks and uncertainties can vary drastically depending on location. Those living in developing countries have significantly different resources and applications than those living in developed countries. The need for financial literacy is especially critical in developing countries as it could be the first step in creating financial stability. However, financial literacy and planning are difficult when living in poverty.

Beyond financial literacy education is the ability to apply financial knowledge. Access to financial institutions and services is a major component of applying financial literacy. Without the modern resources offered in developed nations, those living in developing nations have limited ways to apply their financial literacy (Johnson & Sherraden, 2007). Financial capability should be a significant component of future research studies.

Other future research could include the many new mobile apps and games that promote financial literacy education, especially for those living in poverty as in the Citizens Financial Education Project in Brazil. The timing of financial education is another essential component for future research. Also, including financial literacy on standardized testing requires more research. It is also important to differentiate between knowledge and real-world application in future research. Poverty must also be considered for financial risk and stability. With the information and resources that are available, comparing resources, programs, and surveys would be valuable. Case studies should also be used for a few countries of similar economic status to allow for meaningful evaluation.

CONCLUSION

Financial literacy education is complex. With so many people unprepared and lacking knowledge when it comes to financial security, it is difficult to plan for risks and uncertainties without having a foundation of knowledge and skills. In a world of uncertainty, financial literacy could potentially reduce risk and increase financial stability for individuals. It is clear that many could benefit from financial education, but education does not guarantee good financial practices.

Consistent findings and recommendations are to start financial literacy education early, include programs in the school curriculum, make lessons hands-on, teach professional development, and involve parents. Also consistent were the topics covered in the resources that included banking, saving, credit, credit score, tax, insurance, consumer protections, rent vs. own, investing, higher education, employment, auto, retirement, budget, borrowing, and decision making. Providing financial literacy education seems to be a matter of policy and priority, as there are indeed enough resources. Poverty is certainly a barrier in many parts of the world, but perhaps financial literacy will be part of the solution. Teacher training and time constraints could be limiting factors in developed countries, but as the need for providing financial education becomes clearer worldwide, perhaps policies will change and we will see more priority accorded to financial literacy education. The goal is not only to prepare youth to be capable of making financially responsible decisions and for the risks and uncertainties of the future, but also to create financial stability throughout the world.

REFERENCES

About the OECD. (2018). Retrieved 2 March 2018 from http://www.oecd.org/about/

Benchmarking Financial Knowledge Survey. Research & reports. (n.d.). Retrieved 14 January 2018 from https://www.getsmarteraboutmoney.ca/resources/publications/research/benchmarking-financial-knowledge-survey/

Brown, A., Collins, M., Schmeiser, M., & Urban, C. (2014). *State mandated financial education and the credit behavior of young adults* (Working paper No. 68). Retrieved 14 January 2018 from https://www.federalreserve.gov/pubs/feds/2014/201468/201468pap.pdf

Building Blocks to Help Youth Achieve Financial Capability. (n.d.). *A new model and recommendations*. Retrieved 14 January 2018 from https://www.consumerfinance.gov/data-research/research-reports/building-blocks-help-yout h-achieve-financial-capability/

Canadian Foundation for Economic Education Resources. (n.d.). Retrieved 14 January 2018 from http://www.cfee.org/resources/

Consumer Financial Protection Bureau. (n.d.). Retrieved 14 January 2018 from https://www.consumerfinance.gov/

Council for Economic Education. (2018). Retrieved 14 January 2018 from http://councilforeconed.org/

Curriculum Evaluation. (2016). *Junior Achievement. Finance Park.* Retrieved 3 March 2018 from https://www.juniorachievement.org/documents/20009/133368/JA+Finance+Park+Evaluation+Report

Engard, B. (2016). Benefits of financial literacy for kids. *CU Online*. Retrieved 14 January 2018 from https://online.campbellsville.edu/education/financial-literacy-for-kids/

Federal Deposit Insurance Corporation (FDIC). (n.d.). Retrieved 14 January 2018 from https://www.fdic.gov/

Fernandes, D., Lynch, J. G. Jr, & Netemeyer, R. G. (2014). Financial literacy, financial education, and downstream financial behaviors. *Management Science*, *60*(8), 1861–1883. doi:10.1287/mnsc.2013.1849

Financial Life Stages of Older Canadians. (n.d.). Retrieved 15 January 2018 from https://www.getsmarteraboutmoney.ca/resources/publications/research/financial-life-stages-older-canadians/

Financial Literacy™. (n.d.). Retrieved 14 January 2018 from https://everfi.com/k-12/everfi-k-12-finliteracy/

Financial Well Being Survey. (n.d.). Retrieved 21 March 2018 from https://www.consumerfinance.gov/data-research/financial-well-being-survey-data/

Find out your financial well-being. (n.d.). Retrieved 2 February 2018 from https://www.consumerfinance.gov/consumer-tools/financial-well-being/

Get Smarter About Money. (2018). Retrieved 2 February 2018 from https://www.getsmarteraboutmoney.ca/

Greenspan, A. (2005). *Board of Governors of the Federal Reserve System, Monetary Policy Report to the Congress*. Retrieved 21 March 2018 from https://www.federalreserve.gov/boarddocs/hh/2005/july/fullreport.pdf

International Gateway for Financial Education. (2012). Retrieved 2 March 2018 from http://www.financial-education.org/join_INFE.html

Johnson, E., & Sherraden, M. (2007). From financial literacy to financial capability among youth. *The Journal of Sociology & Social Welfare, 34*(3), 119-146. Retrieved 10 June 2018 from http://scholarworks.wmich.edu/jssw/vol34/iss3/7?utm_source=scholarworks.wmich.edu/jssw/vol34/iss3/7&utm_medium=PDF&utm_campaign=PDFCoverPages

Jump$tart Clearinghouse. (n.d.). Retrieved 15 January 2018 from https://jumpstartclearinghouse.org/

Jump$tart Who We Are. (2018). Retrieved 2 February 2018 from https://jumpstart.org

Junior Achievement Finance Park. (n.d.). Retrieved 15 March 2018 from https://www.juniorachievement.org/web/ja-usa/ja-programs?p_p_id=56_INSTANCE_abcd&p_p _state=maximized&_56_INSTANCE_abcd_groupId=14516&_56_INSTANCE_abcd_articleId=1 9406

Junior Achievement Programs. (n.d.). Retrieved 15 January 2018 from https://www.juniorachievement.org/web/ja-usa/ja-programs

Khan Academy. (n.d.). Retrieved 15 January 2018 from https://www.khanacademy.org/

Lusardi, A., & Mitchell, O. S. (2011). Financial literacy around the world: An overview. *Journal of Pension Economics and Finance*, *10*(04), 497–508. doi:10.1017/S147474721100448 PMID:28553190

Lusardi, A., Mitchell, O. S., & Curto, V. (2010). Financial literacy among the young. *The Journal of Consumer Affairs*, *44*(2), 358–380. doi:10.1111/j.1745-6606.2010.01173.x

Mandell, L., & Klein, L. S. (2009). The impact of financial literacy education on subsequent financial behavior. *Journal of Financial Counseling and Planning*, *20*(1). Retrieved from https://papers.ssrn.com/sol3/papers.cfm?abstract_id=2224231

Master Teacher Program. (n.d.). Retrieved 14 January 2018 from http://councilforeconed.org/master-teacher-program/

McCormick, M. (2009). The effectiveness of youth financial education: A review of the literature. *Journal of Financial Counseling and Planning, 20*(1), 70-83.

Missing Out: Millennials and the Markets. (n.d.). *Research & reports*. Retrieved 14 January 2018 from https://www.getsmarteraboutmoney.ca/resources/publications/research/missing-out-millennials-a nd-the-markets/

Mylenko, N. (2014). *Oversight frameworks and practices in 114 economies - full report*. Retrieved from 14 June 2018 from http://documents.worldbank.org/curated/en/775401468171251449/Oversight-frameworks-and-practices-in-114-economies-full-report

National Strategies for Financial Education. OECD/INFE Policy Handbook. (n.d.). Retrieved 14 January 2018 from http://www.oecd.org/daf/fin/financial-education/national-strategies-for-financial-education-policy-handbook.htm

Never Too Young. (n.d.). Retrieved 3 March 2018 from https://www.councilforeconed.org/programs- 2/never-too-young-personal-finance-for-k-5-learners/

OECD PISA financial literacy assessment of students. (n.d.). Retrieved 14 January 2018 from http://www.oecd.org/finance/financial-education/oecdpisafinancialliteracyassessment.htm

Omnibus poll: Canadians' obstacles to saving and investing. (n.d.). *Research & reports*. Retrieved 14 January 2018 from https://www.getsmarteraboutmoney.ca/resources/publications/research/omnibus-poll-canadi ans-obstacles-saving-investing/

OSC. (2018). *About*. Retrieved 2 February 2018 from http://www.osc.gov.on.ca/en/About_our-structure_index.htm

Sherraden, M. S., & Grinstein-Weiss, M. (2015). Creating financial capability in the next generation: An introduction to the special issue. *The Journal of Consumer Affairs*, *49*(1), 1–12. doi:10.1111/joca.12067

Smart, X. (n.d.). Retrieved 8 March 2018 from https://www.councilforeconed.org/programs-2/smartx/

Survey of the States. (2018). Council for Economic Education. Retrieved 1 March 2018 from https://www.councilforeconed.org/policy-and-advocacy/survey-of-the-states-2/

Surveys. (n.d.). Retrieved from http://responsiblefinance.worldbank.org/surveys

Willis, L. (2008). *Against financial literacy education*. Retrieved 14 January 2018 from https://papers.ssrn.com/sol3/papers.cfm?abstract_id=1105384

Worldwide, J. A. (n.d.). *Who We Are*. Retrieved 3 January 2018 from https://www.jaworldwide.org/aboutja/

ADDITIONAL READING

Arpea, C. (2016). *International handbook of financial literacy*. Singapore: Springer.

Danns, D. E. (2016). *Financial education in U.S. state colleges and universities: Establishing and building programs*. Cham: Springer. doi:10.1007/978-3-319-24430-3

Durband, D. B., & Britt, S. L. (2012). *Student financial literacy: Campus-based program development*. New York: Springer. doi:10.1007/978-1-4614-3505-1

Lawless, R. E. (2010). *The students' guide to financial literacy*. Santa Barbara, CA: Greenwood.

Liebowitz, J. (2016). *Financial Literacy Education: Addressing Student, Business, and Government Needs*. CRC Press.

Lucey, T. A. (2012). *Reframing financial literacy: Exploring the value of social currency*. Charlotte, NC: Information Age Publ.

Ryan, J. S., & Ryan, C. (2017). *Personal financial literacy*. Australia: South-Western Cengage Learning.

Smith, A. O. (2016). *Financial literacy for millennials a practical guide to managing your financial life for teens, college students, and young adults*. Praeger.

KEY TERMS AND DEFINITIONS

Canadian Foundation for Economic Education (CFEE): A Canadian non-profit organization that focuses on individual financial stability and economic education.

Consumer Financial Protection Bureau (CFPB): A United States government agency that protects and educates consumers.

Council for Economic Education (CEE): A United States non-profit organization that focuses on individual financial stability and economic education.

Financial Capability: The idea that financial literacy can only be applied if proper resources are available.

International Network on Financial Education (INFE): A division of OECD that is dedicated to worldwide financial education.

Junior Achievement (JA): A worldwide non-profit organization dedicated to educating youth on financial literacy, preparing for work, and entrepreneurship.

Ontario Securities Commission (OSC): An Ontario corporation that protects consumers and works to ensure financial stability.

Organization for Economic Cooperation and Development (OECD): An intergovernmental organization that works to create policies addressing social and economic concerns worldwide.

Program for International Student Assessment (PISA): An international survey through OECD that tests 15-year-olds every three years in math, problem-solving, reading, science, and financial literacy.

World Bank: An international institution focused on providing financial and technical services to reduce poverty and increase prosperity in developing countries.

Chapter 11
Social Media Analytics for Maintaining Financial Stability

Sebin B. Nidhiri
Delhi School of Economics, India

Sakshi Saxena
Symbiosis International University (Deemed), India

ABSTRACT

Risk and uncertainty are disliked but inevitable. The nature of these has changed and new sources of risk have risen. To mitigate risk and maintain financial stability, the firms need to adapt. The world wide web and, within it, social media have had tremendous growth and wide coverage lately, making them determining forces in any economic activity. This has led to generation of large amount of data on myriad concerns. Recent developments in computing technology has thrown open the possibility of mining useful information from the enormous and dynamic data. The chapter outlines the growth of social media and social media analytics and its financial implications to businesses, consumers, and governments. It details how risk management and social media, two domains earlier considered more diverged than chalk and cheese are now inextricably linked and explains using various cases how social media analytics is used to manage risk and uncertainty. The authors also look at the emerging challenges with these developments.

INTRODUCTION

The Chinese curse, "May you live in interesting times," has never been truer than today. With 'Disruptive Innovation' being the new buzzword, there is rapid change all around. This period of Information Revolution has virtually connected people across the globe. An increasingly large amount of time is spent online today. With the increase in mobile devices and improved access to internet, people today consume most of their information online. This has further created many online businesses as well as driven traditional businesses electronically. More recently, social media has gathered considerable forces online. Young (2017) finds that one in every three minutes spent online is devoted to social media. Enormous amount of data and content is generated through channels of social media like Twitter, LinkedIn, Facebook and

DOI: 10.4018/978-1-5225-7208-4.ch011

Instagram, to name a few, and this data is continually updating in real time. Evidently social media is a vital medium to reach large online audience in their day to day lives with ease. The increasing economic activities and improved means of information transmission have brought in new kinds of uncertainty and risks too. The gargantuan information available can itself be tapped to mitigate these new risks. With such significance of social media in the current scenario, how important is its role to aid risk mitigation decisions is worth researching.

Financial stability can comprise different things for different economic entities — the firm, the government and the household. But across these divides, financial stability can be understood as the resistance to economic shocks and not losing the ability to fulfil its basic functions. Core risks can be classified into four types, namely: Market Risk, Credit Risk, Liquidity Risk and Operational Risk. In layman terms, market risk arises when loss is associated to the factors that affect the market, such as stock prices, foreign exchange rates, etc. (Arshad, Zafar, Fatima, & Khan, 2015; Hull, 2018). Credit risk arises when an entity fails to fulfill its commitments towards its counter parties. Liquidity risk arises when an investment cannot be traded instantaneously to counter or minimize a loss. Operational risk arises when loss is a product of operational failures, which can be external or internal in nature that can include technical failures, frauds because of failed internal processes, and other such events. With the digital socialism in trend, it is imperative to understand these risks in the context of social media.

Thus, there is a need for firms to adapt to maintain financial stability and counter those risks. The present chapter studies how such adaption is worked upon by firms in the present period and how they would for the changing times ahead. The rest of the chapter is organized as follows. The next section looks at the rise of social media, making it an obligatory part of business, and its implications for business. The third section describes the various aspects of social media analytics — both content and structure-based analytics — and looks at the latest inroads into the realm of big data. This is followed by looking at ways in which social media and social media analytics are used for financial stability as well as solutions and recommendations. Lastly, the authors highlight future concerns and challenges for social media analysis in times to come, indicate directions for future research and conclude.

BACKGROUND

Rise of Social Media

Social media is a broad term encapsulating a wide range of online platforms that let users create and exchange content. These websites are constantly evolving and adding functionalities in an attempt to stay relevant. This makes it hard to distinguish between the different options. Nevertheless, Barbier and Liu (2011) categorize social media as:

1. Social networks, E.g.: Facebook, Orkut, LinkedIn
2. Microblogs, E.g.: Twitter, FriendFeed and Tumblr
3. Blogs, E.g.: Blogger and WordPress
4. Social news, E.g.: Digg, Slashdot and Reddit
5. Social bookmarking, E.g.: Delicious, StumbleUpon, etc.
6. Review sites, E.g.: Zomato, TripAdvisor, Glassdoor, Yelp
7. Media sharing, E.g.: Instagram, Snapchat, YouTube, Vimeo

8. Wikis, E.g.: Wikipedia, Wikihow, etc.
9. Question and answer sites, E.g.: Yahoo! Answers, Answerbag and Quora

The existence of social networks can be traced from the mid-1990s, where a social platform Yahoo facilitated communication through chat rooms. With the advancement in visibility of such social networks, platforms like LinkedIn, Orkut etc. emanated in the later years. A more significant development was in 2004, when Facebook emerged. This space has seen many new entrants like Twitter, Instagram, Snapchat, etc. Piskorski (2014) finds that there are many social failures which relate to not just two or more people interacting but also environments where people display information about themselves or collect information about others. These failures also lead to market failures where two parties are not able to engage in a mutually beneficial transaction. Social networks succeed because they work towards reducing these failures. LinkedIn is an excellent case in point.

The internet and mobile technologies are the main reasons for the exponential growth of social media websites (Zeng, Chen, Lusch, & Li, 2010). A report by We Are Social and Hootsuite reveal that 3.819 billion (51% of world population) use internet and 3.028 billion (40% of world population) are active social media users (Kemp, 2017). According to a report by Internet and Mobile Association of India (IAMAI), internet penetration in December 2017 was 64.84% in urban India and 20.26% in the rural areas. The number of internet users stood at 481 million in December 2017, an increase of 11.34% from the earlier year (Agarwal, 2018). The recent fall in price of data, thanks to a price war brought in by the entry of Reliance Jio, has increased the time spent online by Indians particularly on social media. The average internet user consumes more data than what was the case just a couple of years ago. A report released in 2017 by Ericsson, the Swedish phone maker, suggests that the monthly data consumption on every smartphone in India is estimated to grow up to five times from 3.9 GB in 2017 to 18 GB by 2023 (Press Trust of India, 2017).

Social media has brought the world closer and is responsible for a larger and quicker flow of information. Moreover, social media like Facebook, Twitter and Instagram are used not only to keep in touch with friends, but to be au fait with news and current developments. Social media websites have evolved to now become platforms where videos, blog posts and news articles are shared, and not just a means of keeping in touch with friends. They have not just smoothed interaction among people but also served as an interface between companies and the consumers. These social media websites are cashing in on this attention span they have gained by letting businesses advertise their products.

A rising number of people today look through news via social media. News articles are shared or retweeted by users on different social networking sites. As it is a very dynamic medium with large number of posts in short time, the life of an article shared is short. News articles have short time span and hence to become popular, they should be read by many readers in short time. It is evident from existing researches that news articles which become socially popular must have certain scoring criteria which can be identified and classified. Bandari et al. (2012), find that the top news sources whose tweets get circulated (retweeted) the most on Twitter are not necessarily from the conventional news agencies, but from blogs such as Mashable and the Google Blog. These are very widely shared across social media. That apart, it was discovered that one of the most important predictors of popularity of a news article was the source of the article. This is in conformity with the intuition that readers are likely to be influenced by the news source which disseminates the article and an identified source gets more circulation. The study used regression and classification models and achieved 84% accuracy in making proper predictions about the probable popularity of a news article on social media by looking at its characteristics (Bandari,

Asur, & Huberman, 2012). This is further proof of the rising prominence of social media over traditional media and why businesses cannot ignore this medium. YouTube on mobile devices alone reaches more people in the United States than any other TV network (YouTube for Press, n.d.). Apparently, technology acceptance is more evident in young consumers. This was tested in a study which established a relationship between use of social media among young consumers in Latin America using Technology Acceptance Model (TAM) (Bailey, Bonifield & Arias, 2018).

Financial Implications to Business From Social Media

The current form of the internet is what experts call the Web 2.0. Earlier, the web was characterized by static pages dishing out information. Searching for a product would lead you to the product's website which would give information as a traditional product brochure would. Today, most websites allow users to create content and provides platforms for interaction and collaboration. Thus, the online content is generated by the users themselves. This helps one get reviews of products from actual customers and so forth. On the web today, the most popular websites are social media websites. It is a critical part of the information ecosystem, is adopted by all, and has immense reach to consumers, voters, businesses and governments alike. Naturally, there is tremendous interest from businesses, political parties, governments etc. in social media from both application and research perspective. Businesses today use social media as a platform and also a source of information for product design, innovation, customer relationship management (CRM) and marketing.

Global Web Index, the largest study in the world on the digital consumer, finds that 98% of digital consumers are social media users and this is not composed only of the younger cohort of people. 94% of the digital consumers in the age group of 55-64 are active users of social media (Young, 2017). Naturally, social media has become a tool for CRM which no business can ignore. This opportunity has also added a new dimension of risk to businesses which can no longer ignore these media. There are multiple cases of a poor review being posted online by someone, shared by many, and spreading like wildfire causing doom to businesses. The brand's image and outlook online are something to be actively worked on. Every business worth its salt has a team working on its social media presence.

Marketing has been the primary application of social media analytics in recent years. This is only natural and can be attributed to the widespread and growing adoption of social media by people worldwide who are also the consumers to other businesses (He, Zha, & Li, 2013). Forrester Research, Inc. had projected social media to be the second-fastest growing marketing channel in the United States between 2011 and 2016 (VanBoskirk, Overby, & Takvorian, 2011). But, Forrester Research Inc. (2018) predicts that ad spending on social media will be flat in 2018 as customers are increasingly trying to avoid ads and firms are faced with wasted ads. Forrester predicts that businesses will try to advance technology to deliver personalized experiences at a large scale and decode algorithms of other digital platforms to get their product visible. This would mean that businesses would now need a stronger understanding of consumer perception and sentiment of their brand on social media. Pumping in money for advertisements is no longer going to be a solution. The criticality of social media analytics; to better understand one's audience and customizing one's message for targeted advertising, is set to rise. To succeed wooing users on social media, a delicate balance has to be struck between various factors such as user sentiments, target-based user identification, choice of social media platform etc. (Zhu & Chen, 2015). A primary data-based research revealed that electronic word of mouth had an indirect inter-relationship with brand equity. In the context of managerial implications in an organization, it means that the organization would be better off using viral trends as their advertising strategy, while ensuring that their target demography receives the marketing communication at the right time and place (Severi, Ling, & Nasemoadeli, 2014). Furthermore, it has been shown that a consumer trusts electronic word of mouth as a credible source of information (Themba & Mulala, 2013).

In a study, an online beauty product promotion campaign by Neiman and Belk was evaluated using Twitter streaming data. It was evident from the study that an online marketing campaign with a hashtag had positive impact on consumers (Ribarsky, Wang, & Dou, 2014). Moreover, companies want to explore these sentiments to make profits and have competitive edge over others. An effective role of social media was observed through a case study of a small mechanical company called Gamma that faced difficulty in selling its products due to other low-cost Chinese products available in the market. The company shifted strategy and focused on social media and was able to enter new markets; the use of Web for selling products yielded benefits in term of profits and better control over operational processes (Bocconcelli, Cioppi, & Pagano, 2017).

Social media has not just helped firms make marketing gains but has also emerged as a booming platform to connect business partners, thereby broadening the business network. The traceability gap, which exists between the users of social media and the organization, makes it difficult to know if the business has been transacted successfully between them (Grizane & Jurgelane, 2017). However, with the right strategy, social media can be actively leveraged by entrepreneurial firms to establish connections and to ease the operational and logistic processes if actively engaged (Drummond, McGrath, & O'Toole, 2017). Furthermore, social media analytics is also essential for devising competitive advantage. Literature on the application of enactment theory suggests that effective communication between buyer and suppliers might prevent the chances of suppliers to default (Oliveira & Handfield, 2017). This is primarily due to buyer's accessibility and understanding of financial conditions of supplier, thus reducing information asymmetry to a large extent. In such scenarios, social media could help gaining insights.

A case where things went south owing to social media was when Electronic Arts, a game company, hosted a Question and Answer session on the social media platform of Reddit. It went disastrously wrong, as the company's response to criticism was not well received by the users, which resulted in their response being the most down voted comment in the history of the platform. The user sentiments about the organization were affected negatively in light of this situation, hence jeopardizing the sales of the game they were promoting via this Question and Answer session[1]. This fiasco clearly highlighted how the theoretical concepts of financial risks, particularly market risk, can be adaptive to the world of social media. In addition to the external use of social media for interacting with customers and shareholders, the use of social media internally in an organization is also a dual edged sword -- while it can be beneficial to the organization, it can also put the organization at risk owing to the inherent factors of social media, such as hyper-interaction, spontaneity and data permanence (Demek, Raschke, Janvrin, & Dilla, 2018).

A case where social media directly affected the finances was when the Twitter account of Associated Press (AP) was hacked in 2013 to report explosions in White House, which compromised the safety of the then POTUS, Barack Obama. In seconds, the Dow Jones Industrial Average (DJIA) dropped 143.5 points and the Standard & Poor's 500 Index lost more than $136 billion of its value. This goes to show that just one post on a social media platform can majorly affect financial systems (Karppi & Crawford, 2016). Additional research examined the impact of emotional sentiments expressed on social media platform (Twitter) on the Standard & Poor's 500 Index. It was apparent from the research that tweets about an organization are strongly related to the organization's stock returns (Sul, Dennis, & Yuan, 2014). It is evident from a study that negative sentiments of users on social media platforms about an organization can affect and predict the organization's stock prices (He, Guo, Shen, & Akula, 2016). Nevertheless, a study of four business scandals by Jiang and Shen (2017) showed that while Twitter was the earliest source of information on these scandals, traditional media is still critical. Newspaper articles are more important than tweets to explain stock market returns and trading volumes in response to scandals.

Politics, technology, business, and other social areas are all likely to be impacted by social media for the foreseeable future. Data analysis will help quantify and provide useful insights. As the number of social media users continues to grow and it reaches hitherto uncovered areas; most of which traditional media finds hard to reach, there have to be significant changes in the way we communicate and share information. Data analysis will then provide us with an empowering ability to dive deeper into these very large data sets in a more significant manner. Social networking sites, blogs, and other online social media services provide a digital record of social behavior from a multitude of perspectives making it the conclusive data source for analytics and gaining insights on people.

SOCIAL MEDIA ANALYTICS

"Social media analytics is concerned with developing and evaluating informatics tools and frameworks to collect, monitor, analyze, summarize and visualize social media data, usually driven by specific requirements from a target application" (Zeng, Chen, Lusch, & Li, 2010, p. 14). While use of social media for CRM has become a norm, firms are also tapping into emerging techniques of social media analytics to understand and mitigate risk. Improvements in technology have transformed data from a traditional sense of numbers to text and pictures. This has allowed a large amount of information in the form of text and pictures available on social media to be subject to useful analysis. With humongous amount of data being generated every second, analyzing such data and deriving important information, is equally crucial. Consequently, businesses, both data-driven and otherwise, are investing majorly in understanding public perception about their product or service.

Social media analytics broadly uses two sources of information; (1) the relationships and interactions between people, organizations & products and (2) user-generated content (posts, images, videos). Accordingly, the analysis can be classified into two groups:

CONTENT-BASED ANALYTICS

Content-based analytics, as the name suggests, focuses on the contents (or data) posted by users on social media platforms. These are customer feedback, product reviews, subjective opinions, etc. These are unstructured and could be in the form of text, images and/or videos. Such content on social media is often voluminous, unstructured, noisy, and dynamic. Text, audio, and video analytics (discussed later), can also be subjected to analysis in order to derive actionable insights from the data. Given the scale and dynamic nature of the data, big data technologies play a vital part in the analysis. Two types of analysis based on the type of content are explained further.

Text Analysis

There is a lot of text in the posts on social media. The text is much unstructured but can be mined and then molded for different analysis. This is made plausible as people use social sites to express their emotions, beliefs or opinions about things, places or personalities (Hasan, Moin, Karim, & Shamshirband, 2018). Text analysis is concerned with deriving high-quality structured data from unstructured text and thereafter deriving information. Another name for text analytics is text mining. The unstructured data is collected on the item of interest. This may be collected from social media, newspapers or other portals online. The task is to structure the data appropriately and then find patterns, trends and/or relations in the data. These are then interpreted into actionable conclusions. Manually performing text analysis would be a tedious task, and today, software is available that can perform these tasks much more efficiently. Text mining techniques are more cost effective and provide more information than traditional survey methods (Morinaga, Yamanishi, Tateishi, & Fukushima, 2002).

Text analytics can be used to effectively perform sentiment analysis, opinion mining, cluster analysis, categorization, social media monitoring, competitive intelligence, information's extraction, link analysis etc. (Ferguson, 2016). "What others think" is always a curiosity for individuals and for businesses; it is a very useful piece of information that helps make many decisions. Sentiment analysis is the computational study of opinions, sentiments, evaluations, attitudes, views and emotions expressed in the form of text. The analysis classifies a statement by predicting the polarity of words used in it and then classifying the words into positive or negative sentiment (Jose & Chooralil, 2015). With the coming of big data, text analysis has evolved, widening its scope and application. Predictive analytics that uses statistical modelling combined with this helps predict future changes.

Face Recognition and Image Detection

In the field of social media analytics, Face Recognition and Image Detection are other booming areas that can be very helpful in fraud detection and risk mitigation. In a study based on Image Based Fraud Prevention, it was proposed that online fraudulent transactions can be stopped using these technologies (Babu, Bhagyasri, Lahari, Madhuri, & Kumari, 2014). Technological tools behind face recognition and image detection are Hidden Markov Model and Singular Value Decomposition. Hidden Markov Model helps in capturing the image from the source and then matches it with the images in database trying different iterations. This is done by extracting different features from an image like eyes, mouth, hair, eyebrows and chin. Furthermore, Singular Value Decomposition helps in statistical data analysis and signal processing.

STRUCTURE-BASED ANALYTICS

Also known as social network analytics, it is concerned with evaluating the structural attributes of a social network and extracting intelligence from the relationships among the participating entities. This structure is modelled visually with nodes and edges, which stand for participants and relationships respectively. Two such graphs that are popular are social graphs and activity graphs (Heidemann, Klier, & Probst, 2012). While an edge in a social graph depicts the existence of a relationship (like being friends on Facebook or a connection on LinkedIn), in an activity graph it stands for an interaction (liking or commenting on the other person's activity). Therefore, each has its use in differing purposes.

TECHNIQUES OF STRUCTURE BASED ANALYTICS

Community Detection

This is a technique of Structure-based analytics which is very similar to clustering in data analytics (Aggarwal, 2011). Clustering divides data into sub groups based on similarities in the data, and helps understand the large data better. Similarly, community detection analyses one's links and identifies distinct sub groups. It identifies sub networks of users who interact more extensively with each other than with others in the network. This helps summarize online social networks which average millions of nodes and edges, and thereby understand behavioral patterns and predict future properties of the network. Social graphs can help point out communities or determine hubs (i.e., users that may be individuals or pages of organisations who have relatively large number of direct and indirect social links), whereas activity graphs show an active relationship and may sometimes be more relevant than just a connection or acquaintance.

Social Influence Analysis

This involves techniques dealing with understanding and modeling the influence of actors and connections in an online social network. Humans are social animals and their behavior is affected by others' actions both online and offline. Social Influence analysis evaluates participants' influence, quantifies the strength of connections and reveals the patterns of influence diffusion in the network. Quantifying the strength of connections is achieved through quantifying importance of network nodes. Some measures for this purpose are calculating degree centrality (number of edges a node has), betweenness centrality (which is the number of times a node acts as a bridge along the shortest path between two other nodes; was introduced as a measure for quantifying the control of a human in a social network on the communication between other humans in the same social network), closeness centrality (average length of the shortest path between the node and all other nodes in the graph; thus, the more central a node is, the closer it is to all other nodes; the more towards a corner a node is, it may get close to a few other nodes but happens to be much farther than more than half of the total nodes), and eigenvector centrality (assigns a relative score to all the nodes in the network based on the logic that a connection to a high-scoring node contributes more to the score of the node in concern than equal connection to a low-scoring node).

Another aspect of social influence analysis, as mentioned above, is to understand how ideas spread over a network by means of communication among the social entities. This is known as information diffusion and there are models which explain how the process happens. In these models, each node is either active or inactive. Over iterations, inactive nodes become active as more of its neighbors become active. This is the concept behind models like the Linear Threshold Model (LTM) as well as the Independent Cascade Model (ICM) which are two of the most popular information diffusion models (Sun & Tang, 2011).

Link Prediction

No social network is static. It is a dynamic object that is always growing through the creation of new nodes and edges. The idea behind link prediction is to predict future linkages that will arise by studying current linkages. Link prediction techniques predict the happening of interaction, collaboration and/or influence among entities of a network within a given time interval. Link prediction techniques have been found to be better than pure chance, hinting that the current structure of the network contains latent information within future links (Liben-Nowell & Kleinberg, 2007). Link predictions today are also used to unravel potential associations in terrorist, criminal or drug networks. Link prediction is behind how Facebook operates 'People You May Know' where friends are recommended and Youtube's 'Recommended for You' where videos to watch are recommended.

BIG DATA

TechAmerica Foundation's Federal Big Data Commission (2012) defines Big Data as "Big data is a term that describes large volumes of high velocity, complex and variable data that require advanced techniques and technologies to enable the capture, storage, distribution, management, and analysis of the information." Traditionally, data was collected by enterprises from sources like ATMs, Mortgage units, Credit cards, portfolios etc. With the rising complexity of data, data sources now also include news data, trading data, industry data, alerts, reports, advertising response data, customer feedback data and other social media data (Oracle, 2015). 95% of big data is unstructured data. (Gandomi & Haider, 2015). Some of the popular tools that are used in big data analysis are Tableau, Rapid Miner, Hadoop, Project R, IBM Big Data etc.

The Three V's – Volume, Variety and Velocity, are considered the major challenges with and the defining characteristics of Big Data. As the name suggests, big data is in large volumes. With the coming of the Internet of Things, which refers to all the devices other than computers that collect and record data and are connected to the internet, we are surrounded by data. This can be seen in households where there are smart refrigerators, smart air conditioners, smart TVs and with persons using consumer gear like fitness trackers etc. All these interconnected devices create large amounts of data that is measured in Zettabytes (a Zettabyte equals one trillion gigabytes). Owing to the volume, this data is worked on from a distributed processing and storage environment. Social media also generates such large volumes of data. Facebook receives 600 TB of data daily and scans roughly 105 TB of data per hour (Vagata & Wilfong, 2014). Whatever data that businesses are able to subject to analysis, will also be commensurately large. Variety talks about the differing kinds of data that big data refers to. It is very different from traditional data sources which had rows and columns of data. Big data cannot always be fit into a spreadsheet or even in the form database management software usually work with. The posts on social media include photos, videos, and also text which do not follow any specific structure. Also, many actions on social media which users undertake, namely liking a post or retweeting a tweet, are all data. Velocity refers to the speed at which data is flowing. Big data software handles velocities up to 10 Gigabytes per second. The data on social media is increasing every minute. Facebook has 1.44 billion users (that is 7 crore more than the population of China) and receives in excess of 900 million photos in a single day (Miller, 2015).

USE OF SOCIAL MEDIA AND SOCIAL MEDIA ANALYTICS FOR FINANCIAL STABILITY

On the one hand, there is very large and continually growing amount of data on social media, albeit varied, and on the other we now have cheaper and more powerful computational processing and affordable data storage. This is fertile ground to quickly and automatically create models from the analysis of bigger, more complex data and still deliver faster, far more precise results. Building precise models on larger sets of data gives an organization a better chance of identifying profitable opportunities and mitigating risks.

Social media could serve as a channel to mitigate risk and reduce uncertainty in a number of ways. Campbell (2017) puts forth four aspects involved in this. First is modelling of the data. This is probably the most crucial step as data can turn bad and lose its relevance over time. Topic Model is one such method that helps to understand, categorize and organize text available from social media portals. Sentiment Analysis is another technique involved which helps in identification of positive and negative sentiments trolling over the internet about any news or event. Second is credit risk management; after organizing the data into relevant subject related information, risk managers can apply different forecasting tools to minimize future losses and earn operational efficiency related revenue. Through Business Intelligence tools, like word cloud, this information can be presented to different audience in a visually impacting way. Third is Market Risk Management, which is largely based on live data from trading communities about valuation and opening position that is important to have edge over the others and to build strategies to reduce position-based risks. Social media hence is important to provide timely insights to have maximum impact. Last is the technology in use. Machine Learning and Artificial Intelligence technology have come to the mainstream due to their computing power which helps to understand big data that is generated online in various forms like text, images, video etc. Technology, one like Machine Learning and Artificial Intelligence, helps to detect subtle changes in sentiments, which otherwise could have been neglected.

The financial risk that information from social media data can mitigate cuts across various sectors. Banks as well as other businesses in the financial industry can use social media to identify investment opportunities and know when to trade. Algorithms used by traders make buy/sell decisions by watching trends on social media. These algorithms help firms stay abreast of happenings and enable a quick response, thus controlling the damage from adverse scenarios. Social media analysis also helps understand sentiments towards certain companies which can then influence decisions of buying and selling the stocks of that company. There is a technological race wherein hedge funds as well as other deep-pocket investors, with the use of big-data analytics, instantly analyze several lakhs of tweets on Twitter and other non-traditional information sources to buy and sell stocks in a matter of minutes, beating many smaller investors (Weiczner, 2015). Matthew Granade, Managing Director and Chief Market Intelligence Officer at Point 72, a hedge fund company, says, "You have this explosion of other independent real-time sources. It's a lot easier to get to [on-the-ground] truth. Overall, I think this is a golden age for new investment data sources." Liu, Wu, Li & Li (2015) find that there is stock co-movement for firms which have similar metrics (no. of followers and tweets) for their official Twitter handles and these social media data predict co-movement better than even industry categories. Banks in India are currently facing a large problem with the quantum of non-performing assets, a large chunk of which is due to default on loans handed out to institutions. While technology is actively used to credit risk score ratings for individuals, this has not been tapped into well in the case of corporate lending. Social media analytics can supplement this process particularly with respect to detecting credit risk of corporations and small

& medium enterprises. Also, social media interactions of employees can be used to detect tendency to commit fraud and deter them.

Literature on the application of enactment theory suggests that effective communication between buyers and suppliers might prevent the chances of suppliers to default (Oliveira & Handfield, 2017). This is primarily due to buyer regular accessibility and understanding of financial conditions of supplier. In such scenarios, social media could help gaining insights. Communication by the firm with stakeholders via social media can also help attenuate the negative market reactions to news of acquisitions (Mazboudi & Khalil, 2017).

Online review websites like Zomato and TripAdvisor are the latest forms of customer feedback that can make and break businesses, particularly in the hospitality sector. Within a study of the impact of such feedback, performance of leading hotel chain was obtained and the social media data on the hotel chain was purchased from a social media analysis firm. It was evident from an analysis on this data that the overall rating of the hotel on review sites had the largest significant impact on the performance of hotel. The second most important factor was the response rate to negative comments in the online reviews (Kim, Lim, & Brymer, 2015). This shows that it is important to monitor the feedback on your services online and to engage with the feedback.

Social media analysis is increasingly being used by politicians and political parties to help them manage electoral risks and thereby financial risks. It helps monitor, inform, and increase political influence and provides insights into which groups or categories of people to connect with, how to best communicate and engage with the electorate, and increase the overall engagement (Quantzig, n.d.). It enables events to be organized based on what the target group is interested in and customize the outreach to certain demographics based on insights from sentiment analysis as well as social media analysis in politics. The 2016 United States election results which went contrary to the predictions by mainstream media are also touted as one of the successes of an effective social media analysis. The influence social media had on the election cannot be overstated and is easily understood from a finding from a study by Pew Research Centre (2016) which found that 44 percentage of the adults in the United States got all their information about the 2016 presidential election from social media which is higher than the percentage of people who responded for local or national print newspapers or candidate websites and emails put together. Also, 24 percent got news and information from the social media posts put up by Donald Trump and Hillary Clinton themselves. Donald Trump had around hundred lakh Twitter followers and ninety lakh Facebook followers while Hillary Clinton had seventy lakh on Twitter and about half of Trump's number on Facebook in 2016. In May of 2016, the Pew study found that on average the candidates put out 5 to 7 posts daily on Facebook and 11 to 12 daily on their Twitter accounts. Barack Obama's initial election and subsequent re-election campaigns heavily utilized social media and social media analytics to engage and mobilize voters, particularly those who were voting for the first time and young voters. (Williams, 2017).

Social media has played a vital role in political mobilization as well. Social networks like Facebook and Twitter played an undeniable role during the Arab Spring and aided the push to democracy that originated in Tunisia to spread to Egypt, Libya, Lebanon, Syria, Jordan, Algeria, and Bahrain and also into Saudi Arabia. During Tunisia's Jasmine Revolution, there was a blackout in the mainstream media and the government controlled all media platforms. Millions of people organized themselves in this revolution through the news received from social media. The world watched the revolution on their Twitter and Facebook feeds. Mohamed Bouazizi's self-immolation, which triggered the revolution, was not the first case of self-immolation in Tunisia. But this was video graphed and posted to YouTube and was later covered by Al Jazeera and subsequently other news channels. The government's efforts to cut out the flow of information by blocking certain websites, deleting problematic accounts, arresting bloggers and other active people on the social platform could not stop the force (Malhotra, 2011). Social media has played a vital role in converting street movements into larger movements with considerable impact in Romania (Momoc, 2013). In the same passion, during the anti-corruption movement of 2012 in India, social activist and staunch Gandhian, Anna Hazare, used social media to connect people in New Delhi (Meti, Khandoba, & Guru, 2015). The group that rallied around him, 'India Against Corruption,' had a large following on social media and this helped the movement put considerable pressure on the government. The social media has buried the physical and social gaps to a large extent and being a horizontal media, they work a lot like a participatory democracy where everyone has a voice that is heard. Modern political parties have utilized this media to augment their political strategies and gain public support. Political parties have taken up social media channels with a focus to proliferate political transactions and engineer the support of various sources. The emphasis is on the building of long-lasting relationships between political parties and people, which are attempts at social engineering (Meti, Khandoba, & Guru, 2015).

A study analyzing the impact of social media on risk perception during the Middle East Respiratory Syndrome outbreak in South Korea suggests that social media is important due to its role of shaping risk perception about health issues (Choi, Yoo, Noh, & Park, 2017). This can facilitate increase in disease preventive behavior and effective risk communication strategies.

Content-Based Analytics to Reduce Risk

Carolyn Holton (2009) demonstrated the use of text mining as a means to predict fraud by disgruntled employees in an organization. Employee fraud or Occupational fraud is the most prevalent of all frauds faced by a firm (KPMG Forensics, 2003). Occupational fraud causes heavy financial losses to companies and an estimate puts it to the tune of $652 billion per year in the United States alone. This is equivalent to about 5 percent of total corporate revenues and definitely a much larger share of profits (Association of Certified Fraud Examiners, 2006). World over on average, fraud loss per company in the 2004–2007 period is estimated to be at $8.2 million (Kroll Inc., 2008). Holton (2009) collected data from several internet discussion groups (Several Vault.com and Yahoo! Discussion groups) used for intra-company communications but were not on the organizations' network. The sample collected consisted of 50 disgruntled messages and 40 non-disgruntled messages that were so classified by two coders who agreed on each message's classification. The messages were cleaned to remove unnecessary information and words and a clustering method was applied on the cleaned sample. The clustering showed that there was clear distinction between disgruntled and non-disgruntled messages. This upheld the idea that disgruntled messages can be identified and a naïve Bayes model[2] was applied. The sample was divided into training and evaluation[3] sub sets in various ratios ranging from 50:50 to 90:10, and 80:20 was found to be the best with strong and relatively stable results. From an evaluation sample of 18 messages, the code correctly identified and classified 16 as either disgruntled or non-disgruntled. While the act of sending a disgruntled message is by no means validation that the person has committed or will commit fraud, it is a useful indicator to identify the possibilities of fraud. Association of Certified Fraud Examiners (ACFE) point to three factors which come together to lead to fraudulent activity; perceived unshareable financial need, perceived opportunity and rationalization. Rationalization occurs particularly when one feels that he/she is being treated unfairly. These three are known as the fraud triangle, an idea that was first expressed in the book 'Other People's Money' by Donald Cressey (1953). Up to two of these three factors can be identified from disgruntled communication. Also, Securities and Exchange Commission (SEC) mandates public companies for the storage of all documents that influence financial reporting including email communications of employees. The availability of this large data opens up a window for an analytics code to mine the data and detect disgruntled employees, thereby providing scope for detecting and deterring fraud. This reduces a large risk faced by firms.

Eagle Alpha, a research firm from Ireland used text analytics to study 7,416 comments on a Reddit gaming thread in October 2015 and predicted that the Star Wars videogame released by Electronic Arts (EA) would sell much more than the creator had projected; EA soon revised upward its sales forecast, citing "excitement" over the game (Weiczner, 2015). This is a case of a positive uncertainty that could be tapped to make gains in the stock market. Li, Chan, Ou & Ruifeng (2017) studied stock prices of 30 companies listed in NASDAQ and Twitter sentiment related to those companies. Twitter's text data was mined to identify sentiments regarding particular companies and these sentiments derived from the tweets could explain the stock movement of the companies with an average accuracy over 70%. A study of the contents on crowd sourced content service for financial markets 'Seeking Alpha' showed that negative sentiment from the social media site could predict future negative price performance (Chen, De, Hu, & Hwang, 2014).

Security breaches, faced particularly by banks, cause heavy financial losses and social problems to society and people. Hao & Dai (2016) propose the use of social media as a surveillance tool to track security breaches. Their study states "social media monitoring provides a supplementary tool for the more traditional surveys which are costlier and time-consuming." The large unstructured data from 1,13,340 related tweets collected in August 2015 on Twitter were mined and topics, opinions and knowledge about security breaches from the general public extracted. Sentiment score as well as impact factors are good determinants of real-time public opinions and also attitudes to security breaches. Thereby, unusual patterns/events of security breaches can be detected in the early stage itself, and this can prevent further harm by spreading awareness amongst the people.

Dubey et al. (2017) applied text mining on tweets generated on Twitter for two popular Indian politicians; Arvind Kejriwal and Narendra Modi; these revealed areas where they needed to get more involved in. It also revealed how they could deal with their political affairs in a better way. Analysis could provide insights for preventive action before losses politically and financially.

Structure-Based Analytics to Reduce Risk

Community detection has application in marketing to help make product recommendation systems effective (Parthasarathy, Ruan, & Satuluri, 2011). In politics, one of the ways political parties hedge risk uses social media analytics. The analytics is used to identify influential people and to know who to target campaign and support efforts at. Analyzing a celebrity's posts, followers, and social media activity can aid to confirm whether or not their involvement will be beneficial or detrimental to a particular campaign (Williams, 2017).

SOLUTION AND RECOMMENDATIONS

Social media has a widespread role in disparate real time concepts in online space, like real-time marketing, real time communication, real time social engagement and real time information generation. Thus, social media monitoring becomes essential as data generated from it is widely used for research purposes and have real time impact on the audience and the businesses. Consequently it is evident from the existing research work that social media platform can be a potential source of information for business decisions and policy formulation. As financial risk is an important aspect of any business and has a direct link to the usage of social media both: within and outside the organization — it is important to consider few aspects while conducting a social media research.

- Emotional impulses and user psychology matters. A thorough research and understanding on user psychology is essential for succeeding on social media platforms. A better understanding of users' emotional responses can help increase brand likeability, brand reputation and have other such benefits that can directly affect finances of a business (Crowl, 2015).
- Timing matters. It is essential 'when' an organization is active on social media when dealing with existing and potential clients. Posting the right things at the right time significantly affects user engagement, and can hence increase client interaction. As a research points out, the ideal time to post content for maximum user interaction on Facebook, one of the largest social media platforms, is specific, and hence operating actively on those timings can potentially attract more attention to the content, hereby affecting user interaction, engagement, brand awareness and perception (IZEA, 2017).
- In addition to the "how" part of analytics, it is also important to concentrate on the "who" part. Running analytics on a specific data set, or in context of social media — a specific user base, which is carefully selected after ensuring that there is no sort of selection bias and which represents the offline world, is important, as the entirety of social data may not be representative of the ground reality. Hence, overcoming representation issues is one of the essential things in the analytical cycle to even out the data (Carson, 2016).
- Keywords, and now hashtags, directly affect the attention potential of a product or a brand, and hence, they should be carefully and considerably selected, else the content would not be correctly categorized, leading to misinformation. Different platforms have different needs, and hence it is necessary to cater the hashtags and keywords to every social platform. People trend to react differently on different platforms, for example, the more hashtags you use for a post on instagram, the more the chance of user engagement, while having more than two hashtags on twitter results in a significant drop in user engagement (Osman, 2017).
- It is also important to know and understand the language of the audience. In addition to normal filters like regional language, country and other geography-related filters, it is also important to make the posts relatable by being in sync with up-to-date lingo and culture. For example, emojis, which are basically icons used for expressing emotions and things, were a common factor among social media influencers (Crowl, 2015). Big names such as Coca-Cola, Burger King and Comedy Central have already designed custom emojis to keep their content more relatable and approachable (Seiter, 2016).

- Apart from traditional analytical concepts like network analysis, text analysis, analytics of keywords based on frequency of usage and sentiment analysis, it is also quintessential to know latest concepts in the analytics scene such as Social Network maps, Variety Search and other data scraping tools.
- Visualizing data has great benefits that directly and indirectly contribute to the efficiency of social media analytics. Apart from traditional ways of visualizing data such as bar graphs and pie charts, using multi-dimensional graphs, heat maps, map layering etcetera for advanced visualization helps in grasping the inference from the data better. One of the major documented benefits of business analytics, which includes data visualization, is that it results in better distinction of key facts and patterns from the data from the overall noise (Data Visualization's Positive Impact on Decision Making, 2010).
- Thousands of posts on social media get created and deleted every day. Deleted content can reveal hidden facts and patterns which would usually go un-analyzed. Before making a business decision based on social media posts, it is important to ensure that you have a complete data set, which takes into account the hidden or deleted data. From mundane reasons such as typos and spelling errors, to complex issues such as manipulation by big businesses and censorship by governments, there can be a range of reasons why public posts can be hidden or deleted. By comparing the generated model with a model based on hidden or deleted posts, one can ensure the accuracy and reliability of the generated model (Almuhimedi, Wilson, Liu, Sadeh, & Acquisti, 2013).

FUTURE RESEARCH DIRECTIONS

There are multiple challenges that have been foreseen for social media and social media analysis on which offer scope for future research.

Today, a large number of social media websites are using algorithms to customize the user experience. A user's social media page will show him details it thinks are relevant to the user. This has been termed as a 'filter bubble' by activists working towards a free and fair internet. On the basis of the posts you like and share, the website forms an impression of what you like to engage in and begins to show more of such posts. While this may increase interest in the websites, a major pitfall is that it blocks out alternate opinions. If someone likes and shares posts having a leftist ideology, he will never see posts having a right-wing ideology. In an age where most news is consumed and opinions formed from social media, this is an alarming development that needs reckoning. The jury is still out on this whether there should be a programme that selectively shows updates when you login to a social network, or whether updates should just be shown chronologically. With the increasing number of posts and larger number of connections on social network, this might end up scrolling through multiple posts before you see posts relevant to you. There is scope for research on how social media could evolve balancing user experience and the interests of the service provider. A lot of such research is currently proprietary research conducted by social media firms.

False information spreading through such media is also a concern. There have been cases of violence being instigated and being successful to some extent via social media. The widespread violence against Rohingya Muslims in Myanmar in the latter part of 2017 which came as part of an alleged ethnic cleansing was aggravated with fake news circulated on Facebook. Doctored photos and videos that spewed hate against the minority became viral on Facebook. To some extent, Facebook is also responsible for this as just a year ago, Facebook provided Freebasics in Myanmar; a service where users can access few websites including Facebook without costing them data. Freebasics increased the number of Facebook users in Myanmar from around 20 lakhs to over 3 crores (Roose, 2017). It is such concerns of spreading rumor and fake news that internet communication services are regionally cut off during times of crisis to prevent panic. The latest fad Crypto currency, which uses block chain technology spreading far and finding more takers, definitely had a lot to do with the hype on social media. The recent increase in reach of social media and its impacts on risk and financial stability throws open many questions.

Privacy concerns on social platforms, security issues, problems related to negative expression about a product or a service are all byproducts of the opportunities social media presents. With rising popularity of social media, it is equally important to manage the risk and ensure that online behavior is right. In a reading, authors have tried to establish that better personal usage policy and business usage policy can help to ensure using social media data. Firms have faced a lot of problems with some social media savvy employee revealing too much on a social media platform. This can lead to loss of competitive edge and in severe cases, results in cases of insider trading. Chen, Hwang & Liu (2018) contend that the Twitter activity from company executives can help predict abnormal returns by studying the Twitter data from the accounts of CEOs and CFOs of the largest publicly traded companied in the United States. This increased access to information for retail investors poses its own risks. A solution to this would be allowing staff special authorization power to publish data online giving them proper training and guidelines (Chelliah & Field, 2014).

In addition, data generated through social media networks are difficult to access and are mostly unstructured, hence fetching, cleaning and processing such data is cumbersome. A different aspect of social media analytics are the challenges faced by different researchers in the course of identifying topics, collecting data and then extracting relevant data for analysis. Conferring to a study that undertook all these facets, it was found that because of the large amount of data generated from various online platforms, businesses are interested in understanding or discovering trends wandering over the internet and deriving useful insights to mitigate risk and for mass communication (Stieglitz, Mirbabaie, Ross, & Neuberger, 2018). As social media involves concepts of big data, for that reason social media data is also called social media big data. Primarily, using social media data poses one major challenge due to its large volume that is storage space. Second, due to its high speed of data creation, it is actually difficult to analyze that in real time. Third, as the data is in a variety i.e. in unstructured form, it is challenging to derive information from that on time. Moreover, social media is about diffusion of information on the network, hence it becomes necessary to identify the influencers and analyze this information, hence tracking comes to be another challenge. Finally, the ambiguity with regard to data quality is another important constraint. Research on the methodology of doing social media analysis is itself an emerging area.

CONCLUSION

The world as we know it is constantly changing. In these changing times, business cannot survive by resisting change but by adapting. The internet which brought a sea of change in how businesses worked has now molded into Web 2.0 making it a very horizontal medium of exchange. This age is rightly called the information age where everyone has a lot of information at their disposal. There is tremendous data that is available in social media, and the world is getting aware and developing systems to make sense of this data. Social media offers an unprecedented opportunity to connect directly with investors and other stakeholders. Such interactions enhance transparency and accessibility (Alexander & Gentry, 2014). Firms that have recognized the potential and tapped in to social media analytics are reaping its benefits. For some businesses, the social media analytics is yet not financially viable, given the large cost of storage and analysis. With improving technology and decreasing costs, social media analytics will become used widely. There are also new problems arising which the world collectively has to find solutions to. With more and more people getting connected and the power of social media rising, there are ethical responsibilities on whether to and if yes how to regulate the flow of information. While there are purists who argue for the 'wisdom of masses' to be left to itself to work, yet others point to the many pitfalls of this wisdom. One can say that the pace of change is startling, but the opportunities are tremendous.

REFERENCES

Agarwal, S. (2018, February 20). Internet users in India expected to reach 500 million by June: IAMAI. *Economic Times*. Retrieved April 24, 2018, from https://economictimes.indiatimes.com/tech/internet/internet-users-in-india-expected-to-reach-500-million-by-june-iamai/articleshow/63000198.cms

Aggarwal, C. C. (2011). An introduction to social network data analytics. In C. C. Aggarwal (Ed.), *Social Network Data Analytics* (pp. 1–15). Springer. doi:10.1007/978-1-4419-8462-3_1

Alencar, A. B., de Oliviera, M. F., & Paulovich, F. V. (2012). Seeing beyond reading: A survey on visual text analytics. *Wiley Interdisciplinary Reviews. Data Mining and Knowledge Discovery*, *2*(6), 476–492. doi:10.1002/widm.1071

Alexander, R. M., & Gentry, J. K. (2014). Using social media to report financial results. *Business Horizons*, *57*(2), 161–167. doi:10.1016/j.bushor.2013.10.009

Almuhimedi, H., Wilson, S., Liu, B., Sadeh, N., & Acquisti, A. (2013). Tweets are forever: A large-scale quantitative analysis of deleted tweets. *CSCW Computer Supported Cooperative Work* (pp. 897-908). New York. *ACM New York, NY, USA, 2013*. doi:10.1145/2441776.2441878

Arshad, A., Zafar, M., Fatima, I., & Khan, S. K. (2015). The Impact of Perceived Risk on Online Buyg Behavior. *International Journal of New Technology and Research*, *1*(8), 13–18. Retrieved from https://www.ijntr.org/download_data/IJNTR01080013.pdf

Association of Certified Fraud Examiners. (2006). *Report to the nation on occupational fraud and abuse*. ACFE. Retrieved from https://www.acfe.com/uploadedFiles/ACFE_Website/Content/documents/2006-rttn.pdf

Babu, D. M., Bhagyasri, M., Lahari, K., Madhuri, C. H., & Kumari, G. P. (2014). Image Based Fraud Prevention. *International Journal of Computer Science and Information Technologies*, *5*(1), 728–731. Retrieved from http://ijcsit.com/docs/Volume 5/vol5issue01/ijcsit20140501158.pdf

Bailey, A. A., Bonifield, C. M., & Arias, A. (2018). Social media use by young Latin American consumers: An exploration. *Journal of Retailing and Consumer Services*, *43*, 10–19. doi:10.1016/j.jretconser.2018.02.003

Bandari, R., Asur, S., & Huberman, B. A. (2012). *The pulse of news in social media: Forecasting popularity. In Proceedings of the Sixth International AAAI Conference on Weblogs and Social Media* (pp. 26–33). Association for the Advancement of Artificial Intelligence. Retrieved from https://www.aaai.org/ocs/index.php/ICWSM/ICWSM12/paper/viewFile/4646/4963

Barbier, G., & Liu, H. (2011). Data mining in social media. In C. C. Aggarwal (Ed.), *Social network data analytics* (pp. 327–352). Springer. doi:10.1007/978-1-4419-8462-3_12

Bocconcelli, R., Cioppi, M., & Pagano, A. (2017). Social media as a resource in SMEs' sales process. *Journal of Business and Industrial Marketing*, *32*(5), 693–709. doi:10.1108/JBIM-11-2014-0244

Campbell, L. (2017). *The Importance of Social Media in Risk Management*. Retrieved April 30, 2018, from Cube Logic: https://cubelogic.com/white-papers/the-importance-of-social-media-in-risk-management/

Carson, B. (2016). *Social Media as a Research Methodology*. Retrieved from https://blog.marketresearch.com/social-media-as-a-research-methodology

Chelliah, J., & Field, J. (2014). Managing the risks of social media: Ways to ensure that online behavior is always appropriate. *Human Resource Management International Digest*, *22*(5), 39–41. doi:10.1108/HRMID-07-2014-0103

Chen, H., De, P., Hu, Y., & Hwang, B.-H. (2014). Wisdom of Crowds: The Value of Stock Opinions Transmitted Through Social Media. *Review of Financial Studies*, *27*(5), 1367–1403. doi:10.1093/rfs/hhu001

Chen, H., Hwang, H., & Liu, B. (2018). *The Emergence of "Social Executives" and Its Consequences for Financial Markets*. doi:10.2139srn.2318094

Choi, D.-H., Yoo, W., Noh, G.-Y., & Park, K. (2017). The impact of social media on risk perceptions during the MERS outbreak in South Korea. *Computers in Human Behavior*, *72*, 422–431. doi:10.1016/j.chb.2017.03.004

Cressey, D. R. (1953). *Other people's money; a study of the social psychology of embezzlement*. New York: Free Press.

Crowl, J. (2015). *Impulse Behavior: Why Social Media Content is Such a Popular Downtime Activity*. Retrieved from www.skyword.com: https://www.skyword.com/contentstandard/marketing/impulse-behavior-why-social-media-content-is-such-a-popular-downtime-activity/

Data Visualization's Positive Impact on Decision Making. (2010). Retrieved from https://www.mapbusinessonline.com/Whitepaper.aspx/Decision-Making

Demek, K. C., Raschke, R. L., Janvrin, D. J., & Dilla, W. N. (2018). Do organizations use a formalized risk management process to address social media risk? *International Journal of Accounting Information Systems*, *28*, 31–44. doi:10.1016/j.accinf.2017.12.004

Drummond, C., McGrath, H., & O'Toole, T. (2017). The impact of social media on resource mobilisation in entrepreneurial firms. *Industrial Marketing Management*, *70*, 68–89. doi:10.1016/j.indmarman.2017.05.009

Dubey, G., Chawla, S., & Kaur, K. (2017). Social media opinion analysis for Indian political diplomats. In *Cloud Computing, Data Science & Engineering - Confluence, 2017 7th International Conference on* (pp. 681-686). Noida: IEEE. doi:10.1109/CONFLUENCE.2017.7943238

Essays, U. K. (2013, November). *Social Media In The Jasmine Revolution*. Retrieved April 23, 2018, from UK Essays: https://www.ukessays.com/essays/media/effect-of-social-media-on-the-jasmine-revolution-media-essay.php?vref=1

Ferguson, M. (2016, May 19). *What is Text Analytics?* http://www.ibmbigdatahub.com/blog/what-text-analytics

Forensics, K. P. M. G. (2003). *Fraud Survey*. Montvale, NJ: KPMG.

Forrester Research Inc. (2018). *Predictions 2018: A year of reckoning*. Forrester Research Inc. Retrieved from https://go.forrester.com/blogs/predictions-2018-a-year-of-reckoning/

Gandomi, A., & Haider, M. (2015). Beyond the hype: Big data concepts, methods, and analytics. *International Journal of Information Management*, *35*(2), 137–144. doi:10.1016/j.ijinfomgt.2014.10.007

Grizane, T., & Jurgelane, I. (2017). Social Media Impact on Business Evaluation. *Procedia Computer Science*, *104*, 190–196. doi:10.1016/j.procs.2017.01.103

Hao, J., & Dai, H. (2016). Social media content and sentiment analysis on consumer security breaches. *Journal of Financial Crime*, *23*(4), 855–869. doi:10.1108/JFC-01-2016-0001

Hasan, A., Moin, S., Karim, A., & Shamshirband, S. (2018). Machine Learning-Based Sentiment Analysis for Twitter Accounts. *Mathematical and Computational Applications*, *23*(1), 11–26. doi:10.3390/mca23010011

He, W., Guo, L., Shen, J., & Akula, V. (2016). Social Media-Based Forecasting: A Case Study of Tweets and Stock Prices in the Financial Services Industry. *Journal of Organizational and End User Computing*, *28*(2), 18. doi:10.4018/JOEUC.2016040105

He, W., Zha, S., & Li, L. (2013). Social media competitive analysis and text mining: A case study in the pizza industry. *International Journal of Information Management*, *33*(3), 464–472. doi:10.1016/j.ijinfomgt.2013.01.001

Heidemann, J., Klier, M., & Probst, F. (2012). Online social networks: A survey of a global phenomenon. *Computer Networks*, *56*(18), 3866–3878. doi:10.1016/j.comnet.2012.08.009

Holton, C. (2009). Identifying disgruntled employee systems fraud risk through text mining: A simple solution for a multi-billion dollar problem. *Decision Support Systems*, *46*(4), 853–864. doi:10.1016/j.dss.2008.11.013

Hull, J. C. (2015). *Risk Management and Financial Institutions* (4th ed.). John Wiley & Sons. Retrieved from http://www.simonfoucher.com/MBA/FINA%20695%20-%20Risk%20Management/riskmanagementandfinancialinstitutions4theditionjohnhull-150518225205-lva1-app6892.pdf

IZEA. (2017, March). *6 Key Factors That Influence Your Social Media Engagement*. Retrieved from www.izea.com: https://izea.com/2017/03/16/key-factors-affect-social-media-engagement/

Jiang, J., & Shen, M. (2017). *Traditional Media*. Twitter and Business Scandals; doi:10.2139srn.2959419

Jose, R., & Chooralil, V. S. (2015). Prediction of election result by enhanced sentiment analysis on Twitter data using Word Sense Disambiguation. In *Proceedings of the 2015 International Conference on Control Communication & Computing India (ICCC)* (pp. 638-641). Trivandrum: IEEE. 10.1109/ICCC.2015.7432974

Karppi, T., & Crawford, K. (2016). Social Media, Financial Algorithms and the Hack Crash. *Theory, Culture & Society*, *33*(1), 73–92. doi:10.1177/0263276415583139

Kemp, S. (2017, August 7). *Number of social media users passes 3 billion with no signs of slowing*. Retrieved January 10, 2018, from The Next Web: https://thenextweb.com/contributors/2017/08/07/number-social-media-users-passes-3-billion-no-signs-slowing/

Kim, W. G., Lim, H., & Brymer, R. A. (2015). The effectiveness of managing social media on hotel performance. *International Journal of Hospitality Management*, *44*, 165–171. doi:10.1016/j.ijhm.2014.10.014

Kroll Inc. (2008). Economist Intelligence Unit Overview. In *The Kroll Global Fraud Report*. Kroll Inc. Retrieved from https://eiuperspectives.com/sites/default/files/FraudReport_English-UK_Sept08_1.pdf

Li, B., Chan, K. C., Ou, C., & Ruifeng, S. (2017). Discovering public sentiment in social media for predicting stock movement of publicly listed companies. *Information Systems*, *69*, 81–92. doi:10.1016/j.is.2016.10.001

Liben-Nowell, D., & Kleinberg, J. (2007). The link prediction problem for social networks. *Journal of the Association for Information Science and Technology*, *58*(7), 1019–1031. doi:10.1002/asi.v58:7

Liu, L., Wu, J., Li, P., & Li, Q. (2015). A social-media-based approach to predicting stock comovement. *Expert Systems with Applications*, *42*(8), 3893–3901. doi:10.1016/j.eswa.2014.12.049

Malhotra, A. (2011). Social Media: The New Tool of Revolution. *Scholar Warrior*, 74-81. Retrieved April 24, 2018, from http://www.claws.in/images/journals_doc/Spring%202011-%20Final%20Issue.87-94.pdf

Mazboudi, M., & Khalil, S. (2017). The attenuation effect of social media: Evidence from acquisitions by large firms. *Journal of Financial Stability*, *28*, 115–124. doi:10.1016/j.jfs.2016.11.010

Meti, V., Khandoba, P., & Guru, M. (2015). Social Media for Political Mobilization in India: A Study. *Journal of Mass Communication & Journalism*, *5*(9). doi:10.4172/2165-7912.1000275

Miller, R. (2015, June 30). *Inside Facebook's Blu-Ray Cold Storage Data Center*. Retrieved April 29, 2018, from Data Center Frontier: https://datacenterfrontier.com/inside-facebooks-blu-ray-cold-storage-data-center/

Momoc, A. (2013). Social Media- PR Tools for Romanian Politicians? *Procedia: Social and Behavioral Sciences*, *81*, 116–121. doi:10.1016/j.sbspro.2013.06.398

Morinaga, S., Yamanishi, K., Tateishi, K., & Fukushima, T. (2002). Mining product reputations on the web. In *Proceedings of the eighth ACM SIGKDD international conference on Knowledge discovery and data mining* (pp. 341-349). ACM. 10.1145/775047.775098

Oliveira, M. P., & Handfield, R. (2017). An enactment theory model of supplier financial disruption risk mitigation. *Supply Chain Management*, *22*(5), 442–457. doi:10.1108/SCM-03-2017-0121

Oracle. (2015, February). *Big Data in Financial Services and Banking: Architect's Guide and Reference Architecture Introduction.* Retrieved March 13, 2018, from Oracle: http://www.oracle.com/us/technologies/big-data/big-data-in-financial-services-wp-2415760.pdf

Osman, M. (2017). *How to Use Hashtags on Every Social Media Network.* Retrieved from www.sproutsocial.com: https://sproutsocial.com/insights/how-to-use-hashtags/

Parthasarathy, S., Ruan, Y., & Satuluri, V. (2011). Community discovery in social networks: Applications, methods and emerging trends. In C. C. Aggarwal (Ed.), *Social network data analytics* (pp. 79–113). Boston: Springer. doi:10.1007/978-1-4419-8462-3_4

Pew Research Center. (2016, July 18). *Election 2016: Campaigns as a Direct Source of News.* Retrieved April 10, 2018, from Pew Research Center Journalism and Media: http://www.journalism.org/2016/07/18/election-2016-campaigns-as-a-direct-source-of-news/

Piskorski, M. J. (2014). *A Social Strategy: How we profit from Social Media.* Princeton, NJ: Princeton University Press. doi:10.1515/9781400850020

Press Trust of India. (2017, November 28). Data usage per smartphone in India to grow 5-fold by 2023: Ericsson. *Economic Times.* Retrieved April 29, 2018, from https://economictimes.indiatimes.com/tech/internet/data-usage-per-smartphone-in-india-to-grow-5-fold-by-2023-ericsson/articleshow/61838209.cms

Quantzig. (n.d.). *Social Media Analytics and Politics.* Retrieved April 17, 2018, from Quantzig Blog: https://www.quantzig.com/blog/social-media-analytics-politics#

Ribarsky, W., Wang, D. X., & Dou, W. (2014). Social media analytics for competitive advantage. *Computers & Graphics*, *38*, 328–331. doi:10.1016/j.cag.2013.11.003

Roose, K. (2017). *Forget Washington. Facebook's Problems Abroad Are Far More Disturbing.* Retrieved April 30, 2018, from The New York Times: https://www.nytimes.com/2017/10/29/business/facebook-misinformation-abroad.html

Seiter, C. (2016). *The Psychology of Social Media: Why We Like, Comment, and Share Online.* Retrieved from www.blog.bufferapp.com: https://blog.bufferapp.com/psychology-of-social-media

Severi, E., Ling, K. C., & Nasemoadeli, A. (2014). *The Impacts of Electronic Word of Mouth on Brand Equity in the Context of Social Media.* Academic Press. doi:10.5539/ijbm.v9n8p84

Stieglitz, S., Mirbabaie, M., Ross, B., & Neuberger, C. (2018). Social media analytics – Challenges in topic discovery, data collection, and data preparation. *International Journal of Information Management*, *39*, 156–168. doi:10.1016/j.ijinfomgt.2017.12.002

Sul, H., Dennis, A. R., & Yuan, L. I. (2014). Trading on Twitter: The Financial Information Content of Emotion in Social Media. *Proceedings of the 47th Hawaii International Conference on System Sciences.* Conference Publishing Services. doi:10.1109/HICSS.2014.107

Sun, J., & Tang, J. (2011). A survey of models and algorithms for social influence analysis. In C. C. Aggarwal (Ed.), *Social network data analytics* (pp. 177–214). Boston: Springer. doi:10.1007/978-1-4419-8462-3_7

TechAmerica Foundation's Federal Big Data Commission. (2012). *Demystifying bigdata: A practical guide to transforming the business of Government.* Washington, DC: Tech America. Retrieved from http://www.techamerica.org/Docs/fileManager.cfm?f=techamerica-bigdatareport-final.pdf

Themba, G., & Mulala, M. (2013). Brand-Related eWOM and Its Effects on Purchase Decisions: An Empirical Study of University of Botswana Students. *International Journal of Business and Management*, *8*(8), 31. doi:10.5539/ijbm.v8n8p31

Toma, S.-V., Chitiţă, M., & Şarpe, D. (2012). Risk and Uncertainty. *Procedia Economics and Finance*, *3*, 975–980. doi:10.1016/S2212-5671(12)00260-2

Vagata, P., & Wilfong, K. (2014, April 10). *Scaling the Facebook data warehouse to 300 PB*. Retrieved April 28, 2018, from Facebook: https://code.facebook.com/posts/229861827208629/scaling-the-facebook-data-warehouse-to-300-pb/

VanBoskirk, S., Overby, C. S., & Takvorian, S. (2011). *US interactive marketing forecast, 2011 to 2016.* Forrester Research Inc. Retrieved from https://retelur.files.wordpress.com/2012/01/forrester_interactive_marketing_forecast_2011_to_2016.pdf

Weiczner, J. (2015, December 7). How Investors Are Using Social Media to Make Money. *Fortune*. Retrieved from http://fortune.com/2015/12/07/dataminr-hedge-funds-twitter-data/

Williams, C. B. (2017). Introduction: Social Media, Political Marketing and the 2016 US Election. *Journal of Political Marketing*, *16*(3-4), 207–211. doi:10.1080/15377857.2017.1345828

Young, K. (2017, November 14). *The Biggest Social Media Trends Shaping 2018*. Retrieved December 30, 2018, from Global Web Index: https://blog.globalwebindex.com/trends/social-media-trends/

YouTube for Press. (n.d.). Retrieved March 15, 2018, from YouTube: https://www.youtube.com/yt/about/press/

Zeng, D., Chen, H., Lusch, R., & Li, S.-H. (2010). Social media analytics and intelligence. *IEEE Intelligent Systems*, *25*(6), 13–16. doi:10.1109/MIS.2010.151

Zhu, Y.-Q., & Chen, H.-G. (2015). Social media and human need satisfaction: Implications for social media marketing. *Business Horizons*, *58*(3), 335–345. doi:10.1016/j.bushor.2015.01.006

ADDITIONAL READING

Akinkunmi, M. (2018). Data Mining and Market Intelligence: Implications for Decision Making. *Synthesis Lectures on Engineering*, *13*(1), 1–181. doi:10.2200/S00838ED1V01Y201803ENG030

Cheney-Lippold, J. (2017). *We Are Data: Algorithms and the making of our digital selves.* New York: New York University Press. doi:10.2307/j.ctt1gk0941

Fan, W., & Gordon, M. D. (2014). The Power of Social Media Analytics. *Communications of the ACM*, *57*(6), 74–81. doi:10.1145/2602574

Gorodnichenko, Y., Pham, T., & Talavera, O. (2018). *Social media, sentiment and public opinions: Evidence from# Brexit and# USElection. (No. w24631)*. National Bureau of Economic Research; doi:10.3386/w24631

Lal, A. (2017). *India social: How social media is leading the charge and changing country*. New Delhi: Hachette India.

Piskorski, M. (2014). *A social strategy: How we profit from social media*. Princeton: Princeton University Press. doi:10.1515/9781400850020

Schmidt, E., & Cohen, J. (2013). *The new digital age*. New Delhi: Hachette India.

Sponder, M. (2012). *Social media analytics: effective tools for building, interpreting, and using metrics*. New York: McGraw-Hill.

KEY TERMS AND DEFINITIONS

Big Data: This is data characterized by its large volume, wide variety, and high velocity. Volume refers to high quantity of data usually running into terabytes. The data is not only numbers or text, but can include images, videos, etc., making it very varied and the data is generated rapidly which is called its high velocity.

Content-Based Analytics: In social media analysis, content-based analytics involves the analysis on the contents posted by users on social media. This includes text, images, and videos.

Occupational Fraud: Occupational fraud is the use of one's occupation for personal enrichment through the deliberate misuse or misapplication of the organization's resources or assets. It could include any of payment fraud, procurement fraud, and travel and subsistence fraud, personnel management, exploiting assets or information and receipt fraud.

Risk: When the outcome of an event is uncertain, but one is aware of the probabilities of each outcome, the outcome is said to possess risk.

Social Media Analytics: It is the process of gathering, structuring, analyzing and gaining actionable insights from data available on social media. This is data generated from the conversations of stakeholders on social media.

Structure-Based Analytics: In social media analysis, structure based analytics or social network analytics is concerned with evaluating the structural attributes of a social network and extracting intelligence from the relationships among the participating entities. The structures are modelled visually with nodes, and edges connecting the nodes.

Text Analysis: This is the process of creating high-quality structured data for analysis from unstructured and heterogeneous textual data. The structured data is then analyzed to derive usable conclusions. In social media analysis, the raw text could be in the form of tweets, Facebook posts, comments on social media, hashtags, and blog posts.

Uncertainty: When the outcome of an event is uncertain and one doesn't know all possible outcomes and/or their probabilities, then outcome is said to be uncertain.

Web 2.0: As opposed to the traditional world wide web (retroactively called Web 1.0), Web 2.0 has a lot of inputs generated by users. These are in the form of forums, microblogging, social networking and wikis (a server program that allows users to collaborate in forming the content of a website [e.g., Wikipedia]). An information architecture consultant Darcy DiNucci coined the term Web 2.0 in 1999, but it was popularized by Tim O'Reilly, founder of O'Reilly Media.

ENDNOTES

1 This Q&A session on Reddit can be accessed here - https://www.reddit.com/r/StarWarsBattlefront/comments/7d4qft/star_wars_battlefront_ii_dice_developer_ama/?st=JA1BP7F6&sh=f5117ea9.

2 Naive Bayes model is a method of probabilistic classification based on Bayes' theorem and begins with strong independence assumption amongst the features. It is a popular method for text categorization in machine learning. It uses word frequencies to classify text into a category. It is highly scalable and has found application in many fields like automated medical diagnosis, classifying mail as spam or legitimate etc. This model is also known as simple Bayes or independence Bayes.

3 Data that has been already classified as disgruntled on non-disgruntled is fed to the software. In machine learning, the software analyses the text and identifies different features and assigns weights to each feature in classifying the text as disgruntled or non-disgruntled. Before the learning process, the data is divided into two parts. One part is fed in, on which after multiple iterations the machine finds the best factors and weights for them to predict the outcome (classification). This model is then tested on the second part of the data to test its accuracy. So, all machine learning processes involve dividing the data into training data – data used to identify the parameters of the model and evaluation data – data on which the accuracy of the model is tested.

Chapter 12
Farm Debt Waiver in India:
An Ephemeral Palliative or an Enduring Risk Management Tool? A SAP-LAP Analysis

Sushma Nayak
Symbiosis International University (Deemed), India

Shrabana Mukherjee
Association of Indian Forging Industry, India

ABSTRACT

Farm debt waivers have been introduced in India, from time to time, to provide relief to the indebted farmers. The chapter focuses on the viability of farm debt waiver in India—whether it serves as an ephemeral palliative (a temporary reassuring measure) or an enduring risk management tool (a permanent remedy to build resilience against a longstanding debt crisis)—for farmers by employing situation, actor, process, learning, action, performance (SAP-LAP) framework. Loan waivers occasionally appear as a quick fix to alleviate farmers' misery. They trigger moral hazard as the farmers make no attempts to repay the loans themselves with the expectation that an imminent waiver from the government would clear their debts, thus ruining the credit culture of the country. From a policy viewpoint, it is imperative to make agriculture sustainable by lessening inefficiencies, augmenting income, moderating costs, and affording protection through premeditated and well-defined insurance schemes.

INTRODUCTION

India, since the Green Revolution in the 1960s, has incurred rapid gains in agricultural productivity with increased producer incomes, higher labour wages and lowered food prices. With the objective to improve farmers' accessibility to institutional credit and reduce their reliance on informal credit (such as borrowing from moneylenders and kinsfolks), the government has improved the flow of credit through nationalization of commercial banks, establishment of regional rural banks (RRBs) and the institution of National Bank for Agriculture and Rural Development (NABARD). Various farm credit and farm

DOI: 10.4018/978-1-5225-7208-4.ch012

improvement programmes such as the Kisan Credit Scheme – 1998, Interest Subvention Scheme – 2006, Pradhan Mantri Jan-Dhan Yojana (PMJDY) – 2014, Soil Health Card Scheme – 2015, Pradhan Mantri Krishi Sinchai Yojana (PMKSY) – 2015, Paramparagat Krishi Vikas Yojana (PKVY) – 2015, Pradhan Mantri Fasal Bima Yojana (PMFBY) – 2016, have been launched over the years. As an outcome, the percentage of institutional credit to agricultural gross domestic product scaled up to 41% in 2015-16 as against 10% in 1999-2000 (Kumar & Bathla, 2017). However, despite decades of measures in rural development and spending in new agricultural technology, farmer indebtedness continues to plague the rural economy. In an agrarian economy, like India, nearly 70% of the 90 million agricultural households spend more than their income each month resulting in mounting debts (Saha, 2017). The 70th Round of National Sample Survey states that the Incidence of Indebtedness (IOI) was about 31.4% among the rural households as on June 30, 2012; indebtedness within cultivator households was higher by 9 percentage points as compared to non-cultivator households (National Sample Survey Office, Government of India, 2013). In 2013, the average amount of debt (AOD) per indebted household was Rs. 1,03,457 in rural areas (Deccan Chronicle, 2016). However, the fundamental cause of the agrarian crisis is not merely indebtedness – indebtedness is only a cue. "The underlying causes are stagnation in agriculture, increasing production and marketing risks, institutional vacuum and lack of alternative livelihood opportunities" (Ministry of Finance, Government of India, 2007). Nonetheless, indebtedness has been the primary reason for the increasing numbers of farmer suicides across the country. Farmer suicides accounted for about 11.2% of all suicides in India (Nagaraj, Sainath, Rukmani & Gopinath, 2014). Considering the growing indebtedness of farmers, farm debt waiver scheme is reckoned as an important policy measure by the Government of India. Therefore, consideration of farm debt waiver is crucial and a pertinent issue for discussion in the present-day context. The present chapter aims to examine whether farm debt waiver is a lasting solution to India's deepening agrarian distress by employing "Situation, Actor, Process, Learning, Action, Performance (SAP-LAP)" (Sushil, 2000) framework that attempts to adopt a holistic and all-inclusive approach for examining a problem at hand. Through SAP-LAP paradigm, the authors shall not only examine the viability of farm debt waiver in India but also offer recommendations to improve the resilience of farmers against diverse types of agricultural risks.

The rest of the chapter is organized as follows. The background section gives a timeline of farm debt waiver schemes in India, the consequences and associated risks of such schemes, and an overview of SAP-LAP paradigm — the framework used to examine the nuances of waivers. The following segments analyse farm debt waivers in India, using SAP-LAP method, from the standpoint of proposing solutions and recommendations to improve the overall state of farmers in India; identify directions for future research; and offer concluding remarks.

BACKGROUND

Timeline of Farm Debt Waiver Schemes in India

The Government of India, time and again, has announced debt waiver schemes to provide relief to the indebted and burdened farmers and curb the agrarian crisis. In simple words, debt waiver is waiving off or not claiming the real or potential liability of an individual or party who has taken a loan voluntarily. The first ever nation-wide farm loan waiver amounting to Rs. 10,000 crore were announced in the budget of March 1990, under the leadership of Mr. V. P. Singh (Rath, 2008). The scheme was implemented during 1990-91 but resulted in adversely affecting the rural credit scenario with a high incidence of defaults. While the Union government was to compensate commercial banks for the writing off of all agricultural loans, the responsibility of compensating the co-operative credit societies was to be equally distributed by the centre and the state governments. However, almost every state government opposed to the proposal. To ask the states to bear 50% of loans offered by the co-operative societies was unfair. Many of the states were financially incapable of shouldering the responsibility of a burden promised by the Union government. The Reserve Bank of India (RBI) was requested to offer a solution to the problem. RBI offered that the states would be provided a loan to the extent of 50% of the cost of the co-operative loans relinquished through NABARD, but the loan would be repayable in three annual instalments starting from 1991, with 10% interest ("Farm Loan Waiver-Onerous Terms", 1990). To repay loans within three years compelled many states to cut down on their plan size to meet the centre's commitments.

On February 29, 2008, the then Finance Minister, Mr. P. Chidambaram, proposed writing off loans amounting to Rs. 600 billion to credit institutions, focused mainly on providing relief to small and marginal farmers (Rath, 2008). This scheme of the Government, as a part of the Agricultural Debt Waiver and Debt Relief Scheme (AWDRS) for Small and Marginal Farmers, came to be one of the most generous household debt relief programmes in the history. Implemented in June 2008, the program estimated to waive off Rs. 715 billion issued by commercial and co-operative banks from 1997 to 2007 (Kanz, 2012). The actual amount of disbursement towards AWDRS was Rs. 525.16 billion (Table 1).

The scheme covered crop loans, investment loans for direct agricultural purposes or purposes allied to agriculture as well as loans rescheduled under previous programs (Ramkumar, 2017). Loan waiver eligibility required that the loans were disbursed up to March 31, 2007, were overdue as on December 31, 2007 and remained unpaid until February 29, 2008. The scheme stated that a farmer classified as 'small farmer' or 'marginal farmer' would be eligible for fresh agricultural loans once the eligible amount was waived off. A farmer classified as 'other farmer' would be eligible for a one-time settlement (OTS) relief and shall undertake an agreement to pay his share (that is eligible amount minus the amount of OTS relief) in not more than three instalments, where, the first two instalments shall be for an amount not less than one-third of his share. The last dates of payment in the case of three instalments would be September 30, 2008, March 31, 2009, and June 30, 2009. The volume of debt relief granted under this scheme amounted to 1.6% of India's Gross Domestic Product (GDP) (Ramkumar, 2017). The programme is claimed to have affected approximately 45 million households across the country (Kanz, 2012).

Many states have, time and again, announced farm debt waivers to relieve the mounting farmer indebtedness in their states. In 2017, Punjab announced a farm debt waiver of Rs. 10,000 crore, while a waiver of Rs. 8,165 crore were announced in Karnataka; Uttar Pradesh announced a farm loan waiver

Table 1. Amount disbursed year-wise towards AWDRS (2008-2012)

Year	Amount (Rs. Billion)
2008-09	250
2009-10	150
2010-11	113.40
2011-12	11.76
Total	**525.16**

Source: Solanki, 2018

of Rs. 36,359 crore followed by Maharashtra of Rs. 30,500 crore (Ministry of Agriculture & Farmers Welfare, 2018).

Consequences and Associated Risks

Reasons for announcements of farm debt waivers are unassuming and straightforward. Guided by political as well as economic considerations, politicians declare such schemes prior to elections from the standpoint of securing their vote bank. Experts and enthusiasts alike argue that the UPA Government came back to power in 2009 due to the Farm Loan Waiver Scheme announced in 2008 (No Panacea for Agrarian Distress, 2017).

However, there has been a constant debate surrounding the impact of debt waiver schemes in benefitting the agrarian economy. Many suggest that agricultural loan waivers and subsidies do not benefit the poorest in rural India. Loan waivers provide little help to the most vulnerable farmers with no or small landholdings. These farmers are not considered creditworthy and have no access to institutional loans. Loan waiver schemes do little to resolve skewed landownership patterns, uneven access to subsidies and vulnerability to climatic vagaries (No Panacea for Agrarian Distress, 2017). According to a report submitted by a ministerial expert group, chaired by Shri R. Radhakrishnan, indebtedness is a "symptom and not the root cause of India's farm crisis" (Ministry of Finance, Government of India, 2007). The group reported that the average farm household borrowing has not been excessive and is majorly due to factors beyond agricultural credit.

The agrarian crisis has persisted and has become severe. Climate change and risky weather patterns have further worsened the timidities of farmers. The deficiency of quality capital assets in surface irrigation and rainwater harvesting continues to be an experiment. This has led to a growing dependence on diminishing groundwater as the main source of irrigation. About half of the country's cropped area still does not have access to guaranteed irrigation facilities. The initiative to increase the number of workdays under the Mahatma Gandhi National Rural Employment Guarantee Act (MNREGA) to 150 days a year in the drought-affected states has an important bearing by the Union government (Tewari, 2016). Creation of assets that preserve water, improve irrigation and prevent recurring drought-like conditions need to be accelerated. A multitude of other factors have adversely affected the assets-liabilities statement of Indian farmers. Agricultural produce market is characterised by imperfection and volatility in India and the world over. In this scenerio, it is important to understand the detoriorating farm income and rural indebtedness. Unless concerted efforts are made to address these systemic problems, little will be achieved to break this vicious cycle.

After the declaration of the farm debt waiver in 1990, availability of agricultural loans from cooperative credit societies and commercial banks witnessed a decline. The reasons were many. Firstly, it took many years for the governments to compensate the banks or the credit societies. As a result, farmers or societies with defaults were not eligible for fresh loans till the previous ones were written off. Cultivators who had repaid their loans before the announcement felt cheated and denied repaying fresh loans. The beneficiaries realized that the government would announce such waiver schemes from time to time and were unenthusiastic about repayment (Rath, 2008). In addition, the 1991 economic reform policies focused on the profit performance of the state-owned commercial banks and a reduction in non-performing assets (NPAs). The consequences were evident. Amongst scheduled commercial banks, the number of small borrower accounts with credit limits of Rs 25,000 or less had attained a peak of 62.55 million in March 1992, but by March 2001, these had dwindled to one-half at 37.25 million; the percentage share of these small borrower accounts in aggregate bank credit had dropped from the peak of 25.4 per cent to 7 per cent during the period (Hukeri & Prasanth, 2008). A similar decline had occurred in direct finance for agriculture, with the number of loan accounts declining from 27.34 million in March 1992 to a low of 19.56 million in March 2001 and their share in aggregate bank credit receding from a peak of about 15 per cent to 8 per cent (Hukeri & Prasanth, 2008).

The crisis of the rural economy not only needs direct spending on schemes but also on channelizing the rural demand for further diversification of the rural economy into the non-farm sector (Himanshu, 2016). The output of the agriculture sector may rebound in the short-run, but the real challenge is to revive the growth in incomes of farmers in the middle to long-run. Also, the target group must be re-assessed. A small farmer with less land but in a rain-fed area could have higher returns as against a large farmer with more land in an arid or semi-arid region. The idea of identifying the target group through measurement of the size of land is misleading (Joshi, 2008).

These schemes also ignore the importance of informal credit institutions. According to the NSSO, out of the 48.6% of the indebted farm households surveyed, 61% were marginal farmers. Out of the total outstanding loans, 41% of the money was borrowed for purposes other than farm related activities, like, healthcare and domestic needs. 57.7% of the total outstanding debts was borrowed from institutional credit, whereas, 42.3% were taken from informal sources, such as moneylenders, traders, relatives, and friends (National Sample Survey Office, 2013). The farm waiver scheme by the Government did not cover the informal credit borrowings. Cases, where a farmer might have borrowed from a money lender to repay his loans to the bank in time, would be unjustly excluded from the scheme. Furthermore, bankers and agricultural experts point that farmers who have invested their savings instead of borrowings would be excluded from the relief scheme, causing disharmony amidst farmers.

Swaminathan (2008) suggests that the centre, along with the state governments, must set up an Indebted Farmers' Support Consortium, at district levels. The Consortium, comprising farm scientists, financial institutions, panchayat leaders, financial institutions and other relevant people, would assist the farmers to overcome their old debts by augmenting productivity and improving the profitability of their farms in a sustainable manner. This would enable the farmers to incur higher marketable surplus, leading to more cash income. To avoid indebtedness, the smaller farm needs a more marketable surplus. Secondly, despite the Commission for Agricultural Costs and Prices specifying Minimum Support Prices (MSP) for 24 crops, MSPs usually exist for rice and wheat. To elude this scenario, Market Intervention Funds must be set up by the central and state governments to prevent small farmers from selling at lower than MSP at harvest time. Provision of loan waivers can prove to be of some avail, provided the farmers are given access to suitable infrastructure, upgraded technology, services, input-output pricing policies.

SAP-LAP Framework

SAP-LAP (Situation, Actor, Process, Learning, Action, Performance) was first developed by Professor Sushil as a "generic framework which can be used in a variety of contexts, such as problem solving, change management, strategy formulation, supply chain management, marketing management, technology management, human resource management, and so on" (Sushil, 2009). This framework involves two ladders. SAP is an integration of the prevailing *situation* concerning a particular issue; the *actors* (enjoying *freedom of choice*) who influence and act upon the *situation* to bring about the desired change; and the *process* undertaken to manage the *situation*. A fusion of SAP leads to LAP wherein there is

Figure 1. SAP-LAP Framework
Source: Sushil (2000)

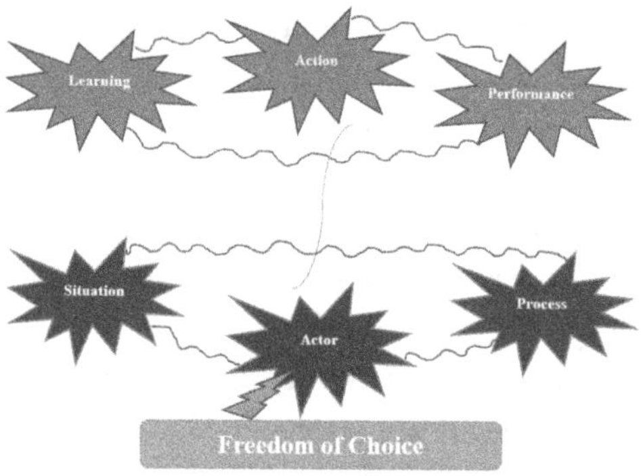

learning for right *action* towards effective *performance* of the *situation* in sight. Figure 1 exhibits a typical SAP-LAP framework.

SAP-LAP framework has been employed to examine and explore a wide range of situations in diverse sectors and industries, few of which have been listed in Table 2.

SAP-LAP analysis allows an extensive inquiry of a subject by delving into its origins and aftermaths, as well as offers a systematic action plan to deal with it. In the present chapter, it is used for exploring one of the most debated policy measures of the Indian government — farm debt waiver — which has its own set of paybacks and pitfalls, and needs to be inspected from the standpoint of retaining it or axing it in the future.

MAIN FOCUS OF THE CHAPTER

The present chapter focuses on the viability of farm debt waiver in India — whether it serves as an ephemeral palliative (a temporary reassuring measure) or an enduring risk management tool (a permanent remedy to build resilience against a longstanding debt crisis) — for farmers. "In India, agricultural risks are exacerbated by a variety of factors, ranging from climate variability and change, frequent natural disasters, uncertainties in yields and prices, weak rural infrastructure, imperfect markets and lack of financial services including limited span and design of risk mitigation instruments such as credit and insurance" (Jain & Parshad, 2006). The numerous risk management tools have either been poorly developed or have not penetrated enough to the needy farmers across the country. In such a scenario, the government on frequent occasions, has employed farm debt waiver as a risk sharing/risk transfer mechanism to alleviate the farmers from cyclical indebtedness. However, such a strategy is inherently loose as it fuels moral hazard and rescinds the credit discipline by encouraging wilful default (Patel, 2017). Furthermore, it also puts additional burden on tax payers as the fiscal deficit in the budget can be overcome only by taxing citizens or by way of public debt. By employing SAP-LAP framework, the present chapter conducts an exhaustive analysis of farm debt waivers in India — the costs involved, the benefits derived, the lessons learnt and the way ahead for sustainable agriculture by augmenting the coping capacities and resilience of farmers. Farm debt waivers have necessitated the urgency of scheming enduring remedies to the structural malaise that distresses Indian agriculture.

Table 2. Fields of research drawing on SAP-LAP inquiry

Authors	Fields of Research Drawing on SAP-LAP Inquiry
Sushil (2000)	Proposed the SAP-LAP framework as a prototypical model for managerial inquiry
Ravi & Shankar (2006)	Reverse logistics in Indian paper manufacturing companies
Arshinder, Kanda & Deshmukh (2007)	Supply chain synchronization issues of a distinguished automotive parts manufacturer in India
Suri & Sushil (2008)	Execution of e-governance applications with regard to Department of Fertilizers in India
Garg & Deshmukh (2010)	Case analysis of a government maintenance organization in India dealing with refurbishment of automobiles
Pramod & Banwet, (2010)	Case analysis of logistics development in telecom service sector in India
Charan (2012)	Status of supply chain performance initiatives pertaining to a prominent equipment manufacturer in India
John & Ramesh (2012)	Apathetic status of humanitarian supply chain management in India
Mangla, Kumar & Barua (2014)	Developing risk mitigating strategies in green supply chain
Iyengar, Behl, Pillai & Londhe (2016)	Case analysis of a palliative care unit involved in improving the quality of lives of patients suffering from terminal illnesses
Chand, Thakkar & Ghosh (2018)	Factors influencing supply chain intricacies for mining equipment manufacturing firms in India
Kumar, Haleem, Qamar & Khan (2018)	Impact of shift from railways to waterways relating to coal carriage and transportation supply chain in India
Anand, Medhavi, Soni, Malhotra & Banwet (2018)	Information security in e-governance in India
Akhtar & Sushil (2018)	Comparative analysis of the performance of oil companies
Gupta & Shri (2018)	Performance assessment of corrugated packaging establishments in India

Source: Various Sources

SAP-LAP PARADIGM OF FARM DEBT WAIVER IN INDIA

Situation

1. It is a widely putative fact that as an economy progresses, the dominance of agriculture dwindles and other sectors, such as industry and services, assume prominence. However, it is correspondingly true that growth in agricultural sector is imperative for industrialization, and empirical evidences clearly demonstrate how agricultural growth is a precursor for growth in manufacturing and services, although the converse is not true (Thirtle, Irz, Lin, McKenzie-Hill & Wiggins, 2001). In India, despite the progress attained in diverse sectors, agriculture continues to be a major source of employment for more than 50 per cent of the total population and contributes nearly 17-18 per cent of the nation's GDP as reported by the Economic Survey 2017-18. Experts and professionals clearly suggest that "agriculture sector needs the much-needed attention and 52% population of the country are looking forward to reforms in this sector for the last 4 years" (Sunder, 2018).
2. Farmers in India are exposed to diverse types of risks as exhibited in Figure 2. Such persistent risks and dismal development and penetration of risk management tools throughout the country signify the enormous opportunities to bring out the cultivators from the poverty trap by cloistering them from income shocks and ensuring a fair price for their produce.

3. Agriculture in India has been appalling and plagued with numerous quandaries — fragmented and stunted land holdings, diminishing water table levels, declining soil condition, escalating input costs and sinking productivity. Monsoons have been erratic. Yield prices have not been always remunerative; if there is bumper crop in a particular season, output prices fall automatically. As mentioned earlier in the chapter, farmers have such limited incomes that they are often compelled to borrow to meet their daily expenses. Furthermore, countless small farmers lacking collateral or ineligible for bank credit, seek loans at extortionate interest rates from private sources. As nature rides roughshod over farmers trapped in a recurring debt cycle in the form of inconsistent rains and crop failures, they face distressing alternatives (Siva, 2017).
4. Policy-driven agrarian affliction and plight of Indian farmers are grim realities. Census of India 2011 reported that there was a drop in the total number of farmers by approximately 15 million than what it was 2 decades prior, thus implying an attrition rate of 2,040 farmers on a daily basis (Sainath, 2018). Most of these farmers got downgraded in their status from farmers to being farm labourers. The costs of cultivation have gone up significantly, but farmers' incomes have not risen at the same time; they have either stagnated or diminished. According to the National Institution for Transforming India (NITI Aayog), the average income ascent for a farming family in India amid 2011-2016 was a meagre 0.44 per cent thus indicating frozen incomes (Giri & Sinha, 2018).
5. Although 18 per cent of the Adjusted Net Bank Credit (of scheduled commercial banks and foreign banks with 20 branches and above) is earmarked for agriculture as an obligatory mandate for priority sector lending, of which 8 per cent is proposed for small and marginal farmers (Reserve Bank of India, 2015), it has been observed that public sector banks have shied away from lending to these farmers, thus compelling them to resort to money lenders charging as high as an upward of 60 per cent yearly interest rate (Sainath, 2018). The excessive defaults by farmers abet money lenders to survive and sustain in the rural agricultural credit market as the organized sector becomes disinclined to extend loans in the backdrop of inveterate non-payments (Balachandran & Dhal, 2018).
6. There is insufficient flow of credit to sensitive and distressed farming regions of the country. As a case in point, in 2017, NABARD apportioned 50 per cent of its credit to Mumbai and its peripheries, while Vidarbha and Marathwada — widely known for their agricultural vulnerabilities — received a paltry 16 per cent (Sainath, 2018).
7. Farmer suicides having been rising in the country and it is reported that "over the past 22 years, more than 330,000 farmers have committed suicide in India" (Giri & Sinha, 2018). Indebtedness is a fundamental reason for scores of farmer suicides in the country (Siva, 2017). Agricultural experts clearly suggest that agrarian crisis is more an outcome of policy paralysis which cannot be attributed to a single government but a series of governments on account of their failure to provide alternative gainful sources of employment by moving people from rural areas to urban areas.

To deal with the longstanding agrarian crisis, farm debt waiver has been of great consequence from the standpoint of liberating the farmers from the clutches of indebtedness. It was first introduced in India in 1990, and since then has been launched at different time periods, the major one being the one in 2008. Since 2008 till March 2017, it is estimated that the central and state governments together have waived approximately Rs. 890 billion (Desai, 2017).

Figure 2. Types of farm risks confronting Indian farmers
Source: Jain & Parshad (2006)

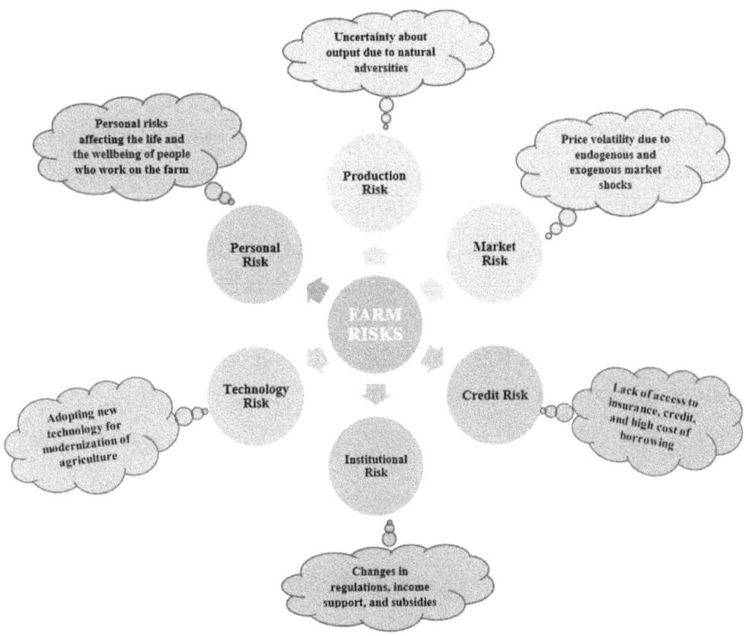

Actors

Farm debt waiver involves five main actors – central government, state government, monetary authority, banks/formal financial institutions and beneficiaries viz. the farmers. The execution of waivers has undergone considerable change ever since it was first introduced in the country in 1990. Today, the exact process of implementing waivers, particularly the terms and provisions for recompensing lenders, is imprecise, as regards who shall eventually bear the cost. In essence, the centre or states may take possession of the liability of farmers and reimburse the banks (Siva, 2017). When it was introduced on a massive scale in 2008, the central government claimed the debt and reimbursed the banks ("FM on whys and hows of farm loan waiver", 2008). Presently, the central government has clearly stated that it shall not reimburse for the waivers (Desai, 2017). Therefore, the onus remains with the state governments to compensate the lending institutions. One way of financing the waiver is issuing farm loan waiver bonds by state governments to banks, which is reckoned to be a weak arrangement as there would be very few investors in the market who would prefer to invest in such bonds; also, central government dissuades states from market borrowing in excess of definite, conventionally established limits (Venu, 2017). Another way of financing the waiver by state governments is the creation of a central account where funds are deposited for the policy enactment; alongside this, an account is opened by the state government with every bank. When a farmer with a loan account in a certain bank is known to be entitled for the waiver, the state government remits funds from the central account to the bank where the beneficiary holds the account. This is done to eschew irregularities and anomalies in the entire process. This is how Maharashtra rolled out the waiver in 2017 (Jain, 2017). The threshold amount of the waiver as well as the number of beneficiaries within a farmer family are announced beforehand by the state government, way prior to the execution of the scheme. However, it has been observed that if the waiver by a state involves a very huge amount, that state government may seek central assistance in the form of partial support; this was done by the Karnataka state government in June 2018 when it was ascertained that the estimated amount of waiver worked out to Rs. 53,000 crore for loans maintained with nationalized banks and co-operative banks (The Hindu, 2018a). Likewise, Uttar Pradesh sought assistance from the central government when it faced a waiver of small loans equivalent to Rs. 36, 000 crore in 2017, which was not welcomed by the centre on the grounds of adverse debt to GDP ratio and colossal fiscal deficit it would result for the centre (Venu, 2017). Thus, the burden of financing a waiver falls more or less on the state government. The nodal agency — institution responsible for coordinating finance and revenue departments — for a waiver could vary depending upon the remitter of funds to the lending institutions. For the 2008 waiver, RBI was the nodal agency with respect to scheduled commercial banks, urban cooperative banks and local area banks while NABARD was the nodal agency with respect to RRBs and cooperative credit institutions (Reserve Bank of India, 2008). It could be the state agricultural department or any other body (as may be decided from time to time) if the waiver is funded by the state government.

Process

The process of steering a loan waiver — nation-wide or state-wide — has been varying each time it has been launched for a definite time period. Waivers are frequently selective — only certain types of loans, particular categories of farmers, specific loan purposes and restricted loan sources may be eligible. For instance, in 2008, direct agricultural loans, short term production loans and investment loans were waived for marginal and small farmers; other farmers were given debt relief through a 25 per cent rebate of the 'eligible amount' (Reserve Bank of India, 2008). In 2017, Maharashtra introduced a conditional loan waiver of up to Rs. 1.5 lakhs for farmers in the state; those, who had their crop loan restructured during the period 2012 to 2016 and were still debtors as on June 30, 2016, were extended incentives up to 25 per cent of the crop loan or Rs 25,000, whichever is less (The Indian Express, 2017). In the same year, Uttar Pradesh announced a waiver of farm loans up to Rs. 1 lakh by lending institutions as on or before March 31, 2016 (The Economic Times, 2017). In July 2018, Karnataka announced a waiver with a ceiling of Rs. 2 lakh for all defaulted crop loans offered up to December 31, 2017; the families of government officials and the cooperative sector, farmers who had paid income-tax for the previous three years were kept outside the ambit of the loan waiver; the government committed to repay Rs. 25,000 or the entire loan amount, whichever is lower, to all farmers who had repaid the loan, as a boost for credible borrowers who had met their debt obligations in time (The Hindu, 2018b). There was also provision for farmers to avail fresh loans through waiving of the arrears form the defaulting account. Thus, the process of execution of a waiver has been contingent upon the need of farmers and the prevailing agrarian situation in the country or each of the states announcing a waiver.

Learning

There are important lessons to learn about the macroeconomic and financial ramifications of farm waivers, their lasting impact on the economy, the probable distortions that they could expose public policies with, and the final incidence of the financial obligation. A few of these are listed as follows:

1. Farm debt waiver has significant ramifications for lending institutions and has systemic consequences. The instant impact is manifested on their balance sheets as a result of time lag in the arrival of

reimbursement from the government. This squeezes the lending capacity of financial institutions, deteriorates their asset quality, pushes up the interest rates and crowds out private borrowers (Patel, 2017). While it serves as an ad hoc initiative for farmers' relief, it ominously adds to the fiscal burden of states and adversely influences their finances in the intermediate term (Prabhu, 2017), which may be translated into a prolonged impact too (Reserve Bank of India, 2017).

2. Albeit a debt waiver is sliced within the budgetary stipulations, it squanders the expenditures from other important heads within the sector. The agricultural sector, as a whole, is likely to suffer as what could have been otherwise spent for irrigation works, infrastructure, warehousing, cold storage chains, etc. is used to wipe off loans taken in an earlier period. In other words, an increase in revenue expenditure dispels capital expenditure (Reserve Bank of India, 2017).
3. An ideal tax system is progressive in nature and is based on the ability to pay principle. While such a system is operational, the tax payers should also be the ones who receive the benefits of government expenditure (tax-financed spending by the government). However, a farm debt waiver involves transfer of benefits from the tax payers to borrowers as the resources tend to be majorly utilized for the benefit of the latter.
4. Farm debt waiver triggers moral hazard as the farmers make no attempts to repay the loans themselves with the expectation that an imminent waiver from the government would clear their debts, thus ruining the credit culture of the country. It encourages the spirit of wilful default, that has led to gargantuan overdues in all sectors of formal financial institutions, particularly the credit cooperatives, which have the highest outreach and accessibility to the rural population. "The deterioration in the cooperative credit system is, in large measure, due to the conscious state policy of interference in the grant and recovery of loans" (Vaidyanathan, 2008). The expectations of future debt waivers also encourage borrowings for non-productive purposes and adversely impacts agricultural investments (Chakraborty & Gupta, 2017).
5. ADWDRS – 2008 brought forth the most startling limitations of farm debt waiver. "Paying those who were ineligible, depriving those who were eligible, overpaying some beneficiaries and paying less than what was due to others, clearly seem to indicate acts of omission as well as of commission. When such acts are found out to affect almost 22 percent of the sample, it raises serious questions about the robustness of governance of agricultural loans and of the monitoring role performed by the RBI and NABARD" (Upadhyaya, 2013).

Action

Regardless of the considerable amount of subsidised and bankrolled credit disbursements as well as the numerous fiscal stimulants, Indian agriculture is plagued with inherent distortions which make it susceptible to risks and extreme volatility. It has been inherently characterised by inadequate investment, antediluvian irrigation procedures, heavy reliance on monsoons, subdivision and fragmentation of land holdings and obsolete technology. Ineffectual property rights and diminutive primary net worth of farmers add to the constrictions. Subsequently, significant fluctuations in output and prices has been enforcing sizeable losses on farmers and potentially incarcerating them in a cycle of indebtedness with ominous frequency. Therefore, in the absence of organized, synchronized and unrelenting efforts to bring into being rudiments of a virtuous pedal of upliftment, loan waivers occasionally appear as a quick fix to alleviate farmers' misery. Farm loan waivers serve as a provisional solution and involve a moral hazard. Loan waivers extend temporary reprieve to farmers, but there are deliberations and arguments about the enduring efficacy of the measure. Experts and detractors alike call for making agriculture sustainable by lessening inefficiencies, augmenting income, moderating costs and affording protection through premeditated and well-defined insurance schemes. "A sustainable and long-term resolution of our farmer community requires concerted and urgent reforms in the areas of agricultural marketing, pricing, credit and extension systems, and an open trading regime" (Reserve Bank of India, 2017). From a policy viewpoint, it is imperative to deviate from palliatives — debt waiver and debt relief — into a more deep-seated resolution that augments welfare all around. Several components of this ideal approach are recognized – "crop insurance, infrastructure, irrigation, technology-enabled productivity improvements, and, opening up the farm economy to market forces and open trade" (Reserve Bank of India, 2017). The Government's efforts to launch a countrywide marketplace for farm produce by means of National Agriculture Market, the PMFBY, the PMKSY, the PKVY, and the general drive for financial inclusion for all, are critical programmes in this regard. The realization of objectives of these programmes holds the prospect of accomplishing the mission of multiplying farmers' income with time. It is necessary to ensure that their paybacks permeate to all the envisioned recipients.

Performance

Farm debt waivers introduced till date have definitely worked in improving the financial condition of farmers. However, waivers are not here to stay. They are only likely to increase the fiscal burden for the benefactors and tax payers eventually. Therefore, waivers, if introduced should be occasional, conditional and rare initiatives; the nature of such waivers should encourage timely future repayments through incentives for credible borrowers. The major emphasis should remain on the effective implementation of newly launched schemes as well meeting the targets of priority sector lending, an aspect that seems to have been relegated by banks.

SOLUTIONS AND RECOMMENDATIONS

Loan waiver, if introduced for a definite time period, must aim at resuscitating the economic health and vitality of farming. Credit should not be a substitute for other policy interventions. Specifically, facets concerning technology, trade and training in the agricultural sector commands attention. Farmers should be educated for climate-efficient farming, and, from farm to fork, the agricultural sector has to be viewed in a rounded and all-inclusive manner. There is need for agriculture that rests on the canons of environment and economics. Furthermore, there should be efficient and effective land use planning ahead of every crop cycle to avoid excess production and glut resulting in crash in prices and lesser returns that create distress for farmers. Farmers should be educated to cultivate crops that are suitable for the soil and climate in a particular region instead of those which are backed by Minimum Support Prices (MSPs). Contract farming can also be a viable solution for sponsors and cultivators alike, which is largely dependent on the effective legislation in the country for scrupulous execution of contracts.

FUTURE RESEARCH DIRECTIONS

There is paucity of recent research in the field of farm debt waivers in India. Considering the fact that the last couple of years have witnessed numerous farm waivers being introduced by states and an upsurge in demand from farmers in other states, it will be of relevance to examine the impact of these waivers from the standpoint of their costs and benefits and their immediate as well as long-run implication for the government, the general public (particularly the tax payers) as well as the economy as a whole.

CONCLUSION

Eligibility of loan waiver liberates farmers from the clutches of longstanding debts and generates hopes of potential credit availability. As an outcome, the willingness to repay loans automatically dwindles. Frequent debt waivers lead to wilful defaults and evasions. Farmers borrow from banks for consumption use or other unproductive purposes. Farm debt waiver serves as an ephemeral palliative (a temporary reassuring measure) and not as an enduring risk management tool (a permanent remedy to build resilience against a longstanding debt crisis) — for farmers. From a policy viewpoint, it is imperative to deviate from palliatives — debt waiver and debt relief — into a more deep-seated resolution that augments welfare all around. An important policy to reconnoitre is agricultural insurance which has limited adoption by farmers so far.

ACKNOWLEDGMENT

The authors express gratitude to Dr. Abhishek Behl of Indian Institute of Technology Bombay for his guidance and support throughout the completion of this chapter.

REFERENCES

Akhtar, M., & Sushil. (2018). Managing strategic performance in a dynamic business environment: A study of two Indian oil companies. *Global Business and Organizational Excellence*, *37*(5), 47–62. doi:10.1002/joe.21876

Anand, R., Medhavi, S., Soni, V., Malhotra, C., & Banwet, D. (2018). Transforming information security governance in India (A SAP-LAP based case study of security, IT policy and e-governance). *Information and Computer Security*, *26*(1), 58–90. doi:10.1108/ICS-12-2016-0090

Arshinder, K., Kanda, A., & Deshmukh, S. G. (2007). Supply chain coordination issues: An SAP-LAP framework. *Asia Pacific Journal of Marketing and Logistics*, *19*(3), 240–264. doi:10.1108/13555850710772923

Balachandran, R., & Dhal, S. (2018). Relationship between money lenders and farmers. *Agricultural Finance Review, 78*(3), 330–347. doi:10.1108/AFR-07-2016-0066

Chakraborty, T., & Gupta, A. (2017). Hazards of farm loan waivers. Retrieved from http://www.ideasforindia.in/topics/agriculture/hazards-of-farm-loan-waivers.html

Chand, P., Thakkar, J., & Ghosh, K. (2018). Analysis of supply chain complexity drivers for Indian mining equipment manufacturing companies combining SAP-LAP and AHP. *Resources Policy*. doi:10.1016/j.resourpol.2018.08.011

Charan, P. (2012). Supply chain performance issues in an automobile company: A SAP-LAP analysis. *Measuring Business Excellence, 16*(1), 67–86. doi:10.1108/13683041211204680

Chronicle, D. (2016, December 12). *Rural indebtedness at 31.4 per cent, Rs 1.03 lakhs per household: NSS*. Retrieved from https://www.deccanchronicle.com/business/in-other-news/121216/rural-indebtedness-at-314-per-cent-rs-103-lakhs-per-household-nss-survey.html

Desai, S. (2017). India's Farm Loan Waiver Crisis [Blog]. Retrieved from https://www.frbsf.org/banking/asia-program/pacific-exchange-blog/indias-farm-loan-waiver-crisis/

Expert Group on Agricultural Indebtedness. (2007). *Report of the Expert Group on Agricultural Indebtedness*. New Delhi: Government of India.

Farm, L. W.-O. T. (1990, July 7). Article. *Economic and Political Weekly, 25*(27), 1428.

FM on whys and hows of farm loan waiver. (2008). Retrieved from http://www.rediff.com/money/2008/may/24spec.htm

Garg, A., & Deshmukh, S. (2010). Engineering support issues for flexibility in maintenance. *Asia Pacific Journal of Marketing and Logistics, 22*(2), 247–270. doi:10.1108/13555851011026980

Giri, A., & Sinha, S. (2018). Devinder Sharma on India's Agriculture Crisis. *The Diplomat*. Retrieved from https://thediplomat.com/2018/06/devinder-sharma-on-indias-agriculture-crisis/

Gupta, M., & Shri, C. (2018). Developing a Conceptual Framework for Performance Evaluation of Corrugated Packaging Firms in India. *Journal of Packaging Technology and Research, 2*(1), 45–60. doi:10.100741783-018-0028-3

Himanshu. (2016, April 16). Rural Push in Budget 2016–17: Rhetoric versus Reality. *Economic and Political Weekly, 51*(16), 36-38. Retrieved from https://www.epw.in/journal/2016/16/budget-2016%E2%80%9317/rural-push-budget-2016-17.html

Hukeri, P., & Prasanth, V. (2008). The Loan Waiver Scheme. *Economic and Political Weekly, 43*(11), 28–34.

Iyengar, V., Behl, A., Pillai, S., & Londhe, B. (2016). Analysis of Palliative Care Process through SAP-LAP Inquiry: Case Study on Palliative Care and Training Centre. *Global Journal of Flexible Systems Management, 17*(4), 403–416. doi:10.100740171-016-0137-1

Jain, B. (2017, October 18). Maharashtra: Farmers rejoice as govt rolls out loan waiver. *The Times of India*. Retrieved from https://timesofindia.indiatimes.com/city/mumbai/loan-waiver-begins-our-diwalis-been-made/articleshow/61137159.cms

Jain, R. C. A., & Parshad, M. (2006). *Report of the working group on risk management in agriculture for the eleventh five-year plan (2007-2012)*. New Delhi, India: Government of India Planning Commission. Retrieved from http://planningcommission.nic.in/aboutus/committee/wrkgrp11/wg11_risk.pdf

John, L., & Ramesh, A. (2012). Humanitarian supply chain management in India: A SAP-LAP framework. *Journal of Advances in Management Research*, *9*(2), 217–235. doi:10.1108/09727981211271968

Joshi, S. (2008, March 5). Debt Relief and Waiver Scheme – Effective only if it is total. *The Hindu Business Line*. Retrieved from https://www.thehindubusinessline.com/todays-paper/tp-opinion/Debt-Relief-and-Waiver-Scheme-mdash-Effective-only-if-it-is-total/article20124871.ece

Kanz, M. (2012). *What does debt relief do for development? evidence from India's bailout program for highly-indebted rural households*. The World Bank. Retrieved from http://documents.worldbank.org/curated/en/589181468044056902/pdf/wps6258.pdf

Kumar, A., & Bathla, S. (2017, November 14). Loan waiver is not the solution. *The Hindu*. Retrieved from https://www.thehindu.com/opinion/op-ed/loan-waiver-is-not-the-solution/article20394319.ece

Kumar, P., Haleem, A., Qamar, F., & Khan, U. (2018). Analysis of maiden modal shift in coal transportation supply chain using SAP-LAP technique. *International Journal of Logistics Systems and Management*, *30*(4), 458. doi:10.1504/IJLSM.2018.093585

Mangla, S., Kumar, P., & Barua, M. (2014). A Flexible Decision Framework for Building Risk Mitigation Strategies in Green Supply Chain Using SAP–LAP and IRP Approaches. *Global Journal of Flexible Systems Management*, *15*(3), 203–218. doi:10.100740171-014-0067-8

Ministry of Agriculture & Farmers Welfare. (2018, July 24). *Waiving off Agricultural loan*. Retrieved from Press Information Bureau: http://pib.nic.in/newsite/PrintRelease.aspx?relid=180924

Ministry of Finance, Government of India. (2007). *Report of the Expert Group on Agricultural Indebtedness*. Retrieved from http://www.igidr.ac.in/pdf/publication/PP-059.pdf

Nagaraj, K., Sainath, P., Rukmani, R., & Gopinath, R. (2014). Farmers' suicides in India: Magnitudes, trends, and spatial patterns, 1997–2012. *Review of Agrarian Studies*, *4*(2), 53–83.

National Sample Survey Office, Government of India. (2013). *Household Indebtedness in India*. Retrieved from http://mospi.nic.in/sites/default/files/publication_reports/nss_577.pdf

No Panacea for Agrarian Distress. (2017). *Economic and Political Weekly*, *52*(15). Retrieved from https://www.epw.in/journal/2017/15/editorials/no-panacea-agrarian-distress.html

Patel. (2017). *Seminar on Agricultural Debt Waiver – Efficacy and Limitations*. Reserve Bank of India. Retrieved from https://www.rbi.org.in/SCRIPTS/BS_SpeechesView.aspx?Id=1045

Prabhu, N. (2017, June 18). RBI sounds the alarm on farm loan waivers. The Hindu. Retrieved from https://www.thehindu.com/news/cities/bangalore/rbi-sounds-the-alarm-on-farm-loan-waivers/article19099356.ece

Pramod, V., & Banwet, D. (2010). System modelling of telecom service sector supply chain: A SAP-LAP analysis. *International Journal of Business Excellence*, *3*(1), 38. doi:10.1504/IJBEX.2010.029486

Ramkumar, R. (2017). *Lessons from Agricultural Debt Waiver and Debt Relief Scheme of 2008.* Reserve Bank of India. Retrieved from https://rbidocs.rbi.org.in/rdocs/content/pdfs/Dr.%20R.%20Ramakumar_Paper(31082017).pdf

Rath, N. (2008). Implications of the loan waiver for rural credit institutions. *Economic and Political Weekly*, 13–16.

Ravi, V., & Shankar, R. (2006). Reverse logistics operations in paper industry: A case study. *Journal of Advances in Management Research*, *3*(2), 88–94. doi:10.1108/97279810680001248

Reserve Bank of India. (2008). *Index to RBI circulars – Agricultural Debt Waiver and Debt Relief Scheme 2008*. Retrieved from https://www.rbi.org.in/scripts/BS_CircularIndexDisplay.aspx?Id=4190

Reserve Bank of India. (2015). *Master circular-priority sector lending-targets and classification.* Retrieved from https://rbi.org.in/scripts/bs_viewmascirculardetails.aspx?id=9857

Reserve Bank of India. (2017). *Seminar on Agricultural Debt Waiver – Efficacy and Limitations.* Retrieved from https://rbi.org.in/Scripts/BS_PressReleaseDisplay.aspx?prid=41530

Saha, D. (2017, July 2). Farmer suicides: 70% of India's farm families spend more than they earn. *Hindustan Times*. Retrieved from https://www.hindustantimes.com/india-news/farmer-suicides-70-of-indias-farm-families-spend-more-than-they-earn/story-GKLoObJeDtbH2Z22csJsxK.html

Sainath, P. (2018, April 13). In India, Farmers Face a Terrifying Crisis. *The New York Times*. Retrieved from https://www.nytimes.com/2018/04/13/opinion/india-farmers-crisis.html

Siva, M. (2017, April 10). All you wanted to know about farm loan waivers. *The Hindu Businessline.* Retrieved from https://www.thehindubusinessline.com/opinion/columns/slate/all-you-wanted-to-know-about-farm-loan-waivers/article21957423.ece1

Solanki, A. (2018, January 25). Anatomy of Agricultural Debt Waivers in India. Vivekananda International Foundation. Retrieved from https://www.vifindia.org/article/2018/january/25/anatomy-of-agricultural-debt-waivers-in-india

Sunder, S. (2018, January 29). India economic survey 2018: Farmers gain as agriculture mechanisation speeds up, but more R&D needed. *Financial Express*. Retrieved from https://www.financialexpress.com/budget/india-economic-survey-2018-for-farmers-agriculture-gdp-msp/1034266/

Suri, P., & Sushil, N. (2008). Towards a strategy for implementing e-governance applications: A case study of integrated fertilisers management information system based on SAP-LAP framework. *Electronic Government. International Journal (Toronto, Ont.)*, *5*(4), 420. doi:10.1504/eg.2008.019527

Sushil. (2000). SAP-LAP models of inquiry. *Management Decision, 38*(5), 347-353. doi:10.1108/00251740010340526

Sushil. (2009). SAP-LAP Linkages — A Generic Interpretive Framework for Analyzing Managerial Contexts. *Global Journal of Flexible Systems Management, 10*(2), 11-20. doi:10.1007/bf03396558

Swaminathan, M. (2008, March 8). Looking beyond Farmers' Suicides and Loan Waivers. *Mainstream Weekly*. Retrieved from https://www.mainstreamweekly.net/article573.html

Tewari, R. (2016, January 6). Centre increases number of work days under MGNREGA. *The Indian Express*. Retrieved from https://indianexpress.com/article/business/economy/centre-increases-number-of-work-days-under-mgnrega/

The Economic Times. (2017, September 13). *Over 11,000 Uttar Pradesh farmers get waiver for loans of Re 1 to Rs 500.* Retrieved from https://economictimes.indiatimes.com/news/politics-and-nation/over-11000-uttar-pradesh-farmers-get-waiver-for-loans-of-re-1-to-rs-500/articleshow/60496814.cms

The Hindu. (2018a, June 18). *Kumaraswamy seeks 50% Central assistance for farm loan waiver.* Retrieved from https://www.thehindu.com/news/national/karnataka/kumaraswamy-seeks-50-central-assistance-for-farm-loan-waiver/article24187796.ece

The Hindu. (2018b, July 5). *Kumaraswamy announces farm loan waiver in Karnataka Budget.* Retrieved from https://www.thehindu.com/news/national/karnataka/kumaraswamy-announces-farm-loan-waiver-in-karnataka-budget/article24337573.ece

The Indian Express. (2017, June 24). *Maharashtra govt announces Rs 34,000-crore farm loan waiver, to benefit 89 lakh farmers*. Retrieved from https://indianexpress.com/article/india/maharashtra-farm-loan-waiver-devendra-fadnavis-farmers-4719925/

Thirtle, C., Irz, X., Lin, L., McKenzie-Hill, V., & Wiggins, S. (2001). *Relationship between changes in agricultural productivity and the incidence of poverty in developing countries*. Retrieved from https://www.odi.org/sites/odi.org.uk/files/odi-assets/events-documents/4086.pdf

Upadhyaya, H. (2013). Caveat from farm debt waiver scheme. *India Together*. Retrieved from http://www.indiatogether.org/farmers-agriculture

Vaidyanathan, A. (2008, March 6). Farm loan waiver: a closer look and critique. *The Hindu*. Retrieved from http://el.doccentre.info/eldoc1/k40_/06mar08h1.pdf

Venu, M. (2017, April 5). Centre Cannot Avoid Fiscal Responsibility of UP Farm Loan Waiver. *The Wire*. Retrieved from https://thewire.in/agriculture/farm-loan-waiver-central-fisc

ADDITIONAL READING

Gill, A. (2016). Agricultural Credit in Punjab: Have Policy Initiatives Made a Dent in Informal Credit Markets? In *Economic Transformation of a Developing Economy* (pp. 165–182). Singapore: Springer. doi:10.1007/978-981-10-0197-0_8

Hoda, A., & Terway, P. (2015). *Credit policy for agriculture in India: An evaluation. Supporting Indian farms the smart way. Rationalising subsidies and investments for faster, inclusive and sustainable growth* (No. 302). Working Paper. Indian Council for Research on International Economic Relations (ICRIER)

Mehta, D. (2012). Crop Insurance in India. *International Journal of Scientific Research, 2*(1), 13–15. doi:10.15373/22778179/JAN2013/5

Moss, T. (2006). *Will Debt Relief Make a Difference? Impact and Expectations of the Multilateral Debt Relief Initiative*. SSRN Electronic Journal; doi:10.2139srn.983182

Neelima, K. (2018). *Widows of Vidarbha*. New Delhi: Oxford University Press.

Salve, T., & Biradar, J. (2014). An Impact of Government's Agricultural Debt Waiver and Debt Relief (ADWDR) Scheme. *Journal of Commerce and Management Thought, 5*(4), 635. doi:10.5958/0976-478X.2014.00010.X

Sane, R. (2018). Loan Waivers as Fresh Start in Bankruptcy. *IndraStra Global, 4*(3), 5.

Shylendra, H. (1995). Farm Loan Waivers: A Distributional and Impact Analysis of the Agricultural and Rural Debt Relief Scheme, 1990. *Artha Vijnana: Journal of The Gokhale Institute of Politics and Economics, 37*(3), 261. doi:10.21648/arthavij/1995/v37/i3/115977

KEY TERMS AND DEFINITIONS

Average Amount of Debt (AOD): Average amount of cash dues per indebted household as on June 30, 2012, according to National Sample Survey Office, 2013.

Incidence of Indebtedness (IOI): The percentage of indebted households to total households.

Marginal Farmer: Refers to a farmer cultivating agricultural land up to 1 hectare (2.5 acres), as owner or tenant or share cropper (NSSO).

Other Farmer: Is a farmer cultivating, as owner or tenant or share cropper, agricultural land of more than 2 hectares (more than 5 acres).

Small Farmer: A farmer cultivating agricultural land of more than 1 hectare and up to 2 hectares (5 acres), as owner or tenant or share cropper.

Chapter 13
Agricultural Risk Management Through Contract Farming Ventures:
An Exploration of Cross-Country Evidences

Isha Gole
Gokhale Institute of Politics and Economics, India

Neha Sharma
Gokhale Institute of Politics and Economics, India

ABSTRACT

To build an agrarian economy that guarantees sustenance and food security to a vast populace, raw material for its growing industrial base, surpluses for exports, and a just, even-handed, and reasonable rewarding system for the farming community, "commitment-driven" contract farming is undoubtedly a feasible unconventional farming model that offers a reliable and consistent input service to farmers and delivers preferred farm produce to the contracting firms. Contract farming is used as a risk management tool. Facilitation of contract farming requires support in terms of flexibility in legislation, offering effective mechanism to resolve conflicts between contracting parties, having an arbitration body for resolving conflicts and providing quality checking facilities. Proper design of the contract is critical in making contract farming more successful. Education and training in connection with contract farming should be provided extensively to companies and other government agencies. Governments should endeavor to encourage contract farming by means of appropriate legislation and facilitation, through a demand-driven approach. The chapter aims to examine contract farming as a risk mitigation tool for farmers in general and small farmers in particular by considering diverse cases of successes/failures in developed and developing countries. While doing so, the authors have also delved into the historical evolution of contract farming, types of contracts, benefits, and apprehensions of the contracting parties, and they offer solutions to make contract farming successful.

DOI: 10.4018/978-1-5225-7208-4.ch013

INTRODUCTION

Agriculture, by its very nature, is prone to a variety of risks, viz., yield risk, market risk, financial risk, institutional risk, etc. With the existence of such perils, farmers are known to evolve different methodologies to mitigate the looming risks. Contract farming – an arrangement that connects producers of farm output with the buyers of such output (companies and/or governments) – has been prevalent in numerous countries across the globe and has been serving as an important risk mitigating strategy for the aggrieved farmers. Such an arrangement ensures a 'mutual benefit' to all parties taking part in the transaction; the farmers enjoy the benefits of an assured buyer and stable prices for their produce, while the buyers, often referred to as sponsors or contractors, are assured of timely produce that serves as an essential input to the products they manufacture. Contract farming not only acts as a mechanism to overcome institutional and market failures for the farmers, but also provides the farmers with the access to a diverse range of managerial, technical and extension services that otherwise may be unobtainable. The sponsors, on the other hand, have access to quality output. For instance, countries like India have enormous population pressures and limited land resources which makes farming estates or the act of purchasing land at economically viable options, unattractive. Corporate farming allows the conglomerates to enter the market with tracts of land, provided either by the government or small farmers, by virtue of lucrative forward agreements entered into by the parties to the contract. The contracting firms get the quantity and quality of supply needed to run for the purpose of their respective business operations, and the farmers on the other hand get an assured market at a predetermined price.

Although this arrangement seems sound and unassailable, it is likely to succeed only when there is a strong sense of commitment on the part of every party involved in the contract. Since the farmer is obliged to cultivate the crop required by the sponsor according to the latter's quality specifications, any shortfall on the part of the farmer may lead to non-compliance of contractual obligations by the sponsor. This poses further risks as the farmer will now be required to look for a new market for the produce. The sponsor, on the other hand, too may face the threat of sale of produce by farmers to a third party, outside the conditions of a contract. Extra-contractual sales are always possible and are not easily controlled when an alternative market exists.

A shift from industry dominated small scale farms to large scale farms is observed in developed nations, with strengthened alignment of the production and distribution chain. Structural adjustments, trade liberalization and changing market trends in developing countries are also the key drivers of integration of world markets. Therefore, the farmers from developing nations are getting linked to corporations and consumers of the rich nations. Even though major changes in agricultural food markets take place in the developed nations, the scope of agricultural development seems to be promising in the developing countries, thus giving a huge scope for contract farming (Kirsten and Sartorius, 2002).

BACKGROUND

In many of the developed countries, contract farming arrangements have now become quite common. It is now seen as the primary driver of competition in the market, which ultimately has resulted in creating a deeply coordinated system (Wang, Wang, & Delgado, 2014). With the development in technology, agriculture in developed countries has experienced significant developments in vertical coordination. This shift has led to decline in the spot markets, which are replaced by contracts, strategic alliances, franchisees and joint ventures. There are several factors that have affected the movement of agriculture away from traditional spot markets. Some of them include the advancement in agricultural biotechnology, advancements in information technology, environmental pressures, credit and risk issues, etc. All of these factors, escalate the relative costs incurred in spot market transactions making them economically unviable (Young and Hobbs, 2002). Contract farming also seems to be preferred due to the contractor's (or the contracting party's) willingness to market the farmers' produce collectively, reducing market risk, even if it leads to reduced control of the farmers on their own crops (Prowse, 2012). The ever-increasing consumer demand for better quality and differentiated products has encouraged the distribution system to be more specialized and integrated.

Given its controversial nature, contract farming has turned out to be one of the most debated institutional arrangements for the production as well as marketing of agricultural commodities in the developing nations. According to the World Investment Report (2009), by UNCTAD, 'contract farming activities by Transnational Corporations (hereinafter referred to as TNCs) are spread worldwide, covering over 110 developing and transition economies, spanning a wide range of commodities' (Oya, 2011).

In developing countries, farmers are exposed to different kinds of risks, which include but are not limited to, changing weather conditions, pest and diseases, and imperfect information in predicting product and farm input prices, etc. These factors in turn have a huge influence on the farm produce as well as the production patterns. The fluctuation in prices of the produce, is also being caused due to factors like global warming, natural disasters like flood and drought, which affect prices both for a particular region, as well as in the international market and these changes can be more adversely seen in the rainfed areas of the developing countries. Changing consumer consumption patterns and preferences also add to the risk factors which indirectly affects the demand for agricultural products and cost of production (Aditto, Gan & Nartea, 2014; Singh, 2013).

In recent decades, contract farming has become more popular in developing countries, whereas it has been well established in developed countries. Even though the concept/origin of contract farming in both developed and developing countries is guided on similar grounds, which primarily aims to achieve economic development and reduce risk, there are other benefits derived by developing countries from the concept of contract farming. Due to lack of education, transportation, infrastructure coupled with small scale farms, management and production technologies tend to be inefficient and underdeveloped. Thus, the only way for farmers to earn higher returns and have access to high end markets may be to pair with the agribusiness firms. Engaging in contract farming can help farmers in developing countries to achieve economies of scale, better technological facilities, improved welfare and standard of living. It is a key to help modernise the agricultural sector. However, contract farming has its obvious concerns in developing countries which include food shortage due to over-reliance on cash crops, instability for non-participants in contracts, exploitation from large agribusiness firms, disturbance in traditional relations etc. (Wang, Wang, & Delgado, 2014). Small scale farmers are most affected due to lack of information about production methods and market opportunities. The non-availability of financial credit or collateral also acts as a hurdle which leads them to become risk averse (Minot, 2007).

One of the key reasons of contract farming gaining a lot of interest in the farming community is because it possesses the potential to solve these problems. Trends in developing countries show that there is wide spread prevalence of agriculture and increase in contract farming (Minot, 2007). The growth and expansion of agricultural activities, aligned chained networks, favourable government policies and increased awareness of quality of food and its safety are major driving factors for high value commodities (Bijman, 2008).

History

Contract farming has been a practice since ages and not a new concept. Historically, sharecropping contracts involving farmers and tenants prevailed in the Greek and Chinese agrarian economies, but the initial formal contracts between companies and farmers found their footing in the late nineteenth and the early twentieth century (Prowse, 2012). For example, in Taiwan, the Japanese adopted contract farming tools to produce sugar in 1885. The beginning of the 20th century saw U.S. companies entering into contract farming ventures in Central America. Contracting was used excessively in various food and fiber sectors. In around 1920, the chain food merchandiser A&P had built a national network to procure vegetables and fresh fruits for its outlets from the farmers (USDA, n.d). According to Little & Watts (1994), as cited in Kirsten & Sartorius (2002), the US and Europe witnessed wide use of contracts in the canning business. Furthermore, the European and the North American merchants entered into seed production contracts with farmers from countries like Australia, Hungary, Holland and Canada. After World War II, several firms expanded significantly to procure directly from farms, asserting on quality and timely supply (USDA, n.d).

After being well established in the developed countries, it rapidly spread over Latin America, Asia and Africa due to the high valued crops being exported for higher returns. In Latin America, contract farming got promoted heavily due to its import substitution programmes since 1945, whereas in Africa, contract farming evolved much before. Colonial Africa saw a rise in contracting of fruits and vegetables during the period 1930-50. The following time frame pertaining to the period 1975-85 had 60 schemes operating in 16 countries in Africa. South Africa's contract farming history can be traced back to the early 20th century which includes variety of sharecropping techniques (Kirsten & Sartorius, 2002). The Indonesian government helped promote contract farming through Federal Land Development Agency (FELDA) which turned out to be a successful scheme. Almost 90% of Vietnamese cotton and fresh milk and over 40% of its tea and rice are produced through contract farming. Malaysia too uses contract farming on a wide scale and it is a predominantly state promoted out grower. Similarly, in China contract farming has been getting support from its government since 1990. In 2001, China saw over 18 million hectares under the arrangement of contract farming. In 1960's, India initially produced seeds under contract farming whereas now it has diversified in expanding the concept of contract farming to poultry, potatoes, rice, dairy, etc. The Sub Saharan Africa had full and partial government ownership in contract farming in the late 1980's, where public sector owned the large projects, but recently, most projects are initiated by the private sector. More than 50% of tea and sugar produced in Kenya are contractual followed by coffee and tobacco. Even though tea contract farming is a huge success, small scale farmers face problems in the system of production (von Bülow & SØrensen, 1993).

Small Scale Farmers and Contract Farming

Critics of contract farming argue that agribusiness firms tend to work with smaller number of large-scale farmers rather than huge number of small-scale farmers. This leads to increased income inequality and poverty which can further increase the tensions in the social groups in rural areas. It is because of the advantage of lower transaction costs like technical assistance, negotiation, monitoring of quality and harvest collection that attract firms to large scale farmers. However, apart from the controversies surrounding contract farming, a case can be made in favour of contract farming supporting the fact that it has indeed benefitted the small-scale farmers. In the event of crop failures, the risk of overall supply is lower with small scale farmers as compared to large scale farmers. Enormous sizes of land getting destroyed in pest attacks etc., yield a greater damage than small sized farms. Due to the labour-intensive nature of small-scale farmers, the quality delivered by small scale farmers is more refined. Lower wage rates are a feature of small-scale farming which results in helping the agribusinesses to lower down their costs (Minot, 2007).

Few examples of countries with small-scale contract farmers in developing economies include Indonesia, Mexico and Kenya. In Indonesia, abundant chillies are produced and it is one of the most important crops, of which a quarter of the total national produce is produced by small scale farmers. Earlier being sold in traditional markets, where the agents displayed lack of coordination, chillies have made their way through to the supermarkets creating new opportunities for farmers. These supermarkets provide a platform for intense coordination with the supply chain agents as compared to the traditional markets. The chilli market undergoes huge price fluctuations, thus making contract farming a viable business for both the parties to mitigate the risk of these fluctuations (Sahara & Gyau, 2014). Mexico, on the other hand, has contract farmers producing a wide range of tomatoes. Previously, the United States' agro processors first collaborated with large farmers but eventually contracted with small-scale farmers because it became difficult on the part of the firms to enforce contract with large growers (Minot, 2007). In Kenya, companies such as Kenya Horticultural Exporters, Kevian Ltd, work with other NGOs like Kenya Gatsby Trust, Drumnet, which connect the agribusiness firms to the small-scale farmers and also offer to handle a part of their finances.

Typology of Contracts

In simple terms, contract farming can be defined as, "Agricultural production carried out according to an agreement between farmers and a buyer, which places conditions on the production and marketing of the commodity" (Shepherd, n.d.). Broadly speaking, contracts can be in the form of a verbal agreement or a formal/ informal written document. The former can be exercised in the court of law subject to fulfilment of certain conditions. When contracts are individually negotiated with the farmer, they may be offered a "take it or leave it" contract by the buyer. Sometimes contracts are also formed for a "single sale" purpose which has a specific time period or may rather continue until either party wants to discontinue the contract. The "evergreen" contract is another type which specifies the conditions regarding the quality, quantity and price of the commodity. It may also hold provisions regarding the sale of the product.

Following contracts made by Mighell & Jones (1963) differ according to their objectives and transfer of risks:

1. **Market Specification Contract:** The agreement between contractors and producers occurs during pre-harvest season. Major condition underlying this contract is the quality of the product which may alter production decisions of the farmer. The contractor has right over most of the decisions on the farming assets and activities, thus making the farmer more prone to risk. A market is well established for the farmer by the contractor to reduce uncertainties.
2. **Production Management Contract:** The contractor receives more control over the farming production than market specification contract. Delegation of decision rights is given by farmer to contractor and he/she decides the amount of inputs to be used in what production methods. Here, more risk is borne by the contractor than the producer.

3. **Resource Providing Contract:** As the name suggests, the contractor not only provides a well-established market but also provides inputs, which are in a way a source of credit to the farmers. The cost of these inputs is recovered when farmer produces its crops. It may include the production management contract, but most of the risks here are transferred to the contractor whereas the production decisions are taken by the farmer (Bijman, 2008)

Use of Contracts in Varied Situations

Entering into contracts can benefit the producers in a number of ways. First, it can take care of price volatility by specifying price or method of determining the price. If a fixed price is specified, then price volatility is completely eliminated for the producer. On the other hand, if final price is determined through premiums or deductions on the spot price, then the farmer would face greater price volatility, though his average return will be higher.

Contracting is especially useful in eliminating the placement risks, more so in the case of perishable commodities. It ensures that the buyer will get all or a part of the grower's production. It also helps the growers to avoid the added marketing costs involved in finding the buyer even while the commodity is in saleable condition. When quality standards are defined in the contract, the growers can benefit and be rewarded by adhering to them. The contract can mention premiums/deductions for delivering the agreed quality standards. When third party grading systems are absent, defining the quality attributes are of immense use as otherwise, the farmers might not get rewarded for the high-quality produce.

Another way contracting helps reduce both quality as well as quantity risks is through the transfer of knowledge from buyers to the producers. This knowledge may be regarding various techniques which would improve quality and/or quality of the output. The farmer can further use this know-how in producing non-contracted crops as well.

Figure 1. Major provisions found in agricultural contracts
Source: Eaton and Shephard (2001)

- the duration of the contract
- the quality standards to be applied
- quality control (when, how, who is responsible, who pays)
- the quantity that the farmer is obliged or allowed to deliver
- the cultivation / raising practices required by the contractor
- the timing of delivery
- packaging, transport and other delivery conditions
- price or price determination mechanism (such as fixed prices, flexible prices based on particular (spot) markets, consignment prices, or split prices)
- technical assistance
- procedures for paying farmers and reclaiming credit advances
- insurance
- procedures for dispute resolution

MAIN FOCUS OF THE CHAPTER

To gain more understanding on the subject matter of contract farming, a comparative analysis of developed and developing countries is achieved in the following section. The study initially focuses to find countries which are performing remarkably well in the contract farming business and compare them with countries which need to strengthen their contract farming roots. After researching and finding relevant literature about the developing countries, it is found that Kenya has achieved success and South Africa needs structural changes in the same. On the contrary, developed nations seem to have a strong foundation in contract farming, thus the two most successful countries in contract farming, US and Netherlands, have been analysed.

BRIEF REVIEW OF CONTRACTING IN THE US AGRICULTURAL SECTOR

The US economy has seen a significant decline in the total value added by farms in the last 150 years. The sector did see an expansion but was over shone by an even greater rate of growth of the economy as a whole.

According to Macdonald and Korb (2011), around 40% of the total agricultural production in USA accounted to formal contracts. Farmers in the US are now placing heavier reliance on contract farming to mitigate their risks. From 1991 to 2007, the contractual production had increased by about 10 percentage points. Also, the use of many of the inputs (including labour and land) has reduced or is constant. This is due to the technological innovations in agriculture. The increased use of chemicals and novel production techniques require the farmers to be especially aware and educated about the use of technology to manage their expanded operations. So, this makes the role of the corporates even more important for (a) providing requisite knowledge and inputs and, (b) spreading risks over a larger number of stakeholders. In USA, the Federal Contract Management programs also help manage the risks. The farms in the US use several types of contractual arrangements that tie them with numerous businesses. They have options for marketing contracts or price contracts to clear up their stocks. Many of the corporates also rent equipment/land to the farmers so that they don't face issues with tied up capital (O'Donoghue et al., 2011).

Contract Designs of Selected Crops

In crop production, marketing contracts used to be more popular than production contracts. According to Macdonald et al. (2004), in 2001, production contracts accounted for only 2.8% of the total crop output whereas marketing contracts constituted 23.4% value of the total crop output.

As of 2008, the use of contracts was more prevalent in livestock (60%) as compared to crops (40%). Contracts in USA are most widely used in poultry production (90%) and hog production (68%). In crops, 90% sugar beet and tobacco were produced under contracts. At the same time, contracts were not used as much for corn, soybeans and wheat. Nevertheless, the application of contracts in these crops indeed rose by at least 10 percentage points during the period of 2001-2008. The latter three commodities are generally produced under marketing contracts by large farmers who focus more on the delivery of their produce along with securing themselves from price risks and managing storage options (Macdonald and Korb 2011).

Tobacco is one of the major crops cultivated in the USA, and it is where all the leading companies have opted for contracts. This is because cigarettes need a set blend of tobacco and contracting out the production enables the companies to procure their desired quantity and quality of several varieties. The US has strict regulations on the quality of the cigarettes. Accordingly, marketing contracts entail several incentives for the farmers to produce better quality crops like greater payment for higher quality and lower return (which acts as a hindrance) for lower quality crops. Since spot markets do not exhibit the true value of quality, the farmers had lesser incentives to produce good quality leaves (Macdonald et al., 2004).

The experience with sugar beet production provides another important insight into the importance of organizational structures to form suitable contract design. The return to farmers on sugar beet depends on the amount of sugar extracted from it. According to Balbach (1998), as cited in Macdonald et al. (2004), if cooperatives owned the processers they had an incentive to improve the quality of the beet and have the terms in their favour to create profits, whereas if another investor owned the processor, there was a substantial drawback to the farmers.

It becomes inevitable for tomato growers to rely on contracts as diverse characteristics are required for varied processed products of the fruit, for example, soup products, sauce, paste, etc. In the contracts for tomato, effectual incentives for quality are achieved by the way of linking the contracts with an assurance from an external agency like the Processing Tomato Advisory Board (Macdonald et al., 2004).

Contracts have most widely been used for the production of identity-preserved corn because they take plenty of time and effort to produce and sell; at times they have lower yield. The higher cost incurred to produce corn increases the risks attached to spot markets. Contracts generally come with a premium to the farmers, but in the cases of low yield, they fail to cover up the costs of production (Macdonald et al., 2004).

Expansion of Contracting During 2005-08

The use of contractual arrangements in soybean, wheat and corn, US's most produced field crops, accelerated sharply in the years starting from 2005 to 2008. This can be attributed to the growing risk in the spot markets due to high fluctuations in prices during the same period. Therefore, in 2008, 37% of farms adopted contracting vis-à-vis 22% in 2005.

Evaluation

The farmers' choice of entering into contracts also depends on the extent of control and regulation that the government exercises over a commodity. For example, when Federal marketing programs existed, price fluctuations in tobacco and peanuts were minimized. Unfortunately, since those policies were recalled by the government in 1998, the exposure of farmers in the spot market rose substantially and hence they turned to contracts to seek relief. The producers wanted marketing contracts as they allowed the prices to be in accordance with quality. Accordingly, the farmers preferred contracts when they found the spot markets to be inefficient and the producers view contracts as a way to urge the farmers to supply the right quality at the right time.

Even with all of the benefits, as compared to meat products, the share of contract farming for field crops like soybean, cotton, corn and rice is still a lot less. It has been observed that the share of production under contracts in total agricultural output is greater than the total percentage of farms that actually produce under contracts. This implies that the small number of farms who actually use contracts use them sizably. So, it is the larger farms that prefer to take up farming on contractual basis than their smaller counterparts.

Of those who engage in contracting, many tend to use contracts as a risk diversifying tool. Therefore, they keep a part of their crops for sales under contract and the other part for the spot market. Many a times, during low production, the share reserved for spot market can also be used to fulfil contract obligations. An exception to this is cotton and rice. Those producers who utilized marketing contracts mostly sold off their cotton by means of contracts. It has also been observed that the farms operating under contracts have a higher debt to net worth ratio as compared to those operating independently.

The study conducted by Rehber (2000) indicates the contents of contracts in vegetables production in the US. Most of the contracts provided only seeds and in some cases provision of services like harvesting. Often, the contractors also prescribe the specific kind of chemicals to be used, or they can provide chemical inputs of their own. Sometimes, the contents of the contracts are immensely detailed and strict. Prices are generally fixed and as mentioned before, the producers can get premiums or discounts based on the quality of the vegetables. There are many conditions which are implicitly understood among the parties and the contractor can assist in the production process if there is continuous contact between the two parties.

Issues

According to Young and Hobbs (2000) despite the positive aspects of contracting in agriculture, there can be serious cases of large corporates exploiting small and individual farmers and make prices advantageous for themselves. As a consequence of the same, the farmers collaborated and formed associations (similar to labour unions) for collective bargaining.

Another concern towards contract farming was the legal disputes regarding the agreement. There had been a lack of transparency concerning the terms of the contract. Many a times, the farmers felt cheated with the complicated and unfair terms in the contract. Evaluation of performance, on which the premiums were dependent, was also a matter of question.

The large corporations are able to use the contracts in their favour. For example, Monsanto in its contracts acknowledges that the seed material can be drifted away to other crops, but takes no responsibility of such contamination. On the other hand, it can easily take actions against farmers if there seems to be any kind of contamination in the fields, even if the contamination is because of the company's own seeds. Farmers don't have adequate resources to challenge such corporations in the court. In some contracts, it is specified that the farmers do not have the title of the crops. But even though these farmers provide only services, the risk factor is imposed on them by the companies (CASFS, n.d.).

The farmers are further vulnerable to investment risks. Some of the short-term contracts require huge investments from the grower's part. And these may have delayed paybacks. So, in case the company refuses to honour the contracts on certain grounds (like the Monsanto case), the farmers can fall into serious indebtedness. Some of the contracts containing confidentiality clauses cause potential harm to the farmers by the way of asymmetry of information. The farmers are not able to approach any third party for help in order to understand or clear the doubts regarding the terms, for the sole reason of maintaining confidentiality. The contractors tend to put the farmers liable for any environmental externality that might occur, even when both the parties are equally liable for any damage to the environment. And the most unsafe ones are those where farmers are obliged to sign the arbitration clause which defines the contract as non-negotiable. This completely blocks the farmers' from taking any recourse to the courts of law in the event of any mishap (Pultrone, 2012).

BRIEF REVIEW OF CONTRACTING IN THE NETHERLANDS

The Netherlands is one of the top exporters of vegetables in the world, second only to the US. A quarter of the vegetables exported from Europe come from the Netherlands. Extensive investment is made in the research and development for agriculture and agribusiness. The country has always had an upper hand in the production and supply chains (Agriculture and food, n.d.). The growers and farmers are complete partners in the agricultural production chains. Overall, the Netherlands exports around 64 billion Euros worth of commodities which include fruits, flowers, dairy, meat products and vegetables. (Agriculture, n.d.). In 2015, the most important exports were fruits, vegetables and potatoes accounting for about 11.1 billion euros in value.

Before the 1990s, for several decades, the cooperatives sold their fruits and vegetables through clock auctions. The market was almost completely competitive and the mechanism provided adequate transparency in pricing. But the '90s saw a shift in the preferences of suppliers from the spot markets to contracting and production of a variety of products. Auctioning was not preferred by the large retailers. It did not let them customize the products, enter into long term contracts with the suppliers (growers and farmers), and there was absence of a centralized purchasing facility. So finally, the cooperatives substantially reduced the auctioning system and introduced bilateral contracting which was applicable for both short term and medium-term contracts. Auctioning has not completely lost its value though (Bijman and Gijselinckx, 2012), it is still used in the trade of potted plants and flowers; however, fruits and vegetables are now sold under contracts to the wholesalers and retailers and prices are determined based on the contracts (Meulenberg and Viaene, 1993). The use of contracts as risk management tools in horticulture is significantly less (only 10%). But in the sector itself, vegetables are contracted more as compared to flowers (Asseldonk and Meer, 2016).

Evaluation

According to a study conducted by Asseldonk and Meer (2016), the arable crop farming in the Netherlands consists of diversified crops like varied kinds of potatoes, seed onions, barley, sugar beet and wheat. Potato is the primary cash crop and it was found that ware potatoes are most prone to price volatilities. Therefore, about 50% of the farmers have adopted some kind of price contract. According to Vaals and Rijske (2001), as cited by Smit et al. (2008), the potato market is fairly open in nature, i.e. entry is almost free. So, a large number of growers are attracted to potato farming. Potential imports of potato would also increase the supply, leading to a downward pressure in prices. So, in order to be certain of realizing a given price, the farmers engage into contracts. Another argument behind increased contracting for potato production is that the market has numerous sellers and oversupply of the crop. At the same time, buyers for the crop are consolidated. According to Smit et al. (2008) there were only five potato processors in the country for French fries, who further sold them to different retailers and restaurants. Around 75-90% of potatoes used for processing were sold under contracts. With growing demand from consumers with respect to certain types of products (example, organic farming), the processors require very specific types of seeds to produce the desired variety. But since specialized seeds are licensed and expensive, independent farms tend to use cheaper varieties. In such cases, the processors have no option other than to engage the farmers into a contract. It is indeed useful for both the parties as the farmer can be certain about the sale of his produce and the processor gets the quality which he desires.

The crop farms which utilized contracts were, on an average, 25% larger as compared to those which did not. Although the level of protection depends on the type of contract and other hedging options, still the volatility in prices was far lesser than the non-contracted farms.

Apart from price and quantity considerations, the contracts may also involve terms regarding logistics, packaging and peak supply. This is done to ensure transparency in supply chain, better product quality and accessibility. The interdependence of the suppliers, processors and supermarket chains has consistently been increasing. Such deep arrangements imply that a customer/ company cannot easily change its supplier with any random producer (Bunte et al., 2009).

In the Netherlands, the prices for different commodities are set differently. For potatoes, vegetables and fruits, the prices may be set weekly, daily or on a monthly basis. Price contracts are also set based on a single harvesting season too. It is a general consensus that a fixed price contract is pretty risky. The crops may be overpaid or underpaid depending on the market conditions.

Issues

Mostly, the negotiating position of the suppliers is weak in the contract. This is because the companies choose suppliers based on the prevailing market conditions. And since there is presence of oversupply and excess capacity, the suppliers compete among themselves to grab the contract. The companies try to fully exploit this competition to secure low cost contracts (Bunte et al., 2009).

In case the producers own a license to any new variety, the negotiating power reverses. Producers have a better say in price terms. The common threat used by the producers (or suppliers) to get a better price is the cancellation of delivery (or non-acceptance of the product). But such threats are realized very occasionally and disputes are generally resolved through mutual understanding and dialogue (Bunte et al., 2009).

Production contracts are also popular because they provide easy access to capital. At the same time, it also involves risks as it might impose several unanticipated requirements from the contractors or companies (Meuwissen et al).

BRIEF REVIEW OF CONTRACTING IN KENYA

The early seeds of contract farming in the Kenyan state were sown by the plantation agriculture in sisal, tea and coffee, which were produced for the purpose of exports. Kenya also included large scale ranches and mixed farms. However, this system had large drawbacks. The modes of production used in the mixed farms proved to be highly inefficient as they were largely dependent from support from the then colonial administration. This system survived till the peasant revolt of 'Mau Mau' in 1951, which was followed by the imposition of emergency during the same period. The colonial administration embarked on a series of reforms after realising that there is a need for a structural change to modernise the system. The Swynnerton Plan was thus designed to specifically create a structural base for capitalistic agricultural development in the country. The colonial administration went through the task in three ways:

1. Land tenure was granted individually to smallholders and cash crop and export production were permitted;
2. Permanent cash crops such as tea, coffee and hybrid maize appeared and substituted the local variety; and
3. Exotic cattle were introduced (Busch-Hansen and Marcussen, 1982).

These reformist measures led to the rapid development in the tea, coffee and pyrethrum production for the purpose of exports along with the dairy production in the domestic market. While there was rapid development in the volume of production of certain crops, it was accompanied with the technological innovations at a larger scale. Rather, it was due to the extension of smallholder land under cash crops, accompanied by family labour. Their share of production largely increased from around a quarter of marketed agricultural production at the time of Kenyan Independence in 1963 to nearly half of the total marketed commodities by the mid-1970s. This is the point when the existing system reached its tipping point. The utilisation of family labour had also reached its limits. As a result of the severe restrictions on the subdivision of the large scale, there was little room for small land holder's expansion. The desire of the Kenyan government to improve the educational status of the country lead to the onset of the scheme which directed towards free primary education. This lead to the youth of the country taking part in the educational system, leading to a boom in white collar job market (Busch-Hansen and Marcussen, 1982).

Another reason for the stagnation of the peasant commodity production was the low rate of return on cash income. It was a tendency of the farmers to spend on consumption goods rather on agricultural production, which set severe limitations on the possibilities of expanded production within the existing system and fuelled the Kenyan agricultural crisis in the mid-seventies.

The Road Towards Contract Farming

The main objectives of the Kenyan government, faced by an imminent agricultural crisis, were clear-

1. Expand the horizon of agricultural production to gain foreign currency, which can be further used to reinvest into industrial development;
2. Reduce starvation and feed the urban population; and
3. To enlarge farm development so as to absorb a growing population (as the stake of population employed in industrial and service sectors was still static).

This is the point where the development strategy adopted tilted towards the most obvious solution: raising the productivity of smallholdings. Agri-business firms, industries and contract farming play a crucial role in this solution (von Bülow & Sorensen, 1993).

Issues

To promote the cash crop production among the smallholders, a Special Crop Development Authority was established in 1960. This organisation greatly dealt with the production of tea, it was subsequently retitled into the Kenya Tea Development Authority (hereinafter referred to as 'KTDA') in 1964.

The main objective of this organisation after its establishment was to break the monopoly of the large-scale plantations, owned by the multi-national corporations such as Brooke Bond and James

Finlay. KTDA, a parastatal organisation, vowed to dismantle this monopoly by promoting smallholder tea production on a contract basis. The assistance of the World Bank, the technical knowledge provided by the multi-national tea producers along with the Commonwealth Development Corporation in Kenya greatly increased the small-holder tea production. This model also spiralled into the production of other crops including tobacco and sugar (which adopted contract farming systems in 1973).

Meanwhile, the rising tea and coffee prices coincided with the increased tea production in Kenya. As a result, nearly 40 per cent of the total tea production in Kenya was produced by the smallholders on contract with KTDA by the 1980's. Similarly, approximately 75-80 per cent of sugar was produced on contract by smallholders. Kenyan tea and sugar production became the most sought-after and important backdrops of the contract farming systems which illustrated the success of agri-business, agro-industrial production and contract farming in Kenya (Busch-Hansen and Marcussen, 1982).

Another successful aspect in the context of contract farming in Kenya was the production of tobacco. In 1974, there was an integration provided by an MNC located in Kenya - the British American Tobacco (Kenya) Ltd. The BAT (K) in partnership with the Ministry of Agriculture, initiated a major leaf development programme in Kenya. By 1983, around 9 years after the birth of the partnership, 10,000 contract farmers in Kenya were producing 6.3 million kgs of leaf tobacco. At that point, it made Kenya self-sufficient in tobacco production, and also enabled Kenya to export small quantities of tea which was produced in the country. This not only encouraged in recruiting farmers to the schemes but also saved the Kenyan Government millions in foreign exchange. According to the *Weekly Review,* around 251 million Kenya Shillings were saved in the period 1980-1983 and nearly 588 million were raised in excise duty and corporate taxes when the fruits of contract farming first began taking fruit (Currie and Ray, 1987).

As a result of the success enjoyed by contract farming in tea and tobacco production, various other sectors such as poultry industries were also taken into purview. This demonstrated how contract farming, transformed Kenya, and turned the tides when the nation was rattling from a severe agricultural crisis.

BRIEF REVIEW OF CONTRACTING IN SOUTH AFRICA

The post-apartheid political landscape in South Africa paved way for a change in the policy relating to agriculture and the environment. Many policy documents in the 1990's showed how the apartheid practices were responsible for the degradation of the rural environments. There was sanguineness about the new culture of democracy in the country that will lead to the reformulation of the environmental policies and the development of a more vibrant and environmental conscious agricultural process (Mather, 1996). This led the young South African democracy to experiment with the concept of contract farming, which at that time had shown its instances of success in nations such as Kenya.

Dakadaka Community Irrigation Project: The Onset of Contract Farming in South Africa

The first step towards the direction of contract farming came in the form of the Dakadaka Community Irrigation Project in the Umvoti valley in 1994. The project was conducted in an area of irrigated sugarcane land just after the 1994 elections, and used contract farming measures as its backdrop, which at the time was hailed as a success by both: the company which operated it and the small famers. However, upon close inspection by researchers like Michael Watts, a geographer, and Peter Little, an anthropologist, cracks began opening up (Porter & Howard, 1997).

Most of the contract farming schemes incorporated some aspect of state ownership or management, whereas there was hardly any African nation where the element of State ownership is not present. With the Dakadaka Community Irrigation Project being South Africa's first contract farming initiative, it was expected this feature would become common there as well. However, it was found by Watts that there was a gross mishandling of the local farmers by the large corporation and there were several problems associated with the project, from the land being appropriated from the local farmers and the resettled farmers receiving inadequate compensation to water ownership issues. Although the famers owned the irrigation system, the water was less likely in their hands, with the mill employing the pump attendants and supervising the water to the farmer's plots. In drought periods, the farmers were given dates as to when they could irrigate. Contract farming works on the underlying principle that contract famers do not rely completely on the company and there is the presence of alternate production possibilities. But the dependence on sugarcane as the only source of production for farmers at Dakadaka was identified as another problem. There had been instances of gender biasness on the part of the company, where the company had stated that the 'expert' farmers would be male (Porter & Howard, 1997).

While it is not correct to state that there were no positive aspects of the Dakadaka Community Irrigation Project, it is incorrect to say that the project was a complete success with major issues being ignored by the South African government in the review of the project.

Issues

There are examples of how countries across the globe have been successful with contract farming as a concept. The instances of success pertaining to it include (i) Brazil, where 75 per cent of poultry and 35 per cent of soya bean are sourced through the means of contract farming; (ii) Kenya, where 60 per cent of tea and sugar and nearly all of cut flower exports are through this method; (iii) Vietnam, where 90 per cent of cotton and fresh milk, 50 per cent of tea and 40 per cent of rice are contract farming sourced; (iv) Zambia, where a staggering 100 per cent of cotton and paprika results as a direct result of contract farming; (v) Mozambique, where most of the cotton and tobacco production is a direct result of contract farming (Oya, 2011).

With these examples of successful advents of contract farming, there are bound to be some failures. The direct contributor behind the low success of South Africa in contract farming has been due to the developed capital agriculture for plantation crops, where the introduction of contract farming schemes does alter the dominance of non-contract farming schemes in large-scale agriculture. As in the case of Transvaal sugar company in South Africa, where the smallholding group including a total of 1000 farmers is only able to supply 10-20 per cent. Similarly, when it comes to South African sugarcane production, the failure of smallholders and the dependence of South Africa on large scale growers is more evident as nearly 70 per cent of sugarcane production is accounted for by only 3 per cent of the large-scale growers in the country (OMR – Observatório do Meio Rural).

The production of horticulture products in South Africa presents a similar story. Today, the dynamic exports of fresh fruits and vegetables remain dominated by the large-scale growers and only a marginal share comes from the smaller contract farming schemes. According to a study conducted by the Food and Agriculture Organisation (FAO), an arm of the United Nations, the vast majority of the supplies came from agribusiness' own estates or from large scale contract growers, with only a small share being sourced from small-scale out growers (OMR – Observatório do Meio Rural).

Thus, the example of Dakadaka Community Irrigation Project highlights how the beginning of contract farming policies was marred by various potential threats which were not properly addressed by the South African authorities. Similarly, the presence of the developed capital agriculture and for plantation crops has been one of the key factors behind the country lagging behind in the contract farming measures.

RISKS INVOLVED IN CONTRACTING

From the above discussion, one can easily understand that while contracting is beneficial for the farmers as well as buyers, it comes with its own set of risks too. A farmer loses his flexibility in exploiting unforeseen opportunities. When contracts follow fixed price system, the growers may lose the potential gains from price spikes in the spot market. However, even more important considerations are those involving the interaction between production risks and the agricultural contract. It might happen that the production practices laid out in the contract would result in variable output or lesser output. This may lead to a greater variability in revenues as the farmer may not be able to fulfil the required delivery quota. He may have to purchase additional output from the spot market to complete the delivery. Further, in case of excess output, the buyer isn't obliged to purchase any quantity more than that mentioned in the contract. This leads to placement risk.

Another category is the relationship risk. This happens when the buyer may not pay timely leading to increased costs for the growers. So, if the grower wants to cease his deliveries, he cannot do so as the previous payments are still left to be received. An extreme case is that the buyer may go bankrupt. In this case, the farmer will have to search for another buyer for the output which was produced according to the specifications of the bankrupt buyer.

Contractual risk mostly occurs in the case of "take it or leave it" contracts, which relieves on party from the liability due to the mistakes of the other party. But the buyer can benefit from such contracts by including dispute resolution clauses, which greatly reduce their financial risks. Therefore, fundamentally reducing risks is never free. The costs and benefits must be evaluated on a case by case basis.

SOLUTIONS AND RECOMMENDATIONS

The first and foremost step that both the contracting parties should take is making the contract as comprehensive as possible. The farmers especially should be aware of the machinery available for redressal of disputes before entering into a contract – further, they should also be aware of the steps to be taken in case of non-compliance, etc.

In the system of contract farming, individual farmers are the weakest participants as they do not possess the market power in their hands. It has been observed that the farm entrepreneurs aren't rewarded appropriately for their contribution due to this lack of power to negotiate. Therefore, it is prudent that these farmers come together to form an institution (in the form of cooperatives or unions) that would act on the behalf of the farmers to bargain with the contracting companies. The Tomato Growers' Association in the USA played the same role – they worked on to limit the imports into the country, further developed into the National Association of Growers and processors of fair trade and henceforth were successful in adjusting consumer demands, regulating political actions, etc. An integrator firm plays a crucial role in determining the conduct and practices of the contractor and the producers. Efficiency of contract farming directly depends on how efficient the contracting firms are. Therefore, every company, regardless of the type of contract, should have a distinct unit which overlooks all the contractual issues and has necessary manpower and equipment to resolve problems arising within the agreements (Rehber, 2007).

The government plays a significant role in providing the guidelines for implementation and the redressal mechanism. Since contracts vary from company to company, it is not possible to have a comprehensive and stringent regulation governing the arrangement. Instead, the governments can provide a framework for the firms to follow in case of disputes. FAO and UNIDROIT are the bodies that periodically carry out research and provide legal and technical advice to the growers as well as processors (Pultrone, 2012). The fruits and vegetables sectors are an important policy area for the European Union. It provides a substantial financial support to the producer organisations of the Netherlands in the fruits and vegetables sector (Bijman, 2012).

Due to racial and gender discrimination in South Africa, the government must ensure and take necessary actions to vouch that everyone, including women, must get a chance and equal opportunity to participate in contract farming. To increase the bargaining power of the farmers, there should be investment in the education of the farmers, which can be done through farmer collective associations. Reliable methodologies including randomized control trials need to be used to evaluate the welfare impact of contract farming. In Kenya, a policy on horticultural development was drafted so as to suggest and incorporate issues that relate to contract farming. A platform such as a contract farming task force can help create a forum for discussion on such matters and help formulate food laws. Due to high common standards for farm management created by several European supermarkets, agribusiness firms find it difficult and costly to implement them. Thus, harmonization of standards is required and donor agencies can underpin the government for harmonization of international trade negotiations (Strohm and Hoeffler, 2006). The contracts must also cover all the important information aspects of contract farming that can be understood by all the stakeholders, so as to promote equity. Farmers need to be trained and provided information on the right inputs to be used in farming. Subsequent interaction about latest information about market prices, costs etc. will help in building mutual trust and integrity among the promoters and farmers as well. (Contract farming offers fresh hope for Africa's declining agriculture, 2018).

FUTURE RESEARCH DIRECTIONS

The authors in this report have explored the experiences of various countries in contract farming ventures and explored the various issues faces by these countries in the process of adapting the contracting culture. A primary study with statistical analysis was not carried out due to distance constraint and lack of secondary data on the same.

In addition, further research can be pursued to:

1. Understand the effectiveness of farmers' organizations in contractual arrangements and also look at the problems arising within the organizations/ cooperatives
2. Delve and explore deeper into the contract farming system in both developed and developing countries to create a wider knowledge base; and
3. The viability and efficacy of contracts in the light of gender and race.

CONCLUSION

Contract farming has now become very popular in developed countries, mostly with the objective of fulfilling ever increasing and diversifying consumption demand as well as to safeguard the farmers from varied risks in the spot market. It has further been observed that, especially in the US, it is mostly the bigger farms that engage into contract arrangements as compared to those in the developing countries, where smaller farms take up contract farming.

Nevertheless, there has been steady increase in the crop production under contracts, majorly as a result of it being the safer alternative of marketing the crops. Regardless of the country being developed or developing, the parties to the contract still suffer from the biasedness that comes with market power. Individual and small farmers are often exploited by the bigger corporations which results into dissatisfaction in the part of the producers.

The problem of gender and race conflicts is being observed by policy makers and planners. Thus, as long as most people are excluded and deprived from the contract farming business, the only way to reduce poverty through contract farming is by increasing labour employment, rather than having a direct influence on the small-scale farmers in South Africa. The correct actions need to be undertaken so as to enforce conditions where the most deprived groups, especially women and small-scale producers can participate in reaping the benefits from the contract farming arrangements. On the other hand, The White Paper on Agriculture, 1995 and other policies are helping in the goal of achieving sustainability post-apartheid rural order in South Africa. It mainly focuses on encouraging sustainable methods of farming, re-orienting of research and moving away from large scale farming to an under developed class of black farmers. Although, the replacement of existing input methods with environmentally sustainable methods is unlikely to work out in the white farming sector.

Involvement of a third party with technical expertise, contract farming models and a good contract design is a key for successful contract farming. They have the necessary negotiation skills. Neutral to both parties, a third party agreeable to all, can act as an arbitrator, contract designer, provider of quality assurance and product characteristics as well as taking care of payment schedules. The essence of contract farming can be improved by advice, encouragement, honest dialogues which increase goodwill and trust. Last but not the least; the government has a vital role to play in providing the public goods and a well-functioning environment, which allows farms and firms to benefit from long term and mutually advantageous contracts.

REFERENCES

Aditto, S., Gan, C., & Nartea, G. (2014). Economic risk analysis of alternative farming systems for smallholder farmers in central and north-east Thailand. *International Journal of Social Economics*, *41*(4), 294–320. doi:10.1108/IJSE-11-2012-0223

Agriculture. (2018). Retrieved from https://www.government.nl/topics/agriculture

Agriculture and food. Retrieved from https://www.hollandtradeandinvest.com/key-sectors/agriculture-and-food

Agriculture and sustainable development in the Netherlands. (n.d.). Retrieved from http://www.un.org/esa/agenda21/natlinfo/countr/nether/agriculture.pdf

Agriculture. Retrieved from https://www.government.nl/topics/agriculture

Asseldonk, M., & Meer, R. (2016). *Coping with price risks on Dutch farms*. Wageningen: LEI Wageningen UR. Retrieved from http://library.wur.nl/WebQuery/wurpubs/507522

Bijman, J. (2008). Contract farming in developing countries: an overview. Wageningen University, Department of Business Administration.

Bijman, J., & Gijselinckx, C. (2012). *SFC Case Study Report. Fruit and Vegetable cooperatives in the Netherlands and Belgium*. Wageningen UR.

Bijman, J., & Hendrikse, G. (2003). Co-operatives in chains: Institutional restructuring in the Dutch fruit and vegetable industry. *Journal on Chain and Network Science*, *3*(2), 95–107. doi:10.3920/JCNS2003.x033

Buch-Hansen, M., & Marcussen, H. (1982). Contract farming and the peasantry: Cases from Western Kenya. *Review of African Political Economy*, *9*(23), 9–36. doi:10.1080/03056248208703486

Center for Agroecology & Sustainable Food Systems. Social Issues in Current U.S. Agriculture [Ebook]. California. Retrieved from https://casfs.ucsc.edu/about/publications/Teaching-Organic-Farming/PDF-downloads/3.2-social-issues.pdf

Contract farming offers fresh hope for Africa's declining agriculture. (2018). Retrieved 25 April 2018, from http://www.worldagroforestry.org/downloads/Publications/PDFS/BR07060.pdf

Currie, K., & Ray, L. (1987). The Kenya state, agribusiness and the peasantry. *Review of African Political Economy*, *14*(38), 89–96. doi:10.1080/03056248708703719

Eaton, C., & Shepherd, A. (2001). Contract farming: Partnerships for growth (No. 145). Food & Agriculture Org. Farming in Developing Economies. *American Journal of Agricultural Economics*, *96*(5), 1257–1271. doi:10.1093/ajae/aau036

James, H. Jr, Klein, P., & Sykuta, M. (2011). The adoption, diffusion, and evolution of organizational form: Insights from the agrifood sector. *Managerial and Decision Economics*, *32*(4), 243–259. doi:10.1002/mde.1531

Kirsten, J., & Sartorius, K. (2002). Linking agribusiness and small-scale farmers in developing countries: Is there a new role for contract farming? *Development Southern Africa*, *19*(4), 503–529. doi:10.1080/0376835022000019428

MacDonald, J., Perry, J., Ahearn, M., Banker, D., Chambers, W., Dimitri, C., & … . (2004). *Contracts, Markets, and Prices: Organizing the Production and Use of Agricultural Commodities*. SSRN Electronic Journal. doi:10.2139srn.754986

MacDonald, J. M., & Korb, P. J. (2008). *Agricultural contracting update, 2005 (No. 58639)*. United States Department of Agriculture, Economic Research Service.

Mather, C. (1996). Towards sustainable agriculture in post-apartheid South Africa. *GeoJournal*, *39*(1). doi:10.1007/BF00174927

McDonald, J., & Korb, P. (2008). Agricultural contracting update: Contracts in 2008. *Economic Information Bulletin, 72*.

Meulenberg, M. T. G., & Viaene, J. (1993). Agricultural marketing in Belgium and The Netherlands. *Journal of International Food & Agribusiness Marketing*, *5*(3/4), 141–161.

Meuwissen, M. P. M., Hardaker, J. B., Huirne, R. B. M., & Dijkhuizen, A. A. (2001). Sharing risks in agriculture; principles and empirical results. *NJAS Wageningen Journal of Life Sciences*, *49*(4), 343–356.

Mighell, R. L., & Jones, L. A. (1963). *Vertical Coordination in Agriculture, Agricultural Economic Report 19*. U.S. Department of Agriculture.

Minot, N. (2007). *Contract Farming in Developing Countries: Patterns*. Impact, and Policy Implications.

O'Donoghue, E. J., Hoppe, R. A., Banker, D. E., Ebel, R., Fuglie, K., Korb, P., & Sandretto, C. (2011). *The changing organization of US farming. United States Department of Agriculture, Economic Research Service*. OMR – Observatório do Meio Rural. Retrieved from http://omrmz.org/omrweb/

Oya, C. (2011). Contract Farming in Sub-Saharan Africa: A Survey of Approaches, Debates and Issues. *Journal of Agrarian Change*, *12*(1), 1–33. doi:10.1111/j.1471-0366.2011.00337.x

Porter, G., & Howard, P. (1997). Contract Farming in South Africa: A Case Study from KwaZulu-Natal. *Geographical Association*, *82*, 38–44.

Prowse, M. (2012). *Contract Farming in Developing Countries - A Review*. Presentation.

Pultrone, C. (2012). An overview of contract farming: Legal issues and challenges. *Unif. L. Rev.*, *17*(1-2), 263–289. doi:10.1093/ulr/17.1-2.263

Rehber, E. (2000). *Vertical coordination in the agro-food industry and contract farming: A comparative study of Turkey and the USA (No. 052). University of Connecticut, Department of Agricultural and Resource Economics, Charles J.* Zwick Center for Food and Resource Policy.

Sahara, S., & Gyau, A. (2014). Contractual arrangements and commitment in the Indonesian supermarket channel. *British Food Journal*, *116*(5), 765–779. doi:10.1108/BFJ-03-2012-0070

Shepherd, A. (n.d.). *An introduction to Contract Farming*. Technical Centre for Agricultural and Rural Cooperation (ACP-EU). Retrieved from http://makingtheconnection.cta.int/sites/default/files/Contract-Farming-Introduction.pdf

Singh, S. (2013). The practice of contract farming in India: Making it inclusive and effective. *Food Chain*, *3*(3), 137 154. doi:10.3362/2046-1887.2013.014

Smit, A. A. H., Driessen, P. P., & Glasbergen, P. (2008). Constraints on the conversion to sustainable production: The case of the Dutch potato chain. *Business Strategy and the Environment*, *17*(6), 369–381.

Strohm, K., & Hoeffler, H. (2006). *Contract Farming in Kenya: Theory, Evidence from selected Value Chain and Implications for Development Cooperations*. Academic Press.

US Agriculture. (n.d.). Retrieved from https://www.statista.com/topics/1126/us-agriculture/

USDA. (1996). *Farmers' Use of Marketing and Production Contracts*. Washington, DC: Economic Research Service. Retrieved from https://www.ers.usda.gov/webdocs/publications/40764/18614_aer747a_1_.pdf?v=41063

von Bülow, D., & Sorensen, A. (1993). Gender and contract farming: Tea out grower schemes in Kenya. *Review of African Political Economy*, *20*(56), 38–52. doi:10.1080/03056249308703984

Wang, H., Wang, Y., & Delgado, M. (2014). The Transition to Modern Agriculture: Contract Farming in Developing Economies. *American Journal of Agricultural Economics*, *96*(5), 1257–1271. doi:10.1093/ajae/aau036

Young, L., & Hobbs, J. (2002). Vertical Linkages in Agri-Food Supply Chains: Changing Roles for Producers, Commodity Groups, and Government Policy. *Review of Agricultural Economics*, *24*(2), 428–441. Retrieved from http://www.jstor.org/stable/1349770

ADDITIONAL READING

Abebe, G., Bijman, J., Kemp, R., Omta, O., & Tsegaye, A. (2013). Contract farming configuration: Smallholders' preferences for contract design attributes. *Food Policy*, *40*, 14–24. doi:10.1016/j.foodpol.2013.01.002

Niu, B., Jin, D., & Pu, X. (2016). Coordination of channel members' efforts and utilities in contract farming operations. *European Journal of Operational Research*, *255*(3), 869–883. doi:10.1016/j.ejor.2016.05.064

Otsuka, K., Nakano, Y., & Takahashi, K. (2016). Contract Farming in Developed and Developing Countries. *Annual Review of Resource Economics*, *8*(1), 353–376. doi:10.1146/annurev-resource-100815-095459

Sanyal, D., & Vijayvargiya, Y. (2014). *Analysing Contract Farming Through the Lens of Impoverished*. SSRN Electronic Journal; doi:10.2139srn.2403642

Tiffen, M. (1995). Living Under Contract: Contract farming and agrarian transformation in sub-Saharan Africa. *African Affairs*, *94*(376), 425–427. doi:10.1093/oxfordjournals.afraf.a098844

Wu, S. (2014). Adapting Contract Theory to Fit Contract Farming. *American Journal of Agricultural Economics*, *96*(5), 1241–1256. doi:10.1093/ajae/aau065

KEY TERMS AND DEFINITIONS

Apartheid: A policy/system in South Africa where segregation or discrimination occurs on grounds of race.

Dakadaka: An irrigated sugarcane scheme in South Africa.

Harmonization: Adoption of a consistent set of international technical standards.

Mau Mau: A war in the British Kenya Colony (1920–1963).

Parastatal: Having some political authority and serving the state indirectly.

Swynnerton Plan: A policy aiming to increase and intensify the development of agricultural practice in Kenya.

Unassailable: Unable to be attacked, questioned, or defeated.

Vertical Coordination: A process where each stage of production is managed and interrelated to the next stage so as to make decisions on what and how much to produce.

Chapter 14
Evaluating Emerging Indian Retail Scenario:
Consumer Preferences, Perceived Risks, and Uncertainties - Store Brands vs. National Brands

Shivali Pande
Indian Institute of Management Bangalore, India

Aishwarya Narayan
National University of Singapore, Singapore

ABSTRACT

Globalization seems to have achieved ultimate penetration—the plethora of choice a consumer faces in any given product or service is only a testament to the fact. Worldwide, consumers are presented the options to choose between store brands (or generic/local brands, as they are sometimes known) and national brands. The choices consumers make are reflective of their perceptions about either brand and thus provide an insight into the perceived risks that consumers associate with store or national brands. This risk creates an uncertainty of consumer base and threatens the stability of market shares for brands. The chapter aims to study the various perceived risks consumers associate with brands across two product categories: consumer goods and hedonic goods. Consequently, solutions to change consumer perceptions or brand strategies have been provided so that brands may be able to reduce perceived risk associated with themselves and create a stable consumer base.

DOI: 10.4018/978-1-5225-7208-4.ch014

INTRODUCTION

The narrative of the Indian retail market in the coming years will be entirely influenced by the metastasis in consumer behavior. India ranks highest worldwide in terms of consumption growth among countries ranked by household final consumption expenditure (PricewaterhouseCoopers, 2017). Per capita income has also quadrupled since 2000, leaving considerable disposable income in the pockets of consumers (World Bank, 2014). These macroeconomic factors construct the ideal environment for the growing willingness to pay for goods and services. A growing class of young, affluent, Indians seeking better quality and aware of global trends, increases the pressure on brands to evolve to suit the preferences of what will become their most important consumer base.

At this juncture, a clarification of the term 'store brand' and its alternatives is due. As retail culture grew, one of the most important trends has been marked by the rise of the retailer as a brand in and of itself (Grewal, Levy, & Lehmann, 2004). A store brand is distinct in that it is exclusively branded and sold (and occasionally produced) by the retailer. The retailer draws on the existing loyalty of customers to the store, which marks an important advantage to the former. In India, Pantaloons, Big Bazaar, More, Reliance and Trent are some of the largest retail-brands which have witnessed enormous success. Baltas (1997) likens the producer of store brand goods to the perfectly competitive firm from classic microeconomic theory. The supplier accepts a fixed price, and there is no reward for either advertising or innovation. Large retailers, with the power to economize their scales of production, are able to procure products based on marginal costs of producers – allowing consumers the benefit of low shelf prices.

The traditional brands, produced and marketed under an umbrella brand, with nation-wide distribution networks are more commonly known. Often, their extensive marketing and advertising along with superior product quality is what establishes them as market leaders. While initially, store brands were developed to be low-cost alternatives to national brands (Oldenberg, 2005), today many store brands are able to compete with national brands on several fronts. In the Indian retail scenario, consumers often find themselves unknowingly choosing store over national brands, especially in certain product categories. In other categories, however, the humble (low cost, low quality) origins of store brands are a cause of worry for many consumers. The consumer is apprehensive of the quality of product a store brand is capable of offering, in comparison to the well marketed (and hence considered trustworthy) alternatives of national brands (Mieres, Martín, & Gutiérrez, 2006). It is this perception of risk associated with purchase that poses a concern to store brands – will this image negatively impact their chances of being worthy opponents to national brands? It is this question that forms the axis of this chapter and makes relevant the theme of the book.

This chapter aims to offer insight on behalf of both store and national brands to mitigate the risk of consumer perception.

BACKGROUND

A vast majority of literature exists between the period 1994-2006, likely when the prevalence of store brands as a viable buying choice became widespread in developed countries as the US, UK and Germany. Most research is limited to studies in developed countries (Baltas, 1997). India's consumer culture had not yet caught up to this trend by this point, especially not to the extent that it demanded in-depth research into the matter. One may wonder the point of looking into a supposedly outdated trend. In India, penetration of store brands is a relatively recent phenomenon, making the angle of related risk relevant today. The store brands as they evolve today, are important competitors to existing national brands. This chapter may hence be considered a call to re-open investigation regarding the competition between store and national brands, in an Indian context.

Perceived Risk and Decision Making

A purchasing decision for a consumer involves a risk, as the outcome of his purchase (measured in terms of satisfaction) can only be determined ex-post. The uncertainty faced herein, and the possibility that the consumer may not attain an optimal utility outcome constitute the risk incurred by any consumer (Mieres et al., 2006). The concept of perceived risk often creates distinction between 'inherent risk' (the risk present in any product category) and 'handled risk' (the risk specific to the situation the consumer puts themselves in, by choosing a particular product/brand) (Mitchell, 1998). Perceived risk theory has long been utilized in understanding consumer buying behavior. The most famous application is to purchasing decisions of food. For example, when the American public believed that eggs contained salmonella, the consumption of eggs plunged (Mitchell, 1992). The perceived health risk of consuming eggs prevented their consumption on a large-scale basis. While this example tends toward the more apparent and brazen, contemporary literature is around subtler perceived risks. The commonly identified types of perceived risks are financial, social, physical, performance, safety, time and psychological (Mitchell, 1992). In the choice between national and store brands, performance, social and financial risks seem to be the most relevant. The differentiating factors between national brands and store brands are a constituent of these factors, accordingly, this study shall progress along these lines.

In the context of the Asian region (and developing countries at large), the perceived risk approach is considered of vital importance. The phenomenon of store brands is inchoate in comparison to the developed markets of North America and Europe. As with any nascent product, the inherent risk of sampling new products would hinder consumers from choosing store brands (Sheau-Fen, Sun-May, & Yu-Ghee, 2012).

Generally, consumers expect that store brands would be of a poor quality, and tend to avoid those (Mierez et al., 2006). This perception of quality is one of the main determinants due to which consumers consider store brands riskier than their national counterparts. Mieres et al. (2006) concludes that financial risk is lower for even those national brands that are priced higher than store brands. Such a result indicates that consumers may envision links between price and quality – a lower price signals that the product is of inferior quality, and that the consumer would have to spend on the replacement or repair of the product. While this seems fairly intuitive, there are other determinants of risk also, as detailed below.

Consumers have consistently been found to prefer store brands over national ones, in those product categories wherein the consequences associated with a wrong purchase are lower (Batra & Sinha, 2000). For example, in product categories such as baby food, there are severe impacts in case of a wrongful purchase. However, categories such as bread, milk and other grocery items are considered less risky. Batra & Sinha (2000) and (Hsu & Lai, 2008) identify another determinant of risk, specific to store brands: the degree of expected variability of quality across products. In those product categories where, lower variability of quality is expected, store brands would be preferred.

Another aspect along which risk is observed is the 'information search vs. purchase experience' perspective. Those products which must be possessed to understand the involved risks are usually considered less risky than others (Hsu & Lai, 2008). In the former product category, store brands would be preferred over national brands.

While all these observations are supported by sufficient empirical evidence, store brands possessing improved quality of products may have altered the notion that store brands are low price, low-quality options. Hence, to revisit the qualities that affect perceived risk and store brand proneness/inclination in an Indian context is best. Additionally, existing literature fails to take into consideration the Indian consumer specifically, something this chapter will aim to do.

Store Brand Proneness

Store brand proneness is defined as the degree to which consumers are inclined to actually purchase store brand grocery items (Richardson, Jain, & Dick, 1996). A large portion of marketing literature is focused on identifying the characteristics of the average customer that prefers store brands. Early literature in the field was focused on identifying the demographic markers (age, income, gender, etc.) that described the average.

The risks associated by consumers to store brands is vital in determining store brand proneness. Most consumers explicitly attach lower levels of risk whilst purchasing a national brand – which come with the promise and goodwill associated with a large, well-marketed brand (Mierez et al., 2006). This leads one to an important conclusion – a consumer who considers himself risk averse will tend away from store brands, and stick to the safe choices of the national brands. Baltas (1997) recognizes store brand customers to be wary of price, but not swayed by advertising. An important conclusion to be drawn from this is the permanently low price such a consumer necessitates. It becomes challenging for a store brand to break out of a particular price point, especially to one greater than that of national brands. Erdem, Zhao, & Valenzuela (2004) establish three tenets for the success of store brands:

- Consumer is not a-prior uncertain about the brand.
- The product is constant in its qualities over time.
- Consumers are more price sensitive, less quality sensitive and less risk averse.

Familiarity to store brands is often considered to be a contributing factor to proneness. Consumers that are familiar with store brands are more likely to perceive them as value for money products, while those with limited experience would likely perceive them as riskier (Richardson, Jain, & Dick, 1996). As a customer interacts more with the store brand, their knowledge of it is greater, and hence the associated uncertainty falls.

Sethuraman & Cole (1999) envision consumer characteristics as influencing the amount of price premium a consumer is willing to pay for a national brand over a store brand. Average purchase price, purchase frequency, annual household income, age, education, gender and family size are some of the important variables. While such studies are important, potential for managerial influence in such factors is limited. It is important to note that the characteristics associated with store brand proneness are contingent upon the context within which such purchasing decisions are made – brands, product categories and behavioral context (Mieres et al., 2006). Hence, while consumer characteristics are important to understand consumer mind set, the brand role is vital in determining how managers can engineer better growth trajectories.

Consumers face a risk while making purchasing decisions, which they transfer to brands, in terms of the uncertainty – that the brand will have a stable consumer base/market share. Especially in times of financial crisis, the first area where consumers cut down on expenses is the retail market for Fast Moving Consumer Goods (FMCG) goods. The uncertainty of consumer retention hence becomes an even more pressing concern. The proper management of the brand can potentially ensure consumer loyalty even during trying times. The brand is technically a mitigation mechanism for this transferred risk; the manner in which a brand is wielded fundamentally determines its perception, and by extension its perceived risk. The brand is capable of bestowing prestige, image and market positioning through subtle cues to the consumer. Hence, the brand management for both national and store brands will determine their survival in the market. Accordingly, this chapter provides directions for brand managers of both store and national brands to survive in a competitive market.

Indian Retail Market Overview

The Indian Brand Equity Foundation (2017) describes the retail sector as one of the largest sectors of the Indian economy. Though the organized retail penetration is low at a meagre 8% as of 2015, the scope for growth is enormous (India Brand Equity Foundation, 2016). In fact, organized retail is expected to account for 24% of the overall retail market by 2020 (India Brand Equity Foundation, 2016).

The private label strategy has begun to create a significant impact in the organized retail industry. In developed markets, the share of private label sales is as high as 40% (The Nielsen Company, 2018). Currently, Indian private label penetration stands at just 6% (Subha, Kirthika, & Narayanaswamy, 2018). However, individual brands like Shoppers Stop and Lifestyle (both retail fashion brands) attribute nearly 20% of their revenue to store brand products (Subha, Kirthika, & Narayanaswamy, 2018). E-Retailers such as Myntra and Nykaa have based their business models around their store brands. BBlunt (salon and personal care) has launched a range of beauty products under the name Ikonic, and has revolutionized the purchase of professional styling products from salons. However, the trend is not just in pleasure-based products, but those of sheer utility as well. Packaged groceries alone accounts for around 53% of total sales (Dhaktod & Chib, 2016). Packaged rice, lentils, atta and ghee have garnered the highest value sales. Godrej Interio (a niche high end grocery store) has witnessed a shift in consumer perception of store brand, with the private label often being preferred to the national brands, as reported by Mohit Khattar (Managing Director) (Pani, 2015).

CONSUMER PREFERENCES, RISKS AND UNCERTAINTIES: A PRIMARY STUDY

The primary study for this chapter is aimed to establish the perceived risks Indian households associate with store and national brands. An online questionnaire was administered, the target audience being middle class households spread over Tier-1 cities in India. One possible limitation of the survey is the inadvertent sample bias arising from the small sample size. The sample comprised 100 survey responses.

The questionnaire collects data for two product categories: consumption-based products or consumer goods and preference-based products or hedonistic goods. Consumer goods are typically purchased out of need and hence involve a well-thought-out purchasing decision in terms of price & associated quality or utility. Hedonistic goods tend to be purchased on more emotional grounds and are very often guided by perceived quality and status symbol associated with certain products.

An important distinction between the two arises from the different risk associations consumers make. In this study, groceries have been used to represent the former while shoes have been used to represent the later. We assume, for the purpose of this study, that the choices consumers make in groceries and shoes respectively represent their preferences across consumer and hedonistic goods respectively.

The products have been identified on the basis of purpose of purchase. In the hedonistic products category, the authors have: an 'everyday use footwear,' an 'occasional/partywear footwear,' and 'special occasion footwear.' These products differ in their hedonistic and preferential utilities to different consumers. Hence, this distinction is important. While 'everyday use footwear' is representative of daily use hedonistic purchases, which also tend to be consumer goods; a 'special occasion footwear' (e.g.: bridal shoes) have exceptionally limited use, and therefore purchases may be heavily influenced by brand perceptions and associated social status conveyed by the product.

In the consumer goods category we have: 'everyday groceries' (oil and wheat flour), 'occasional groceries' (biscuits and breads), 'premium groceries' (exotic vegetables and salad sauces). The first category represents consumer products of absolute daily need and utility which are necessary, frequent purchases. On the other hand, 'premium groceries' are rare consumer products which are purchased for a very limited use and their consumption is usually based in a social setting or influenced by social factors.

The choice of store brand or national brand as made by the respondents is studied against the natures of the buyers and their perceptions to identify the existing profile of buyers of either kind of product categories. The current literature identifies a low correlation between demographic features and consumer preference while identifying a high correlation between behavioral, attitudinal and perception variables and consumer choice (Baltas, 1997). Thus, the study focuses on the latter. Based on this profile the possible perceived risks with either kind of brands is identified and consequently, plausible solutions are suggested.

Preferences in Consumption-Based Products Based on Nature of Buyer

It is observed that regardless of the nature of the buyer, when it comes to the purchases of premium groceries, national brands are preferred by more than three quarters of the entire sample. A plausible explanation for the same is the implicit social context associated with premium consumer goods. This category includes products such as exotic vegetables, salad dressings, premium chocolates, cheese etc. The consumption of these products is influenced by several social factors, for example: the salads available in a restaurants tend to influence the choice of dressings purchased for home cooking, the brand of cheese or chocolates shown frequently on cookery shows or television shows tend to be more preferred due to the greater number of people who would acknowledge the brand or the international packaged food brands for eatables that consumers learn about from social settings (such as pastas or dim sums- those which are not a part of native consumption) tend to be more purchased due to the sheer popularity of the same stemming from social media interactions between global consumers. This is an area where national brands clearly dominate the market thanks to their widespread marketing efforts along with the conscious marketing strategy of appealing to emotions (example- salad dressings or oils are often linked to a healthy lifestyle and chocolates are linked to special occasions or relations).

A brand conscious customer does not rely on the advertisements or promotions available in the store at the time of purchase i.e. the purchase decision is not based on spontaneous or impromptu factors but instead their decisions are guided by an ingrained understanding of the cumulative characteristics of each brand such as the price ranges, available varieties, perceived qualities and importance of a brand name/ status symbol associated with any product's consumption. On the other hand, consumers who do not plan their brands before-hand tend to be influenced by spontaneous factors such as promotions, lower prices and targeted promotions by in-house sales agents.

When it comes to occasional groceries more than half of the respondents who pre-decide the brands to be purchased always or sometimes tend to opt for store brands. Those who never decide their brands before-hand show an equal likeliness for opting store brands and national brands (Refer to Figure 1). These products are purchased for limited usage of an individual. Thus, any kind of a loss in terms of poor quality, bad taste or non-suitability to preferences of consumer will have to be borne for a limited period only. Thus, a consumer is more willing to take the risk of trying store brands. In fact, the store brands offer the same varieties in products at relatively lower prices due to cost savings in packaging or marketing. This makes the purchases of store brands for occasional consumer products a wise decision.

As observed in Figure 2, in case of daily groceries, nearly two thirds of those who pre-decide their brands opt for national brands whereas more than half of those who do not pre-plan tend to buy store brands. The loss associated with adverse purchases in this category is very high (due to the daily consumption and absolute need to utilize these products) and thus planned buyers tend to account for these losses and thus opt for national brands that are often associated with a greater quality and improved standards. On the other hand, spontaneous buyers tend to get attracted to the cheaper variants made available by store brands. Another factor contributing to the preference of store brands by buyers who are not brand conscious is that the perceived quality differential is increasingly being reduced between the two brands due to the retailers' efforts of promoting their quality standards and safety measure with respect to the products.

Figure 1. Brand consciousness and choice of brand for occasional groceries
Source: Authors

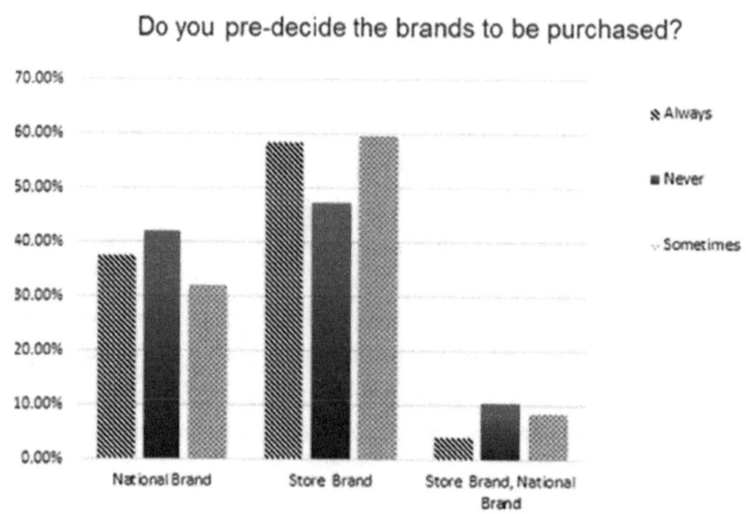

Figure 2. Brand consciousness and choice of brand for daily groceries
Source: Authors

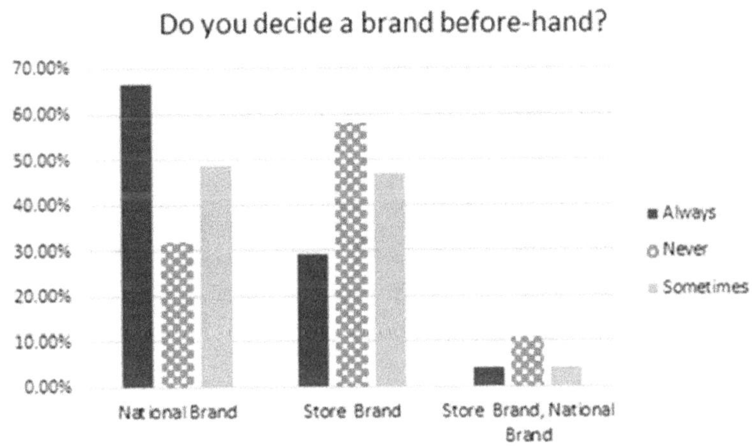

Trying multiple brands helps create a better and more accurate understanding of actual quality differentials and therefore risks associated with different brands. Typically, experimental consumers are more open to the idea of adopting store brands once they realize that store brands also offer products at par quality minus the marketing extravaganza. However, these are the customers who cannot be accounted as loyal to any particular brands due to their preference for experimenting.

Experimental buyers of the sample show a clear preference for store brands in case of occasional grocery purchases but tend to prefer national brands when it comes to daily groceries (Refer Figure 3). Thus, the generic view that national brands are safer purchases when it comes to high frequency consumptions tends to be reinstated by the preference made by experimental buyers. For the buyers who are strictly not experimental, national brands are preferred for occasional as well as daily purchases. These buyers are analogous to risk averse individuals who will prefer to opt for the national brands under the widely established presumption that they guarantee better quality.

In case of discount preference, nature does not seem to hold much of an influence on the choice of brands for occasional purchases because regardless of whether or not a respondent bases his purchases on discounts and promotional offers, store brands are preferred. When it comes to everyday grocery items, a discount-seeking customer would opt for a store brand whereas the one who never decides what to purchase based on promotions will prefer the national brand. The observation for everyday items is a simple consequence of store brands offering the price benefit to consumers who are primarily concerned with the amount of money they spend on their purchases.

Like the previous category of buyer's nature, whether or not a consumer is informed about products does not seem to affect the preferences in case of occasional grocery purchases. However, in case of everyday groceries, nearly half of the surveyed people who collect information before making a purchase opted for a store brand. This is contrary to popular perception that store brands are a risky purchase for items that are used every day. The increased confidence in store brands probably stems from positive reviews that other customers give who have tried the products and have realized that the quality differential is extremely narrow or even non-existent in the current scenario. Also, the targeted promotions inside the retail store could be an important influencing factor as they tend to be more informative and

Figure 3. Experimental nature of buyer and choice of brand
Source: Authors

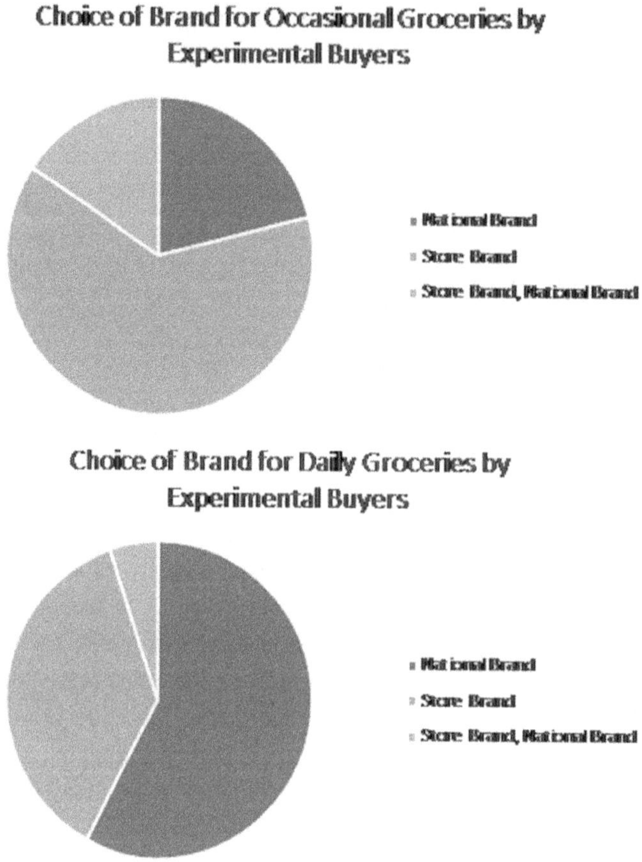

**For a more accurate representation see the electronic version.*

personalized than national-level ad-campaigns and hence, grab the attention of consumers who are interested in acquiring information.

Preferences in Consumption-Based Products Guided by Perceptions

Just as the nature of buyer has no influence on choice of brand in case of premium groceries, no matter what the perception of the buyer, national brands are preferred by an absolute majority in case of premium consumer products because these purchases are predominantly guided by social and sensory factors - an arena well controlled by the national brands.

A majority of the respondents who believe that price is an indicator of quality invariably opt for national brands in case of both occasional as well as daily grocery purchases (Refer Figure 4). This is a direct consequence of the higher prices of national brands signaling a superior quality for those who believe in a price-quality link. However, amongst those who disagree with the idea that price can indicate quality, a major chunk of the respondents opted for a store brand for both - daily as well as occasional uses. This observation is indicative of the emerging success of the new narrative that retailers have developed about store brands: products which provide quality at par with any other brand minus the

Figure 4. Price quality perception and choice of brands
Source: Authors

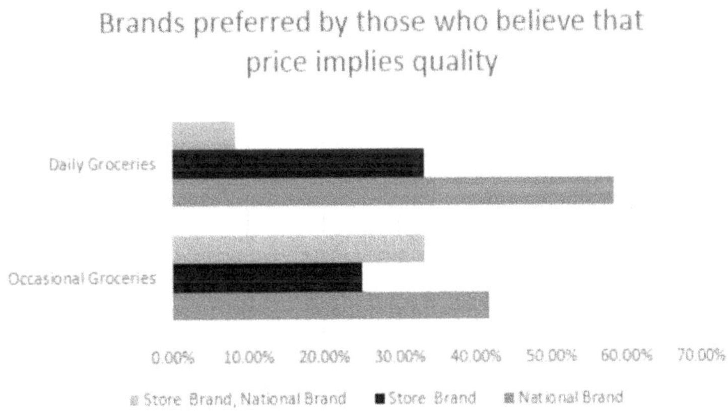

fluff of marketing. Buyers who do not have a preconceived notion of quality based on prices are more accepting of this new worldview.

Regardless of the view of the customer about advertisement being a source of information, a store brand is preferred in case of occasional purchases. This is a typical observation for this category as the purchases tend to be very casual and not a lot of thought is put into the choice made, thus usefulness of advertisements for any other perception for that matter tend to have very little impact on the ultimate choice. In case of everyday purchases, more than half of those who consider advertisement as a source of information opt for national brands whereas those who do not view advertisements as an information source opt for store brands. This is an obvious consequence of the widespread use of advertisements by national brands as opposed to the minimal use of the same by store brands in this category.

The perceptive link between the packaging & display and quality of products does not impact the occasional grocery purchases. Store brands are wholly preferred by consumers for this category. However, in case of everyday groceries, a majority of the customers who agree to a positive relation between packaging, display and superiority in quality prefer the national brands which invest huge amounts of money to ensure an attractive packaging and alluring display. On the contrary, those who disagree with this relation opt for store brands as they do not believe that the superior packaging of national brands is indicative of a superior quality of the component within.

Preferences in Preference-Based Products Based on Nature of Buyer

The purchase of premium footwear or preference-based products that are specifically bought to be used on a single and special occasion such as graduation or wedding are unaffected by the nature of the buyer. Regardless of the purchasing habits, more than half of the respondents exhibiting different natures prefer national brands for such purchases. This is because single-occasion hedonistic products have a very high level of emotional and social context associated with themselves. For example, the bridal shoes purchased are not merely for the purpose of comfort of walking, these shoes are considered to be symbolic of the occasion and must make the bride stand out; thus, the social status value of these shoes must be high and there should be an emotional connotation associated with the shoes by the brand so that it appeals to the purchaser. National brands typically create such an emotional imagery for their products and also generate mass appreciation, thereby becoming status symbols, and thus they dominate this sector.

In fact, not only single-occasion use but also party-wear or occasional footwear purchases are not affected by the nature of the buyer. A majority of all kinds of buyers opt for national brands when it comes to occasional footwear purchases (Refer Figure 5). These include shoes worn for formal events or parties or festivities. They are not meant for a single special occasion but are often used in multiple occasions that mark a social gathering and signify a certain kind of celebration and thus have an important social connotation which favors national brands.

Also, hedonistic purchases tend to be consumption beyond necessity. Individuals indulge in these purchases after having met their needs and seek pleasure from such shopping experiences. Hedonistic products also tend to have art characteristics in that they are not simple commodities that can be easily replicated, each shoe or perfume or dress is distinct and the purchases are often based on consumer's personality and preferences getting resonated with a particular fragrance or design. Thus, unlike groceries, where distinguishing products on any basis other than the outer packaging can be difficult, hedonistic product qualities can be markedly different. The shine on an Italian shoe brand is very evident and so is the softness of pure silk used by a well-established national saree brand. The inherent importance of the raw material used in hedonistic purchases means that a better quality will have to be highly priced as it will involve the use of the costlier inputs and greater craftsmanship. Together, the well-established social image of a national brand, higher perceived quality and sensory appeal created by these brands, ensure the dominance of national brands in case of rare and occasional use hedonistic products.

More than half of both the kinds of buyers: those who pre-decide brands to be purchased as well as those who do not decide their brands prior to a purchase, opt for national brands and therefore the inherent hedonistic appeal of national brands tends to be a stronger influence on all customers regardless of the importance they personally associate with brands. While those who are consistent planners naturally tend to prefer the national brands, spontaneous buyers become an easy target audience to appeal to for national brands with their sophisticated branding and display.

Figure 5. Preference for national brands in single occasion use footwear regardless of consumer's nature
Source: Authors

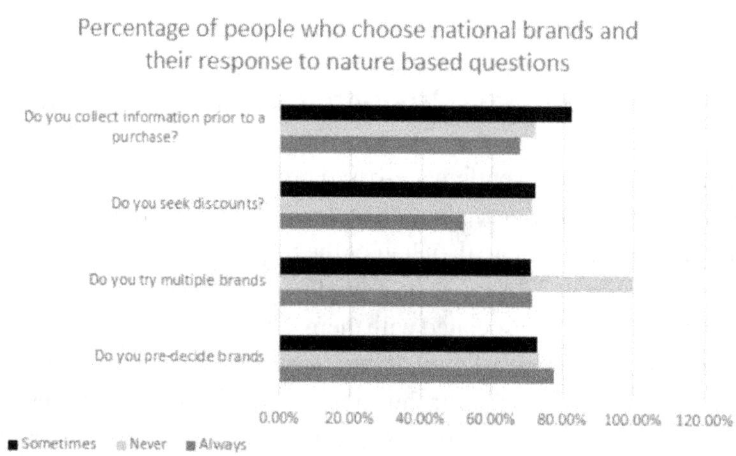

Nearly sixty percent of the respondents who always experiment with multiple brands prefer store brands. This trend bolsters the idea that when multiple brands are tried, the actual awareness about the quality and usefulness of products improves and the perceived risk associated with store brand products declines. Experimental buyers identify that for everyday use footwear (such as home slippers or office use sneakers) do not exhibit a great quality differential across national or store brands because the commodity nature of products is more pronounced in this category than the hedonistic nature.

More than half of the customers who seek discounts and promotions opt for store brands. This is an obvious observation given the cheaper prices offered by store brands. In case of those customers who do not look out for discounts, an equal likeliness to buy store brands and national brands is shown. A possible reason for this behavior is that such customers actively do not base their purchasing decisions on price-based factors. Thus, their preference for national brands stems from conventional factors whereas the preference for store brands might be stemming from the fact that these brands also provide utility at par with national brands in everyday product categories and hence can appeal to customers competitively even when the customers are not seeking lower prices.

Majority of the customers who acquire information before buying a product opt for national brands. Typically, the sources of information used are advertisements, consumer magazines and peers. The media sources have an inherent bias towards national brands because these are the sources that act as the marketing playground for national brands. And peers tend to suggest national brands in order to assert their own social status which is often associated with the brand a person uses in today's context. Thus, unlike consumer goods where the primary information sought is objective in nature (such as weight, nutrition levels, cleanliness and taste), the primary information asked for in case of hedonistic purchase is subjective or opinion-based (such as design, craft, social appeal etc.) and hence the information seeking itself is biased towards national brands. In case of those respondents who never seek a priori information more than half prefer store brands. This is mostly because they can objectively observe the competitive products that store brands provide in everyday use category at lower prices and hence view store brand purchases as a wiser deal.

Preferences in Preference-Based Products Based on Perceptions

As with the nature of products, perceptions do not seem to influence the choice of brands in case of premium footwear (single-occasion use) or occasional footwear. National brands are preferred by an absolute majority regardless of the view of consumers. The reasons for this are the same as those mentioned above while discussing choice of brand based on the nature of buyer.

A greater proportion of individuals who believe that price implies quality strictly prefer a national brand to a store brand for their everyday footwear purchases (Refer Figure 7). This is understandable since the higher prices of national brands signal a better quality to customers with such a perception. On the other hand, more than half of the customers who disagree to the link between price and quality opt for store brands. This is because these customers do not use the price ranges as indicators of the product's inherent usefulness or quality.

A majority of both kinds of customers- those who view advertisements as a source of information as well as those who disagree to advertisements being a source of information- prefer store brands to national brands for everyday footwear purchases. A likely reason for this observation is that not a lot of individuals would base their purchases for such products on advertisements. An everyday footwear is more about comfort and durability than being about the style or emotion. Thus, the traits relevant to the

Figure 6. Choice of brands by customers who acquire information prior to purchase for everyday footwear
Source: Authors

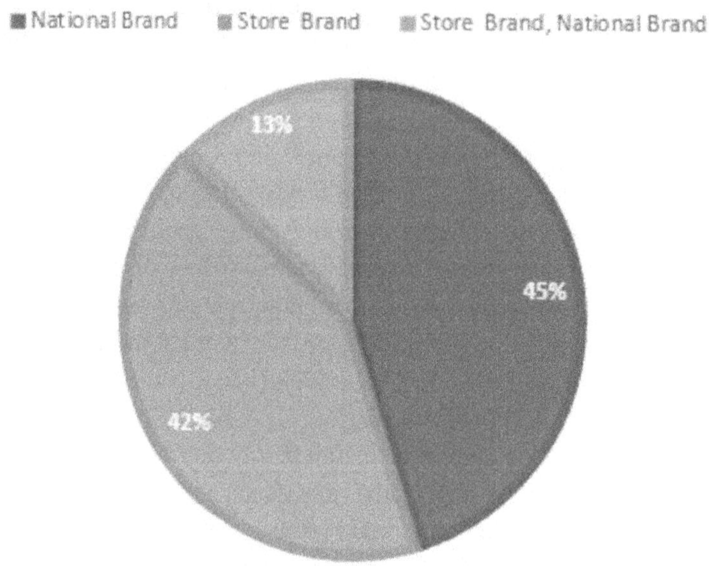

Figure 7. Price quality perception and choice of brand
Source: Authors

purchases for every day hedonistic products are often not captured by advertisements and therefore the usefulness of advertisements is not a very relevant influencer of the choice of brand.

When it comes to packaging and display, half of those who agree to it being an indicator of quality opt for store brands whereas more than half of those who disagree to such a relation prefer national brands. Refer Figure 8. This is contrary to the fact that store brands invest very little in packaging while national brands invest heavily in the same. The possible explanation then for this observation is that, everyday use products tend to be displayed or packed in more or less a similar fashion by either kind of brands- slippers and flip flops are simply hung on racks and packed in plastic or cloth covers, plain polo t-shirts (such as those used for gym wear) do not have a lot of design differentiation and are organized in stacks by color by either brand. Thus, while consumers may have an opinion about whether or not packaging and display indicate quality, the packaging and display is not a distinguishing factor between the two kinds of brands and the choice is thus characterized by the factors and perceptions listed above.

Perceived Risks for Store Brands and National Brands

The current preferences, as indicated in Figure 9, indicate that national brands enjoy dominant market shares in case of premium groceries and a marginally superior share in case of everyday grocery items. As far as occasional grocery purchases are concerned, store brands enjoy a greater preference. A similar analysis in case of hedonistic purchases reveals that national brands enjoy a dominant preference in case of single-occasion/premium as well as occasional/party wear products. Store brands have developed a marginal superiority in case of everyday use footwear. Thus, national brands enjoy a secure market position as far as premium groceries, premium footwear and occasional footwear is considered; they ought to reinforce and maintain the perceptions that yield this preference. Likewise store brands enjoy secure market position as far as occasional groceries is concerned.

The preference for national brands in case of everyday groceries is very marginal and thus any adverse change in perceptions or composition of the nature of buyers can lead to store brands becoming dominant in the market. Thus, national brands need to take continuous efforts to maintain the perceptions and differentials while store brands must seize the competitive opportunity that this field provides by changing

Figure 8. Perception of packaging & quality relation and choice of brand
Source: Authors

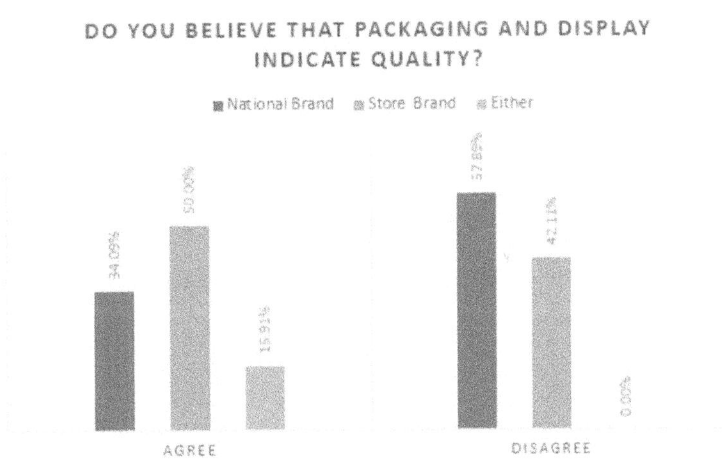

their product qualities or influencing the consumer perception in a manner that lures customers on the threshold away from national brands. Similarly, the preference for store brand in everyday footwear or hedonistic products is marginal and there is dire need to reinforce the image or perception that leads to this choice on the part of store brands. Also, national brands must take note of the perceptions that turn away customers and must take appropriate measures to change their products or their marketing strategies to win customers for such product categories. Therefore, everyday groceries and everyday hedonistic purchases are the two areas where there exists uncertainty as to who will be the dominant player and thus there is scope for strategizing in a way that perceived risks associated with different brands can be minimized in order to improve customer base.

Perceived Risks and Associated Preferences

Brand conscious customers tend to opt for national brands in case of everyday groceries however, the proportion of buyers who pre-decide on the brands to be purchased is only marginally more than those who never decide before-hand. Also, most of the people decide on brands to be purchased before-hand only occasionally. Thus, store brands have ample scope to influence the buyers because a greater proportion of buyers buy spontaneously rather than buying in a planned manner (a trait of brand conscious buyers). However, this creates an uncertain market base for national brands who need to ensure that their perceived image in market is successful enough to create brand loyal customers who would always wish to buy their brands and also, their promotional strategies need to be strong enough to compete with store brands and attract spontaneous buyers. Brand consciousness is not an influential trait for everyday footwear products.

Experimental buyers opt for store brands in case of everyday footwear due to a fall in the perceived risk that occurs when customers realize that the quality differential is low. Since most of the buyers of this category tend to like to try new brands, national brands face the risk of losing customers in this category. In case of everyday groceries, national brands are preferred regardless of the experimental nature

Figure 9. Brand preference across product categories
Source: Authors

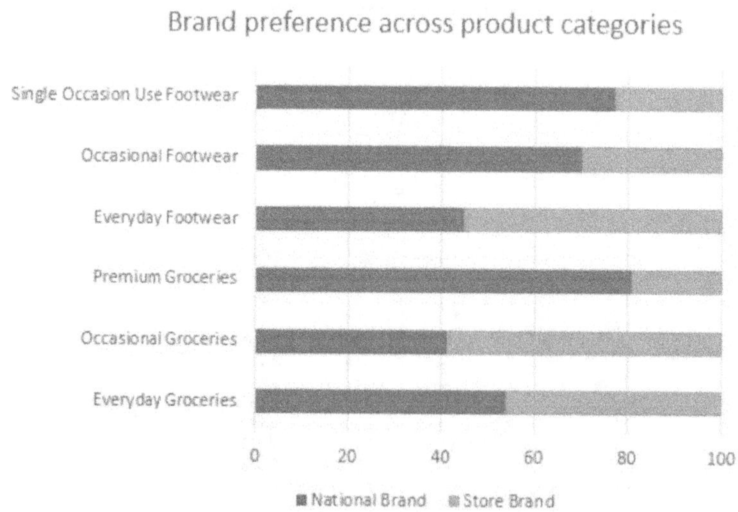

due to the associated high perceived risk. The only way store brands can break through this preference is by reducing the perceived quality differential and convincing customers that there is no risk or loss associated with the consumption of their products. Figure 10 summarizes the perceived risks and their associated preferences.

Those who do not seek discounts adopt national brands for their everyday grocery purchases, however a major proportion of people seek for discounts at least occasionally and national brands are thus threatened to lose their share unless they incorporate price-based promotions and reduce the price differential between themselves and store brands without signaling a drop-in quality. Regardless of whether a customer looks for discounts, store brand footwears are preferred for daily use and thus non-price-based solutions need to be adopted by national brands to break through the current preferences.

The informed buyers tend to adopt store brands for everyday groceries as they get to know that there isn't much difference in either brand's product except the marketing activities. However, a greater proportion of buyers tend to not collect information and thus national brands can continue to enjoy preference as long as a perceived difference is maintained. However, creating an actual quality differential or reducing the price differential may help convert informed buyers into national brand loyalists also. The information-seekers in case of everyday footwear tend to prefer national brands and most of the buyers seek information always or at least sometimes. Thus, a successful advertisement strategy can help develop a positive review for the national brand and can increase the customer base significantly because media is the most often used source of information for these products. In order to compete, store brands need to increase their presence across such media to ensure that informed buyers consider their brands.

Figure 10 shows that those who believe that price indicates quality opt for national brands however the proportion of people who actually believe in this link is much lower as compared to the proportion of people who have a neutral or negative stance with respect to the relation between price and quality. Thus, the new narrative being constructed by retailers which aims at deconstructing the link between price and quality while guaranteeing safe qualities at lower prices acts as a successful crowd puller and national

Figure 10. Summary of consumer perceptions
Source: Authors

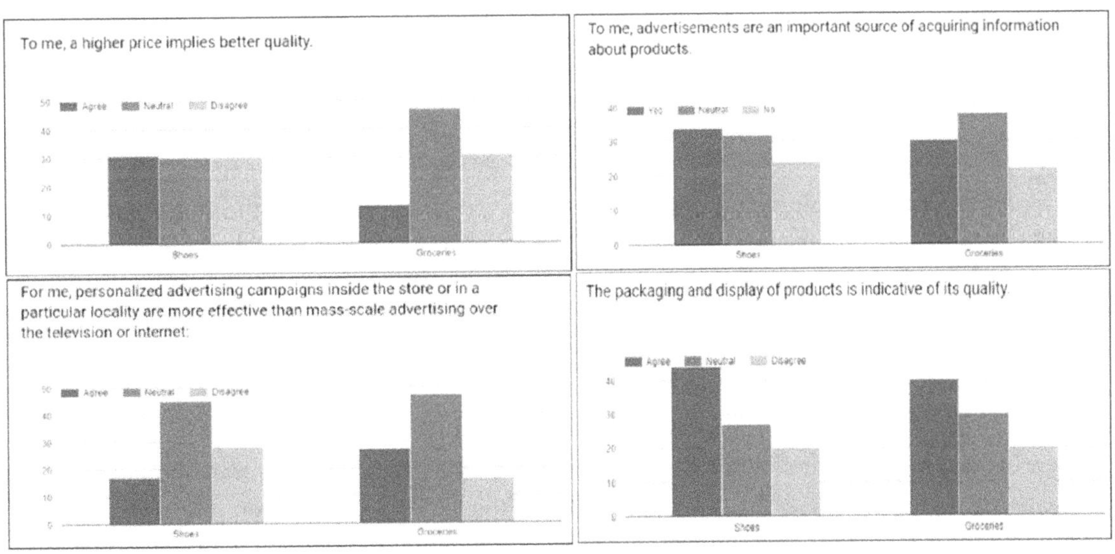

brands need to substantially improve their product qualities commensurate to the prices or reduce the price differential to avoid the risk of losing customers. A similar trend is seen in everyday footwear where those who judge quality by price adopt national brands. However, in this case the number of people who believe in such a link, those who do not and those who are neutral is almost equal and hence store brands will lose their share if they do not focus on the other factors that favor their brands. Likewise, national brands must be opportune to use price differentials to create a greater perceived benefit for their product. Also, other strategies should be adopted to attract customers who do not use price as a judgment factor.

Those who use advertisements as a source of information tend to prefer national brands for every-day groceries and thus it becomes imperative that national brands continue to maintain a strong and carefully researched marketing strategy and at the same time they should also sufficiently respond to the marketing strategies that store brands are now adopting. Particularly in the scenario that the lines between store brands and national brands are diminishing for several products, store brands stand an optimistic opportunity to step into the game of advertising and branding and allure customers by not only promoting their actual benefits of low prices, decent qualities and no-frills approach but also appealing to the sensory experience of the new retail market format of departmental stores and malls. This is particularly important because a large number of people believe advertisements to be an informative source and the next largest proportion as neutral - these can be tapped by appealing to facets other than product information in advertising campaigns because these people do not use advertisement for information but may be influenced by the same. The advertisements, however, are not a great influencer for everyday footwear category.

The store brands in general should consider shifting their marketing scale from localized and targeted to more generic for either product category because majority of the respondents are neutral towards the effectiveness of the localized ad campaigns conducted in localities or residential housing societies in status quo.

Consumers using packaging and display to ascertain quality choose national brands in case of every day groceries. Also, a major proportion of consumers tend to believe that packaging and display indicate quality and therefore national brands should emphasize on their merchandising, packaging and print branding to maintain consumer trust. However, the differentiation in products of national and store brands using packaging or display for every day footwear is minimal and thus its influence on choice of brands is also insignificant.

Summarizing the Perceived Risks

The analysis presented above indicates that the typical choices made between national and store brands depend upon the product being considered. The perceived risks change as the frequency of using a product increases and as the price ranges change. There are three major risks that are associated with such a choice in retail market: performance, financial and social risk.

- For the products that are used rarely and hence often those which belong to the higher-end in terms of prices, it is the social risk which is most considered by individuals. This risk is represented in terms of the social factors considered while making a purchase; for example, the social risk of wearing a store brand product on your wedding is very high due to the status symbol regarded to the products in addition to their utility purpose or the social risk of consuming a premium/exotic grocery from a store brand generates a risk of not fitting into the socially approved choices.

- In case of the products that are used everyday i.e. in greater frequency, consumers are primarily considered with the performance risks of products: the quality of nutritional value of groceries, durability of footwear etc. It is observed that the performance risks associated with store brands for grocery products is high whereas that associated with store brands in case of footwear is negligible. These are the products which have to be consumed or used every day and hence any performance failure will entail greater inconvenience and will create an urgency to replace the product which means a financial burden is imposed immediately. Consequently, it is performance that most concerns individuals in this field.
- In case of products used occasionally, the products are neither primarily supposed to serve utility nor are they supposed to act as a status symbol. Thus, the price shelled out for these products commensurate to the quality is important in case of consumer goods and the price spent commensurate to the pleasure experienced is important for hedonistic goods. Therefore, financial risk is of greater importance. Consumers associate a very low financial risk in using store brands for occasional grocery purchases because the prices are sufficiently reasonable for the quality expected. However, in case of hedonistic purchases, the financial risk is higher because the prices of such products are significant but the corresponding pleasure or experience is considered to be lower. In such occasional purchases, the financial risk is often measured relative to the performance risk and social risk associated with consumer goods and hedonistic goods respectively.

SOLUTIONS AND RECOMMENDATIONS

The strategies should be an optimal combination of three components: pricing & promotion, value perception management and retailer-manufacturer relationship (Alliance Consulting Group, n.d.). The relative importance of these components will depend on the particular risk that a brand is trying to tackle which in turn depends on the perception of a consumer about the value of any product. A solution or strategy is needed only when the perceptions are adverse, however an adverse perception need not always be accurate. When an adverse perception is accurate, brands should focus on improving the associated value whereas when the adverse perception is inaccurate, brands must focus on managing the perception (Alliance Consulting Group, n.d.). Mostly, store brands adopt price-based solutions and national brands adopt value-based perception/retailer-manufacturer relationship related solutions. However, with the changing retail market scenario, brands need to experiment with newer strategies.

Solutions and Strategies for Store Brands

As the link between price and quality gets eroded, consumers become more receptive towards the idea of trying store brands. While retailers have actually improved the quality of the products they provide (particularly consumer goods which are commodities that can be easily replicated), in order for the consumers to identify this, a strong marketing strategy aimed at deconstructing the positive relation between price and quality is needed. An effective strategy for this purpose would be to target the customers who do not enter a store already having planned the brands they want to purchase - these are the customers who would be accepting trial packs and listen to sales persons to make a choice. Thus, a combination strategy can be used wherein a salesperson convincing and price-based promotions and discounts can be used to attract a customer and then trial packs can be used to allow a customer an opportunity to test the quality and assure himself of the same. Thus, a loyal and informed consumer base can be created.

Another important change in the retail market scenario that retailers must leverage upon to expand the consumer base for store brands is the new format of retail shopping. Shopping is no longer a daily chore for individuals, it has become a pleasurable or sensorial experience with the rise in air-conditioned malls and departmental stores spread over large areas offering endless varieties of products, opportunity to interact with other consumers while making purchases and several anecdotal experiences such as discount contests, samples and trials, play areas for kids, food arenas etc. (Dhaktod & Chib, 2015). Nowadays retailers such as Reliance Smart, Reliance Trends, Reliance Footprints, Big Bazaar, Tata Star Bazaar, Aditya Birla Group's More and several others have become the de-facto shopping destination for households across product categories. The exposure to international lifestyle, global online consumerism, increased proportion of young earners who have rising disposable incomes contribute to this new style of retail (Ranga, 2017). All in all, retailers have created a brand identity for themselves in the market. This brand identity that retailers have created for themselves as sellers of products can be utilized to launch private labels and store brands also (Dhaktod & Chib, 2015). The trust which consumers repose in the retailers by favoring them as shopping destinations reveal the satisfaction and loyalty of the consumer base towards a retailer's identity. A store brand launched under the same identity is most likely to enjoy these ready-made perceptions. This strategy will help eliminate the perceived performance risk associated with store brands.

Additionally, retailers also have access to massive volumes of customer data from the sales counter records - these can be used to understand the daily changes in demands, preference for different varieties/flavors/designs, relations between purchases of different products, impact of advertising strategies (not just of own brands but all brands being marketed by the retailer) (Alliance Consulting Group, n.d.). This data can provide invaluable insights in designing accurate and targeted brand strategies in order to create store brands that are carefully constructed keeping in mind all perceptions and demands of a customer. An example that illustrates the importance of scanner data is given by Baltas (1997) wherein it was identified using scanner data that consumers who tend to make bulk purchases usually opt for store brands due to larger amounts of money that can be saved, therefore, store brands introduced family packs across multiple product categories to increase convenience of shopping and attract greater number of bulk purchasers. In fact, using appropriate advertisement, price promotions and quality improvement strategies can convert store brands into strong and independent identities which in turn will contribute to the image and brand identity of a retailer (Baltas, 1997). Thus, store brands and retail brand names can benefit from the positive circular causation.

Also, the current market scenario is one which is heavily dependent on marketing, branding and narrative creations. Once store brands have successfully established a hold in the currently vulnerable areas by leveraging tangible features and benefits in terms of prices and quality, diversification can be undertaken to upscale products by launching advertising campaigns that appeal to consumers emotionally (Baltas, 1997). This can increase the hedonistic value of store brand products which is useful because hedonistic products are often purchased in a loyal or consistent form and a consumer once convinced of a brand with regards to a hedonistic purchase, finds it difficult to convert to another brand due to the emotional association (Sethuraman & Cole, 1999). This strategy also mitigates the perceived social risk of store brands.

Solutions and Strategies for National Brands

The national brands must have two-pronged strategies to deal with two important objectives: firstly, maintaining the dominant hold in case of hedonistic products or premium products and secondly, capturing the vulnerable product categories by competing with store brands continuously.

In order to capture consumers who have recently turned to store brands, national brands can either reduce the price differential or increase the quality differential commensurate to prices. Cutting down prices in product categories where customers are price conscious could be more helpful. However, prices should not be cut down to the point that they signal a deterioration in quality. Very often a cut in prices by national brands does more harm than good. For example, when Marlboro cut prices in 1993 to reclaim market shares from cheaper variants, it resulted in a stock price fall worth 14 billion dollars due to the adverse perception it created for the brand (Sethuraman & Cole, 1999). Thus, rather than cutting prices permanently, national brands should use occasional discounts and promotions to attract customers and simultaneously a perceived quality differential must be created in order to ensure that the customers who adopt national brands become loyalists.

Creating a quality differential is important to ensure that customers are willing to pay a price premium i.e. customers are accepting the higher prices charged by national brands when offers are not provided. An acceptance for paying higher price commensurate to the benefits received or quality perceived implies a decline in the perceived financial risk that national brands tend to face. This quality differential can be created using non-price-based strategies such as advertising campaigns. National brands should reinforce the sensory appeal and emotional tangent associated with their products. This is an effective strategy for product categories that are inherently brandable i.e. where there is a possibility of associating products with emotions or qualities. For example, cookies and biscuits are often depicted to be consumed in times of happiness or perfumes are associated with love and romance; on the contrary products such as soaps and laundry detergents lack brandability (Alliance Consulting Group, n.d.). However, national brands can easily associate all the products that they manufacture with the general ethics and values associated with the brand identity to increase the feel-good factor or hedonistic value of products, which as mentioned before adds to overall brand building. A recent example of this practice would be Ariel's share-the-load campaign wherein the laundry detergent's use has been associated with the idea of gender equality within a household - this directly connects to the gender equality ethic of Procter & Gamble (the national brand managing Ariel). In fact, national brands should not only create a perceived quality differential but should also bring about an actual improvement in qualities by altering its inputs or packaging practices to justify the price premium. For example, in the everyday footwear category, multiple colors, designs and patterns of slippers can be manufactured and the display can be changed from simple rack hangers to fancy stands in shapes of feet or clouds (anything indicative of relaxation and comfort) that are positioned around seats and sofas for consumers to be able to try them conveniently. Another example could be the use of reusable, high-grade plastic covers for selling food grains such that the packets can be resealed and used for storing other food items also - this not only convinces customers of safer food quality but also creates a link between the brand's products and its environmental conscience.

The Emergence of Co-Opetition

In the current retail market framework, it is impossible to eliminate either the store brands or the national brands, and in fact, it might even be undesirable due to the interdependence that these brands now experience. National brands usually have excess production capacity that they tend to utilize for production of commodities or goods for retailers which then become store brand products. Such retailer-manufacturer relations often become an important determinant of efficiency in production, profits and trade terms for selling & distribution of retail products. Also, retailers cannot solely depend on store brands for success; the primary reason behind the emergence of retailers as important market players is the availability of large-scale variety of brands and products. Customers very often are attracted to retail stores for the national brands that they can access under a single roof. Even the profits of retailers across product categories depends on the sale of national brands products along with own label products. This interdependence forms the basis for co-opetition (Alliance Consulting Group, n.d.).

Co-opetition can be realized through several retail strategies that involve effective management of the manufacturer-retailer relation. Retailers must realize that the shoppers base is calculated as a product of the number of shoppers and trips per shopper. Presence of national brands attracts a greater number of shoppers and expands consumer base. This increased consumer base can also contribute to a greater pool of people who can be targeted for store brand purchases. Thus, an adequate number of national brands must be stored and merchandised in a way that their visibility captures customers. Value bundles can be created between complementary products of either kinds of brands; for example, various varieties of spreads and jams created by national brands can be offered as a combined pack with store brand breads - this will not only increase the sales of either, but also maintain the current preference profiles.

Thus, while the two brands are competitors, they also must co-exist and co-operate to ensure mutual existence and success while extracting marginal gains wherever possible using the aforementioned strategies.

FUTURE RESEARCH DIRECTIONS

Store brands have now started venturing into newer product categories and in order to ensure success in the same, an in-depth evaluation of consumer preferences, perceptions and retail trends must be conducted for these newer categories. Along with this product diversification, store brands are also broadening their marketing strategies and increasingly projecting themselves as at-par competitors of national brands. Thus, the distinction between the two brands is becoming hazy and a new perspective of study needs to be developed wherein rather than the inherent distinction of the brands, the apparent differences in their positioning is focused upon. This can help create new strategies that will help both the brands sustain in the rapidly changing Indian retail scenario.

CONCLUSION

The collective impact of demographic shifts, rise in disposable incomes, increased exposure to an international lifestyle, intensive marketing and spread of consumerism in general, has definitely changed the retail landscape. Today, shopping is no longer an everyday chore that must be performed, instead it has become an activity enjoyed by individuals just like going to the cinema or travelling. As a result, the sensory value associated with retail has increased manifold. The emergence of store brands in competition with the national brands in fact is not an isolated event. This emergence is more a response to the variety of consumers that have emerged and the different demands that they create. The age of globalization and information has led to the birth of an individualistic customer i.e. each customer has a different set of perceptions, expectations, needs, preferences and budget. To cater to the multifaceted demands that such individualistic customers present, products must be available across price ranges, designs, varieties and brands. The battleground that retail market has become between national and store brands is then a mere consequence of suppliers trying to address emerging demands. The horizontal diversification of customers has also been accompanied by a vertical increase in the number of each kind of customer - while on the one hand the young earners are rising in numbers and demand cheaper products with high hedonistic value, on the other hand are the middle-aged high earners who demand social satisfaction and their incomes, and therefore purchases continue to ascend. Consequently, there is ample scope for either kinds of brands to make use of several strategies mentioned above (price-based, quality-based, marketing oriented or co-opetition-based) to expand, co-exist and yet compete to be successful in areas where consumer preferences favor a particular kind of brand.

However, it's not only products whose demands have risen, the demand for experiential satisfaction has also gone up. As a result, retailers have become sellers of not just goods but also experiences and services. Thereby the inherent sensory appeal of retailers is increasing. Add to this the ever-booming importance of advertisements and brand constructions - the sharp lines between store brands and national brands based on packaging, marketing and prices are fast blurring. The only way brands can then construct and retain a unique position in market is by establishing a stable and loyal customer base. This invariably calls for greater attention to be paid to the perceptions which customers form, risks they perceive and decisions they take. Ultimately, consumer and his preferences form the fiber of the retail fabric and an in-depth understanding of the same is the only way to preserve stability in times of uncertainty and change.

REFERENCES

Agarwal, S. (2018). *Big consumer brands losing market share to smaller rivals.*[REMOVED HYPERLINK FIELD] Retrieved 1 April 2018, from https://www.livemint.com/Industry/GtuYtAhywKgkyuNNyDBa2J/Big-consumer-brands-losing-market-share-to-smaller-rivals.html

Alliance Consulting Group. (n.d.). *How National Brand Manufacturers Can Protect Their Brands and Profits*. Retrieved from http://www.alliancecg.com/uploads/the_threat_of_retailer_brands.pdf

Baltas, G. (1997). Determinants of store brand choice: A behavioral analysis. *Journal of Product and Brand Management*, *6*(5), 315–324. doi:10.1108/10610429710179480

Batra, R., & Sinha, I. (2000). Consumer-level factors moderating the success of private label brands. *Journal of Retailing*, *76*(2), 175–191. doi:10.1016/S0022-4359(00)00027-0

Dhaktod, P., & Chib, S. (2015). Private Labels: A Changing Perspective in Indian Retailing. *International Journal of Management and Commerce Innovation*, *3*(2), 282–288.

Erdem, T., Zhao, Y., & Valenzuela, A. (2004). Performance of Store Brands: A Cross-Country Analysis of Consumer Store-Brand Preferences, Perceptions, and Risk. *JMR, Journal of Marketing Research*, *41*(1), 86–100. doi:10.1509/jmkr.41.1.86.25087

González Mieres, C., María Díaz Martín, A., & Trespalacios Gutiérrez, J. (2006a). Antecedents of the difference in perceived risk between store brands and national brands. *European Journal of Marketing, 40*(1/2), 61–82. doi:10.1108/03090560610637310

González Mieres, C., María Díaz Martín, A., & Trespalacios Gutiérrez, J. (2006b). Influence of perceived risk on store brand proneness. *International Journal of Retail & Distribution Management, 34*(10), 761–772. doi:10.1108/09590550610691347

Grewal, D., Levy, M., & Lehmann, D. (2004). Retail Branding and Customer Loyalty: An overview. *Journal of Retailing, 80*(4), ix–xii. doi:10.1016/j.jretai.2004.10.001

Hsu, H., & Lai, C. (2008). Examination of Factors Moderating the Success of Private Label Brands: A Study of the Packaged Food Market in China. *Journal of Food Products Marketing, 14*(4), 1–20. doi:10.1080/10454440801986256

India Brand Equity Foundation. (2016). *Retail.* Retrieved from https://www.ibef.org/download/Retail-January-2016.pdf

Mitchell, V. (1992). Understanding Consumers' Behaviour: Can Perceived Risk Theory Help? *Management Decision, 30*(3), 00251749210013050. doi:10.1108/00251749210013050

Mitchell, V. (1998). A role for consumer risk perceptions in grocery retailing. *British Food Journal, 100*(4), 171–183. doi:10.1108/00070709810207856

Oldenburg, D. (2005). *Store Brands vs. National Brands. Washingtonpost.com.* Retrieved 14 February 2018, from http://www.washingtonpost.com/wp-dyn/content/article/2005/06/20/AR2005062001146.html

Pani, P. (2015). *Godrej Nature's game plan is to be around for a long time: Mohit Khattar.* Retrieved from https://www.thehindubusinessline.com/companies/godrej-natures-game-plan-is-to-be-around-for-a-long-time-mohit-khattar/article7261214.ece

PricewaterhouseCoopers. (2017). *The promise of Indian retail: From vision to execution.* PWC. Retrieved from https://www.pwc.in/assets/pdfs/publications/2017/the-promise-of-indian-retail-from-vision-to-execution.pdf

Ranga, M. (2017). Private label brands retailers in India: Food and grocery sector. *International Journal of Multidisciplinary Research and Development, 4*(5), 143–145.

Retailers Association of India. (2017). *Think India. Think 'connected' retail.* Knight Frank. Retrieved from https://kfcontent.blob.core.windows.net/research/317/documents/en/think-india-think-connected-retail-2017-4441.pdf

Richardson, P., Jain, A., & Dick, A. (1996). Household store brand proneness: A framework. *Journal of Retailing, 72*(2), 159–185. doi:10.1016/S0022-4359(96)90012-3

Sethuraman, R., & Cole, C. (1999). Factors influencing the price premiums that consumers pay for national brands over store brands. *Journal of Product and Brand Management, 8*(4), 340–351. doi:10.1108/10610429910284319

Sheau-Fen, Y., Sun-May, L., & Yu-Ghee, W. (2012). Store brand proneness: Effects of perceived risks, quality and familiarity. *Australasian Marketing Journal*, *20*(1), 48–58. doi:10.1016/j.ausmj.2011.10.014

Subha, T., Kirthika, R., & Narayanaswamy, P. (2018). Private Label Brands in Indian Retail Industry. *International Journal of Research and Development - A Management Review*. Retrieved from http://www.irdindia.in/journal_ijrdmr/pdf/special_iss_1/10.pdf

The Nielsen Company. (2018). *The rise and rise again of private label*. Nielsen. Retrieved from https://www.nielsen.com/content/dam/nielsenglobal/ru/docs/2018.02%20-%20Global%20-20The%20Rise%20and%20Rise%20Again%20of%20Private%20Label.pdf

Wahi, R. (2017). *The rise of private label brands - Re-Tales by Rajat Wahi*. Retrieved 19 April 2018, from https://retail.economictimes.indiatimes.com/re-tales/the-rise-of-private-label-brands/2241

ADDITIONAL READING

Dursun, İ., Kabadayı, E., Alan, A., & Sezen, B. (2011). Store Brand Purchase Intention: Effects of Risk, Quality, Familiarity and Store Brand Shelf Space. *Procedia: Social and Behavioral Sciences*, *24*, 1190–1200. doi:10.1016/j.sbspro.2011.09.133

Glynn, M., & Chen, S. (2009). Consumer-factors moderating private label brand success: Further empirical results. *International Journal of Retail & Distribution Management*, *37*(11), 896–914. doi:10.1108/09590550910999343

Hoch, S. (1996). How Should National Brands Think about Private Labels? *Sloan Management Review*, *37*(2), 89. doi: https://ais.ku.edu.tr/course/12481/hoch%201996.pdf

Quelch, J., & Harding, D. (1996). Brands Versus Private Labels: Fighting to Win. *Harvard Business Review*, *74*(1), 99–109.

Rao, A., & Monroe, K. (1989). The Effect of Price, Brand Name, and Store Name on Buyers' Perceptions of Product Quality: An Integrative Review. *JMR, Journal of Marketing Research*, *26*(3), 351. doi:10.2307/3172907

Sethuraman, R., & Raju, J. (2012). The Competition between National Brands and Store Brands: Models, Insights, Implications, and Future Research Directions. *Foundations and Trends® In Marketing*, *7*(1), 1-108. doi:10.1561/1700000029

Vahie, A., & Paswan, A. (2006). Private label brand image: Its relationship with store image and national brand. *International Journal of Retail & Distribution Management*, *34*(1), 67–84. doi:10.1108/09590550610642828

KEY TERMS AND DEFINITIONS

Co-Opetition: The phenomenon of several entities (store brands and national brands in this case) competing in an area where they must co-exist for sustenance.

Consumer Goods: These are typically mass-market items that consumed out of necessity rather than want. Their utilitarian purpose is of greater importance than social or emotional appeal.

Consumer Purchasing Behavior: It refers to the decision-making process of consumers wherein they choose from the multiple products and varieties available in order to meet their needs, minimize costs and maximize satisfaction. The behavior is reflective of consumers preferences, nature and budget constraints.

Hedonic Goods: These are goods which are desirable and yield satisfaction or a sense of happiness to the consumer but cannot be termed as necessities. The social and emotional value of these goods exceeds the utilitarian value.

Perceived Risk: Any adverse view that consumers associate with a product based on the perception they have formed about it. Any perceived risk is viewed as leading to a plausible loss that consumers will bear from consumption.

Pricing Strategy: The use of price changes and discounts to manage the appeal and preference for products to achieve certain levels of sales and profits.

Private Label: Products under these labels are manufactured by a third-party (usually national brand manufacturers) under contract but sold by label owners (retailers) under their brand names and identities.

Retail Market: It refers to the interactions between buyers and sellers of goods in market space.

Value Perception Management: The techniques used to influence a consumer's perception about the value that any product offers by controlling product features, prices, advertisements, packaging, etc.

Chapter 15
Financial Risk Analysis for Crude Oil Buried Pipeline System

Narendra Rajaram Gade
Mahatma Gandhi Mission's College of Engineering and Technology, India

Ravi Dhondiba Suryavanshi
Bharati Vidyapeeth College of Engineering, India

Pravin Suryawanshi
Indian Institute of Technology Bombay, India

Arati Barik
Mahatma Gandhi Mission's College of Engineering and Technology, India

Rahul Bhalerao
Petrofac Engineering India Pvt. Ltd, India

ABSTRACT

Buried pipelines are the most lucrative deal in today's transportation for transmission of vital fluids and liquids. However, with the advent of disasters, the continuous flow through these indispensable systems gets hampered. The purpose of this chapter is twofold: one is to develop a simulation approach to capturing the effect of risk/disaster due to unforeseen events on buried pipeline, and the second is to gauge financial losses due to such uncertain events. A simulation model considering hoop, longitudinal, and radial stresses on continuous flow carrying buried pipeline subjected to uncertain and risky events is developed in CAESAR II engineering software. The authors performed statistical analysis to carry node-based analysis to describe the repair cost associated with the individual node or throughout the whole pipeline system under study. Although with a limitation in terms of model accuracy and reliability as the actual scenario could differ from the simulated model, the study outlines financial gain over total repair cost using simulation modeling approach in face of disruptions.

DOI: 10.4018/978-1-5225-7208-4.ch015

INTRODUCTION

Keeping in concern the economic, safety, speed and pollution aspects, every year crude oil and gas are transported in heavy quantities to different demand points. The activity of transportation involves the transfer via trucks, barge, and rail, and pipeline, sea/river ways transport as a ship, underwater pipeline transport and under-earth transport. Moreover, for long distance transports, pipelines are the best suitable and cheap option. Such transport is safe (less prone to accidents), fast, and continuous and significant in terms of volume transportation. Such system not only carries petroleum products, crude oil, and natural gas but other essential liquids but also it is more eco-friendly and leaves a low carbon footprint.

However, the pipelines are affected by the different geological conditions, under various regions and under different seismicity. Thus, it is acknowledged as reliable, economic and efficient means for the transportation of water and other commercial fluids such as oil and gas (Shah, 2016). Many times booster pumps are used to facilitate the flow in the piping system by maintaining the integrity and need of the nation's (Riegel et al, 2007; Mehrishi, 2017). To ensure the maximum degree of safety, it is important to design the pipeline to ensure a uniform approach to the problem (Kumar, 2016). Majorly, any pipeline system is subjected to the static and dynamic forces; however, the system is required to have the flexible and expansion capabilities for sustainable flow of crude oil. Because as these forces increases, there excessive bending, unusual loads at joints, or undesirable forces or moments at points puts pressure on the points of connection of the systems (Kumar, 2016). Majorly two types of the loading are affected by the pipeline system and are classified as primary loads and secondary loads. Also when the failure is sudden, it attributes to primary and loadings primary loadings. Every piping system goes through the life cycle where in it has to face different potential loads. Therefore, ignoring any such loads poses challenges to the designers such as excessive erection, hydro-testing issues, and automatic shut-up and down, abnormal operation, and heavy maintenance etc. to the piping system. At times, due to dominos effect the pipeline might break down. The Present work intended to study stress analysis of the buried Pipeline (at construction stage) with a practical solution and to reduce stress and to increase the life of pipeline with an appropriate design for the pipelines so that they can withstand these stresses (Green et al, 2015; Anderson, 1994; Azevedo, 2007). The piping system consists of pipe, fixtures such as nuts and bolts, valves, and joints to handle the flow due to other portions of the piping components. Apart from these, other items are also required such as components which help to reduce excessive pressure and stress. Thus, pipe is just an element or a part of piping. Thus, pipes should be tightly fit to the valves and other joints properly in order to hang and support to the other mechanical equipments (Shah, 2016; Riegel, 2007).

Pipeline Network in India

Presently, the pipelines exist across India spreads over 15000 km. The authority which looks over the working and design of the network in India is GAIL ltd (India) (Kumar, 2016). Currently, Bokaro-Ranchi-Talcher-Paradip-Angul pipeline is implementation. Also, a project named Coal Bed Methane (CBM) of 312 km is in process to connect to the existing Hazira-Vijyapur-Jagdishpur pipeline at Phulpur, Uttar Pradesh. Apart from these big projects, small projects such as Phulpur (UP) to Dobhi (Bihar) of 414 km, are taken under by the respective oil and gas corporations (Kumar, 2016).

Figure 1. Typical mode wise transportation crude oil and petroleum products industry
(Source: PPAC, 2016)

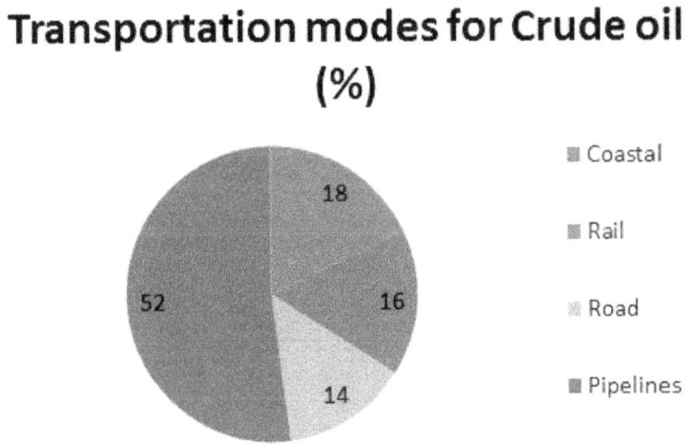

In India Gas Authority of India Limited (GAIL), Reliance Gas Transportation Infrastructure Limited (RGTIL), and Gujarat State Petronet Limited (GSPL) has captured the whole pipeline transportation. Figure 1 explains the different proportion of modes of transport in India for the crude oil. GAIL pipeline constitutes to about 68.59% followed by RGTIL about 9.16% and rest is captured by GSPL (16.17%).

This pipeline passes through Andhra Pradesh, Maharashtra and, Gujarat and integrated with GAIL's and GSPL's network to reach Northern and Western Indian market. GSPL is mainly focused in the state of Gujarat consisting about 2612 km (about 16.17%) (Kumar, 2016).

All the sources for these gas is primarily from KG-D6 (Krishna-Godavari-Dhirubhai6), Mumbai offshore, Cambay Basin, Ravva Offshore, KG Basin, Cauvery basin and Imported LNG [4]. Moreover, looking at the consumption side, 80% of gas is consumed by the western and northern parts of the country. The Table 1 and Figure 2 depicts the explanation as mentioned above. Also, Figure 2 shows the Crude oil and LPG pipeline of India (Chen et al, 2002).

It may trigger domino effect and cause the major disaster so it's very important to take note of all potential loads that piping system may occur. Out of a total job man-hour for a particular project, engineering man-hour contributes to 40 to 48% and piping man hour contribute to 20 to 25% of total man hours to engineering. Stress analysis contributes to 8 to 12% of total piping man hours. Stress analysis constitutes to rather an insignificant amount of total job man-hour, piping begins most dedicated com-

Table 1. Spread of pipeline network of different transporter network

Sr. no.	Transporter	(Length km)	(% share)
1	GAIL	11077	68.59%
2	RGTIL	1480	9.16%
3	GSPL	2612	16.17%
4	AGCL/OIL/DNPL	817	5.06%
5	IOCL	140	0.87%
6	ONGC	24	0.15%
Total		16150	100%

(Source: PPAC, 2016)

Figure 2. Crude oil and LPG pipeline of India
(Source: National Energy Map for India)

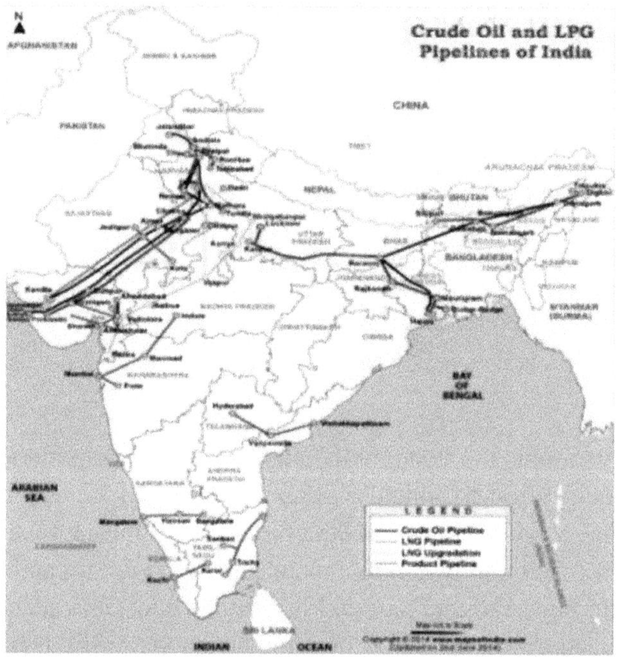

ponent in any Process Plant. Also, the business entity is subjected to almost all kind of load ignoring or misleading any such, while designing, erection, hydro testing, startup, shutdown, normal operation maintenance etc. can lead to inadequate design and engineering of piping system the system may fail at first occurrence of this overload failure of piping system. It may trigger domino effect and cause the major disaster so it's very important to take note of all potential load that piping system may occur (Teri, 2006).

Figure 3. Stress at different nodes (without Kflex)

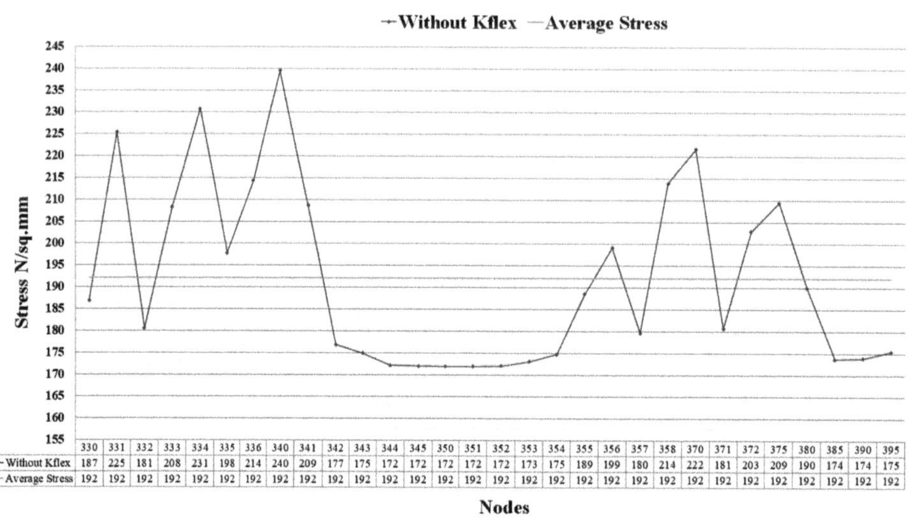

	330	331	332	333	334	335	336	340	341	342	343	344	345	350	351	352	353	354	355	356	357	358	370	371	372	375	380	385	390	395
Without Kflex	187	225	181	208	231	198	214	240	209	177	175	172	172	172	172	172	173	175	189	199	180	214	222	181	203	209	190	174	174	175
Average Stress	192	192	192	192	192	192	192	192	192	192	192	192	192	192	192	192	192	192	192	192	192	192	192	192	192	192	192	192	192	192

Nodes

Output result obtained for different code stresses by "CAESAR II basic model" modeling approach shown in Table 5. It is evident from Table 5 that buried pipeline system gets failed at node number 340,334,370,331,375,331, 341,341,356. The results obtained from the simulation study within node number from 330 to 342, stress is fluctuating as shown in Figure 3 and Table 5. After node number 342, stress generated is almost constant till node 354 and it is again fluctuating from node 355 to 395. Working stress is in the range of 171.98 to 239.56 N/mm^2. At different nodes, the failure exits due to the pipe wall and soil interaction. Sohail (et al, 2017) performed stress analysis for pump discharge system and reported that the code stress at each node is less than the allowable stress as per ASME (Guerrero, 2015). The stress values obtained for the case of without Kflex and corresponding allowable stress limit have been presented in Table 5. It is unsafe at 8 out of 30 nodes. Base on allowable for each load case exceeded beyond ASME limit. To control stress value within code limit we have different methods they are below (Antaki, 2003; Alliance, 2001, Guerrero, 2015).

- Changing material of construction (MOC)
- Change pipeline routing
- Change soil property
- Shifting anchor location
- Concrete trench / Coating
- Wrapping of polyurethane

Changing Material of Construction (MOC)

While manufacturing the pipe itself, different materials can be used. These materials can provide better performance and desirable safety. Considering the dynamic demand, it is unadvisable to experiment with such activity as every time it is required that the for procurement dept. has to get a license and the project management (PMC) approval.

Change Pipeline Routing

Selecting the pipeline routes plays major role as these routes act as the vein for oil industry. It is recommended that to avoid the risky paths while establishing a channel for the pipelines. Currently, various factors such as shortest distance, environmental factors, approachability and governmental rules are considered while designing a pathway for the pipeline system. Moreover, it is infeasible at time to change the pathway for the pipeline as doing so lead delays in the erection activities.

Change Soil Property

It is common that the pipelines and soil interaction are subject to a combination of tension, blending, and external pressure etc. loads. This load either individually or in combination can be more severe than operational loads and may govern drilled path design or specification (Cochetti et la, 2009; Yuain et al, 2012). With activity if changing the soil around buried pipeline might affect the pipeline and change its properties and reliability over the part of the entire pipeline. Digging soil from one end and filling to pipeline network will cause environmental issues which are not advisable.

Concrete TRENCH / COATING

One of the know industry standard that is followed to avoid breakdown in thepiepline system is usage of concrete trench. Costs analysis suggested by the Zarghamee et al., (2012) reported the costs associated with identifying distressed pipeline sections vary widely depending on the method selected by the water utility, length of pipe, diameter, and access to the pipeline, environmental concerns, and many other factors. Table 3 reflects the cost associated with the different strategies carried to safeguard the piping system (Zarghamee et al., 2012).

Table 2 & 4 represents the Cost data, along with the technical benefits and limitations of the three renewal options discussed in this study were obtained as part of the 2012 industry questionnaire and survey conducted by WRF (Zarghamee et al., 2012) (see Appendix)

Wrapping of Polyurethane Material (Kflex)

Kflex provides high structural support to the pipeline via high compressive strength. The bond between the polyurethane foam and carbon steel service provides a higher resistance to differential movement (Shear) from thermal expansion or soil stresses (Antaki, 2003; Alliance, 2001).

Table 2. Approximate Costs Associated with Identifying Distressed Pipeline Sections

Item	Unit	Approximate Cost
Internal visual and sounding inspection	Per mile	$2k to $3k
External visual and sounding inspection	Per pipe	$10k
Electromagnetic Inspection	Per mile	$12.5k to $56k
Over-the-line corrosion/corrosively survey	Per mile	$0.5k to $3k
Acoustic Fiber Optic Monitoring	Per mile / year	$70k to $170k
Dewatering	Per mile / inch diameter	$300 to $500

Source: Zarghamee et. al., 2012, p. 30

Table 3. Comparison of renewal strategies

Repair Method	Traffic Disruption	Environmental / Social Impact	Construction Duration
Pipe Section Replacement	High	High	High
Carbon-fiber-reinforced polymer (CFRP) Lining	Low	Low	Moderate
Steel Slip lining	Moderate	Moderate	Moderate

Source: Rahman et. al., 2012, p. 499

Table 4. Renewal cost data based on 2012 WRF industry survey

Renewal Strategy	Technical Benefits	Technical Limitations	Comparative Cost
Pipeline Section Replacement	Effective for repair of pipeline sections. No reduction in internal diameter.	Requires excavation of the pipe. May require field welding of the closure piece. Requires an extensive work the area along the pipeline alignment.	$$$ $20 per LF – inch diameter
CFRP Lining	Requires a limited work area. Minimal reduction of the internal diameter. Reduction of surface roughness.	Requires monitoring of CFRP installation.	$$$$ $40 to 50 per LF – inch diameter
Slip Lining of Pipe Section	Effective for repair of nearly straight sections of pipelines. Minimized welding inside the pipe.	Reduction of diameter may results in loss of flow capacity. Requires extensive work area and removal of several pipe sections.	$ $14 per LF – inch diameter

Source: Zarghamee et. al., 2012, p. 120

Listing few of the advantages of using polyurethane

- Increases the cross-sectional area to sustain more stress
- Good and easy local solution for effective reducing the stresses
- Inexpensive and time-saving
- Prevents pipelines from corrosion and rusting

Guan et al. (2007) performed efficiency of Kflex compared to other methods and demonstrated the same using a numerical studies with a view to prevent unexpected failure of flexible pipes at minimal cost by prioritizing maintenance based on failure severity and system reliability.

Polyurethane

Polyurethane foam has a high strength, durable, with moderate density of 2.2 pcf i.e. 35.2 kg/m^3. The foam has its own advantages such as shock absorbent, insulator, buoyancy during flotation, vibration reducer etc. One of the most important properties of this foam is its loading capacity, it can hold up to 2.5 psi (17.5kPa) (Tian-bo et al, 2006; Alliance, 2001). Foam properties are shown in appendix Polyurethane Appendix.

The polyurethane foam has wide application apart from the piping system including computer hardware, infrastructure projects, automotive business and recreation. However, the optimum performance is achieved with expert's hands designing the total packaging solution. The widely used type of polyurethane wrapping available in the market is called as "K-flex" and it is insulation with an extruded polyurethane coating available in different sizes as per requirement from industry (Tian-bo, et al, 2006).

SOLUTIONS AND RECOMMENDATIONS

Mathematical Groundwork

Out of a total job man-hour for the particular project engineering man-hour contribute to 40 to 48% and piping man hour contributed to 20 to 25% of total man hours to engineering. Stress analysis contributed to 8 to 12% of total piping man hours but stress analysis constituted to rather an insignificant amount of total job man-hour, piping begins most dedicated component in any Process Plant (Nayyar et al, 1994). A pipeline system is subjected to static and dynamic loads due to local environmental and operating conditions, and provision must be made for the system to have flexibility and expansion capability to prevent excessive stresses in the pipe or components, excessive bending or unusual loads at joints, or undesirable forces or moments at points of connection to equipment. The types of loadings which will affect the flexibility and expansion of the pipeline as a system include (Jayadevan et al, 2004; Wang et al, 2002).. The piping system taken for the case study is pipeline launcher and receiver area unit of a petroleum refinery (at construction stage) the pipeline is analyzed for stress analysis which consists of the crude oil as the fluid for a constant temperature of 120°C. The material used for the pipeline was made of Carbon steel API-5LX42.The discussions for the analysis consists of determining the nodes, where the stress exceeds the allowable limits for different values. Many times, the underground pipelines are subjected to severe loading conditions such as the length of the pipe, the fluid pressure generated due to its weight and thermal loads etc.

Above (Figure 4) loads which effect pipeline system lead exceeded the American Society of Mechanical Engineers (ASME) allowable limit, these standards are referred for designing pipeline systems (ASME B31.3 and ASME B31.4). For the mathematical understanding, we have listed the formulas required while doing the analysis as below; Firstly, we derive for nominal wall thickness. Secondly, we calculate the respective allowable stress denoted 'S';

$$t_n \geq t + A$$

Where,

A=Sum of allowances for threading, grooving, corrosion, and erosion as required by ASME standards.
t_n=Nominal wall thickness for pressure and allowances
t = Pressure design wall thickness as calculated in. (mm) in accordance with the following

Figure 4. Types of loadings/ stresses affects the pipeline

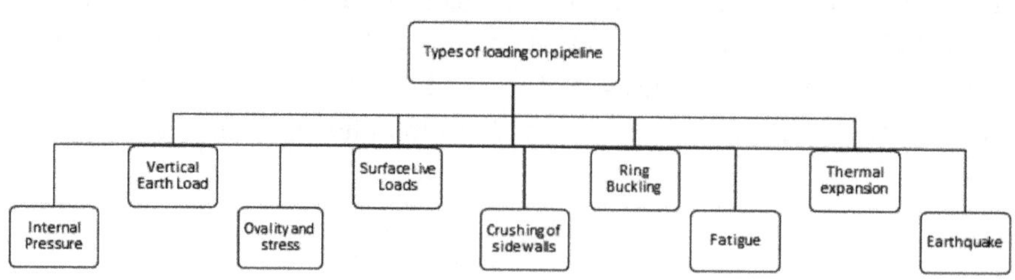

$$t = \frac{D \times P_i}{20 \times S} \; t = \frac{D * P_i}{20 * S}$$

where,

D = Outer diameter of the pipe, in. (mm)
Pi = internal design gauge pressure, psi (bar)
S = applicable allowable stress value, psi (MPa),

As determined by the following equation:

$S = F \times E \times S_y$

where

E = Weld joint factor as per ASME standards
F = Design factor based on nominal wall thickness
S_y = Specified minimum yield strength of the pipe, psi (MPa)
S = applicable allowable stress value

Thus, the allowable expansion stress, SA, is as follows:

$S_A \leq f\,[1.25\,S_c + S_h - S_L]$

where,

f = fatigue factor calculated as f p 6.0N-0.2, (not exceed 1.2)
N= equivalent number of full displacement cycles during the expected service life of the pipeline system
S_c =2/3SY at the lower of the installed or minimum operating temperature
S_h = 2/3SY at the higher of the installed or maximum operating temperature [2, 3]. S_L = Longitudinal stress
S_A = Allowable Stress

Soil Models

The CAESAR II software has the module where a designer can add the soil model structure and provide the user defined inputs. The software gives a provision for estimating soil stiffness and ultimate loads for inadequate data using appropriate methods. There are two modeling algorithms CAESAR II Basic Model and American Lifelines Alliance.

We have used CAESAR II Basic Model "Stress Analysis Methods for Underground Pipelines," as suggested by L.C. Peng (1978) for Pipeline system. American Lifelines Alliance" In the Appendix we gave soil spring representation" from the Guidelines provided by the design of buried steel pipe by the American Lifelines Alliance.

III PIPE STRESS ANALYSIS

Caesar II Model

For the modeling purpose, we have used piping software called CAESAR II (V 7.0.2014). The geometric properties for the pipe and the soil properties are selected directly in the modeling software, this creates the soil model. The soil material used in the software is APL-5L X42. For the understanding purpose we have captures the window during the modeling phase and is shown in Figure 5

- **Load Cases:** To meet these objectives several load cases are required during stress analysis (Riegel, 2007; Mehrishi, 2017; Kumar, 2016). Operating case: When the operation starts working fluid will flow through the piping at a temperature and pressure. So accordingly, our operating load cases will be as mentioned below:

L1= W+T1+P1

- **Sustained Load Case:** These are the case types where the support configuration of a converged operating condition is required. These cases also help to address the non-linear conditions active in some operating situations and inactive in others.

L2 = W+P1

- **Expansion Load Case:** It is obtained by subtracting sustained case form the operating case. The expansion the case represents the change in the piping system due to the effect of temperature,

Figure 5. Parameter specification

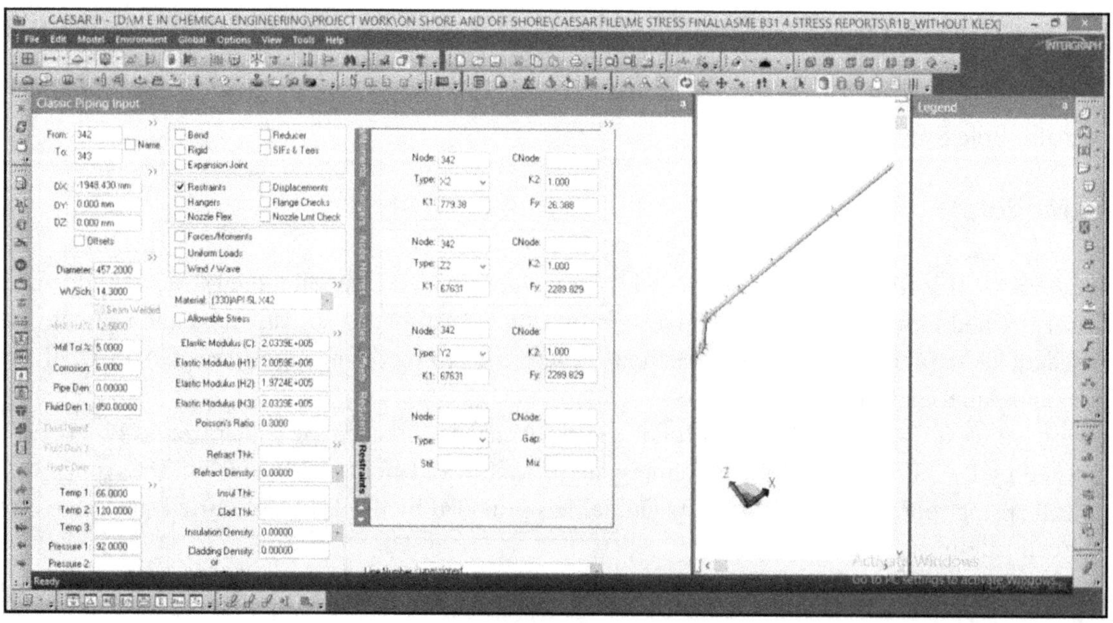

with the presence of other loads. This is important because the restraint status of the operating and sustained cases can be different if there are nonlinear restraints (such as +Y, -Z, any restraint with a gap, etc.), or boundary conditions (friction). Therefore expansion loads case:

L4=L1-L3

The ratio of pipe routing is defined as code stress to allowable stress and signifies the amount by which the code stress has to less than the allowable stress or vice versa (Riegel, 2007; Mehrishi, 2017).

Ratio = code stress/ allowable stress

Allowable stress is the pressure per unit area quality and is the maximum load a pipe can withstand. It is the most important parameter in the piping system and is varied material wise. Therefore, as the name suggests the working stress (code stress) in the piping system should not exceed an allowable stress of the material for the selected code and standard. The CAESAR software takes cares of the nodal displacement denoted as (DXin, DYin, DZin,) and (RXdeg, RYdeg, RZdeg) in all the three directions.

Stress Analysis (With 50 mm Kflex)

As discussed in the methodology section, the first step done was wrapping the Polyethylene foam with 50 mm thickness to the buried pipeline. The obtained result of code stress analysis at different nodes is shown in Figure 5. It can be seen from the Figure 5 that the obtained stresses at different node number are less in comparison with the stresses obtained in the case of without Kflex. With the dynamic nature of flows in the pipeline and other forces on soil along with the interaction results in transfers of the load from one node to another. In this case, the nodes at which the propensity to fail is incurred as 353,356,357,358, 370,371,372 of the buried pipe and acceptance/non-acceptance of the nodes is as per the allowable stress by the American Society of Mechanical Engineers (ASME) (Guerrero, n.d.). The stress values obtained for the case of with Kflex and corresponding allowable stress limit have been presented in Figure 6.

As shown in Figure 6, the average stress lies at 194 N/mm2. For Kflex 50, the stress at nodes after node number 356, exceeds the Allowable Stress value of 208.49 N./mm2 along with fluctuating results with highest as 249 N/mm2 at node number 358.Since at most of the nodes crosses the allowable stress limit (9 out of 30) Table 5, it is not acceptable to use the Kflex 50 mm for wrapping of the given pipeline. One very common standard followed in industries to minimize the stress effect is to provide anchor support the buried pipeline. Anchor support is one of important factor of crossing allowable stress limit as per the study conducted by Sohail et al (2017). In the present work, the analysis was done during construction or erection phase of the buried pipeline as providing anchor support at the time of construction or erection phase may lead delay in erection activity and repetition of work which is not advisable (from the economical point of view.)

Stress Analysis (With 25 mm Kflex)

The further thickness of wrapping reduced from 50 mm to 25 mm (50% of reduction) and the obtained result of code stress analysis at different nodes is shown in Figure 6. From the Figure 6, it can be seen

Figure 6. Stress at different nodes (for 50mm Kflex)

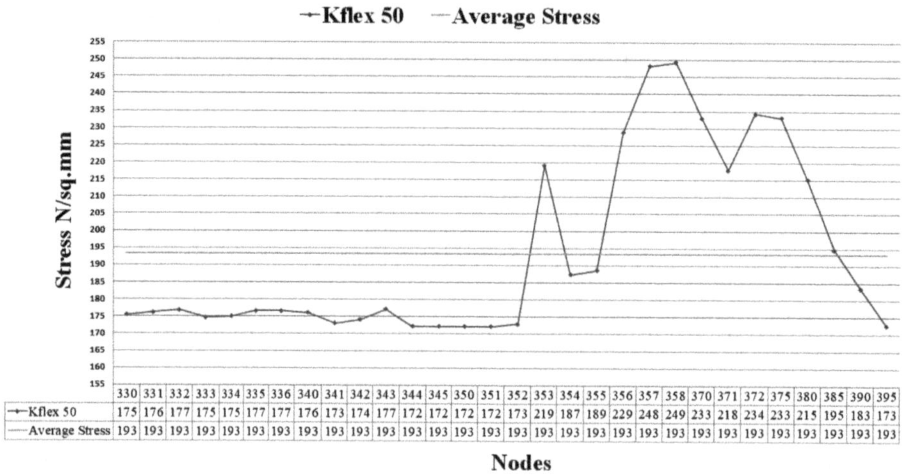

that the stresses at different nodes are less as compared to the wrapping for Kflex-50. Moreover, the average stress value for Kflex-50 and Kflex-25 is 194 N/mm2 and 184 N/mm2 respectively.

It is evident from the Figure 6 that the stress value after node number 354 exceeds the average value of 184 N./mm2 with the highest value of 209.18 N/mm2 at node number 357. Table 5 represents the obtained stress values for Kflex 25 along with the allowable stress limit values from the simulation study. The Table 5 also indicates the nodes which are safe/unsafe keeping allowable stress value as the bench mark. There is only one node that crosses the allowable stress limit value whereas there are five nodes out of 30 having values near to the allowable limit. These are at node number 356, 358, 370, 372, and 375. The overall stress values are near the average of 184.27 N./mm2 and within the range of 150 to 200 N./mm2. The ratio for code stress and allowable stress for node number 357 is more than one, therefore the node number 357 is declared as unsafe so Kflex 25 mm is not suitable for wrapping for the given pipeline system. Hence, the need for further fine-tuning is required to reduce stress at different nodes to safeguard pipeline system.

Stress Analysis (With 15 mm Kflex)

As per the wrapping method explained above for Kflex 25, the same process is implemented to wrap the pipeline system with Kflex 15 and the simulation results obtained are shown in Figure 7. Figure 7 shows the obtained results for different code stresses. The allowable stress limit, in this case, is at 208.49 N./mm2. The results obtained out of the simulation study is in the range of 170 and 200 N./mm2. For Kflex 15 all the code stress values are within the safe range and are not exceeding the allowable limit of 208.49 N./mm2. Therefore, to obtain better results, usage of Kflex 15 is recommended. Comparing the code stress value with the average values, there are nodes which exceed the average value at node number 357, 358, 372, and 375. The value for stresses at different nodes never crosses the allowable limit and the ratio of code stress to allowable stress for all the nodes is within 95%. Henceforth, the Kflex at 15 mm is found to be safe for all nodes as per the simulation study. All the interpreted conclusion is derived from the Table 5.

Figure 7. Stress at different nodes (for 15mm Kflex)

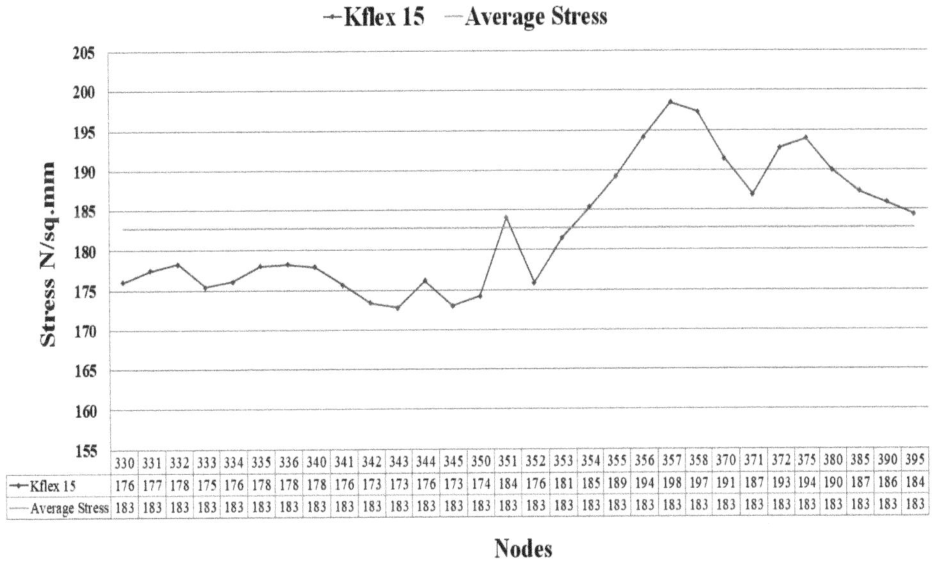

Even though the results obtained from the wrapping of 15 mm Kflex were satisfactory. The similar analysis is performed with Kflex 10, to check for achieving better results as compared to wrapping with Kflex 15.

Stress Analysis (With 10 mm Kflex)

The results obtained for Kflex 10 does not perform satisfactorily as compared to Kflex 15. The applied polyurethane foam of 10 mm thick to buried pipe shows that at node number 330 to 350, the values for code stress are drastically different. However, these values are within the allowable limit of 208.49 N./ mm^2. All the results obtained from the simulation study are presented in Table 5.

Comparison of Different Wrapping Strategies

Figure 8 represents the bar chart for values for the number of cases at the different percentage for given piping system with and without Kflex. The values at the top of bar charts at 85% for Kflex-15, 25 and 50 mm as well as without Kflex represents a number of nodes for which the code stress exceeds the respective allowable stress limit value. Though in Figure 8 the number of exceeded cases is high for Kflex 15 compared with the Kflex 25, the failure rate is higher for Kflex 25 compared with the Kflex 15. Therefore, usage of wrapping at 15 mm Kflex is recommended.

Table 5 (Appendix) presents the consolidated table for all the entries for code stress at different wrapping strategies i.e. Kflex 10, 15, 25, 50 and without Kflex along with the node numbers. Figure 8 depicts the overall analysis for different series, comparing all of them at a time. Where each series represent individual line for different wrapping strategies implemented on the given piping system. The maximum deviation for code stress values for given piping system is without Kflex whereas the stable values are obtained for Kflex 15 and Kflex 10. However, the stress code values for Kflex 15 are

Figure 8. Bar chart showing cases where the code stress value exceeds the variable allowable limit

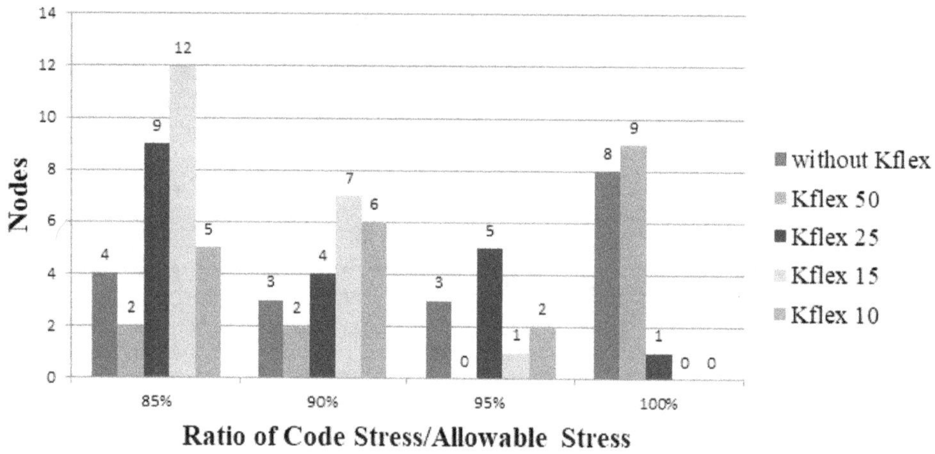

comparatively lesser than the allowable limit as compared to the Kflex 10. Thus from the CAESAR II simulation and analysis, it is recommended to use a foam of polyurethane with a wrapping of 15 mm thickness to given piping system.

FUTURE RESEARCH DIRECTIONS

Pipeline engineering is a vast field with hidden potential. The number of improvements based on performance condition and efficiency is yet to be discovered. Some of the activities such as buckling and upheaval or lateral buckling in pipelines, reducing earthquake effect on the pipeline, soil properties are major influencing factors in the buried pipeline system. So, changing soil can be checked for reducing stress. Waste plastics can also be utilized in making outer wrapping of buried pipelines to prevent frictional stress with soil.

This thesis bridges the gap between theoretical understanding and practical implementation for a buried pipeline under various stresses. We have provided the engineering solution for the model under study with sufficient and accurate analysis. However, from a research perspective, there are several matters which require further research, namely:

1. The time-dependent behavior of the soil should be investigated, to incorporate the effect of the same on the buried pipeline.
2. A more detailed parametric study should be carried out to investigate the influence of the following factors:
    a. Burial depth of the pipe
    b. Initial properties of soil
    c. The diameter of the pipe
    d. Position of anchor
3. Thermal analysis to be carried on wrapped polyethylene to facilitate the transportation of media inside the pipeline.

4. To elucidate the effect of wrapping polyethylene without using anti-corrosion coating and Nanoparticle coting to check anti-corrosion behavior.
5. Testing the life expectancy of the pipeline when wrapping is done throughout instead on selected terminals.

Further study can be conducted on overall performance wrapping of polyurethane to evaluate its corrosion prevention measures and its efficiency in reducing the dead load for the pipe. We can also study its efficacy in reducing the buckling effect or in the absorption of sudden loads.

CONCLUSION

A present study devoted to analyzing the buried pipeline system by "CAESAR II basic model" modeling approach. Study subjected to static as well as dynamic forces, under various operating events like erecting, hydro-testing, start-up, shut-down, normal operation, maintenance etc. The buried pipeline systems have different working conditions than above ground pipeline systems. Maintaining the stresses in buried pipeline system within the allowable stress limit can be done using several different methods. But, considering the feasibility and the economical limitations, we use the method of wrapping of polyurethane material (Kflex) to reduce stresses on the buried pipeline system.

Polyurethane wrapping increases the cross-sectional area to sustain more stress. Providing wrapping of polyurethane gives us a good and easy local solution and effectively reduces the stresses on the buried pipeline system. It reduces the cost of erection along with time to implement reduces drastically. Comparative to other methods, present wrapping of polyurethane material (Kflex) very inexpensive and time-saving. This wrapping also prevents the pipeline from corrosion and can act as a cushion over the pipeline.

First, we had identified the potential loads that would act on the buried pipeline system over its entire life. Then, the loads with the considerations of earthquake, wind or shock loadings are used to compute the stresses and strains that would be developed in the pipeline system. The methods used in the completion of these tasks were done primarily using the software "CAESAR II 2014 Version 7.00" accompanied with various other calculations which were not completed using the software. All the required parameters and data was entered as input in this software. As the output of this software, we obtained the necessary data for further calculations. The stress analysis was carried out in accordance with ASME standards.

After these calculations, we obtained the result that required critical thickness, or the closest value, for the wrapping with several iterations. We calculated stresses for wrapping thickness of four types and compared these stresses. Obtained results found the thickness value closest to the critical thickness, which corresponds to the minimum stresses generated as compared to the stresses generated by the other thickness values. We calculated the ratio of code stress to allowable stress, to check which nodes are unsafe.

Present investigation calculated stresses for different wrapping thickness of four types, namely 50 mm, 25 mm, 15 mm and 10 mm, we found that the thickness of 15 mm, gives us the best possible results for the stress analysis (i.e code stress to allowable stress ration with ASME limit). The stresses generated at the nodes for the thickness of 15 mm are less than 95% of the allowable stress limit. While 10 mm thickness provides almost as good results as 15 mm thickness, but it does cross the level of 95% of the allowable stress. So, 15 mm must be the critical thickness for the wrapping or very close to that value.

In our study, we found that the stresses reduce drastically with respect to the thickness of the wrapping, as it almost reduces stresses by approximately 35%.

Also, comparing all the nodes with each other, for all the wrapping thickness types, we find that highest level of stress is generated in the node 357, even if it doesn't cross the allowable stress limit in some cases. Incidentally, for the case of without any wrapping of polyurethane, this node does not even cross the 90% of the allowable stress. But, since it generated the maximum stress in all the other cases we can make it an anchor node (anchor support), to keep it constrained and keep the stresses to a minimum. Therefore, we can increase our efficiency even more.

Thus, results obtained using the wrapping of polyurethane we can reduce stresses generated in the pipeline system considerably as an inexpensive and time-efficient method. We found the critical thickness of the wrapping of polyurethane material (Kflex) to reduce stresses on the buried pipeline system.

ACKNOWLEDGMENT

The authors express heartfelt gratitude to their kin for their constant inspiration, guidance, and support right through the completion of the chapter. The authors further wish to express gratitude to the managing committee, staff, members and customers of BhaginiNiveditaSahakari Bank Ltd., Pune, for their patience and co-operation while providing necessary information and statistics relevant to the study. We are also glad to share our journey with IGI Global team, as their constant support and co-ordination has helped us to articulate our study into more systematic and organized manner.

REFERENCES

Alliance, A. L. (2001). Guidelines for the design of buried steel pipe. In American Society of Civil Engineers. American Society of Civil Engineers. doi:10.1061/9780784413074

Anderson, R. A. (1994). Electrostatic Forces in an Ideal Spherical-particle Electrorheological Fluid. *Langmuir, 10*(9), 2917–2928. doi:10.1021/la00021a013

Antaki, G. A. (2003). *Piping and Pipeline Engineering: Design, Construction, Maintenance, Integrity, and Repair*. New York: CRC Press; doi:10.1201/9780203911150

Atten, P., & Aitken, F. (2007). Electro Coalescence Criterion for two Close Water Drops. *Industry Applications Conference, 2007, 42nd IAS Annual Meeting, Conference Record of the 2007 IEEE*, 452-456. 10.1109/07ias.2007.7

Azevedo, C. R. (2007). Failure Analysis of a Crude Oil Pipeline. *Engineering Failure Analysis, 14*(6), 978–994. doi:10.1016/j.engfailanal.2006.12.001

Blake, T. D., Clarke, A., & Ruschak, K. J. (1994). Hydrodynamic assist of dynamic wetting. *AIChE Journal. American Institute of Chemical Engineers, 40*(2), 229–242. doi:10.1002/aic.690400205

CAESAR II. (2014). *Design Manual of software CAESAR II*. Intergraph Corporation. doi:10.1016/0010-4485(85)90100-9

Chaudhary, V., Pasupuleti, V. D. K., & Ramancharla, P. K. (2012). 3D FE Modelling of Buried Continuous Pipeline Exposed to Fault Motion with Material Nonlinearity and large Deformation. *Fourth International Conference on Structural Stability and Dynamics ICSSD 2012*, 6-8. 10.1504/ijstructe.2013.056981

Chaudhary, V., Pasupuleti, V. D. K., & Ramancharla, P. K. (2014). *Finite Element Analysis of Buried Continuous Pipeline Subjected to Large Ground Motion*. Centre for Earthquake Engineering International Institute of Information Technology Hyderabad. doi:10.1504/ijstructe.2013.056981

Chen, W. W., Shih, B. J., Chen, Y. C., Hung, J. H., & Hwang, H. H. (2002). Seismic Response of Natural Gas and Water Pipelines in the Ji-Ji earthquake. *Soil Dynamics and Earthquake Engineering*, *22*(9), 1209–1214. doi:10.1016/S0267-7261(02)00149-5

Cocchetti, G., di Prisco, C., Galli, A., & Nova, R. (2009). Soil–Pipeline Interaction Along Unstable Slopes: a Ccoupled Three-dimensional Approach. Part 1: Theoretical Formulation. *Canadian Geotechnical Journal*, *46*(11), 1289–1304. doi:10.1139/T09-028

Cooperation, A. P. E. (2002). *Earthquake Disaster Management of Energy Supply System of APEC Member Economies*. Taipei, China: Energy Commission, Ministry of Economic Affairs.

Cosham, A., & Macdonald, K. A. (2008). January. Fracture Control in Pipelines under High Plastic Strains–A Critique of DNV RP-F108. *International Pipeline Conference*, 625-638. 10.1115/ipc2008-64348

De Luna, S., Fernández-Sáez, J., Pérez-Castellanos, J. L., & Navarro, C. (2000). An Analysis of the Static and Dynamic Fracture Behaviour of a Pipeline Steel. *International Journal of Pressure Vessels and Piping*, *77*(11), 691–696. doi:10.1016/S0308-0161(00)00058-2

Dey, P. K., Ogunlana, S. O., Tabucanon, M. T., & Gupta, S. S. (2001). Multiple Attribute Decision Making Approach to Petroleum Pipeline Route Selection. *International Journal of Services Technology and Management*, *2*(3-4), 347–362. doi:10.1504/IJSTM.2001.001608

Green, K. P., & Jackson, T. (2015). *Safety in the Transportation of Oil and Gas: Pipelines or Rail?* Fraser Institute.

Guan, S., Mayes, P., Andrenacci, A., & Wong, D. (2007). Advanced two-layer polyethylene coating technology for pipeline protection. *International Corrosion Control Conference*, 5-7. 10.1115/iogpc2017-2453

Guerrero, J. C. (2015). *ASME B31.4 Pipeline Transportation System for Liquid Hydrocarbon & other Liquid*. New York: Two Park Avenue. doi:10.1016/b978-0-12-813045-2.00007-7

Jayadevan, K. R., Ostby, E., & Thaulow, C. (2004). Strain-Based Fracture Mechanics Analysis of Pipelines. *Proceedings of the International Conference on Advances in Structural Integrity*, 14-17. 10.1115/omae2005-67518

Jones, L. M., Bernknopf, R., Cox, D., Goltz, J., Hudnut, K., Mileti, D., ... Seligson, H. (2008). The Shakeout Scenario. *U.S. Geological Survey Open-File Report*, *1150*, 308. doi:10.1193/1.3563624

Kumar, V. (2016). *Indigenous Crude Oil Production and Import and Processing by Petroleum Planning & Analysis Cell (PPAC)*. New Delhi: Ministry of Petroleum & Natural Gas, Government of India.

Mehrishi, R. (2017). *India Yearbook 2017*. New Delhi: Publications Division Ministry of Information and Broadcasting.

Meyer, K., Comhome, D., & In, L. (2016). *Composites World: Polyurethanes-Collaboration and Adaptation for Optimal Application*. Florida State University. doi:10.1016/0956-7143(90)90258-x

Modine, J. D. (2009). *American Petroleum Institute Handbook Specification for Line Pipe. American Petroleum Institute*. doi:10.3403/00259052

Nayyar, M. L. (1994). *Piping handbook*. New York: McGraw-Hill Handbooks.

Nayyar, M. L. (1999). *Piping handbook*. New York: McGraw-Hill Handbooks.

Ogawa, Y., & Koike, T. (2001). Structural Design of Buried Pipelines for Severe Earthquakes. *Soil Dynamics and Earthquake Engineering*, *21*(3), 199–209. doi:10.1016/S0267-7261(01)00005-7

Østby, E., Jayadevan, K. R., & Thaulow, C. (2005). Fracture Response of Pipelines Subject to Large Plastic Deformation Under Bending. *International Journal of Pressure Vessels and Piping*, *82*(3), 201–215. doi:10.1016/j.ijpvp.2004.08.012

Riegel, E. R. (2007). Kent and Riegel's Handbook of Industrial Chemistry and Biotechnology (Vol. 1). Academic Press.

Shah, A. P. (2016). The Status of Pipelines Carrying Petroleum Products by Refineries and Ports in South India. Ministry of Petroleum & Natural Gas, Bangalore Zonal Office.

Sohail, M., Venukumar, S., & Reddy, M. V. (2017). An Outline of Piping Design Using CAESER II-Case Study. *Materials Today*, *4*(8), 8269–8278. doi:10.1016/j.matpr.2017.07.169

Song. (2006). External Fusion Bonded Epoxy Coating for Steel Pipeline. *Corrosion & Protection, 7*, 17. doi:10.12999/awwa.c213.07

Taylor, J. R. (2003). *Risk Analysis for Process Plant and Pipelines and Transport*. Routledge. doi:10.4324/9780203474914

Teri, G. (2006). National Energy Map for India: Technology Vision 2030. The Energy and Resources Institute, TERI Press. doi:10.15676/ijeei.2010.2.3.3

Wang, S. H., & Chen, W. (2002). A study on the Pre-cyclic-load-induced Burst of Creep Deformation of a Pipeline Steel Under Subsequent Static Load. *Materials Science and Engineering A*, *325*(1), 144–151. doi:10.1016/S0921-5093(01)01458-7

Xue, Z., Foster, E., Wang, Y., Nayak, S., Cheng, V., Ngo, V. W., ... Johnston, K. P. (2014). Effect of Grafted Copolymer Composition on Iron Oxide Nanoparticle Stability and Transport in Porous Media at High Salinity. *Energy & Fuels*, *28*(6), 3655–3665. doi:10.1021/ef500340h

Yuan, F., Wang, L., Guo, Z., & Xie, Y. (2012). Analytical Analysis of Pipeline–soil Interaction During J-lay on a Plastic Seabed with Bearing Resistance Proportional to Depth. *Applied Ocean Research*, *36*, 60–68. doi:10.1016/j.apor.2012.02.004

Zarghamee, M. S., Ojdrovic, R. P., & Nardini, P. D. (2011). Prestressed concrete cylinder pipe condition assessment—what works, what doesn't, what's next. In Pipelines 2011: A Sound Conduit for Sharing Solutions (pp. 182-194). Academic Press. doi:10.1061/41187(420)18

Zarghamee, M. S., Ojdrovic, R. P., & Nardini, P. D. (2012). Prestressed concrete cylinder Pipe Condition Assessment–What Works, What Doesn't, What's Next. *WaterResearch Foundation, 2012*. doi:10.1061/41187(420)18

ADDITIONAL READING

Azevedo, C. R. (2007). Failure analysis of a crude oil pipeline. *Engineering Failure Analysis*, *14*(6), 978–994. doi:10.1016/j.engfailanal.2006.12.001

Nayyar, M. L. (1992). Piping handbook: Vol. 1. *No. 45370771* (p. 1). New York: Mcgraw-hill.

Standard, A. S. M. E. (1984). Measurement of fluid flow in pipes using orifice, nozzle and venturi. In ASME MFC-3M (pp. 1-56). United Engineering Center 345 East 47th Street, New York.

Wu, X., Shu, H., Shen, K., Zan, L., Jiang, X., & Hu, D. (2013). Stress Analysis of Gas Pipeline in Tunnels on Pressure Testing Condition. In ICPTT 2012: Better Pipeline Infrastructure for a Better Life (pp. 238-247).

KEY TERMS AND DEFINITIONS

CAESAR: Within industry, piping is a system of pipes used to convey fluids (liquids and gases) from one location to another. CAESAR is automated computer-aided drawing software used by engineers to draw basic layout of piping structure.

Circumferential or Hoop Stress: This is the stress which is set up in resisting the bursting effect of the applied internal pressure and can be most conveniently treated by considering the equilibrium of the cylinder.

Longitudinal Stress: Longitudinal stress is the stress in a pipe wall, acting along the longitudinal axis of the pipe. And it is produced by the pressure of the fluid in the pipe.

Polyurethane: Same as natural polymers such as amber, wool, silk, and rubber with advance properties of adhesiveness. It is an organic group of Carbamates joined together in chemical process.

Radial Stress: The radial stress for a thick-walled cylinder is equal and opposite of the gauge pressure on the inside surface, and zero on the outside surface.

APPENDIX

Stress Summary report for Kflex 15 mm thickness:

LOAD CASE DEFINITION KEY
CASE 1 (OPE) W+T1+P1
Piping Code: Multiple Codes
B31.4 = B31.4 -2006, October 20, 2006
B31.3 = B31.3 -2012, Jan 10, 2013
CODE STRESS CHECK PASSED:
LOADCASE 2 (OPE) W+T1+P1
Highest Stresses: (N./sq.mm) LOADCASE 2 (OPE)
W+T1+P1
Ratio (%): 77.7 @Node 20050
OPE Stress: 202.5 Allowable Stress: 260.6
Axial Stress: 66.8 @Node 20060
Bending Stress: 69.6 @Node 200
Torsion Stress: 7.1 @Node 4709
Hoop Stress: 147.2 @Node 20040
OCTAHEDRAL Stress: 115.3 @Node 358
LOAD CASE DEFINITION KEY
CASE 2 (SUS) W+P1
Piping Code: Multiple Codes
B31.4 = B31.4 -2006, October 20, 2006
B31.3 = B31.3 -2012, Jan 10, 2013
CODE STRESS CHECK PASSED:
LOADCASE 4 (SUS) W+P1
Highest Stresses: (N./sq.mm.) LOADCASE 4 (SUS) W+P1
Ratio (%): 37.7 @Node 4570
Code Stress: 52 Allowable Stress: 137.9
Axial Stress: 66.8 @Node 20060
Bending Stress: 40.6 @Node 351
Torsion Stress: 4.9 @Node 370
Hoop Stress: 147.2 @Node 20040
OCTAHEDRAL Stress: 110.8 @Node 351
LOAD CASE DEFINITION KEY
CASE 3 (EXP) L5=L2-L4
Piping Code: Multiple Codes
B31.4 = B31.4 -2006, October 20, 2006
B31.3 = B31.3 -2012, Jan 10, 2013

CODE STRESS CHECK PASSED : LOADCASE 5 (EXP) L5=L2-L4
Highest Stresses: (N./sq.mm) LOADCASE 5 (EXP)
L5=L2-L4
Ratio (%): 53 @Node 20015
Code Stress: 110.4 Allowable Stress: 208.5
Axial Stress: 33.7 @Node 1125
Bending Stress: 63.9 @Node 200
Torsion Stress: 6.2 @Node 4709
Hoop Stress: 0 @Node 20
OCTAHEDRAL Stress: 46.6 @Node 200

Table 5 shows the node analysis (without Kplex) and sorting for the Safe/Unsafe scenarios generated from the simulation model. The similar analysis is carried for the data generated for Kplex 10, 15, 25 50.

Table 5. Summary of stress analysis code stress ratio

			Code Stress Ratio				
Sr. Number	Node Number	Allowable Stress N./mm².	without Kflex	Kflex 50	Kflex 25	Kflex 15	Kflex 10
1	330	208.49	89.62	84.15	84.44	84.43	84.69
2	331	208.49	108.11	84.49	85.06	85.12	83.81
3	332	208.49	86.61	84.8	85.42	85.52	83.78
4	333	208.49	99.91	83.78	84.18	84.13	84.09
5	334	208.49	110.69	83.94	84.45	84.45	83.8
6	335	208.49	94.83	84.71	85.31	85.38	83.85
7	336	208.49	102.77	84.72	85.38	85.51	83.6
8	340	208.49	114.9	84.47	85.17	85.33	83.33
9	341	208.49	100.08	83.01	83.89	84.24	82.75
10	342	208.49	84.82	83.5	82.9	83.15	82.68
11	343	208.49	83.9	84.98	83.79	82.87	82.61
12	344	208.49	82.57	82.6	83.57	84.49	82.59
13	345	208.49	82.5	82.58	83.26	82.97	82.58
14	350	208.49	82.48	82.58	83.88	83.56	82.73
15	351	208.49	82.49	82.59	84.92	88.27	83.96
16	352	208.49	82.53	82.97	88.8	84.36	86.34
17	353	208.49	83.02	105.14	82.63	87.05	88.19
18	354	208.49	83.8	89.82	86.94	88.87	83.08
19	355	208.49	90.43	90.45	91.3	90.73	87.08
20	356	208.49	95.51	109.74	96.82	93.1	93.55
21	357	208.49	86.16	119.05	100.33	95.19	96.91
22	358	208.49	102.59	119.6	99.95	94.62	96.89
23	370	208.49	106.32	111.69	96.15	91.81	93.66
24	371	208.49	86.64	104.48	91.99	89.64	91.59
25	372	208.49	97.36	112.4	95.8	92.46	94.82
26	375	208.49	100.46	111.8	96.16	93.01	94.85
27	380	208.49	91.1	103.22	93.08	91.13	91.72
28	385	208.49	83.34	93.39	90.23	89.85	88.49
29	390	208.49	83.45	87.98	88.65	89.14	86.72
30	395	208.49	84.16	82.78	87.08	88.44	84.95

Compilation of References

Abid, L., Ouertani, M. N., & Zouari-Ghorbel, S. (2014). Macroeconomic and bank-specific determinants of household's non-performing loans in Tunisia: A dynamic panel data. *Procedia Economics and Finance*, *13*, 58–68. doi:10.1016/S2212-5671(14)00430-4

About the OECD. (2018). Retrieved 2 March 2018 from http://www.oecd.org/about/

Ackert, L., Church, B., & Deaves, R. (2003). *Economic Review Section Quarterly*. Federal Reserve Bank of Atlanta.

Aditto, S., Gan, C., & Nartea, G. (2014). Economic risk analysis of alternative farming systems for smallholder farmers in central and north-east Thailand. *International Journal of Social Economics*, *41*(4), 294–320. doi:10.1108/IJSE-11-2012-0223

Agarwal, S. (2018). *Big consumer brands losing market share to smaller rivals.*[REMOVED HYPERLINK FIELD] Retrieved 1 April 2018, from https://www.livemint.com/Industry/GtuYtAhywKgkyuNNyDBa2J/Big-consumer-brands-losing-market-share-to-smaller-rivals.html

Agarwal, S. (2018, February 20). Internet users in India expected to reach 500 million by June: IAMAI. *Economic Times*. Retrieved April 24, 2018, from https://economictimes.indiatimes.com/tech/internet/internet-users-in-india-expected-to-reach-500-million-by-june-iamai/articleshow/63000198.cms

Aggarwal, C. C. (2011). An introduction to social network data analytics. In C. C. Aggarwal (Ed.), *Social Network Data Analytics* (pp. 1–15). Springer. doi:10.1007/978-1-4419-8462-3_1

Agriculture and food. Retrieved from https://www.hollandtradeandinvest.com/key-sectors/agriculture-and-food

Agriculture and sustainable development in the Netherlands. (n.d.). Retrieved from http://www.un.org/esa/agenda21/natlinfo/countr/nether/agriculture.pdf

Agriculture. (2018). Retrieved from https://www.government.nl/topics/agriculture

Agriculture. Retrieved from https://www.government.nl/topics/agriculture

Akerlof, G. (1991). Procrastinantion and Obedience. *The American Economic Review*, *81*(2), 1–19.

Akhtar, M., & Sushil. (2018). Managing strategic performance in a dynamic business environment: A study of two Indian oil companies. *Global Business and Organizational Excellence*, *37*(5), 47–62. doi:10.1002/joe.21876

Alandejani, M., & Asutay, M. (2017). Nonperforming loans in the GCC banking sectors: Does the Islamic finance matter? *Research in International Business and Finance*, *42*, 832–854. doi:10.1016/j.ribaf.2017.07.020

Alencar, A. B., de Oliviera, M. F., & Paulovich, F. V. (2012). Seeing beyond reading: A survey on visual text analytics. *Wiley Interdisciplinary Reviews. Data Mining and Knowledge Discovery*, *2*(6), 476–492. doi:10.1002/widm.1071

Alexander, R. M., & Gentry, J. K. (2014). Using social media to report financial results. *Business Horizons, 57*(2), 161–167. doi:10.1016/j.bushor.2013.10.009

Allen, K., Davidson, T., Hein, S., & Whitledge, M. (2017). Dodd–Frank's federal deposit insurance reform. *Journal of Banking Regulation*, 1-16. doi:10.105741261-017-0050-3

Allen, F., & Carletti, E. (2008). *The Role of Liquidity in Financial Crises*. SSRN Electronic Journal. doi:10.2139srn.1268367

Allen, F., Carletti, E., Goldstein, I., & Leonello, A. (2015). Moral Hazard and Government Guarantees in the Banking Industry. *Journal of Financial Regulation, 1*(1), 30–50. doi:10.1093/jfr/fju003

Alliance Consulting Group. (n.d.). *How National Brand Manufacturers Can Protect Their Brands and Profits*. Retrieved from http://www.alliancecg.com/uploads/the_threat_of_retailer_brands.pdf

Alliance, A. L. (2001). Guidelines for the design of buried steel pipe. In American Society of Civil Engineers. American Society of Civil Engineers. doi:10.1061/9780784413074

Almuhimedi, H., Wilson, S., Liu, B., Sadeh, N., & Acquisti, A. (2013). Tweets are forever: A large-scale quantitative analysis of deleted tweets. *CSCW Computer Supported Cooperative Work* (pp. 897-908). New York. *ACM New York, NY, USA, 2013*. doi:10.1145/2441776.2441878

Altman, A. (2008). A Brief History of Ponzi Schemes. *Time*.

Álvarez, J. A. (2008). La banca española ante la actual crisis financiera. *Estabilidad Financiera, 15*, 21–38.

Amidzic, G., Massara, A., & Mialou, A. (2014). *Assessing Countries' Financial Inclusion Standing—A New Composite Index* (IMF Working Paper No. 14/36). Retrieved from International Monetary Fund website: https://www.imf.org/en/Publications/WP/Issues/2016/12/31/Assessing-Countries-Financial-Inclusion-Standing-A-New-Composite-Index-41385

Anand, R., Medhavi, S., Soni, V., Malhotra, C., & Banwet, D. (2018). Transforming information security governance in India (A SAP-LAP based case study of security, IT policy and e-governance). *Information and Computer Security, 26*(1), 58–90. doi:10.1108/ICS-12-2016-0090

Andersen, T. B., & Tarp, F. (2003). Financial liberalization, financial and economic growth in LDCs. *Journal of International Development, 15*(2), 189–209. doi:10.1002/jid.971

Anderson, C., Getmansky, A., & Hirsch-Hoefler, S. (2017). Burden Sharing: Income, Inequality, and Willingness to Fight. *British Journal of Political Science*.

Anderson, R. A. (1994). Electrostatic Forces in an Ideal Spherical-particle Electrorheological Fluid. *Langmuir, 10*(9), 2917–2928. doi:10.1021/la00021a013

Andolfatto, D., Nosal, E., & Sultanum, B. (2017). Preventing bank runs. *Theoretical Economics, 12*(3), 1003–1028. doi:10.3982/TE1970

Anginer, D., Demirguc-Kunt, A., & Zhu, M. (2014). How does deposit insurance affect bank risk? Evidence from the recent crisis. *Journal of Banking & Finance, 48*, 312–321. doi:10.1016/j.jbankfin.2013.09.013

Antaki, G. A. (2003). *Piping and Pipeline Engineering: Design, Construction, Maintenance, Integrity, and Repair*. New York: CRC Press; doi:10.1201/9780203911150

Arcand, J.-L., Berkes, E., & Panizza, U. (2012). *Too much finance?* (IMF Working Paper WP/12/161). Retrieved from International Monetary Fund website: https://www.imf.org/external/pubs/ft/wp/2012/wp12161.pdf

Arestis, P., Demetriades, P. O., & Luintel, K. B. (2001). Financial development and economic growth: The role of stock-markets. *Journal of Money, Credit and Banking*, *33*(1), 16–41. doi:10.2307/2673870

Arshad, A., Zafar, M., Fatima, I., & Khan, S. K. (2015). The Impact of Perceived Risk on Online Buyg Behavior. *International Journal of New Technology and Research*, *1*(8), 13–18. Retrieved from https://www.ijntr.org/download_data/IJNTR01080013.pdf

Arshinder, K., Kanda, A., & Deshmukh, S. G. (2007). Supply chain coordination issues: An SAP-LAP framework. *Asia Pacific Journal of Marketing and Logistics*, *19*(3), 240–264. doi:10.1108/13555850710772923

Asian Development Bank Institute. (2014). *Financial Inclusion in Asia*. Asian Development Bank.

Asseldonk, M., & Meer, R. (2016). *Coping with price risks on Dutch farms*. Wageningen: LEI Wageningen UR. Retrieved from http://library.wur.nl/WebQuery/wurpubs/507522

Association of Certified Fraud Examiners. (2006). *Report to the nation on occupational fraud and abuse*. ACFE. Retrieved from https://www.acfe.com/uploadedFiles/ACFE_Website/Content/documents/2006-rttn.pdf

Atten, P., & Aitken, F. (2007). Electro Coalescence Criterion for two Close Water Drops. *Industry Applications Conference, 2007, 42nd IAS Annual Meeting, Conference Record of the 2007 IEEE*, 452-456. 10.1109/07ias.2007.7

Ayyagiri, M., & Beck, T. (2015). *Financial Inclusion in Asia: An Overview*. Asian Development Bank.

Ayyildiz, F. V. (2017). *Gelir Adaletsizliginin Sebeplerinin Arastirilmasi*. Ampirik Analiz.

Azevedo, C. R. (2007). Failure Analysis of a Crude Oil Pipeline. *Engineering Failure Analysis*, *14*(6), 978–994. doi:10.1016/j.engfailanal.2006.12.001

Babu, D. M., Bhagyasri, M., Lahari, K., Madhuri, C. H., & Kumari, G. P. (2014). Image Based Fraud Prevention. *International Journal of Computer Science and Information Technologies*, *5*(1), 728–731. Retrieved from http://ijcsit.com/docs/Volume 5/vol5issue01/ijcsit20140501158.pdf

Bağce, H. E. (2017). Parlamenter ve Başkanlık Sistemiyle Yönetilen Ülkelerde Gelir Dağılımı Eşitsizliği ve Yoksulluk. *İnsan&İnsan*, 5.

Bailey, A. A., Bonifield, C. M., & Arias, A. (2018). Social media use by young Latin American consumers: An exploration. *Journal of Retailing and Consumer Services*, *43*, 10–19. doi:10.1016/j.jretconser.2018.02.003

Balachandran, R., & Dhal, S. (2018). Relationship between money lenders and farmers. *Agricultural Finance Review*, *78*(3), 330–347. doi:10.1108/AFR-07-2016-0066

Baltas, G. (1997). Determinants of store brand choice: A behavioral analysis. *Journal of Product and Brand Management*, *6*(5), 315–324. doi:10.1108/10610429710179480

Bandari, R., Asur, S., & Huberman, B. A. (2012). *The pulse of news in social media: Forecasting popularity. In Proceedings of the Sixth International AAAI Conference on Weblogs and Social Media* (pp. 26–33). Association for the Advancement of Artificial Intelligence. Retrieved from https://www.aaai.org/ocs/index.php/ICWSM/ICWSM12/paper/viewFile/4646/4963

Banerjee, A. V., & Newman, A. F. (1993). Occupational choice and the process of development. *Journal of Political Economy*, *101*(2), 274–298. doi:10.1086/261876

Bank of Spain. (2017). *Informe sobre la Crisis Financiera y Bancaria en España. 2008-2014*. Retrieved from https://www.bde.es/f/webbde/Secciones/Publicaciones/OtrasPublicaciones/Fich/InformeCrisis_Completo_web.pdf

Banking Regulation & Supervision Agency of Turkey (BRSA). (2017). *Financial Sector Report.* Istanbul: BRSA. Retrieved from: https://www.bddk.org.tr/WebSitesi/turkce/Raporlar/TBSGG/16031tbs_temel_gostergeler_raporu_mart_2017.pdf

Barber, B., & Odean, T. (2007). All that Glitters: The Effect of Attention and News on the Buying behavior of Individual and Institutional Investors. *Review of Financial Studies*, *21*(2), 785–818. doi:10.1093/rfs/hhm079

Barbier, G., & Liu, H. (2011). Data mining in social media. In C. C. Aggarwal (Ed.), *Social network data analytics* (pp. 327–352). Springer. doi:10.1007/978-1-4419-8462-3_12

Başçı, E., & Kara, H. (2011). Finansal İstikrar ve Para Politikası. *İktisat, İşletme ve Finans, 26*, 9-25.

Basel Committee on Banking Supervision. (1993). *The supervisory treatment of market risks.* BIS. Retrieved from: https://www.bis.org/publ/bcbs11a.pdf

Basel Committee on Banking Supervision. (2001). *The New Basle Capital Accord: an explanatory note.* BIS. Retrieved from: https://www.bis.org/publ/bcbsca01.pdf

Basel Committee on Banking Supervision. (2016). *RCAP Report, Assessment of Basel III risk-based capital regulations in Turkey.* BIS. Retrieved from: https://www.bis.org/bcbs/publ/d359.pdf

Basle Committee on Banking Supervision. (1988). *Internal Convergence of Capital Measurement and Capital Standards.* BIS. Retrieved from: https://www.bis.org/publ/bcbs04a.pdf

Batra, R., & Sinha, I. (2000). Consumer-level factors moderating the success of private label brands. *Journal of Retailing*, *76*(2), 175–191. doi:10.1016/S0022-4359(00)00027-0

Bauer, P. W. (1998). *Currency: time for change?* Federal Reserve Bank of Cleveland, Economic Commentary.

Beasley, M. S., Branson, B. C., & Hancock, B. V. (2011). *Developing Key Risk Indicators to Strengthen Enterprise Risk Management.* Retrieved December 21, 2017 from https://mgt.ncsu.edu/vol2/erm/ee/i/weblogs/research-documents/coso-kri-paper-jan2011.pdf

Becker, W. E. (1999). Carl Shapiro and Hal R. Varian. Information Rules: A Strategic Guide to the Network Economy. *The Journal of Economic Education*, *30*(2), 189–190. doi:10.1080/00220489909595956

Beck, R., Georgiadis, G., & Straub, R. (2014). The finance and growth nexus revisited. *Economics Letters*, *124*(3), 382–385. doi:10.1016/j.econlet.2014.06.024

Beck, T., Demirgüç-Kunt, A., & Levine, R. (2007). Finance, inequality and the poor. *Journal of Economic Growth*, *12*(1), 27–49. doi:10.100710887-007-9010-6

Beck, T., Demirgüç-Kunt, A., & Martínez Peria, M. S. (2007). Reaching Out: Access to and Use of Banking Services across Countries. *Journal of Financial Economics*, *85*(2), 234–266. doi:10.1016/j.jfineco.2006.07.002

Beck, T., & Levine, R. (2004). Stock markets, banks, and growth: Panel evidence. *Journal of Banking & Finance*, *28*(3), 423–442. doi:10.1016/S0378-4266(02)00408-9

Belsky, G., & Gilovich, T. (2010). *Why Smart People make Big Money Mistakes.* New York: Simon and Schuster.

Benartzi, S., & Thaler, R. (1995). Myopic loss aversion and the equity premium puzzle. *The Quarterly Journal of Economics*, *110*(1), 73–92. doi:10.2307/2118511

Benartzi, S., & Thaler, R. (2007). Heuristics and biases in retirement savings behavior. *The Journal of Economic Perspectives*, *21*(3), 81–104. doi:10.1257/jep.21.3.81

Benchmarking Financial Knowledge Survey. Research & reports. (n.d.). Retrieved 14 January 2018 from https://www.getsmarteraboutmoney.ca/resources/publications/research/benchmarking-financial-k nowledge-survey/

Berger, A., & Turk-Ariss, R. (2014). Do Depositors Discipline Banks and Did Government Actions During the Recent Crisis Reduce this Discipline? An International Perspective. *Journal of Financial Services Research*, *48*(2), 103–126. doi:10.100710693-014-0205-7

Berges, A., & Ontiveros, E. (2013). Sistema bancario español: Una transformación sin precedentes. *Harvard Deusto Business Review*, *229*, 16–28.

Berisha, E., Meszaros, J., & Olson, E. (2015). Income inequality and household debt: A cointegration test. *Applied Economics Letters*, *22*(18), 1469–1473. doi:10.1080/13504851.2015.1039698

Berthelemy, J., & Varoudakis, A. (1996). Economic growth convergence clubs and the role of financial development. *Oxford Economic Papers*, *48*(2), 300–328. doi:10.1093/oxfordjournals.oep.a028570

Bessis, J. (2010). *Risk management in banking*. Wiley.

Beyes, P., & Bhattacharya, R. (2016). *India's 2016 demonetisation drive: A case study on innovation in anti-corruption policies, government communications and political integrity*. OECD Global Anti-Corruption Integrity Forum. Retrieved from https://www.oecd.org/cleangovbiz/Integrity-Forum-2017-Beyes-Bhattacharya-India-demonetisation-drive.pdf

Bijman, J. (2008). Contract farming in developing countries: an overview. Wageningen University, Department of Business Administration.

Bijman, J., & Gijselinckx, C. (2012). *SFC Case Study Report. Fruit and Vegetable cooperatives in the Netherlands and Belgium*. Wageningen UR.

Bijman, J., & Hendrikse, G. (2003). Co-operatives in chains: Institutional restructuring in the Dutch fruit and vegetable industry. *Journal on Chain and Network Science*, *3*(2), 95–107. doi:10.3920/JCNS2003.x033

Bishop, W. (2013). The Role of Ethics in 21st Century. *Journal of Business Ethics*, *118*(3), 635–637. doi:10.100710551-013-1618-1

Blake, T. D., Clarke, A., & Ruschak, K. J. (1994). Hydrodynamic assist of dynamic wetting. *AIChE Journal. American Institute of Chemical Engineers*, *40*(2), 229–242. doi:10.1002/aic.690400205

Blanchard, O., Dell'Ariccia, G., & Mauro, P. (2010). *Rethinking Macroeconomic Policy: Getting Granular. IMF Staff Position Note* (Vol. 10). IMF eLibrary. doi:10.1111/j.1538-4616.2010.00334.x

Blanco, F. (2017). *Cognitive Bias. In Encyclopedia of Animal Cognition and Behavior*. Springer International.

Bocconcelli, R., Cioppi, M., & Pagano, A. (2017). Social media as a resource in SMEs' sales process. *Journal of Business and Industrial Marketing*, *32*(5), 693–709. doi:10.1108/JBIM-11-2014-0244

Bolton, P., Freixas, X., & Shapiro, J. (2007). Conflicts of interest, information provision, and competition in the financial services industry. *Journal of Financial Economics*, *85*(2), 297–330. doi:10.1016/j.jfineco.2005.06.004

Bonini, S., & Boraschi-Diaz, D. (2013). The Causes and Financial Consequences of Corporate Frauds. In R. Cressy (Ed.), *C. D & M. C, Entrepreneurship, Finance, Governance and Ethics* (pp. 295–314). Springer. doi:10.1007/978-94-007-3867-6_13

Bordo, M., & Haubrich, J. (2010). Credit crises, money and contractions: An historical view. *Journal of Monetary Economics*, *57*(1), 1–18. doi:10.1016/j.jmoneco.2009.10.015

Borio, C., & Drehmann, M. (2009). *Towards an Operational Framework for Financial Stability: 'Fuzzy' Measurement and Its Consequences* (Working Paper No. 284). BIS. Retrieved Dec 12, 2017, from https://www.bis.org/publ/work284.htm

Bosch, E., Eckard, W., & Singal, V. (1998). The Competitive Effect of Air Crashes: Stock Market Evidence. *The Journal of Law & Economics*, *41*(2), 503–519. doi:10.1086/467399

Bose, P. (2017, December 27). *FRDI Bill, 2017: Inducing Financial Instability*. Retrieved from http://www.epw.in/engage/article/frdi-bill-2017-issues-and-concerns

Bourgeois, D., Kanoute, A., & Faye, D. (2014). Strategies to promote better research on oral health in Africa: A Delphi consensus study. *Contemporary Clinical Dentistry*, *5*(1), 13. doi:10.4103/0976-237X.128654 PMID:24808689

Boyle, G., Stover, R., Tiwana, A., & Zhylyevskyy, O. (2015). The impact of deposit insurance on depositor behavior during a crisis: A conjoint analysis approach. *Journal of Financial Intermediation*, *24*(4), 590–601. doi:10.1016/j.jfi.2015.02.001

Brodeur, A., Buehler, K., Patsalos-Fox, M., & Pergler, M. (2010). *A Board Perspective on Enterprise Risk Management*. McKinsey Working Papers on Risk, Number 18. Retrieved December 15, 2017 from https://www.mckinsey.com/~/media/mckinsey/dotcom/client_service/risk/working%20papers/18_a_board_perspective_on_enterprise_risk_management.ashx

Brown, A., Collins, M., Schmeiser, M., & Urban, C. (2014). *State mandated financial education and the credit behavior of young adults* (Working paper No. 68). Retrieved 14 January 2018 from https://www.federalreserve.gov/pubs/feds/2014/201468/201468pap.pdf

Bryant, J. (1980). A model of reserves, bank runs, and deposit insurance. *Journal of Banking & Finance*, *4*(4), 335–344. doi:10.1016/0378-4266(80)90012-6

Buch, H. (2017). *As stock market heats up retail investors slake thirst with mutual fund sips*. Retrieved from https://www.moneycontrol.com/news/business/mutual-funds/as-stock-market-heats-up-retail-investors-slake-thirst-with-mutual-fund-sips-2385439.html

Buch-Hansen, M., & Marcussen, H. (1982). Contract farming and the peasantry: Cases from Western Kenya. *Review of African Political Economy*, *9*(23), 9–36. doi:10.1080/03056248208703486

Building Blocks to Help Youth Achieve Financial Capability. (n.d.). *A new model and recommendations*. Retrieved 14 January 2018 from https://www.consumerfinance.gov/data-research/research-reports/building-blocks-help-yout h-achieve-financial-capability/

Bumann, S., & Lensink, R. (2016). Capital account liberalization and income inequality. *Journal of International Money and Finance*, *61*, 143–162. doi:10.1016/j.jimonfin.2015.10.004

Bureau, E. T. (2012, November 26). *What is a Ponzi Scheme and how investors are trapped*. Retrieved from The Economic Times: https://economictimes.indiatimes.com/analysis/what-is-a-ponzi-scheme-and-how-investors-are-trapped/articleshow/17348270.cms

Bureau, E. T. (2014). Financial inclusion can curb ponzi schemes: RBI Governor Raghuram Rajan. *The Economic Times*.

Businessworld. (2017). *Investors prefer equities survey*. Retrieved from http://www.businessworld.in/article/84-Retail-Investors-Prefer-Equities-Survey/19-07-2017-122408

CAESAR II. (2014). *Design Manual of software CAESAR II*. Intergraph Corporation. doi:10.1016/0010-4485(85)90100-9

Calomiris, C., & Jaremski, M. (2016). Deposit Insurance: Theories and Facts. *Annual Review of Financial Economics*, *8*(1), 97–120. doi:10.1146/annurev-financial-111914-041923

Calomiris, C., & Wilson, B. (2004). Bank Capital and Portfolio Management: The 1930s "Capital Crunch" and the Scramble to Shed Risk. *The Journal of Business*, *77*(3), 421–455. doi:10.1086/386525

Calvo Bernardino, A., & Martín de Vidales Carrasco, I. (2014). Crisis y cambios estructurales en el sector bancario español: Una comparación con otros sistemas financieros. *Estudios de Economía Aplicada*, *32*(2), 535–566.

Calvo, G. (2012). Financial crises and liquidity shocks a bank-run perspective. *European Economic Review*, *56*(3), 317–326. doi:10.1016/j.euroecorev.2011.12.005

Cámara, N., & Tuesta, D. (2014). *Measuring Financial Inclusion: A Muldimensional Index* (BBVA Working Paper No. 14 (26)). Retrieved from BBVA website: https://www.bbvaresearch.com/wp-content/uploads/2014/09/WP14-26_Financial-Inclusion2.pdf

Campbell, L. (2017). *The Importance of Social Media in Risk Management*. Retrieved April 30, 2018, from Cube Logic: https://cubelogic.com/white-papers/the-importance-of-social-media-in-risk-management/

Canadian Foundation for Economic Education Resources. (n.d.). Retrieved 14 January 2018 from http://www.cfee.org/resources/

Caprio, G., Hunter, W., Kaufman, G., & Leipziger, D. (Eds.). (1999). Preventing banking crises: lessons from recent global bank failures. Economic Development Institute of WB.

Caprio, G., & Klingebiel, D. (2003). *Episodes of systemic and borderline financial crises*. World Bank.

Carbó Valverde, S., & Rodríguez Fernández, F. (2014). Has bank restructuring in Spain and Europe paid off? *Spanish Economic and Financial Outlook*, *3*(3), 5–13.

Carson, B. (2016). *Social Media as a Research Methodology*. Retrieved from https://blog.marketresearch.com/social-media-as-a-research-methodology

Caruana, J. (2010). Grappling with systemic risk. *The Finsia Journal of Applied Finance*, *2*, 6-10. Retrieved Dec 5, 2017, from https://www.finsia.com/docs/default-source/jassa-new/jassa-2010/6_10.pdf?sfvrsn=bec1de93_6

Cecchetti, S., & Kharroubi, E. (2012). *Reassessing the impact of finance on growth* (BIS Working Papers No 381). Retrieved from Bank for International Settlements website: https://www.bis.org/publ/work381.pdf

Center for Agroecology & Sustainable Food Systems. Social Issues in Current U.S. Agriculture [Ebook]. California. Retrieved from https://casfs.ucsc.edu/about/publications/Teaching-Organic-Farming/PDF-downloads/3.2-social-issues.pdf

Cerutti, E., Claessens, S., & Laeven, L. (2017). The Use and Effectiveness of Macroprudential Policies: New Evidence. *Journal of Financial Stability*, *28*, 203–224. doi:10.1016/j.jfs.2015.10.004

Chakraborty, T., & Gupta, A. (2017). Hazards of farm loan waivers. Retrieved from http://www.ideasforindia.in/topics/agriculture/hazards-of-farm-loan-waivers.html

Chakravorti, B. (2016). *The Cost of Cash in the United States*. The Fletcher School Tufts University. Retrieved from http://fletcher.tufts.edu/CostofCash/~/media/Fletcher/Microsites/Cost of Cash/CostofCashStudyFinal.pdf

Chand, P., Thakkar, J., & Ghosh, K. (2018). Analysis of supply chain complexity drivers for Indian mining equipment manufacturing companies combining SAP-LAP and AHP. *Resources Policy*. doi:10.1016/j.resourpol.2018.08.011

Chant, J., Lai, A., IIling, M., & Daniel, F. (2003). *Essays on Financial Stability* (Technical Report No. 95). Bank of Canada, Retrieved from https://www.bankofcanada.ca/wp-content/uploads/2010/01/tr95.pdf

Charan, P. (2012). Supply chain performance issues in an automobile company: A SAP-LAP analysis. *Measuring Business Excellence, 16*(1), 67–86. doi:10.1108/13683041211204680

Chaudhary, V., Pasupuleti, V. D. K., & Ramancharla, P. K. (2012). 3D FE Modelling of Buried Continuous Pipeline Exposed to Fault Motion with Material Nonlinearity and large Deformation. *Fourth International Conference on Structural Stability and Dynamics ICSSD 2012*, 6-8. 10.1504/ijstructe.2013.056981

Chauhan, S., & Kaushik, N. (2016). Impact of Demonetization on Stock Market: Event Study Methodology. *Indian Journal of Accounting*, 127.

Chelliah, J., & Field, J. (2014). Managing the risks of social media: Ways to ensure that online behavior is always appropriate. *Human Resource Management International Digest, 22*(5), 39–41. doi:10.1108/HRMID-07-2014-0103

Chen, H., Hwang, H., & Liu, B. (2018). *The Emergence of "Social Executives" and Its Consequences for Financial Markets.* doi:10.2139srn.2318094

Cheng, S. (2012). Substitution or complementary effects between banking and stock markets: Evidence from financial openness in Taiwan. *Journal of International Financial Markets, Institutions and Money, 22*(3), 508–520. doi:10.1016/j.intfin.2012.01.007

Chen, H., De, P., Hu, Y., & Hwang, B.-H. (2014). Wisdom of Crowds: The Value of Stock Opinions Transmitted Through Social Media. *Review of Financial Studies, 27*(5), 1367–1403. doi:10.1093/rfs/hhu001

Chen, W. W., Shih, B. J., Chen, Y. C., Hung, J. H., & Hwang, H. H. (2002). Seismic Response of Natural Gas and Water Pipelines in the Ji-Ji earthquake. *Soil Dynamics and Earthquake Engineering, 22*(9), 1209–1214. doi:10.1016/S0267-7261(02)00149-5

Chen, Y., & Hasan, I. (2008). Why Do Bank Runs Look Like Panic? A New Explanation. *Journal of Money, Credit and Banking, 40*(2-3), 535–546. doi:10.1111/j.1538-4616.2008.00126.x

Cheung, F., & Lucas, R. E. (2016). Income inequality is associated with stronger social comparison effects: The effect of relative income on life satisfaction. *Journal of Personality and Social Psychology, 110*(2), 332–341. doi:10.1037/pspp0000059 PMID:26191957

Choi, D.-H., Yoo, W., Noh, G.-Y., & Park, K. (2017). The impact of social media on risk perceptions during the MERS outbreak in South Korea. *Computers in Human Behavior, 72*, 422–431. doi:10.1016/j.chb.2017.03.004

Choudhury, S. D. C., & Dwarakanath, B. (2017, January 16). India central bank relaxes cash withdrawal limit with immediate effect. *Reuters*. Retrieved from https://in.reuters.com/article/us-india-modi-corruption-withdrawal/india-central-bank-relaxes-cash-withdrawal-limit-with-immediate-effect-idINKBN1501GQ

Chow, E. (2018, March 9). *Why China keeps falling for pyramid schemes*. Retrieved from The Diplomat: https://www.realclearworld.com/2018/03/09/why_china_keeps_falling_for_pyramid_schemes_190718.html

Christensen, G. (2012). Allocating loss in Securities Fraud. *William & Mary Business Law Review, 3*(2), 310-339.

Chronicle, D. (2016, December 12). *Rural indebtedness at 31.4 per cent, Rs 1.03 lakhs per household: NSS*. Retrieved from https://www.deccanchronicle.com/business/in-other-news/121216/rural-indebtedness-at-314-per-cent-rs-103-lakhs-per-household-nss-survey.html

Çifter, A. (2015). Bank concentration and non-performing loans in Central and Eastern European countries. *Journal of Business Economics and Management, 16*(1), 117–137. doi:10.3846/16111699.2012.720590

Claessens, S., Ghosh, S. R., & Mihet, R. (2013). Macro-Prudential Policies to Mitigate Financial System Vulnerabilities. *Journal of International Money and Finance*, *39*, 153–185. doi:10.1016/j.jimonfin.2013.06.023

Clark, A., & D'Ambrosio, C. (2013). *Attitudes to income inequality: experimental and survey evidence*. Academic Press.

Clement, P. (2010). The term "macroprudential": Origins and Evolution. *BIS Quarterly Review*. Retrieved Feb 18, 2018, from https://www.bis.org/publ/qtrpdf/r_qt1003h.pdf

Cocchetti, G., di Prisco, C., Galli, A., & Nova, R. (2009). Soil–Pipeline Interaction Along Unstable Slopes: a Ccoupled Three-dimensional Approach. Part 1: Theoretical Formulation. *Canadian Geotechnical Journal*, *46*(11), 1289–1304. doi:10.1139/T09-028

Commander, S. J., & Mumssen, C. (1998). *Understanding barter in Russia*. Academic Press.

Consumer Financial Protection Bureau. (n.d.). Retrieved 14 January 2018 from https://www.consumerfinance.gov/

Contract farming offers fresh hope for Africa's declining agriculture. (2018). Retrieved 25 April 2018, from http://www.worldagroforestry.org/downloads/Publications/PDFS/BR07060.pdf

Cooperation, A. P. E. (2002). *Earthquake Disaster Management of Energy Supply System of APEC Member Economies*. Taipei, China: Energy Commission, Ministry of Economic Affairs.

Cooper, R., & Kempf, H. (2015). Deposit insurance and bank liquidation without commitment: Can we sleep well? *Economic Theory*, *61*(2), 365–392. doi:10.100700199-015-0897-4

Corral Delgado, S., Domínguez Martínez, J. M., & López del Paso, R. (2011). El nuevo mapa del sistema financiero español. *Extoikos*, *3*, 65–77.

Cortes, D., Santamaria, J., & Vargas, J. (2016). *Economic Shocks and Crime: Evidence from the crash of Ponzi Schemes*. Bogota: Universidad del Rosario. Retrieved from http://repository.urosario.edu.co/bitstream/handle/10336/11880/dt185.pdf?sequence=3

Cosham, A., & Macdonald, K. A. (2008). January. Fracture Control in Pipelines under High Plastic Strains–A Critique of DNV RP-F108. *International Pipeline Conference*, 625-638. 10.1115/ipc2008-64348

Council for Economic Education. (2018). Retrieved 14 January 2018 from http://councilforeconed.org/

Cowell, F. (2011). *Measuring inequality*. Oxford University Press. doi:10.1093/acprof:osobl/9780199594030.001.0001

Cressey, D. R. (1953). *Other people's money; a study of the social psychology of embezzlement*. New York: Free Press.

Criste, A., & Lupu, I. (2014). The Central Bank Policy Between the Price Stability Objective and Promoting Financial Stability. *Procedia Economics and Finance*, *8*, 219–225. doi:10.1016/S2212-5671(14)00084-7

Crowl, J. (2015). *Impulse Behavior: Why Social Media Content is Such a Popular Downtime Activity*. Retrieved from www.skyword.com: https://www.skyword.com/contentstandard/marketing/impulse-behavior-why-social-media-content-is-such-a-popular-downtime-activity/

Cull, R., Ehrbeck, T., & Holle, N. (2014). *Financial inclusion and development: Recent impact evidence*. Retrieved from http://www.cgap.org/publications/financial-inclusion-and-development-recent-impact-evidence

Cull, R., Senbet, L., & Sorge, M. (2002). The effect of deposit insurance on financial depth: A cross-country analysis. *The Quarterly Review of Economics and Finance*, *42*(4), 673–694. doi:10.1016/S1062-9769(02)00120-5

Curriculum Evaluation. (2016). *Junior Achievement. Finance Park*. Retrieved 3 March 2018 from https://www.junior-achievement.org/documents/20009/133368/JA+Finance+Park+Evaluation+Report

Currie, K., & Ray, L. (1987). The Kenya state, agribusiness and the peasantry. *Review of African Political Economy, 14*(38), 89–96. doi:10.1080/03056248708703719

D'Onofrio, A., Minetti, R., & Murro, P. (2017). Banking development, socioeconomic structure and income inequality. *Journal of Economic Behavior & Organization*. doi:10.1016/j.jebo.2017.08.006

Dabla-Norris, M. E., Kochhar, M. K., Suphaphiphat, M. N., Ricka, M. F., & Tsounta, E. (2015). *Causes and consequences of income inequality: A global perspective*. International Monetary Fund.

Damasio, A. (1994). *Descartes' Error: Emotion, Reason and the Human Brain*. New York: Putnam Publishing.

Data Visualization's Positive Impact on Decision Making. (2010). Retrieved from https://www.mapbusinessonline.com/Whitepaper.aspx/Decision-Making

de Haan, J., & Sturm, J. E. (2017). Finance and income inequality: A review and new evidence. *European Journal of Political Economy, 50*, 171–195. doi:10.1016/j.ejpoleco.2017.04.007

De Luna Martinez, J. (2000). *Management and resolution of banking crises*. WB Discussion Paper, 413. doi:10.1596/0-8213-4723-3

De Luna, S., Fernández-Sáez, J., Pérez-Castellanos, J. L., & Navarro, C. (2000). An Analysis of the Static and Dynamic Fracture Behaviour of a Pipeline Steel. *International Journal of Pressure Vessels and Piping, 77*(11), 691–696. doi:10.1016/S0308-0161(00)00058-2

Deason, S., Rajgopal, S., & Waymire, G. (2015). *Who Gets Swindled in Ponzi Schemes?* Atlanta: Emory University. Retrieved from https://www0.gsb.columbia.edu/mygsb/faculty/research/pubfiles/12962/ponzi%20draft%20may%2013%202015.pdf

Dedola, L., Karadi, P., & Lombardo, G. (2013). Global Implication of National Unconventional Policies. *Journal of Monetary Economics, 60*(1), 66–85. doi:10.1016/j.jmoneco.2012.12.001

Dell'Ariccia, G., Igan, D., Laeven, L., Tong, H., Bakker, B., & Vandenbusseche, J. (2012). *Policies for Macrofinancial Stability: How to Deal with Credit Booms?* IMF Staff Discussion Note. Retrieved from https://www.imf.org/external/pubs/ft/sdn/2012/sdn1206.pdf

Deloitte & Touche LLP. (2012). *Risk Assessment in Practice*. Retrieved December 6, 2017 from https://www2.deloitte.com/content/dam/Deloitte/global/Documents/Governance-Risk-Compliance/dttl-grc-riskassessmentinpractice.pdf

Deloitte & Touche LLP. (2015). *Türkiye*. İstanbul: Türkiye'de Borsaya Kote Olmayan Şirketlerde Kurumsal Yönetim Uygulamaları.

Demek, K. C., Raschke, R. L., Janvrin, D. J., & Dilla, W. N. (2018). Do organizations use a formalized risk management process to address social media risk? *International Journal of Accounting Information Systems, 28*, 31–44. doi:10.1016/j.accinf.2017.12.004

Demirgüç-Kunt, A. & Huizinga, H. (1999). Determinants of commercial bank interest margins & profitability: An international evidence. *WB Economic Review, 13*, 379-408. doi:10.1093/wber/13.2.379

Demirgüç-Kunt, A., & Detragiache, E. (1997). The Determinants of Banking Crises: Evidence From Developing and Developed Countries. *IMF Working Papers, 97*(106), 1. doi:10.5089/9781451947175.001

Demirgüç-Kunt, A., Kane, E., Karacaovali, B., & Laeven, L. (2008). Deposit Insurance around the World: A Comprehensive Database. *Deposit insurance around the world: Issues of design and implementation*, 363. doi:10.7551/mitpress/9780262042543.003.0011

Demirguc-Kunt, A., Klapper, L., Singer, D., & Van Oudheusden, P. (2015). *The Global Findex Database 2014* (World Bank Policy Research Working Paper No 7255). Retrieved from World Bank website: http://documents.worldbank.org/curated/en/187761468179367706/pdf/WPS7255.pdf

Demirgüç-Kunt, A., & Kane, E. (2002). Deposit Insurance Around the Globe: Where Does It Work? *The Journal of Economic Perspectives*, *16*(2), 175–195. doi:10.1257/0895330027319

Demirgüç-Kunt, A., Kane, E., & Laeven, L. (2015). Deposit insurance around the world: A comprehensive analysis and database. *Journal of Financial Stability*, *20*, 155–183. doi:10.1016/j.jfs.2015.08.005

Demirgüç-Kunt, A., & Klapper, L. (2013). Measuring Financial Inclusion: Explaining Variation Across and Within Countries. *Brookings Papers on Economic Activity*, *44*(1), 279–321. doi:10.1353/eca.2013.0002

Department of Economic Affairs, Government of India. (2016). *The Financial Resolution and Deposit Insurance Bill, 2016*. Delhi: Ministry of Finance, Government of India. Retrieved from https://dea.gov.in/sites/default/files/FRDI%20 Bill-27092016_1.pdf

Desai, S. (2017). India's Farm Loan Waiver Crisis [Blog]. Retrieved from https://www.frbsf.org/banking/asia-program/pacific-exchange-blog/indias-farm-loan-waiver-crisis/

Destek, M. A., Okumus, İ., & Manga, M. (2017). Türkiye'de Finansal Gelişim ve Gelir Dağılımı İlişkisi: Finansal Kuznets Eğrisi. *Dogus University Journal, 18*(2).

Dewitte, S., & Schouwenberg, H. (2002). Procrastination, Temptation and Incentives: The struggle between the present and the future in procrastinators and the punctual. *European Journal of Personality*, *16*(6), 469–489. doi:10.1002/per.461

Dey, P. K., Ogunlana, S. O., Tabucanon, M. T., & Gupta, S. S. (2001). Multiple Attribute Decision Making Approach to Petroleum Pipeline Route Selection. *International Journal of Services Technology and Management*, *2*(3-4), 347–362. doi:10.1504/IJSTM.2001.001608

Dhaktod, P., & Chib, S. (2015). Private Labels: A Changing Perspective in Indian Retailing. *International Journal of Management and Commerce Innovation*, *3*(2), 282–288.

Diamond, D., & Dybvig, P. (1983). Bank Runs, Deposit Insurance, and Liquidity. *Journal of Political Economy*, *91*(3), 401–419. doi:10.1086/261155

Diamond, D., Kashyap, A., & Rajan, R. (2017). Banking and the Evolving Objectives of Bank Regulation. *Journal of Political Economy*, *125*(6), 1812–1825. doi:10.1086/694622

DICGC. (2017). *A Guide to Deposit Insurance*. Retrieved from https://www.dicgc.org.in/FD_A-GuideToDepositInsurance.html

Dijk, O. (2017). Bank run psychology. *Journal of Economic Behavior & Organization*, *144*, 87–96. doi:10.1016/j.jebo.2017.08.005

Dimitrios, A., Helen, L., & Mike, T. (2016). Determinants of non-performing loans: Evidence from Euro-area countries. *Finance Research Letters*, *18*, 116–119. doi:10.1016/j.frl.2016.04.008

Dinçer, H., Yuksel, S., & Adalı, Z. (2018). Relationship Between Non-Performing Loans, Industry, and Economic Growth of the African Economies and Policy Recommendations for Global Growth. In *Globalization and Trade Integration in Developing Countries* (pp. 203–228). IGI Global. doi:10.4018/978-1-5225-4032-8.ch009

Dobler, M. (2008). Incentives for Risk Reporting – A Discretionary Disclosure and Cheap Talk Approach. *The International Journal of Accounting*, *43*(2), 184–206. doi:10.1016/j.intacc.2008.04.005

Donohoe, H., Stellefson, M., & Tennant, B. (2012). Advantages and Limitations of the e-Delphi Technique. *American Journal of Health Education, 43*(1), 38–46. doi:10.1080/19325037.2012.10599216

Donou-Adonsou, F., & Sylwester, K. (2016). Financial development and poverty reduction in developing countries: New evidence from banks and microfinance institutions. *Review of Development Finance, 6*(1), 82–90. doi:10.1016/j.rdf.2016.06.002

Dornbusch, R. (2001). *A primer on emerging market crises (No. w8326)*. National Bureau of Economic Research. doi:10.3386/w8326

Drummond, C., McGrath, H., & O'Toole, T. (2017). The impact of social media on resource mobilisation in entrepreneurial firms. *Industrial Marketing Management, 70*, 68–89. doi:10.1016/j.indmarman.2017.05.009

Dubey, G., Chawla, S., & Kaur, K. (2017). Social media opinion analysis for Indian political diplomats. In *Cloud Computing, Data Science & Engineering - Confluence, 2017 7th International Conference on* (pp. 681-686). Noida: IEEE. doi:10.1109/CONFLUENCE.2017.7943238

Dumitrescu, E. I., & Hurlin, C. (2012). Testing for Granger non-causality in heterogeneous panels. *Economic Modelling, 29*(4), 1450–1460. doi:10.1016/j.econmod.2012.02.014

Durusu-Ciftci, D., Ispir, M. S., & Yetkiner, H. (2017). Financial development and economic growth: Some theory and more evidence. *Journal of Policy Modeling, 39*(2), 290–306. doi:10.1016/j.jpolmod.2016.08.001

Eaton, C., & Shepherd, A. (2001). Contract farming: Partnerships for growth (No. 145). Food & Agriculture Org. Farming in Developing Economies. *American Journal of Agricultural Economics, 96*(5), 1257–1271. doi:10.1093/ajae/aau036

Egbuna, E., Oduh, M., Ujunwa, A., & Okoyeuzu, C. (2018). Does deposit insurance promote moral hazards and adverse selection? Evidence from Sub-Saharan Africa. *International Journal of Managerial Finance, 14*(2), 150–169. doi:10.1108/IJMF-10-2016-0196

Ellsberg, D. (1961). Risk, Ambiguity and the Savage Axioms. *The Quarterly Journal of Economics, 75*(4), 643–669. doi:10.2307/1884324

Elster, J. (1998). Emotions and economic theory. *Journal of Economic Literature, 36*(1), 47–74.

Engard, B. (2016). Benefits of financial literacy for kids. *CU Online*. Retrieved 14 January 2018 from https://online.campbellsville.edu/education/financial-literacy-for-kids/

Engineer, M. (1989). Bank runs and the suspension of deposit convertibility. *Journal of Monetary Economics, 24*(3), 443–454. doi:10.1016/0304-3932(89)90031-7

Ennis, H., & Keister, T. (2009). Bank Runs and Institutions: The Perils of Intervention. *The American Economic Review, 99*(4), 1588–1607. doi:10.1257/aer.99.4.1588

Epley, N., & Gilovich, T. (2010). Anchoring unbound. *Journal of Consumer Psychology, 20*(1), 20–24. doi:10.1016/j.jcps.2009.12.005

Epley, N., & Golivich, T. (2001). Putting adjustment back in the anchoring adjustment heuristic: Differential processing of self-generated & experimenter provided anchors. *Psychological Science, 12*(5), 391–396. doi:10.1111/1467-9280.00372 PMID:11554672

Erdem, T., Zhao, Y., & Valenzuela, A. (2004). Performance of Store Brands: A Cross-Country Analysis of Consumer Store-Brand Preferences, Perceptions, and Risk. *JMR, Journal of Marketing Research, 41*(1), 86–100. doi:10.1509/jmkr.41.1.86.25087

Ertekin, M., & Kırca, M. (2017). Türkiye'de Kentleşme ve İktisadi Büyüme İlişkisinin Zamanla Değişen Nedensellik Analizi Yöntemiyle İncelenmesi. *Journal of Emerging Economies and Policy*, *2*(2), 44–63. Retrieved from http://dergipark.gov.tr/download/article-file/430140

Essays, U. K. (2013, November). *Social Media In The Jasmine Revolution*. Retrieved April 23, 2018, from UK Essays: https://www.ukessays.com/essays/media/effect-of-social-media-on-the-jasmine-revolution-media-essay.php?vref=1

European Central Bank (ECB). (2012). *Financial Stability Review, What is Financial Stability*? Financial Stability Report. Retrieved Feb 15, 2018, from https://www.ecb.europa.eu/pub/pdf/other/ecb.financialstabilityreview201711.en.pdf?7a775eed7ede9aee35acd83d2052a198

European Central Bank. (2018). *European Central Bank Database*. Retrieved June 1, 2018 from https://www.bis.org/publ/work381.pdf

European Central Bank. (2018). *What are non-performing loans (NPLs)?* European Central Bank. Retrieved from https://www.ecb.europa.eu/explainers/tell-me/html/npl.en.html

Evans, D. S. (2002). The Antitrust Economics of Two-Sided Markets. *Ssrn*, *20*, 325. doi:10.2139srn.332022

Expert Group on Agricultural Indebtedness. (2007). *Report of the Expert Group on Agricultural Indebtedness*. New Delhi: Government of India.

Fama, E. (1970). Efficient capital markets: A review of theory and empirical work. *The Journal of Finance*, *25*(2), 383–417. doi:10.2307/2325486

Farhi, E., & Tirole, J. (2012). Collective Moral Hazard, Maturity Mismatch, and Systemic Bailouts. *The American Economic Review*, *102*(1), 60–93. doi:10.1257/aer.102.1.60

Farm, L. W.-O. T. (1990, July 7). Article. *Economic and Political Weekly*, *25*(27), 1428.

Federal Deposit Insurance Corporation (FDIC). (n.d.). Retrieved 14 January 2018 from https://www.fdic.gov/

Ferguson, M. (2016, May 19). *What is Text Analytics?* http://www.ibmbigdatahub.com/blog/what-text-analytics

Fernandes, J. (2013). *Chit fund scam: How Saradha duped its investors?* Retrieved from http://www.ndtv.com/india-news/chit-fund-scam-how-saradha-duped-its-investors-520076

Fernandes, D., Lynch, J. G. Jr, & Netemeyer, R. G. (2014). Financial literacy, financial education, and downstream financial behaviors. *Management Science*, *60*(8), 1861–1883. doi:10.1287/mnsc.2013.1849

Fernández de Lis, S., & Rubio, A. (2013). *Tendencias a medio plazo en la banca española* (BBVA Working Paper No. 13/33). Retrieved from BBVA website: https://www.bbvaresearch.com/publicaciones/tendencias-a-medio-plazo-en-la-banca-espanola/

Ferrari, J., Mason, C., & Hammer, C. (2006). Procrastination as a predictor of task perceptions: Examining delayed and non-delayed tasks across various deadlines. *Individual Differences Research*, *4*(1), 28–36.

Financial Life Stages of Older Canadians. (n.d.). Retrieved 15 January 2018 from https://www.getsmarteraboutmoney.ca/resources/publications/research/financial-life-stages-older-canadians/

Financial Literacy™. (n.d.). Retrieved 14 January 2018 from https://everfi.com/k-12/everfi-k-12-finliteracy/

Financial Stability Board, International Monetary Fund and Bank for International Settlements. (2009). *Guidance to Assess the Systemic Importance of Financial Institutions, Markets and Instruments: Initial Considerations*. Washington, DC: IMF. Retrieved from https://www.imf.org/external/np/g20/pdf/100109.pdf

Financial Well Being Survey. (n.d.). Retrieved 21 March 2018 from https://www.consumerfinance.gov/data-research/financial-well-being-survey-data/

Find out your financial well-being. (n.d.). Retrieved 2 February 2018 from https://www.consumerfinance.gov/consumer-tools/financial-well-being/

Fletcher, C., & Herrmann, D. (2012). *The Internationalisation of Corruption*. Surrey: Gower.

Florida, R., & Mellander, C. (2016). The geography of inequality: Difference and determinants of wage and income inequality across US metros. *Regional Studies*, *50*(1), 79–92. doi:10.1080/00343404.2014.884275

FM on whys and hows of farm loan waiver. (2008). Retrieved from http://www.rediff.com/money/2008/may/24spec.htm

Foot, M. (2003). *What is 'Financial Stability and How Do We Get it?* The Roy Bridge Memorial Lecture. Financial Services Authority.

Forensics, K. P. M. G. (2003). *Fraud Survey*. Montvale, NJ: KPMG.

Forrester Research Inc. (2018). *Predictions 2018: A year of reckoning*. Forrester Research Inc. Retrieved from https://go.forrester.com/blogs/predictions-2018-a-year-of-reckoning/

Frankel, T. (2012). *The Ponzi Scheme Puzzle*. New York: Oxford University Press. doi:10.1093/acprof:osobl/9780199926619.001.0001

Froese, A., Nisly, S., & May, R. (1984). The effects of task interest and difficulty on Procrastination. Kansas Academy of Science, 87(3-4), 119-128. doi:10.2307/3627847

Furness, W. H. (1910). *The island of stone money, Uap of the Carolines, by William Henry Furness, 3d ... with illustrations from photographs by the author*. London: J.B. Lippincott Company.

Furnham, A., & Boo, H. C. (2002). A literature review of the anchoring effect. *Journal of Socio-Economics*, *40*(1), 35–42. doi:10.1016/j.socec.2010.10.008

Gabel, J. (2011). Midnight in the Garden of Good Faith: Using Clawback Actions to HArvest the Equitable Roots of Bankrupt Ponzi Schemes. *Case Western Reserve Law Review, 62*(1), 19-79.

Galati, F., & Moessner, R. (2011). *Macroprudential Policy-A Literature Review* (Working Paper No. 337). BIS. Retrieved from https://www.bis.org/publ/work337.pdf

Gallego, S., Herrero, A. G., & Salas, J. S. (2002). *The Asian and European Banking Systems: The case of Spain in the quest for development and stability* (No. 217). Banco de España, Servicio de Estudios. Retrieved from http://econwpa.repec.org/eps/fin/papers/0304/0304007.pdf

Galor, O., & Zeira, J. (1993). Income distribution and macroeconomics. *The Review of Economic Studies*, *60*(1), 35–52. doi:10.2307/2297811

Gambacorta, L., Hoffman, B., & Peersman, G. (2014). The Effectiveness of Unconventional Monetary Policy at the Zero Lower Bound: A Cross- Country Analysis. *Journal of Money, Credit and Banking*, *46*(4), 615–642. doi:10.1111/jmcb.12119

Gandomi, A., & Haider, M. (2015). Beyond the hype: Big data concepts, methods, and analytics. *International Journal of Information Management*, *35*(2), 137–144. doi:10.1016/j.ijinfomgt.2014.10.007

García Montalvo, J. (2014). Crisis financiera, reacción regulatoria y el futuro de la banca en España. *Estudios de Economía Aplicada*, *32*(2), 497–528.

Garcia-Swartz, D. D., Hahn, R. W., & Layne-Farrar, A. (2004). *The economics of a cashless society: An analysis of the costs and benefits of payment instruments.* AEI- Brooking Joint Center For Regulatory Studies.

Garg, A., & Deshmukh, S. (2010). Engineering support issues for flexibility in maintenance. *Asia Pacific Journal of Marketing and Logistics*, *22*(2), 247–270. doi:10.1108/13555851011026980

Gastwirth, J. L. (2017). Is the Gini index of inequality overly sensitive to changes in the middle of the income distribution? *Statistics and Public Policy (Philadelphia, Pa.)*, *4*(1), 1–11. doi:10.1080/2330443X.2017.1360813

Genç, E., & Sasmaz, M. Ü. (2016). Takipteki Banka Kredilerinin Makroekonomik Belirleyicileri: Ticari Krediler Örnegi/ Macroeconomic Determiners Of Non-Performing Loans: Commercial Loans Sample. *Selcuk Üniversitesi Sosyal Bilimler Enstitüsü Dergisi*, (36), 119.

Gennaioli, N., Shleifer, A., & Vishny, R. (2013). A Model of Shadow Banking. *The Journal of Finance*, *68*(4), 1331–1363. doi:10.1111/jofi.12031

Gertler, M., & Karadi, P. (2011). A Model of Unconventional Monetary Policy. *Journal of Monetary Economics*, *58*(1), 17–34. doi:10.1016/j.jmoneco.2010.10.004

Gertler, M., & Kiyotaki, N. (2015). Banking, Liquidity, and Bank Runs in an Infinite Horizon Economy. *The American Economic Review*, *105*(7), 2011–2043. doi:10.1257/aer.20130665

Get Smarter About Money. (2018). Retrieved 2 February 2018 from https://www.getsmarteraboutmoney.ca/

Ghosh, A. (2015). Banking-industry specific and regional economic determinants of non-performing loans: Evidence from US states. *Journal of Financial Stability*, *20*, 93–104. doi:10.1016/j.jfs.2015.08.004

Ghosh, A. (2017). Sector-specific analysis of non-performing loans in the US banking system and their macroeconomic impact. *Journal of Economics and Business*, *93*, 29–45. doi:10.1016/j.jeconbus.2017.06.002

Gilovich, T., & Medvec, V. (1995). The experience of Regret: What, when and why. *Japanese Psychological Review*, *102*(2), 519–595. doi:10.1037//0033-295x.102.2.379 PMID:7740094

Giri, A., & Sinha, S. (2018). Devinder Sharma on India's Agriculture Crisis. *The Diplomat*. Retrieved from https://thediplomat.com/2018/06/devinder-sharma-on-indias-agriculture-crisis/

González Mieres, C., María Díaz Martín, A., & Trespalacios Gutiérrez, J. (2006a). Antecedents of the difference in perceived risk between store brands and national brands. *European Journal of Marketing*, *40*(1/2), 61–82. doi:10.1108/03090560610637310

González Mieres, C., María Díaz Martín, A., & Trespalacios Gutiérrez, J. (2006b). Influence of perceived risk on store brand proneness. *International Journal of Retail & Distribution Management*, *34*(10), 761–772. doi:10.1108/09590550610691347

Gorton, G. (1985). Bank suspension of convertibility. *Journal of Monetary Economics*, *15*(2), 177–193. doi:10.1016/0304-3932(85)90063-7

Gough, J. (1988). *Risk and uncertainty. Information Paper no.10.* Center for Resource Management, University of Canterbury and Lincoln College.

Graham, A. (2008). *Integrated Risk Management - Implementation Guide*. Retrieved December 1, 2017 from http://post.queensu.ca/~grahama/publications/TEXTPDF.pdf

Granger, C. (1969). Investigating Causal Relations by Econometric Models and Cross-Spectral Methods. *Econometrica*, *37*(3), 424–438. doi:10.2307/1912791

Green, K. P., & Jackson, T. (2015). *Safety in the Transportation of Oil and Gas: Pipelines or Rail?* Fraser Institute.

Greenspan, A. (2005). *Board of Governors of the Federal Reserve System, Monetary Policy Report to the Congress.* Retrieved 21 March 2018 from https://www.federalreserve.gov/boarddocs/hh/2005/july/fullreport.pdf

Greenwood, J., & Jovanovic, B. (1990). Financial development, growth, and the distribution of income. *Journal of Political Economy, 98*(5), 1076–1107. doi:10.1086/261720

Grewal, D., Levy, M., & Lehmann, D. (2004). Retail Branding and Customer Loyalty: An overview. *Journal of Retailing, 80*(4), ix–xii. doi:10.1016/j.jretai.2004.10.001

Griffin, D., Dunning, D., & Ross, M. (1990). The role of construal processes in overconfident predictions about the self and others. *Journal of Personality and Social Psychology, 59*(6), 1128–1139. doi:10.1037/0022-3514.59.6.1128 PMID:2283587

Grizane, T., & Jurgelane, I. (2017). Social Media Impact on Business Evaluation. *Procedia Computer Science, 104*, 190–196. doi:10.1016/j.procs.2017.01.103

Group of Thirty (G-30). (2010). *Engancing Financial Stability and Resilience - Macroprudential Policy, Tools and Systems for the Future.* Retrieved from http://group30.org/images/uploads/publications/G30_EnhancingFinancialStabilityResilience.pdf

Guan, S., Mayes, P., Andrenacci, A., & Wong, D. (2007). Advanced two-layer polyethylene coating technology for pipeline protection. *International Corrosion Control Conference*, 5-7. 10.1115/iogpc2017-2453

Guerrero, J. C. (2015). *ASME B31.4 Pipeline Transportation System for Liquid Hydrocarbon & other Liquid.* New York: Two Park Avenue. doi:10.1016/b978-0-12-813045-2.00007-7

Guiso, L., Sapienza, P., & Zingales, L. (2013). *Time varying risk aversion.* CEPR Working Paper.

Gupta, M., & Shri, C. (2018). Developing a Conceptual Framework for Performance Evaluation of Corrugated Packaging Firms in India. *Journal of Packaging Technology and Research, 2*(1), 45–60. doi:10.100741783-018-0028-3

Gutiérrez Fernández, M., Fernández Torres, Y., & Palomo Zurdo, R. (2016). De la Transformación a la Bancarización de las Cajas de Ahorros españolas: Un análisis de los resultados perseguidos. *REVESCO, 122*, 86–109.

Hacker, R. S., & Hatemi-J, A. (2006). Tests for Causality between Integrated Variables Using Asymptotic and Bootstrap Distributions: Theory and Application. *Applied Economics, 38*(13), 1489–1500. doi:10.1080/00036840500405763

Halan, M. (2017, December 13). *FRDI Bill is not going to hike the risk to your deposits.* Retrieved from https://www.livemint.com/Opinion/WHC48EQMgIucC8ve5d38FM/FRDI-Bill-is-not-going-to-hike-the-risk-to-your-deposits.html

Hannoun, H. (2010). *Towards A Global Financial Stability Framework.* (Working Paper No. 284). BIS. Retrieved from https://www.bis.org/speeches/sp100303.pdf

Hao, J., & Dai, H. (2016). Social media content and sentiment analysis on consumer security breaches. *Journal of Financial Crime, 23*(4), 855–869. doi:10.1108/JFC-01-2016-0001

Hari, G. R. (2017). *Demonetisation.* Retrieved from http://www.mca.co.in/images/Demonetisation_MCA.PDF

Hasan, A., Moin, S., Karim, A., & Shamshirband, S. (2018). Machine Learning-Based Sentiment Analysis for Twitter Accounts. *Mathematical and Computational Applications, 23*(1), 11–26. doi:10.3390/mca23010011

Havrylchyk, O., & Verdier, M. (2018). The Financial Intermediation Role of the P2P Lending Platforms. *Comparative Economic Studies, 60*(1), 115–130. doi:10.105741294-017-0045-1

Hayes, S. C. (2004). Acceptance and commitment therapy, relational frame theory and the third wave of behavioral and cognitive therapies. *Behavior Therapy*, *35*(4), 639–665. doi:10.1016/S0005-7894(04)80013-3 PMID:27993338

Heidemann, J., Klier, M., & Probst, F. (2012). Online social networks: A survey of a global phenomenon. *Computer Networks*, *56*(18), 3866–3878. doi:10.1016/j.comnet.2012.08.009

Her Majesty's Treasury. (2004). *The Orange Book: Management of Risk-Principles and Concepts*. Retrieved December 21, 2017 from https://assets.publishing.service.gov.uk/government/uploads/ system/uploads/attachment_data/file/220647/ orange_book.pdf

He, W., Guo, L., Shen, J., & Akula, V. (2016). Social Media-Based Forecasting: A Case Study of Tweets and Stock Prices in the Financial Services Industry. *Journal of Organizational and End User Computing*, *28*(2), 18. doi:10.4018/ JOEUC.2016040105

He, W., Zha, S., & Li, L. (2013). Social media competitive analysis and text mining: A case study in the pizza industry. *International Journal of Information Management*, *33*(3), 464–472. doi:10.1016/j.ijinfomgt.2013.01.001

Himanshu. (2016, April 16). Rural Push in Budget 2016–17: Rhetoric versus Reality. *Economic and Political Weekly*, *51*(16), 36-38. Retrieved from https://www.epw.in/journal/2016/16/budget-2016%E2%80%9317/rural-push-budget-2016-17.html

Holton, C. (2009). Identifying disgruntled employee systems fraud risk through text mining: A simple solution for a multi-billion dollar problem. *Decision Support Systems*, *46*(4), 853–864. doi:10.1016/j.dss.2008.11.013

Hoskisson, R. E., Eden, L., Lau, C. M., & Wright, M. (2000). Strategy in emerging economies. *Academy of Management Journal*, *43*(3), 249–267.

Hsu, H., & Lai, C. (2008). Examination of Factors Moderating the Success of Private Label Brands: A Study of the Packaged Food Market in China. *Journal of Food Products Marketing*, *14*(4), 1–20. doi:10.1080/10454440801986256

Hukeri, P., & Prasanth, V. (2008). The Loan Waiver Scheme. *Economic and Political Weekly*, *43*(11), 28–34.

Hull, J. C. (2015). *Risk Management and Financial Institutions* (4th ed.). John Wiley & Sons. Retrieved from http:// www.simonfoucher.com/MBA/FINA%20695%20-%20Risk%20Management/riskmanagementandfinancialinstitution-s4theditionjohnhull-150518225205-lva1-app6892.pdf

IMF. (1998). *World Economic Outlook*. International Monetary Fund. Retrieved from:http://www.imf.org/en/Publications/WEO/Issues/2016/12/31/Financial-Crises-Causes-and-Indicators

India Brand Equity Foundation. (2016). *Retail*. Retrieved from https://www.ibef.org/download/Retail-January-2016.pdf

India Today. (2015, January 21). *Pradhan Mantri Jan Dhan Yojana Made it to the Guiness Book of World Records*. Retrieved from India Today: https://www.indiatoday.in/education-today/gk-current-affairs/story/pradhan-mantri-jan-dhan-yojana-made-it-to-guinness-world-records-a-record-11.5-cr-accounts-opened-236741-2015-01-21

Institute of Chartered Accountants in England and Wales. (2011). *Reporting Business Risks: Meeting Expectations*. Retrieved December 2, 2017 from http://www.icaew.com/~/media/corporate/files/technical /financial%20reporting/ information%20for%20better%20markets/ifbm/rbr%20final.ashx.

Institute of Risk Management (IRM). (2002). *A Risk Management Standard*. Retrieved January 1, 2018 from https:// www.theirm.org/media/886059/ARMS_2002_IRM.pdf

International Association of Deposit Insurers. (2014). *IADI Core Principles for Effective Deposit Insurance Systems*. IADI. Retrieved from https://www.iadi.org/en/assets/File/Core%20Principles/cprevised2014nov.pdf

International Gateway for Financial Education. (2012). Retrieved 2 March 2018 from http://www.financial-education.org/join_INFE.html

International Monetary Fund (IMF). (2011). *Macroprudential Policy: An Organizing Framework*. Washington, DC: IMF. Retrieved from https://www.imf.org/external/np/pp/eng/2011/031411.pdf

International Monetary Fund (IMF). (2013). *Key Aspects of Macroprudential Policy-Background Paper*. Washington, DC: IMF. Retrieved from https://www.imf.org/external/np/pp/eng/2013/061013C.pdf

International Monetary Fund. (2015). *World Economic Output*. International Monetary Fund.

International Organization for Standardization. (2018). *ISO 31000 Risk management — Guidelines*. Retrieved August 28, 2018 from https://www.iso.org/obp/ui#iso:std:iso:31000:ed-2:v1:en

International, Nigeria Watch. (2017, January 23). *MMM Nigeria Ponzi Scheme And the Curse of 'Herd Mentality'*. Retrieved from Vigilance-Security Magazine: http://www.vigilance-securitymagazine.com/news/general/nigeria-watch-international/8722-mmm-nigeria-ponzi-scheme-and-the-curse-of-herd-mentality

Investment Company Institute. (2017). *US mutual funds, Chapter 3*. Investment Company Fact Book. Retrieved from http://www.icifactbook.org/ch3/18_fb_ch3

Investopedia. (2017). *Ponzi Scheme*. Retrieved from Investopedia: https://www.investopedia.com/terms/p/ponzischeme.asp

Iyengar, V., Behl, A., Pillai, S., & Londhe, B. (2016). Analysis of Palliative Care Process through SAP-LAP Inquiry: Case Study on Palliative Care and Training Centre. *Global Journal of Flexible Systems Management*, *17*(4), 403–416. doi:10.100740171-016-0137-1

Iyer, R., Jensen, T., & Johannesen, N. (2016). *The Run for Safety: Financial Fragility and Deposit Insurance*. SSRN Electronic Journal. doi:10.2139srn.2780073

Iyer, R., & Puri, M. (2012). Understanding Bank Runs: The Importance of Depositor-Bank Relationships and Networks. *The American Economic Review*, *102*(4), 1414–1445. doi:10.1257/aer.102.4.1414

IZEA. (2017, March). *6 Key Factors That Influence Your Social Media Engagement*. Retrieved from www.izea.com: https://izea.com/2017/03/16/key-factors-affect-social-media-engagement/

Jacobs, P., & Schain, L. (2011). *The Never Ending Attraction of the Ponzi Scheme*. Fairfield: Sacred Heart University.

Jain, B. (2017, October 18). Maharashtra: Farmers rejoice as govt rolls out loan waiver. *The Times of India*. Retrieved from https://timesofindia.indiatimes.com/city/mumbai/loan-waiver-begins-our-diwalis-been-made/articleshow/61137159.cms

Jain, R. C. A., & Parshad, M. (2006). *Report of the working group on risk management in agriculture for the eleventh five-year plan (2007-2012)*. New Delhi, India: Government of India Planning Commission. Retrieved from http://planningcommission.nic.in/aboutus/committee/wrkgrp11/wg11_risk.pdf

James, H. Jr, Klein, P., & Sykuta, M. (2011). The adoption, diffusion, and evolution of organizational form: Insights from the agrifood sector. *Managerial and Decision Economics*, *32*(4), 243–259. doi:10.1002/mde.1531

Jarell, G., & Peltzman, S. (1985). The Impact of Product Recalls on the Wealth of Sellers. *Journal of Political Economy*, *93*(3), 512–536. doi:10.1086/261313

Jauch, S., & Watzka, S. (2016). Financial development and income inequality: A panel data approach. *Empirical Economics*, *51*(1), 291–314. doi:10.100700181-015-1008-x

Jayadevan, K. R., Ostby, E., & Thaulow, C. (2004). Strain-Based Fracture Mechanics Analysis of Pipelines. *Proceedings of the International Conference on Advances in Structural Integrity*, 14-17. 10.1115/omae2005-67518

Jenkins, S. (2017). The measurement of income inequality. In *Economic inequality and poverty: International perspectives* (pp. 17–52). Routledge.

Jiang, J., & Shen, M. (2017). *Traditional Media*. Twitter and Business Scandals; doi:10.2139srn.2959419

Jiwarajka, G. (2017). *Increasing the base of retail investors*. Retrieved from http://www.primedatabase.com/article/2017/41. Article-Gopal%20Jiwarajka.pdf

John, L., & Ramesh, A. (2012). Humanitarian supply chain management in India: A SAP-LAP framework. *Journal of Advances in Management Research*, *9*(2), 217–235. doi:10.1108/09727981211271968

Johnson, E., & Sherraden, M. (2007). From financial literacy to financial capability among youth. *The Journal of Sociology & Social Welfare, 34*(3), 119-146. Retrieved 10 June 2018 from http://scholarworks.wmich.edu/jssw/vol34/iss3/7?utm_source=scholarworks.wmich.edu/jssw/vol34/iss3/7&utm_medium=PDF&utm_campaign=PDFCoverPages

Jones, L. M., Bernknopf, R., Cox, D., Goltz, J., Hudnut, K., Mileti, D., ... Seligson, H. (2008). The Shakeout Scenario. *U.S. Geological Survey Open-File Report*, *1150*, 308. doi:10.1193/1.3563624

Jorion, P. (2006). *Value At Risk: The new benchmark for controlling market risk*. McGraw-Hill.

Jose, R., & Chooralil, V. S. (2015). Prediction of election result by enhanced sentiment analysis on Twitter data using Word Sense Disambiguation. In *Proceedings of the 2015 International Conference on Control Communication & Computing India (ICCC)* (pp. 638-641). Trivandrum: IEEE. 10.1109/ICCC.2015.7432974

Joshi, S. (2008, March 5). Debt Relief and Waiver Scheme – Effective only if it is total. *The Hindu Business Line*. Retrieved from https://www.thehindubusinessline.com/todays-paper/tp-opinion/Debt-Relief-and-Waiver-Scheme-mdash-Effective-only-if-it-is-total/article20124871.ece

Joshi, V. (2018). Impact of Demonetization on Indian Economy with Respect to Real Estate Sector. *Ssrn*, *7*(3), 20–28. doi:10.2139srn.3120188

Jump$tart Clearinghouse. (n.d.). Retrieved 15 January 2018 from https://jumpstartclearinghouse.org/

Jump$tart Who We Are. (2018). Retrieved 2 February 2018 from https://jumpstart.org

Junior Achievement Finance Park. (n.d.). Retrieved 15 March 2018 from https://www.juniorachievement.org/web/ja-usa/ja-programs?p_p_id=56_INSTANCE_abcd&p_p_state=maximized&_56_INSTANCE_abcd_groupId=14516&_56_INSTANCE_abcd_articleId=1 9406

Junior Achievement Programs. (n.d.). Retrieved 15 January 2018 from https://www.juniorachievement.org/web/ja-usa/ja-programs

Kahneman, D. (1994). New Challenges to the Rationality Assumption. *Journal of Institutional and Theoretical Economics*, *150*(1), 105–124.

Kahneman, D. (2011). *Thinking Fast and Slow*. New York: Farrar, Straus and Giroux.

Kahneman, D., Knetsch, J., & Thaler, R. (1991). Anomalies: The endowment effect, loss aversionand status quo bias. *The Journal of Economic Perspectives*, *5*(1), 193–206. doi:10.1257/jep.5.1.193

Kahneman, D., & Lovallo, D. (1993). Timid choices and bold forecastes: A cognitive perspective on risk taking. *Management Science*, *39*(1), 17–31. doi:10.1287/mnsc.39.1.17

Kahneman, D., & Tversky, A. (1979). Prospect Theory: An analysis of decision under risk. *Econometrica, 47*(2), 263–291. doi:10.2307/1914185

Kahneman, D., & Tversky, A. (1984). Choices, Values and Frames. *The American Psychologist, 39*(4), 341–350. doi:10.1037/0003-066X.39.4.341

Kane, E. (2000). *Designing Financial Safety Nets to Fit Country Circumstances.* World Bank. Retrieved from http://documents.worldbank.org/curated/en/423381468764432839/pdf/multi-page.pdf

Kanz, M. (2012). *What does debt relief do for development? evidence from India's bailout program for highly-indebted rural households.* The World Bank. Retrieved from http://documents.worldbank.org/curated/en/589181468044056902/pdf/wps6258.pdf

Karluk, S. R., & Unal, U. (2017). *Türkiye Ekonomisinde Yoksulluk.* Yolsuzluk ve Gelir Dağılımı İlişkisi.

Karppi, T., & Crawford, K. (2016). Social Media, Financial Algorithms and the Hack Crash. *Theory, Culture & Society, 33*(1), 73–92. doi:10.1177/0263276415583139

Kashyap, A., Rajan, R., & Stein, J. (2002). Banks as Liquidity Providers: An Explanation for the Coexistence of Lending and Deposit-taking. *The Journal of Finance, 57*(1), 33–73. doi:10.1111/1540-6261.00415

Kaufman, G. (2000). Banking and currency crises and systemic risk: Lessons from recent events. *Economic Perspectives, 24*(3), 9–20. Retrieved from https://www.chicagofed.org/publications/economic-perspectives/2000/3qepart2

Kaufman, G., & Scott, K. (2003). What is systemic risk and do bank regulators retard or contribute to it? *Independent Review, 7*(3), 371–391. Retrieved from http://www.independent.org/pdf/tir/tir_07_3_scott.pdf

Kauko, K. (2012). External deficits and non-performing loans in the recent financial crisis. *Economics Letters, 115*(2), 196–199. doi:10.1016/j.econlet.2011.12.018

Kaul, V. (2014). *Another Sahara: How Sahara built a 'brand' and duped people.* Retrieved from http://www.firstpost.com/investing/another-sahara-how-saradha-built-a-brand-and-duped-investors-724287.html

Kawai, M., & Morgan, P. J. (2012). *Central Banking for Financial Stability in Asia* (Working Paper No. 377). ADBI. Retrieved from https://www.adb.org/sites/default/files/publication/156232/adbi-wp377.pdf

Kawai, M., & Takagi, S. (2008). *A Survey of The Literature on Managing Capital Inflows* (Discussion Paper No. 100). ADB. Retrieved from https://www.adb.org/sites/default/files/publication/156738/adbi-dp100.pdf

Kawai, M., & Morgan, P. (2014). *Regional Financial Regulation in Asia.* Asian Development Bank Institute. doi:10.4337/9781783472208.00012

Keeley, M. C. (1990). Deposit insurance, risk, and market power in banking. *The American Economic Review*, 1183–1200. Retrieved from https://www.jstor.org/stable/2006769?seq=1#page_scan_tab_contents

Kemp, S. (2017, August 7). *Number of social media users passes 3 billion with no signs of slowing.* Retrieved January 10, 2018, from The Next Web: https://thenextweb.com/contributors/2017/08/07/number-social-media-users-passes-3-billion-no-signs-slowing/

Kempson, E., Atkinson, A., & Pilley, O. (2004). *Policy level response to financial exclusion in developed economies: Lessons for developing countries.* Retrieved from http://www.bristol.ac.uk/media-library/sites/geography/migrated/documents/pfrc0409.pdf

Kennedy, T., Smyth, R., Valadkhani, A., & Chen, G. (2017). Does income inequality hinder economic growth? New evidence using Australian taxation statistics. *Economic Modelling, 65*, 119–128. doi:10.1016/j.econmod.2017.05.012

Khan Academy. (n.d.). Retrieved 15 January 2018 from https://www.khanacademy.org/

Khedekar-Swaminathan, A., & Kulkarni, S. (2018). Behavioral challenges for retirement planning: A study of employees of the Information Technology industry in Pune, Maharashtra. *International Journal of Applied Behavioral Economics*, *7*(2), 15–29. doi:10.4018/IJABE.2018040102

Kibritcioglu, A. (2002). *Excessive risk-taking, banking sector fragility and banking crises*. University of Illinois, Commerce and Bus. Admin. Working Paper No. 02-0114. doi:10.2139srn.317491

Kim, I., Kim, I., & Han, Y. (2014). Deposit Insurance, Banks' Moral Hazard, and Regulation: Evidence from the ASEAN Countries and Korea. *Emerging Markets Finance & Trade*, *50*(6), 56–71. doi:10.1080/1540496X.2014.1013875

Kim, W. G., Lim, H., & Brymer, R. A. (2015). The effectiveness of managing social media on hotel performance. *International Journal of Hospitality Management*, *44*, 165–171. doi:10.1016/j.ijhm.2014.10.014

Kirsten, J., & Sartorius, K. (2002). Linking agribusiness and small-scale farmers in developing countries: Is there a new role for contract farming? *Development Southern Africa*, *19*(4), 503–529. doi:10.1080/0376835022000019428

Kleftouri, N. (2013). Deposit protection system's design and effectiveness. *Journal of Banking Regulation*, *16*(1), 51–63. doi:10.1057/jbr.2013.21

Knight, F. (1921). *Risk, Uncertainty and Profit*. Boston: Houghton Mifflin.

Knütter, R., Mohr, B., & Wagner, H. (2011). *The Effects of Central Bank Communication on Financial Stability: A Systematization of the Empirical Evidence* (Discussion Paper No.463). FernUniversitat in Hagen. Retrieved from http://www.fernuni-hagen.de/wirtschaftswissenschaft/download/beitraege/db463.pdf

Koehler, D. (1991). Explanation, Imagination & Confidence in Judgment. *Psychological Bulletin*, *110*(3), 499–519. doi:10.1037/0033-2909.110.3.499 PMID:1758920

Koehler, D., & Poon, C. (2006). Self-predictions overweight strength of current intentions. *Journal of Experimental Social Psychology*, *42*(4), 517–524. doi:10.1016/j.jesp.2005.08.003

Köllner, S., & Gründler, K. (2016). *Determinants of Governmental Redistribution: Income Distribution*. Development Levels, and the Role of Perceptions.

Konstantakis, K. N., Michaelides, P. G., & Vouldis, A. T. (2016). Non-performing loans (NPLs) in a crisis economy: Long-run equilibrium analysis with a real time VEC model for Greece (2001–2015). *Physica A*, *451*, 149–161. doi:10.1016/j.physa.2015.12.163

Krige, D. (2012). Fields of dreams, fields of schemes: ponzi finance and multi-level marketing in South Africa. *International African Institute, 82*(1), 69-92.

Kroll Inc. (2008). Economist Intelligence Unit Overview. In *The Kroll Global Fraud Report*. Kroll Inc. Retrieved from https://eiuperspectives.com/sites/default/files/FraudReport_English UK_Sept08_1.pdf

Krugman, P. (2014, April 26). Is a banking ban the answer? [Blog]. Retrieved from https://krugman.blogs.nytimes.com/2014/04/26/is-a-banking-ban-the-answer/

Kumar, A. (2017b). *Understanding the Black Economy and Black Money in India*. RUA Publications. Retrieved from https://books.google.co.in/books?id=DB6UnQAACAAJ

Kumar, A., & Bathla, S. (2017, November 14). Loan waiver is not the solution. *The Hindu*. Retrieved from https://www.thehindu.com/opinion/op-ed/loan-waiver-is-not-the-solution/article20394319.ece

Kumar, A. (2017a). Economic Consequences of Demonetisation Money Supply and Economic Structure. *Economic and Political Weekly*, *150*(1).

Kumar, P., Haleem, A., Qamar, F., & Khan, U. (2018). Analysis of maiden modal shift in coal transportation supply chain using SAP-LAP technique. *International Journal of Logistics Systems and Management*, *30*(4), 458. doi:10.1504/IJLSM.2018.093585

Kumar, V. (2016). *Indigenous Crude Oil Production and Import and Processing by Petroleum Planning & Analysis Cell (PPAC)*. New Delhi: Ministry of Petroleum & Natural Gas, Government of India.

Kusairi, S., Sanusi, N., & Ismail, A. (2018). Dilemma of deposit insurance policy in ASEAN countries: Does it promote banking industry stability or moral hazard? *Borsa Istanbul Review*, *18*(1), 33–40. doi:10.1016/j.bir.2017.08.006

Laeven, M. L., & Valencia, F. (2008). The use of blanket guarantees in banking crises (No. 8-250). International Monetary Fund.

Laeven, L., & Levine, R. (2007). Is there a diversification discount in financial conglomerates? *Journal of Financial Economics*, *85*(2), 331–367. doi:10.1016/j.jfineco.2005.06.001

Laeven, L., Ratnovski, L., & Tong, H. (2014). *Bank Size, Capital, and Systemic Risk: Some International Evidence*. SSRN Electronic Journal. doi:10.2139srn.2508910

Lahiri, A. K. (2016). *Demonetization, the Cash Shortage and the Black Money*. Academic Press.

Lambert, C., Noth, F., & Schüwer, U. (2017). How do insured deposits affect bank risk? Evidence from the 2008 Emergency Economic Stabilization Act. *Journal of Financial Intermediation*, *29*, 81–102. doi:10.1016/j.jfi.2015.07.001

Lee, C. C., & Lee, C. C. (2018). The Impact of Country Risk on Income Inequality: A Multilevel Analysis. *Social Indicators Research*, *136*(1), 139–162. doi:10.100711205-016-1534-8

Lerner, J., Small, D., & Loewnstein, G. (2004). Heart strings and purse strings. *Psychological Science*, *15*(5), 337–341. doi:10.1111/j.0956-7976.2004.00679.x PMID:15102144

Levine, R. (2005). Finance and growth: theory and evidence: 12. In P. Aghion & S. Durlauf (Eds.), *Handbook of economic growth* (pp. 865–934). Amsterdam: Elsevier; doi:10.3386/w10766

Levmore, S. (2012). Rethinking Ponzi-Scheme Remedies in and out of Bankruptcy. *BUL Review*, *92*, 969.

Lewis, M. (2015). *Understanding Ponzi Schemes: Can Better Financial Regulation Prevent Investors from Being Defrauded?* Edward Elgar Publishing. doi:10.4337/9781782549109

Li, B., Chan, K. C., Ou, C., & Ruifeng, S. (2017). Discovering public sentiment in social media for predicting stock movement of publicly listed companies. *Information Systems*, *69*, 81–92. doi:10.1016/j.is.2016.10.001

Liben-Nowell, D., & Kleinberg, J. (2007). The link prediction problem for social networks. *Journal of the Association for Information Science and Technology*, *58*(7), 1019–1031. doi:10.1002/asi.v58:7

Lim, C., Columba, F., Costa, A., Kongsamut, P., Otani, A., Saiyid, M., ... Wu, X. (2011). *Macroprudential Policy: What Instruments and How to Use Them? Lessons from Country Experiences. (Working Paper No. 238)*. Washington, DC: IMF. Retrieved from https://www.imf.org/external/pubs/ft/wp/2011/wp11238.pdf

Lindauer, D. L. (2017). Maintaining Perspective on the Economic Issues of Today. *Society*, *54*(1), 2–3. doi:10.100712115-016-0090-9

Linsley, P. M. (2011). *UK Bank Risk Disclosures in the Period Through to The Onset of the Global Financial Crisis – Briefing*. Retrieved December 10, 2017, from https://www.icaew.com/-/media/corporate/files/ products/financial-services/cbp-uk-bank-risk-disclosures-in-the-period-through-to-the-onset-of-the-global-financial-crisis.ashx

Linstone, H. (1978). *The Delphi technique. In Handbook of Futures Research* (pp. 271–300). Westport, CT: Greenwood.

Linstone, H., & Turoff, M. (1975). *The Delphi method*. Reading, MA: Addison-Wesley Pub. Co., Advanced Book Program.

Litwack, J. M., & Sutherland, D. (2000). The Demonetisation of the Russian Economy: Causes and Policy Options. *OECD Economic Survey of Russia: 1999-2000*. Retrieved from https://www.imf.org/external/pubs/ft/seminar/2000/invest/pdf/litwack.pdf

Liu, L., Wu, J., Li, P., & Li, Q. (2015). A social-media-based approach to predicting stock comovement. *Expert Systems with Applications*, *42*(8), 3893–3901. doi:10.1016/j.eswa.2014.12.049

Loewenstein, G., Weber, E., Hsee, C., & Welch, N. (2001). Risk as feeling. *Psychological Bulletin*, *127*(2), 267–286. doi:10.1037/0033-2909.127.2.267 PMID:11316014

Lotto, B. (2017). *Deviate: The science of seeing differently*. London: Weidenfeld & Nicolson.

Louzis, D. P., Vouldis, A. T., & Metaxas, V. L. (2012). Macroeconomic and bank-specific determinants of non-performing loans in Greece: A comparative study of mortgage, business and consumer loan portfolios. *Journal of Banking & Finance*, *36*(4), 1012–1027. doi:10.1016/j.jbankfin.2011.10.012

Luo, G. Y. (1998). The evolution of money as a medium of exchange. *Journal of Economic Dynamics & Control*, *23*(3), 415–458. doi:10.1016/S0165-1889(98)00029-3

Lusardi, A., & Mitchell, O. S. (2011). Financial literacy around the world: An overview. *Journal of Pension Economics and Finance*, *10*(04), 497–508. doi:10.1017/S1474747211000448 PMID:28553190

Lusardi, A., Mitchell, O. S., & Curto, V. (2010). Financial literacy among the young. *The Journal of Consumer Affairs*, *44*(2), 358–380. doi:10.1111/j.1745-6606.2010.01173.x

Lussardi, A. (2003). *Planning and Saving for Retirement*. Dartmouth College Working Paper.

Lynch, J. Jr, & Zauberman, G. (2007). Construing consumer decision making. *Journal of Consumer Psychology*, *17*(2), 107–112. doi:10.1016/S1057-7408(07)70016-5

MacDonald, J. M., & Korb, P. J. (2008). *Agricultural contracting update, 2005 (No. 58639)*. United States Department of Agriculture, Economic Research Service.

MacDonald, J., Perry, J., Ahearn, M., Banker, D., Chambers, W., Dimitri, C., & ... . (2004). *Contracts, Markets, and Prices: Organizing the Production and Use of Agricultural Commodities*. SSRN Electronic Journal. doi:10.2139srn.754986

Mahama, W. (2016, February 4). *Ponzi Schemes and Financial Literacy in Ghana*. Retrieved from Ghana Web: https://www.ghanaweb.com/GhanaHomePage/features/Ponzi-schemes-and-financial-literacy-in-Ghana-412808

Maierbrugger, A. (2015). *South Asia has world's lowest financial literacy*. The Gulf Times.

Malhotra, A. (2011). Social Media: The New Tool of Revolution. *Scholar Warrior*, 74-81. Retrieved April 24, 2018, from http://www.claws.in/images/journals_doc/Spring%202011-%20Final%20Issue.87-94.pdf

Mali, V. (2016). Demonetization: A step towards modified India. *International Journal of Commerce and Management Research International Journal of Commerce and Management Research Issue*, *2*(12), 2455–1627.

Mandell, L., & Klein, L. S. (2009). The impact of financial literacy education on subsequent financial behavior. *Journal of Financial Counseling and Planning, 20*(1). Retrieved from https://papers.ssrn.com/sol3/papers.cfm?abstract_id=2224231

Mangla, S., Kumar, P., & Barua, M. (2014). A Flexible Decision Framework for Building Risk Mitigation Strategies in Green Supply Chain Using SAP–LAP and IRP Approaches. *Global Journal of Flexible Systems Management, 15*(3), 203–218. doi:10.100740171-014-0067-8

Mantel, B. (2001). *Why Don't Consumers Use Electronic Banking Products? Towards a Theory of Obstacles, Incentives, and Opportunities*. doi:10.2139srn.256736

Maroto, R., Mulas Granados, C., & Fernández Álvarez, J. (2012). *Crisis financiera y rescates bancarios en Europa. Ideas sobre el caso español*. Madrid: Fundación Ideas.

Martinez Peria, M., & Schmukler, S. (2001). Do Depositors Punish Banks for Bad Behavior? Market Discipline, Deposit Insurance, and Banking Crises. *The Journal of Finance, 56*(3), 1029–1051. doi:10.1111/0022-1082.00354

Masiero, S. (2017). New routes to cashlessness ? ICTs, demonetisation, and the Indian informal economy. *Dsa2017*.

Master Teacher Program. (n.d.). Retrieved 14 January 2018 from http://councilforeconed.org/master-teacher-program/

Mather, C. (1996). Towards sustainable agriculture in post-apartheid South Africa. *GeoJournal, 39*(1). doi:10.1007/BF00174927

Mattana, E., & Panetti, E. (2017). *The Welfare Costs of Self-Fulfilling Bank Runs* (No. 2017/17). ISEG-Lisbon School of Economics and Management, REM, Universidade de Lisboa. Retrieved from https://rem.rc.iseg.ulisboa.pt/wps/pdf/REM_WP_017_2017.pdf

Matten, C. (2000). *Managing bank capital: Capital allocation and performance measurement*. John Wiley & Sons, Ltd.

Maudos, J. (2012). El impacto de la crisis en el sector bancario español. *Cuadernos de Información Económica, 226*, 155–163.

Mazboudi, M., & Khalil, S. (2017). The attenuation effect of social media: Evidence from acquisitions by large firms. *Journal of Financial Stability, 28*, 115–124. doi:10.1016/j.jfs.2016.11.010

McCormick, M. (2009). The effectiveness of youth financial education: A review of the literature. *Journal of Financial Counseling and Planning, 20*(1), 70-83.

McDonald, J., & Korb, P. (2008). Agricultural contracting update: Contracts in 2008. *Economic Information Bulletin, 72*.

Mehrishi, R. (2017). *India Yearbook 2017*. New Delhi: Publications Division Ministry of Information and Broadcasting.

Merna, T., & Al-Thani, F. (2008). *Corporate Risk Management*. West Sussex, UK: John Wiley & Sons Ltd.

Meti, V., Khandoba, P., & Guru, M. (2015). Social Media for Political Mobilization in India: A Study. *Journal of Mass Communication & Journalism, 5*(9). doi:10.4172/2165-7912.1000275

Meulenberg, M. T. G., & Viaene, J. (1993). Agricultural marketing in Belgium and The Netherlands. *Journal of International Food & Agribusiness Marketing, 5*(3/4), 141–161.

Meuwissen, M. P. M., Hardaker, J. B., Huirne, R. B. M., & Dijkhuizen, A. A. (2001). Sharing risks in agriculture; principles and empirical results. *NJAS Wageningen Journal of Life Sciences, 49*(4), 343–356.

Meyer, B. D., & Sullivan, J. X. (2017). *Consumption and Income Inequality in the US Since the 1960s (No. w23655)*. National Bureau of Economic Research. doi:10.3386/w23655

Meyer, K., Comhome, D., & In, L. (2016). *Composites World: Polyurethanes-Collaboration and Adaptation for Optimal Application*. Florida State University. doi:10.1016/0956-7143(90)90258-x

Micajkova, V. (2013). Deposit insurance in times of financial crisis. *South Eastern European Journal of Economics, 2*, 165–176. Retrieved from https://ojs.lib.uom.gr/index.php/seeje/article/viewFile/5502/5530

Mighell, R. L., & Jones, L. A. (1963). *Vertical Coordination in Agriculture, Agricultural Economic Report 19*. U.S. Department of Agriculture.

Miller, R. (2015, June 30). *Inside Facebook's Blu-Ray Cold Storage Data Center*. Retrieved April 29, 2018, from Data Center Frontier: https://datacenterfrontier.com/inside-facebooks-blu-ray-cold-storage-data-center/

Ministry of Agriculture & Farmers Welfare. (2018, July 24). *Waiving off Agricultural loan*. Retrieved from Press Information Bureau: http://pib.nic.in/newsite/PrintRelease.aspx?relid=180924

Ministry of Electronics & Information Technology. (2015). *Digital India*. Retrieved April 16, 2018, from http://digitalindia.gov.in/content/introduction

Ministry of Electronics and Information Technology (MeitY). (n.d.). *Cashless India*. Retrieved April 16, 2018, from http://cashlessindia.gov.in

Ministry of Finance, Government of India. (2007). *Report of the Expert Group on Agricultural Indebtedness*. Retrieved from http://www.igidr.ac.in/pdf/publication/PP-059.pdf

Minot, N. (2007). *Contract Farming in Developing Countries: Patterns*. Impact, and Policy Implications.

Mishkin, F. S. (2000). *Financial Stability and the Macroeconomy (Working Paper No. 9)*. Central Bank of Iceland. Retrieved from http://hpi.uw.hu/pdf/wp9.pdf

Missing Out: Millennials and the Markets. (n.d.). *Research & reports*. Retrieved 14 January 2018 from https://www.getsmarteraboutmoney.ca/resources/publications/research/missing-out-millennials-a nd-the-markets/

Mitchell, V. (1992). Understanding Consumers' Behaviour: Can Perceived Risk Theory Help? *Management Decision, 30*(3), 00251749210013050. doi:10.1108/00251749210013050

Mitchell, V. (1998). A role for consumer risk perceptions in grocery retailing. *British Food Journal, 100*(4), 171–183. doi:10.1108/00070709810207856

Modine, J. D. (2009). *American Petroleum Institute Handbook Specification for Line Pipe. American Petroleum Institute*. doi:10.3403/00259052

Mohan, R. (2006, November). *Economic growth, financial deepening and financial inclusion*. Paper presented at the Annual Bankers' Conference 2006. Retrieved from http://rbidocs.rbi.org.in/rdocs/Speeches/PDFs/73697.pdf)

Momoc, A. (2013). Social Media- PR Tools for Romanian Politicians? *Procedia: Social and Behavioral Sciences, 81*, 116–121. doi:10.1016/j.sbspro.2013.06.398

Monroe, H., Carvajal, A., & Pattillo, C. (2010). *Perils of Ponzis*. IMF.

Moon, W. (2017). A Coinless Society as a Bridge to a Cashless Society: A Korean Experiment. In *Cash in East Asia* (pp. 101–115). Springer; doi:10.1007/978-3-319-59846-8_7

Morinaga, S., Yamanishi, K., Tateishi, K., & Fukushima, T. (2002). Mining product reputations on the web. In *Proceedings of the eighth ACM SIGKDD international conference on Knowledge discovery and data mining* (pp. 341-349). ACM. 10.1145/775047.775098

Mounika, D., & Kadhirvel, R. (2017). Impact Of Demonetization In E-Banking. *International Journal of Trend in Research and Development*, 1–3.

Mukhopadhaya, P. (2013). Trends in income inequality in China: The effects of various sources of income. *Journal of the Asia Pacific Economy, 18*(2), 304–317. doi:10.1080/13547860.2013.778158

Mylenko, N. (2014). *Oversight frameworks and practices in 114 economies - full report*. Retrieved from 14 June 2018 from http://documents.worldbank.org/curated/en/775401468171251449/Oversight-frameworks-and-practices-in-114-economies-full-report

Naceur, S. B., & Zhang, R. (2016). *Financial Development, Inequality and Poverty: Some International Evidence* (IMF Working Papers No. 16/32). Retrieved from International Monetary Fund website: https://www.imf.org/en/Publications/WP/Issues/2016/12/31/Financial-Development-Inequality-and-Poverty-Some-International-Evidence-43718

Nagaraj, K., Sainath, P., Rukmani, R., & Gopinath, R. (2014). Farmers' suicides in India: Magnitudes, trends, and spatial patterns, 1997–2012. *Review of Agrarian Studies, 4*(2), 53–83.

Nam, R., & Bhat, S. (2016, December 21). FACTBOX - RBI rolls back curbs on cash deposits. *Reuters*. Retrieved from https://in.reuters.com/article/india-demonetisation-latest/factbox-rbi-rolls-back-curbs-on-cash-deposits-idINKBN14A12A

National Sample Survey Office, Government of India. (2013). *Household Indebtedness in India*. Retrieved from http://mospi.nic.in/sites/default/files/publication_reports/nss_577.pdf

National Strategies for Financial Education. OECD/INFE Policy Handbook. (n.d.). Retrieved 14 January 2018 from http://www.oecd.org/daf/fin/financial-education/national-strategies-for-financial-education- policy-handbook.htm

Nayyar, M. L. (1994). *Piping handbook*. New York: McGraw-Hill Handbooks.

Neaime, S., & Gaysset, I. (2017). Financial inclusion and stability in MENA: Evidence from poverty and inequality. *Finance Research Letters*.

Nerkar, A. D. (2016). Demonetisation: Impact on Indian Economy. *International Journal of Advanced Engineering Research and Science, 3*(12), 281–283. doi:10.22161/ijaers.3.12.50

Never Too Young. (n.d.). Retrieved 3 March 2018 from https://www.councilforeconed.org/programs- 2/never-too-young-personal-finance-for-k-5-learners/

Newby Clark, I., Ross, M., Buehler, R., Koehler, D., & Griffin, D. (2000). People focus on optimistic scenarios and disregard pessimistic scenarios while predicting task completion times. *Journal of Experimental Psychology. Applied, 6*(3), 171–182. doi:10.1037/1076-898X.6.3.171 PMID:11014050

Neyapti, B., & Dincer, N. (2004). *Measuring the quality of bank regulation and supervision, with an application to transition economies. Discussion Paper, Turkish Economic Association, No. 2004/2*. Ankara: Turkish Economic Association. Retrieved from https://www.econstor.eu/bitstream/10419/83282/1/dp_2004-02.pdf

Ngalawa, H., Tchana, F., & Viegi, N. (2016). Banking instability and deposit insurance: The role of moral hazard. *Journal of Applied Econometrics, 19*(2), 323–350. doi:10.10161514-0326(16)30013-7

Ngamaba, K. H., Panagioti, M., & Armitage, C. J. (2017). Income inequality and subjective well-being: A systematic review and meta-analysis. *Quality of Life Research: An International Journal of Quality of Life Aspects of Treatment, Care and Rehabilitation*, 1–20. PMID:29067589

Ning, D. (2017, September 12). *Owner of China's Biggest Ponzi Scheme Sentenced to Life in Jail.* Retrieved from Bloomberg News: https://www.bloomberg.com/news/articles/2017-09-12/owner-of-china-s-biggest-ponzi-scheme-sentenced-to-life-in-jail

Nkusu, M. M. (2011). Nonperforming loans and macrofinancial vulnerabilities in advanced economies (No. 11-161). International Monetary Fund.

O'Donoghue, E. J., Hoppe, R. A., Banker, D. E., Ebel, R., Fuglie, K., Korb, P., & Sandretto, C. (2011). *The changing organization of US farming. United States Department of Agriculture, Economic Research Service.* OMR – Observatório do Meio Rural. Retrieved from http://omrmz.org/omrweb/

O'Donoghue, T., & Rabin, M. (1998). *Procrastination in preparing for retirement.* UCLA Berkley Working paper.

Ochsner, K., & Gross, J. (2003). *Thinking makes it so: a social cognitive neuroscience approach to emotion regulation. In The Handbook of Self-Regulation.* The Guilford Press.

Odean, B., & Barber, T. (2000). Trading is hazardous to your wealth: The common stock investment performance of individual investors. *The Journal of Finance*, *55*(2), 773–806. doi:10.1111/0022-1082.00226

OECD PISA financial literacy assessment of students. (n.d.). Retrieved 14 January 2018 from http://www.oecd.org/finance/financial-education/oecdpisafinancialliteracyassessment.htm

OECD. (2001). Policy reassessment in the light of the end-2000 financial crisis. In *OECD Economic Surveys: Turkey.* Paris: OECD. Retrieved from: http://www.oecd.org/turkey/1886247.pdf

OECD. (2011). *Financial Inclusion as Defined by RBI.* OECD.

OECD. (2011). *Mesauring Financial Literacy.* OECD.

Ogawa, Y., & Koike, T. (2001). Structural Design of Buried Pipelines for Severe Earthquakes. *Soil Dynamics and Earthquake Engineering*, *21*(3), 199–209. doi:10.1016/S0267-7261(01)00005-7

Ognjenovic, D. (2017). *Deposit Insurance Schemes: Funding, Policy and Operational Challenges* (1st ed.). Palgrave Macmillan. doi:10.1007/978-3-319-51143-6

Oldenburg, D. (2005). *Store Brands vs. National Brands. Washingtonpost.com.* Retrieved 14 February 2018, from http://www.washingtonpost.com/wp-dyn/content/article/2005/06/20/AR2005062001146.html

Oliveira, M. P., & Handfield, R. (2017). An enactment theory model of supplier financial disruption risk mitigation. *Supply Chain Management*, *22*(5), 442–457. doi:10.1108/SCM-03-2017-0121

Omnibus poll: Canadians' obstacles to saving and investing. (n.d.). *Research & reports.* Retrieved 14 January 2018 from https://www.getsmarteraboutmoney.ca/resources/publications/research/omnibus-poll-canadi ans-obstacles-saving-investing/

Oracle. (2015, February). *Big Data in Financial Services and Banking: Architect's Guide and Reference Architecture Introduction.* Retrieved March 13, 2018, from Oracle: http://www.oracle.com/us/technologies/big-data/big-data-in-financial-services-wp-2415760.pdf

OSC. (2018). *About.* Retrieved 2 February 2018 from http://www.osc.gov.on.ca/en/About_our-structure_index.htm

Osman, M. (2017). *How to Use Hashtags on Every Social Media Network.* Retrieved from www.sproutsocial.com: https://sproutsocial.com/insights/how-to-use-hashtags/

Østby, E., Jayadevan, K. R., & Thaulow, C. (2005). Fracture Response of Pipelines Subject to Large Plastic Deformation Under Bending. *International Journal of Pressure Vessels and Piping*, *82*(3), 201–215. doi:10.1016/j.ijpvp.2004.08.012

Oya, C. (2011). Contract Farming in Sub-Saharan Africa: A Survey of Approaches, Debates and Issues. *Journal of Agrarian Change*, *12*(1), 1–33. doi:10.1111/j.1471-0366.2011.00337.x

Paliwal, B. (2017, April). 30 Days of Demonetization in India. *Cornell Policy Review*. Retrieved from www.cornellpolicyreview.com/30-days-of-demonetization-in-india/?pdf=3449

Pani, P. (2015). *Godrej Nature's game plan is to be around for a long time: Mohit Khattar*. Retrieved from https://www.thehindubusinessline.com/companies/godrej-natures-game-plan-is-to-be-around-for-a-long-time-mohit-khattar/article7261214.ece

Parthasarathy, S., Ruan, Y., & Satuluri, V. (2011). Community discovery in social networks: Applications, methods and emerging trends. In C. C. Aggarwal (Ed.), *Social network data analytics* (pp. 79–113). Boston: Springer. doi:10.1007/978-1-4419-8462-3_4

Patel. (2017). *Seminar on Agricultural Debt Waiver – Efficacy and Limitations*. Reserve Bank of India. Retrieved from https://www.rbi.org.in/SCRIPTS/BS_SpeechesView.aspx?Id=1045

Pedroni, P. (2001). Fully modified OLS for heterogeneous cointegrated panels. In *Nonstationary panels, panel cointegration, and dynamic panels* (pp. 93–130). Emerald Group Publishing Limited.

Peersman, G. (2011). *Macroeconomic Effects of Unconventional Monetary Policy in The Euro Area. (Working Paper No. 1397)*. ECB. Retrieved from https://www.ecb.europa.eu/pub/pdf/scpwps/ecbwp1397.pdf?99ef78cb1aa613f60d8716d0db59b585

Pennacchi, G. (2006). Deposit insurance, bank regulation, and financial system risks. *Journal of Monetary Economics*, *53*(1), 1–30. doi:10.1016/j.jmoneco.2005.10.007

Pesaran, M. H. (2007). A Simple Panel Unit Root Test in the Presence of Cross-Section Dependence. *Journal of Applied Econometrics*, *22*(2), 265–312. doi:10.1002/jae.951

Pew Research Center. (2016, July 18). *Election 2016: Campaigns as a Direct Source of News*. Retrieved April 10, 2018, from Pew Research Center Journalism and Media: http://www.journalism.org/2016/07/18/election-2016-campaigns-as-a-direct-source-of-news/

Piskorski, M. J. (2014). *A Social Strategy: How we profit from Social Media*. Princeton, NJ: Princeton University Press. doi:10.1515/9781400850020

Podpiera, J., & Weill, L. (2008). Bad luck or bad management? Emerging banking market experience. *Journal of Financial Stability*, *4*(2), 135–148. doi:10.1016/j.jfs.2008.01.005

Porter, G., & Howard, P. (1997). Contract Farming in South Africa: A Case Study from KwaZulu-Natal. *Geographical Association*, *82*, 38–44.

Prabhu, N. (2017, June 18). RBI sounds the alarm on farm loan waivers. The Hindu. Retrieved from https://www.thehindu.com/news/cities/bangalore/rbi-sounds-the-alarm-on-farm-loan-waivers/article19099356.ece

Pramod, V., & Banwet, D. (2010). System modelling of telecom service sector supply chain: A SAP-LAP analysis. *International Journal of Business Excellence*, *3*(1), 38. doi:10.1504/IJBEX.2010.029486

Press Information Bureau. (2018, February 20). *Cabinet approves New Bill to ban Unregulated Deposit Schemes and Chit Funds (Amendment) Bill, 2018*. Retrieved from Press Information Bureau: http://pib.nic.in/newsite/PrintRelease.aspx?relid=176677

Press Trust of India. (2014). *Formal Finance to curb ponzi schemes*. Business Standard.

Press Trust of India. (2017, November 28). Data usage per smartphone in India to grow 5-fold by 2023: Ericsson. *Economic Times*. Retrieved April 29, 2018, from https://economictimes.indiatimes.com/tech/internet/data-usage-per-smartphone-in-india-to-grow-5-fold-by-2023-ericsson/articleshow/61838209.cms

PriceWaterhouseCoopers. (2008). *A Practical Guide to Risk Assessment*. Retrieved December 15, 2017 from https://web.actuaries.ie/sites/default/files/erm-resources/a_practical_guide_to_risk_assessment. pdf

PricewaterhouseCoopers. (2017). *The promise of Indian retail: From vision to execution*. PWC. Retrieved from https://www.pwc.in/assets/pdfs/publications/2017/the-promise-of-indian-retail-from-vision-to-execution.pdf

Prowse, M. (2012). *Contract Farming in Developing Countries - A Review*. Presentation.

Pultrone, C. (2012). An overview of contract farming: Legal issues and challenges. *Unif. L. Rev.*, *17*(1-2), 263–289. doi:10.1093/ulr/17.1-2.263

Quantzig. (n.d.). *Social Media Analytics and Politics*. Retrieved April 17, 2018, from Quantzig Blog: https://www.quantzig.com/blog/social-media-analytics-politics#

Rabin, M., & Thaler, R. (2001). Anomalies: Risk Aversion. *The Journal of Economic Perspectives*, *15*(1), 219–232. doi:10.1257/jep.15.1.219

Rajagopal, K. (2016). *Ponzi schemes not under our purview: SEBI*. Retrieved from http://www.thehindu.com/news/national/Ponzi-schemes-not-under-our-purview-SEBI/article14559017

Rajan, R., & Dhal, S. C. (2003). Non-performing loans and terms of credit of public sector banks in India: An empirical assessment. *Occasional Papers, 24*(3), 81-121.

Rajha, K. S. (2016). Determinants of Non-Performing Loans: Evidence from the Jordanian Banking Sector. *The Journal of Finance*, *4*(1), 125–136.

Ramkumar, R. (2017). *Lessons from Agricultural Debt Waiver and Debt Relief Scheme of 2008*. Reserve Bank of India. Retrieved from https://rbidocs.rbi.org.in/rdocs/content/pdfs/Dr.%20R.%20Ramakumar_Paper(31082017).pdf

Ramsay, F. P. (1926). Truth and Probability. In R.B. Braithwaite (Ed.), The Foundations of Mathematics and other logical essays. New York: Harcourt Brace.

Ranga, M. (2017). Private label brands retailers in India: Food and grocery sector. *International Journal of Multidisciplinary Research and Development*, *4*(5), 143–145.

Rath, N. (2008). Implications of the loan waiver for rural credit institutions. *Economic and Political Weekly*, 13–16.

Ravi, V., & Shankar, R. (2006). Reverse logistics operations in paper industry: A case study. *Journal of Advances in Management Research*, *3*(2), 88–94. doi:10.1108/97279810680001248

Read, D., Loewenstein, G., & Rabin, M. (1999). Choice bracketing. *Journal of Risk and Uncertainty*, *19*(1), 171-197.

Rehber, E. (2000). *Vertical coordination in the agro-food industry and contract farming: A comparative study of Turkey and the USA (No. 052). University of Connecticut, Department of Agricultural and Resource Economics, Charles J.* Zwick Center for Food and Resource Policy.

Reserve Bank of India. (2008). *Index to RBI circulars – Agricultural Debt Waiver and Debt Relief Scheme 2008*. Retrieved from https://www.rbi.org.in/scripts/BS_CircularIndexDisplay.aspx?Id=4190

Reserve Bank of India. (2015). *Master circular-priority sector lending-targets and classification.* Retrieved from https://rbi.org.in/scripts/bs_viewmascirculardetails.aspx?id=9857

Reserve Bank of India. (2017). *Seminar on Agricultural Debt Waiver – Efficacy and Limitations*. Retrieved from https://rbi.org.in/Scripts/BS_PressReleaseDisplay.aspx?prid=41530

Retailers Association of India. (2017). *Think India. Think 'connected' retail.* Knight Frank. Retrieved from https://kfcontent.blob.core.windows.net/research/317/documents/en/think-india-think-connected-retail-2017-4441.pdf

Rhee, R. (2009). *The Madoff Scandal, Market Regulatory Failure, and the Business Education of Lawyers*. Gainesville, FL: University of Florida.

Ribarsky, W., Wang, D. X., & Dou, W. (2014). Social media analytics for competitive advantage. *Computers & Graphics*, *38*, 328–331. doi:10.1016/j.cag.2013.11.003

Ricciardi, V. (2017). The Role of Group Psychology in Behavioural Finance: A Research Starting Point for Banking, Economic, and Financial Historians. In K. Schönhärl (Ed.), *Decision Taking, Confidence and Risk Management in Banks from Early Modernity to the 20th Century.* Cham: Palgrave Macmillan. doi:10.1007/978-3-319-42076-9_12

Richardson, P., Jain, A., & Dick, A. (1996). Household store brand proneness: A framework. *Journal of Retailing*, *72*(2), 159–185. doi:10.1016/S0022-4359(96)90012-3

Riegel, E. R. (2007). Kent and Riegel's Handbook of Industrial Chemistry and Biotechnology (Vol. 1). Academic Press.

Rigotti, L., & Shannon, C. (2005). Uncertainty and risk in financial markets. *Econometrica*, *73*(1), 203-243. doi:.00569.x doi:10.1111/j.1468-0262.2005

Rizzi, J. (2008). Behavioral bias of the financial crisis. *Journal of Applied Finance (JAF)*, *18*(2), 84–96.

Rogoff, K. (2014). *Costs and Benefits to Phasing Out Paper Currency*. doi:10.3386/w20126

Rogoff, K. (1998). Blessing or curse? Foreign and underground demand for euro notes. *Economic Policy*, *13*(26), 261–303. doi:10.1111/1468-0327.00033

Rogoff, K. (2015). Costs and Benefits to Phasing out Paper Currency. *NBER Macroeconomics Annual*, *29*(1), 445–456. doi:10.1086/680657

Roose, K. (2017). *Forget Washington. Facebook's Problems Abroad Are Far More Disturbing*. Retrieved April 30, 2018, from The New York Times: https://www.nytimes.com/2017/10/29/business/facebook-misinformation-abroad.html

Rougoor, W., & Van Marrewijk, C. (2015). Demography, growth, and global income inequality. *World Development*, *74*, 220–232. doi:10.1016/j.worlddev.2015.05.013

Roy, I. (2015). *The Saradha chit fund scam*. Retrieved from http://www.rediff.com/news/special/explained-the-saradha-chit-fund-scam/20150107

Saha, D. (2017, July 2). Farmer suicides: 70% of India's farm families spend more than they earn. *Hindustan Times*. Retrieved from https://www.hindustantimes.com/india-news/farmer-suicides-70-of-india-s-farm-families-spend-more-than-they-earn/story-GKLoObJeDtbH2Z22csJsxK.html

Sahara, S., & Gyau, A. (2014). Contractual arrangements and commitment in the Indonesian supermarket channel. *British Food Journal*, *116*(5), 765–779. doi:10.1108/BFJ-03-2012-0070

Sainath, P. (2018, April 13). In India, Farmers Face a Terrifying Crisis. *The New York Times*. Retrieved from https://www.nytimes.com/2018/04/13/opinion/india-farmers-crisis.html

Samartin, M. (2002). Suspension of Convertibility versus Deposit Insurance: A Welfare Comparison. *Review of Finance*, *6*(2), 223–244. doi:10.1023/A:1020147632508

Sarma, M. (2008). *Index of financial inclusion* (ICRIER Working Paper No. 215). Retrieved from Indian Council for Research on International Economic Relations website: http://www.icrier.org/pdf/Working_Paper_215.pdf

Sarma, M., & Pais, J. (2011). Financial inclusion and development. *Journal of International Development*, *23*(5), 613–628. doi:10.1002/jid.1698

Schich, S. (2008). Financial crisis: Deposit insurance and related financial safety net aspects. *OECD Journal: Financial Market Trends, 2008*(2), 1-39. doi:10.1787/fmt-v2008-art12-en

Schinasi, G. J. (2004). *Defining Financial Stability*. (Working Paper No. 04/187). Washington, DC: IMF. Retrieved from https://www.imf.org/en/Publications/WP/Issues/2016/12/31/Defining-Financial-Stability-17740

SEC.gov. (2013). *Pyramid Schemes*. Retrieved from https://www.sec.gov/answers/pyramid

Seiter, C. (2016). *The Psychology of Social Media: Why We Like, Comment, and Share Online*. Retrieved from www.blog.bufferapp.com: https://blog.bufferapp.com/psychology-of-social-media

Senior Supervisors Group. (2008). *Observations on Risk Management Practices during the Recent Market Turbulence*. Retrieved January 12, 2018 from https://www.sec.gov/news/press/2008/report 030608.pdf

Sethuraman, R., & Cole, C. (1999). Factors influencing the price premiums that consumers pay for national brands over store brands. *Journal of Product and Brand Management*, *8*(4), 340–351. doi:10.1108/10610429910284319

Seven, U., & Coskun, Y. (2016). Does financial development reduce income inequality and poverty? Evidence from emerging countries. *Emerging Markets Review*, *26*, 34–63. doi:10.1016/j.ememar.2016.02.002

Severi, E., Ling, K. C., & Nasemoadeli, A. (2014). *The Impacts of Electronic Word of Mouth on Brand Equity in the Context of Social Media*. Academic Press. doi:10.5539/ijbm.v9n8p84

Shah, A. P. (2016). The Status of Pipelines Carrying Petroleum Products by Refineries and Ports in South India. Ministry of Petroleum & Natural Gas, Bangalore Zonal Office.

Sheau-Fen, Y., Sun-May, L., & Yu-Ghee, W. (2012). Store brand proneness: Effects of perceived risks, quality and familiarity. *Australasian Marketing Journal*, *20*(1), 48–58. doi:10.1016/j.ausmj.2011.10.014

Shefrin, H., & Statman, M. (1985). The disposition to sell winners too early and ride losers too long: Theory and evidence. *The Journal of Finance*, *40*(3), 777–790. doi:10.1111/j.1540-6261.1985.tb05002.x

Shekhar, P. (2016, November 18). Demonetisation: Could private hospitals have saved 55 lives with old notes? *India Today*. Retrieved from https://www.indiatoday.in/india/story/demonetisation-private-hospitals-old-currency-notes-352711-2016-11-18

Shelor, R., Anderson, D., & Cross, M. (1992). Gaining from Loss: Property Liability Insurer Stock Values in the aftermath of the 1989 California Earthquake. *The Journal of Risk and Insurance*, *59*(3), 476–488. doi:10.2307/253059

Shepherd, A. (n.d.). *An introduction to Contract Farming*. Technical Centre for Agricultural and Rural Cooperation (ACP-EU). Retrieved from http://makingtheconnection.cta.int/sites/default/files/Contract-Farming-Introduction.pdf

Sherraden, M. S., & Grinstein-Weiss, M. (2015). Creating financial capability in the next generation: An introduction to the special issue. *The Journal of Consumer Affairs*, *49*(1), 1–12. doi:10.1111/joca.12067

Shiller, R. (1987). Fashions, fads and bubbles in financial markets. In J. Coffee (Ed.), Knights, Raiders and Targets: The impact of the hostile takeover. Oxford, UK: Oxford University Press.

Shiller, R. (1998). *Human Behavior and the Efficiency of the Financial System.* NBER Working Paper.

Shiller, R., Fischer, S., & Friedman, B. M. (1984). Stock prices and social dynamics. *Brookings Papers on Economic Activity*, *2*(2), 457–498. doi:10.2307/2534436

Shin, H. S. (2013). Adapting Macroprudential Approaches to Emerging and Developing Economies. In O. Canuto & S. R. Ghosh (Eds.), *Dealing with the Challenges of Macro Financial Linkages in Emerging Markets* (pp. 17–55). Washington, DC: World Bank.

Shleifer, A., & Vishny, R. (2010). Unstable banking. *Journal of Financial Economics*, *97*(3), 306–318. doi:10.1016/j.jfineco.2009.10.007

Shleifer, A., & Vishny, R. (2011). Fire Sales in Finance and Macroeconomics. *The Journal of Economic Perspectives*, *25*(1), 29–48. doi:10.1257/jep.25.1.29

Shrivastava, B., & Chakraborty, S. (2014). *Sahara to Saradha spur SEBI's Rs.64,000 crore Ponzi Schemes Crackdown.* Retrieved from http://www.livemint.com/Money/74gd93JfsVVrUZKCj0ABXL/Sahara-to-Saradha-spur-Sebis-Rs64000-crore-Ponzi-schemes-c

Silver, M., & Sabini, J. (1982). When it's not really procrastination. *Psychology Today*, *16*(1), 39–42.

Simon, H. (1956). Rational choice and the structure of the environment. *Psychological Review*, Vol.63, compiled in, and quoted from, de. *Simon*, *1957*, 241–260.

Simonsohn, U., & Loewenstein, G. (2006). Mistake #37: The effect of previously encountered prices on current housing demand. *Economic Journal (London)*, *116*(508), 175–199. doi:10.1111/j.1468-0297.2006.01052.x

Singh, B., & Roy, I. (2017). *Mint Street Memo No. 01 Demonetisation and Bank Deposit Growth.* Academic Press.

Singh, J. (2015). *Changing Mandate of Deposit Insurance Systems*. Retrieved from https://www.dicgc.org.in/pdf/Speeches/ChangingMandatesOfDepositInsurance.pdf

Singh, R. (2017, November 27). Demonetisation: Why the challenge to take digital payment to rural India is as huge as the opportunity. *Economic Times*, pp. 1–10. Retrieved from http://economictimes.indiatimes.com/news/economy/policy/sunday-et-making-rural-india-pay-digitally-and-challenges-post-demonetisation/articleshow/55640316.cms

Singh, R. K. (2016, November 30). Indian economy racing before Modi removed oxygen of cash. *Reuters*. Retrieved from https://in.reuters.com/article/us-india-economy-gdp/indian-economy-racing-before-modi-removed-oxygen-of-cash-idINKBN13P1X8

Singh, S. (2013). The practice of contract farming in India: Making it inclusive and effective. *Food Chain*, *3*(3), 137–154. doi:10.3362/2046-1887.2013.014

Siva, M. (2017, April 10). All you wanted to know about farm loan waivers. *The Hindu Businessline*. Retrieved from https://www.thehindubusinessline.com/opinion/columns/slate/all-you-wanted-to-know-about-farm-loan-waivers/article21957423.ece1

Skinner, J. (2007). *Are you sure you're saving enough.* NBER, Working Paper 12981.

Slovic, P., Finucane, M., Peters, E., & MacGregor, D. (2002). The Affect Heuristic. In Heuristics and Biases: The Psychology of Intuitive Judgment (pp. 397–420). New York: Cambridge University Press. doi:10.1017/CBO9780511808098.025

Slovik, P. (2011). Market uncertainty and market instability. IFC Bulletin No. 34, Bank for International Settlements.

Smart, X. (n.d.). Retrieved 8 March 2018 from https://www.councilforeconed.org/programs-2/smartx/

Smit, A. A. H., Driessen, P. P., & Glasbergen, P. (2008). Constraints on the conversion to sustainable production: The case of the Dutch potato chain. *Business Strategy and the Environment*, *17*(6), 369–381.

Sohail, M., Venukumar, S., & Reddy, M. V. (2017). An Outline of Piping Design Using CAESER II-Case Study. *Materials Today*, *4*(8), 8269–8278. doi:10.1016/j.matpr.2017.07.169

Solanki, A. (2018, January 25). Anatomy of Agricultural Debt Waivers in India. Vivekananda International Foundation. Retrieved from https://www.vifindia.org/article/2018/january/25/anatomy-of-agricultural-debt-waivers-in-india

Solli, J. (2017, March 15). *'Buyer Beware' is insufficient financial protection*. Retrieved from Center for Financial Inclusion: https://economictimes.indiatimes.com/news/economy/finance/financial-inclusion-can-curb-ponzi-schemes-rbi-governor-raghuram-rajan/articleshow/40906102.cms

Somoza López, A. (2015). Algunas consideraciones sobre el proceso de reestructuración en las cajas de ahorro españolas: Una referencia al caso alemán. *Análisis Financiero*, *129*, 20–33.

Song. (2006). External Fusion Bonded Epoxy Coating for Steel Pipeline. *Corrosion & Protection*, *7*, 17. doi:10.12999/awwa.c213.07

Sridhar, G. (2018, July 19). FRDI Bill fiasco: More caution needed in policy-making. *The Hindu Businessline*. Retrieved from https://www.thehindubusinessline.com/economy/policy/frdi-bill-fiasco-more-caution-needed-in-policy-making/article24464067.ece

Steel, P. (2007). The Nature of Procrastination: A meta analytical and theoretical review of quintessential self-regulatory failure. *Psychological Bulletin*, *133*(1), 65–74. doi:10.1037/0033-2909.133.1.65 PMID:17201571

Steel, P. (2010). Arousal avoidant and decisional procrastinators: Do they exist? *Personality and Individual Differences*, *48*(8), 926–934. doi:10.1016/j.paid.2010.02.025

Stieglitz, S., Mirbabaie, M., Ross, B., & Neuberger, C. (2018). Social media analytics – Challenges in topic discovery, data collection, and data preparation. *International Journal of Information Management*, *39*, 156–168. doi:10.1016/j.ijinfomgt.2017.12.002

Strohm, K., & Hoeffler, H. (2006). *Contract Farming in Kenya: Theory, Evidence from selected Value Chain and Implications for Development Cooperations*. Academic Press.

Stucky, T. D., Payton, S. B., & Ottensmann, J. R. (2016). Intra-and inter-neighborhood income inequality and crime. *Journal of Criminal Justice*, *39*(3), 345–362.

Subha, T., Kirthika, R., & Narayanaswamy, P. (2018). Private Label Brands in Indian Retail Industry. *International Journal of Research and Development - A Management Review*. Retrieved from http://www.irdindia.in/journal_ijrdmr/pdf/special_iss_1/10.pdf

Sul, H., Dennis, A. R., & Yuan, L. I. (2014). Trading on Twitter: The Financial Information Content of Emotion in Social Media. *Proceedings of the 47th Hawaii International Conference on System Sciences*. Conference Publishing Services. doi:10.1109/HICSS.2014.107

Sunder, S. (2018, January 29). India economic survey 2018: Farmers gain as agriculture mechanisation speeds up, but more R&D needed. *Financial Express*. Retrieved from https://www.financialexpress.com/budget/india-economic-survey-2018-for-farmers-agriculture-gdp-msp/1034266/

Sun, J., & Tang, J. (2011). A survey of models and algorithms for social influence analysis. In C. C. Aggarwal (Ed.), *Social network data analytics* (pp. 177–214). Boston: Springer. doi:10.1007/978-1-4419-8462-3_7

Suri, P., & Sushil, N. (2008). Towards a strategy for implementing e-governance applications: A case study of integrated fertilisers management information system based on SAP-LAP framework. *Electronic Government. International Journal (Toronto, Ont.)*, *5*(4), 420. doi:10.1504/eg.2008.019527

Survey of the States. (2018). Council for Economic Education. Retrieved 1 March 2018 from https://www.councilforeconed.org/policy-and-advocacy/survey-of-the-states-2/

Surveys. (n.d.). Retrieved from http://responsiblefinance.worldbank.org/surveys

Sushil. (2000). SAP-LAP models of inquiry. *Management Decision, 38*(5), 347-353. doi:10.1108/00251740010340526

Sushil. (2009). SAP-LAP Linkages — A Generic Interpretive Framework for Analyzing Managerial Contexts. *Global Journal of Flexible Systems Management, 10*(2), 11-20. doi:10.1007/bf03396558

Swaminathan, M. (2008, March 8). Looking beyond Farmers' Suicides and Loan Waivers. *Mainstream Weekly*. Retrieved from https://www.mainstreamweekly.net/article573.html

Szyszka, A. (2011). Behavioral anatomy of the financial crisis. *Journal of Centrum Cathedra*, 121–135.

Tajadura Garrido, C. (2015). El sistema financiero español tras la crisis: Menor en tamaño. más seguro y menos rentable. *Análisis Financiero*, *127*, 1–19.

Tanner, M. (2011). *Social Security, Ponzi Schemes, and the Need for Reform*. Washington, DC: Cato Institute. Retrieved from https://object.cato.org/sites/cato.org/files/pubs/pdf/PA689.pdf

Tao, Y., Wu, X., Zhou, T., Yan, W., Huang, Y., Yu, H., . . . Yakovenko, V. M. (2016). *Universal Exponential Structure of Income Inequality: Evidence from 60 Countries*. arXiv preprint arXiv:1612.01624

Tarchouna, A., Jarraya, B., & Bouri, A. (2017). How to explain non-performing loans by many corporate governance variables simultaneously? A corporate governance index is built to US commercial banks. *Research in International Business and Finance*, *42*, 645–657. doi:10.1016/j.ribaf.2017.07.008

Taylor, J. R. (2003). *Risk Analysis for Process Plant and Pipelines and Transport*. Routledge. doi:10.4324/9780203474914

TechAmerica Foundation's Federal Big Data Commission. (2012). *Demystifying bigdata: A practical guide to transforming the business of Government*. Washington, DC: Tech America. Retrieved from http://www.techamerica.org/Docs/fileManager.cfm?f=techamerica-bigdatareport-final.pdf

Teri, G. (2006). National Energy Map for India: Technology Vision 2030. The Energy and Resources Institute, TERI Press. doi:10.15676/ijeei.2010.2.3.3

Tewari, R. (2016, January 6). Centre increases number of work days under MGNREGA. *The Indian Express*. Retrieved from https://indianexpress.com/article/business/economy/centre-increases-number-of-work-days-under-mgnrega/

Thaler, R. (1980). Toward a positive theory of Consumer Choice. *Journal of Economic Behavior & Organization*, *1*(1), 39–60. doi:10.1016/0167-2681(80)90051-7

Thaler, R. (1999). Mental accounting matters. *Journal of Behavioral Decision Making, 12*, 183–206. doi:10.1002/(sici)1099-0771(199909)12:3<183:aid-bdm318>3.0.co;2-f

Thaler, R. (2015). *Misbehaving: The making of behavioral economics*. New York: W.W. Norton & Company.

Thangaratinam, S., & Redman, C. (2005). *The Delphi technique*. Retrieved from https://obgyn.onlinelibrary.wiley.com/doi/pdf/10.1576/toag.7.2.120.27071

The Banks Association of Turkey (TBAT). (2000). *The Banking Sector Report*. Istanbul: TBAT.

The Banks Association of Turkey (TBAT). (2009). *The Financial system and banking sector in Turkey*. Istanbul. TBAT. Retrieved from: https://www.tbb.org.tr/Dosyalar/Arastirma_ve_Raporlar/The_Financial_System_and_Banking_Sector_in_Turkey.pdf

The Central Bank of the Republic of Turkey (CBRT). (2015). *Finansal İstikrar - Türkiye'de Finansal İstikrar Gelişmeleri*. Ankara: CBRT.

The Committee of Sponsoring Organizations of the Treadway Commission. (2009). *Strengthening Enterprise Risk Management for Strategic Advantage*. Retrieved December 5, 2017 from https://www.coso.org/documents/COSO_09_board_position_final102309PRINTandWEB FINAL_000.pdf

The Economic Times. (2017, September 13). *Over 11,000 Uttar Pradesh farmers get waiver for loans of Re 1 to Rs 500*. Retrieved from https://economictimes.indiatimes.com/news/politics-and-nation/over-11000-uttar-pradesh-farmers-get-waiver-for-loans-of-re-1-to-rs-500/articleshow/60496814.cms

The Economic Times. (2018, March 29). *What is a bank run? It's in full swing in Telangana and Andhra Pradesh*. Retrieved from https://economictimes.indiatimes.com/news/politics-and-nation/what-is-a-bank-run-its-in-full-swing-in-telangana-and-andhra-pradesh/articleshow/63531528.cms?utm_source=WAPusers&from=mdr

The Economist. (2018). Pyramid schemes cause huge social harm in China. *The Economist*.

The Hindu. (2018a, June 18). *Kumaraswamy seeks 50% Central assistance for farm loan waiver*. Retrieved from https://www.thehindu.com/news/national/karnataka/kumaraswamy-seeks-50-central-assistance-for-farm-loan-waiver/article24187796.ece

The Hindu. (2018b, July 5). *Kumaraswamy announces farm loan waiver in Karnataka Budget*. Retrieved from https://www.thehindu.com/news/national/karnataka/kumaraswamy-announces-farm-loan-waiver-in-karnataka-budget/article24337573.ece

The Indian Express. (2017, June 24). *Maharashtra govt announces Rs 34,000-crore farm loan waiver, to benefit 89 lakh farmers*. Retrieved from https://indianexpress.com/article/india/maharashtra-farm-loan-waiver-devendra-fadnavis-farmers-4719925/

The Nielsen Company. (2018). *The rise and rise again of private label*. Nielsen. Retrieved from https://www.nielsen.com/content/dam/nielsenglobal/ru/docs/2018.02%20-%20Global%20-20The%20Rise%20and%20Rise%20Again%20of%20Private%20Label.pdf

The Reserve Bank of India. (2013). *Financial Inclusion in India - An Assessment*. Mumbai: RBI.

The World Bank. (2018, April). *Asia Pacific Economic Update*. Retrieved from The World Bank: http://www.worldbank.org/en/region/eap/publication/east-asia-pacific-economic-update

Themba, G., & Mulala, M. (2013). Brand-Related eWOM and Its Effects on Purchase Decisions: An Empirical Study of University of Botswana Students. *International Journal of Business and Management, 8*(8), 31. doi:10.5539/ijbm.v8n8p31

Thirtle, C., Irz, X., Lin, L., McKenzie-Hill, V., & Wiggins, S. (2001). *Relationship between changes in agricultural productivity and the incidence of poverty in developing countries*. Retrieved from https://www.odi.org/sites/odi.org.uk/files/odi-assets/events-documents/4086.pdf

Times of India. (2017). *19 lakh new investors in mutual funds added in April-May*. Retrieved from https://timesofindia.indiatimes.com/business/india-business/19-lakh-new-investors-in-mutual-funds-added-in-april-may/articleshow/59161430.cms

Toda, H. Y., & Yamamoto, T. (1995). Statistical Inference in Vector Autoregressions with Possibly Integrated Processes. *Journal of Econometrics*, *66*(1-2), 225–250. doi:10.1016/0304-4076(94)01616-8

Todaro, M., & Smith, S. (2014). *Economic Development (12 b.)*. Pearson.

Toma, S.-V., Chitiţă, M., & Şarpe, D. (2012). Risk and Uncertainty. *Procedia Economics and Finance*, *3*, 975–980. doi:10.1016/S2212-5671(12)00260-2

Tovar, C. E., Escribano, G. M., & Martin, V. M. (2012). *Credit Growth and the Effectiveness of Reserve Requirements and Other Macroprudential Instruments in Latin America* (Working Paper No. 12/142). Washington, DC: IMF. Retrieved from https://www.imf.org/external/pubs/ft/wp/2012/wp12142.pdf

Tuesta, D., Sorensen, G., Haring, A., & Cámara, N. (2015). *Financial inclusion and its determinants: The case of Argentina* (BBVA Research Working Paper No. 15/03). Retrieved from the BBVA website: https://www.bbvaresearch.com/wp-content/uploads/2015/01/WP_15-03_Financial-Inclusion-in-Argentina.pdf

Tversky, A., & Fox, C. (1995). Weighing risk and uncertainty. *Psychological Review*, *102*(2), 269–283. doi:10.1037/0033-295X.102.2.269

Tversky, A., & Kahneman, D. (1974). Judgment under Uncertainty: Heuristics and Biases. *Science New Series*, *185*(4157), 1124–1131. doi:10.1126cience.185.4157.1124 PMID:17835457

Tversky, A., & Kahneman, D. (1992). Advances in prospect theory: Cumulative representation of uncertainty. *Journal of Risk and Uncertainty*, *5*(4), 297–323. doi:10.1007/BF00122574

Tvesky, A., & Kanheman, D. (1981). Framing decisions & the psychology of choice. *Science New Series*, *211*(4481), 453–458. doi:10.1126cience.7455683 PMID:7455683

U.S. Securities and Exchange Commission. (2018). *Ponzi Scheme*. Washington, DC: U.S. Securities and Exchange Commission.

Ulrich, C. W. (2008, December 15). *Ponzi Schemes: Know How To Protect Yourself*. Retrieved from CNBC: https://www.cnbc.com/id/28239456

UNDP. (2016). *Human Development Report 2016*. Author.

Unnikrishnan, D. (2016, April 8). *Jan Dhan Reality Check*. Retrieved from First Post: https://www.firstpost.com/business/jan-dhan-reality-check-manmohan-singhs-criticism-is-indeed-right-but-only-partially-2718642.html

Upadhyaya, H. (2013). Caveat from farm debt waiver scheme. *India Together*. Retrieved from http://www.indiatogether.org/farmers-agriculture

Urbaneja Cillán, J. (2014). La Reestructuración del Sistema Financiero Español. El proceso de reforma tras la asistencia financiera a la Banca Española. *Revista Jurídica de Castilla y León*, *32*, 1–46.

US Agriculture. (n.d.). Retrieved from https://www.statista.com/topics/1126/us-agriculture/

US Legal. (2018). *Financial Regulation Law and Legal Definition*. Retrieved from US Legal: https://definitions.uslegal.com/f/financial-regulation/

Us, V. (2017). The Determinants of Non-Performing Loans Before and After the Crisis: Challenges and Policy Implications for Turkish Banks. *Emerging Markets Finance and Trade*.

USDA. (1996). *Farmers' Use of Marketing and Production Contracts*. Washington, DC: Economic Research Service. Retrieved from https://www.ers.usda.gov/webdocs/publications/40764/18614_aer747a_1_.pdf?v=41063

Usta, Ö. (2012). *İşletme Finansı ve Finansal Yönetim*. Ankara: Detay Yayıncılık.

Vagata, P., & Wilfong, K. (2014, April 10). *Scaling the Facebook data warehouse to 300 PB*. Retrieved April 28, 2018, from Facebook: https://code.facebook.com/posts/229861827208629/scaling-the-facebook-data-warehouse-to-300-pb/

Vaidyanathan, A. (2008, March 6). Farm loan waiver: a closer look and critique. *The Hindu*. Retrieved from http://el.doccentre.info/eldoc1/k40_/06mar08h1.pdf

Van Greuning, H., & Bratanovic, S. B. (2009). *Analyzing banking risks: A new framework for assessing risk management*. World Bank. doi:10.1596/978-0-8213-7728-4

VanBoskirk, S., Overby, C. S., & Takvorian, S. (2011). *US interactive marketing forecast, 2011 to 2016*. Forrester Research Inc. Retrieved from https://retelur.files.wordpress.com/2012/01/forrester_interactive_marketing_forecast_2011_to_2016.pdf

Venu, M. (2017, April 5). Centre Cannot Avoid Fiscal Responsibility of UP Farm Loan Waiver. *The Wire*. Retrieved from https://thewire.in/agriculture/farm-loan-waiver-central-fisc

Vilhjalmsdottir, A., Gardarsdottir, R. B., Bernburg, J. G., & Sigfusdottir, I. D. (2016). Neighborhood income inequality, social capital and emotional distress among adolescents: A population-based study. *Journal of Adolescence*, *51*, 92–102. doi:10.1016/j.adolescence.2016.06.004 PMID:27337213

Villamil, A. (1991). Demand deposit contracts, suspension of convertibility, and optimal financial intermediation. *Economic Theory*, *1*(3), 277–288. doi:10.1007/BF01210565

Vithessonthi, C. (2016). Deflation, bank credit growth, and non-performing loans: Evidence from Japan. *International Review of Financial Analysis*, *45*, 295–305. doi:10.1016/j.irfa.2016.04.003

von Bülow, D., & Sorensen, A. (1993). Gender and contract farming: Tea out grower schemes in Kenya. *Review of African Political Economy*, *20*(56), 38–52. doi:10.1080/03056249308703984

Wadhwa, V. (2017). Why Bitcoin is the largest ponzi scheme in human history. *The Hindustan Times*.

Wahi, R. (2017). *The rise of private label brands - Re-Tales by Rajat Wahi*. Retrieved 19 April 2018, from https://retail.economictimes.indiatimes.com/re-tales/the-rise-of-private-label-brands/2241

Walker, A., & Selfe, J. (1996). The Delphi method: A useful tool for the allied health researcher. *British Journal of Therapy and Rehabilitation*, *3*(12), 677–681. doi:10.12968/bjtr.1996.3.12.14731

Wang, S. H., & Chen, W. (2002). A study on the Pre-cyclic-load-induced Burst of Creep Deformation of a Pipeline Steel Under Subsequent Static Load. *Materials Science and Engineering A*, *325*(1), 144–151. doi:10.1016/S0921-5093(01)01458-7

Weiczner, J. (2015, December 7). How Investors Are Using Social Media to Make Money. *Fortune*. Retrieved from http://fortune.com/2015/12/07/dataminr-hedge-funds-twitter-data/

Wilber, D. Q. (2009, June 12). *Economic Downturn Speeds Collapse of Ponzi Schemes*. Retrieved from Washington Post: http://www.washingtonpost.com/wp-dyn/content/article/2009/06/11/AR2009061103993.html

Williams, C. B. (2017). Introduction: Social Media, Political Marketing and the 2016 US Election. *Journal of Political Marketing*, *16*(3-4), 207–211. doi:10.1080/15377857.2017.1345828

Willis, L. (2008). *Against financial literacy education*. Retrieved 14 January 2018 from https://papers.ssrn.com/sol3/papers.cfm?abstract_id=1105384

Wilson, T., & Brekke, N. (1994). Mental contamination and mental correction: Unwanted influences on judgment and evaluations. *Psychological Bulletin*, *116*(1), 117–142. doi:10.1037/0033-2909.116.1.117 PMID:8078969

Wingfield, B. (2016). *The relationship between demographic factors and financial literacy among students at a South African University*. Pretoria: University of Pretoria.

Wood, C. (2006). *Federalism in Securities Regulation: A Brief Introduction and Reflection*. San Francisco: University of San Francisco.

World Bank. (2018a). *Bank nonperforming loans to total gross loans (%)*. World Bank Open Data. Retrieved from https://data.worldbank.org/indicator/FB.AST.NPER.ZS

World Bank. (2018b). *GINI index (World Bank estimate)*. World Bank Open Data. Retrieved from https://data.worldbank.org/indicator/SI.POV.GINI

World Bank. (n.d.). *Current Developments in Deposit Insurance*. Retrieved from http://pubdocs.worldbank.org/en/586861477065128589/16-Current-Development-in-Deposit-Insurance.pdf

Worldwide, J. A. (n.d.). *Who We Are*. Retrieved 3 January 2018 from https://www.jaworldwide.org/aboutja/

Worthington, S. (2006). *The cashless society The European plastic payment card*. The Cashless Society; doi:10.1108/09590559510095260

Xue, Z., Foster, E., Wang, Y., Nayak, S., Cheng, V., Ngo, V. W., ... Johnston, K. P. (2014). Effect of Grafted Copolymer Composition on Iron Oxide Nanoparticle Stability and Transport in Porous Media at High Salinity. *Energy & Fuels*, *28*(6), 3655–3665. doi:10.1021/ef500340h

Yagcilar, G. G., & Demir, S. (2015). Türk Bankacılık Sektöründe Takipteki Kredi Oranları Üzerinde Etkili Olan Faktörlerin Belirlenmesi. *Uluslararası Alanya İşletme Fakültesi Dergisi*, *7*(1).

Yang, Y., & Greaney, T. M. (2017). Economic growth and income inequality in the Asia-Pacific region: A comparative study of China, Japan, South Korea, and the United States. *Journal of Asian Economics*, *48*, 6–22. doi:10.1016/j.asieco.2016.10.008

Yoshina, N., Morgan, P., & Wignaraja, G. (2015). *Financial Education in Asia: Assessment and Recommendations*. Asian Development Bank Institute.

Young, K. (2017, November 14). *The Biggest Social Media Trends Shaping 2018*. Retrieved December 30, 2018, from Global Web Index: https://blog.globalwebindex.com/trends/social-media-trends/

Young, L., & Hobbs, J. (2002). Vertical Linkages in Agri-Food Supply Chains: Changing Roles for Producers, Commodity Groups, and Government Policy. *Review of Agricultural Economics*, *24*(2), 428–441. Retrieved from http://www.jstor.org/stable/1349770

YouTube for Press. (n.d.). Retrieved March 15, 2018, from YouTube: https://www.youtube.com/yt/about/press/

Yuan, F., Wang, L., Guo, Z., & Xie, Y. (2012). Analytical Analysis of Pipeline–soil Interaction During J-lay on a Plastic Seabed with Bearing Resistance Proportional to Depth. *Applied Ocean Research*, *36*, 60–68. doi:10.1016/j.apor.2012.02.004

Yüksel, S. (2016). *Bankacılık Krizlerinin Erken Uyarı Sinyalleri: Türkiye Üzerine Bir Uygulama*. Ankara: Akademisyen Yayınevi.

Yüksel, S. (2017). Determinants of the Credit Risk in Developing Countries After Economic Crisis: A Case of Turkish Banking Sector. In *Global Financial Crisis and Its Ramifications on Capital Markets* (pp. 401–415). Cham: Springer. doi:10.1007/978-3-319-47021-4_28

Zarghamee, M. S., Ojdrovic, R. P., & Nardini, P. D. (2011). Prestressed concrete cylinder pipe condition assessment—what works, what doesn't, what's next. In Pipelines 2011: A Sound Conduit for Sharing Solutions (pp. 182-194). Academic Press. doi:10.1061/41187(420)18

Zeng, D., Chen, H., Lusch, R., & Li, S.-H. (2010). Social media analytics and intelligence. *IEEE Intelligent Systems*, *25*(6), 13–16. doi:10.1109/MIS.2010.151

Zhang, D., Cai, J., Dickinson, D. G., & Kutan, A. M. (2016). Non-performing loans, moral hazard and regulation of the Chinese commercial banking system. *Journal of Banking & Finance*, *63*, 48–60. doi:10.1016/j.jbankfin.2015.11.010

Zhu, Y.-Q., & Chen, H.-G. (2015). Social media and human need satisfaction: Implications for social media marketing. *Business Horizons*, *58*(3), 335–345. doi:10.1016/j.bushor.2015.01.006

Zuckoff, M. (2006). *Ponzi Schemes: The True Story of a Financial Legend*. Random House.

About the Contributors

Abhishek Behl is a Research Scholar at Shailesh J. Mehta School of Management, Indian Institute of Technology Bombay, Mumbai, India. He is pursuing his second PhD in the area of Decision Sciences and Business Analytics at IIT (B); he has successfully completed his first PhD in the area of Technology Diffusion for Financial Inclusion and Rural Development from Symbiosis International University in 2015. He has also enjoyed the honor of being 'Emerald Research Scholar' awarded by Emerald Publishing House, UK, and Symbiosis International University, for notable contribution in research (2014-2016). He has served as a Resource Person for renowned educational institutions in India and conducted numerous Management Development Programmes in India and overseas. He has published several papers in journals indexed in prominent indices. Presently, he is serving as one of the Editors for a book titled Maintaining Financial Stability in Times of Risk and Uncertainty, anticipated to be released in 2019 by IGI Global. He has also presented papers at a number of national and international conferences. His research interests are primarily focused on actionable inquiries and exploration mostly in the area of management, with stems in Economics and social sciences.

Sushma Nayak is a Visiting Fellow at Symbiosis School of Economics (SSE) and a Doctoral Scholar with Symbiosis International (Deemed University), India. In addition to M.Phil. (Economics), she also holds a Post Graduate Diploma in Supply Chain Management. She has nine years of teaching experience and has taught fourteen different courses relating to Economics, Banking, Finance and Political Economy. Presently, she teaches Indian Banking & Financial System and Economic Journalism at SSE. She is a key member of the Center for Academic Writing at SSE. She also works towards the making of Oeconomica Scriptis — an in-house publication of SSE — which is a compilation of outstanding academic writings by students. She has been honored at the hands of Dr. Bibek Debroy, Economist and Member of NITI Aayog — the think tank of Indian Government, for her contribution to the Center for Academic Writing at SSE. She is serving as a reviewer for three IGI Global journals viz. International Journal of Civic Engagement and Social Change (IJCESC), International Journal of Information Systems and Supply Chain Management (IJISSCM) and International Journal of Distance Education Technologies (IJDET). Her subjects of interest include Population Studies, Agricultural Economics, Economics of Social Sector, Banking & Finance, Managerial Economics, Public Finance, Theory of Political Economy and Supply Chain Management.

* * *

Arati Barik has completed her PhD from Institute of Chemical Technology, Matunga, Mumbai. Her research interest includes topics such as Waste Water Treatment, Sonolysis, and Ozonation. Currently, she is working as an Assistant Professor at Mahatma Gandhi Mission's College of Engineering and Technology, Kharghar, Navi Mumbai.

Aastha Behl is an Assistant Professor at Pranveer Singh Institute of Technology (PSIT), Kanpur, India, teaching various subjects (Accounts, Law & Economics) for the Masters of Business Administration (MBA) program. She has more than two years of teaching experience. Prior to joining PSIT, she was with Axis College of Planning and Management, Kanpur, as Assistant Professor with the MBA department. She is a qualified Company Secretary professional and has also cleared UGC NET. Her research interests include broad areas of Law and Economics.

Rahul Bhalerao is a Consultant Engineer at Petrofac Engineering India Pvt Ltd. He provides consultancy relating to oil field services to international oil and gas industry. His expertise includes designing disruption and stress-free pipelines under low and high temperatures according to American Society of Mechanical Engineers (ASME) standards.

Ipek Tamara Cetiner is a Doctoral Scholar with Medipol University focusing on Strategy and Management. Before pursuing her academic career, she worked with various international companies in management teams.

Çağla Demir Pali works as a Cost Controller and Internal Auditor with an international textile company. She received her PhD degree in Accounting from Istanbul University in 2018. Her research focuses on Risk Management, Cost Management and Financial Reporting.

Hasan Dinçer is an Associate Professor of Finance at Istanbul Medipol University, Faculty of Economics and Administrative Sciences, Istanbul, Turkey. Dr. Dincer has Bachelors in Financial Markets and Investment Management at Marmara University. He received PhD in Finance and Banking with his thesis entitled "The Effect of Changes on the Competitive Strategies of New Service Development in the Banking Sector." He has work experience in the finance sector as a portfolio specialist and his major academic studies focus on Financial Instruments, Performance Evaluation, and Economics. He is the Executive Editor of the International Journal of Finance and Banking Studies (IJFBS) and a founder member of the Society for the Study of Business and Finance (SSBF).

Narendra Gade is a Master's student at MGM College of Engineering and Technology, Kharghar, Navi Mumbai. He has been working as a Piping Consultant for oil, gas and refinery industry for nearly ten years. During his career, he has also visited industries abroad and provided consultancy services to numerous firms.

Begoña Alvarez García is a lecturer in the Department of Business at the University of A Coruña (Spain). She has also been a lecturer at the University of Paris IX-Dauphine (France) and the Coordinator of Master's in Banking and Finance at the University of A Coruña. She holds a PhD degree in Economy and Management from the University of A Coruña and was given an Extraordinary Doctorate Award.

She has completed several research stages in the Universities of Paris-Dauphine and the Massachusetts Institute of Technology (MIT). She has participated in several European and national research projects and has published numerous books related to Finance. She is currently working on two lines of research: the first one focused on financial domain, and the second one on social innovations.

Sümeyra Gazel is an Assistant Professor in the Faculty of Economics and Administrative Sciences at the Bozok University in Turkey where she has been a faculty member since 2007. She was awarded the PhD in Behavioral Finance from Erciyes University in 2013. Her research interests include Financial Management, Behavioral Finance and Financial Econometrics.

Isha Gole is pursuing her Masters in Agribusiness Economics from Gokhale Institute of Politics and Economics. Prior to this, she graduated from Symbiosis International University with a Bachelors in Economics (Hons) degree. It was during this period where she discovered her passion and love for economics. She has a keen interest in subjects like Macroeconomics, Statistics and Econometrics. She has also been involved in another publication that has been internationally recognised.

Meltem Gurunlu is an Assistant Professor of Finance at the Department of International Trade & Finance in Istanbul Arel University, Turkey. She has received her PhD degree in Accounting & Finance from Marmara University in Istanbul in 2008. Her research interests include Corporate Finance, Corporate Governance and Strategic Decision Taking (such as IPOs and FDI), Capital Structure Decisions, Emerging Markets Finance and Ownership Structure.

Tarun Khandelwal is an Assistant Professor at Symbiosis School of Economics, a department of Symbiosis International (Deemed University), India.

Ashlesha Khedekar-Swaminathan is an Adjunct Faculty at Symbiosis School of Economics, a department of Symbiosis International (Deemed University), India. Her areas of interest include Behavioral and Gender Economics.

Danielle McKain is a High School Mathematics Teacher at Beaver Area High School. She has taught numerous courses including Algebra I, Algebra II, Integrated Math, Probability and Statistics, Trigonometry, and Computer Assisted Algebra. Additionally, she has years of experience preparing students for the SAT. Dr. McKain earned her PhD in Instructional Management and Leadership from Robert Morris University. She holds a Master of Science degree in Instructional Leadership with a specialization in Mathematics Education and a Bachelor of Science degree in Applied Mathematics. Her research interests include Real World Math, Math Anxiety, Remedial Math, and preparing future teachers.

Sourya Mookerjee is currently pursuing M.Sc. Finance at Trinity College in Dublin, Ireland. Prior to this, he graduated from Symbiosis School of Economics in Pune, India with B.Sc. Hons. in Economics. During his undergraduate studies, he has held the post of student representative for two academic years, and presented his dissertation titled 'Is India an Undertaxed Nation?' in the final year. He intends to build his career in equity research and is currently working for his masters' thesis in this domain.

Shrabana Mukherjee is currently working as the Deputy Secretary, Association of Indian Forging Industry, Pune. She has completed B.Sc. Economics from Lady Brabourne College, Calcutta University, Kolkata, and M.Sc. Economics from Symbiosis School of Economics, Symbiosis International (Deemed University), Pune. She is also working as a Visiting Faculty at Symbiosis College of Arts and Commerce, Pune, where she teaches Industrial Economics for Bachelors in Economics (Hons) program. Her areas of research interest include Microeconomics, Development Economics and Econometrics.

Aishwarya Narayan is rooted in Chennai, Tamil Nadu. She is currently pursuing her postgraduate studies in Economics from National University of Singapore. She was the president of the debating society and also an active member of the student government in her capacity as member of placement committee. She has been an ardent leader in organizing events in college. Although versatile in various fields, her interest leans towards Development Economics. She hopes to, in the future, end the vicious cycle of poverty straps that exist in Indian slums.

Sebin B. Nidhiri is a Research Scholar at Department of Economics, Delhi School of Economics, Delhi, India. He was an Assistant Professor at Symbiosis School of Economics, Pune, and the Programme In-Charge of the B.Sc. Economics programme at the School prior to which he was a Programme Officer at Public Affairs Centre (PAC), Bangalore, India. He has taught courses on Statistics and Econometrics at the undergraduate level and a course on Land Economics at the postgraduate level. He has co-authored a manual on 'Citizen Monitoring of Pradhan Mantri Gram Sadak Yojana (PMGSY) Roads' and has published papers in the area of development studies. He has worked on consultancy projects with the industry: one on 'Using Behavioral Economics to Curb Employee Absenteeism in a KPO Firm,' another on 'Estimating the Socio-Economic Cost of COPD in Pune' with Chest Research Foundation, and lastly on 'Creating an Index on SDG Achievement for Maharashtra's Districts.' He has an M.Sc. in Economics with specialization in Development Studies and is also UGC NET qualified.

Abhinav Pal is currently pursuing his PhD in Economics. He has three years of teaching experience at Symbiosis International (Deemed University). He has cleared UGC NET in Economics in 2014.

Shivali Pande is currently pursuing an MBA at IIM Bangalore. Her major areas of interest include Marketing Management, Brand Management, Luxury Retail Management and Retail Strategies. She wishes to pursue her further studies in the field of Marketing Management which will help her to eventually develop successful brand names and strategies in the corporate sector.

Fatih Pınarbaşı is a Research Assistant at Istanbul Medipol University and a Doctoral Scholar with Yıldız Technical University.

Varun Sardesai is a student at Symbiosis School of Economics (SSE), a department of Symbiosis International (Deemed University), pursuing B.Sc. Economics (Hons). His areas of interest include Political Science, Public Policy and Administration, and Finance.

Sakshi Saxena is currently associated with Symbiosis Centre for Management and Human Resource Development (SCMHRD) as a Research Assistant. She has diverse research experience of working with various research and educational institutes like Giri Institute of Development Studies, Teach for India, and Indian Institute of Education. Her core areas of research include Development Economics and Marketing. She has presented her research in several national and international conferences and has two publications to her credit. She teaches courses like Business Statistics and Managerial Economics to the postgraduate students. After completing her Bachelors of Arts from Lucknow University, she pursued M.Sc. in Economics from Symbiosis International (Deemed University).

Neha Sharma graduated from Symbiosis International (Deemed University) with Bachelors in Economics (Hons) degree and is pursuing MSc in International Business Economics and Finance from Gokhale Institute of Politics and Economics. During the span of her college career, she has probed into the Indo-Carribean relations and the Agri-Tech industry in India. She is currently working in the sphere of International Relations and exploring Indo-Japanese association. Her non-academic activities include swimming and loves scouting Indian Polity in her leisure time.

Pravin Suryawanshi is a Research Scholar at Shailesh J Mehta School of Management, IIT Bombay. Currently, he is pursuing research in the area of Decision Making and Supply Chain (SC) Optimization. His expertise includes designing a complex SC structure with the help of fundamentals of Operations Research, solve them using appropriate software packages such as CPLEX or Matlab. Although a naive researcher, he has publications in conference proceedings, book chapters and a journal publication.

Ravi Suryavanshi is an Assistant Professor in Applied Sciences Department for the subject of Applied Mathematics at Bharati Vidyapeeth College of Engineering, Kharghar, Navi Mumbai, since 2009. He is undertaking research in topics relating to Algebra at Department of Mathematics, University of Mumbai. He has eight years of experience teaching subjects such as Algebra, Probability and Statistics, Calculus and Mathematical Sciences.

Chandan K. Tiwari received his PhD from RTM Nagpur University. An MBA from University of Pune, India, he has over six years of teaching and research experience at reputed B-Schools in India. An active researcher, he has presented papers in several international conferences, and published papers in reputed international journals. Presently, he is an Assistant Professor (Banking and Finance) at Symbiosis Centre for Management Studies, Noida.

José Pablo Abeal Vázquez is a lecturer in the area of Financial Economics and Accounting of the Department of Business of the University of A Coruña (Spain). He has also taught at several University Schools linked to the University of A Coruña and other Private Universities. He holds a PhD Degree in Economics from the University of A Coruña and he was given an Extraordinary Doctorate Award. He completed a Management Development Program by IESE Business School and he holds a Master in Commercial Management and Marketing from the Caixanova Business School. He frequently collaborates in economic studies for companies and institutions, and as a speaker in courses and specialized seminars. He has various publications in journals and congresses in the economic field.

Serhat Yüksel is an Assistant Professor of Finance with İstanbul Medipol University. Before holding this position, he worked as a Senior Internal Auditor for seven years in Finansbank, Istanbul-Turkey and one year in Konya Food and Agriculture University as an Assistant Professor. Dr. Yüksel has a BS in Business Administration (in English) from Yeditepe University (2006) with full scholarship. He got his Master's degree in Economics from Boğaziçi University (2008). He also has a PhD in Banking from Marmara University (2015). His research interests lie in Banking, Finance and Financial Crisis. He has more than 70 publications (books, book chapters, scientific articles, etc) to his credit.

Index

E

F

G

H

I

J

K

L

M

U

V

W

www.ingramcontent.com/pod-product-compliance
Lightning Source LLC
LaVergne TN
LVHW060406300926
849162LV00006B/1363